USE OF INTERPRETATION
IN TREATMENT
Technique and Art

USE OF INTERPRETATION
IN TREATMENT
Technique and Art

EMANUEL F. HAMMER, Ph.D., *Editor*

GRUNE & STRATTON • **NEW YORK and LONDON**

Library of Congress Catalog Number 68-13194

Printed in the United States of America
(K-A)

TO LILA

Contents

PREFACE xi

SETTING THE STAGE

1. INTERPRETATION: WHAT IS IT?
   Emanuel F. Hammer, Ph.D. 1

2. THE ROLE OF INTERPRETATION IN THERAPY
   Emanuel F. Hammer, Ph.D. 5

THE BASIC ISSUES

3. SOURCES OF GAIN IN PSYCHOTHERAPY
   Nicholas Hobbs, Ph.D. 13

4. INTERPRETATIONS: WHERE AND WHEN
   Emanuel F. Hammer, Ph.D. 22

SPECIFIC DIMENSIONS AND TECHNIQUES

5. INTERPRETATION IN THE EARLY PHASE OF THERAPY
   Max Cooper, Ph.D. 27

6. INTERPRETATION TECHNIQUE: A PRIMER
   Emanuel F. Hammer, Ph.D. 31

7. INTERPRETATION IN RELATIONSHIP THERAPY
   William U. Snyder, Ph.D. 43

8. CONFESSIONS OF AN EX-NONDIRECTIVIST
   Rosalea A. Schonbar, Ph.D. 55

9. INTERPRETATION AND THE INTERPERSONAL INTERACTION IN
      PSYCHOTHERAPY
   Sol L. Garfield, Ph.D. 59

10. INTERPRETATION AS INTERPERSONAL STRUCTURING
    Emanuel F. Hammer, Ph.D. 62

11. INTERPRETATION AND EGO FUNCTION. .
    Esther Menaker, Ph.D. 67

12. SPONTANEITY IN THE ANALYTIC INTERPRETATION
    Harold Lindner, Ph.D. 71

13. INTERPRETATION AND INSIGHT IN PSYCHOTHERAPY
    Rosalea A. Schonbar, Ph.D. 74

14. SOME PSYCHOECONOMIC ASPECTS OF ANALYTIC INTERPRETATION
       IN THE LIGHT OF INTRASYSTEMIC CONFLICT
    Stanley Berger, Ph.D. 81

15. INTERPRETATION AND THE THERAPEUTIC ACT
Jule Nydes, M.A. 91

16. THE ANALYST'S ROLE, TO INTERPRET OR TO REACT?
Bertram Pollens, Ph.D. 101

17. THE MATURATIONAL INTERPRETATION
Hyman Spotniz, M.D. 107

18. INTERPRETATION: THE PATIENT'S RESPONSE
Reuben Fine, Ph.D. 110

19. THE THERAPEUTIC ACT
John L. Herma, Ph.D. 121

20. ON THE DIALOGUE IN CLASSIC PSYCHOANALYSIS
Donald M. Kaplan, Ph.D. 129

21. INTERPRETATION AND LANGUAGE
Susan Deri 141

22. THE USE OF IMAGERY IN INTERPRETIVE COMMUNICATION
Emanuel F. Hammer, Ph.D. 148

23. VARYING TECHNIQUE IN TREATMENT
Emanuel F. Hammer, Ph.D. 156

VIEWPOINTS

24. TWO PROPOSED ALTERNATIVES TO PSYCHOANALYTIC INTERPRETING
Harry Bone, Ph.D. 169

25. SULLIVANIAN: Interpretation as Active Nurture: An Interpersonal
Perspective
Edwin Kasin, M.D. 197

26. CLIENT-CENTERED: The Experiential Response
Eugene T. Gendlin, Ph.D. 208

27. TRANSACTIONAL: A Transactional View of Interpretation
Lawrence Edwin Abt, Ph.D. 228

28. RATIONAL THERAPY: A Rational Approach to Interpretation
Albert Ellis, Ph.D. 232

29. EXISTENTIAL: The Problem of Interpretation from the Point of
View of Existential Psychoanalysis
Herbert Holt, M.D. 240

30. FREUDIAN: Remarks on Insight and Interpretation
Paul Cornyetz 253

31. PARADIGMATIC: ". . . More Than One Way to Skin a Cat"
Marie Coleman Nelson 260

DREAM ANALYSIS

32. FREE ASSOCIATION AND INTERPRETATION OF DREAMS: HISTORICAL
    AND METHODOLICAL CONSIDERATIONS
    Martin S. Bergmann 270

33. THE PLACE AND USE OF DREAM INTERPRETATIONS IN THERAPY
    Richard C. Robertiello, M.D. 280

34. INTERPRETATION OF DREAMS ON THE SUBJECTIVE LEVEL:
    ITS APPLICATION IN DIAGNOSIS
    Renee Nell, Ed.D. 285

THERAPY MODIFICATIONS AT DIFFERENT AGE LEVELS

35. INTERPRETATIONS AND CHILD THERAPY
    Haim G. Ginott, E.D. 291

36. THE USE OF INTERPRETATION IN THE PSYCHOANALYTIC TREATMENT
    OF CHILDREN
    Dorothy Bloch, M.A. 300

37. SPECIFIC FORMS OF INTERPRETATION IN PSYCHOTHERAPY WITH
    ADOLESCENTS
    Ernest Harms, Ph.D. 321

38. THE ROLE OF INTERPRETATION IN PSYCHOTHERAPY WITH THE AGED
    Robert L. Wolk, Ph.D. 332

GROUP THERAPY

39. SOME ASPECTS OF INTERPRETATION IN GROUP THERAPY
    Leslie Rosenthal 339

HYPNOTHERAPY

40. CLINICAL INTERPRETATION IN HYPNOANALYSIS
    Milton V. Kline, Ed.D. 344

ON THE THERAPIST'S SIDE

41. INTERPRETATION: A PSYCHOANALYTIC DIALOGUE
    Stephen A. Applebaum, Ph.D. 351

42. THE RELUCTANCE TO INTERPRET
    Erwin Singer, Ph.D. 364

43. INTERPRETATION: SCIENCE OR ART?
    Emanuel F. Hammer, Ph.D. 372

INDEX 375

Preface

Confronting pain, conflict and emotional complexity in troubled people, the psychotherapist struggles to perform his work. At the same time, he struggles with the rationale of his own procedures. For this volume, a number of articulate and reflective therapists were asked to take some hard looks at what they do.

This book is a broad-ranged appraisal of one of the more dramatic tools utilized by therapists—interpretation in treatment. It is readily noticed that the vast majority of therapists employ interpretations to varying degrees and in different styles; yet, surprisingly little agreement has been reached with respect to their place, role, depth, timing or art of interpretation. Therefore, perspectives from a wide range of theoretical vantage points are focused on these central dimensions. The chapters include both the uses to which interpretations are put by the patient and the particular needs of the therapist in interpreting or not interpreting.

This book pursues the goal of assembling viewpoints which embody specificity and operationalism in therapeutic work, and this aim requires no defense. Although it is somewhat difficult to find a desirable path between the frequent ambiguities of clinical exposition and the equally frustrating papers so molecular and scientific that they cease almost to have any relevancy to people, the contributors aim for the target of this difficult middle ground.

To a degree, the secret of being an editor is the ability to marry a timely idea with the right writers, and then stay out of the way. The chapters vary in length in that, as editor, I preferred to set no rules other than that each contributor allow his chapter to unfold naturally to cover, but not exceed, what he had to say.[1]

To write about psychotherapy is never simple. To write simply about the vicissitudes in the process, the collaborative coping of patient and therapist with the mass of often refractory material and involved problems, the orderliness beneath the accidents and haphazardness, and the intricacy of interaction in an uncovering procedure is always incredibly difficult. I was understandably pleased when prominent psychologists, who are almost always very busy psychologists, were interested enough to undertake one or another aspect of this challenge and to write about what they do when they treat people.[2]

Before each chapter I have tried to tell the reader who an author is, where he came from, what his job history is, what his expertness is, and what he has written

---

[1] I claimed the same privilege in introducing each chapter.

[2] As editor, I found the bulk of the contributed chapters very satisfying. An occasional one, however, suggests to us that an expanding field needs a big figure to serve as a universal landmark, an unmistakable North by which every compass could be regulated, and for this Freud becomes the natural choice. In this sense, he is at times studied not so much to be understood but to be *used*. At such times, it is important to determine if the system attacked is one set up as a straw man—to evaluate if there is any specification of whether one is talking about, as Hans Strupp puts it, "Freud$_{1912}$ or Freud$_{1937}$." Freud, it seems, more than any other in our field, rarely had students; he had (and still has) partisans and detractors, both equally uncompromising. What is needed, along with what are most important—innovations—are also efforts to rescue what is serviceable in Freud from his adulators and denigrators alike.

or done—in short, who and what he is professionally. Contributors address predominantly the practicing therapist as the intended audience. One chapter, however, is slanted, on the one side, to the therapy trainee and, on the other, to his supervisor.

In reporting on British laboratories, Turner (1966) asserts that many pieces of apparatus are infernally noisy by American standards and vibrate when turned on. This is caused by a "dithering device" installed in these pieces of equipment merely to shake the apparatus while it is in operation, much as one kicks a machine to make it work more readily, to insure against any sticking of parts. It may be that this principle used in the assemblage of parts called a machine may also be used in a collection of people called a profession, and thus by a jolting process may activate what otherwise might grow stagnant. One of the purposes of the present book is to inform and educate; another is to serve as a "dithering device." With some chapters to kick up the dust, the aim is to stimulate discussion, thinking, controversy, agreement or dissent. I, for one, would feel this book a disappointment if—at this stage in the growth of our field—some questions were not answered, but I would also feel disappointment, in relative comparison, if more questions were not raised than answered.

While the focus of this book is the dimension of the exchange between therapist and patient that we call "interpretation," I wish to emphasize what I hope should be obvious: that this is by no means the whole of that exchange which produces alteration in patients.

Appreciative acknowledgement is made to the *American Psychologist,* the *Psychoanalytic Review,* the New York Society of Clinical Psychologists, and the American Psychological Association, the journals for permission to reproduce several of the papers, and to the Society and the Association for hosting the symposium at which some others were read. The bulk of the contributions, however, were written for, and are presented for the first time, in this work. Appreciation is deeply extended to Esther Breitman and Hannelore Goldman for editorial assistance. Warmest thanks for their sensitive reading of the manuscript and their many fruitful suggestions are expressed to Drs. Daniel W. Schwartz, Robert L. Wolk, and Dorothy Bloch, and to Jerome Ben Rosen, writer and friend, and to Lila, wife, colleague and friend.

E. F. H.

REFERENCE

Turner, R. H., Dithering devices in the classroom: How to succeed in shaking up a campus by really trying. *Amer. Psychol.,* 1966, 12, 957-964.

SETTING THE STAGE

CHAPTER 1

Interpretation: What is It?

EMANUEL F. HAMMER, PH.D.

Hammer, the editor, describes Hammer, the contributor, as a psychoanalyst in private practice in New York City and as a Supervisor at the New York University Graduate School of Arts and Sciences, Clinical Doctoral Program. He is a faculty member and training analyst at both the National Psychological Association for Psychoanalysis and the Metropolitan Institute for Psychoanalytic Studies, and Director of Research at the latter institution. A Liaison Fellow of the American Anthropological Association, a Fellow of the American Psychological Association, and a Diplomate in Clinical Psychology of the American Board of Examiners in Professional Psychology, Dr. Hammer has written approximately 50 professional publications, including several books, the most recent of which is Creativity, Random House. *He has held the office of Secretary of the Society of Projective Techniques and Personality Assessment and recently was President of the New York Society of Clinical Psychologists.*

In this, and in a few of the other of his own chapters, he attempts to cut across some of the schools of therapy to get at what he considers the essentials in interpretation.

Ever since Freud's earliest contributions to technique, the use of interpretation in treatment has demonstrated a staying power at the center of the dynamically-oriented psychotherapeutic procedures. It may be easily observed that whether the therapist is a Freudian or an Adlerian, a Jungian or a Sullivanian, a Transactionalist or an Rankian, an Existentialist or a Rational Therapist, a Paradygmatist, a Neo-Classisist, or an Eclectic, the use of interpretation is a common tool. The content of the interpreted material may differ from one theoretical school to another, but the same considerations of the *technique* of interpreting cut across all of them. "To be sure, interpretation is not the only procedure used in bringing about change, but it is certainly one of the major ones, and quite likely one of the most powerful ones" (Levy, 1963). For such diverse theorist-therapists as Fenichel (1945), Fromm-Reichmann (1950), and Rosen (1953), interpretation is one of the nodal points of the entire psychotherapeutic encounter.

There is some experimental support. In contrast to Roger's view that "interpretations are usually threatening and tend to slow rather than speed the process of therapy" (Rogers, 1961, p. 13), Auld and White (1959) at Yale found no evidence that the patient's resistance increased following interpretation. Dittman (1952) at the University of Michigan found therapeutic movement to be associated with interpretations somewhat deeper than pure "reflection." But much more experimental work awaits doing.

In practice, when a patient enters treatment, he feels a vague mixture of varying degrees of courage and fear, of being both intrigued and intimidated at the prospect of entering a relationship which at the same time promises and threatens to reveal to him secrets of his deeper self. Whatever else he expects therapy to be, he anticipates—unless he consults a Non-Directivist or one of the "behavior modifiers," and knows something about their respective approaches—some interpretation, some illumination from the therapist in the interest of gaining a little more of an inner sense of what his life, below the surface, is actually all about.

The unexamined experience endows little wisdom. "Experience is not what happens to a man," Aldous Huxley has written, "it is what a man does with what happens to him."

While the extrovertive patient may look for therapy to supply little more than symptom removal, the more introspective individual hopes for more, including the possibility of an inward vision. In the atmosphere of therapy, if treatment takes at all, the sometimes bracing, sometimes unsettling, but always involving ring of truth hovers in the air between patient and analyst. At times it is defeated and at times it is cut around, but it is always the pivotal point, the one which makes sense of therapist and patient's being together at all. Thus, the collaboration takes place around a value system shaped by Freud, Plato, Aristotle, and others before and after them. Such a system embraces the convictions that knowledge is better than ignorance, that awareness is better than self-deception, that an approach toward truth offers more than retreat from it, that Shakespeare's injunction, "To thine own self be true," if followed, expands life today as it did when it was first offered.

*

Those therapists who practice a more or less classic procedure, and those who deviate only partially from it, tend to forget, over the years, how extraordinary a situation the patient finds upon weathering the initial interview and then settling down for the beginning phase of treatment. The patient comes predominantly for the relief of his psychic pain. He is generally invited to lie down or to sit and talk about his problems or anything else he chooses. As Menninger (1958) describes it, the patient "may talk about himself, his neighbors, his wife, his friends, or his parents. He may talk about the present, the past, the future. He doesn't even have to be fair, he doesn't have to be considerate, he doesn't have to be objective." He only has to try to be honest in reporting everything he feels and thinks.

For the initial phase, the analyst listens, but makes few responses except to indicate his close attention. The patient leaves having received little or no suggestions, no criticism, and few comments. The patient, Menninger continues, "returns; reclines; recites." Again the analyst listens and is for the most part silent. This is repeated for many sessions. This is the "dialogue" for the long, beginning period.

Then when the analyst or analytically-oriented therapist does enter into a more active role (still parsimoniously and probably talking no more than about ten per cent of the time), it is, among other things, as often as not in an interpretative stance. At various times he interprets resistance, transference, and content having to do with the past and the present, with the surface and the underlying. "Whatever more an interpretation is, suffice it to say it is at least thoughtful and verbal. It is also declarative, as against, say, hortatory, inspirational or parabolic" (Kaplan, 1966).

The dialogue becomes now and then searching, at other times merely expressive. The therapist is highly attentive—and the patient senses this—to what is being said and what he, the patient, is going through. The therapist does not just listen, he is *absorbed* in listening and very much with the patient.

Since the place where the analyst (and that of the other psychodynamically-oriented therapists with him) most actively enters the dialogue is often enough around some interpretative exchange, what then is interpretation in actuality? "Interpretation begins when we ask the question: What does this mean?" says Levy (1963, p. viii). "It ends when we no longer feel the need to ask this question."

We might operationally define interpretation as the offering to the patient of an *alternate* view of some datum or data of feeling or behavior. The implicit assumption behind many interpretations is that, in the long run, some desired change can be enabled if some feeling or behavior of the patient is viewed in a new or broader perspective. Is the art of interpretation really anything more than the appropriate tilting of some data so that, for the patient, it can better catch the light?

Another way of describing it is offered by Fenichel (1953), who states Freud's view of the essence of interpretation as similar to "the indication given by the teacher of histology to the student as to what he will see in the microscope, without which the student's eye, which is not yet set for microscopic vision, would not see anything." In connection with this, Kaiser (1934) adds, "Even the most exact and most apposite anticipatory idea we might give to the searcher could not facilitate his search as long as he is searching in a space which does not contain the object sought."

In describing interpretations, Bellak (1954) classifies them into two broad types, the *horizontal* and the *vertical*. Horizontal interpretations are those in which a common denominator is pointed out involving those behavior patterns and interpersonal relationships of the patient's contemporary life, such as similar reactions to bosses, teachers, parents, and the therapist. The relationship to the therapist is particularly focused upon as a special case of the current life situation within the horizontal pattern.

Vertical interpretations concern the historical development: those patterns of the patient which pertain to his past, particularly his early years of development. Relating past to present is the core of the vertical interpretation. Frequently, of course, it is the combined pointing out of both vertical and horizontal relationships which leads to the more integrated insights. Many analysts, in fact, consider that the only complete interpretation is one which connects the three aspects of the patient's feelings or behavior: transference, present reality, and past experience.

In psychodynamically-oriented treatment, the ultimate goal of interpretation—its basic aim and its rationale—has to do with enabling insight and expanding self-knowledge. This, in turn, serves to place the conscious self, the ego, in a more commanding position in the personality system. From this position it is possible to deal with the rigidity, pressures, demands, and sometime tyranny of the "should's" and "should not's" of the superego; at the same time, it is possible to deal with the clamoring appetites and the incessant "I want what I want because I want it" of the id. All this takes place while honoring the firm requirements of reality on the third side.

The explanation of *why* insight is helpful is that it expands the realm and the freedom of the ego. The patient extends his boundaries of awareness by being both more of an observer and an experiencer of himself. He develops a mental standing ground, at the same time *both* inside and outside his experience. Interpretation, according to Paul (1966), "creates an opportunity to experience the feelings under the aegis of one's self-regulatory powers, the observing 'ego.' This is a combined, double-barreled movement in the direction of more power (self-direction) *and* more contact with feeling."

The intent of uncovering therapy is to broaden the ego so that a portion of it can stretch away from the other portions to attain enough distance for an observing function to emerge and look at the experiencing functions. This can exert a modifying influence as the patient establishes more *self*-direction from above rather than remaining uncritically subject to influence by the irrational operations below. Thus, in widening the range of options, we may assist the patient to become a more choosing and deciding individual.

REFERENCES

Auld, F., Jr., and White, Alice M., Sequential dependencies in psychotherapy. *J. Abnorm. Soc. Psychol.* 1959, 58, 100-104.

Bellak, L., *The TAT and CAT in clinical use.* New York: Grune & Stratton, 1954.

Dittman, A. T., The interpersonal process in psychotherapy: Development of a research method. *J. Abnorm. Soc. Psychol.* 1952, 47, 236-244.

Fenichel, O., *The psychoanalytic theory of neurosis.* New York: Norton, 1945.

——, *The collected papers of Otto Fenichel: First Series.* New York: Norton, 1953.

Fromm-Reichman, Frieda, *Principles of intensive psychotherapy.* Chicago: University of Chicago Press, 1950.

Kaiser, H., Probleme der technik. *Internat. J. Psychoanal.* 1934, 20, 490-522.

Kaplan, D. M., Classical psychoanalysis: policies, values and the future. *Psychoanal. Rev.,* Spring 1966, 99-111.

Menninger, K., *Theory of psychoanalytic technique.* New York: Basic Books, 1958.

Paul, L., Nonregressive ahistorical means of transference examination. *Psychoanal. Rev.* 1966, 53, 99-106.

Rosen, J. N., *Direct analysis.* New York: Grune & Stratton, 1953.

CHAPTER 2

The Role of Interpretation in Therapy

Emanuel F. Hammer, Ph.D.

HOW MUCH OF ME IS ME?—Abner Dean

"Every extension of knowledge arises from making conscious the unconscious."

"Those who cannot remember the past are condemned to repeat it."

Whose insights are these? Psychoanalysts'? Freud's or one of his disciples? Actually, this wisdom comes from an entirely different vantage point: from the philosophers, Nietzche and Santayana.

Before moving toward therapeutic considerations within the art and what there is of the science of psychotherapy, let us first take a long step back from the subject to early man. Man, the inward-seeing, became different from the other creatures. Anthropologist Loren Eiseley has commented that ancestral man entered his own head; and since then he has been trying to adapt to what he found there. What would he have found there if he could have descended deeply enough? The turbulence, confusion, irrationality, wish fulfillment, primitive and primary process thinking—all contained beneath the secondary process thinking which tried sometimes heroically, sometimes vainly, to cope with his needs, with the clash and storm of conflicting promptings inside and with the immediate environment outside.

Sir Julian Huxley (1967) points out, "In the natural sciences, man has learned the technique of 'reality thinking'—of accepting the facts and phenomena of external nature, in trying to understand them objectively, without bias. But he still has to tackle the more difficult task of abandoning primitive for reality thinking in dealing with . . . [the] mechanisms for thinking about himself." With those people who consult him, the therapist attempts just this latter goal, to explore with a patient his way of coping with his existence.

Imprisoned, to varying degrees, in a mental cage whose walls are made of the forces of his inner desires and his defenses against them, whose bars are the constructions of his own limited knowledge of himself, his irrational anxieties and overloads of guilt, the patient commits himself in therapy to the assumption that understanding himself more deeply will be of some advantage in his coping with himself and his problems.

Other than the relationship-therapy aspects (the patient feeling a sense of support, a relationship with someone who cares, a sense of trust), one of the first gains the patient generally struggles to acquire is being able to *identify* what is going on, affectively *and* rationally. Fenichel (1945) says, "The verbalization of unclear worries alone brings relief, because an ego can face verbalized ideas better than unclear emotional sensations." Until one learns the face of one's private furies, one fears them excessively as nameless dreads. "Now it has a name," a patient in treatment once said to me with deep relief.

To order one's sense of self or one's world is a fundamental need of man. In his

5

important book, *The Savage Mind,* Levi-Strauss (1966) quotes a native as saying, "All sacred things must have their place." The author comments: "It could even be said being in their place is what makes them sacred for if they were taken out of their place, even in thought, the entire order of the universe would be destroyed. Sacred objects therefore contribute to the maintenance of order in the universe by occupying places allocated to them." To take Levi-Strauss' insight about human nature back into the therapy room, interpretation to a patient with disordered feelings or thoughts represents an attempt at bringing about a more appropriate alignment of things.

Using linguistics as his model, Levi-Strauss demonstrates that man has always been the great pattern-maker. Such patterns are arbitrary systems of representation, more obedient to logic than to nature. Man's mastery of nature depends upon his ability to manipulate symbolic logic in abstract form, that is, upon mathematics and upon language. The ultimate roots of these mathematical and linguistic transformations are found in tribal societies. People everywhere classify, not only that which is useful, but also that which is known. No matter how naked a people, it cannot live in a world of disorder. But a condition of neurosis is, among other things, just such a state of disorder.[1] Interpretive ordering of the patient's disordered feelings, impulses, and ideas—upheaved in a churning, ongoing, active neurosis—may add sense to the patient's view of self and more security to his self-experiencing.

Beyond this there is another value to identifying what is going on within the patient, one which we can also learn from anthropological sources. For example, the Eskimo language does not simply label things already there. Words are like the knife of the carver: they free the idea, the thing, from the general formlessness of the context. This idea is reflected in the manner in which the Eskimo names a child. When the mother is in labor, an old woman stays by her and says as many different eligible names for the baby as she can associatively think up. The child, it is felt, comes out of the womb when its name is called. Thus the naming and the giving birth to the new are inextricably bound together. Similarly, the therapist's naming of what is going on within the patient can assist the patient to deliver the sensations up to consciousness, where then it can more easily be dealt with. Thus, a sensitive and appropriately-timed interpretation of material at the preconscious edge constitutes a sort of small "action," one which actually produces some change in the relative depth where a thought, feeling or wish bobbles. Thus, an idea under the idea, or a feeling beneath the feeling, can be assisted to emerge, and the process becomes more than an intellectual exercise; it produces an actual shift. As what was within is brought up, the therapist, assisting the patient's ego, now collaborates with it to face what it had previously warded off.

As we can learn from the philosophers and anthropologists in areas adjacent to ours, we can also profit from the truths offered by writers. In an article some years ago, Philip Roth spoke for a number of his fellow novelists in declaring that since contemporary life has become grotesque and unreal, the only subject matter re-

---

[1]It may be for just this reason that any structuring or interpretation, whether relatively valid or not, may prove helpful. It is this which partially may explain the reported success of such diverse structurings of the individual's situation as are offered by Christian Science, by Dianetics, by movements or cults of all sorts, or even by any explanation. The child who suffers from enuresis and who is told by the pediatrician that he merely has a "weak bladder" feels better about it, as do his parents.

maining to the writer—the one thing whose motions and urgings he could trust and take hold of—was his personal self. This is becoming increasingly so not only for the writer, but for modern man in general. As the outer world loses more and more reality, reality—if it is to be sensed at all—must be sensed within. It is for that much-discussed sense of alienation that increasingly the patient today seeks the therapist's assistance. The neurotic problems of patients in Freud's Vienna have given way to those of a deeper sort today—those of a sense of emptiness, of uncertainty as to the very nature of one's being.

While there have always been men who did not believe in God, we live in the first age in which it has been proposed that "God is dead." Holmes (1966) writes that "the valueless abyss of modern life is unbearable." Some, in desperate recoil from this vacuum, search out therapy. This constitutes a tall order for therapy to fill. This type of patient, described as "new" by Esther and William Menaker (1965), comes to analysis searching for a new ego-integration, not just for the removal of symptoms. He reaches for expansion and resynthesis.

Automation, as almost no one needs to be reminded, has brought about a loss of dignity and satisfaction in work. Most of our patients have lived through the years of World War II, the Korean War and the Viet Nam "non-war." One resonates to the horrors of only yesterday: Jews, more than the mind can contemplate, gassed to death; women and children destroyed in the atomic bombings of Hiroshima and Nagasaki; Vietnamese made into flaming torches by napalm; our country swept by McCarthyism and its lingering malignancy; a young, vigorous President of grace and intelligence who became emblematic of hope senselessly assassinated. The impact of tragedy today is communicated by television with all its immediate vividness. We are inundated by the sheer availability of the instant image, the instant sound, the instant news in an electronic world of simultaneity.

This is the context in which we treat suffering people today. Against the torrent of these events, it is our challenge to help an individual construct his personal world a bit more solidly and with a sense of meaning. This we must attempt when he feels the frustration, in regard to the broader world, of being able to do no more than all he can.

To rightly live, an individual today must preserve himself through sanctifying his humanity and individual freedom. For the younger male patient, the ominous prospect of being drafted into a war he frequently doesn't believe in is one more problem in which the social infuses into the personal. In addition, individuals no longer feel the strong, stabilizing influence of the family unit. Never before have the difficulties of those who consult us regarding their problems in living been so complex; never has the treatment been so involved.

The repeatedly-demonstrated capacity of man to destroy what he builds, to build again, and to destroy again is inescapable. The reflective individual observes this, and the one honest with himself cannot blink away the reality that the balance is not at all decisively tipped toward the constructive forces winning ultimately over the destructive.

With the ever-present nuclear threat, with air pollution, water contamination, and the population explosion as dire dangers to the very survival of both patient *and* therapist, the therapist is often called upon, not only to mirror reality, but also to free the patient in a temporary stepping back from the oppressive encroachment of things as they externally are, to enable him to dip within himself for some sense of enriched existence, to embark upon the controlled descent to, and return from, the inner state. Often what is enlivening to the modern patient is the gaining of the capacity for an expansion of self, not from "pot" and not from acid "trips," but from a liberating of greater creativity within himself via learning the freedom of free-association and, in Kris' sense, "regression in the service of the ego." We can here lend our services, as therapists, to the patient's profound yearning to come close to the core of himself, to the layers of authenticity that are within him and that are beneath the outer roles society demands be played.

Here the therapist serves a function, although in a more personal and hopefully deeper way, to that provided by literature or art. Therapy, if it also is at all creative, seeks to enrich experience by expanding and intensifying consciousness.[2] An individual attains a degree of wisdom and a greater sense of mastery in the process of facing, gradually, the truth in himself and in engaging in a more basic inspection of his predicament. An additional yield is that once he recognizes more of who he really is, once he realizes his distortions and misconceptions, he is less easily taken in by them.

The goals of therapy are divided and are moved by the two broad camps in directions of polarities, one aiming at assisting the patient to unfold and to enrich himself, and the other at more surface symptom treatment. If the former type of therapist diminishes the patient's respect for surface illusion and for conscious intention, what does he offer in return? The central promise of depth therapy is that it makes engagement with the emotional workings of one's life more possible and more precise.

Singer (1965) in his recent book, *Key Concepts in Psychotherapy,* quotes Goethe's *Faust:*

> "This is the highest wisdom that I own,
> The best that mankind ever knew;
> Freedom and life are earned by those alone
> Who conquer them each day anew."

This affirmation of life, battle and all, this gritted determination to live and to experience, to take on the struggle with the contradictions of one's own nature, offers a striking contrast to the aim of symptom removal which the Behavior Modifiers settle for as the be-all and end-all of therapeutic collaboration. Menninger (1958), espousing the deeper goal, speaks of the patient emerging "weller than well." He says, "The patient who has fully recovered from an illness with the aid of psychoanalysis will not have become his old self again; rather he has become (we trust) an enlarged, an improved, indeed a *new* self." He adds, however, another distinguishing characteristic of the two schools of therapeutic goals. "But it is hard to say in advance how long this will take." Hence the investment and the yield are strikingly different.

Erik Erikson, in his dialogue with Richard Evans (1967), refers to psychoanalysis as the principal modern form of introspection and meditation. He continues in agreement with Menninger: "It is not all a matter of being cured of isolated symptoms [that kind of cure one may sometimes buy more cheaply], but of learning to become aware of your elemental conflicts. . . . [The

---

[2]Erik Erikson, referring to analysis as the "first systematic and active 'consciousness-expansion,'" adds that such expansion may be necessary in the technological world "as man concentrates on the conquest of matter and is apt to over-identify with it" (Evans, 1967).

THE ROLE OF INTERPRETATION IN THERAPY

goal is one of being] really healthy, that is, more than not-sick . . . [and thus attain] a certain liveliness and spirited quality which is more than a mere absence of severe conflict."

Attempting to bridge the gap between the divergent viewpoints, there are those who espouse the current reasoning circulating in our field, one which includes the following logic: If all therapeutic techniques have some success, then all must have something in common, that is, all must work by the same mechanism—being nice and friendly to the patient, which Fiedler has cited as a denominator common to all psychotherapy. This is like saying that there is no difference between reward and punishment, since both methods make a child study more. Similar results are not identical results, especially if they are not viewed shallowly. The child studies more under both conditions; but what he gets out of it, what he assimilates, and how much of what he learns he uses to extend himself may be strikingly different in the two situations of reward and punishment. If the current spurious line of reasoning about the various psychotherapies were valid, clinicians might well be absolved of investigating the different factors responsible for the results of varied therapies. If there is actually little difference between suggestion and analysis, between support and uncovering, and if the Rogerian reflection of feeling is, in effect, the same as interpretation of resistance, then there is little need to learn the refined skills of the interpretive (or any other) therapeutic tools. But life for the therapist is, unfortunately, not that simple.

In insight therapy (to restate the basic) the objective is to help the patient achieve maximum degrees of independence and self-realization via an increase in the scope of his awareness of himself. In pursuing this end the therapist strives to assist the patient resolve defenses and resistances and to bring unconscious conflicts into awareness. This he does predominantly by guiding the patient through the reexperiencing of the repressed through the transference. By recreating the ingredients of these conflicts in the context of the relationship with the analyst, the attempts to achieve a resolution are now more feasible.

Symptom relief, on the other hand, may be the principal goal of either supportive therapy or the behavioral therapies. The alleviation of symptoms and behavioral change is pursued on levels which do not undertake the goal of modification of deeper personality elements or of resolution of the underlying conflicts. Toward the more modest goal, no special effort is made to assist the patient in the reexperiencing of that which is repressed. London (1966) speaks of this latter group of treatment approaches as the "action therapies." They derive their therapeutic principles from the empirical and theoretical precepts of conditioning and learning, particularly as represented by Salter, Wolpe, Stampfl and Skinner. These approaches tend to "actively impose treatment procedures rather than passively await the introspection of the patient" as the psychodynamic or insight therapies would. Although this differentiation is meaningful, as Freudenberger (1967) points out, it cannot be accepted as a clear-cut dividing line. Certainly the classical analyst, for example, does more than merely await introspections from his patients. He, at times, intervenes in seeking to understand with the patient the meaning and the sense of the transference distortions, the resistances and defenses, and the cathecting of people and things. He also actively seeks to clarify the patient's reality and his perceptions of his environment as well as of himself.

At this point, perhaps it is time to ask the basic question: What is psychotherapy? On one level, is it not essentially a partnership between two people, one a pro-

fessional and one an amateur (although the latter is not invariably the less potentially able at this human art); is it not a partnership aimed at getting the respective
elements of the microcosmic world called the "therapy relationship" to interact
together, to achieve more and more effective communication on increasingly deeper
levels, to establish interpersonal genuineness—with a gradually lessened need for
the defenses and maneuvers which get between people and keep them out of touch?
Interpersonally between therapist and patient, and intrapsychically within the patient, everything that occurs is utilized to get close to experience and to assist one to
stop interposing walls, screens and filters between what is happening and what one
allows oneself to know about the inner or the outer experience.

As a patient develops an inwardness and acquires a more open receptivity to
what he feels inside himself—both the particulars of what he finds and, perhaps
even more, the *process* of experiencing a less defended phenomenological state
toward what is—both tend to lift him toward self-discovery. The sense of adventure
in the process is rewarding, in the reinforcement-theory sense, and operates to spur
on increasing openness and further inroads into awareness. This is a yield in its own
right, whether or not symptoms abet (although we hope in the process they do), and
it is no trivial gain for one to increase in emotional richness, perceptiveness, and a
deepening down into what he is.

As therapists we soon learn how sheerly *experienceable* the inner world is, and on
how many levels. The repressed is active and alive under the surface. It presses
forward for expression. If what is dealt with by the clinician is always that part of
the material already available in preconscious derivatives and, in Fenichel's (1941)
words, "striving to break through to consciousness," then these elements
generally understand, to varying degrees, how to answer when questions are rightly
put.

Ruesch (1965) defines communication as the central ingredient in all forms of
mental healing. Attentive listening, occasionally offering support or direction, patient waiting for free association, focused interpreting, sensitive observation, casual
conversation, and even silence belong to the sphere of therapeutic communication.
To illustrate the multifaceted nature of what might ordinarily be taken to be the
simplest of these (silence) in the subtle dialectics between patient and therapist, we
need only recall Reich's (1933) dichotomy between a patient's "spiteful silence"
and his "anxious silence." To this categorization we can also add withdrawn
silences, thoughtful silences, awkward or uncomfortable silences, and even cozy
ones. Therapists are not alone in sensing the nuanced differences in silences. John
Browning, the concert pianist, states, "You can judge the audience by the quality of
silence when you're playing. There are all kinds of silence: electric, absorbed, or
one just barely not snoring."

With his patients, the therapist should thus hear their silences as well as their
thoughts. Silences in therapy are sometimes handled one way and sometimes
another. Silence is at times to be met with patient silence; at other times, by inquiry
or by interpretation; occasionally, by reflection or by support.

One patient repeatedly lapsed into an "obedient" silence; that is, she appeared to
be unable to talk until she "knew" what it was she thought the therapist wanted
her to talk about. The writer related her silence to the demands she had experienced at home by commenting that she seemed to feel in therapy as if she were a
child, and children "should not speak until spoken to." With another patient who
manifested a hostile silence, it was helpful to inquire, moving toward the

transference, *"Who* used to give you the silent treatment?" As it turned out, the patient was treating me as he wished to treat his father, who had earlier thus treated him. In a third patient, a silence appeared which reflected a state of being almost literally frozen in fear. What was offered therefore was reassurance and structure, rather than interpretation at this point. I told her, "It is all right to be silent, and it is all right to talk. When you want to be silent, I will be with you by being quiet. And when you think of something to say, I will be with you listening." This gave her two-way license and tended to soften her isolation and immobilization.

With another patient, a woman in group therapy who would not speak and who would turn her back toward the group, pick up reading matter to flip noisily through, or would scowl and otherwise engage in an "attention-getting" silence, the therapist partially reflected and partially reacted with, "You keep interrupting us with your silence." At other times, a patient will grow quite "comfortable" in silence, and this may be an index that a positive transference has settled in. When a patient moves into such a peaceful silence with "nothing to say," the therapist might then settle into the mellow mood, sharing it with the patient.

At other times the silence may be a clue to the fact that the patient is feeling something toward the therapist about which he is blocked. If the therapist has the feeling that this may be what is going on in the silence, and if asking the patient what he is thinking produces no breakthrough, one might then offer direction by suggesting that the patient talk about feelings toward the therapist.

But if the silences are complex, the other communications are infinitely more so. When therapy really gets under way, it does so when the patient has learned to, and dares to, let his mind rove. That starts it. Selected scenes are dipped out of the flow of the span of his life. He remembers first one thing long forgotten and then another; he thinks of something current that is similar; he goes back and forth between past and present and is alerted to relate things to the events and feelings of the therapy session as well.

In this sometimes bewildering array of sensations, memories and feelings, the therapist's synthesizing statements help to organize the chaotic impressions. The therapist accompanies the patient through a maze that leads, at the end, to greater understanding and functional mastery. Attempts are made to order the confusion and the multifarious impressions which those who are not too threatened see and know and feel. The therapist serves as guide, as someone who knows something about the direction. Hopefully, in part out of his own psychotherapeutic experience or analysis, he has found his own way and is now more familiar with the dark pathways. As a patient, upon completing analysis, said on a card accompanying his first published poem, "To my analyst who has found his way, and in helping others to find their way, finds with them hidden corners."

Before reaching this terminal phase, that patient who has entered an analytic experience has in the process become able to free-associate rather than only to talk more directedly and conventionally. This is a most important cause *and* effect of successful treatment. When he does so, the patient will move on. His pattern will shift from one course to another, and the larger absurdities will rearrange themselves. He will understand the previously-obscured factors in his coming to his present tangle at this point in his life. Some of the elements he will resolve; some he will learn to live with. Hopefully there will be more of the former than the latter. The experiences in therapy will be assimilated and become very much a part of his life. As Fisher (1964) describes it: "The patient tells what bothers him, his pains, despairs, fears, and why—in his mind—he came to have them. The analyst listens, wondering: 'What is it that he is blind to, such that he lives with so little sense and satisfaction?' To be sure, the patient's problems are illuminated and clarified, but is this the only purpose in therapy? Perhaps human difficulties are never really solved—short of death—but only become incorporated in larger frames of reference. If we faithfully study the details of his subjectivity, thereby brightening his awareness, the so-called problems often take care of themselves. In going back to the troublesome situation, he can now see what to do."

The poet-patient previously mentioned spoke of this "seeing" what to do in a fragment of a poem:

> "The blind see with eyes reversed what the seeing cannot see.
> The deaf hear with ears reversed what the hearing cannot hear.
> The sick become well and for having been sick feel what the always-well
>   cannot feel for having been never-sick."

In this process of assisting the patient thus to *see better* and to *see more,* therapy inevitably comes up against the outward mask which the patient earlier in life donned in self-defense against childhood threats, a defense once necessary when he was small, weak, dependent, and vulnerable, and when he existed as a pygmy in a world of giants. But if the entire nature of the threat was pushed underground to be locked in repression, it now fuels the neurotic defenses—neurotic because, while once necessary, they are still automatically retained against phantoms of the past transformed into distortions of current figures in the patient's life. Interpretive uncovering of the once-real threat, exposing it to the light of current evaluation, can enable the patient to see the inappropriateness of a defense employed today which was necessary against those who were once stronger or more in charge than he, figures upon whom he was, at the same time, totally dependent for love, if not his very survival.

As Richfield (1954) states, "The conscious personality cannot learn to handle a need of which it is unaware." Thus the patient, when his pattern of living is better understood, may make his future beginnings and endings more constructive ones. On a deeper and more vibrant level of his being, perhaps the basic measure of the patient's success in analysis is his ability to live with self-knowledge—effectively, actively and, in a more positive sense beyond the mere alleviation of symptoms, with delight.

REFERENCES

Evans, R., *Dialogue with Erik Erikson.* New York: Harper & Row, 1967.
Fenichel, O., *The psychoanalytic theory of neurosis.* New York: W. W. Norton & Co., 1945.
Fisher, K., Stanislavsky and psychotherapy. *J. Hum. Psychol.* 1964, 4, 130-138.
Freudenberger, H., Review for The Behavioral Science Book Service, 1967.
Holmes, J. C., *Nothing more to declare.* New York: E. P. Dutton & Co., 1966.
Huxley, J., The Crisis in man's destiny. *Playboy,* 1967, 14, 93-217.
Levi-Strauss, C., *The savage mind.* Chicago: University of Chicago Press, 1966.
London, P., *The modes and morals of psychotherapy.* New York: Basic Books, 1966.
Menaker, Esther and Wm., *Ego in evolution.* New York: Grove Press, 1965.
Menninger, K., *Theory of psychoanalytic technique.* New York: Basic Books, 1958.
Reich, W., *Character analysis* (1933), 3rd ed. New York: Orgone Institute Press, 1949.
Richfield, J., An analysis of the concept of insight. *Psychoanal. Quart.* 1954, 23, 390-408.
Ruesch, J., *Therapeutic communication.* New York: Norton, 1965.
Singer, E., *Key concepts in psychotherapy.* New York: Random House, 1965.

THE BASIC ISSUES

CHAPTER 3

Sources of Gain in Psychotherapy

NICHOLAS HOBBS, PH.D.

Dr. Nicholas Hobbs is one of American psychology's outstanding figures and is a Past-President of the American Psychological Association. He was recently appointed Provost of Vanderbilt University and, at the same time, Director of The John F. Kennedy Center for Research on Education and Human Development, George Peabody College. In 1954 he was Visiting Professor of Psychology at Harvard. In addition, he has served as Consulting Editor on the Journal of Counseling Psychology, *the* Journal of Abnormal Psychology, *and* Contemporary Psychology. *A Diplomate in Clinical Psychology of the American Board of Examiners in Professional Psychology, a member of the President's Panel on Mental Retardation, and the author of over 30 professional publications, Dr. Hobbs is listed in* American Men of Science *and in* Who's Who in America.*

Hence, when he takes a blast at the efficacy of interpretation and insight in psychotherapy, as he does below, they stand indicted. His paper, and the one which immediately follows his, constitute a dialogue around the crucial points on which he focuses.

This paper needs a subtitle. Let it be: "Five Hypotheses in Search of a Theory." One of the firmly rooted assumptions in psychotherapeutic practice is that the development of insight on the part of the client is both a major goal of the therapeutic endeavor, intrinsically worth promoting, and a primary means of achieving, step by step in the therapeutic process, the overall objective of more effective functioning. If a client can be helped to understand why he behaves as he does or to recognize and understand the origin of the neurotic tactics that continually defeat him, he will gradually abandon the inappropriate behavior and sustitute therefore more rational tactics in the management of his life. Increased self-understanding is regarded as inherently good and as a means to the end of good psychological health.

The promotion of insight is thus the tactic most heavily relied upon by most therapists who write about their work. Other strategies—the encouragement of catharsis, of abreaction, of transference—are valued to the extent that they lay the groundwork for the achievement of insight. The interpretation of behavior, perhaps the most widely used tactic of all, is aimed directly at the promotion of self-understanding. Furthermore, the achievement of insight by a client is a welcomed signal to the therapist that his efforts are paying off, and that his client, armed with new understanding, will gain a new measure of control over his life. All of this is a part of the folklore, both amateur and professional, of helping people by talking with them. But I have come seriously to doubt the presumed relationship between the achievement of insight and the achievement of more effective functioning.

This paper was presented as the Presidential Address to the Division of Clinical Psychology at the 1961 meeting of the American Psychological Association.

My doubts about the efficacy of insight as a change agent were first aroused a number of years ago while working in a clinic with a staff with diverse theoretical persuasions. In staff discussions of therapy cases, the occurrence of a significant insight on the part of a client was greeted with approval and satisfaction and with the expectation that there should follow some change for the better in the client's behavior. When anticipated changes did not occur, there was general discomfort. If the client persisted in behaving contrary to theory, as some obstinate clients did, we countered with a very useful, theory-preserving gambit. We said, "Well, it is obvious that the client did not have real insight. He may have had 'intellectual insight'," we said, "but he did not have 'emotional insight'." This was always an after-the-fact adjustment. We were not attracted to the obvious alternate interpretation, namely, that insight need not lead to changes in behavior. We were too much part of our culture, both general and professional, to question the time-honored relationship between self-understanding and effective functioning.

I began to wonder why we never examined the alternate explanation of the failure of insight to produce changes in behavior. Once jarred from the point of usual perspective on this issue, I began to see a number of arguments for an alternate explanation, namely, that insight may have nothing to do with behavior change at all, or is, at best, an event that may or may not occur as a result of more fundamental personality reorganizations. Here are some of the arguments:

Item 1. In interpretive therapies, great stress is placed on the exquisite timing of interpretations. The thought occurs that an interpretation may be acceptable to a client only after he has achieved sufficient self-reorganization for the interpretation no longer to be relevant. He can accept, but he no longer "needs," the interpretation.

Item 2. In play therapy with young children most therapists do not bother to try to develop insight. Rational formulations are adult fare, a consequence of the adult's addiction to words. Instead, therapists provide children concrete experiences in relationship with a particular kind of adult and get good results.

Item 3. The equipotentiality of diverse interpretations is a bothersome thing. It is quite apparent that therapists of different theoretical persuasions seem to promote different but equally effective insights. An Adlerian interpretation based on assumed relationships between organ inferiority and life style seems just as effective as a Freudian interpretation based on disjunctions among id, ego, and superego requirements. A Jungian interpretation based on the relationship between the individual and the cosmos seems as effective as an existential interpretation of the estrangement of man resulting from the subject-object dichotomy, currently described as an invention of Descartes. Or the therapist can get equally good results by making no interpretations at all, as Rogers has shown. All this suggests that the occurrence of an insight merely means that the client is catching on to the therapist's personal system for interpreting the world of behavior. The therapist does not have to be right; he mainly has to be convincing.

There are other arguments, but these will suffice. They do not, of course, disprove the accepted relationship between insight and change in behavior but they do suggest that one should give serious consideration to an alternate hypothesis. It seems to me that the traditional formulation of the relationship between self-understanding and effective behavior may be backwards. I suggest that insight is not a cause of change but a possible result of change. It is not a source of therapeutic gain but one among a number of possible consequences of gain. It may or may not occur in therapy; whether it does or not is inconsequential, since it reflects only the preferred modes of expression of the therapist or the client. It is not a change agent, it is a by-product of change. In a word, insight is an epiphenomenon.

The role of insight in therapeutic progress has probably escaped detailed analysis because we have no good definitions of what is meant by the term. Particularly are we lacking in criteria for differentiating between intellectual insight and emotional insight, if there are, indeed, two such entities, which I doubt.

The best definition that I have been able to come up with is this: Insight is manifested when a client makes a statement about himself that agrees with the therapist's notions of what is the matter with him. This is not a particularly useful formulation.

The acceptance of insight as the sovereign remedy for all neuroses represents both an unwarranted extrapolation from Freud's position and a failure to take into account the kinds of neuroses generated by Viennese life at the turn of the century and by American or European life today. Freud could not have been more explicit in insisting that his method worked best, if not solely, in cases of massive repression with accompanying conversion symptomatology. Contemporary culture often produces a kind of neurosis different from that described by Freud. Contemporary neuroses are frequently characterized not so much by repression and conversion as by an awful awareness and a merciless raw anxiety. The problem of the contemporary neurotic is not lack of insight but lack of a sense of identity, of purpose, of meaning in life. Because of a dehumanization of existence, as Kierkegaard pointed out, he has a sickness unto death. Indeed, in many of the people I work with there seems to be a substantial component of realism in their neurotic condition. Nothing can make a person more anxious, or more guilty, than an unrelentingly clear appreciation of the absurd and desperate condition of man today.

Let us suppose for the moment that insight plays no significant role in the therapeutic process. How then does change come about? What are the sources of gain in psychotherapy? My effort will be to identify sources of change that are common to all approaches to therapy, with the hope that the analysis will provide a theoretical matrix for more adequate quantitative and comparative studies of the therapeutic process. At present it seems to me that there are five major sources of gain, five kinds of experiences that are the wellsprings of personality reorganization. I might add that these experiences often occur in daily life quite apart from psychotherapy and are the sources of healthy integrations and reintegrations that develop throughout the life span. Psychotherapy is a unique life situation deliberately designed to make these five sources of gain available in an intense and usable form in a compressed time span, especially for those people who are unable, because of their neurotic tendencies, to avail themselves of the normal healing and nurturing experiences of life. Psychotherapy may thus be practiced, as indeed it is, by anyone who comes into intimate contact with a client on a professional basis.

The first source of gain is in the therapeutic relationship itself. This is a widely accepted notion, and I only wish to specify, which is seldom done, what it is about the relationship that has therapeutic impact. It is this: The client has a sustained experience of intimacy with another human being without getting hurt. He has an experience of contact, of engagement, of commitment. He learns directly and immediately, by concrete experience, that it is possible to risk being close to another, to be open and honest, to let things happen to his feelings in the presence of another, and indeed, even to go so far as to dare to include the therapist himself as an object of these feelings. The neurotic, on the basis of earlier attempts, at intimate relationships with important life persons, primarily his mother and father, has come to the deep-seated conviction that other people cannot be trusted, that it is terribly dangerous to open oneself up to them. This conviction may well have a very realistic basis: When he reached out to his parents he was rebuffed. When he made tentative, affective overtures to other important life persons, he got clobbered. On the basis of these hurtful experiences, he has adopted the tactic of alienation that is so characteristic of the neurotic. He may simply withdraw from significant human contacts. He may live and work in proximity with others, but let it be known that the relationship stops where his self begins. Or he may get engaged with others in intense relationships that should lead to intimacy but always with reservations, always on terms that guarantee that he is not really exposed. These are the counterfeit friendships and marriages of the neurotic. And in all this, of course, he will not even be intimate with himself; he cannot let himself feel how he actually feels about himself and others. Now I argue that human intimacy is necessary for human survival. Intimacy may be an instinctual, a biological requirement. But even if it is not a built-in requirement, the prolonged period of dependency of the human infant with its all but inevitable experience of some sustaining intimacy provides ample time to acquire, to learn a need to be close to others. The risking and handling of intimacy are learned by immediate experiencing; talking about intimacy, acquiring insight about intimacy, do not help much.

Now psychotherapy is a situation carefully designed to make it possible for a client to learn to be close to another person without getting hurt. For example, the therapist does not, or should not, punish the client's tentative and fearful efforts at being open and honest about his feelings. On the contrary, he is alert to and reinforces any reaching-out behavior. The therapist permits the client to use him to learn how to be intimate, but he does not make reciprocal demands of a personal character, such as those inevitably involved in friendship or marriage, for these would be too threatening to the client. The therapist may make formal demands but not personal ones. In this special accepting situation, where the ground rules are clear, the client dares to establish a fully honest relationship with another person, and finds it a tremendously reinforcing experience. He is encouraged on the basis of this concrete learning experience to risk more open relationships outside of therapy. Of course, he takes the chance of getting hurt again, as in childhood, but more likely than not he finds that others are responsive and that he is after all capable of richer, of more giving and more sustaining relationships with other people. This first source of gain lends itself readily to analysis in learning theory terms.

Now, source number two. Much of the time in psychotherapy is spent, or should be spent, in helping the client divest verbal and other symbols of their anxiety producing potential. Shaffer is the author of the rich declarative sentence: "Man is forever signalling to himself." It is man's ability to acquire, store, and manipulate symbols, and signal to himself in symbolic form, that makes him so distinctive, and so interesting. It also makes him uniquely susceptible to neurosis. Each of us has a tremendous store of symbols that are the residuals of experiences with which they were originally associated. In the domain of interpersonal relationships, some people have a collection of symbols that, for the most part, set off in them at the deepest and most pervasive somatic level feelings of well being, of comfort, of safety, of assurance. Other people, the ones we call neurotic, have a collection of symbols that set off in them, for the most part, feelings of anxiety and guilt or of somatic distress of specific or pervasive character. Actually, most of us have a mixed collection of distressing and sustaining symbols, and we call ourselves psychologically healthy if we have a clearly favorable algebraic balance of the positive and the negative. The negative symbols, associated with earlier life experiences of a hurtful nature, tend to stick tenaciously with us. In ordinary life circumstances we do not have an opportunity to learn new and more appropriate responses to them. Here is what seems to happen. A child suffers more than he can tolerate at the hands of his father. The concrete experiences get associated with specific symbols that are a product of this unique relationship and its attending circumstances. As an adult, even after his father has long been dead, experiences with authority figures evoke the symbols which evoke anxiety, guilt, hostility, or perhaps headaches, nausea, or other somatic reactions. Because of the distress that has been aroused, he retreats either literally or psychologically from the situation. His distress diminishes, thus reinforcing the avoidance of the authority relationship, and leaving the symbols as strong as ever. But authority cannot be avoided, and the cycle gets repeated over and over again. The crucial thing to note is that he never has an opportunity to learn new and more appropriate responses to the symbols that are evoking in him what we call neurotic behavior. The conditioned response cannot get extinguished.

The task of the therapist is not to help the client gain insight into the fact that he has trouble with authority figures because of his unfortunate experiences with his own father. This is far too abstract a formulation to be of help. He has got to be helped to identify and use comfortably the specific symbols that are elicited in him by authority figures. The symbols must be divested of their anxiety-producing potential.

At this point my communication problem becomes exceedingly difficult because there is no general way to identify or categorize these symbols. They are all highly personal, highly concrete, highly specific to the particular individual. And they have got to be talked about by the client in highly specific, hot, personal, intimate terms. The terms used must get as close as possible to the client's own idiosyncratic symbol system. A bright girl who had frequent attacks of nausea explained early in therapy that she feared she was homosexual and that she recognized the unsatisfactory character of her relationship with her mother, a fine insightful statement. Much later, after she was sure that it was safe to talk to the therapist using the same symbols that she used when talking to her most private self, she described in specific detail the experiences she felt had warped her relationship with her mother. At the end of the very difficult hour, she said, "This is the blackness that I have been trying to vomit."

The transference relationship is a third source of gain in psychotherapy. It also provides the clearest illustration of the differences between therapies which stress, respectively, the rational, abstract, and verbal, or the nonrational, concrete, and experiential components of the therapeutic process. Freud's discovery of the transference situation was a brilliant achievement. It made available to the therapist a most valuable instrument, comparable to the microscope or telescope in its clarifying powers. The essence of the situation is this: The client does not talk about his neurosis, he acts it out. His neurotic stratagems are no longer filtered through semantic screens; they are tried out in concrete, specific acts of hostility, overdependency, seduction, dissimulation, and so on. The therapist and the client are both immediately involved in the client's desperate and always self-defeating and yet so very human ploys and gambits.

In the Freudian prescription for the handling of transference one finds the great psychoanalytic paradox: The cure for unreason is reason. Freud gave us a twentieth-century discovery that unreasonable (i.e., neurotic) behavior is determined by specific life experiences, thousands of them probably, and that neurotic behavior is unconscious and preeminently nonrational in origin. He could have said that neurosis is a summary term describing an extensive matrix of conditioned responses built up in a lifetime of hurtful relationships with important life persons, hardened around an armature of assumed guilt. He might further have observed that no man by taking thought becomes neurotic. But for this twentieth-century diagnosis, Freud had a nineteenth-century prescription: Be rational. Transference represents the neurosis in microcosm; when transference appears it should be interpreted. As Fenichel so clearly instructs us, the client should be shown that he is behaving in an irrational manner.

Now I think it likely that this tactic will result in the client's learning that certain neurotic stratagems are not approved of, and they may well be abandoned in favor of other protective mechanisms. In the face of repeated interpretations, he may learn to repress particular transference symptoms. But nothing has been done about his need for these symptoms; his underlying distrust of himself and of other people remains untouched by the therapist's efforts to promote insight by interpreting the transference.

Transference develops when the client feels that the relationship with the therapist is becoming too dangerous, that he is losing control of the situation. He does not know how to handle the growing intimacy of the relationship without resorting to well established neurotic defenses. He does not need to be told that his tactics are inappropriate, that they are characteristic of his way of life, but he needs to learn through an immediate experience with another human being that the tactics are not necessary. Transference is best handled by providing the client with the kind of understanding and unqualified acceptance that have been so notably absent in his life. Transference stratagems disappear when the client has an opportunity to learn through concrete experience that it is possible to establish a simple, honest, open relationship with another person.

A fourth source of gain is available in those therapies which place the locus of control of the situation in the client rather than in the therapist. The client has hundreds of opportunities to practice decision making, to learn to be responsible for himself, to develop a concept of himself as a person capable of managing his own life. Here again, you will note the emphasis not on insight but on specific opportunities for the acquisition of new ways of behaving.

Before proceeding to examine a fifth source of gain which seems to be different in character from the four already mentioned, I should like to discuss briefly two possible explanations for our confident advocacy of insight as a primary change agent in psychotherapy.

Insight and understanding appeal to us as central mechanisms in therapy because of our strong general commitment to rationality in problem solving. As F. S. C.

Northrup has pointed out, western culture (in spite of its immense irrationalities) has a deeply ingrained rational component. For us, reason is a faith. From earliest childhood we are taught to apply rational principles to the solution of many kinds of problems. If our automobile breaks down, we do not ordinarily kick it, pray over it, or assume that its spirit has departed, as a person from a primitive culture might do. We first try to discover what is wrong and then make appropriate interventions to correct the difficulty. It is perhaps the very strength of our faith that has led to a curious short-circuiting in the domain of psychotherapy. Faced with a breakdown of personal functioning, we seem to assume that the development of understanding itself is a sufficient intervention to correct the difficulty. If a person can be helped to understand the origins and current manifestations of his neurotic behavior, particularly if he feels deeply while he is gaining this insight, the neurotic behavior should disappear. A good rational question is: Why should it disappear unless appropriate learning experiences follow?

Even if we do have a cultural bias regarding the importance of insight and understanding, our convictions would gradually be extinguished in the therapy situation if they were not occasionally reinforced. And they are. Insight sometimes does lead to changes in behavior—but not for the reasons commonly assumed. Insight is usually thought of as a freeing or releasing mechanism. I think it may actually operate through the facilitation of repression and the elimination of a particular symptom. A good example is provided by Dollard and Miller. A girl had a habit of thumbing rides with truck drivers at night and then being surprised when men "took advantage of her." The therapist pointed out to her what she was doing and she stopped doing it, thus seeming to validate the assumption of insight as a releasing influence. But Miller's conflict theory provides a better explanation of her behavior, I think. She could either give up hitch hiking or run the risk, as she would see it, of incurring the disappointment of her valued therapist. She might be expected to repress her hitchhiking symptom. But nothing would have been done about her neurotic need for affection.

The same insight-related mechanism may operate outside of therapy to change behavior through repression. A person who expresses his hostility through malicious gossiping reads in a newspaper column that if he gossips he will inevitably alienate all his friends. If this prospect arouses enough anxiety, he will feel much in conflict and may repress his tendency to gossip. But since he is as hostile as ever, he may now become sarcastic or learn to excel at bridge. Again nothing would have been done about his neurotic need to be hostile. It should be pointed out that the repression of some symptoms may have subsequent therapeutic benefits if the person is thereby brought into more intimate human relationships that are intrinsically healing in accordance with the four sources of gain already described. Some symptoms are better than others. The worst symptoms are those that engender most alienation from significant others, for this cuts the person off from the normal sources of therapeutic gain in daily living.

There is a fifth source of gain common to all psychotherapies that is qualitatively quite different from the four sources that have already been described. You may have noted in the preceding arguments not only a disavowal of the efficacy of insight as a change agent, but also the strong emphasis on specific and concrete opportunities for learning new ways of responding, new ways of relating to other people, and new ways of perceiving oneself. The stress is on immediate experience and specific behaviors. Throughout the discussion there is an implicit invitation to recast the analysis in terms of learning theory of a general reinforcement type. Now the fifth source of gain involves a different level of abstraction and can best be talked about in terms of cognitive process. I, of course, imply no disjunction between learning and cognition, but simply accept the fact that, at its current stage of development, psychology tends to use different constructs to describe these two aspects of human behavior.

All approaches to psychotherapy seem to have a more or less elaborated conception of the nature of man, which they, in essence, teach to the client. In doing so, they tie in with an ongoing process which is a unique and most exciting and engaging characteristic of man. Man constantly engages in building and repairing and extending and modifying cognitive structures that help him make personal sense of the world. The individual has got to have a cognitive house to live in to protect himself from the incomprehensibilities of existence as well as to provide some architecture for daily experiencing. He has to build defenses against the absurd in the human condition and at the same time find a scheme that will make possible reasonably accurate predictions of his own behavior and of the behavior of his wife, his boss, his professor, his physician, his neighbor, and of the policeman on the corner. He must adopt or invent a personal cosmology. When he invests this cosmology with passion, we may call it his personal mystique.

There are many available cosmologies for ordering the universe and increasing predictive efficiency in daily life. One of the first of these was provided by Pythagoras, some 3,000 years ago. Contemporary religious systems seem useful in reducing uncertainty in at least some realms of experience, and for some people. Religions with established dogmas, elaborated rituals, and extensive use of personification appear to have widest appeal, as one would expect. Those with almost no formal doctrine probably appeal most to people who have at hand alternate systems for construing the world. Psychoanalysis provides a cognitive structure of remarkable cogency. Its range of applicability is not cosmic but mundane, which is one source of its appeal among pragmatic people. Its metaphor is engaging; its extensive use of reification simplifies matters, but not too much; its formulation of behavior dynamics is occasionally useful in predicting ones' own behavior and the behavior of others. On the other hand, existential therapies would seem to be most acceptable to people who have come to suspect all institutionalized solutions (such as psychoanalysis) to the problem of meaning. Albert Ellis' rational therapy seems eminently suited to his clientele. I would guess that he works largely with bright, articulate, nonreligious, and reasonably well-educated but not too disenchanted people who find the process and the model of rational analysis appealing and convincing. Client-centered therapy probably works best with clients who already have well developed but conflicting cognitive structures; they do not need to be taught a system for bringing order into their lives, but rather need to be helped to discover which system makes sense and feels right to them. George Kelly's fixed role therapy is, of course, the most forthright and charming method for providing a client with a cognitive structure for construing his world.

I think it possible to identify some criteria for assessing the adequacy of a personal cosmology and thus provide a therapist with some guidelines for dealing with the cognitive structures of the individual. Above all a person's cosmology must be convincing to him; when doubt occurs, anxiety mounts. Second, it should overlap reasonably well with the cosmologies of the people with whom he associates. If a person adopts a too divergent cosmology, he runs the risk of being declared psychotic and incarcerated. Then it should be perceived by the individual as internally consistent—or relatively so. When there is too great a discrepancy between self and self-ideal, for example, discontent ensues. It should contain, on the other hand, some dissonances of either internal or external origin. With a bit of dissonance, the individual will work to strengthen his major propositions about himself and his world. In addition, it should bring him into more intimate relationships with other people, for without such sustenance the spirit withers. Finally, it should have built in requirements for revision, for to live is to change, and to remain static is to die.

The individual seeks psychotherapy (or some other source of cognitive control) when his cosmology, his personal system for imposing order on the world, breaks down to an alarming degree. With increasing anxiety, order must be restored.

There are two summary points that I would make about this fifth source of gain in psychotherapy: (a) Man by his nature is going to erect cognitive structures to increase his feeling of control over his destiny, and (b) there is no way of establishing the validity of a particular order-giving structure independently of the individual who is going to use it. The concept of insight can have meaning only as a part of the process of elaborating on some particular system for interpreting events. There are no true insights, only more or less useful ones.

All systems of psychotherapy involve in varying measures the five kinds of experiences that I have described. Their effectiveness will depend on the extent to which they provide an opportunity for the client to experience closeness to another human being without getting hurt, to divest symbols associated with traumatic experiences of their anxiety producing potential, to use the transference situation to learn not to need neurotic distortions, to practice being responsible for himself, and to clarify an old or learn a new cognitive system for ordering his world. I am not prepared at the moment to assign beta weights to these several functions.

CHAPTER 4

Interpretations: Where and When

EMANUEL F. HAMMER, PH.D.

This book was, in actuality, stimulated by the jolting run-in the utility of interpretative interventions has experienced with Nicholas Hobbs in his paper which precedes.

Hobbs' charges are several:

1. He points out that interpretation is perhaps the most widely used therapeutic tactic and is one aimed directly at the promotion of self-understanding. He further points out that the achievement of insight by a client is taken as an index that, armed with new understanding, this client may be gaining an increased measure of control over his life. Hobbs then, however, refers to this as the "folklore" of helping people, and asserts, "I have come seriously to doubt the presumed relationship between the achievement of insight and more effective functioning."

2. "The therapist does not have to be right; he mainly has to be convincing. . . . There are no true insights, only more or less useful ones." Thus, Hobbs also asserts that there is no correlation between the validity of insight and its relative usefulness.

3. Hobbs takes the view that the traditional formulation of the relationship between self-understanding and effective behavior "may be backwards." He suggests that insight is not a cause of change, but a possible result of change. Insight "may or may not occur in therapy; whether it does or not is inconsequential . . . insight is an epiphenomenon."

4. He sees interpretation as serving, at best, merely to chase one symptom away, only to be replaced by another.

5. Hobbs ends with the challenge that the technique of therapy will remain inconsequential until we "recast . . . analysis in terms of learning theory of a general reinforcement type."

Hobbs' position, frank and forthright, cuts to the bone. It raises questions of such basic importance to both *technique* and to the *theory of technique* that we must react to it as setting the stage for, and inviting, a dialogue of exchange of experience.

His paper is certainly one which makes an incisive contribution, and his five factors of what cause change are apt, sensitive and rather basic in terms of the therapy process. My only quarrel with his view is that my experience suggests that the five variables he proposes operate in addition to—not, as Hobbs maintains, instead of—the gains attributable to the bringing about of insight.

The issues raised provide pivotal points for some of what follows, and certainly his dismissal of the role of insight requires a confrontation. Since the other chapters will be addressing the topic of the use of interpretations in general, I would like here to answer Hobbs' charges specifically. Agreeing with his long-needed deemphasis of the role of insight in successful therapy, I cannot go along with the sweeping totality of his view which approaches, and falls just short of, giving insight the value of ir-relevancy. Hobbs even speaks of the need for a "disavowal of the efficacy of insight as a change agent."

There are a number of specific answers to this basic indictment of the interpretive technique:

1. In psychotherapy, interpretation can make a basic contribution to the task of *stripping away the self-deceptive function of the symptom*. This, in its own right, is at times an important step in the patient's beginning to get better. Reich's con-tribution to the area of interpreting the character armor stands as one monumental illustration.

For example, I remember one particular patient, a college teacher who was refer-red to me because of ineffectiveness in his work, uncertainty and hesitancy in front of the class, and sexual troubles in his marriage. In beginning to work with him, I gradually became aware of a certain characteristic of his. He was always cordial and pleasant and would seemingly agree with things I said by beginning each of his replies with "Yes." He would then finish the sentence in such a way as to express some contradiction of what had been said to him. It was as if he were not capable of directly saying "No," as if he could not openly oppose others. His manner was mild, friendly and ingratiating. His relentless affability, which at first puzzled me, was now understood as a front he was frightened to drop. In situations which would have angered or saddened others, as when criticized by the Dean, the Department Chairman, or his wife, he merely became more kindly.

The interpretive approach focused upon this mask he employed to cover the com-ponents of rage and fury within. This gradually produced a change, initially a feeble effort on the patient's part at assertion. His first efforts in this direction concerned a request for a change in appointment time, but for once his interaction was unac-companied by facial muscles frozen in a smile of amiability. It was, of course, the success he experienced at *living* out his efforts at assertion, initially tentative and eventually more confident, which allowed him to learn that his character armor was less necessary than he had been automatically assuming. Finding this true first in therapy, he eventually put it to the test in the outside world. There, certainly, oc-curred the more important experience that the characterologic defenses once necessary in handling his parents were not necessary in handling his contemporary relationships with others.

It was, however, the *interpretation* that the patient had to be continually docile in appearing to accept interpretations which first allowed him to dare an attempt to be more direct. It was an interpretive approach which focused and began the resolution of his misperception of disagreement as a forbidden aggressive act.

Similarly, interpretations aimed at the character armor of intense modesty behind which lies conceit, interpretation of an outer role of innocuousness and in-effectuality as a protective disguise for secret ambitiousness, interpretive uncovering of exaggerated humbleness and humility used to deny underlying arrogance, of fears masquerading as aggressions and vice versa, of the virtue of powerlessness, of the power of helplessness, of the illumination of a patient's cloak of bristling an-tagonism employed to ward off people and the dangers of experiencing closeness with others—all are examples wherein the experience which enables people to change is initially launched by the interpretive dissolving of the patient's self-decep-tive outer role.

2. Interpretation may be used to shed light on not only the defenses, but also those submerged wishes under the defenses which are irrationally forbidden and which produce guilt and tension within. Once these layered-over needs are uncovered and then accepted by the therapist, the patient—identifying with the therapist as a more tolerant superego figure—gains in self-acceptance and in reduced feelings of inner dirtiness and sinfulness. By means of the process of the patient's identifying with him, the *interpreting therapist endorses the patient's ego as liberator.*

3. If interpretations are made directly from the living content experienced, the understanding attained has, to use Symonds' phrase, "the feel or ring of reality." Something inside the patient clicks, and regardless of his outer response there is an "Oh yes" in a secret place. The combined free-associative and interpretive connecting of the various affective components works toward a synthesis. This integration, at the same time, *orders and illuminates one's sense of self.*

4. It is frequently the *blend* of sparingly used interpretation by the therapist and his interaction with the patient which sets the latter an example of, as well as more directly unites in him, the *capacity to feel and think as one, instead of separately.* E. M. Forster stated it as to "live in fragments no longer."

5. We might also remember that not all emotional states are genuine. Affect may at times be employed as a diversionary tactic, as in hystrionic weeping, mock anger, or exaggerated woe. One 30-year-old woman was going through session after session of inflated agony over what it was like to live at home with her parents. The interpretation, that she had to demonstrate that the situation was utterly intolerable before she felt she had the right to raise the issue of moving out, put her in touch with her underlying wish. Interpretations and the glimmer of insight which may follow can be *a way of cutting through emotional pyrotechnics.*

6. Interpretations are also helpful in *linking up dissociated actions which have become automatic.* A social worker in analysis had, as a child, been harshly punished for saying "shit" in front of his father. He could easily say "shit" today, but the analyst noticed that he couldn't pronounce the *sh* sound correctly when it appeared in the middle of words. While the client's *idealized image,* in part influenced by his professional training, required that he say such words as "shit" naturally, the inhibition went underground and expressed itself surreptitiously, outside of awareness.[1] *Interpretation brings dissociative material into awareness and places it at the control of the ego.*

7. The introduction of rational interpretation into the treatment interaction frequently serves another end. It opens the door to the patient through which he must then, of course, dare to venture through to the emotional experience. Interpretation and understanding intrigue a patient (as understanding does people generally); they beckon him to try an otherwise avoided experience, to find out emotionally (in his guts, where it really counts) the truth or falsity of the rational view proposed. The interpretation, based on therapeutic insight, provides support and reassurance to a patient in his effort to try an experience, to dare the awesome. *A known fear is easier to tackle than is some nameless anxiety.*

The interpretation may thus at times facilitate a new kind of human experience. A young man, living at home with his parents, expressed a continuing inhibition about telling me something in therapy. My interpretation that perhaps he feared that

---

[1]While the example is trivial, the principle is significant.

I would violate his confidence and tell his father, as his mother had once done after promising to respect a secret he had (as a child) confided to her, helped him over the threshold. Seeing what he feared, and that what he feared seemed irrational, allowed him to put the fear to the test.

It was the subsequent months, following his daring to confide the "secret" to me, which was, of course, the therapeutic experience. As his trust was kept, he learned from the experiment which the interpretation helped him inaugurate that not all people would let him down, and that he did not have to defend himself unselectively and continuously against openness to others. The yield of this lesson had to be rewon many times; but this was the beginning, and the interpretation was the beginning of the beginning. Interpretation may at times lead to daring, daring to trust, and trust to lessened defensiveness and more relaxed interpersonal comfort.

8. It might also be observed that among the symptomatic defenses it is (at first glance perhaps somewhat paradoxically) rationalization for which rational understanding is particularly helpful. To peer interpretively through the "good" reasons in which he cloaks his actions allows the patient to address himself to the "real" reasons; *seeing beyond the secondary reasons he puts forward can help a patient deal with, and more constructively handle, the primary situation.*

9. Although isolated adult patients can only be reached by an emotional encounter, nondetached adolescents and young adults, particularly undergraduate and graduate students, *cathect ideas.* They are frequently excited by understanding, enthused by illumination, and hence *emotionally* responsive to interpretations.

10. There is another place in which awareness has decided value: *short-term therapy.* We have only to recall what the technique of therapy has here profited from Alexander and French. Here, of necessity, focus must be shifted to the ego resources that the client possesses.

11. Self-understanding, sometimes if only on a cognitive level, provides comfort to the acutely-anxious patient. I think particularly of one adolescent boy who was experiencing all sorts of seemingly bizarre symptoms and feelings. In this case interpretations went a long way toward making sense out of his experienced chaos. Supplying understanding of his behavior added structure and support to his shaky view of himself, reduced his secondary anxiety, and eased things considerably. *It made sense of his irrational world.* To be helped to see the underlying reasons for his actions enabled him to feel less "crazy" and to experience himself as reasonable, if not rational.

SUMMARY

Thus, while of admittedly less value than has been traditionally maintained, interpretations *are* of value (a) in the task of stripping away the self-deceptive function of symptoms; (b) in opening a door to an experience in therapy or outside it; (c) in endorsing the patient's ego as liberator (via the patient's identifying with the interpreting therapist); (d) in supporting a patient's attempt to dare to put false, old assumptions and realistic new ones to the experiential test; (e) in handling rationalization; (f) in enabling a shift to a constructive handling of real issues rather than screen ones; (g) in dealing with bright adolescents and young adults; (h) in uniting the feeling and thinking levels; (i) in cutting through emotional pyrotechnics; (j) in reintegrating dissociated areas; (k) in short-term therapy in which the goal is frequently the more limited one of managing more than resolving symptoms; (l) in shifting ego-syntonic symptoms out to an ego-alien position;[1] and (m) in dealing with acute borderline states in helping the patient make sense of his chaotic, seemingly irrational world.

Now, none of this is to imply that interpretation is the principal ingredient of therapy. The more basic factor is the therapist's capacity to be "with it," to be with the patient at the unfolding feelings of his inner world: sharing his understanding in a way the patient can hear, at a time when the patient can listen; paying attention, caring, and being there himself. But a sensitive, perceptive, accurate interpretation, on a level to which the patient can resonate, is one way of demonstrating this.

James Baldwin said something which pertains to the therapist's role, as it does to human nature in general: "To get, you have to give, and giving, baby, isn't a day at a bargain counter but a total risk of who you are and what you think you want to be." Freud was touching one extension of the same insight when he offered us his early injunction that the analyst would have to tolerate learning from his patients a measure of truth about himself. This is what is decisive, what is above and beyond the question of interpretation.

One maxim emerges as therapist and client, collaborators in the human growth process, participate in that curious relationship our field has shaped! The best psychoanalyst, I think, is not the most brilliant interpreter; like the good novelist or poet, he is one who sees few wounds which he does not also know as his own.

REFERENCE

Hobbs, N., Sources of gain in psychotherapy. *Amer. Psychol.* 1962, 17, 741-747.

---

[1]For an interesting illustration of this goal of interpretation, the reader is referred to the example at the end of the section, "The Ego-Alien and the Ego-Syntonic," in Chapter 15, "Interpretation and the Therapeutic Act."

SPECIFIC DIMENSIONS AND TECHNIQUES

CHAPTER 5

Interpretation in the Early Phase of Therapy

Max Cooper, Ph.D.

Max Cooper is a Fellow of the American Psychological Association and Diplomate in Clinical Psychology of the American Board of Examiners in Professional Psychology. After obtaining his bachelor's degree from City College in 1931 and his master's degree from that institution in 1934, Dr. Cooper was granted the Ph.D. degree by New York University in 1944. At the present time he is Associate Clinical Director of the Fifth Avenue Center for Counseling and Psychotherapy, and Secretary of the Metropolitan Institute for Psychoanalytic Studies. In the past Dr. Cooper has organized, directed and supervised several training and service programs in psychology for New York State and the Veterans Administration. He has published reports of research and theoretical discussions in the areas of individual and group psychotherapy and the relationship between personality and psychogenic and psychosomatic factors. Dr. Cooper has been engaged in the practice of clinical psychology for the past 30 years and has conducted a private practice for the past 15 as a psychotherapist, psychoanalyst and supervisor of psychotherapy.

Dr. Cooper here provides a discussion, to use a chess term, of the "opening" phase. Consideration is given to the structuring of the relationship, the contract between patient and therapist, and issues of interpretive technique during the early sessions of the therapeutic encounter.

In psychoanalysis or in various forms of psychoanalytic therapy (and for that matter in most methods of psychotherapy), the therapist's interpretations are the major instruments or avenues for leading the patient to adequate insights into his neurotic conflicts. It is generally assumed that the analyst will make his interpretations in an atmosphere of impartiality; that the goal of the analysis is the ultimate resolution by the patient himself of his neurosis and the achievement of certain permanent changes in the patient's pattern of behavior and life. There would, of course, also be certain associated changes in the patient's ego, id and superego attitudes which, in turn, free and extend the power of the ego. The structure and content of the analytic relationship should, for the most part, involve free verbalization by the patient without guidance or direction from the analyst. The analyst's interpretations should be directed primarily toward enabling insight into the influence past conflicts have had on the current life-pattern of the patient and toward insight into his needs in his day-to-day living, as well as future aspirations related to such needs.

Under the heading of "interpretation," the writer broadly includes all statements or comments made by the analyst to the patient for the purpose of clarifying or enabling recognition of the overt or covert meaning of behavior, thought or feeling at any particular time, or statements for the purpose of intervention.

In the classic analytic method the analyst is primarily silent in the early stages of the relationship and rarely offers any comment or interpretation except in the few instances when there is crisis involving the life or health of the patient. The rule of abstinence was long paramount in the classic method. However, more recent approaches and developments in psychoanalytic methods have become more liberal and with remarkably good results for progress of the analytic relationship.

There is here no quarrel or dispute with the basic tenet of analytic therapies that the role of the analyst must be established, as early as possible, as that of the impartial observer rather than the omnipotent or authoritative figure which most patients tend to view him at the beginning. Frequently, the rule of relative abstinence of comments by the analyst can be practiced, as in the case of the well-motivated patient who is eager to begin the analytic work; here, certainly, the analyst's silence is of value in creating the atmosphere conducive to free association. But in the case of the poorly-motivated patient or the one suffering from severe symptoms, the therapist should be more active and make whatever early interpretations might be related to the specific material presented by the patient—for example, as in the case of the low self-esteem of the depressed patient.

Let us now look for a moment at the patient who has completed the first series of visits. The analyst may have by now determined that the patient is suitable for analytic therapy and is reasonably certain that he is himself comfortable with the patient and does not anticipate any unusual countertransference reaction which could interfere with the analytic work.

One of the first tasks facing the patient and analyst involves the clarification of what the patient seeks from the analytic relationship. Most patients who come to therapy are hoping to find in the analyst the oracle or the omnipotent figure who will guide and direct them through life or relieve their symptoms promptly. The patient has usually been exposed to extensive therapeutic efforts, at the hands of various practitioners, involving drugs and superficial reassurances to relieve his symptoms and anxiety. Let us also remember that it is very likely that the patient has gone through a long period, perhaps years, of self-debate as well as intense suffering prior to coming to the therapist. The patient is often in a state of depression or panic and has finally gathered the courage to acknowledge to himself his need for help. It is usually reassuring to the patient at this point when the analyst demonstrates his role as the observer rather than the authority, parent or judge the patient had anticipated.

The analyst must also at this time explain the importance of free association and verbal interaction, and interpret the patient's skepticism concerning such methods, especially where he seeks *prompt* relief from his symptoms. For example, the patient who comes to therapy with a long history of somatic symptoms will inevitably present doubt about a verbal technique. "How is talking going to relieve the pain in my belly?" he is likely to ask. Some blend of interpretation and reassurance on the part of the analyst is important at this juncture. It is at this point that the analyst can, with good result, interpret the patient's fears and doubts as to the analyst's competence. The analyst would, of course, reserve for a later occasion any attempt to interpret the basic meaning of the patient's symptom. It is often such interpretive intervention by the analyst which uncovers the patient's initial anxiety in associating freely as being linked to his fear of rejection by the authority figure involved in the etiology of the patient's neurosis.

Another problem arising early in the analysis has to do with the structure of the relationship between patient and analyst with respect to appointments, lateness, cancellations, and fees. The analyst will again be called upon to make the interpretations, where appropriate, of the hostile feelings which generally appear in relation to these matters and which the patient may repress or act out in various forms. For the most part they are designed by the patient (usually on an unconscious covert level, but occasionally overtly) to test the analyst's interest and concern and the patient's fear of rejection by the analyst. If the analysis is to move ahead, the analyst cannot overlook handling these behavior manifestations of the patient.

It is sometimes helpful to describe the analytic relationship to the patient as a type of contract in which it is agreed that the analyst will provide his attention, time (usually 45 minutes), and office to the patient at a certain time, day and frequency. The patient, on the other hand, agrees to pay the analyst a sum of money and to utilize the time as his own and as he sees fit (within certain limits and rules which are set by the analyst and to which the patient acquiesces). This usually simplifies matters when the patient is silent, refuses to lie on the couch, comes late for or cancels his appointments, or otherwise acts out in therapy. It also provides the analyst with frequent opportunities to interpret the patient's fears of rejection or the patient's attempts to test the limits in the early stages of the analysis. Frequently, in the early phases, the patient will become hostile and verbalize his feelings in relation to the difficulty in obtaining early relief of his symptoms. Here again it is valuable for the analyst to interpret either the patient's wish for the omnipotence of the analyst or the related need.

I am sure most of us are familiar with the analytic patient who after five to ten sessions announces that he feels so much better that he doesn't any longer feel the need for continuing the analysis. This is often described as a "flight into health." Frequently, however, there is some basis in reality for such feeling on the patient's part, and then the analyst finds himself in a difficult situation. Or the patient may make a similar announcement and realistically give as his reason financial difficulties in paying the agreed fee. The interpretation of the resistance mechanism must be utilized in spite of the early stage of the analysis, since to delay will lose the patient his chance at more fundamental gains. The interpretations made by the analyst in the early stages of analysis may often also produce a favorable result even on those occasions when the patient may terminate prematurely. In such cases the patient often resumes the analysis (perhaps not with the original analyst) and then goes on to a more adequate result.

In many cases, often during the first or second interview, the patient (either because he has read or heard of dream analysis or because he is sufficiently motivated) will describe a dream he has recalled. Usually the dream is replete with dynamic material, and the alert therapist will often get from it a clear picture of the dynamics. But what is he to do with it? Certainly the patient is not ready for dream work, and even if the analyst understands the material being communicated to him via the dream, his interpretation of the dream to the patient will accomplish very little in the way of insight for the patient. Nevertheless, there is much use to be made of the dream when so presented. In the first place, it provides the therapist (since it usually recapitulates the patient's neurosis) with valuable diagnostic information. He may then utilize the dream as a basis for reassuring the patient—e.g., as to his ego strength and the probability of a good result from the analysis. He might even go so far as to make certain interpretations of the patient's personality structure based on the dream material—e.g., that the patient has a strong need for success or is hampered by low self-esteem.

There are instances in which the analyst might feel that early interpretation would be of significant value in clarifying the relationship or in reassuring the patient—e.g., when the analyst in response to a hostile comment from the patient interprets the comment and also indicates the value of such behavior on the patient's part in clarifying the role of the analyst. That the latter does not assume a punitive or judgmental role in therapy, is common, especially when we consider that in the beginning the patient is expected to confide the most intimate details of his past and present life to a comparative stranger. The task is a difficult one for every one entering analysis, and the analyst should utilize every opportunity to interpret this state to the patient.

We are familiar, also, with the analytic patient who, after three or four sessions, will endeavor to engage the analyst in a discussion of the oedipus complex, ego, id, libido, superego, etc. He most likely has come across these terms in books or in a lecture or course. Here the rule of abstinence is usually effective. But the questions might also provide a suitable opportunity to interpret the patient's need to make a test of the analyst's competence, or to invite inquiry into what makes the patient ask and as to whether the particular complex asked about is one he wonders about in himself. This may also be the time to urge upon the patient the importance of avoiding books and technical literature which deal with psychoanalysis.

Then there is the complication of the patient who happens to be taking a course in psychology, in which case he is bound to come across textbook materials and become involved in classroom discussions concerning psychoanalytic theory and psychotherapy techniques. Should the analyst advise the patient to drop the course lest it interfere with his analytic work? Should the role of the analyst become that of the authority figure who orders and directs, or should the problem be left to the patient's own exploration and decision? Experience indicates that the latter is usually the preferred method. If the patient then brings into the analytic work some theoretical concept or term, the analyst remains in a favorable position to interpret the behavior for what it is: whether as a test of the analyst, or as an attempt to view his analyst as better than the one some friend or relative might be seeing. The significance of the resistance mechanism in these situations must also be considered and, if perceived as present, interpreted to the patient. Does the patient wish the analyst to assume the role of teacher and provide a course in psychoanalysis instead of making the patient work on his conflicts?

To conclude, the use of interpretation in the early stages of psychotherapy and psychoanalysis can be of major effectiveness in establishing the roles of patient and therapist. The appropriate use of the rule of abstinence and silence cannot be evaded in most analytic work situations, but there are many instances which constitute an exception, even in the early stages of therapy. In such instances the analyst would do better to make an appropriate interpretation, or to utilize intervention and confrontation, all of which often enhance the attainment of the goals the patient has set for himself in the work of the analysis.

CHAPTER 6

Interpretive Technique: A Primer

EMANUEL F. HAMMER, PH.D.

This particular chapter is written primarily for the beginning therapist. It may, at the same time, be of interest to his supervisor as a summary of those principles which tend to come up frequently for discussion in control or supervisory work. A marshalling and discussion of the basic principles below pertain to complications which, while rudimentary to the experienced therapist, loom as emanating from a befuddling and unstructured field of uncertainties into which the beginner must move.

> TO STUDY THE PHENOMENA OF DISEASE WITH-
> OUT BOOKS IS TO SAIL AN UNCHARTED SEA,
> WHILE TO STUDY BOOKS WITHOUT PATIENTS
> IS NOT TO GO TO SEA AT ALL.
>
> —Sir William Osler

On one level, interpretations—whether of resistance, of transference, or of context—relate to that which the patient is unaware of, and are thus in the service of eventually expanding consciousness. Interpretations, experience suggests, are more effective if based on an understanding of questions of level or depth, of timing, and of manner or style of phrasing.

DEPTH AND TIMING OF INTERPRETATION

In terms of depth, there is more or less agreement that the surface of the unconscious is the level to be sought (Bullard, 1959; Fenichel, 1953; French, 1958; Freud, 1924; Fromm-Reichmann, 1950; Hammer, 1968; Horney, 1933; Levy, 1963; Loewenstein, 1957; Menninger, 1958; Nydes, 1968; Reik, 1949; Strachey, 1934; Wolberg, 1966). One communicates to the patient what the patient is *almost* ready to see for himself, that which is just outside awareness. This allows an approach toward the optimal balance between the considerations of (1) time-saving provided by short cuts, and (2) minimal stirring up of greater resistance and defense. Above and beyond the factor of time-saving, interpretations make a more decisive contribution in those instances in which, without the initial illumination by the therapist, some patients would not find the awareness breaking through at all.

Dollard and Miller (1950) also observe that interpretations are best when of material below the surface, but yet not too deep. "The *time* to make an interpretation is when the behavior in question is occurring, when the patient is unlikely to see the point for himself, but when he is near enough to it so that undue fear will not be aroused" (p. 402). Thus, by drawing the near, but unseen, closer to its ultimate elucidation, we put within the patient's grasp that which is just beyond it.

Freud (1913) early suggested that important interpretations should not be made until the patient is almost ready, of his own accord, to understand that which the analyst is about to interpret to him. Both Horney (1933) and Reik (1949) in-

31

dependently have arrived at an obstetrical analogy. They advise that the therapist interpret the thoughts and wishes that are almost ready to emerge, to be born to consciousness. French (1958), too, speaks of dealing interpretively with that "just below the surface of consciousness." Colby's (1951) analogy is: "Like pushing a playground swing at the height of the arc for optimum momentum, the best-timed interpretations are given when the patient, already close to it himself, requires only a nudge to help him see the hitherto unseen." Fenichel (1953) advises that the analyst focus upon that which the patient is barely aware of "and *just a little bit more.*" In terms of timing, then, there is general agreement that the therapist would do well not to precede the patient by more than a half-step, and thus offer understanding at a time when the patient can listen.

INTERPRETATION OF RESISTANCE

Another guiding principle is to focus on resistances before content. Since resistances hinder the patient from assimilating other types of interpretation, any content interpretation will only be defended against by the resistance maneuvers employed. Thus, until the type of resistance is illuminated and resolved, there is little point in offering other types of interpretive interventions with this obstacle in the way. The patient may defend himself by immediate denial of any interpretive clue offered him, without giving it a consideration. To offer an opposite example, he may submissively concur just as automatically without really weighing the matter and inwardly exploring the interpreted possibility. Hence, whatever his manner of deflecting interpretations, it must be dealt with before content can be addressed.

It is Reich's (1933) contribution in the area of character analysis which became the foundation of the theory and the practice of later interpretation of resistance. We can still profit today from the general approach he formulated three and a half decades ago. In approaching from the resistance side, we attempt, first, to make it clear to the patient that he is warding off something; next, how he is doing it; and finally, we engage him in the question, "Against what is the defense directed?"

FREQUENCY OF INTERPRETATION

Another clue is that interpretations are to be used sparingly. The inexperienced therapist is usually sufficiently trained so that his difficulty is not apt to be one of not perceiving the meaning behind some material the patient presents. His difficulty is more likely to be one of managing his impulse to interpret to the patient as soon as something is sensed. Questions, too, should not be too numerous, particularly in the initial sessions when they are prone to be more frequent. Their infrequency is recommended in order to avoid dampening the patient's spontaneity or taking out of his hands the initiative for an appropriate degree of self-direction.

In response to his feeling of inexperience, youthful appearance, or general insecurity, the beginner sometimes grows a mustache or beard, begins to smoke a pipe, or tries too hard to be helpful. The danger in this latter instance is one of the therapist employing compensation to demonstrate his capability, frequently by over activity in questioning or interpreting. Too-frequent interpretation runs the risk of heightening the patient's resistances, of making the process an intellectual one, of inculcating passivity, of infantalizing the patient, or of leaving him feeling confused, inundated, drained, or with intuition dulled. Levy (1963) points out that every interpretation involves a suggested exchange of the therapist's point of view for that of the patient. Therefore, the interpretation usually encompasses a challenge to the validity of the patient's viewpoint. Too-frequent interpretation hence may cause the patient to protect himself by heightened resistance, or else to panic as if "on a sea of shifting sands" (p. 333). Ideally, interpretations are a cooperative venture; and to the degree to which this ideal is approached, to that degree is threat softened.

STYLE OF INTERPRETATION

Next, it is the therapist's purpose to share his awareness in a form the patient can hear (see also Chapter 22). The manner of phrasing interpretations is a question of style, a question of how something is put, and of the meaning of that *how*. We usually pay more attention to the content of an interpretation than to its manner. The "style," however, is a psychological factor of influence in its own right. It supplies both verbal and affective texture. The therapist learns the substance to interpret to his patients long before he learns the *way* to put it, the technique of shaping a careful, usable interpretation. Levy (1963) speaks of style as the existence of a "personal element . . . which may, in the final analysis differentiate between the successful and the unsuccessful, the mediocre and the brilliant . . . and may often count for as much as, if not more than, content in making the difference."

Style, however, is not only, in part, a function of one's personality, but even at times of one's transient mood: exuberant or dampened, playful or sombre, energetic or passive, whimsical or matter-of-fact, expansive or constricted. In constructing the therapeutic relationship, the therapist (even *if* on theoretical ground he feels he should not) inevitably draws on his way of being, his personality and his mood, and his particular method of making relationships work; in so doing, he endows the relationship with some tone of consequence. In this regard, we will be particularly interested in Freud's comment regarding the therapist's personal involvement when he writes that the therapist should "not entirely give up one's personal note" (Meng and Freud, F., 1964).

Within the scope allowed by both one's personality and by one's mood, there is a segment within this range where one may *elect* to function, where one may call forth something which exists within, where one can give license to the emergence of one or another component. Each therapist shapes his own style from the interaction of *his* personality with *his* experience. Are there, however, any common denominators left when experiences are pooled and the individualistic elements subtracted? Are there any guidelines to be distilled, even in terms of style, which if they cannot quite be "taught," can at least be passed on as time-saving "hints" to those who have the particular *potentials* themselves for one or another style? One might think there are. If an art can't exactly be taught, at least a direction can be pointed for those who *can* follow.

Style, as indicated above, is the manner of a communication, not its matter. Yet the distinction between manner and matter is a slippery one; manner affects matter. Donald Hall (1967), the poet, discussing this issue in a literary context, points out that one linguist took Caesar's "I came—I saw—I conquered," and revised it into "I arrived on the scene of the battle, I observed the situation, I won the victory." Here the matter is the same, but the tone of arrogant dignity in Caesar disappears into the pallid pedantry of the longer version. It is impossible to say that the matter is unaffected.

Jonathan Swift, perhaps among the best prose stylists, offers reassurance, when we transpose his observation into the deduction that, in the therapist who knows what he is talking about, the issue of the manner employed generally takes care of itself. "When a man's thoughts are clear, the properest words will generally offer themselves first, and his own judgement will direct him in what order to place them, so as they may be best understood." This is to some degree so.

Interpretive style should ordinarily, however, in terms of language, be molded by considerations of conceptual economy, precision and clarity of communication. Colby (1951) conveys the concentrated advice. "Effective interpretations are concise, simply phrased, and few in number, begin as approximations on the periphery, and end as convergences on the center" (p. 90).

In affective tone, we might observe that the *style of interpretation is often best when both astringent and tender, astringent in content and tender in manner*: when an attitude of calling it as the therapist sees it is combined with some sympathetic tuning in on the patient having to receive the new. In speaking of desirable qualities in men who treat the mind, Plato mentioned boldness and benevolence.

In a relative sense, the interpretation is more usable and capable of touching feelings if aimed toward a point of emotional relevance, that is, toward what the patient is experiencing right *now*, not what he experienced last session or earlier. This, however, is not to say that reference to what happened previously should not be combined with what is happening currently. But there is little therapeutic advantage in going back to a stale, past occurrence when it is not echoing in some event in the present. It is for this reason, as will be discussed later, that transference interpretations are more mutative than are interpretations of general content.

The underlying model is one of two collaborators working with each other, not that of a doctor working *on* a patient. "The analyst should be," as Robertiello, Friedman, and Pollens (1963) put it, "a human being working *with* another human being, not doing something *to* another human being" (p. 119). On the basis of this model, interpretative *possibilities* offered to the patient might convey a certain tentativeness. Therefore the therapist would do well to begin an interpretation with some phrase such as, "Could it be that . . ." or "Perhaps . . ." This offers three advantages: (1) It permits the patient to refute an interpretation with less timidity or possible feeling that he may be threatening the relationship. (2) It allows the patient to more easily revise, change a nuance or an emphasis, or accept part and reject another part of the interpretation. (3) It puts the patient in an active posture in the beginning of the treatment enterprise, rather than defines him as a passive recipient, someone who "receives" treatment.

Similarly, if the patient gives a rationalization, the therapist might say, "Yes, and for what other reasons?" Or, "Yes, and what else?" This doesn't make the patient feel he has been called a liar, and yet shows the therapist not to be naïve. At the same time, it moves the patient forward toward the more basic reason behind the secondary or "good" reason he initially offered.

Another suggestion is to employ the patient's own words wherever possible: "mishigas" for his obsession, "habit" if this is the way he refers to his tic, "fiddling" as the child may term his masturbating, and so on.

On the other hand, in those instances where the patient is euphemizing, the young therapist might be instructed not to accept the patient's terms, but to employ a more direct one. If the patient says, "We were doing it," the therapist might ask, "Intercourse?" or use the vernacular; and if the patient refers to someone "passing away," the therapist might use the more direct term "died." The therapist should demonstrate that the facts of human experience are not to be avoided, that issues or feelings can be addressed without prissiness—close up, not at arm's length. Thus the therapist, in the directness of his words when commenting or interpreting, sets an example for the patient of honesty in expressing oneself. In the process, the patient might, for example, come to find that this principle of authenticity extends to many things. It applies to his no longer having to think in such terms as, "I didn't *mean* to hurt your feelings," when there really existed a desire to hurt. It means not resorting to generalities in order to attribute to no one in particular opinions that one is unwilling to call one's own. It means not disguising lack of feeling by cliches which purport to display feeling.

Thus the intent is to break through the barrier of the surface noises people ordinarily make to fend off relating rather than to relate. In the therapeutic experience, the patient is exposed to the hard actuality, on both sides, of genuine statements. He learns, thereby, eventually to truly communicate "of himself." He gains the courage to tell it like it is.

The therapist might early be taught to stay away not only from technical words, but from formal words as well. Aristotle in his *Rhetoric* advised, "Clearness is secured by using the words . . . that are current and ordinary." Rather than speak of the patient's need to be "controlling," the therapist might better refer to his need "to call the shots" or to "hold the reins," particularly if the patient does not come from an educated background. Even with sophisticated people, rather than saying "compulsive" the therapist might speak of the patient "liking everything in its place before he begins" when he straightens the ashtray and then himself very fastidiously on the couch. The advantage is that this style is more personal and closer to the patient's feelings, and that it conveys that the therapist is speaking *of* the patient, not from a textbook.[1]

Beyond using the patient's own words where possible and common parlance at all times, when interpreting or commenting we must, to reach the patient more than intellectually, translate our observation into the patient's concrete experience. The patient's individualistic or characteristic phrases might be adopted by the therapist in the interests of also furthering an intimate, personal communication system, much like that which builds up between long-time friends. The common, private, "in-group" aspects of language established between patient and therapist afford not only short cuts, but also a more affect-toned idiom and a closeness in communicative exchange. It is thus helpful for the therapist to know and make use of the particular phrases which trigger those special images and meanings to which the patient most personally relates.

One woman in treatment had been brought up by a mother who always gave her, beneath acceptable dresses, the most shabby and torn of undergarments to wear, relegated her to the least expensive activities, and saved money on small things as well as large—all this in spite of the fact that the family was that of an upper middle-class physician. Now, as an adult, the patient felt guilty whenever she took pains with her appearance, whenever she obtained a good grade in school, whenever she accomplished, succeeded or otherwise came out well. In her case, the therapist

---

[1]This principle pertains particularly to psychologists, psychiatrists, or psychology majors in treatment. It is important to pull these patients away from the academic or technical terms, to have them talk the language they grew up with before entering professional training.

commented: "Could it be you feel afraid when you dare to dress in feminine un-
derwear, not the *torn undergarments* your mother prescribed?" She seemed to experience a flash of insight in which she suddenly *really* knew, at a gut level, what she
had "known" all along. There was an "aha" moment, beyond seeing, at the *sensing*
of a connection.

A male patient who entered therapy because of an impotency problem and its interference with his marriage had lost his father when he was seven. His mother had
remarried a man shortly thereafter who wore a prosthetic device in place of a missing hand. When therapy was under way, the patient seemed to explore whatever the
therapist said to underscore for himself the therapist's capability, knowledge,
perceptiveness, and mastery. What the patient appeared to be looking closely for
here were positive aspects, not the more usual negative ones with which to disqualify the therapist or reduce him as a "rival." At one point, when there was cause
to refer to this, it was done in the form of the patient's desire to reassure himself that
the therapist "has two good hands." This said it for the patient, briefly and in a
way he could experience.

A similar effect was obtained in the following instance. A young man was quite
ambivalently involved in competitive relations with peers and in rivalry with an in-
timidating father. The father had been a professional minor league baseball player
and had pressured his son to play initially in the Little League and then on the high
school and college baseball teams. When the patient's acute rivalrous wishes and
fears were reexperienced toward me in the transference, the comment that he seemed to be contending "to see who had the more powerful bat" was something he
could emotionally relate to more than to any other way it had previously been expressed. When interpreting, we must, if we are to reach the patient, retranslate
meanings back into his specific experience.

As an extension of this point, the most basic precondition for psychotherapy is
that therapist and patient speak the same language. I remember an incident years
ago when, as an intern, I was asked to fill out a research form on an adolescent patient in the hospital. I asked him, when I came down to that question, whether he
had ever had intercourse.

"No", he said.

Something about him and his background stirred in my mind, and I asked, "Have
you ever been laid?"

"Oh yes, lots of times, since I was fourteen."

I've remembered this lesson. When an adolescent in group therapy jumps up to
punch another, an analyst should have ready at hand the words "Cool it!" We can
sense how much more authority there is in speaking the patient's language at this
critical moment than there would be in the words, "No fighting allowed." Speaking
the patient's vernacular allows the therapist to step closer to the patient when this is
suddenly (or otherwise) needed.

UNDERSCORING OF TEMPORAL SEQUENCE

The underscoring of a time sequence, whenever this can be discerned in the reactions of a patient, may be especially helpful in the interpretive work. To a young
man, it proved effective to point out that his frequent headaches seemed to begin
when he moved back home to live with his parents. Lowenstein (1957) offers an instructive example: A girl at an out-of-town college was her father's favorite. A

temporal connection made brought up for her consideration the reasons for her sudden decision to leave school. The decision to quit college and go home coincided with a letter she had received from her father explaining that the relationship between him and her mother had suddenly gotten noticeably better.

A temporal relationship is particularly persuasive in providing the opening to further exploration, in pointing the general direction.

TRANSFERENCE INTERPRETATION

In terms of priority of material, Fromm-Reichmann speaks for the Sullivanian viewpoint, although happily on this issue all schools of therapy would tend to converge: "The investigation of the interaction between patient and doctor should take precedence over . . . all other aspects of the patient's communication" (Bullard, 1959). Using analytical terms, Fenichel (1945) asserts that the "pathogenic conflicts, revived in the transference, are now experienced in their full emotional content . . . [and this] makes the transference interpretation so much more effective than any other interpretation." Freud observed, in this connection, that one cannot conquer an enemy in absentia. Strachey (1934) elaborates that the extratransference interpretation is less likely to be given "at the point of urgency." This is because the object of the patient's feelings, in the extratransference interpretation is not present. The nontransference interpretation tends to be concerned with those matters distant in both time and space, and is hence less immediate and therefore less effective.

Strachey (1934) explains further: "Instead of having to deal as best we may with conflicts of the remote past, which are concerned with dead circumstances and mummified personalities, and whose outcome is already determined, we find ourselves in an actual and immediate situation in which we and the patient are the principal characters."

It is a not uncommon experience to find a patient with an adequate prognosis showing no shift at all in response to an extended period of receiving interpretation after interpretation in months, if not years, of therapy. One factor, among others, to explore in such an instance is whether the focus of the interpretive work has been an extratransference one. The missing ingredient frequently turns out to be one of proper attention to the ongoing, present relationship, the therapy situation itself.

Extensive activity involving extratransference interpretation has been referred to as "interpretation-fanaticism" by Ferenczi and Rank (Strachey, 1934) and is included under "wild" analysis by Freud (1910).

There are few more opportune times to place a patient's finger on the pulse of an underlying feeling than when it is pulsating. It is one thing to point out to a patient, for example, that the more his boss bawled him out in some incident recounted, the more fearful and/or angry he (the patient) may have felt beneath his reported calming appeasements. But it is quite another thing to help him to sense, to actually feel, something while it is going on: a tone, say, of underlying resentment or irritation toward the therapist at some point when the patient's surface behavior is one of an increasingly bigger smile of ingratiation. Once the patient can get in touch with the buried feelings while they are activated, then, of course, the similar occurrence of the submerged anger in the situation with the boss can be linked up with the underside of the two-layered experience in the therapy session. Once he gets in contact with his hidden hostility in a session—and has the therapist's support for accepting an affect he now feels less impelled to reject because the therapist does not reject him for it—then, and only then, is he in a better position to taste the similar sensations of anger when they move up within him in situations outside therapy.

Another patient, a female, responded to situations which would have angered others by instead feeling a desire to urinate. When she reported such outside incidents, the writer made no mention of the angry idioms, "Piss on him" or "Piss on that," and its implications for hostility and dismissal. Waiting until the sensation to urinate came up one session, it was then explored. The patient had asked for a change in appointment time for the following session, but had asked for it to be scheduled on a day the therapist found he had no opening. She quite blandly and casually accepted this fact of life, but next reported the sensation to urinate. At this point, when the interpretation was offered, she was able to get in touch with her actual sensation of underlying resentment and irritation at the therapist. This, in turn, served as a breakthrough to feeling the rage on the outside which accompanied and, in the long run, replaced her desire to urinate when frustrated.

Capitalizing upon the transference in still another way, Freud (1924) shares with us a basic therapeutic suggestion, namely, that the important interpretations should not be offered until a dependable positive transference has been established. Thus, the relationship to the analyst—both transference and real—may be available to sustain and support the patient through any possible anxiety stirred up by confrontations or interpretations.

At this point, the question arises as to when the work of transference interpretation should be inaugurated. This issue of timing is a complex one, but there is at least one general guidepost. The time to move to the transference, interpretively, is when the resistances mount. Until then, while the patient is able to express himself freely about the things that matter to him, the transference feelings need not yet be addressed. At the point, however, at which the patient's efforts are diverted or blocked, his thoughts and feelings about the therapist should be invited. One procedure is to ask about feelings toward the therapist. If he has feelings which he is not expressing, the patient's inhibition about verbalizing them may, if not handled, become the center of expanding blocking and resistance.

One patient, referring to her former analytic experience, explained: "During my previous therapy go-around, I had some absolutely magnificent dreams—both nightmares and the pleasant variety—in which I learned a helluva lot. Finally, when I developed a rage at the doctor, I stopped remembering my dreams, and have remembered very few ever since—or usually just brief flashes from what I know was a long, complex dream. I hope I'll soon begin to remember my dreams again; I've been irritated at having cut myself off from my psychic innards."

At this point we might turn to examine something the Existentialist analysts advocate: that the therapist actively express himself in order to "gain the advantage that he does not become the passive object of fantasy-projection on the part of the patient. . . . As a consequence the transference problem is minimized" (Holt, this book). So too, we might note that in the process the transference advantage is lost. This advantage includes the use of a relatively uncontaminated transference as (a) an investigative instrument reinstituting etiological factors in the patient's neurosis, and (b) a leverage of treatment.

The neurotic is an individual who reacts as if imagined or past events are a real and continuing part of his present. He is more prone to engage in parataxic distortions. It is when these distortions occur in his perception of the therapist that it is called transference. It is, then, the transference, more than any other tool, which allows the patient eventually to understand his difficulties with others, his neurotic patterns while experiencing them. This understanding on the patient's part (granted that he has the capacity for an observing as well as experiencing ego function) is accomplished through his investigation with the therapist of his mode and style of relating to the therapist. When this is not diluted or distorted by the therapist's affects, and allowed to unfold in its own characteristic manner from within the patient (whether compliant, combatative, provocative, ingratiating, accusatory or whatever), it best serves this purpose. Thus, if the patient is not prodded, as the Existentialist advocates he should be, by the therapist's anger, loneliness, ego needs, seductiveness, or other intruding stimuli, it is the patient's characteristic patterns which emerge in the relatively neutral atmosphere provided. It does, of course, take patience on the therapist's part to await the unprovoked emergence of this more natural transference. Then, through observation and investigation of the relationship between patient and therapist—a relationship established in the patient's mode, not in the therapist's—what the patient contributes to his difficulties with others can be experienced and clarified.

Then, and only then, if the therapist wishes to feed one or another emotional ingredient into the relationship, to allow this or that reaction on his part to emerge, that is another matter. He now already has been painted as being like the significant figure(s) in the patient's formative development. Once the therapist wears these parental robes, once the patient is, for example, relating to the therapist as he once did as a child to his father (and still subtly does as an employee to his supervisor, etc.), then the therapist can—in the context of the patient reliving a formative relationship—supply positive endings to the old conflicts. Here, positive endings, in the concept of Alexander and French (1946), move toward replacing the more destructive ones which earlier shaped the patient's pattern.[2] Unless the transference is established, what the therapist provides in the relationship does not replace or dilute the previous destructive counterpart, but is merely grafted on top.

To consider a highly simplified example, a boy was found masturbating by a puritanical mother who heaped upon him a tirade of moralistic abuse. He was a "little beast," both "wicked and sinful."

Years later, now a young adult in treatment, unmarried and living at home, he dared to "confess" his masturbatory practices. In doing so, he confided as he lay on the couch, that it was as if he were being "caught" doing so all over again, and the above story of his mother's reactions was stammered out. The transference was developed by this time and he felt that I, too, must view him as a reprehensible and "dirty" person. Let us now compare the effect in two different therapy settings of my response to his confessed masturbation, a response viewing his desires and activities naturalistically, not moralistically.

If the therapist's response were offered to a patient before a transference had developed, then it would have only educational value, a value not much deeper than that of hearing from one's psychology teacher in class, or reading in a book, that

---

[2]Alexander's phrase for this positive ending is a "corrective emotional experience." Here he breaks with Freud in that this approach deliberately cuts off the emergence of the patient's ambivalent feelings.

masturbation is a natural, substitutive response occurring, according to the Kinsey figures, in close to 99 per cent of males. The patient is then in a position where one authority figure (the therapist, or teacher, or Kinsey) says masturbation is nothing to feel guilty about, but his mother—an earlier, more influential, personal figure—says it is! The patient is left in the position where he now knows one thing intellectually, but feels another emotionally. The guilty feelings, the sense of himself as soiled and condemnable, are not so much reduced as layered over by the information.

But if the therapist's reaction is received by the patient in transference, then the therapist is not just another authority figure; he *is* psychologically (regardless of his sex) the authoritarian mother here, and for the patient the situation is one of being detected again masturbating. Now it is the "parent" who accepts the patient and his impulses. The previous situation is *relived*, via the transference setting, and now the symbolic parent (not just his therapist) understands and receives him—not conditional upon rigid, untenable standards which he must live up to, but as he humanly is.[3] Sullivan (1947) observed that as soon as a patient has understood *one* parataxic distortion in the transference and accepted it as such, there is hope for a successful outcome of the treatment.

INTERFERING NEEDS OF THE THERAPIST

Menninger (1958) advises that the patient be given an interpretative lead "in such a way that the patient—not the analyst—takes the 'credit' for the discovery" (p. 134).[4] In line with this he points out that "young analysts . . . need to be reminded that they are not oracles, not wizards, not linguists, not detectives, not great wise men who, like Joseph and Daniel, 'interpret' dreams—but quiet observers, listeners, and occasionally commentators" (p. 129).[5] The therapist thus at times points to the existence of a possible connection or draws an implication or an inference which escapes the patient. His comments may pull together the varied and fractionated material of the patient's associations or sort out an underlying theme from the apparently diversified aspects presented. He may remind the patient of forgotten statements or point out a contradiction or an apparent but unrecognized omission. The proper role, then, is one of a quiet sharing (although this does not rule out occasional emotional tones of circumscribed intensity or affect) of a feeling or observation about something the patient said, did or underlyingly feels.

Interfering needs which the therapist has to guard against also come from a number of other possibilities we can add to Menninger's list above: a tendency to be

---

[3]The approach employed here is, strictly speaking, not quite the Alexanderian procedure. While it does involve a "corrective emotional experience," what he advocates is that the therapist play a role, rather than respond with what he naturally feels. Alexander's is a very active, deliberate process in which the therapist acts the opposite way the parent did. He does so by intentional role-playing, rather than responding differently as a function of being freer and more enlightened than were the patient's parental figures.

[4]Often we find, after a patient will reject an interpretation suggested by the therapist, he (the patient) will then sometimes later make the same connection spontaneously, stating it as his derived awareness; i.e., "You know, it just occurred to me, that . . . ." The novice should be cautioned against taking credit: "Don't you remember my indicating that last week?"

[5]Fenichel remarked that the wish of the patient to be cured by a magician was sometimes equalled by the wish of the therapist to be such a magician.

the friendly advisor, to play God, to observe patients as if they were under a microscope; to marshal a secret inner superiority by ferreting out weaknesses or "flaws" in patients; to feed narcissistic needs by claiming credit for the patient's improvement; to bask in the positive transference of a patient as if it represented a realistic appraisal of the therapist as "simply wonderful"; to be threatened by negative transference attitudes of the patient as if they represent a failure on the part of the therapist (this by no means implies the therapist should not face his real mistakes and shortcomings); to maintain subtly the patient's dependency; or to be the benevolent father. The therapist should also be free to remain silent much of the time, to be free of the need to be as all-knowing or "almost perfect in every way" as Mary Poppins.

Thus a therapist who is insecure, rather than omnipotent or hostile, may block treatment in *his* way; by his continual needs to be perceived as benevolent or giving, by his desire to be liked. This therapist may prove unreceptive to those ideas which flash through his mind which he feels to be indelicate, difficult to speak about, or apt to displease his patient. He may brush aside such ideas as unlikely, silly, or inappropriate. Here, he may use defenses in order to block out the negative as he collaborates with the patient to cut around the unpleasant.

Reik's (1949) advice to the young analyst is apt here: "Tell the truth . . . no qualifications, and no 'watering down'! Call a spade a spade and do not speak of an agricultural instrument! Your patient will be able to stand the truth when he feels you mean well toward him. To tell him the truth amounts to a compliment to his intelligence and to his moral courage. . . . It is not always easy to detect a lie behind its myriad masks. But truth is unmistakable; its note cannot be counterfeited. He who is courageous in the face of the hidden shock of thought, makes others courageous. . . ." (p. 502). There is no deeper wisdom upon which a chapter may draw to a close.

Lastly, however, and of equal importance, the effective therapist is the one who keeps his theory and his ideological spectacles in his pocket as he listens to people and tries to understand them. Like Freud before him, who described himself as not a Freudian, he is humble before the facts.

REFERENCES

Alexander, F., and French, T. M. *Psychoanalytic therapy.* New York: The Ronald Press, 1946.

Bullard, D. (Ed.). *Psychoanalysis and psychotherapy: Selected papers of Frieda Fromm-Reichmann.* Chicago: University of Chicago Press, 1959.

Dollard, J., and Miller, N. E., *Personality and psychotherapy.* New York: McGraw-Hill, 1950.

Colby, K. M., *A primer for psychotherapists.* New York: Ronald Press, 1951.

Fenichel, O., *The psychoanalytic theory of neurosis.* New York: W. W. Norton, 1945.

——, *The collected papers of Otto Fenichel.* New York: W. W. Norton, 1953.

French, T. M., Art and science in psychoanalysis. *J. Amer. Psychoanal. Ass.* 1958, 6, 197-214.

Freud, S., Further recommendations in the technique of psychoanalysis (1913). *Collected Papers,* Vol. 2. London: Hogarth Press, 1924.

——, "Wild" psychoanalysis (1910). *Standard Edition,* 11:221-227. London: Hogarth Press, 1957.

Fromm-Reichmann, Frieda, *Principles of intensive psychotherapy.* Chicago: University of Chicago Press, 1950.

Hall, D., Speaking of books, a clear and simple style. *New York Times Book Review,* May 7, 1967.

Hammer, E. F., The role of interpretation in psychotherapy. In Hammer, E. F. (Ed.), this book, 1968.

Horney, Karen, Seminar of the Chicago Institute for Psychoanalysis, 1933.

Levy, L. H., *Psychological interpretation.* New York: Holt, Rinehart & Winston, 1963.

Lowenstein, R. M., Some thoughts on interpretation in the theory and practice of psycho-analysis. *Psychoanalytic Study of the Child,* Vol. XII, 1957.

Meng, H., and Freud, Ernst, *Sigmund Freud and Oscar Pfister: psychoanalysis and faith.* New York: Basic Books, 1964.

Menninger, K., *Theory of psychoanalytic technique.* New York: Basic Books, 1958.

Nydes, J., Interpretation and the therapeutic act. In Hammer, E. F. (Ed.), this book, 1968.

Reich, W., *Character analysis.* New York: Orgone Institute, 1933.

Reik, T., *Listening with the third ear.* New York: Ferrar, Straus & Co., 1959.

Robertiello, R., Friedman, D., and Pollens, B., *The analyst's role.* New York: Citadel Press, 1963.

Sullivan, H. S., *Conceptions of modern psychiatry.* Washington, D.C.: Wm. A. White Psychiatric Foundation, 1947.

Strachey, J., The nature of the therapeutic action of psychoanalysis. *Internat. J. Psychoanal.* 1934, 15, 127-159.

Wolberg, L. R., *Short-term psychotherapy.* New York: Grune & Stratton, 1966.

CHAPTER 7

Interpretation in Relationship Therapy

WILLIAM U. SNYDER, PH.D.

*Dr. William U. Snyder is Professor and Chairman of the Psychology Depart-
ment at Ohio University in Athens, Ohio. He also serves as director of clinical
training, a post he formerly held at the Pennsylvania State University, where he
was on the psychology faculty for 17 years. He had previously held positions at
Ohio State University, and as director of the Des Moines (Iowa) Child Guidance
Center. His Master's degree in psychology was from Duke University, and his
Ph.D. from Ohio State. Dr. Snyder's principal teaching and research interest
has been in the area of psychotherapy, which is understandable, since he was one
of Carl Rogers' first doctoral students. He has written three books, numerous
chapters in other books, and about 50 professional articles dealing almost exclusively with research in psychotherapy. His early interest in, and practice of, the
client-centered methods has broadened, ultimately, to cover a more eclectic
approach, which is still a relationship-type therapy but which also draws upon
the concepts found in learning theory and psychoanalysis.*

*Out of his years of seasoned experience in both areas, Professor Snyder effec-
tively bridges therapeutic practice and research, bringing both together into a
harmonious unit. His paper also charts the history of growth in the United
States—and its illustration by the development of one of its significant therapists—
from a minimally interpretive to a more actively interpretive stance on the part
of the clinician in the therapeutic encounter.*

Among the first research efforts to define interpretation were those of Rogers and
his students (1942, 1951), and my own definitions became the more-or-less standard ones of much of the research and therapeutic work, particularly of that conducted by the client-centered therapists trained by Rogers. My definition of interpretation (1943, 1953) was as follows: "Any counselor statement which indicates, even vaguely, a causal relationship in the client's behavior, points out a
characterization, explains, or informs the client as to his patterns or personality,
provided he has not specifically mentioned it in previous statements. These (interpretive) statements frequently represent the counselor's attempt to impose his
'diagnostic' concepts."

The definition of clarification of feeling developed at that time is also relevant
here: "A statement by the counselor which puts the client's feeling or affective tone
in a clearer or more recognizable form; or any effort to show that the counselor is
accurately recognizing the feelings of the client's statement by understanding it."

Later the Psychotherapy Research Group at Pennsylvania State University
(Snyder, 1953) modified the above definition by distinguishing between accurate
and inaccurate clarifications, and they also identified the concept of clarification of
unverbalized feelings, which, in fact, comes very close to interpretation: "A statement by the counselor which expresses unverbalized attitudes or feelings of the
client. A recognition or clarification of a feeling or an attitude which the client has
not verbalized but which is clearly implied in the client's previous statements and is

in context with these previous statements. . . . Shrewd guesses of the client's attitudes which are obtained from the counselor's knowledge of the total situation are coded in this category."

Bordin and his students (Harway *et al.*, 1955) invented a classification of subdivisions labeled "depth of interpretation," which constituted an important refinement of the concept of interpretation and which has been widely employed in the literature and research on this concept. His levels of interpretation are as follows:

XIT_1 The therapist merely repeats the material of which the client is fully aware. (This is comparable to Snyder's restatement of content.)

XIT_2 Restatement of material of which the patient is aware.

XIT_3 Implied focusing with regard to material of which the client is unaware. (Somewhat similar to my own clarification of feeling).

XIT_4 Therapist connects two aspects of the contents of previous client statements.

XIT_5 Therapist reformulates the behavior of the client during the interview in a way not explicitly recognized previously by the client.

XIT_6 Therapist comments on the client's bodily or facial expressions as manifestations of the client's feelings.

XIT_7 Therapist uses a preceding client statement to exemplify a process that has been building up during the interview, and of which the client is seemingly unaware.

XIT_8 Therapist speculates as to the possible childhood situation which might relate to current client feelings.

XIT_9 Therapist deals with inferences about material completely removed from the client's awareness.

My introduction of the concept of discussing the relationship (XRL), meaning the interpersonal relationship between therapist and client, constitutes a recent development (1961, p. 44*ff.*) in my thinking, but I believe it is a very important and special aspect of interpretation, and I chose to label it as a separate type of therapist intervention rather than simply classifying it as only another aspect of interpretation. This reflects my bias that the interpersonal relationship between the therapist and the client is the most important aspect of the therapeutic process. I also believe, and have demonstrated by research (1963), that a client's responses to a relationship intervention by the therapist (XRL) are quite different in character from his responses to other forms of interpretations. This matter is discussed further below.

Wolberg (1954, p. 439*ff.*) has defined interpretation as "seeing beyond the facade of manifest thinking, feeling and behavior, into less obvious meanings and motivations." However, it is really more than just seeing beyond the facade; it also incorporates the act of the therapist's conveying his insights to the repressing client. In most of the relationship therapies, but not in the client-centered therapy of Rogers, interpretation is a valuable tool and one which is employed often, although judiciously. In a typical case of mine (Quinn case in *Dependency in Psychotherapy*, 1963), "pure" interpretations comprised 18 per cent of the therapist's interaction, but some other types of response were utilized in such a manner as also to comprise interpretive action. These included discussing the relationship (8 per cent), calling attention (1.6 per cent), and challenging (5 per cent); some of the questions asked by the therapist were also interpretive in character (15.5 per cent). Clarification of feeling is a mildly interpretive activity, but since it usually stays rather close to the expressed and conscious response, we do not generally classify it as interpretive, although there are occasions when the feeling reflected by the therapist is definitely an unrecognized one, as the client often quickly admits. Thus it is apparent that about half of my responses in a typical case could be classified as interpretations or interpretive in character (not counting clarifications of feeling).

Early in my history as a therapist (1943), the proportions of interpretive and reflective responses were quite different; at that time "pure" interpretation comprised only 8.5 per cent, and direct questions only 4 per cent, whereas clarification of feeling constituted almost one-third of the therapeutic interventions. (Simple acceptance, the "mm-hmm" type of response, accounted for a great proportion of the therapist's activity at that time.) "Relationship" responses were not counted at that time, but probably occurred as clarification of feeling. A case conducted by Rogers in 1941 (Herbert Bryan) contained 12 per cent interpretations, 26 per cent clarifications, and 6 per cent direct questions. By 1946 Rogers had perfected his client-centeredness to the point where, in one of his "best" cases (Mary Jane Tilden), interpretations were down to 1.3 per cent of the published portion of the case, and clarifications of feeling were up to 73 per cent. There were no direct questions or other somewhat interpretive types of responses.

Of interest is the question of whether throughout the therapy process the amount of interpretation varies, and the answer is that in general my use of interpretation increases as therapy progresses. Five out of six cases studied in detail in 1943 revealed that the majority of the interpretations occurred in the second half of the therapy series of interviews. This phenomenon appeared to be consistent, in that it held true for 20 cases studied in 1958. The Quinn and Jones cases (1963) illustrate this situation, in which the more interpretive and reflective responses comprised, for them, about 35 per cent of the therapist's responses in the beginning of therapy; but in the second half of therapy these same types of responses averaged about 50 per cent of the responses.

What is the purpose of interpretation? It must be considered primarily as an aid to the induction of insight or self-understanding. The therapist, in making an interpretation, must assume that the information he is giving (usually an explanation of the client's unrecognized psychodynamics) is an accurate one, that it will be helpful to him in eliminating certain undesirable instrumental or emotional behaviors, and that presenting the concept interpretively is more likely to produce insight than would be the process of waiting for the client to arrive at the understanding "on his own." Or at least this understanding may be reached more efficiently, if not necessarily in a better manner. The interpretation must be a shortcut to the production of self-insight on the part of the client. Or perhaps it is often assumed that the client will never, or at least only very tardily, arrive at the insight by himself—i.e., that he needs to be told, if he is *ever* to perceive the dynamic.

I personally view interpretation as a very valuable tool of the therapist. This point of view constitutes a genuine positional evolution for me, since I was trained (by Rogers) to view interpretation as an error, and can easily recall the rather scornful, or at least chiding, way in which I would classify my own or one of my students' responses in this category.

Actually it makes a lot of sense to assume that the therapist is in a better position to perceive the unconscious dynamics of the client than is the latter. First, the therapist usually has no subjective or defensive reason for repressing or failing to recognize the dynamic, except in those cases where negative transference on the part of the client might, of course, be threatening to the therapist himself. Second, the therapist is extensively trained and schooled in the analysis of dynamics, including his own, whereas the client, by virtue of the usual social conventions, has had almost no training in self-examination, and may, indeed, have received a lot of rein-forcement in the process of repression. Furthermore, the therapist has probably en-countered many times an identical situation of the dynamic which the client is un-consciously displaying. So by reasons of both training and experience the therapist is in a better position to understand the dynamic which is occurring.

There are a number of different varieties of interpretation. In traditional psychoanalysis the primary form is the interpretation of the resistances and/or transference, or of those instances when the patient is finding it difficult to analyze further because his defenses are being threatened. This is a valid sort of in-terpretation and one which I use frequently. However, I typically point out first the resistance *and then* inquire whether the client has some negative feeling about me of which he is not aware. Actually this constitutes a second form of interpretation, i.e., discussion about the therapeutic relationship. I consider this the most important form of interpretation, because I also consider the *relationship* the principal medium of therapeutic progress. Almost invariably this analysis of the resistance in terms of understanding the therapeutic relationship proves to be a very effective way of overcoming the resistance and of moving ahead to new therapeutic goals.

Another common form of interpretation is the pointing out of unrecognized client psychodynamics and their meanings for the client's behavior. This kind of in-terpretation is usually believed by the layman to be the principal therapeutic in-tervention. It is an important way of moving the client toward his therapeutic goals. The client may, for example, never have heard of oedipal strivings, which may con-stitute an important part of his problem. Actually, labeling such strivings as "oedipal" is not very important, but getting the client to recognize their character usually *is* very important if he is to arrive at self-understanding.

Another form of interpretation constitutes the integrating of formerly un-connected items of information revealed by the client which in their new jux-taposition have an important, meaningful relationship. For example, the client, a student, may not have recognized the similarity between his responding to pro-fessors and other authority figures with hostility, and his previous responses to his authoritarian parent.

Sometimes an interpretation may be based on a gesture, action, or facial ex-pression of a client, frequently one of which he is unaware. The client's superior feelings toward others may be revealed in a sort of smirking manner, his tenseness may be observed in the unrelaxed way in which he sits; or his generally frightened approach to life may be observed in his hand-wringing or handkerchief-twisting. An extreme of this behavioral counterpart for emotional responses was revealed by the behavior of one young woman client who stood in a distant corner of the office with her arms folded tightly over her bosom. Another client, a young male with homosexual feelings, would blush and breathe very hard when he felt under any pressure from the therapist, and he described a concurrent sensation of "chills"; later he was able to identify these with homosexual wishes directed toward the therapist, but meanwhile the therapist had interpreted their relationship to the client's being in the presence of older males toward whom he felt passive-submissive urges combined with some hostility and resentment. The client indicated his awareness, then, of homosexual urges toward the therapist, and the fear that they would become evident to the therapist.

A point which perhaps needs defending is whether it is better for the client to learn about his dynamics through having them interpreted to him, or through arriving at an awareness of them by means of his own processes of self-analysis and searching while under the guidance of the therapist. This question must be answered pragmatically and by empirical testing. Much of what has been discovered about the learning process seems to indicate that information acquired by effort on the part of the learner is better retained than that obtained by the simple process of "being told." The "digging through" to the insight seems to flex the intellectual and emotional muscles, and the exercise produces, perhaps, sounder growth.

Many times, however, the self-examination is a process of circular mislogic, and the same errors may be repeated if there is no intervention from a therapist to start the thinking process along a new channel. It is similar to an intellectual problem-solving situation, such as solving an algebraic problem; the learner may repeatedly make the same error and thereby make absolutely no progress at all. This behavior is witnessed very frequently in the academic situation, and any experienced therapist sees it occur almost as often when his client is wrestling with an emotional problem. It is not an unusual experience to have a client respond to an interpretation with a statement like, "You know, I never thought of that," or "What has prevented me from seeing such an obvious relationship all this time?" Some clients are even quite embarrassed by this experience of having their obvious repression uncovered. In fact, it often leads to a form of resistance if the interpretation has been too threatening or made too early by the therapist.

This raises the question of the client's usual response to interpretation. Many times clients accept an interpretation readily, but on other occasions they may be quite resistant. The resistance may be because the therapist's interpretation is wrong, or it may be (and more often is) because the interpretation is *too* correct and happens to concern ego-threatening or ego-damaging material for the client. A study of the response sequences of Quinn and Jones in my book (1963) reveals that Quinn most frequently responded to interpretation with resistance ($r = .457 \pm .127$), while Jones' typical response was a dependent reaction ($r = .227 \pm .228$). Furthermore, the affective responses of clients to interpretations may vary somewhat, both among different clients and for the same client with regard to different interpretations. Both Quinn and Jones responded much more favorably to the giving of information or advice than they did to interpretation. Quinn's responses to interpretation (based on my Client Affect Scale administered after each interview) was rather neutral, but Jones' response was mildly negative ($r = -.183 \pm .231$).

Regarding the actual client activity, in contrast to the *emotional* response, Quinn leaned strongly toward use of statements classified as resistance ($r = .457 \pm .127$), with this being the only type of response he used significantly often. Jones, on the other hand, gave responses demonstrating dependency, consideration of the therapy relationship, resistance, anxiety, and self-insight *about* equally often, although in the above order of frequency. None of these types of responses was used significantly more often than any other. Evidently Jones' resistance to interpretation was not nearly as intense as was Quinn's, and he was more willing to face certain unpleasant or repressed aspects of his personality. It was also true, however, that more interpretation was used with Quinn than with Jones, but this was because

Jones was more adept at making his own interpretations. Our data also suggest that Quinn was a more dependent person than Jones and moved toward independence with much more difficulty.

Consideration should now be given to how effective interpretation is in producing insight. Much attention is currently given to the concepts of operant conditioning, direct psychotherapy, and other learning therapies. All of these are based on information learned from the psychological laboratory, usually with animals as subjects, regarding the use of conditioning in modifying lower-order types of behavior, such as motoral habits and responses of the autonomic nervous system. A few of the studies, such as the operant conditioning ones, have also been directed toward the modification of verbal behavior in the human. It has been clearly demonstrated, since the time of Pavlov, that conditioning procedures can be quite effective with this level of behavioral response. A natural tendency has been to move from the autonomic behavior to the area of conditioning of the emotional and even the cognitive response—at least in theory. Actually there is still an unresolved issue regarding how much higher-order cerebral and cognitive behavior patterns differ from those coming under the control of the lower brain. Usually, however, in human beings the term "learning" is applied to modification of higher order responses, as differentiated from the conditioning of lower order responses. While there is some tendency to use these terms interchangeably in the less-precise situation, this tendency may lead to a trend toward overgeneralization of the process of conditioning and to the observation that all learning follows the same rules—that there are no different sorts of learning.

The assumption that all learning is alike has, in turn, led to the easy generalization that all behavior is the result of conditioning, and that whatever behavior has been acquired as the result of conditioning can just as readily be deconditioned. So deconditioning or reconditioning has tended to become a popular concept and, to some extent, is enjoying a fad in the field of psychotherapy at present. The logical jump implied from conditioning to cognitive learning is not yet, however, warranted to the extent to which it is often made. Learning at the cognitive level is usually recognized now to be different in character, or at least much more complex, than conditioning at the autonomic level. It is practically indisputable that many habits can be deconditioned, although sometimes only with a considerable amount of difficulty. Unfortunately for this theory, however, the majority of problems for which clients seek psychotherapy are not ones which relate solely to autonomic behavior, but rather to cognitive and/or emotional misperceptions. Eliminating or modifying a fixed idea would appear to be a rather different order of behavior modification. It is in this fact that interpretation finds its justification.

Insight *is* necessary if much of the erroneous emotional sensitivity of the neuroses is to be overcome, and insight requires a higher level of mental behavior. Thinking and other cognitive behaviors are almost certainly more influenced by the cognitive process of interpretation than by mere conditioning procedures. One can easily decondition tic-like automatic acts, but it is a very different matter to decondition an insecurity feeling or an anxiety associated with the sexual function. Sexual behavior in humans, for instance, is a much more complex type of activity than is copulation in animals. Almost all the way up the phylogenetic scale the animal apparently does not *think* about sex, he merely responds to stimuli, and he usually copulates. Some of the higher mammals, however, and particularly the highest primates, have *ideas* about sex, and their sexual responses involve both physiological and cognitive behaviors. In the case of the human being this behavior is incredibly complex, and there is some evidence to suggest that among some of the apes it is more complex than we have previously realized.

The human being is capable of ideation; he is responsive to the linguistic stimulus. Much of his therapy, therefore, is most profitably conducted at the linguistic level. This is not to deny the efficacy, in many cases, of such phenomena as hypnosis, autosuggestion, relaxation therapy, and other reconditioning processes. It is simply to assert that when one is dealing with what is primarily a cognitive process, it is very appropriate to use cognitive methods, and that, in fact, many times these are the *most* appropriate. It is for this reason that interpretation, along with suggestion, persuasion, encouragement, clarification, and a host of other cognitive "persuaders" are efficacious in the psychotherapy process and should not be either ignored or derogated.

How does interpretation fit into the rubrics of learning theory? Dollard and Miller (1951), in what is probably the classic attempt to apply learning theory to psychotherapy, equate interpretation with what they call "labeling," or "teaching the patient to think about new topics." As they say, "The neurotic person does not know the answer, and furthermore he does not know that there is a question. Eventually the therapist will supply the question and, if need be, the answer." Interpretation, then, is the attaching of verbal cues to the neurotic behavior or erroneous jumps of logic, and the inference is drawn that only that which is labeled can be understood, and only the understood behavior can be acted upon in a less neurotic or maladjusted manner. Dollard and Miller contend that if a patient cannot arrive at new insights about the dynamics of his behavior, the therapist who does not actively teach the client, by labeling the behavior, must be content with inferior results. The therapist cannot help the patient repeat ideas which have not yet occurred to him. Thus, they believe that if the therapist's theory prevents him from originating and offering "new verbal units" (interpretations) when appropriate, he will probably end up with a confused patient at the end of therapy.

Dollard and Miller hold that there may be a slight tendency in all patients to resist interpretation because of the feeling that they should solve their own problems, and those authors associate that feeling with a "drive for independence" which is acquired in most social training. They feel, however, that if the patient greatly needs help, he will not feel that he is being unduly influenced by the therapist when the latter makes an interpretation.

In terms of learning theory, what is the specific mechanism which occurs during interpretation? The therapist suggests new labels for the pain-producing (neurotic) behavior. The client tries out ("rehearses") these labels and is rewarded because of their plausibility. The interpretation may also produce a drive-reducing discrimination, as when the client says something such as, "Yes, I'm not afraid of *all* women, but only of girls of my own age. As you say, I find it easy to relate to older, more maternal, women." Pain reduction and drive-reduction are the usual precursors of reinforcement, or repetition of the newly learned behavior response. It really makes the patient "feel good" when he receives an appropriate interpretation, and this feeling good is followed fairly automatically by action directed toward continuing or retaining the good feeling by repeating the stimulus which produced it. Thus one might use the analogy of suggesting that the patient "eats up" the interpretation because it tastes good!

Is there any tendency for certain other therapeutic techniques always to be used in conjunction with interpretation? Obviously there might be a considerable number of differences among different clients. We found that in Quinn's case interpretation correlated most often in frequency with a tendency to attenuate an interpretation ($r = .684 \pm .063$). This was probably due to the fact that Quinn resisted interpretation so frequently and that the therapist often felt the need to retreat from his position, at least temporarily. However, it was also true that the technique most commonly associated with interpretation in the Jones case was also attenuation, although to a less marked degree ($r = .213 \pm .230$). Attenuation is by nature a sequel to interpretation, however, and seldom can occur at any other time than after an interpretation, so it is quite logical that attenuation and interpretation are so highly correlated in frequency.

Other techniques which correlated fairly frequently with interpretation in the Quinn case were asking direct questions, clarifying feeling, being supportive or reassuring, and discussing the relationship. All but the supportive category here are, of course, the techniques which I have classified as being similar to interpretation in character, so their correlation is not surprising. Unfortunately, the Jones case gives us little effective information by way of answer to this inquiry, since practically all the other techniques studied did not correlate very highly with interpretation in that case. It should be recalled that not very much interpretation was used with him, however. Most of the correlations with interpretation were negative in character.

Perhaps the question most often asked of therapists who employ interpretative techniques is how they know when to use this method. It is difficult to give any rules for this art, and any attempt to do so sounds somewhat like a sort of cookbook approach. However, there are some generalizations which one can make that might be helpful. One rule I follow regularly is to introduce a discussion of the relationship whenever there is resistance on the part of the client. This relationship discussion is itself somewhat interpretive in character and is usually followed by more strictly interpretive material. In Quinn's twenty-seventh interview, for example, he was being extremely resistant and had arrived a half-hour late for therapy, I asked him, "How do you feel toward me today?" Later in the discussion I commented, "I've been wondering whether the difficulty that you're experiencing is due to the fact that the motivation is down to the point where maybe you're coming here because of a sense of obligation, but not because you're really getting too much any more."

Another frequent stimulus for interpretation is the situation in which the client misses an obvious connection between two similar events and fails to make the generalization which should be made. Recognizing something as obvious is, of course, an individual matter and is perhaps best based on extensive therapeutic experience (plus the experiences of living, in general) and on simultaneously analyzing the meaning of the behavior one observes and/or manifests. Dollard and Miller (1951) speak of "playing the notes over mentally on one's own piano," and listening for the disharmonies. When something just doesn't "make sense" or seems unnatural to the therapist, there may be reason to interpret this fact, or at least to call attention to it. When Quinn described an incident of being slapped at the age of 21 by his father and seemed to accept this in due course, the therapist immediately sensed that this was an abnormally passive attitude for a young man to take. Almost anyone would probably have struck back, or at least have felt a very strong urge to do so!

Sometimes a facial expression or a gesture is the clue for an interpretation. One patient always flushed and cleared his throat when he was feeling tense, and many clients exhibit the behavior of having tears come to their eyes, even though they do not actually cry. Either of these behaviors are excellent clues for an interpretation, or at least for a clarification of feeling.

Sometimes a contradiction in the client's verbal account is a clue for an interpretation. Quinn, who had been asserting for 27 interviews that one of his strongest needs was to have a close buddy or a benign father-figure, suddenly denied that he felt any such need and blamed the therapist for pushing him to establish more such friendships. In this case the therapist said, "Well, you see, when during the previous interviews you've been crying out for a close affectional relationship with a strong male figure, then I tend to believe that this is a basic need for you. . . ."

A frequent clue for the use of interpretation is the omissions in an account which the client gives. He tells part of a story, but obviously not the *whole* story. If, for example, a married client goes through ten interviews and does not discuss marital or sexual matters, he is omitting an important area for discussion by reason of repression or suppression. The notion that perhaps he has no problems in this area is really a rationalization, for it is virtually impossible for an individual not to have experienced some problems in this important aspect of his life. On the other hand, an unmarried client who does not discuss the problems involved in finding a mate, or problems concerned with obtaining satisfactory sexual and emotional outlets, is again "glossing over" an area of significance.

Overly strong denial is another cue. The young unmarried male who denies any masturbatory activity, or who says that his masturbation never produced any guilt or anxiety, is probably either concealing the truth or repressing it, or else he is schizophrenic! An interpretation in the former instances is probably called for in this case. The member of a minority group who never discusses his experiences in being Negro, Jewish, or handicapped is similarly withholding significant material. This therapist worked with a paranoid Jewish immigrant from central Europe who spent 20 interviews discussing his feelings of persecution in America but never implied that his homelife was anything but ideal. Several years after therapy he divorced his wife and several years later he committed suicide!

Freud called attention to some classic signs of break-through from repression: slips of the tongue, jokes and puns, and dreams. Each of these may in turn be a sign for the use of an interpretation of the repressed. Quinn uttered an exclamation, almost out of context: "Do you still love me, mother?" The therapist, at that point, first realized that in terms of transference, he probably symbolized the client's mother rather than his father, or at least that he symbolized aspects of both parents and not just of the father, as he had formerly believed. An interpretation was helpful.

Mrs. Long dreamed about, and described in detail, an event of having intercourse with her former boyfriend, Bill. She described experiencing the semen squirting out over a plastic-like diaphragm covering her face. The fact that she was seriously contemplating reviving an affair with Bill, and was very unhappy with her husband, was known to the therapist, and interpretation was called for. The unusual character of the sexual event had great significance, the therapist felt, and deserved interpretative exploration. Also, for that matter, the fact that her fantasied (and actual) lover had the same first name as the therapist was, it seemed, not without significance, particularly since Mrs. Long denied strenuously that she was experiencing any transference; yet she could not bring herself to leave therapy, cried when it was over, and asked for an extra interview. Here, again, the appropriateness of making interpretations and discussing the relationship seemed abundantly obvious.

Another client told the therapist a joke about the hospital patient who, hearing a knock on the door, replied, "Who is it, friend or enema?" This client had problems in the areas of both hostility-control toward women and passive homosexual urges, and interpretation eventually became appropriate in regard to the area reflected in the joke.

The above examples do not exhaust the possible clues for the use of interpretation; they merely present some of the more frequent ones. Only experience with therapy really teaches a therapist how to recognize these signs. Having seen a symptom many times before in other clients, he is well attuned to its probable meaning and can then make the interpretation both with conviction as to its correctness and with proper timing.

An important matter is one of how far to go in making an interpretation. Since interpretation is so often followed by resistance, which in turn may slow therapeutic progress, there should be guidelines concerning how to make an interpretation without inducing strong resistance, but rather producing primarily acceptance. One procedure is to keep the interpretation tentative. If it is phrased in the interrogative form, the client has a chance to deny the validity of the interpretation—although the seed may have been planted, and he may come to recognize its validity later on. Thus, I very often phrase an interpretation in the form starting, "Is it possible that . . . ?" or "Do you think perhaps you might really feel that. . . ?"

Another important rule of thumb is to make interpretations go just a bit beyond the level of consciously admitted ideas—i.e., to interpret what Freud would have said lay within the preconscious, or what the learning theorist might say was immediately subliminal. Of course, one may ask, "If interpretations are made of material this close to the level of the client's awareness, would he not be likely to arrive at them himself anyway?" The answer is not always yes. The client might arrive at the interpretations spontaneously, but more time would probably be involved and perhaps he might not be as accurate in his conclusions.

Finally, the therapist can use attenuation if he feels he has gone too rapidly for the client. I advocate a sort of trial and error procedure, where the interpretation just below the limen of consciousness is presented. If the client resists it at all strongly, the therapist can back up and say, "Well, perhaps I'm wrong about that." Such an attenuated interpretation has still been made and the client may not actually dismiss it, even though the therapist makes it appear that he has done so. It may be accepted at a later point.

At other times it is appropriate to make fairly strong interpretations and to hold one's ground, even though the client may resist rather vigorously. Mr. Young, while reporting a state of virtual impotence in his sexual relationship with his wife, contended always that he knew he could easily have intercourse with other women. While it was certainly possible that this was true, the therapist felt that he protested too strongly, and after about the tenth time that Mr. Young had asserted this "fact," the therapist challenged it, saying he was not sure that there was any evidence to

support the contention. He was, in fact, correct that Mr. Young's extramarital activities were strictly at the fantasy level. The therapist felt it important to challenge
the assertion of virility, not because he believed that the truth should always come
out, but because he felt that the client's allegations were really a denial of his greatly
feared propensity toward homosexual situations. This later proved to be true, and
the client quite openly admitted it.

Similarly, Quinn always contended that he should never do anything to jeopardize
his marriage, particularly in the form of criticizing his wife's flirtatious activities
with other men, because this might break up the marriage. On the other hand, his
wife was constantly stretching the limits of the marital relationship, as well as
criticizing her husband in very humiliating ways. Finally the therapist interpreted
that he felt Quinn was really *afraid* to be more forceful in the marriage and to take a
firmer hand, that such a position from him was exactly what his wife was provoking
and really wanted. The interpretation proved to be correct. Quinn became more aggressive and his wife responded in a positive manner, implying that she had not
really been sure before whether her husband really cared for her.

SUMMARY

In this chapter we have reviewed some of the literature pertaining to research on
the use of interpretation in the relationship-type psychotherapies. While interpretation tended to be avoided in the earlier days of the practice of
psychotherapy by clinical psychologists in the United States, there is a considerable
body of evidence to indicate that it is now used rather extensively in this type of
therapy. This is not inconsistent with the theories of behavior which derive from
learning theory and the psychology laboratory; in fact, the latter laboratory work
may have considerably influenced the progression toward the use of more interactive and reconstructive processes in the relationship therapies. Among the different types of interpretation used by relationship therapists are interpretation of
resistance and transference; pointing out unrecognized psychodynamics of the
client; the integration of formerly nonconnected items of information revealed by
the client; the identification and labeling of the meaning of gestures, actions, or
facial and bodily expressions of the client; and the interpretation of puns, jokes, and
slips of the tongue.

Some discussion was directed to the question of how the therapist knows when to
use interpretation. The author proposed that it should be used whenever resistance
occurs or whenever a discussion of the interpersonal relationship between the client
and therapist seems relevant. Other times when interpretation is appropriate are
when the client misses an obvious connection between two similar events and fails to
make the appropriate generalization, when the client contradicts himself, and when
he offers overly strong denial to a motive which seems likely to be present. We also
discussed how far to go with interpretations while still being able to avoid excessive
resistance, and when to make rather "deep" interpretations despite resistance.

REFERENCES

Dollard, J., and Miller, N., *Personality and psychotherapy.* New York: McGraw-Hill Book
Co., 1950.

Harway, N. I., et al., The measurement of depth of interpretation. *J. Consult. Psychol.,*
1955, 19, 247-253.

Psychotherapy Research Group (W. U. Snyder, Ed.), *Group report of a program of research in psychotherapy*. University Park, Pa.: Pennsylvania State University, 1953.

Rogers, C. R., *Client-centered therapy*. Boston: Houghton Mifflin Co., 1951.

——,*Counseling and Psychotherapy*, Boston: Houghton Mifflin Co., 1942.

Snyder, W. U., An investigation of the nature of non-directive psychotherapy. *J. Gen. Psychol.*, 1945, 33, 193-224. (Or see unpublished doctoral dissertation under same title, Ohio State University, 1943.)

——, *Dependency in psychotherapy*. New York: The MacMillan Co., 1963.

——, *The psychotherapy relationship*. New York: The MacMillan Co., 1961.

Wolberg, L. R., *The technique of psychotherapy*. New York: Grune & Stratton, 1954.

CHAPTER 8

Confessions of an Ex-Nondirectivist

ROSALEA ANN SCHONBAR, PH.D.

Rosalea Schonbar is well-known as a full Professor in the Clinical Psychology Training Program at Teachers College, Columbia University, and as President of the Division of Clinical Psychology of the New York State Psychological Association.

What she offers us here is an absorbing personal document. It is a statement of one person's involvement as a therapist, an experience given serious reflection and probing examination. Her paper illustrates the proposition that to be bound within any tight theory of technique is to be reduced to operating in a manner which stifles rather than liberates the patient's movement in therapy. As Dr. Schonbar contrasts her self-definition as a therapist with the Rogerian, one infers from her presentation the important distinctions that one can be interpretive without being directive, and—in Nyde's words later in this book—"an authority without being authoritative."

As indicated by the title, my earliest training and supervision in psychotherapy were in client-centered therapy. I worked as a nondirectivist for about four years; during this period, I saw, among others, two long-term patients, at least one of whom contributed substantially to my ultimate development as an interpretive therapist.

This was a young woman who took her therapy very seriously; she worked hard, and so did I. Make no mistake about it: Rogerian therapy is not for passive therapists. This young woman was a dependent girl, and she experienced acutely what she saw as my lack of interest in and participation with her. *I* knew I was interested, *I* knew I cared, but she experienced me as indifferent. Obviously, something was wrong; as predicted by Rogers, she did accept responsibility for these feelings, but she went on feeling them. There were only two alternatives, or some combination of the two: either I was communicating an indifference I did not feel, or she was expressing transference feelings which, according to Rogers, should not have persisted.

She further confounded me by reporting a dream one day. As a client-centered therapist I'd had little experience with dreams. It is of interest that about seven years ago, in preparing to teach a course, I asked Rogers for a transcript of a client-centered interview in which dream material was dealt with; he replied that he couldn't find one, that dreams were seldom brought to client-centered therapy. One such tape is available now, but the scarcity is certainly understandable, for there is little impetus for the patient to consider dreams of importance. When my patient told me her dream I felt handcuffed; my limited armamentarium gave me no way to deal with it meaningfully, apart from a comment on the mood or feeling of the dream. I felt as if something valuable had been brought into the room and just shoved aside into a corner—or, more properly, that it lay between us untouched, thus depriving her of its potential values, and confirming her experience of my not caring. I was indeed rejecting a part of her.

Shortly after this incident, she married and moved out of town. I had by this time begun my own personal therapy with a therapist who had had some Rogerian training but who was interpretive. Contrary to my expectations, I did not feel him to be evaluative, authoritarian, judgmental, disrespectful, or unaccepting; rather, I experienced his active participation in my psychic world, and, far from feeling threatened, I felt hopeful. This further shook my client-centered convictions. Moreover, I discovered increasing discomfort with what I grew to feel as limitations upon my therapeutic behaviors imposed by the Rogerian structure. I found that, as I began to grow more comfortable with myself, I also needed to grow freer in my work with patients, as well as more able to do so. I felt I had more to offer. To move from a client-centered approach to an interpretive one, however, required an intellectual as well as an emotional soul-searching, since I did not feel any less committed to the underlying philosophy of client-centered therapy.

Let us then review briefly that philosophy. Rogers states that client-centered therapy is not a technique, but "a system of attitudes" toward people "which is implemented by techniques and methods consistent with it" (1951, p. 19). These attitudes can be summarized as respect for the individual's capacity and right for self-direction, belief in the worth and dignity of the individual, and unconditional positive regard (1957), defined in terms of a "prizing" of the individual. The therapist implements these attitudes by divesting himself as far as possible of his own self, and, by empathic reflection, providing an atmosphere in which the patient's growth drive can operate fully, unhampered by external evaluations like those which contributed to his difficulties in the first place.

For Rogers, interpretation is a technique which violates these conditions, because it is, as he sees it, rooted in an external frame of reference, is judgmental in nature, and violates the client-determined rate of exploration, thus, from his point of view, "creating" the need for resistance and transference; in addition, it communicates a lack of faith in the patient's capacities.

Is it possible to value the patient, genuinely respect him and his capacity for growth, to be empathic and acceptant, to be guided by his inner experience and readiness, and still be an interpretive therapist? I came to the conclusion that it is possible, that most of the attitudinal aspects of Rogerian theory are probably basic to becoming an effective therapist of any kind, and that the restriction of the implementation thereof to reflection and clarification of feelings is not intrinsic to the basic theory or attitudes, and may, in fact, be in part based upon some assumptions which are not valid. Let me briefly discuss two of these considerations.

THE THERAPIST AS AUTHORITY FIGURE

Rogers believes that, to the degree that the therapist views himself as having more insight into the client than the client does, he is being disrespectful of him, thus inhibiting his growth. The client's difficulties have arisen in relation to authority figures, and for the therapist to be another authority figure is therefore antitherapeutic. This is in direct contrast to Sullivan's description of the therapist as "an expert in interpersonal relations" (1954, p. ix), and for this reason uniquely suited to help troubled people. What Rogers fails to see, I think, is that there are authority figures and authority figures. Fromm (1941, 1947) differentiates rational from irrational authority, describing rational authority as rooted in competence and characteristic of relationships of unequally competent people where the interests of both lie in the same direction. Surely this is characteristic of the therapeutic relationship. Moreover, experience with a person exhibiting rational authority gives the patient an opportunity to learn this important distinction through direct contact. To be expert, to be more competent than another, is not, therefore, to be judgmental of him. One can be an authority *with* him. It can also be argued that to deny one's expertness, to withhold an objective perspective, is to deny that part of the patient which is damaged and needs help. The client-centered therapist accepts and respects the patient's ego strengths, but he rejects its weaknesses.

REFLECTION AND INTERPRETATION

If respect for the patient is not violated by interpretation, what then about the remaining problems concerning the two techniques? Rogers has presented these techniques as a dichotomy. But are they? Whatever the therapist does, he first makes a choice as to whether to remain silent or to speak; and then if he chooses to speak, he must select that part of the patient's communication to which to respond, even *within* the affective area to which Rogers directs himself. For any therapist, part of this selection lies in the question, "What is the patient experiencing, what does he mean, what is he trying to tell me?" The interpretive therapist then has the additional choice of what kind of response to make. But, in any event, a response may refer to the immediate and particular statement of the patient, as in reflection, or it may arise out of the total history of this particular therapeutic relationship. It may be at a relatively low level of inference, as in reflection, or at a relatively high one. These are continua, not dichotomies.

Interpretation includes more than the patient has just said, or fully realizes he has said, and may involve various levels of inferential complexity. Rogers is quite right in asserting that the client's state of readiness should determine the therapist's response. But it was, after all, Fenichel who noted that interpretation could be effective only to the extent that it dealt with material already present in preconscious derivatives and "striving to break through to consciousness" (1939, p. 25). However, this readiness is not a single point in time, as Rogers suggests, but rather a finite region or range. Nor is it specifically related only to what the client is actually saying now: the relationship between what he is focused on now and other material previously discussed may also be workable with and of use to the patient. Also, the patient frequently seems able to make good use of a new formulation of material he has tried many times to make sense of.

All this implies that the therapist must indeed be in close empathic contact with the patient and that his interpretation must grow out of this empathic contact. Empathy may also be concerned with the state of readiness itself; this is what timing is all about. Levy makes the observation that "just as 'damn Yankee' has become a single word for the Southerner, so has 'intellectualizedinterpretation' become a single word for the Rogerian" (1963, p. 246). Actually, the only argument on this score is against Rogers' notion that all interpretation is intellectualized; few of us would support the view that intellectualized interpretations are helpful. And who, after all, would doubt the empathic basis of Frieda Fromm-Reichmann's interpretive therapy?

SUMMARY

I have shared with the reader some of the aspects of my development from a client-centered to an interpretive therapist. For me, at least, some of these aspects were related to my decreased need to escape from freedom (to coin a phrase) and to my increased need for a more flexible repertoire of techniques. With respect to the latter, a study by Strupp shows that I am not alone. He found that, among Rogerians as well as others, "Increase in experience leads to a diversification of therapeutic technique" (1955, p. 7). In addition, I have tried to show that, while my commitment to those attitudes toward people which Rogers states are necessary for a therapist has not decreased, I have come to believe that the technical implementation he proposes is unnecessarily limiting and may indeed be genuinely depriving to the patient. I have also pointed out some conceptual differences.

Rogers has stated that interpretations are generally threatening and that, when the therapist is interpreting, he "is viewing the person as an object, rather than as a person. . . ." (1951, p. 45). The patient I spoke of earlier moved back to town and resumed therapy with me after I had changed my approach. After a few months, she said, "You know, these new things you're doing—well, it's pretty confusing sometimes, but at least I feel you're interested in me now."

REFERENCES

Fenichel, O., *Problems of psychoanalytic technique*. Albany: Psychoanal. Quart., 1939.

Fromm, E., *Escape from freedom*. New York: Rinehart, 1941.

——, *Man for himself*. New York: Rinehart, 1947.

Levy, L. H., *Psychological interpretation*. New York: Holt, Rinehart & Winston, 1963.

Rogers, C. R., *Counseling and psychotherapy*. Boston: Houghton Mifflin, 1942.

——, *Client-centered therapy*. Boston: Houghton Mifflin, 1951.

——, The necessary and sufficient conditions of therapeutic personality change. *J. Consult. Psychol.* 1957, 21, 95-104.

——, *On becoming a person*. Boston: Houghton Mifflin, 1961.

Strupp, H., An objective comparison of Rogerian and psychoanalytic techniques. *J. Consult. Psychol.*, 1955, 19, 1-8.

Sullivan, H. S., *The psychiatric interview*. New York: Norton, 1954.

CHAPTER 9

Interpretation and the Interpersonal Interaction in Psychotherapy

SOL L. GARFIELD, PH.D.

*Sol L. Garfield received his Ph.D. from Northwestern University in 1942 and
has functioned in a variety of professional settings since that time. In addition to
serving as a clinical psychologist in the army during World War II, he has worked
as chief psychologist in V.A. hospitals and clinics in Illinois and Wisconsin.
After leaving the Veterans Administration in 1957, he held the position of Chief,
Psychology Division, Nebraska Psychiatric Institute, and Professor of Medical
Psychology at the University of Nebraska for six years. For a year he functioned
as Principal Research Scientist at the Missouri Psychiatric Institute and as Research
Professor of Psychology at Washington University in St. Louis, leaving that setting
in 1964 to accept his current position as Professor of Psychology and Director
of the Clinical Psychology Program at Teachers College, Columbia University.*

*Dr. Garfield's primary interests are in the education of clinical psychologists
and in research in psychotherapy and psychopathology. He is an ABEPP Diplomate in Clinical Psychology and a Fellow of the American Psychological Association. He is a past president of the Division of Clinical Psychology and currently
is an Advisory Editor of the* Journal of Consulting Psychology *and the* Journal
of Abnormal Psychology. *He is the author of over 50 publications, including*
Introductory Clinical Psychology, Macmillan, 1957.

*In this chapter, he presents a closely-reasoned, sound and solid treatment of
the context of the interpersonal relation between therapist and patient in which
an interpretation is offered.*

I am one of those who believe that interpretation is an aspect of psychotherapy
which has been overemphasized and the significance of which is secondary to the
relationship which has developed between therapist and client. As I see it, whatever
value interpretation may be said to have is conditioned by this relationship and by
the perceptions of the client of what is taking place. If interpretations are viewed by
the client as a manifestation of the sincere interest and understanding which the
therapist has for him, then they will tend to be received positively, and perhaps contribute to positive movement in therapy. If, on the contrary, the interpretation is
viewed as somewhat derogatory and critical in nature, and as a manifestation of the
therapist's negative evaluation of the client, then it more likely will have a negative
impact on therapy. In the latter instance, the client is likely to reject or otherwise defend himself against these threats to his self-worth. Thus, I do not believe it is the
interpretation or the accuracy of the interpretation which is important for positive
movement in therapy, but the quality of the relationship in which it is imbedded. In
terms of this, I feel that Freud (1950) was essentially correct when he emphasized
that some degree of transference had to exist before interpretations could be offered
effectively by the therapist. However, I would interpret this phenomena somewhat
differently by making the impact of the interpretation secondary to the manner and
setting in which it is offered.

Another aspect of this concerns *how* an interpretation is offered to the client. In this connection the concept of "Expression-Content Balance," offered by Holland (1965) is useful. This refers to the fact that most communications have both an expressive (affective) and a content (cognitive) aspect. It is not just the verbal symbols which the listener perceives, but also the manner in which the symbols are communicated. The latter is also part of a larger whole or context, namely, the relationship which has developed in therapy.

Having stated my position, I would like now to make reference to some observations and comments of others. Meehl (1960) reported, in a study which he and Glueck conducted on a sample of 168 psychotherapists covering a wide spectrum of orientation, that about half the therapists surveyed believed, "Interpretation as a tool is greatly overrated at present." In fact, "Two out of five go as far as to say that 'Under proper conditions, an incorrect interpretation, not even near to the actual facts, can have a real and long-lasting therapeutic effect' " (p. 20). If this is so, it would imply that the actual verbal content of the interpretation is of relatively little significance. What is important is the context and relationship within which the verbal statements are made.

Some observations reported by Wolberg (1954) also appear pertinent to the view presented here. Wolberg (1954) states, "Interpretation is most effective where there is good rapport between patient and therapist. Where a patient feels negatively toward the therapist, he will usually be unable to accept interpretation" (p. 445). I would not disagree with this observation but would change the emphasis. It is not the interpretation which is really important, but the relationship and what is taking place within it. If the interpretation is viewed by the client as a manifestation of the interest and understanding which the therapist has for him, then it will not only be accepted, but he will feel freer both to explore his own feelings and attitudes and to be more accepting of himself. What the therapist says may, of course, have value, but of greater significance is the context in which it is said and the manner in which it is communicated. I see this view as also explaining, in part, the fact that interpretations from very diverse orientations all claim to be effective. Thus, it would appear as if the giving of interpretation, rather than the specific content, is what is apparently important, and the *giving* is a manifestation or aspect of the relationship in therapy.

In terms of what I have said, therefore, a number of problems which have been emphasized in the past concerning interpretation are really of secondary importance. Is it timing which is important, or is it the quality of the interpretation and its implications for what is currently occurring between therapist and client? Most interpretations appear to have a negative or critical connotation and thus have both indications for the self-regard of the client and for the inferred views of the therapist toward the client. A corollary has to do with what one is focusing on in therapy. If one is concerned primarily with the here-and-now of the behaving and experiencing of the client in the therapeutic situation, then one is not really concerned with interpretation in the traditional sense as I understand it—e.g., making conscious what was unconscious—but rather in focusing on what is currently going on and being experienced.

One does not have to refer to this as interpretation, which somehow has overly cognitive and "expert-like" connotations, but as focusing on, and directing attention to, what the client is currently experiencing. This is not something outside the ken of the individual's awareness which needs to be interpreted. Rather, the therapist is trying fully to understand and to focus on what is going on currently. He may, perhaps, call attention to, or attempt to clarify, the behavior of the client or the kinds of feelings the client is experiencing, but the material is not of an abstract or historical nature. The observations or comments of the therapist, whether they be referred to and conceptualized as interpretations, confrontations, reflection of feeling or clarification, take on significance in terms of the existing relationship and in terms of how the therapist is perceived. If the therapist's comments derive from the here-and-now, if he is clearly sensitive to what the client is trying to communicate, and if he manifests interest in what the client is saying, then his comments will have a reality to them and will tend to be viewed by the client as attempts by the therapist to really understand him and to help him. If this is so, then problems of timing and premature or resistance-inducing interpretations should probably not arise.

Unfortunately, what I am discussing here rests more on opinion and belief than on research data. I did look through studies pertaining to our topic but found it difficult to evaluate them adequately or to integrate their findings in terms of this discussion. Too many of them were limited by their particular design or by a particular theoretical framework, and since such terms as "interpretation" may take on different meanings in different theoretical orientations, the evaluation becomes difficult. For example, in a study by Frank and Sweetland (1962) of therapy carried out within a Rogerian framework, both interpretation *and* clarification of feeling, which might be seen as different therapist behaviors, led to increased understanding and insight on the part of the client. Speisman (1959) found that therapists' interpretations systematically influence patient responses, and that "moderate interpretations" were more effective than either superficial or deep interpretations in resolving resistance.

It is tempting to reinterpret the findings of these studies as lending support to the point of view expressed here. Similar findings for interpretation and clarification of feeling may be a function of how these responses by the therapist are perceived by the client, and "moderate interpretation" may be a more clear reflection of the therapist's understanding and interest in the patient then superficial or deep interpretation. However, tempting though it be, I won't make this interpretation. Instead, I would like to end by reemphasizing the need for research on such problems, so that in the future our work in this area may rest more on substantive findings than on theoretical views.

REFERENCES

Frank, G. H., and Sweetland, A., A study of the process of psychotherapy: the verbal interaction. *J. Consult. Psychol.,* 1962, 26, 135-138.

Freud, S., Further recommendations in the technique of psycho-analysis. In *Collected papers,* Vol. II. London: Hogarth Press, 1950, pp. 342-365.

Holland, G. A., *Fundamentals of psychotherapy.* New York: Holt, Rinehart & Winston, 1965.

Meehl, P. E., The cognitive activity of the clinician. *Amer. Psychol.,* 1960, 15, 19-27.

Wolberg, R., *The technique of psychotherapy.* New York: Grune & Stratton, 1954.

Speisman, J. C., Depth of interpretation and verbal resistance in psychotherapy. *J. Consult. Psychol.,* 1959, 23, 93-99.

CHAPTER 10

Interpretation as Interpersonal Structuring

EMANUEL F. HAMMER, PH.D.

Psychotherapy, Fromm says (Evans, 1966), has as its "fundamental aspect the reality of two people talking together . . . about something serious—the life of this patient." The therapist's comments, if sensitive, accurate, and aimed at the patient's expanding efforts to sense and know, convey to the latter that in this relationship he may experience not only understanding (sympathy), but may be deeply understood (comprehended).

The interpersonal schools of therapy might be reminded of what Freud said before them: "Psychoanalysis is an exquisitely social undertaking" (Coles, 1965). After Freud, others of the classic as well as the Sullivan and Horney positions have similarly underscored the interpersonal. "The psychoanalytic situation," Erikson has written, does service as "a model of 'competent' behavior . . . true for all other relationships: mutuality, competence, and the development of capacities go together" (Evans, 1967). Colby (1951) comments, "For him [the patient] to talk to someone who does not nag and moralize is a special experience which can permit him to grow to feel that he is a responsible adult rather than a naughty child."

Treatment is obviously a matter of two people coming to terms with one another in a rather special way. Questions might ordinarily be raised about the nature of the treater as well as the nature of the patient when they come into contact. This is also so when they meet in the type of engagement provided by the offering of that move on the therapist's part we call an "intervention," a "confrontation" or an "interpretation."

"Psychoanalytic therapy started with catharsis and shifted to insight" (Alexander, et al., 1966). As early as 1904, however, Freud asserted that "there is . . . the greatest possible antithesis between suggestion and analytic technique." Following this, we have come to distinguish between rapport therapies (also called "anaclitic"—after the Greek, "to lean upon"), in which the patient learns by emulating and feeling close to the therapist, and psychoanalytic therapies, in which the patient learns to scrutinize his relationship to the therapist, i.e., by analyzing with him the transference and also his type of resistances in the process. It is this latter approach which utilizes, as its pivotal tool in the process, the interpretive modalities. It is these modalities which all uncovering schools of therapy employ in common. Furthermore, "All schools of psychotherapy which claim allegiance to what is called 'dynamic psychology' fundamentally maintain that lack and avoidance of self-knowledge are the core of psychopathology" (Singer, 1966).

In the pursuit of self-knowledge by and for the patient, however, advances in the therapist's technique and in the theory of technique have gone beyond "content" analysis to the use and illumination of the interpersonal relationship existing between clinician and client. It had been customary, at one time, merely to scrutinize and interpret the "content of the patient's conflicts, defenses, symptoms, etc." (Bromberg, 1962). In considering that which is central to all therapeutic transactions today, from Freudian through the spectrum of theories to Rogerian, one might start with the situation between therapist and patient, akin to the "encounter" of the Existentialists—the "fact of the reality of two persons in the room," as Rollo May expresses it. In this context, where does interpretation fit in?

Every interpretation is custom-fashioned for the individual patient; it is a unique hypothesis about a unique sequence of data. This is why an interpretation is difficult to arrive at and to render and also why its achievement imparts a freshness and vitality to the patient-therapist interaction, which no amount of tricks, provocation or high-spirited running-off-at-the-mouth can ever duplicate. Indeed, I should go so far as to say that any patient of any amount of sophistication who is being subjected to the grab-bag stunts and homilies of a therapist who himself has never really learned to listen knows with the anxiety and bitterness of secret envy that somewhere there are patients blessed with the fortune of being listened to with a shrewd and practiced attention (Kaplan, 1966).

Thus, as an interpretive approach is initiated by the therapist, something important beyond the content of what is said is communicated. The focus of what brings the patient and therapist together, and what they do, becomes then a search for the causes of the patient's problems and for illumination. The mere utilization of interpretive and analytic efforts by the therapist, regardless of the content or theoretical orientation behind them, has this one special, and important effect: It demonstrates that behavior and feelings (and he, the patient as a person) are to be understood rather than judged. It provides an example of a naturalistic stance, much like that of the botanist, astronomer, or historian, rather than the moralistic one of a judge, as a model for the patient's frequently too rigid, tyrannical, provincial or narrow-minded superego. An interpretive orientation conveys to the patient that his nature and problems are in essence a human condition, one upon which light is to fall rather than criticism meted out.

The interpretive search for meaning, in a setting of acceptance, elicits the varied pictures which the patient eventually focuses for himself: to some degree, a sense of what he is, is sorted from what he says he is, what he thinks he is, and what he would like to be. This search, in a setting of acceptance, enables the patient to shed reserves and be more completely himself.

At this point, the theory of interpretation encounters one of the Rogerian invectives against it: interpretation is threatening to a patient. If this be so, we might well recognize that without pain there is often no growth. To the client-centered therapist or anyone else dealing in the process of emotional reeducation, this should be a truism.

In practice, moreover, factors such as (a) the possible degree of threat of the interpretation, (b) an estimate of the patient's ability to utilize it, and (c) an expectation of the attitudes or behavior it is likely to evoke are, of course, all considerations when we try to judge (and *sense*) the appropriateness and timing in offering interpretative understanding.

In addition, we may deduce from our observation of people, not only in the therapy room, but also on the broader plain outside, that the presence of stress, tension, or discomfort is not necessarily harmful nor undesirable. A mild degree of external threat can, at times, give the patient something to work against when a locked equilibrium otherwise establishes a state of stagnation in therapy. Tension, whether internal or external, can sometimes stimulate growth, or cause invention, discovery, creation, or reform. Tensions brought to the fore around an interpretation invite the patient to struggle with them, and in doing so attain mastery, if not at times wisdom. As brief examples of the principle from the well-known, tension motivated Toulouse-Lautrec and Van Gogh to paint, Freud to analyze himself and reveal his insights to society, and Kafka and countless others to share their inner worlds with us.

Could it be that there is an *optimal* level of tension for each of us relative to our degree of personality strength? Might too little lead to complacency and stultification in the therapy session or outside it in life in general? Might too much lead to paralysis, defensive symptoms, a retreat from progress, spontaneity or originality? An approach to the optimal ratio of stress, on the one hand, and the capacity to handle and master this tension, on the other, may be at the core of an individual's ability to evolve, unfold, and move forward. It is certainly dangerous to employ interpretations which produce more stress than the patient's strength can match. It is also disadvantageous, on the other side, not to mobilize judiciously that degree of tension which can be motivating and effectively used. This balance, admittedly, at times may be a difficult one to assess, but the concept is there and stands available as a guiding principle. The desired degree of anxiety, then, is one which serves to spur the patient to address his problems and do the work in therapy, but is not of such a magnitude as to incapacitate these efforts.

There is another line of reasoning we might also put alongside the Rogerian challenge. Beyond interpretations not being contraindicated *if* threatening, there is a more preliminary consideration: many interpretations are not threatening. In fact, interpretations are sometimes reassuring and relieving. To begin with, we have the obvious example of a psychological interpretation of the dynamic meaning of a cancerphobia. The terrified patient finds it reassuring, in that it makes one thing plausible as an alternative: The more persuasive the relationship uncovered between the irrational fear that one must be dying of cancer and the underlying network of dynamic needs and meanings, the more relief there is for the patient in the heightened plausibility that the fear of cancer has merely a psychological basis.

As another example, one woman, during her session, spoke of her reaction upon the death of her child several years before. She had begun cleaning the floors and straightening the pictures on the walls, mending and darning, and washing dishes. As she lay on the couch, recalling her activities, she condemned herself bitterly for being heartless and unfeeling for "thinking of housework at a time like that." The need to busy herself in distracting chores, was interpreted as an effort to make the awful feelings less immediate, to blanket them under the routine, the familiar and the manageable.[1] She could then, she said with a vast and heaving sight, understand her reaction. She could begin to set aside this painful accusation of herself as a mother.

An adolescent boy was talking of his fear of failing an impending college entrance examination the following week. Later on in the session he suddenly had, and reported, a fantasy of wanting to eat feces out of a toilet bowl. He stammered out this "confession" as a strange thought that had just come into his mind, one which he said must mean he was an "awful pervert," if not actually "crazy."

---

[1]Such an approach may serve as an example of what is sometimes referred to as the use of the "inexact interpretation." This may be employed at a point in the treatment where a reassuring and calming effect is what is wanted. It is "inexact" in the sense of being incomplete rather than invalid. The interpretation here included no nudging in the direction of any exploring yet behind her accusation of herself as an awful mother, possibilities which may have embodied unconscious hostile wishes toward her child.

In the preceding months we had been uncovering masochistic defenses he utilized. At this point, relating his masochism to his need to degrade himself and appease the Fates into allowing him to pass the college examination, it was commented on that his demonstration that he is only a "shit" who even eats the same was in the service of presenting himself as a harmless, lowly entity who would really be no threat to anyone, even if allowed success and college status. As we pursued the problem further, he visibly relaxed under the understanding of this mechanism of his, and of the dismissal of the self-accusations of insanity and of being a pervert.

As a last example, we might turn to a situation handled by a cluster of interpretations rather than a single one. The patient, a woman in her thirties, was a career woman and mother of several children. Soon after beginning analysis she became particularly blocked and hesitant to talk This lasted several months, during which time a picture emerged of the patient's having been squelched, stifled, intimidated, and hemmed-in by an exceedingly authoritarian, dogmatic, righteous, intellectualized, and controlling mother. One day she confided that the reason she felt unable to talk in sessions was because there was one "secret" on her mind she always came to the verge of telling, but from which until now she had backed away. The secret she now braced herself to tell was that she had, during high school and college, engaged in thievery. The thefts ranged from small change and candy to clothing from a department store where she worked, an offense in which she was caught and for which she was then dismissed. After blurting out this last incident, she then lay on the couch paralyzed with fear and dire expectations concerning my reactions.

My first reaction was to comment on her sturdiness in being able to finally tell me something she found so difficult. Then, across the span of this and the subsequent sessions, we went on to work out the following interwoven possibilities: (1) It seemed that she was giving to herself in order to feel less ungiven to. (The candy she stole she experienced as substitutes for the indulgence her mother didn't extend.) (2) She evidently had a need to give herself something she had not earned, whereas her mother gave to her (approval, recognition) *only* what she had over-earned (through good grades, obedience, conformity). (3) The behavior in some way represented spurts at self-assertion and rebellion against the tyranny of the continual "should not's" and "do not's" lest she go down altogether in spirit-broken submission. (In this manner she pushed against the yoke of the "good-little-girl" role her mother had placed so heavily upon her.) (4) At the same time, the stealing allowed her to release her resentment, to hit back at her mother on the latter's high-bound morality, by doing exactly what would have made her mother most aghast *if she but knew*.

But what was the main communication? It was none of the above interrelated and overlapping ones. The most basic was the unstated one between the lines of the others: that (5) the therapist was seeking to understand a bit of behavior, not judge a crime—that as collaborators we were addressing something to cast light upon, not something to pass sentence upon. While the first four interpretations provided more of the instant easing of her acute self-condemnation, it was the last-named demonstration of the atmosphere of our relationship which provided the security for her to proceed from this point less encumbered with her previous incapacity to dare to talk, share, and face things.

Thus, interpretations, while sometimes threatening, are sometimes reassuring and sometimes (particularly with patients who have oral needs) gratifying. These latter patients feel they are given something or, on deeper levels, fed. This very definition of theirs in turn, of course, requires therapeutic focus.

In terms of the range of reactions to interpretations, Horney offers a similar observation: that within the patient's reactions to interpretation there can be anxiety, attack, or relief (Slater, 1956). In this noting of the latter reaction, Levy (1963) concurs. He offers the following construct: In interpreting, "generalizations reduce dissonance primarily through demonstrating that there is order of a sort; constructions reduce dissonance through explaining why the order is of the sort that it is."

Sometimes what is interpreted seems only surface deep and almost touchable, and although there is considerable overlap, I find that these allow the more relieving interpretive exchanges. At other times what is interpretively probed for lies hidden and may reveal itself at some time after the interpretation has been given, or in sudden insight in a subsequent session or between sessions.

Thus, the direction of the unfolding capacities for communication is twofold. It is not only interpersonal, but it is intrapsychic as well. Feeling his way into the labyrinthine maze of his own nature puts an individual in touch with himself. In the process he may develop an inwardness and deepening, as he lays his ghosts to rest by discovering what he is. But he may do more than this. He may expand his being and learn to know not only his wound but also his gifts. As Maslow (1965) states: "As we learn steadily that the depths are not only the wellsprings of neurosis, but also of *health,* of *joy,* of *creativeness,* we begin to speak of the healthy unconscious, of healthy regression, of healthy instincts, of healthy non-rationality, of healthy intuition. And we begin to desire to salvage these capacities for ourselves."

There is another gain along the way. The patient is encouraged to examine his situation both from within and from without. He explores with the inner eye the messages shared with him by the analyst who can listen with a "third ear." In those collaborations where both analyst and patient have the necessary depth and sensitivity, they embark upon an absorbing quest into both psychic interiors and interpersonal subtleties. The quest, in itself, is intrinsically liberating. Introspective adventuring limbers and expands the personality. The collaboration is, at the same time, interpersonally unfolding, an "opening-up" process for both patient and therapist.

REFERENCES

Alexander, F., Eisenstein, S., and Grotjahn, M., *Psychoanalytic pioneers.* New York: Basic Books, 1966.

Bromberg, W., *The nature of psychotherapy. A critique of the psychotherapeutic transaction.* New York: Grune & Stratton, 1962.

Colby, K. M., *A primer for psychotherapists.* New York: Ronald Press, 1951.

Coles, R., The wild analyst: The life and work of Georg Groddeck. *New York Times Book Review,* May 30, 1965.

Evans, R. I., *Dialogue with Erich Fromm,* New York: Harper and Row, 1967.

Evans, R. I., *Dialogue with Erik Erikson.* New York: Harper and Row, 1967.

Kaplan, D. M., Classical psychoanalysis, *Psychoanal. Rev.,* Spring 1966. 99-111.

Levy, L. H., *Psychological interpretation.* New York: Holt, Rinehart & Winston, 1963.

Maslow, A. H., Isomorphic interrelationships between knower and known. In G. Kepes, (Ed.), *Sign, image and symbol.* New York: Braziller, 1965.

Singer, E., *Key concepts in psychotherapy.* New York: Random House, 1966.

Slater, R., Karen Horney on psychoanalytic technique: Interpretations. *Amer. J. Psychoanal.,* 1956, 16, 118-124.

CHAPTER 11

Interpretation and Ego Function

ESTHER MENAKER, PH.D.

Esther Menaker is adjunct Professor of Psychology at New York University and has been in private practice as a psychotherapist and psychoanalyst in New York City for more than 30 years. She received her Ph.D. at the University of Vienna and was trained concurrently at the Vienna Psychoanalytic Institute. In addition to articles in professional journals, she is co-author with her husband of a recent book, Ego in Evolution. *Her paper below reflects her work at its height—scholarly, incisive, thoughtful, and at times, inspiring.*

We pay too little attention to the implications of some of the miracles of life that surround us. One of these miracles is the phenomenon that one individual can influence the behavior, thinking, attitude and feeling of another. Pragmatically, we make use of this fact in countless aspects of our daily lives—in child rearing, in education, in social encounters, in politics, in business—and certainly in our own field of psychotherapy. In fact, the "influenceability" of human personality is the indispensable condition for any psychotherapeutic intervention.

Yet, perhaps because of the dangers implicit in the misuse of the power to influence, the issues surrounding the factors of influence in human interaction have been side-stepped; even more, they have generally been disparagingly dismissed as "suggestion," and the technique of interpretation has been advanced as an antidote to the possible dominance of any element of suggestion in the therapeutic procedure.

In the early days when psychoanalysis was being born out of the techniques of hypnosis, Freud was aware of the inevitable factor of suggestion that played a part in the efficacy of interpretation, as well as in mass psychology and certain ego phenomena. However, because of the transitory and limited effects of hypnosis as a therapeutic method, the discovery of the dynamic unconscious and the phenomenon of repression, Freud regarded suggestion and interpretation as antithetical therapeutic techniques. Suggestion, whether implemented by the authoritative or lovingly persuasive stance of the therapist, placed the ego of the patient under his domination, whereas the uncovering and consequent interpretation of hitherto repressed impulses made available for the patient new self-knowledge, thus expanding the boundaries of his ego and creating opportunities for new integrations. The emphasis, therefore, in the classic psychoanalytic technique was on the uncovering of unconscious content, be it of drives or of defenses, and the interpretation of these to the patient.

To the extent that this viewpoint seeks to increase the patient's ego autonomy, it is valid in its *intention,* for it corresponds to the patient's own conscious motivation to alter his behavior, thinking and feeling. However, it rests on a limited technical definition both of suggestion and of interpretation and on an assumption that they are opposing phenomena relative to the human ego.

I should like to advance a different view: that interpretation involves much more than the uncovering of the unconscious; that it is possible as a tool of psychotherapy, first because of the suggestibility of the human psyche, and second because of the innate tendency of ego to synthesize meaningful wholes, to integrate inner and outer experience at increasingly higher levels of significance. Thus interpretations—sometimes irrespective of their validity but given a positive, trusting and viable atmosphere between therapist and patient—may become foci around which the patient structures new meanings that satisfy the ego's need for oneness. These human attributes are the evolutionary product of our neurophysiological history as a species, and attest to our plasticity and ego-growth potential as individuals.

The term "suggestibility" is used here in its broadest sense. It appears in infancy in its earliest and most primary form as *receptivity* to the loving ministrations of the nurturing mother. As we know from the studies of Spitz, Bowlby, Escalona and others, such loving care, which involves much more than the giving of nourishment, is essential for the development of the nervous system, the emergence of consciousness and the ultimate structuring of ego. It is important to remember that the interaction system, mother-child, is a crucial communication system in which the child's capacity to receive is as important as the mother's ability to give. One possibility of influencing the development, formation and direction of human personality rests in this capacity to receive communications—be they tactile, kinesthetic, auditory, visual or verbal—and first to convert them into neurological structure and subsequently to integrate them into psychic functions. Specifically, the processes of introjection, imitation and identification—which are innate, primary capacities of the human psyche—are responsible for the efficacy of personal interactions in promoting new and higher levels of ego integration and functioning.

We have addressed ourselves to the question of interpretation and ego function. Implied in this juxtaposition is the rather obvious fact that the purpose of interpretation is to improve ego function, whether such function is impaired by anxiety, inhibition or the formation of neurotic symptoms or character disorders. As we have already indicated, in the Freudian view the value of interpretation in meeting these ends lies in the fact that by making conscious what had previously been unconscious, a shift of energy takes place within the psychic systems, making energies previously associated with unconscious processes now available to the ego. Thus the Freudian conception of change or cure depends on a redistribution of energy within a *closed system,* and the function of interpretation is to bring about this redistribution.

When one views personality, and ego as its essential psychological core, not as a closed system seeking stabilization through the reduction of tension within its confines, but as an *open system* striving expansively toward optimal realization of its potentialities, then one's view of the nature and function of communication between individuals changes and a new perspective on the therapeutic interaction appears.

Classic psychoanalysis has found major support for a conception of personality as a closed system in the repetitive phenomena of the transference, of the repetition compulsion in the recurrence of neurotic, often self-destructive, life patterns. These phenomena undoubtedly do exist. They must be among the things dealt with—i.e., appropriately interpreted—in the psychotherapeutic situation; but they do not necessarily argue for a conception of personality as a closed energy system. There are other phenomena which we observe in the therapeutic situation that bespeak the expanding, evolving nature of the human ego as a part of the total life process, which is an open system. As an example, we can cite the operation of *choice* in the patient's motivation toward therapy as a means of achieving a higher level of ego-integration, optimal expressiveness and self-realization, thereby striving to achieve a self-conception more consistent with his ethical goals and his conception of, and need for, love and relatedness. It is important to bear in mind that not only *conflict* can motivate a patient toward therapy, but also *ego-ideal aspiration.* When the therapist has an awareness of this fact, even though it remains unexpressed or even unconscious on the part of the patient, his interpretations are geared toward the support of such strivings and aspirations. He approaches the therapeutic task with a belief in the patient's capacity to transcend himself. Such belief is as crucial for the patient's betterment as the young mother's belief in her infant's capacity to grow is for his actual development. The transmission of this belief—this basic trust in the life process—be it by implication or explicit statement, is a crucial, curative aspect of interpretation.

Empirically the application of classic forms of interpretation has had only limited effect (i.e., in the uncovering of unconscious defenses and the corresponding unconscious impulses which it has been their function to ward off, together with the discharge of affects appropriate to such conflict and the working through of this process on successive levels of libido organization). To my mind, such failure has its roots in two main causes. One lies in the Freudian deterministic, mechanistic conception of personality which, when transposed into the act of interpretation, presents to the patient, from a position of authority, a partial truth about himself as if it were a whole truth, thereby doing violence to his ego, restricting its operation within a given system of thought, and inhibiting its expansive potential to new and higher levels of integration. In essence it is a misuse, however benignly motivated, of the suggestive capacities of the ego. Inadvertently, by leaving no room for the human equality of patient and therapist, the authoritative stance perpetuates what is an inevitable, yet hopefully temporary, dependent, submissive position of the patient in the therapeutic encounter. An interpretation which points up the possibility of a true insight to the patient, thus catalyzing his own ego processes, has an entirely different appeal to his ego than a flat statement designed to expose a defense or an unconscious impulse.

A second source of therapeutic failure in the classic psychoanalytic approach was the assumption that change in thought, feeling or action follows *automatically,* if not directly, upon the interpretation of the unconscious, then certainly upon the working through of the interpretation and the discharge of appropriate affect. In actuality this rarely happens.

Following is an example of what I would regard as the essential and positive contribution of the interpretation of the unconscious, as well as its limitations and what might be added to bring about greater autonomy of the patient's ego.

An attractive and intelligent young man of approximately 25 had been consulting me throughout the past academic year because of feelings of estrangement, fears pertaining to his sexual identity and acceptability to women, and certain inhibitions in his work life. He was a graduate student in one of the arts, was living away from home, but was being supported by his parents. He was in a total state of rebellion; he wished to do almost none of the things that one is supposed to do, and did practically all the things that the conventional adult world frowns upon, from smoking marijuana to being irresponsible about his studies. Such negativism obviously presents the therapist with serious problems. An important asset of the patient, however, enabled me to achieve excellent rapport with him. He possessed a high degree of creative psychological imagination and was motivated by a great desire to understand—to uncover the meanings of perplexing emotional experiences and to reintegrate these into a unified account of his life. Despite his estrangement, he tried to reach out to people, and his wish to love and to be loved belonged to his almost explicitly stated aspirations. It was a pleasure to share his joyous sense of wonder when he made a discovery about himself. We made some of the usual discoveries: among them his unexpressed anger, sometimes even rage, toward parents who meant well, but whom he experienced as controlling and dominating; his highly ambivalent attitude toward an older brother whom he at once loved, was dependent upon, yet hated, and with whom he feared to compete. He saw his insufficiency at work and school as expressions of his anger; he saw his difficulties with peers, both men and women, as in large measure influenced by the unresolved conflicts in his brother relationship, which precipitated passivity, guilt and powerful feelings of inferiority. At times he expressed hostility toward me, and he was able to understand this as a projection of his feelings toward his mother. Yet none of these insights appreciably influenced his overt behavior.

As we approached his final sessions before the summer holiday, it became clear that he had mismanaged his attempts to get a summer job so successfully that he had nothing lined up for the ensuing months. This young man who complained so bitterly about his dependence on parents, was so in the grip of rebellious anger against them that, at the cost of suffering great guilt and feelings of worthlessness, he was impelled to make them pay.

At this point in his treatment, however, I did not reinterpret his inhibition as resulting from the passive, aggressive impulses based on revengeful feelings toward his parents and brother or from defenses against the fear of his own hostilities against them. These connections, which had originally been unconscious, were now known to him but they were not operative. Instead I said: "I suggest that you try to get some kind of work for the summer. You will feel much better with money in your pocket that you have earned; you will be your own man. There are so many things you could do with your talents and experience (and I enumerated some of them for him). You know what will happen if you don't work; you will only feed your feelings of worthlessness and guilt, and that doesn't help in any of your relationships, especially with women. I hope I'm not reminding you of your mother when I say these things."

He assured me that I was not reminding him of his mother, that he felt what I described was right, that he did in fact want to get a job and that he appreciated my urgings.

Can these simple, common-sense suggestions and depictions of the consequences of action or inaction be properly called interpretations? Perhaps not in the usual usage of that term. Yet I would like to speak of a hierarchy of interpretation, in the course of which having gone the accepted Freudian pathway from unconscious ego defense to deeper unconscious impulse, one again returns to address the ego—not the ego that institutes and executes defenses, nor even the inherent conflict-free ego sphere that guarantees the autonomous development of certain ego functions, but rather the ego that is motivated by striving and aspiration to fulfill its optimal potentiality, to achieve a higher, more autonomous degree of integration, to participate more completely in human interaction. In a therapeutic atmosphere in which the therapist conveys his trust in this progressive capacity of ego, as well as an empathic understanding of the patient's conflict and anxiety, and in which the ground has been prepared by making available and meaningful for the ego that which was previously unconscious and unknown, an interpretation which might otherwise be regarded as simple exhortation becomes a catalyst for the self-realization of the patient. Thus applied, the function of interpretation goes beyond its content, to the expression of the capacity of one human being to bring influence to bear upon the expansive ego potential of another.

CHAPTER 12

Spontaneity in the Analytic Interpretation

Harold Lindner, Ph.D.

Dr. Lindner is in the private practice of psychotherapy, psychoanalysis and hypnoanalysis in Washington, D. C. He is Past President of the Society of Clinical and Experimental Hypnosis, Past President of the Washington Society of Clinical Psychologists, and a Diplomate in Clinical Hypnosis of the American Board of Examiners in Psychological Hypnosis. He is also active in national and regional professional and psychotherapeutic associations.

Having written widely on hypnosis and psychotherapy, he has contributed to three books and has published numerous papers in professional journals. Presently he is an associate editor of both The International Journal of Clinical and Experimental Hypnosis *and of* Voices: The Journal of the Art and Science of Psychotherapy.

The concept of spontaneous interpretation within the psychoanalytic relationship, as I have come to understand and practice it over a developmental span of some 12 years, is heavily invested in the psychodynamics of the unconscious. I tend to view the interpretative role of the analyst as meaningful, or even at all possible, only to the degree that his own unconscious motivations have been sufficiently analyzed to allow him reasonable freedom from irrational needs and to make his unconscious readily understandable to him. (Of course, such contact with the unconscious can only be derived from extensive personal and didactic, intensive, therapeutic experience.)

I define interpretative spontaneity as synonymous with deep personal contact with one's own unconscious motivations. I define the freedom to emote spontaneously as synonymous with the enriched capacity to feel deeply through prior exposition and successful resolution of one's own narcissistic drives. I define spontaneity as related to realistically honest and objective self-appraisal, with the humility that follows the acceptance of one's own limitations and imperfections. I define spontaneity as synonymous with the freedom concomitantly to articulate and feel oneself in intimate relationship with the other person in the synthesis of the analytic relationship, to a degree most closely related to a melding of the two persons into a symbiotic one person. Finally, I define spontaneity as synonymous with the analyst's adeptness in the necessary identification with the analysand so that he can meaningfully choose the precise "erlebnitz" interpretation at the moment in time and feeling that the analysand is gropingly preparing himself to discover, comprehend and work with it.

To this analyst interpretative spontaneity is not a gimmick; it is not a volitional, rational or tactically decisional ploy. It is simply and completely the end-product of the search for the inner experience, the existential symbiosis of the two-party unconscious into the one-party unconscious.

To the degree that this is achieved within the psychoanalytic experience, I believe the analysis will prove meaningful and successful. To the degree that it is not achieved, less is accomplished in the analysis, and it is to this that the interminable character of many such experiences is attributable.

From this elucidation of a concept of therapy one might surmise that many of my analytic hours are rather stormy and brutally frank. Such a surmise is correct. I feel free to say verbally and posturally anything my feelings might dictate at the moment within the analytic experience. Likewise, this freedom permits me many hours of silence or of personal rumination. I impose no conscious inhibitions on the amount of physical movement I or my analysand might desire: I might sit in my chair, move to another, or pace the room or sit on the floor, whatever the directive of my inner feeling at the moment. If bored, I might do some paperwork at the desk or read. If stimulated by a fantasy, an insight, or a dream report, I might spend the hour in total examination of it through my unconscious. The analysand has equal freedom and might vary his posture or associative flow in similar fashion. The essential ingredient is that we, *together,* explore all these reactions and analyze them to relatively complete understanding and resolution.

In order to grasp this concept—and to differentiate it from other therapeutic concepts that merely rationalize unconscious needs to act out and propel oneself into a primary narcissistic image of megalomanical proportions through quasi-therapeutic role-playing under the guise of being rational—it is essential to understand that my reactions are interpretative, not instructive; that my responses are free and personal and need not be accepted by the analysand; and that the essence of my position is one of "this is me" or "this is how I feel" or "I feel you feel." The analysand working with me develops the identical freedom to express himself similarly whenever, and if ever, he chooses to do so. Again, there is no short-cutting of ego analysis and no undercutting of ego defenses. Rather, through the spontaneous freedom of the relationship the ego defenses are analyzed and the ego forces are gradually but decisively aligned with the developing integrated ego. The patient then needs no alter ego or rationalizing mentor to define the world for him—whether he likes it or not! Consequently, the analysand develops his strengths himself, develops his freedom to feel and to experience and to learn himself because he knows that his choices will be the honored ones. If the analyst feels differently from him, there will ensue a mutually respected and mutually indulgent attempt to resolve the differences in order to achieve the most meaningful choice for the individual, regardless of the therapist's preconceived notions and no matter how emotionally or rationally camouflaged.

Some ten years ago while I was in the process of formulating these considerations, I was seeing an obsessively rigid, phobic woman who found it terribly difficult to work within the free-associative frame of reference of the analytic situation. She used words precisely and demanded elaborate and carefully defined use of language from me. Typically, she had developed the obsessive's defense against feeling; also typically, she early made those transference projections of her own desires for eminence and perfection upon the analyst. Words were spilled and wasted over more than a year of time in the attempt to cut through the ego defense of demanding that the therapist be not only omnipotent, but just as necessarily her perfect model—such projections, of course, being in the service of her unacceptable anxieties about her own hostilities and inadequacies.

At the time, she was using the couch in her analysis, and on one occasion she was articulating, in stream of consciousness fashion, her strong positive and admiring perceptions of me as compared with her husband, whom she caricatured as a "half-man." Then, as on many previously similar occasions with her when I had attempted to cut through these perceptions with verbal interpretations of what I considered their real meaning and try repeatedly to establish that I was not God but only a fellow mortal, I privately screamed out in silent anger at the subtle persistence of her attempts at castration. Without being consciously aware of it that time, however, I started to relieve a persistent itching sensation in my nostril, at which point she turned her head toward me and I found myself staring into her eyes. Initially her glance seemed jolly, but almost immediately it turned wide-eyed and hostile. She continued to observe me picking my nose for a second or two and then returned to her prone position, facing away from me, and retreated into a silence that lasted the remainder of the session.

At our session the next day, she was able to express for the first time in almost a year very angry feelings about me and to cast aspersions on my omnipotence. I supported her expressions and reinterpreted those relevant ego-defense mechanisms that I had previously attempted. Now, however, indications of success in reaching her were evident, and she commenced to make the first hesitant attempts at working with them herself. It was the spontaneity of the activity and the nondefensive reaction followed by the correct interpretation that had reached her. My action had the effect of saying, "I am only a filthy human; do not make me a God and do not demand so much from yourself and everyone else." One simple exercise in personal freedom proved more meaningful than a whole litany of psychonalyese or cognitive injunction.

That type of experience, common in every psychotherapeutic relationship, if only one becomes attuned to it, was germinal in the development of my concept of interpretative spontaneity. I learned to make my interpretations within the psychoanalytic relationship spontaneously free and always responsive to my inner feelings, to my identifications with the analysand. My interpretations, articulated or not, are always carefully inspected by me. I have learned that this is one very good way to check on the transference situation and my own countertransference feelings. These then provide me with a more highly-sensitized awareness of the immediate status of the therapeutic relationship.

In substance, then, I lean heavily on my ability to take an accurate reading of my inner pulsations. I rely on this reading to stimulate and to direct the spontaneity of my analyst-analysand reactions. My interpretations, within the therapeutic situation, are responsive to these feelings in myself which, in my relationship with the analysand, I try to make as symbiotic as possible in order to develop the working therapeutic relationship.

CHAPTER 13

Interpretation and Insight in Psychotherapy

ROSALEA ANN SCHONBAR, PH.D.

The purpose of this paper is to review, explore, and clarify some issues pertaining to the relationships among interpretation, insight, and psychotherapeutic change. At one time it was believed that to bring about change one needed only to "make the unconscious conscious": interpretation led to the conscious grasp of unconscious conflicts (i.e., insight), and it was assumed that change would automatically follow. With the recent emphasis on ego functions has come a widened appreciation of the complexity of relationships among unconscious and behavioral factors. It was observed that patients with a good grasp of their dynamics nevertheless continued to behave neurotically. Rogers (1951), while not questioning the function of insight, is nevertheless sharply critical of what he sees as the undesirable aspects of interpretation. Hobbs (1962) questions the utility of insight itself and of interpretation as its instrument.

While patients still value insight as a therapeutic gain, their psychotherapists value it far less than symptom relief and behavioral change (Feifel and J. Ellis, 1963). New forms of psychotherapy like those of Ellis (1962) and of Wolpe (1958), while very different, share the characteristic of being primarily engaged in symptom alleviation and direct behavior change through techniques essentially classifiable as persuasion, suggestion, and counterconditioning.

Some of the doubts concerning the interpretation-insight-change paradigm are based upon the following observations:

1. Not all change is attributable to insight.
2. Not all insight leads to change.
3. Not all insight is attributable to interpretation.
4. Not all interpretation leads to insight.

These statements are obviously all true. Also, as Hobbs (1962) suggests, the occurrence of insight may indicate that some change has already taken place. But it is also true that some change does result from insight, and that interpretation and insight are sometimes related. The danger of throwing these babies out with the bath arises in part from a tendency to oversimplify the psychotherapeutic process, and to demand that a single explanatory concept or a single phenomenon or a single technique account for its effectiveness. Complexity frustrates us, but human beings are complex, and psychotherapy, a process involving two human beings over time, is even more complex. A single-factor theory won't account for psychotherapeutic change. We need to reexamine the many factors which may contribute, and the relationships among them.

Criteria for change are anything but clear. Patients' statements are usually not trusted, nor are those of therapist, because both have considerable investment in success. The validity of many relevant tests is questioned; the relevance of many valid tests is dubious. Changes in feelings of internal freedom, reduced anxiety or anger are private and untappable except as verbalized, so they are considered nonexistent or (in the behaviorist tradition) changes in verbal behavior are considered equivalent in all respects to whatever intervening processes they may represent.

Despite the above considerations, there is wide agreement that as a result of therapy more of the patient should become accessible to himself, so that his feelings and behavior may be more genuinely free and reality-oriented. One aspect of greater accessibility of self is insight into self, and one function of interpretation is the facilitation of insight.

Sullivan (1947) and Levy (1962) define interpretation as a restructuring or redefining of the patient's situation by the therapist. While Rogers (1951) assumes that this always represents an external evaluation of the patient, it is worth noting that an interpretation is seldom evaluative, that its "externalness" is a matter of degree, and that "externalness" *per se* is not necessarily undesirable. The most effective interpretations must arise from the therapist's empathic contact with his patient, his intuitive grasp of factors in the situation related to timing, his noninvolvement in the neurotic conflict of the patient—all of these influenced to some degree by his conceptual view of man.

Insight, on the other hand, is a process within the patient. No therapist ever gives the patient insight; he merely offers an interpretation. For Sullivan an interpretation is the offering of a hypothesis for further exploration. Fromm-Reichmann suggests that if the therapist offers interpretations in the form of questions, "he addresses himself to a psychotherapeutic co-worker, as it were, and so, by implication, invites further interpretive collaboration on the patient's part" (1950, p. 132). Interpretation, then, is not something we do *to* the patient; it is part of a cooperative enterprise in which, hopefully, the patient can be helped to develop a new view of himself partly through the process of insight within him.

THE NATURE OF INSIGHT

What kind of process is insight? In 1927 Kohler observed that, when a banana was placed outside the cage of an ape, too far away to be reached by either of the sticks at the ape's disposal, the animal would try over and over to reach it with the inadequate tools; he might try to utilize other equally useless objects in the cage. He was quite obviously involved in a problem-solving endeavor. At some point, after turning his attention to something else, or playing seemingly aimlessly, or during the process of striving, the ape brought the two poles together end to end and discovered that one fitted inside the other, making a long pole; immediately he ran to the front of the cage and obtained his banana. From that moment his behavior in this situation was entirely predictable; he had, in a sense, learned completely in one trial, on the basis of a single success. The animal was experiencing insight, which may be described as a reorganization of the field such that the familiar takes on new meanings with the result that new solutions to formerly impossible problems become available. The reorganization has a quality of suddenness, the situation has irreversibly changed, although all the necessary elements were present from the beginning. In the field of creativity, there have been many accounts of problem-solution following immersion in attempts to solve the problem and a period of incubation, followed by the sudden appearance of the desired solution. Insight seems to be the end of a process of motivated and active problem-solving behavior in which the familiar elements become reorganized in such a way that the individual reacts with confidence, sureness, and conviction. After having tried and tried, some interruption of the unsuccessful process allows the pieces to fall into place, so to speak, and allows the individual to experience the new organization with a sense of "This is it!"

In the classical gestalt consideration of insight, there are two factors of particular relevance to our concerns:

First, Koffka (1935) states that consciousness itself is of little importance; it is the organization and meaning of what is conscious that matters. Thus, in therapy, simple knowledge—even if new—may be accepted by the patient as fact, even as personally relevant fact; but unless there is an opportunity for the new knowledge to be incorporated in some new way, it is of little use. This is related to his momentary dynamic balance between resistance and readiness, the state, in short, of his internal psychic organization at the moment.

Second, Koffka notes something he calls partial insight. There may be no overwhelming "Aha!" experience, but rather a series of smaller, more gradual reorganizations. This fits psychotherapy, a slow, painstaking process in which therapist and patient struggle together toward the corner against the wind, making inch-by-inch, almost imperceptible progress until suddenly both realize that that particular corner has been turned. Strachey (1963) points out that a sudden large change is more likely to be a response to suggestion than a genuinely insightful change. Strachey believes that each small change is a direct result of a particular interpretation, another version of the tendency toward oversimplification already discussed. Nevertheless, it is certainly true that the therapist must always remain closely in touch with the states of minimal reorganization within the patient, so that any interpretation can refer to something immediate or potentially immediate in the patient's experience.

The "Truth" of Insight

One conclusion is that useful interpretation must be intrinsically related to the patient's specific history, current construction of the world, and immediate emotional state. It is therefore not true that insight, as described by Hobbs, is "manifested when a client makes a statement about himself that agrees with the therapist's notion of what is the matter with him" (1962, p. 742). Nor is it correct, as suggested by both Hobbs and Levy (1962), that insight need not be true, but need only be useful. To effect change within a particular psychic configuration, the insight must already in some way be present in it, just as the two short rods were always available to Kohler's apes; it must therefore be "true" in the sense that it can only emerge, it cannot be imposed.

Both Hobbs and Ellis (1964) note the troublesome paradox that the different therapies report similar success rates despite their differing conceptual frameworks. How can similar outcomes be related to interpretation based on different explanatory concepts? How can insight be anything other than acceptance of the therapist's view? How can it bear much of a relation to anything inside the patient? Hobbs concludes that what is therapeutic is simply the patient's contact with someone who offers him an integrated, functional view of life, and that it doesn't really matter what that view is or whether it is right or wrong. But this is not the only possible explanation. We do not really know whether all therapeutic approaches have similar outcomes. There may be differences in goals from orientation to orientation. A patient described as improved by one group may be quite different from one similarly described by another. Also, while the major theories differ in their concepts of healthy development, they are remarkably similar in their views of neurotic behavior. Such disparate theorists as Freud, Rogers, and Sullivan all posit a system of defenses developed and maintained in order to minimize the experience of anxiety arising from conflicts of considerable duration. Moreover, since the development of ego psychology, with its concomitant emphasis on resistance, there has been an even greater convergence among formerly divergent approaches.

Thus, the question may be more correctly conceived as: why the similar proportion of failures? Some kinds of damage may preclude the patient's being helped by any known psychotherapeutic approach. In every orientation some therapists are poor or limited in range. Also, each therapeutic orientation arose from someone's experience with a particular cross section of man. Perhaps theories afford the patient a variety of opportunities, in that some may be more sensitive than others to his particular set of difficulties.

The particular conceptual view held by the therapist is only one of the many factors affecting his response to the patient. For the effective therapist the specific theoretic content is of far less importance than his attention to the particular structure, history and immediate emotion of the individual patient. The assumption that the interpretative therapist recasts each patient in the mold of his theoretical formulation is true only of the therapist who would be ineffective regardless of orientation.

Intellectual and Emotional Insight

Hobbs raises a valid point with respect to the distinction between emotional and intellectual insight. The former, he says, is believed to lead to change, but the distinction is usually made *after* the fact, thus maintaining the belief regardless of what happens. This is not an easy problem to solve, because much of the criterion for the affective meaning component of the insight resides within the patient and may be invisible to the therapist, or confused by the patient with his desire for knowledge. I don't know whether it simplifies or complicates the situation to note that both types of insight may contribute to change.

Richfield (1963) points out that both kinds of insight are forms of cognition, and that both or neither may refer to an emotion. Intellectual insight is basically a descriptive cognition: the patient learns something new *about* something. Emotional or, as Richfield calls it, "ostensive" insight is a direct cognition: the patient learns something new through direct acquaintance with or experience of the content, referents, and meaning of the knowledge. Thus, while we may not be able to distinguish one from the other as it is occurring, we can certainly assume that the more intellectual the interpretation, the more distant *its* referents from the immediately present complex affective state of the patient, the less likely that interpretation is to produce meaningful ostensive insights. Fromm-Reichmann (1950) distinguishes between descriptive and meaningful interpretations. I do not agree with Rogers (1951) that we must not move beyond the patient's current awareness; his potential readiness for meaningful insight extends well (but finitely) beyond his awareness. But Rogers is correct in emphasizing an empathic stance on the part of the therapist: the more he learns about his patient from direct experience, rather than from thinking *about* him, the more his interpretations are likely to produce meaningful emotional insights in the patient.

Some intellectual interpretations and intellectual insights may be useful, too. If I indicate that not all people believe that anger is bad, this is an educational or intellectual statement, intended to offer the patient a new cognition about the world he lives in to lay the groundwork for later experiential cognitions. Similarly, I have occasionally found it useful with suicidal patients to tell them something about the dynamics of depression and suicide, not in any belief that this will bring about immediate emotional insight, but because some sense of intellectual control may be temporarily useful to the patient—and perhaps lead to some working through that can produce in him a sense of emotional truth. Intellectual insights may comprise part of what Koffka has called "partial insights."

In this regard I think of one patient whose most effective defense was intellectualization. During several years of treatment, he had recognized many times over his anger at his psychotic mother's unpredictable shifts between affection and hostility; his relationship with her did indeed change during these years. One day he started to relate his feelings about women to his experience with his mother. "What about your mother?" I asked. This was old hat, and made him angry; he launched into the familiar list of complaints, and then suddenly began to sob. At that moment he was experiencing the feelings we had talked about many times. And I rather doubt that he could have reached this experience without all the previous bits and pieces of partial intellectual and emotional insights he had achieved in a meaningful relationship.

Similarly, another patient who worked very hard at remembering interpretations would solemnly recite them back to me several weeks later, with obvious distance between the words and any experience on his part. He became angry when I suggested that *he* work on his dreams, that he expected magic answers from me, that he disclaimed responsibility both for his current difficulties and for his therapy. I interpreted several times that he was demanding that I *do* something for him, that I change him. He seemed only baffled by the whole thing, stating that, if true, he was not aware of it. One evening, as he was haranguing me on this issue, I interrupted to inquire about how he was feeling "right now." "Helpless," he said. I asked how that felt. There was a pause, and he said, "I feel shitty." I had an image of him as an infant standing in his crib, with dirty diapers, screaming his head off for an absent mother, and said, "You're crying for your mother to change you , and you're furious that she doesn't—that I don't." He visibly relaxed, and was able to feel his anger at his mother and its connection with what had been going on between us, as well as to arrive at some sense of what lay behind his fierce competitiveness with his 15-month younger brother. Would all this, even his experience of helplessness, have been possible without the previous reluctant intellectual cognitions? I doubt it. At least with an intellectualizing patient, this may be his only way of making a connection with the rest of himself. There is a danger here, since the intellectualizing is also used as resistance. With this kind of patient the therapist has even fewer cues than usual to the patient's emotional state, and it is even more important that he identify them and respond experientially and sensitively to them so as to give the patient the greatest possible opportunity for direct experiential response.

It has already been suggested that the disparate elements which become reorganized in the process of insight are already present within the patient, but in a different configuration (the two sticks in the ape's perceptual field). But the apes were not in a conflict situation; no internal opposing force was active in their problem-solving endeavor. By definition the neurotic patient is engaged in defending himself against anxiety, and this anxiety might be released were he to experience prematurely the function of a need for aspects of his defensive structure. Hence, insight, even insight into resistances, must be achieved against resistance, against the tendency to selective inattention toward something which, to the therapist, is undeniably present in the patient's current formulation and behavior. One aspect, then, of the therapist's function is to provide a relationship in which the patient can gradually release his grasp on his defenses. The therapist's interest, respect, and desire to help contribute to this relationship, as does his realistic, nonpunitive stance. To some extent, the offering of interpretations implements certain aspects of these attitudes. In addition, the interpretation may be the contribution which helps tip the scale in favor of facing the conflict instead of defending against it.

This is a delicate interaction. While premature interpretation may destroy the therapeutic endeavor (Reich, 1949), it may sometimes be a therapist's deliberate attempt to "get something on the record," as it were, to make some possibility available to the patient for future use.

In the last analysis, timing and depth are determined by the patient. Fenichel points out that effective interpretation deals with material that is in the process of "striving to break through to consciousness" (1939, p. 25). This implies that the therapist must be in close intuitive touch with the momentary organization of the patient's ever-shifting psychic equilibrium. He must "listen with the third ear" (Reik, 1954), be in continuous empathic contact with his patient, open in a very primitive sense to emotional communion. He must be aware of and responsive to the associations and feelings aroused in himself by the patient's communications. These will arise from the whole history of his relationship with this patient, what has been said and not said, from the whole body of data offered consciously and unconsciously by the patient and noted consciously and unconsciously by the therapist; they will arise from the therapist's openness to his own feelings and fantasies in response to the particular communication to which he is listening. The therapist's theoretical orientation plays a part here to the degree that it has become congruent with his total responsiveness, and, of course, there are cognitive aspects of his sense of the structure and direction of the therapy. The myriad of cues from these sources may be reacted to without full awareness of their individual contributions, but they provide in the therapist a reorganization of *his* field of understanding the patient, including the sense of "rightness" concerning whether or not to respond and, if so, in what manner.

Interpretations offered as "Could it be . . .", or "I think I hear you saying . . .", or "I get the feeling that you . . ." communicate that the interpretation is the outcome of parallel but interacting processes within and between therapist and patient, thus facilitating insight and the mutuality of the therapeutic endeavor. It is not only the content or the affect to which the therapist is empathically attuned, but, through the intuitive process, he is also attuned to the patient's state of readiness itself.

INSIGHT AND CHANGE

If the patient achieves meaningful insights into many areas of his life and into the complex functional relationships between past and present, content and function, into the differences between present and past, between rational and irrational authority, what then? Certainly more of himself is available to himself, and changes in anxiety, attitudes toward self, and the like may be real and yet relatively private.

A study by Feifel and Ellis (1963) showed that therapists cite behavioral change and symptom alleviation as the major gains of the therapy; patients at the end of therapy referred to increased self-understanding and attitude changes, internal factors related to insight. Questioned again four years later, the patients valued insight no less, but now it took second place to behavior change, and symptom relief is also cited significantly more often.

Is it possible that successful patients leave therapy potentially more improved than their therapists will admit because the latter devalue what they cannot immediately see? Could the later behavior changes have occurred without the process having been set in motion by the previously experienced insights? Perhaps some of our distrust of the efficacy of insight arises from impatience, from a desire to see immediate results.

It is reasonable that behavioral changes (and the patient's admission of them into awareness) will take time. Insight is achieved against the opposing forces of anxiety, defense, and years of motivated clinging to a different view. Actual behavioral change may occur in minimal quantities, accompanied by discomfort and unsureness. Moreover, the patient has experienced developmental lags which must be made up for, producing additional discomforts. Freud's (1955) belief that resynthesis would automatically follow analysis does not take these factors into account. The belief that the lifting of repression automatically and immediately allows for the blossoming of new and effective behavior overlooks the fact that the patient must learn how to implement his new views of himself and his world and that this takes time. The patient's life situation is, after all, more complex than that of Kohler's apes.

REFERENCES

Ellis, A., *Reason and emotion in psychotherapy,* New York: Lyle Stuart, 1962.

——, Thoughts and theory versus outcome in psychotherapy. *Psychotherapy,* 1964, 1, 83-87.

Feifel, H., and Ellis, Janet. Patients and therapists assess the same psychotherapy. *J. Consult. Psychol.,* 1963, 27, 310-318.

Fenichel, O., *Problems of psychoanalytic technique.* Albany: Psychoanal. Quart., 1939.

Freud, S., Lines of advance in psycho-analytic therapy (1919). In J. Strachey (Ed.), *The complete psychological works of Sigmund Freud.* Vol. XVII. London: Hogarth, 1955. Pp. 157-168.

Fromm, E., *Man for himself.* New York: Rinehart, 1947.

Fromm-Reichmann, Frieda, *Principles of intensive psychotherapy.* Chicago: University of Chicago Press, 1950.

Hobbs, N., Sources of gain in psychotherapy. *Amer. Psychol.,* 1962, 17, 741-747.

Koffka, K., *Principles of gestalt psychology.* New York: Harcourt, Brace, 1935.

Kohler, W., *The mentality of apes.* New York: Harcourt, Brace, 1927.

Levy, L., *Psychological interpretation.* New York: Holt, Rinehart & Winston, 1962.

Reich, W., *Character analysis* (3rd Ed.) New York: Orgone Inst. Press, 1949.

Reik, T., *Listening with the third ear.* New York: Farrar, Strauss, 1954.

Richfield, J., An analysis of the concept of insight (1954). In L. Paul (Ed.), *Psychoanalytic clinical interpretation.* New York: Free Press of Glencoe, 1963, pp. 93-111.

Rogers, C. R., *Client-centered therapy.* Boston: Houghton-Mifflin, 1951.

Strachey, J., The nature of the therapeutic action of psycho-analysis (1934). In L. Paul (Ed.), *Psychoanalytic clinical interpretation.* New York: Free Press of Glencoe, 1963, pp. 1-41.

Strupp, H., An objective comparison of Rogerian and psychoanalytic techniques. *J. Consult. Psychol.,* 1955, 19, 1-8.

Sullivan, H. S., *Conceptions of modern psychiatry.* Washington, D.C.: W. A. White Psychiatric Foundation, 1947.

——, *The interpersonal theory of psychiatry.* New York: Norton, 1953.

Wolpe, J., *Psychotherapy by reciprocal inhibition* Stanford: Stanford University Press, 1958.

CHAPTER 14

Some Psychoeconomic Aspects of Analytic Interpretation in the Light of Intrasystemic Conflict

STANLEY BERGER, PH.D.

Dr. Stanley Berger is Dean of the Institute for Psychoanalytic Training and Research and is in private practice in New York City. In addition, he is a research psychologist on the staff of the Consultation Clinic for Alcoholism, New York University Medical Center. Earlier clinical experience included positions at Grasslands Psychiatric Hospital, Veteran's Administration Hospital at Montrose, and the Institute of Physical Medicine & Rehabilitation as Chief Clinical Psychologist. Previous teaching assignments were at New York University and the National Psychological Association for Psychoanalysis. Dr. Berger is a member of the American Psychological Association, New York State Psychological Association, New York Society of Clinical Psychologists, Association for Applied Psychoanalysis, and a Fellow of the Institute for Psychoanalytic Training and Research.

The difficulty in presenting any discussion on a topic so inclusive as interpretation is in delimiting the area of concentration in such a way as to manage clarity and elucidation without ignoring or devaluating material essential to a meaningful exploration. As we know, the initial purpose of interpretation was to make the unconscious conscious (speaking in loose terms), when the psyche was considered largely in topographic terms centering about the mechanism of repression. As difficulties arose in getting at this unconscious material, an awareness of inner-directed resistances brought under increasing scrutiny certain forces and functions which necessitated a reformation of the view of the psyche in metapsychological terms. In this regard, the dynamic aspect of interpretation remained in its original position of primary importance, understandable in a doctrine founded upon the genetic concept of psychological development. In order to achieve fuller grasp of the dynamics underlying human functioning and pathology, the structural aspects of psychic organization came under increasing study.

Freud's initial division of the psyche in terms of id, ego and superego (Freud, 1923) depicted the ego as relatively weak and helpless (and therefore of lesser importance) in the face of id forces pushing up and demanding gratification and superego commands pushing down and requiring conforming obedience and restriction. It was not until considerably later that Freud (1937) explicitly acknowledged not only the strength of ego forces, but ascribed to it an existence and even inheritance of drives very much in its own right. The original impetus toward regarding the ego as a legitimate and highly profitable area for psychoanalytic exploration was provided by Anna Freud (1946) and extends through the numerous writings of Greenacre (1952), Rapaport (1958), Jacobson (1954), Kris (1955), Lowenstein, Hartmann (1946, 1948, 1949, 1952) and others who are presently interested in the reformulation of psychoanalytic theory in terms of the newer findings in ego psychology. It is precisely because of the new insights provided by ego psychology that the economic aspect of psychic functioning has gained increasing concern and importance.

THE INTRASYSTEMIC PROBLEM

The broad view of economic factors operating in id-ego and ego-superego conflicts provides an examination of interpretation in terms of aligning and realigning forces. The early dictum, "Where id was, there shall ego be," can be approached, in one sense, by strengthening the mechanisms of defense to master or encapsulate the unbound energies of the id; in another sense, by directing unacceptable or "unhealthy" drives toward aims more easily manageable or attainable, and by enhancing the forces operating under the influence of the reality principle so as to achieve dominance over the primitive pleasure-principle forces. The struggle of the ego with superego pressures invited interpretations from the analyst aimed at alleviating the usurption of ego energies in archaic identifications, and fruitless attempts to gratify impossible narcissistic demands of the ego ideal. In and of its own right, the ego, comprised of primary and secondary autonomous forces (whether operating in a nonconflictual sphere or converted to the handling of early developmental conflicts), attracted interpretations whose purpose was to liberate or reactivate such mechanisms as could then be more directly applied to "perception, anticipation, objectivation, intentionality, and neutralization of energy" (Hartmann, 1950).

Speaking broadly, interpretation would be along those lines promising to liberate in the patient energies in the most utilizable forms, including facilitation of "change of function" (Hartmann, 1947). Our present state of knowledge indicates that certain ego functions can best use, and be served by, energies that are more or less neutralized, i.e., divested of their earlier libidinal and aggressive derivations. The entire problem of neutralization of energies requires considerable discussion, much of which lies outside the scope and purpose of this paper. We are first of all concerned with the still-unfathomable transformations of energies, libidinal and aggressive, in order to determine specifically how interpretation may facilitate such changes. Whether libidinal sublimation—which may require several intermediate alterations such as those involved in the process of identification (Freud, 1915) is identical with the deaggressivization of destructive drives poses only one important, and as yet unanswered, problem. Again, the nature and degree of neutralization will vary from individual to individual and from drive to drive. The accessibility of orally (gastrointestinal) organized drives, for example, may very likely have its own valences and predispositions to alteration and divestment, as contrasted with drives on any of the other psychosexual levels.

Further examination of the ego suggests energies which may be a part of the ego from its inception. That an ego originally exists in the form in which we describe it metapsychologically is very unlikely, but that certain archaic or primitive ego potentials or nuclei are present from the beginning is much more probable. It is the id-ego matrix (after Hartmann) which deserves greater consideration from an economic point of view. Not only is the primitive ego initially a part of the later-developed ego, but also it is very likely endowed with some of the libidinal energy of the id (which is essentially what I consider Freud to mean by primary narcissism). That primary narcissism is an obscure clinical problem does not preclude it from being of considerable importance during the envolvement of the ego into a mature form.

Once fractionated out from the id-ego matrix, the recall of libido from objects is clearly discernible in the clinical manifestation of secondary narcissism—wherein its importance, from an ego developmental aspect, is likewise secondary.

If the primitive ego, lacking in any degree boundaries which would distinguish it as a system in its own right, can be the recipient of the libidinal cathexes of the id, why would it not then follow that aggressive energies would likewise be involved in the later coalescence of an ego structure? This would lead us to infer that any of the autonomous ego functions could, very early, come under the influence of id drives. While we are aware, however, that sexualization or aggressivization of autonomous factors interferes with their remaining in the nonconflictual sphere, I do not believe the precociousness of this process has been really appreciated. This would mean that we should consider not only a primary narcissistic or libidinal influencing of the autonomous factors of ego development, but also a primary aggressivization as well. After all, it is highly improbable that an undeveloped ego would be capable of such selectivity as would require the influx of certain libidinal energies as opposed to the exclusion of the aggressive-destructive energies. In fact, it is generally held that the aggressive drives are essential to the development of the psychic structures in and of themselves, and that healthy id-ego-superego boundaries may require a certain degree of neutralized aggressive energy to evolve and maintain themselves.

What this amounts to is a picture of the developing ego as very much involved in the libidinal and aggressive endowment of the individual, long before defensive and countercathetic factors have been called into play. Within this framework then there evolves a potential for integration and synthesis. Perhaps in this area, the *unifying* aspects of libidinal drives as well as the *disintegrative* effects of the aggressive drive (in Freud's description of this balance, Eros and Thanatos) would have to be evaluated.

To this early dynamic balance must then be added the cathetic and countercathetic energies of conflicts between developing ego and id and superego forces, as well as the external forces of reality. How the individual proceeds to this task seems already to be largely determined by the internal stresses and strains in the id-ego matrix.

Now I would put the problem precisely in this order: Before there exists any real *intersystemic* conflict, there is already in significant operation a series of profound *intrasystemic* conflicts, and while it has been stated that ego syntonicity consists not only of freedom from conflict in the intersystemic sense, but also in the intrasystemic sense (Hartmann, 1955), I do not believe the proper respect has been paid to the enormous effects of the latter.

Before developing this theme further, I would like to point out that while this discussion has so far been attending to intrasystemic conflicts in the ego, such conflicts are a distinct possibility in the superego (after A. Reich's [1954] superego nuclei). Such intrasystemic conflicts are also of some possibility "in the id, depending on how one thinks about the question of 'structures in the id,' and on the concept of 'defense' one uses" (Hartman, 1965).

I would here mention what appears to me to be one of the most blatant examples of an intrasystemic conflict, that is, between superego and ego ideal. In refining the conflict, the problem could be seen further to exist among aspirations, ideals, and perfections, all within the one system (See Lampl-De Groot, 1964).

The first suggestions for this concept were offered by Freud in an unfinished fragment 1938 ("Splitting of the Ego in the Defensive Process"), which even then he was to think of as "something entirely new and puzzling." While Freud understood the conditions requisite to producing such a splitting of the ego as occurring under the influence of a psychical trauma, I would prefer to regard it as the product of more or less normal ego development. However, it is Freud's (1938) conclusion about the significance of such a mechanism that is most noteworthy: "The whole process seems so strange to us because we take for granted the synthetic nature of the workings of the ego. But we are clearly at fault in this. The synthetic function of the ego, though is is of such extraordinary importance, is subject to particular conditions and is liable to a whole series of disturbances."

A reexamination of this problem by Hartmann (1951) resulted in a renewed appreciation of the important role of intrasystemic conflicts. He says, "No definition of ego strength would I consider complete which does not refer to the intrasystemic structures, that is, which does not take into account the relative preponderance of certain ego functions over others. . . ." It would seem that Freud looked to psychical trauma to explain this phenomenon, while Hartmann (1951) regards it more as the product of struggles among the segregated ego components, "for instance, whether or not autonomous ego functions are interfered with by the defensive functions, and also the extent to which the energies the various ego functions use are neutralized". Both appear to be phenomenological explanations of a developmental dilemma which subsume the synthetic and integrative attempts of the ego.

I prefer to regard the intrasystemic conflict as the embodiment of the struggle between pleasure-principle and reality-principle factors in ego development. With this as a basic premise, one could then categorize the large number of ego functions in terms of their serving, in part, both masters. Because the processes referred to occur so early, it would perhaps be more meaningful to speak in terms of pleasure and pain (*Lust-Unlust,* Freud, 1911). Also, in this light it is advantageous to bear in mind Freud's early formulation, "The ego's objects are presented to it from the outside world in the first instance by the instincts of self-preservation, and it is undeniable also, that hate originally betokens the relation of the ego to the alien external world with its afflux of stimuli" (Freud, 1915).

The various id-ego components are involved in the seeking after pleasure (discharge patterns effective in bringing about bearable or desirable degrees of psychic tension), the avoidance of pain (the damning up of psychic tensions and noxious stimuli), and self-preservation. Naturally, the earliest conflicts would be largely concerned with biological factors.

Whenever psychological functions are traced back to their earliest conditions, we arrive at the physiological basis of life, and at this point unfortunately regard the problem as falling in the province of the physiologist or biochemist. However, recognizing the biological aspects of human functioning (actually the basic premise of Freudian psychoanalysis) does not preclude studying those features which are more psychological in nature, or have developed to the extent where psychological aspects become prevalent. In this regard Glover (1947) utilizes the concept of "ego nuclei," while Hendrick (1951) employs the term "partial ego-functions of infancy," to refer to such phenomena as ocular fixation, feeding, the rudiments of language, and the control of such elementary responses of hands, arms, and legs in reaching and crawling. On this very primitive level maturational struggles take place with regard to the biological and psychological needs involved.

It may very well be that the greater the disparity between these biological and psychological needs, the less the neutralization of the aggressive and libidinal drives with which they are cathected. Here we are dealing with bound and unbound energy fluxes. Energy, in a more or less unbound state is first available as the primary process of the id, a process with which we are all familiar. In the transformation of primary to secondary process, we see a binding of the id drives, but now integrated and synthesized under the organization of a developing ego—that is, under the aegis of an ego capable (through perceptions and learning) to organize and synthesize under the reality principle.

In pursuing an understanding of drives ontogenetically, Murphy (1947) states: "We are speaking now, of course, of very raw impulse. Mankind puts an incredible amount of effort into shaping this mass of impulse into integrated and symbolic activities adapted to fantastically complicated social requirements. Everyone born into this world, however, begins with a set of tissues which goes back far beyond the ice age in their primordial demands, their basic insistences, their raw impressions as to what life is about. To forget the stuff of which man, the organism, is built may facilitate the construction of ideal patterns—in both senses of the term—but adjustment to these patterns may involve tensions, or, often enough, biological contradictions."

That we understand the development of psychic structures and forces as evolving from this raw-impulse (id-ego) matrix is consistent with the earliest conceptions of Herbert Spencer (1888) who speaks of "differentiation from a homogeneous matrix." At these earliest expressions of life, we *actually* are dealing with thresholds of stimulus reception, a concept promulgated by Lashley (1924), who held "that a drive consists of a bodily mechanism which lowers the threshold for a behavior pattern, i.e., permits the appearance of synergic responses." Here, then, we are dealing with shifts in energy quanta; and displacements and summation effects are subsumed under the concept of organization (or integration).

It should be emphasized that we are not speaking of synthesizing functions which require fusion or blending of the several disparate energy components. Such synthetic activity would in all probability follow the law of dominance, which, on such a physiological basis, would indicate the preference of one specific drive or need, or one mode of response over the several others operating at the time. The fact that there are these several other drives still very much in operation is important, because underlying this conceptualization is the premise that drives do not or cannot be extinguished. The most that can be done is rearranging of the force fields, a fusing of them to one degree or another, and later subjecting them to aim-inhibition or change in cathexis. (More will be said about this later.)

The facility with which certain fusions or displacements can take place, and the dominance of certain drives over others, is probably best considered as a sort of psychological disposition. These would include those characteristics inherent in the id-ego matrix on a constitutional, psychobiological level, in what we have to accept as "psychic-givens." Included here are all involuntary response patterns, autonomic, sympathetic-parasympathetic enervation patterns, muscle activity (including striped-muscle), glandular activity, and the like. Later activity of emotional learning would then represent the accumulation of specific response patterns into relatively stable behavior traits, coalescing quantitative, qualitative, temporal and spatial stimulations and need gratifications. This process of early learning would, again, be based on the primitive pleasure-pain principle and is in keeping with Holt's (1931) idea that any stimulus which elicits a positive response tends eventually to be sought simply because it is present at the time the seeking movements occur. Murphy (1947) relates this to Freud's repetition compulsion.

This suggests intrasystemic conflict between repetition compulsion, on the one hand, and reality testing, or self-preservation, or even specific mechanisms of defense, on the other. While this kind of problem has received greater attention with the development of ego psychology, it appears that this was the same problem Freud was attempting to answer in his *Project for a Scientific Psychology* (1895), in which he made use of a quantity theory based on the principle of neuronic inertia, contact-barriers (that is, the overcoming of synaptic resistance), and the relation of quantity and quality neuronic discharge patterns, particularly in terms of temporal factors (e.g., "pain" consists in the irruption of large quantities [Q] into γ). It was here, of course, that Freud first promulgated the concept of pleasure as the sensation of discharge, a concept only to be renewed in a more or less rudimentary form in *Beyond the Pleasure Principle,* and then in a rather highly refined form in *Inhibition, Symptom and Anxiety.*

At our present level of understanding, it would appear that intrasystemic conflicts subsume intersystemic conflicts, and that the integrative and synthesizing functions of the ego, so essential to psychic stability and adaptability, are most vulnerable to disruption and, ultimately, disorganization, if resolution of intrasystemic conflicts fails. Further, it would appear that structural and dynamic metapsychological anomalies are the results of economic distress in terms of energic disbalance brought about through intrasystemic conflict. And again, "the flexibility and displacement of pre-genital and aggressive drives, love and the opportunity to identify, all indispensable to the process of sublimation" (Hart, 1948), are seriously jeopardized by irreconcilable intrasystemic drives. It would appear that neutralization must require resolution of energy disbalances in these intrasystemic conflicts before the coalescence requisite to ego formation can take place. Later superego formations (through resolution of oedipal conflicts) must, perforce, derive in part from energic sources initially bound up in ego-ideal structurization, and released only as the intrasystemic conflicts here are resolved. What I believe to be the major unanswered problem is the determination of what constitutes functional autonomy of need or drive, and/or functional autonomy of structure.

INTERPRETATION

In the light of intrasystemic conflict, the question of the nature and teleology of interpretation in treatment requires investigation. In very general terms, interpretation has been utilized to enable the ego to achieve further awareness. At the same time, we recognize that what is ego dystonic cannot enter full awareness because of the countercathectic energies which prevent it. "Voluntary effort or concentration of attention does not always succeed in recapturing elusory thought. But when such an attempt fails, self-observation may be successful in pitting one ego function against another , . ." (Kris, 1951). In like manner, where we are dealing with incomplete recall, "Interpretation may assist in achieving fuller recall, particularly where historical interpretations . . . stimulate memory to recognition leading to recall" (Kris, 1952). "Under this heading also fall those interventions which have an educational effect upon the patient" (Loewenstein, 1951).

"The theoretical psychoanalytic explanation of the relationship between recognition and recall is that the *synthetic* [italics mine] function of the ego, establishing a context, is in the case of recognition facilitated by the help of perception (in our example, the analyst's interpretation)" (Kris, 1952). Therefore, the interpretations of intra-systemic conflict facilitates the synthesizing function of the ego, enabling it then to perform this vital task. In other words, the psychic energies diverted (and consumed) in intrasystemic conflicts, as contrasted with intersystemic conflicts, are precisely those energies required by the ego in carrying out its *synthetic*[1] functions. This is not to say that certain integrative or organizing capacities of the ego are not completely, or perhaps even largely, affected as much as is its ability to synthesize. To this extent we are in accord with Hartmann (1950), who feels that "ego syntonicity consists not only of freedom from conflict in the intersystemic sense (id and superego), but also in the intrasystemic sense in relation to the various ego functions." However, I would include the differentiation processes of the ego under its integrative and organizing aspects, reserving the term "synthesis" for ego processes tending more toward metamorphic alterations with subsequent coalescence.

Further, it seems feasible to regard the capacity of the ego to neutralize sexual and aggressive drives as dependent upon relative resolution of intrasystemic conflicts. It is feasible, in turn, to regard intrasystemic conflicts as very much an expression of the struggle between pleasure-principle and reality-principle factors in ego development. The failure of the ego to effect a suitable resistance to regression (a breakdown of "secondary autonomy of the ego") is very much involved in this primitive struggle of pleasure-pain and reality. Not only regressive features, but untoward rigidity of cathexis (fixation) is likewise involved. "The formation of constant and independent objects, the institution of the reality principle with all its aspects, thinking, action, intentionality all depend on neutralization" (Hartmann, 1955).

The concept of sublimation had been formulated by Hart (1948) as a compromise between instinct and reality, a concept I would reformulate only to the extent that the compromise required be initially conceptualized in terms of intrasystemic conflict. In this regard, interpretation is of value in retarding, halting, and eventually reversing the regressive forces operating in the ego. Furthermore, interpretations directed toward intrasystemic conflicts (which may arise in any personality configuration, although certainly of paramount concern in the narcissistic neuroses) bring about shifts in energy distributions. I would suggest that on this level, more than dynamic insight must be provided. As with any structural conflict—and I believe there exists some distinction between structural and instinctual conflicts, though not always as clearly demarked as Alexander (1933) would have it—the major concern is in penetrating rigidly cathected and consolidated defense systems. "The ability to love . . . comes in analysis from the removal of guilt and repression, together with identification with the mature, objective, and reasonable analyst" (Hart, 1948).

One must not lose sight of the necessary irrationalism and geneticism which subsumes the entire process of identification within the framework established by Freud, else we fall into the pit of "functional autonomy of motives," wherein Allport (1960) fails to give full value to the early infantile needs and distortions in perceptions of the object world. In this regard, then, interpretation must be geared to facilitate identification, rather than incorporation. Hendrick (1942) feels that "identification is a normal and essential factor in development, an inevitable consequence of inevitable relationships with other people, a basic mechanism in the

---

[1]The difference between ego integration and ego synthesizing can be seen in the chemical analogy between an emulsion and a solution.

maturation and molding of personality which is initiated by the impact of other people upon it, but that 'transient identifications' are common during analytic treatment."

The reason for stressing the role of interpretation in and about the processes of
object-recognition, object-cathexis, and the introjective-projective mechanisms is
that the primary (i.e., early developmental status) nature of intrasystemic conflicts
requires dealing with biophysical-psychological energy components, wherein
dynamic and structural aspects are still very much interspersed, ego-id boundaries
are obfuscated, and psychological needs are not disengaged from physical needs. It
is in the perception and response to the external environment, and in particular to
those objects which elicit cathexis as well as provoke aggressive reactions, that
energic redistributions are made possible. It is here, in the human interaction, that
they also are made desirable. Fenichel (1937) states:

> The primitive reactions of assimilation to, and oral introjection of, what is perceived
> are obviously closely related. Freud had always stressed that what is recognized by
> normal psychology and pathopsychology in later periods as "identification" gives the
> impression of a regression, of a "secondary" identification, which was preceded by a
> "primary identification" as the first attempt at coming to terms with the world of
> objects. In this primary identification, instinctual behavior and ego behavior are not
> yet differentiated; it is at one and the same time the first oral object love, the first
> perception (involving assimilation and introjection), and the first motor reaction to
> external stimuli.

The precise language of the interpretation would, of course, vary with the individual situation, but the overall goal should be clear: to penetrate to the early intrasystemic conflicts underlying the intersystemic metapsychological difficulties.
Then, further interpretation is utilized to facilitate object-cathexis (drawing upon
primary narcissistic and aggressive energies as they can be distinguished and
separated from primitive biological needs) to redistribute the psychic energies,
enhancing the establishment of a strong (reality-oriented) integrated ego, and providing it with further neutralized energies to maintain the necessary synthesizing
capacities. The more the patient can be assisted to synthesize the pleasure-ego needs
into reality-ego needs, the greater his capacity grows to maintain a stronger
coalescence of psychological forces, relatively free from regressive tendencies.

Special emphasis should be given to interpretations centering around the
transference relationship, making the analyst the focus of the reexperiencing of ob-
ject-relatedness. This is not unlike Nacht's (1963) emphasis upon the analyst—not
in terms of what he says, but rather what he is.

One of the therapeutic aims is to get the patient to accept limitations, much as
Rapaport (1958) felt "that freedom is the acceptance of the restraints of the law."
This is probably what Hart (1948) had in mind when he saw the need for the patient to "renounce" certain primitive drives. While this term may suggest a conscious selection, the process must be much more involved in unconscious psychic
forces. In fact, the previously discussed pleasure-pain conflict can now be restated
in terms of "getting and giving up." Wherein receiving is pleasure, loss or deprivation is pain. Such a restatement is not only dynamically meaningful, but also is in
keeping with "adding the adaptive and genetic points of view to that of the classic
triad of dynamic, economic, and structural" (Gill, 1964).

In essence, the analyst attempts to manipulate the cathexes brought forth in the transference, keeping in mind, of course, the many images and needs projected and reintrojected. He utilizes interpretation to bring into the intrasystemic conflicts the weight (energies) of reality, effecting through dominance (and "renunciation") a shift in conflicting forces (such as autonomous and defensive ego functions, regressive and progressive pulls), and thereby bringing these forces more under the sway of the reality principle. This process is precisely also the one which should take place in the normal development of every child.

Here, then, we may hope to achieve what can be described as the "ideal psychological man," made up of a predominance of neutralized narcissistic ego-directed libido and sublimated drives. Then as libidinal and aggressive energies build up (either as the result of biological or social forces), they reach a discharge limen and are released in goal-directed action (under ego domination), in which the fused instinctual drives are thereby reduced to a nonthreatening, tolerable level. Treatment then is directed toward extending this sublimated, narcissistic-neutralized state, and in the end enabling the patient to maintain it.

SUMMARY

The problems presented in psychoanalysis, metapsychologically in terms of intersystemic conflicts, are actually the result of very early intrasystemic conflicts emanating from the id-ego matrix. These intrasystemic conflicts have their roots in primary integumented biopsychological needs, operating under the influence of the pleasure-pain principle and later under the pleasure-reality principle. Within the id-ego matrix reside potentially autonomous ego nuclei and defense mechanisms, whose energies are available for integrative-synthesizing ego activity to the extent that they are disengaged from tissue needs and neutralized of libidinal and aggressive cathexes. This early neutralization probably precedes the later binding of energies in the secondary ego process and the secondary utilization of drive energies in sublimations and symbolic activity. The primary, relative freeing from pleasure-pain conflict, the neutralization of these liberated forces, and the rebinding in an organizing, integrated, ego effort permit the release of energies to a synthesizing ego. The ego, through its synthesizing capacity, can now manage a normal libidinal-aggressive economy under the dominance of the reality principle.

In the light of intrasystemic conflicts, interpretation is aimed at facilitating energy redistributions in the id-ego matrix. This can be achieved through the transference relationship, in which the analyst must make use of his image as an object cathected with primary libidinal and aggressive energies, to entice these early, primitive needs to operate under the dominance of reality. While such primitive needs are seen most impressively in the narcissistic neuroses, they appear, to some extent, in every analytic case. To deal adaptively with these drives, a resolution of the underlying intrasystemic conflict is a prerequisite. To that end interpretation can be most effective when concerned with managing the transference relationship and with highlighting those energies derived from primitive psychoanalytical needs and bound up in intrasystemic conflicts.

REFERENCES

Alexander, F., The relation of structural and instinctual conflicts. *Psychoanal. Quart.*, 1933, 2.

Allport, G. W., *Personality and social encounter.* Boston: Beacon Press, 1960.

Fenichel, O., Early stages of ego development. Imago, 1937, 23.

Freud, A., *The ego and the mechanisms of defense.* New York: Int. Univ. Press, 1946.

Freud, S., Project for a scientific psychology. In *The origins of psychoanalysis.* New York: Basic Books, 1954.

——, Formulations on the two principles of mental functioning. *Standard Edition,* 12 (1911). London: Hogarth Press.

——, Instincts and their vicissitudes. *S.E.,* 14 (1915).

——, The ego and the id. *S.E.,* 19 (1923).

——, Analysis terminable and interminable. *S.E.,* 23 (1937).

——, Splitting the ego in the defensive process. *S.E.,* 23 (1938).

Gill, M., and Klein, G. S., The structuring of drive and reality. *Internat. J. Psychoanal.,* 1964, 45 (Part 4).

Glover, E., Basic mental concepts: their clinical and theoretical value. *Psychoanal. Quart.,* 1947, 16.

——, Sublimation, substitution, and social anxiety. *Internat. J. Psychoanal.* 1931, 12.

Greenacre, P., *Trauma, growth, and personality.* New York: Norton, 1952.

Hart, H. R., Sublimation and aggression. *Psychiat. Quart.,* 1948, 22.

Hartmann, H., Comments on the psychoanalytic theory of instinctual drive. *Psychoanal. Quart.* 1948, 17.

——, Comments on the psychoanalytic theory of the ego. *Psychoanal. Stud. Child,* 1950, No. 5.

——, Technical implications of ego psychology. *Psychoanal. Quart.* 1951, 20.

——, The mutual influences in the development of ego and id. *Psychoan. Stud. Child,* 1952, No. 7.

——, Notes of the theory of sublimation. *Psychoanal. Stud. Child,* 1955, No. 10.

——, Rational and irrational action In *Psychoanalysis and the social sciences.* New York: Int. Univ. Press, 1947.

——, *Ego psychology and the problem of adaptation.* New York: Int. Univ. Press, 1958.

——, Personal communication, 1965.

——, Kris, E., and Loewenstein, R. M., Comments of the formation of psychic structure. *Psychoanal. Stud. Child,* 1946, No. 2.

——, ——, and ——, Notes on the theory of aggression. *Psychoanal. Stud. Child,* 1949, No. 3/4.

Hendrick, I., Instinct and ego during infancy. *Psychoanal. Quart.* 1942, 11.

——, Early development of the ego: identification in infancy. *Psychoanal. Quart.,* 1951, 20.

Holt, H. G., *Animal drive and the learning process,* 1931.

Jacobson, B., The self and the object world: vicissitudes of their infantile cathexes and their influence on ideational and affective development. *Psychoanal. Stud. Child,* 1954, No. 9.

Kris, E., Ego psychology and interpretation in psychoanalytic therapy. *Psychoanal. Quart.* 1951, 20.

——, On preconscious mental processes. In *Psychoanalytic explorations in art.* New York: Int. Univ. Press, 1952.

——, Neutralization and sublimation: observations on young children. *Psychoanal. Stud. Child,* 1955, No. 10.

Lampl-De Groot, J., Remarks on genesis, structuralization, and functioning of the mind. *Psychoanal. Stud. Child,* 1964, No. 19.

Lashley, K. S., Experimental analysis of instinctual behavior. *Psychol. Rev.* 1938, 45.

——, Physiological analysis of the libido. *Psychol. Rev.* 1924, 31.

Loewenstein, R. M., The problem of interpretation. *Psychoanal. Quart.* 1951, 20.

Murphy, G., *Personality.* New York: Harper Bros., 1947.

Nacht, S., *La presence du psychoanalyste.* Paris: Press Universitaires de France, 1963.

Nunberg, H., The synthetic function of the ego. In *Practice and theory of psychoanalysis.* New York: Int. Univ. Press, 1960.

Rapaport, D., The theory of ego autonomy: a generalization. *Bull. Menninger Clin.* 1958, 22.

Reich, A., Early identifications as archaic elements in the superego. *J. Amer. Psychiat. Ass.* 1954, 2.

Spencer, H., *First principles,* 1888.

CHAPTER 15

Interpretation and the Therapeutic Act

JULE NYDES, M.A.

Jule Nydes is one of the leading training analysts in New York. He serves on the faculty of the National Psychological Association for Psychoanalysis and as Clinical Professor in the Post-Doctoral Program of Adelphi University. He is also an Editor of Psychoanalytic Review. *In addition to his keenly perceptive analytic capacities, his exact ear for the elusive subtleties of a patient's personal style, and the relentless intelligence at the core of his work, he is also known as one of those rare writers in our field who can bring a presented case to life. If Reik is the most artful writer in psychoanalysis after Freud, Nydes, I believe, is next after Reik. There is also a direct line in the fact that Nydes was analyzed by Reik, as Reik was by Freud.*

Of special interest is this chapter's treatment of the use of fables, proverbs and quotations as part of the interpretive approach, Nydes' affirmation of the value system (that much-debated concept) implicit in the psychoanalytic treatment situation, his discussion of the contraindications of premature reassurance, the place for reality confrontations, and the offering of that which he terms "therapeutic love."

He differentiates interpretation from therapeutic acts, and illustrates the interpretive moving of ego-syntonic symptoms to an ego-alien position. Featured here is his evaluative reaction to the popularly growing existential movement in therapy; in addition, he ranges over a number of critical moments in therapy and the interpretive strategy to be employed—the varied ingredients of his presentation all stitched together against the backdrop of an uncovering orientation.

In Memoriam: Since the above was written, Jule was struck down by untimely illness and death. His passing away followed by a few months that of another contributor, John Herma. Everyone's death is to some degree outrageous, but there are people who, by virtue of their energy and talent and our affection for them, make the outrage of their deaths felt like a raw wound. The growth of Jule Nydes and John Herma, as analysts and as men, was so continuous and inevitable that their deaths seem to have cut into the natural order of things.

But this is Jule's chapter. He wrote on masochism better than any man after Freud, Reik and Menninger, and on paranoia second only to Freud. Those who knew him at work or experienced the fruit of his effort were awed at his natural skill and the fascinating complexity of his personality. Rare gifts, skill and knowledge were richly present, but we who knew him knew that the talent was the man, Jule himself. To his colleagues, his students and his friends, nothing is left now of the man—nothing but his work, his memory, and his example. But these will be a long time echoing away.

Some years ago Marie C. Nelson, John L. Herma and I conducted a research seminar at the NPAP Institute. Our main endeavor was to attempt some definition of a psychoanalytic interpretation and to distinguish it, if possible, from other kinds of verbal and nonverbal behavior which (by design or otherwise) yield positive

---

This is an expanded version of a paper presented at the Professional Meeting, New York Society of Clinical Psychologists, New York City, E. Hammer, Chairman.

therapeutic effects. The latter we termed "therapeutic acts."[1] Since traditional therapeutic intervention has been in the form of interpretation, some of our group contended that all therapeutic acts were *ipso facto* interpretations. My own view (the implications of which I will attempt to explore in this essay) was and remains that, while all interpretations are or should be therapeutic acts, not all therapeutic acts are necessarily interpretations. Silence or a cordial greeting, to use simple illustrations, often have undeniable therapeutic effects and may have an unformulated interpretative significance, but in and of themselves are no interpretations.

REDUCTIONISM

Interpretations take many forms, but all of them involve the reduction of diversity to uniformity. Such reduction is clearly implied in the very name, "psychoanalysis." By discovering motives, patterns of character and defense, and inner relationships, and by relating particulars to general determining principles, the highly diversified material presented by a patient is reduced in some measure to a statement which is uniform in that it is applicable to many patients. For example, one may say, in truth and triviality, to almost anyone, "You are in need of approval." A diagnosis such as schizophrenia is another example of a brief interpretation which reduces a complex array of psychological data to a single word or label. I am not suggesting that diagnostic categories be abandoned. They are the ciphers of psychological stenography; but some interpretations, such as the "need for approval," do carry reductionism to meaningless lengths and serve only to obscure the richness and variety of human experience in a cloud of pervasive generalization and ambiguity.

Existential psychotherapists in particular have championed the cause of anti-reductionism. Interpretations (especially Freudian interpretations), in their view, violate the uniqueness of individual experience. What a person feels here and now in the present moment is all important. What is essential in therapy is the human encounter. The therapist must accompany the patient through the vicissitudes of his own psyche. The therapist neither leads nor follows, but in the course of his venture with the patient into the unknown he confronts the patient with the separate, though allowably similar, human condition of the therapist. Diagnosis or a label which applies to the patient or even to the therapist is deplored. It serves only to stultify the flux of unceasing growth.

But the existentialists are not alone. As recently as August 30, 1965, in *The New York Times* under the title of "In Fear of Reductionism," J. G. Herzberg quotes the declaration of the Study Group of Foundations of Cultural Unity at Bowdoin College as follows:

Since the 17th century the kind of knowledge afforded by mathematical physics has come more and more to furnish mankind with an ideal for all knowledge. This ideal also carries with it a new conception of the nature of things: All things whatsoever are held to be intelligible ultimately in terms of the laws of inanimate nature.

In the light of such a reductionist program, the finalistic nature of living things, the sentience of animals and their intelligence, the responsible choices of man, his moral and aesthetic ideals, the fact of human greatness seem all of them anomalies that will be removed eventually by further progress.

---

[1]The designation, "therapeutic act," was suggested by Dr. Herma.

Their existence—even the existence of science itself—has no legitimate grounds; our deepest convictions lack all theortical foundation.

This movement claims to unify science and to comprehend in it all subjects of study. But, since its ideal is fundamentally mistaken, the result has been to debase the conception of man entertained by the psychological and social sciences and at the same time to isolate the humanistic core of history and criticism.

It has displaced the traditional endeavor of philosophy to comprehend the whole domain of human thought and produced instead distortion and fragmentation.

Such is the truly commendable denunciation of reductionism by a group of eminent scholars and scientists. Surely psychoanalytic psychology will fight shoulder to shoulder with any movement that takes a firm position against the quantitative debasement of the conception of man. But does this mean that all reduction and therefore all psychoanalytic interpretation must be discredited? Does nothing but the existential encounter remain if the uniqueness of individual experience is to be respected and nurtured? Does some similarity to other human beings really deny individual identity? Would not the feeling of deep isolation, which the existentialists deplore, be somewhat modified by some sense of consanguinity with others? On the other hand, does not the insistence on one's difference serve the self-preciousness of a narcissistic defense? Following is an example of what I mean.

Narcissistic Defense

Some time ago I was consulted by a man in his forties who had had many years of analysis with several previous therapists. He was rather ordinary looking, though highly intelligent, sensitive and endowed with an exceptionally keen critical faculty. This talent helped him to belittle and disqualify almost any statement that might be made about him. Whenever I made some observation or responded to something that he had said, he would counter with some remark such as, "That comes straight out of Fenichel!" or "Have you been reading Horney lately?" or "You know, I have read your articles. Do you really think it is helpful to paraphrase them during these sessions?" or "I'll bet your last patient was really impressed when you said that to him." It was a perfect defense. When I asked him why he continued to see me in view of my obvious incompetence, he replied that as a matter of fact he had been thinking of quitting and that he kept coming only because of some kind of inertia. For a period of quite a few months he would begin every session by announcing his termination, and then he would end the session by saying he would see me again the next time. He thought that it was possibly his need to indulge his masochism that compelled him to continue to subject himself to my psychoanalytic cliches. On several occasions he succeeded in provoking me to some expression of exasperation. When this happened, he would smile and say, "I really do succeed in needling you, don't I?" Then, before I had a chance to reply, he would add, "Oh, please don't tell me that what I really want is for you to punish me."

Finally I said to him, "You are so precious, so special, so unique, that it is almost impossible for you to believe that anything that applies to another human being could possibly have application to you. Your only purpose here seems to be to demonstrate that I am incapable of communicating with you. And yet if I should communicate with you, I think you would resent it. You would feel that some exquisite inaccessibility which you treasure had been desecrated." There was a long silence and then he said in a subdued tone of voice, "You are right, I hate to admit that you are right. You did reach me. While I was silent I kept thinking of how I felt when I was in the subway a few hours ago. I looked all around me and all the people seemed very ugly to me. They were like a herd of beasts. All of them were so ugly and I was so beautiful." But then he could not help asking, "What you just said to me about being so special. Did you ever say that to anyone else?" It still seemed most important that my remarks be reserved exclusively for him.

One might inquire why, in the example cited above, I did not interpret his wish for my love and his homosexual fear against which he had raised so many defensive barriers. Such an interpretation, which he had heard from other therapists and which he repeated to me, served only to mobilize his cynical disdain. One of the principles of interpretation is that we direct our attention to matters that are *available* to the patient's consciousness—*to his preconscious,* rather than attempt to breach his defenses with an insight which would only heighten his resistance.

POSITIVE EFFECTS OF GENERALIZATION

I learned from Theodor Reik, who in turn says that he learned from Freud, how effective it is to convey interpretations in the form of anecdotes, fables, proverbs or quotations. There are some patients who find it very difficult to tolerate a statement designed specifically for them. Far from cherishing a feeling of uniqueness, they feel uniquely degenerate. A direct interpretation, no matter how carefully worded, is almost invariably construed as personal accusation, which serves only to confirm a feeling of morbid guilt or to provoke a defensive counterattack. A statement which serves to identify such a patient's problem as one of the foibles of mankind reduces guilt and liberates greater freedom of expression. If, for example, a man feels very guilty about numerous extramarital relationships, it would serve only to inhibit him further to refer (even if—*especially* if—valid) to his latent homosexuality. Would it not be better to quote Polgar who said, "Many women are too few. One is too much!" A more detailed example follows.

An attractive 40-year-old woman, who had been in analysis with me for several years, reported that while she was having intercourse with her husband, she had a fantasy of which she was quite ashamed. She felt most reluctant to tell me about it. The fantasy, however, was of importance because it helped her in some strange way to overcome her sexual inhibitions. For the first time in many months, she reached a satisfactory climax. She was ashamed of the fantasy because it seemed so completely lacking in self-respect. After several more evasive and anxious introductory statements of this kind, she finally related that the picture that came to mind was that her husband was having highly enjoyable sexual relations with a beautiful girl of about 18. At first she tried to put it out of her mind and was somewhat shocked that she was in effect surrendering her husband to another woman. But since she found the fantasy sexually stimulating, she permitted it to persist and then discovered to her surprise that she felt very free, highly excited, and was able to achieve orgasm without difficulty. Both openly and implicitly she pleaded for reassurance that her fantasy was not a symptom of some kind of degrading perversion.

The fantasy combined within itself a variety of determinants: It was in the nature of a masochistic atonement. By enduring the pain of giving her husband to the young woman, she was then liberated to enjoy the sin of satisfaction.

It had homosexual implications on several levels. Her husband had recently told her in a somewhat jocular way of how attractive some of the girls were at his place of business. In this fantasy, rather than being jealous of the young women, she was identifying with her husband and enjoying his satisfaction vicariously. She was also identifying with the girl and in a very specific way with her own mother. But first a few facts about her background must be related.

The patient's mother was an attractive woman who divorced her husband when the patient was a child. During the patient's adolescence the mother had sexual relations with a friend of the family, an affair of which the patient had full knowledge. The patient was conscious that the family friend was an extremely handsome man and recalled vividly times when, finding her alone, he would hug and kiss her passionately and tell her that she was the most beautiful girl in the world. She found his attentions highly stimulating and there were periods during her adolescence when she was obsessed with sexual desires.

When she began to have dates, she recalls that her mother would question her avidly about the kind of experience she enjoyed with the young men who took her out. Her mother's questioning, she said, was by no means intended to be punitive. It was rather as if her mother wanted to enjoy vicariously what the patient was enjoying with her boyfriends. Her mother would ask how far she let them go. Did they kiss her? Did they feel her breasts? Did they manage to get their hands under her skirt? Was she aware of the young man's sexual excitement? Did he press up against her, etc.? The patient found her mother's questioning both annoyingly intrusive and exciting. She felt that there was some kind of sexual intimacy between herself and her mother, both as a result of this kind of questioning and also because they shared the attentions of her mother's lover.

In view of the above, the patient's fantasy while having intercourse with her husband also represented an unconscious guilt-free revival of the wish for oedipal gratification with her mother's lover. It was guilt-free because she was the onlooker rather than the participant; but it was gratifying because she was witnessing, in the experience of the girl with her own husband, what she had often wished might happen between her, when she was a girl, and her mother's lover.

It was also in the nature of a reversal of roles. She was now, in her fantasy, intruding through voyeurism on the experience of the girl, just as her mother attempted to intrude on her when her mother questioned her about her own experiences with boyfriends.

There were numerous possibilities of interpretation that were open to me. To what aspect of the meaning of the fantasy should I devote myself? Should I speak of its masochistic significance? If so, should I reflect her identification with her mother, with the girl, or with the husband? Or should I attempt to reveal the oedipal gratifications that become possible through watching this tableau while at the same time enjoying the act of intercourse? When it is possible to say so many things, all of them true, how do we determine what is most appropriate? Rather than devote myself to any or all of the possibilities outlined above, I felt that it was much more important at the moment to reduce the patient's feeling of shame about her enjoyment of such a fantasy and about her reliance on it for sexual satisfaction with her husband. The fantasy in and of itself was quite harmless. It served to release the patient sexually, so I addressed myself to her embarrassment about telling me the fantasy rather than to its content. I remarked that the fantasy seemed to me to be "a source of innocent merriment." The patient laughed with relief and then, as her discomfort was reduced, was able freely to associate and to produce the material referred to above, much of which she had already related previously and in other contexts.

In the above example, the statement quoted from *The Mikado,* "a source of innocent merriment," reflects one of the values implicit in psychoanalysis: we are responsible only for our behavior, not for our thoughts or fantasies.[2] As such, it counters her shame and divers other feelings with an observation concerning the harmlessness of fantasies in general. It also reflects the fact that her fantasy helped

---

[2]Only the thoughts and fantasies of God had power to create the world, and to wreak destruction upon the wicked. Those who would be pure in heart permit their seeming modesty to hide their aspirations to His throne.

her to be more responsive to her husband. "To let the punishment fit the crime" also means: no crime, no punishment.

SOME NEGATIVE ASPECTS OF REASSURANCE

On the other hand, interpretation is too often employed almost exclusively in the service of reassurance, so much so that the patient is being reassured concerning certain guilt-laden wishes before he even knows that he has them. This is particularly true with regard to homosexuality or homosexual feelings. Often the analyst, sensing that the patient is anxious about a homosexual impulse that has barely reached awareness, rushes in with the explanation concerning the "usualness or normality" of such feelings in an effort, not only to allay or forestall possible anxiety on the part of the patient, but also to dispel the analyst's apprehension when confronted by the problems presented by the patient's anxiety.

Interpretations that serve to short-circuit or dampen the patient's experience of his own feelings are, in effect, rationalizations which heighten the patient's defenses and promote detachment. It is, to be sure, often essential to engage in that kind of anxiety-allaying, defense-building interpretation in order to prepare the patient ultimately for a greater acceptance of his own inner feelings. If, however, interpretation serves only a defensive purpose, the patient is pushed by the analyst's fears, as well as his own, further away from his acceptance of unconscious forces as they become conscious. It is part of the *art* of interpretation to know when it is advisable to refrain from allaying possible anxiety and to permit the patient to be aware of what he feels, even though such awareness may be painful. In terms of psychic economy, an interpretation is often most effective when the pain of the patient's symptoms rises in intensity so that it becomes greater than the pain of the interpretation. The interpretation is then welcomed not only for the illumination it affords, but also for the distress that it alleviates. It is a healthy sign on the part of the patient when he rejects the analyst's explanations concerning his desires and protests that he would like to have the desires before he has them explained. Recently, a patient in effect said as much to me: "Everything you say when a homosexual thought, feeling or bodily sensation arises is true, and I am so absorbed in the truth of your statement and so comforted by it that I often stop experiencing the very feeling that gave rise to your statement. You have helped me not to be afraid of my homosexual feelings. But, whatever they are right now, I don't want to know what they mean. I want to be able to feel them, to experience them, very fully, regardless of what they mean. I am no longer afraid. It is almost because I am so convinced that I am not a homosexual, and that I have learned with your help that such feelings are not so terrible, that I want to be able to really feel them when and if I have them."

SOME VALUES IMPLICIT IN PSYCHOANALYSIS

It is by now generally recognized that the tradition of analytic neutrality is, for the most part, a fiction. It is not only that analysts have values of their own, but that there is implicit in the very process of psychoanalytic therapy a set of values, to several of which I have already referred. The structure of the therapeutic relationship and the role of the analyst are bound by values, the affirmation of which either openly or implicitly often gives rise to therapeutic acts which are very clearly not interpretations. Such therapeutic acts generally reflect the rational reality limits of the therapeutic relationship and of the powers and responsibilities of the analyst.

They also reflect a respect for individual differences and the patient's right as well to choose not to be helped, or to reject the kind of help the analyst is prepared to offer in keeping with the definition of his function.

Here I would like to stress that the values implicit in the therapeutic approach cannot be regarded as "technique, tactics, or strategy." They are more in the nature of the attributes that are implicit in the kind of psychotherapy in which I believe. Hopefully, they also characterize the therapist as a person. Such values form the foundation of *principles* governing the therapeutic process. In addition to those mentioned above, some of the other values implicit in psychoanalysis are: that life is better than death; that health is better than sickness; that truth is better than falsehood; that healthy fulfillment is better than neurotic deprivation—and its obverse, that healthy renunciation is better than neurotic gratification. A great deal, of course, depends on how the words "healthy" and "neurotic" are defined, but the guidelines are there. Just as the analyst must respect the autonomy of his patient, so we must require that the patient respect the autonomy of the analyst. In other words, neither patient nor analyst belongs to the other; each belongs to himself. The principles derived from such values also establish the conditions of therapy. The analyst owes it both to himself and to his patient to comply with such conditions and to refrain from encouraging, even if in the name of therapy, any behavior which violates them.

An Example of Reality Confrontation

Early in my professional career when I had only recently been discharged from the army after World War II, I had the good fortune to share an office with my supervisor. At that time, a patient who was borderline and with considerable talent as a writer was confronting me with somewhat more than my usual problems as a therapist.

It was shortly before my first vacation after my discharge from the army that I began to notice that his symptoms were growing worse and worse. He would leave my office and then telephone me from the mouth of the Holland Tunnel that he was in a state of desperation. "I cannot get through this tunnel," he cried. "It is a tunnel of love and it scares me. I don't know what to do." I would spend a long time with him on the phone giving him comfort and reassurance. He would get through the tunnel, reach his home and telephone me again to berate me for the terrible experience which he had endured. It wasn't long before he began to manifest more serious psychotic signs. He would call me and complain of feelings of disintegration and explain in detail how he was doing everything in his power to help himself. He drank tomato juice to strengthen his blood, grape juice to improve the sweetness of his spirit; milk to make him feel at one with mother, the source of life; beef broth to endow him with iron and give him the stern determination of manhood. You may gather that as a relatively inexperienced therapist I was becoming more and more anxious. One day he called and the anxiety in his voice was so massive it made the phone quiver in *my* hand. "It's no use," he cried. "Something has to be done. Talking doesn't help. I am desperate. You must do something." I didn't know what to say to him and so I told him that I was busy and that I would call him back. Luckily, my supervisor friend with whom I shared the office had some free time, and I told him my troubles. He looked at me and said, "Your condition is worse than your patient's." Then, and I thank him for this, he refused to discuss the case with me. He said simply, "I am giving you orders. Call him up, tell him to come to see you, and when he comes act bored. If he behaves in a crazy way, tell him that he would feel safer if he went to Bellevue and committed himself." I felt as if I were being directed to kill another human being, but my supervisor friend said, "Simply do as I say. I don't have the time or the patience right now to explain it to you."

I called the patient, who was unable to travel alone, and directed his wife to bring him to my office in a taxi.

When he came in, his shirt was unbuttoned down to his navel and his shoelaces were untied. His eyeglasses, which hung from one ear, accented his glazed eyes and disheveled hair. I lit a cigarette and pretended to be calm. Meanwhile, my heart was pounding with agitation. I asked him why he had come to see me and what he thought the trouble was. He gazed distractedly about the room and with a choked voice he said, "I don't know, I don't know." I said to him, "Do you think you are crazy?" and he replied, "Crazy, yes, that's what it is, crazy, crazy, crazy." I took myself in hand, and looked at him sternly and said, "If you really think you are crazy, you would undoubtedly feel safer if you confined yourself to an institution. Your wife is in the waiting room. Would you like me to suggest that she take you to Bellevue?" He sat up, buttoned his shirt, straightened his eyeglasses, brushed back his hair, looked at me sheepishly and in a little-boy, plaintive voice asked, "Are you mad at me?" I answered, "Do you think I should be?"

He was silent for a few moments and then murmured, "I guess so," but he didn't want to say any more for the time being. He remarked apologetically that he had already taken up too much of my time and that he would like to leave and return when his regular session was scheduled. The next time he came in, he was well-groomed and composed. He cordially wished me a very happy vacation and said that he did not realize fully how desperately he was trying to keep me from going away.

Much has been said about the clairvoyant intuitiveness of the schizophrenic. One might argue that whether I manifested it openly or not, the patient must have sensed my anxiety. I think it is true that he sensed my anxiety and recognized it as a vulnerability which he could exploit to gratify his own infantile needs, so long as I was permitting myself to be governed by it in my relationship to him. But when I acted as I had to in spite of anxiety, it was my manifest firmness and strength to which he responded rather than to my inner trepidation. Is not this the difference between the coward and the man of courage? Both are frightened, but the crucial difference is that the coward surrenders to his fear. The courageous person is not governed by his fear but acts as he must in spite of it.

The patient had been acting out a wish to control me through a display of suffering and psychotic desperation. The frustration of that wish and the assertion of my independence, terrible as that seemed to me at first, proved to be therapeutic acts which yielded greater insight on the part of the patient. His need to control was not resolved, but he had taken a big step in that direction by identifying his wish to keep me from taking a vacation as part of his problem. It was a problem which now was becoming ego-alien. It no longer carried the conviction of complete justification which is so typical of problems that are ego-syntonic.

THE EGO-ALIEN AND THE EGO-SYNTONIC

One of the complexities involved in the process of therapy is that when a problem is too ego-alien, it is almost completely devoid of affect and is subjectively experienced by the patient as having nothing whatever to do with him. Many patients regard their dreams in this light. But when in the course of therapy a problem which was formerly ego-alien becomes charged with emotion, it then becomes too ego-syntonic and is often even more difficult to reach therapeutically. The patient seems most available to insight only as his ego-syntonic problems become sufficiently ego-alien to permit him to identify them as an obstructing part of himself which he would like to overcome. The healthy part of the patient then finds it more possible actively to enlist the collaboration of the analyst against their common enemy, the patient's neurosis. At such times the analyst can be therapeutically effective even when he is ruthless and scathing. The patient knows that it is his problem rather than himself that is under attack.

I am thinking of a patient who suffered from very severe conversion symptoms—so much so, that his hands and other parts of his body would become paralyzed when he was "threatened" by success. He had a father who was relentlessly critical of him. When he was ten years old, he beat the captain of the Rutgers' chess team. Quite naturally he felt exhilarated and triumphant. When he came home, he ran to his father and said, "Hey Pop, I just beat the captain of the Rutgers chess team." His father looked at him scornfully and replied, "Some captain!"

In the course of therapy he finally developed enough courage to start his own small factory. At one point he called me up and cried over the phone, "Nydes, it is terrible. You have to help me. I can't unclutch the phone. I am getting orders from everywhere. I am scared. My eyes are shutting tight and my hand is getting tight on the phone. I can't unclutch it. Please say something." Since desperate situations require desperate remedies, I shouted over the phone in a harsh voice, "Sidney, you and I know that you are a shmuck. Those people who are giving you orders are even worse shmucks. Don't worry about it. We've got them fooled." There was a sigh of relief on the other end. He said, "Oh, please keep talking, I am feeling so much better."

Such a therapeutic act was made possible only by the development of a rapport between the patient's healthy ego and me, over a period of years.

The following is an example of the transformation of ego-syntonic behavior into ego-alien behavior, which then become available to insight:

A young man, who had been in therapy with a number of therapists since he was nine years old, began to consult me when he had reached his early twenties. In the first interview he informed me that when he was 15 years old he became so frightened of school that he ran home and defecated on the kitchen floor and then proceeded to smear feces all over himself. As he recounted this episode, he remarked with a bright smile, "But I didn't have the courage to eat it." I replied at once, unsmiling, "You talk as if that were a defect in your character." Such firm rejection of his delight in his capacity to act on any impulse defined the pattern of the first part of our relationship.

In the course of therapy it was necessary to restrain him from throwing a soaking raincoat and umbrella on my chair, from using the carpet as an ash tray, and from throwing checks at me as if they were spitballs. On each occasion he was deeply wounded and would remain silent for the remainder of the session and sometimes for the next session as well. This would be followed by a prolonged explosion of hatred and contempt.

One day, after several years of analysis, he began to play with the ash tray, throwing it up into the air and catching it again. I asked him to stop, since it kept me from listening to him. He was quiet for about five minutes and then said, "I am very annoyed at myself, because I still feel so wounded by your very reasonable request." I congratulated him by pointing out that he had come a great distance, since now he was no longer insisting on his right to be unrestrained, but was rather annoyed that he was still unable fully to tolerate restraint. His irrational demand for gratification, still emotionally alive, was becoming ego-alien. He was now collaborating with me against his impulsiveness. My firmness in not permitting him to impose on me represented a kind of self-respect in me, which he unconsciously sought to emulate. This was in sharp distinction to the way in which he related to his father. He said after two and a half years, "I like you and I trust you maybe 55 or 60 per cent because I can't convince you that I'm very fragile."

HEALTHY IDENTIFICATION AND THERAPEUTIC LOVE

Identification with the analyst as the analyst is self-respecting and frustrating of the patient's neurotic needs is a function of what might be termed "therapeutic love." The analyst's indulgence of the patient's needs, out of the analyst's insecurity or fear of disappointing or losing the patient (and for many other reasons as well), is in effect profoundly disrespectful of the patient's strength. As the analyst refuses to permit the patient to impose on him or to accept the patient's problems as his own, as he does not yield to the temptation to control or be controlled by the patient, no matter how insistently it is demanded, he is endowing the patient's strength rather than subsidizing his weakness.

I remember a man whose main problem was a kind of compulsive gambling, in the course of which he would lose large sums of money. Even though I had originally, in response to his inquiry, told him what my fee would be for the consultation, as I listened to him talk I had a very strong impulse not to charge him for the visit. My awareness of this impulse made me attentive to his problem which, as it unfolded, revealed an almost unbelievable capacity to enlist—without openly asking for it—the help of other people. Again and again when he was on the brink of desperation during the course of his life, friends or relatives would come to his rescue. Obviously my wish not to charge him was not in the nature of a therapeutic act, but rather an unconscious compliance with his need to be taken care of.

But if adequate allowance is made for all distortions of feeling on the part of both patient and therapist, does nothing remain? Are there no emotions that are appropriate and in consonance with the actual nature of the therapeutic relationship? I am thinking, for example, of the genuinely appreciative warmth that the patient may feel as he experiences the therapist as an understanding person. I am thinking of the delight—the therapeutic love—that the therapist experiences as he witnesses and participates in the growth and happiness of another human being. Such love may be therapeutically shared with the patient, with all respect for his autonomy, when patient and therapist are in open and firm collaboration against the mutual adversary, the patient's neurotic affliction.

I reject the stereotype that if he is Freudian, the analyst must be a cold, blank wall. In terms of closeness and distance I think it is possible for the therapist to be friendly though not a friend; to be firm but not rigid; to be frustrating but not punitive; to be an authority but not authoritarian; to be responsive but not uncontrolled; to be accepting but not compliant; to be reserved but not rejecting; to be understanding but not gratifying.

I believe that the realities of the professional relationship are an integral part of therapy. To deny or attempt to "transcend" such realities supports the fiction of personal intimacy between therapist and patient and transforms the therapeutic relationship into an end in itself rather than a means through which the patient is more effectively enabled to resolve his conflicts and to transcend his stereotyped frames of reference outside the consulting room. Therapy in and of itself does not cure. Hopefully, it helps the patient to respond more positively to the therapeutic power of his life experience. A therapeutic act is a kind of love which, as the patient feels it for himself, permits the patient, not to find himself, but to lose himself in the celebration of the grace and enjoyment of life.

CHAPTER 16

The Analyst's Role: To Interpret or to React?

BERTRAM POLLENS, PH.D.

Dr. Bertram Pollens is a practicing psychoanalyst in New York City who is known for his originality in the development of techniques in psychotherapy. He describes himself as an experiential, action-oriented psychoanalyst who believes that Freud's discoveries, in order to reach patients, must be communicated to them predominantly through nonintellectual methods in order to help them grow. He is on the faculty of the Metropolitan Institute for Psychoanalytic Studies and is a consultant for the Center for Creative Living and for Mobilization for Youth. He is a Certified Psychologist and a Diplomate in Clinical Psychology, ABEPP.

Dr. Pollens is a Past President of the New York Society of Clinical Psychologists, and of the Clinical Division of the New York State Psychological Association. He was formerly on the faculties of CCNY, Queens College of the City University of New York, and the Institute for Practicing Psychotherapists. He has served as Chief Psychologist for the New York City Department of Correction, Chief Psychologist of the U. S. Army Rehabilitation Center, psychologist with the Veterans Administration, where he organized the Group Therapy program, and supervisor of psychotherapy at the Community Guidance Service. He is the author of The Sex Criminal, *co-author with Richard Robertiello and David Friedman of* The Analyst's Role, *and has published a number of articles in professional journals. He is also known for his "live" demonstrations of techniques of psychotherapy at professional symposiums.*

Not so many years ago we were taught by our training analysts that we were to communicate insight to patients through correct technical interpretations offered in an objective, dispassionate manner. A neutral, emotionless, monotonous tone of voice was considered a virtue. Countertransference feelings or reactions, positive or negative, were bad and were to be eliminated or suppressed. In more recent years, among certain groups, the pendulum has swung almost to the opposite extreme. Any evidence of intellectuality is considered bad and to be avoided or suppressed. It is now fashionable to be free and spontaneous, to react, to mature and grow together with the patient, and to become as much as possible his equal. Discussions and debates are carried on about the correctness or incorrectness of these points of view. These arguments are just as meaningless as debates that once waged so fiercely around the "heredity vs. environment" or "nature vs. nurture" controversy. Unfortunately, we are still seeking simple, one-dimensional rules or generalizations in an area of work so complex that almost no rules bear the test of time.

It is difficult to approach the question of interpretation without reference to the infantile authority problem and its basic influence on the therapist-patient relationship. Much of our confusion results from the failure to distinguish between the two kinds of authority roles in which the therapist is placed. On one hand, the

This paper was presented at the Spring 1964 Professional Meeting, E. F. Hammer, Chairman, New York Society of Clinical Psychologists, New York City.

therapist is in reality an authority, an expert in his knowledge about the workings of the mind, especially the unconscious. This may earn for him a healthy respect from the patient for his opinions, but it gives him no actual power of decision over the patient. The second authoritative role in which he is cast by the patient is that of an omnipotent parent with the power to decide life and death for the patient. Most frequently this authority role is actualized only in the mind of the patient. In certain instances, however, it is not entirely unreal. For example, if a patient is suicidal, the therapist has the power to arrange for his commitment against his will. If a patient needs depositions to draft boards, insurance companies, employers and the like, the therapist has the power to influence important and realistic decisions by other authorities which seriously affect the patient's life. In general, for immature and helpless patients the therapist is called upon to exercise a greater degree of parental authoritative control. The more independent and mature patient can utilize the therapist as an expert consultant whose opinion becomes one determining factor in reaching his own decisions.

An illustration of the difficulties in which analysts and physicians find themselves because of this dual role is the case of a 30-year-old female patient whom I am now helping to arrive at what on the surface looks like a medical decision. However, many psychological factors are involved.

This patient has been in therapy with me for two years. Her chief complaint was the difficulty of getting married. Engaged three times for long periods, in each instance the fiancé backed out on the eve of marriage. The patient had developed the "baby-doll" design for living as her goal in life. She relied exclusively on her physical charm, focusing particularly on her shapely breasts as the way to attract "Prince Charming" and "live happily ever after." She involved herself repeatedly, however, with sadistic men who fed her the fantasy she was seeking, thus inducing her to subject herself to long periods of masochistic exploitation that ended in rejection. Very recently she discovered a lump on her breast. Biopsy revealed malignancy in the lining of the tumor. The patient's mother had a similar problem about five years ago and was operated on by a different surgeon who removed the mother's breast during the first surgery while she was on the operating table. Because of fear that this might happen to her, my patient chose a different surgeon who, she reports, has given her the option of removal of the breast to prevent further infection, or radium treatment. Her family physician was critical of this surgeon's procedure on the ground that this should be a medical decision; that the patient is not qualified to make such a critical decision and that it is unfair for her to be tortured with such a burdensome responsibility.

In discussing the pros and cons with my patient, I asked if she would have preferred the surgeon to have made the decision and she said, "Two years ago before therapy I would have preferred that he make it, but I would have fallen apart either way. Today, right or wrong, I want to make the decision myself; better this than the way my mother is constantly blaming her surgeon these past five years that he should have saved her breast." The patient's answer indicates that she realizes how, when she was more infantile, she would have wanted to empower the surgeon, as a parental authority, to make the decision for her and then to be able to blame him if it suited her infantile emotional needs. Today, having gained strength and maturity, she would resent any attempt on the part of the surgeon to usurp her power to make decisions affecting her life; she will bear the responsibility herself. In her own words "Even if removing the breast were 90 per cent preventive and radium only 75 per cent preventive, I still have the right to take the gamble on the 15 per cent if I so choose. The bad feelings I would have about being disfigured and the problems I'd run into with dating may be a lot worse than the extra 15 per cent safety advantage against recurrence of cancer. Anyway, only I can decide whether it's worth the gamble just as I have to decide whether it's worth my while to travel in traffic on the 4th of July week-end when 500 people get killed."

If the question were posed as to which attitude is generally more correct for the analyst to adopt toward patients—the attitude of this patient's family physician or the attitude of the second surgeon—the answer would necessarily be that neither invariably is correct. What is appropriate for one patient is not appropriate for another; furthermore, what is appropriate for a patient at one point in his development is no longer appropriate at another point. The position taken toward making a decision for a patient should be based on thorough understanding of the patient's level of development and unconscious dynamics, in the context of all surrounding circumstances. No mechanical rule can replace a careful personality evaluation and the exercise of the therapist's good judgment.

When Freud practiced, problems of decision and authority did not involve the complexities that we face now, in a different age and culture. In Freud's day it was generally accepted that the doctor stood close to God. Although the physician was trained only in the narrow discipline of medicine, he was called upon to solve all sorts of life problems for the patient. Even though Freud recognized the values of self-determination for the patient and freedom from hypnotic influence, he did in fact devise a method wherein the behavior and "invisibility" of the therapist was similar to that of the priest in the confessional booth. Even though the priest's replies may differ in content from the analyst's and be punitive or judgmental while the analyst's may not, the image of the analyst, as seen by the patient, is still that of the aloof authority who, though he sound neutral or even benevolent, may still not be trusted by the patient, since who can tell at what point he may decide to be the God of Wrath instead of the God of Mercy!

This factor, among others, makes it understandable why Freud (1913) experienced most of his success with patients suffering from symptom neuroses and why he failed with psychosis, character and behavior disorders. Perhaps it also explains why he concentrated on the oedipal problem as the core pathology in human beings and kept distance from the preoedipal disturbances. While it may be possible to communicate successfully on a verbal adult level with a patient at advanced stages of development, it is almost impossible to use this method successfully where fear and mistrust of the preoedipal mother is at its height.

Because of this limitation in the therapist-patient relationship, as structured by Freud, later schools of psychotherapy gradually modified his technique by making the analyst less and less the traditional image of the aloof paternal authority and bringing him closer to equality in power to the patient. Ferenczi (1926) was the first to advocate two important changes in the analyst's role. First, he stressed more active participation. Second, he pointed out that the analyst must change roles and must "let himself go during the treatment as psychoanalysis requires of him." Following Ferenczi we have had a succession of new schools developing modifications in the interaction between the analyst and patient. Some of the most outstanding in this respect were Wilhelm Reich (1949), Harry Stack Sullivan (1940), Frieda Fromm-Reichmann (1943), Marie Coleman Nelson (1957), John Rosen (1953) and the existentialists, represented by Whitaker and Malone (1953). The themes stressed by these different schools emphasize (1) interpersonal reactions with the patient on a level of more equality, (2) reduction of authoritative omnipotent aspects of the therapist's role, (3) humanization of the therapist, (4) deliberate communication with the patient on other than the verbal levels, (5) "tuning in" with the patient on his particular channel (i.e., "going along" with the resistances), (6) role-playing by the therapist in one form or another, (7) varying the procedure from patient to patient and with the same patient during different phases of therapy.

As we move from classical analysis toward the other extreme, existential analysis, we gradually abandon intellectually organized, rational explanations and resort to words, phrases, gestures, tones and mannerisms to register an emotional communication. This latter method becomes such an individual matter and depends so much on the therapist's personality that only protocols of specific incidents can be used to convey exactly how it is effected by any individual therapist. Let me cite a couple of examples to describe how I put these principles into practice.

A 25-year-old ex-drug addict and homosexual, with a history of violent aggressive outbursts as well as suicidal attempts, said in a group therapy session that he suddenly realized his mother was out to destroy him and that he felt furious with me because, "Bert is my mother." He added, "I just feel it. This may be crazy and I should be locked up but I just feel he's my mother. I was scared shit of him all weekend— he's evil and I've been tight and depressed and miserable, not able to go near a girl or fuck, because he's made me scared. And I don't want to analyze this or understand it or rationalize it. Shit, I just want to say it."

During this recital the patient's voice was getting stronger and stronger and his mood was getting gayer. He was saying all these negative things about me, yet he alternately smiled and cried and looked at me with affection and relief. It was obvious from his facial expressions that he *felt* what he was saying was irrational and that it was a relief for him to be able to say irrational, negativistic things about me and know, at least on a conscious level, that he would not be punished. His side glances, however, indicated that he was looking for some response or reaction from me and that in part he feared I might embark on some explanation that he was wrong and that he shouldn't feel this way about me.

I responded very spontaneously to him with the first reaction that came to my mind out of my own unconscious. In about a split second I thought that this was no time for logical explanations; that I should join with him and play the role of the bad mother, but by burlesquing it. In addition to my thought that it was correct from a technical, psychodynamic standpoint, I also *felt* that it would be very enjoyable—not unlike psychodrama. I said, "Now, don't forget, I want you to be loyal to me, don't you go out with any other women." Even though I maintained a serious face, I felt that everyone in the group knew I was acting and that this patient also knew, but that at the same time my act felt real to him. The group burst into laughter. His response was immediate. He said, "Keep talking like that, Bert, please. I love it. It feels so good. I know it's crazy but I just love this crazy talk. I don't want any fucking explanations. Just go on, keep talking like that. My depression just went away entirely. I feel light as a feather."

Let us analyze the meaning of my reaction and why it struck such a responsive chord in the patient. If we translate my communication into traditional interpretation, I would have told him that he was having a negative transference onto me as his mother; that he was afraid that I wanted to overpower, possess and swallow him; that I would be angry if he went out with, loved or had sex with a woman because I wanted to keep him to myself, and that this was unreal because, in fact, I was not his mother and did not have such feelings; that he was projecting feelings he had about his mother during his early childhood onto me.

From my experience with this patient, I know that an interpretation in this traditional manner not only would not have reached him emotionally, it would have frightened him and made him suspicious and angry at me. He would have seen me in the image of the anal mother who, while pretending to be permissive, was mechanically reciting a text and instructing him as to how he must think and feel. It would, therefore, only have strengthened his negative transference. The reason he said, "I don't want to analyze this," is that he was afraid someone in the group would tell him that he should not feel this way, that it was wrong.

My response worked well because I was completely in tune with the patient at the moment. I was happy that he was able to express such feelings openly and freely even though, as he said, these feelings were "crazy." I really enjoyed hearing him and felt like reciprocating his feelings by playing a game. Even though this was a spontaneous emotional response on my part, it was made possible only by the fact that I had already studied and thought out the dynamics of this patient carefully on an intellectual level and made the image of his pathology a part of me. I do not go along with the extreme existentialist who contends that a knowledge of the dynamics is not necessary, that all the patient requires to get well is to have a genuine sharing and honest response from a therapist. Some patients may derive benefit from such a relationship, but it is similar to the catharsis derived from talking with a good friend; it may miss entirely the important area of pathology where the patient needs the most help.

In another case, a woman of 25 who had just broken up with her husband and was suffering from an acute reaction of separation anxiety, impulsively quit her job, came back to live with her mother, and lapsed into an oral regression. Prior to this, she had been compulsive, dependable, hard-working, and conscientious—a person who defended herself against oral wishes by a very strong reaction-formation of excessive service to others and self-denial. When she started the session she said, "I'm very afraid to tell you what I'm doing." She told about all these orally regressive actions and complained that she was falling apart and that she would become a "piece of shit." At the same time I noticed that she was talking in a gay, hopeful and optimistic tone; occasionally a smile would unintentionally break through. Knowing her defenses, I felt that there was little chance of her altering her character to such a degree and so suddenly that she would become a "piece of shit." It was more likely that she was secretly enjoying the fact that she was becoming freer and following her feelings for the first time. My immediate reaction was that she was glad to be able to function more freely and indulge herself, but that she was afraid I would disapprove of her for it. She was unconsciously testing me to see if I would be like her prohibitive parents who subjected her to severe discipline. My response was: "Somehow, what you told me doesn't come across as real. I may be all wrong, but despite your complaints, the *feeling* you communicate is that you're glad you found the courage to act like a baby for a change, and that you know you'll go back to work in a couple of weeks anyway but are afraid that I'll think that your behavior is sinful." Her response was a gratified smile and, "You know, you're really smart."

It should be noted that even though my response was based in part on a careful analysis of her behavior and content in the light of her dynamics, my observation was characterized as a personal reaction; I described it as merely my "feeling"—a subjective feeling.

This mode of communication does not invite an argument or debate about the correctness or incorrectness of my judgment. I like to call this type of communication an educated emotional reaction to distinguish it from a primitive non-purposive, nontherapeutic emotional reaction which a person ventilates merely for his own gratification and without consideration for the effect it may have on the listener. We must bear in mind that the purpose of the therapeutic relationship is primarily to benefit the patient, not for the gratification of the therapist. The therapist must therefore be able to formulate a mental set in which only those emotional reactions which will cause no harm to the patient are released.

Knowing this patient as allergic to domination and strongly inclined to argument, I feel certain that, had I communicated my thought in a mode of unqualified conviction, her response would have been an antagonistic, "I think you're full of shit."

Returning to the original question of whether the analyst's role should be to interpret or to react, I believe no generalization is possible. There are still patients who respond favorably only to aloof, intellectualized analysts. Others respond best to an analyst who seems hostile. Some patients can get along only with a female analyst who acts like a wet nurse or a baby-sitter. Still others work well with analysts who are in fact severely disturbed themselves and whose behavior is unconventional and even verges on the bizarre. (I know of one analyst who sees patients at 2 or 4 a.m. and whose sessions last sometimes for three hours.) The role that works best for me is the adoption of emotional reactions which are based on thorough study and understanding of the patient's psychodynamics and unconscious needs. That is, a fusion between the intellectual understanding and the personal emotional reaction seems to bring the best results. Sullivan (1940) first defined the role of the therapist as that of the participant-observer. I prefer moving the concept of participation one big step further and regard the therapist as the reacting participant who continues also to be a scientific observer. The responses that result from such interaction with the patient are "educated emotional reactions."

REFERENCES

Coleman, M. L., and Nelson, B., Paradigmatic psychotherapy in borderline treatment. *Psychoanalysis*, 1957, 5 (3).

Ferenczi, S., *Further Contribution to the theory and technique of psychoanalysis*. London: Hogarth Press, 1926. See also Rank, O., *The development of psychoanalysis*. New York: Nervous and Mental Diseases Publishing Co., 1925.

Freud, S., Further recommendations in the technique of psychoanalysis (1913). *Collected Papers*, II. London: Hogarth Press, 1940, pp. 342-365. See also Turnings in the ways of psychoanalytic therapy (1919). *Ibid.*, pp. 392-402; Recommendations for physicians on the psychoanalytic method of treatment (1912). *Ibid.*, pp. 323-333.

Fromm-Reichmann, F., Psychoanalytic psychotherapy with psychotics. *Psychiatry*, 1943, 6. See also Transference problems in schizophrenia. *Psychoanal. Quart.*, 1939, 8.

Mullan, H., and Sangiuliano, I., Existential matrix of psychotherapy. *Psychoanal. Rev.*, 1960, 47 (4).

Reich, W., *Character analysis*. New York: Farrar, Straus and Cudahy, 1949.

Robertiello, R., Friedman, D. B., and Pollens, B., *The analyst's role*. New York, Citadel, 1963.

Rosen, J. N., *Direct analysis*. New York: Grune & Stratton, 1953.

Sullivan, H. S., Conceptions of modern psychiatry. *Psychiatry*, 1940, 3, 1-117.

Whitaker, C. A., and Malone, T. P., *The roots of psychotherapy*. Philadelphia: The Blakiston Company, 1953.

CHAPTER 17

The Maturational Interpretation

Hyman Spotnitz, M.D., Med. Sc.D.

Dr. Spotnitz is a research psychiatrist engaged in private psychoanalytic practice. As a frequent contributor to professional journals and as a lecturer and teacher, he has covered a variety of topics in both individual and group psychotherapy. His forthcoming book on the theory of psychoanalytic technique in schizophrenia will follow. The Couch and the Circle (*1961*) *and* (*with Lucy Freeman*) The Wandering Husband (*1964*).

A native of Boston and a graduate of Harvard University, Dr. Spotnitz received his M.D. in 1934 from Friedrich Wilhelms University in Berlin, and his Med. Sc.D. in 1939 from Columbia University. Research in neurophysiology at the Neurological Institute, and in psychiatry at the New York State Psychiatric Institute, preceded his entrance into clinical practice. He has held the appointment of Adjunct Psychiatrist at both Mount Sinai Hospital and the Hospital for Joint Diseases, and has served as Consulting Psychiatrist to the Jewish Board of Guardians. He is a Fellow of the American Psychiatric Association, the American Orthopsychiatric Association, the American Group Psychotherapy Association, the New York Academy of Medicine, and the American Association for the Advancement of Science.

Significant stages in the growth of understanding about the curative factors in analytic psychotherapy are reflected in changing emphases in interpretation. Half a century ago it was thought that what healed a patient was the recall of memories. Treatment was then regarded as incomplete unless "all obscurities in the case are explained, the gaps in memory filled out, and the original occasions of the repressions discovered," as Freud stated in the Introductory Lectures. When it became evident that the memories were less important than what prevented their recall, interpretations were made to overcome the repressive forces in the guise of resistance. Later resistance was recognized as an essential source of interpretive data because it told the story of the ego's development. The focus shifted to the constrictive influence that resistance had exerted, and the need to modify it. The analyst worked to resolve resistance, in order to create more favorable psychological conditions for ego functioning. Explanations were oriented toward the integration of the ego and the acquisition of insight.

More recently, widening appreciation of the communication function of resistance has stimulated other approaches to interpretation. As yet, these have not dispelled the misleading notion that therapeutic change issues primarily from objective understanding of one's behavior. In the professional literature, "interpretation" is still commonly laced together with such verbs as "convince," "point out," "demonstrate," "prove," "confront," and "unmask." But the use of interpretation primarily for veil-lifting purposes is waning, with the recognition that

This paper is a revision of one presented in April 1964 at a meeting of the New York Society of Clinical Psychologists, E. Hammer, Chairman, panel on "Interpretations in Treatment".

other aspects of the treatment relationship are often more significant than the development of self-understanding. The patient usually acquires this, but it is rarely the decisive factor in the case.

Objective understanding of his behavior does not invariably make it easier for him to change it. Of course, the therapist has to understand what motivates this behavior, but he does not intervene just to transmit insight. Scientific understanding is the raw data for therapeutic understanding, that is, some knowledge of what goes on in the patient which is given to him if and when it will unlock the door to personality change. Instead of trying to overcome resistance by explaining problems, the analyst uses interpretation to create the precise emotional experience which will resolve the problems.

In many cases I find it helpful to operate on the hypothesis that interpretation is consistently employed for maturational purposes. The treatment itself is conceptualized as a growth experience. In this context, the problems which motivate a person to undergo treatment are attributed, to some extent, to inadequacies in his interchanges with the environment from conception onward. These interchanges—physiochemical and biological as well as psychological—are with different configurations of environmental forces which, in a sense, constitute maturational teams. During infancy, mother and child form the team. When the oedipal level is reached, the child's maturational interchanges are more specifically with his family. Then the social team takes over and the reciprocal processes encompass an expanding circle of peers and adults.

The candidate for psychotherapy is viewed as a person who is unable to deal comfortably with the exigencies of his life because he sustained some damage in these early maturational interchanges. He commits himself to a supplementary series of interchanges with a therapeutic object because he suffers from the effects of failures, or memories of failures. Deleterious experiences with his natural objects caused fixations or arrests in growth. In attempting to cope with them, he developed maladaptations: certain repetitive patterns that drained off energy needed for maturation into circuitous processes. Consequently, he presents two distinctly different problems. One is that his maturational needs were not met. The other is that his maladaptations prevent him from effectively assimilating the experiences that would reduce these needs. The operation of these patterns block maturation.

Maladaptations are not totally reversible, but it is sufficient for the analyst to intervene to loosen their compulsive grip and to nullify the effects of the original blockages. If he does so, the patient usually requires little help in obtaining and assimilating experiences that will reduce his maturational needs.

In theory, therefore, the therapist does not intervene to reduce maturational needs directly; nor does he address himself to maladaptations (defenses) that do not interfere with maturation. Rather, he intervenes to lay the foundation for new growth by freeing the patient from the strangle-hold of pathological maladaptations. As these patterns are reactivated in the relationship (transference) they are studied until the analyst understands how they were set up and why they come into play in a given situation. He relates to the patient in terms of this understanding but does not share it unless the patient desires an explanation that would facilitate his talking and cooperative functioning. In that case, an interpretation is indicated. By and large, maladaptation patterns are dealt with when they have been reactivated with sufficient intensity to be reducible.

Although patients enter treatment in different degrees of immaturity, there are few who do not require some period of preparation before they reach the stage in which interpretation alone will resolve maturational blockages. Preverbal patterns are responsive only to symbolic, emotional, and reflective interventions. Affective nonverbal communications, even the analyst's state of being, give the preoedipal personality freedom to grow. During this preparatory period, the emotional logic of the patient's behavior on the couch is not explained to him. The therapist listens to him, silently analyzes, and generally maintains the attitude of the thoughtful parent with a young child. Intimacy may flow out of this attitude, but it is not fostered deliberately.

After the preoedipal maladaptations are more or less resolved, the patient becomes accessible to verbal interpretation. Thereafter the analyst gives the response which, in his opinion, will resolve whatever maturational blockages are hampering the patient at that moment.

In my experience, interpretation is ineffective unless it is motivated by a specific therapeutic intent. The response of the patient is a more important consideration than the accuracy of the explanation. The analyst should be able to anticipate the patient's reaction to an interpretation, and then voice it only if the anticipated reaction would be desirable at that time.

The hit-or-miss effect of interpretation given to convey the general understanding of a problem is illustrated by a report which recently came to my attention. The patient was a young man who had been brought out of the depths of a severe depression. While the more serious factors in his case were dealt with, the analyst had withheld comment on the patient's disclosures regarding his perverse tendencies. Then one day the analyst decided that he ought to call attention to their implications. In an absolutely correct, even brilliant interpretation, he pointed out the harmful consequences of the perverse behavior. The patient agreed that it was interfering with his recovery. He went on to say that the perverse activity gave him little gratification, and that the time had come for him to give it up.

In recalling what happened, the therapist said, "He knew exactly what I meant, and thanked me for opening his eyes, but I never saw him again."

The interpretation, which would probably have been helpful at another time, apparently stimulated an unconscious battle to defeat the therapist, whatever the cost. The patient was in such an intense state of negative suggestibility that, had he been told that giving up the perverse activity forthwith would make him miserable and mobilize his old suicidal urges, he might still be in treatment. That, at any rate, would have been the maturational interpretation at that time.

I have focused in this discussion on the science of interpretation. Its skillful use takes us into another realm. Intuition, inspiration, and empathy are among the personal qualities which are entailed in the sensing of the exact constellation in which an interpretation will be dynamically effective, and in expressing it in words that will ring bells at the patient's own level of communication. The art of interpretation cannot be taught. It can, however, be nurtured by mastery of the scientific principles.

CHAPTER 18

Interpretation: The Patient's Response

Reuben Fine, Ph.D.

Dr. Fine has achieved prominence as a psychoanalyst, teacher and writer, and as a psychologist who is dedicated to professional affairs. He came to psychoanalysis through the disciplines of philosophy and mathematics. Internationally known as one of the great chess masters of the twentieth century, his books on chess are translated into six languages. Dr. Fine is President of the psychotherapy section of the American Psychological Association and Director of The Center for Creative Living, a low-cost treatment service. He is in charge of training at the Metropolitan Institute for Psychoanalytic Studies and is Adjunct Professor at Long Island University. His forthcoming book on technique of psychoanalysis will be the successor to his Freud, a Critical Re-Evaluation of his Theories, *so well received for its scholarship and clarity.*

Fine's breakdown of so complex a process as the patient-therapist one into the six dimensions below is, I think, a most noteworthy accomplishment.

His excellent section on thought-feelings as one of the goals in analytic therapy reminds one of Bergson's phrase, that individuals should learn to think "as men of action and act as men of thought."

In the analytic process there is an ongoing interaction between the patient and therapist. Every activity, big or small, of the therapist is attended to by the patient, who reacts to it in his own idiosyncratic way. To the analyst, who is able to observe a series of patients, this is easily noticeable; it becomes the basis for his understanding of the transference. The patient, however, for a long time looks upon every interaction as a form of current reality.

The need to take into account the reactions of the patient to whatever the analyst does results in a constant patient-therapist dialogue. In fact, it may be said that there are really two major schools of psychotherapy: the dialogue school and the monologue school. Obviously my efforts in this paper will be devoted to exploring the ramifications of the dialogue approach. While there are many aspects to this dialogue, only those related to interpretation will be considered here.

The interpretation dialogue can be considered along six different dimensions. A careful examination of these dimensions may help to provide a meaningful classification of the clinical material, and perhaps form the basis for a more adequate theory of the process of psychotherapy.

I. Listening

The first dimension is the simplest, that of listening. Before any possible effect of any interpretation can be entertained, it must be determined whether the patient has listened to what has been said.

The question is by no means trivial. Some patients do not listen at all to what the analyst says and others listen partially; still others gather from the interpretation whatever they please, or, more precisely, whatever the ego will permit them to hear at that moment.

There is ample evidence in the literature of experimental psychology that people do not listen impartially and objectively to emotion-laden material. In addition, our whole theory of projective techniques is based on this fact of selective perception (or misperception).

Even the analyst, who is professionally trained to listen, has considerable difficulty in mastering the art. Some years ago Kubie, in work on supervision of psychiatric residents at Yale, had them bring in recordings of sessions with their patients. In a number of cases it turned out that the psychiatrist's report of what had happened was widely at variance with the recording. Thus it should come as no surprise to discover that patients do not listen carefully to interpretations. What is surprising is only that this has not been given adequate weight in the theory of psychotherapy.

Patients who do not listen at all are presumably completely schizophrenic; they do not hear anything of what goes on in their surroundings. Yet even here a more careful analysis forces a correction of this statement. The schizophrenic selects out of his environment certain trivial data or observations which he reacts to entirely out of proportion to their significance. Thus he is listening, but in a most autistic manner. The whole basis of our therapy technique with the schizophrenic is to find out what he is attaching so much importance to, and then to help the patient put these in the proper perspective.

A schizophrenic woman, delusional and hallucinatory, was being seen analytically in daily sessions. There seemed to be some improvement. Then one day she came in terribly frightened. The voices were not hallucinations, she insisted; they were real. Last night there were musicians in the courtyard who were there just to mock her. Army planes flew over and clinked (her word) her. A few days ago the police had really stopped her and called her a clinker.

I inquired what had happened the past day to frighten her so. Yesterday when she left, she said, there was a silly grin on my face and she knew that she had upset me. If even an analyst could not get along with her, what was the use? (The patient suffered from the delusion that she harmed everybody she came in contact with.)

At this point I realized what she was reacting to. At the end of the session the previous day her pack of cigarettes was finished, and she wanted to take the empty box along. I laughingly suggested that she leave the empty box in my trash basket, to which she reluctantly agreed. But she had noticed my laugh, and the intensification of her hallucinations followed.

Searles describes a paranoid man whom he was treating in the hospital. The patient was uncommunicative, and spent all his time lying in bed. Each day Searles visited him and offered explanations of his conduct. The patient did not seem to listen and made no apparent response. As time went on, Searles became rather discouraged and began to offer more and more brief interpretations. Finally he only came in, said hello, stayed awhile, and then said goodbye.

One day he came in, gave his usual hello, and left in a little while without saying goodbye. At this the patient suddenly said, "You didn't say goodbye."

Severe pathology is always extremely illuminating about the less obvious processes that go on in the neurotic. These two examples show that even when the patient does not seem to be paying attention, he picks out some obscure detail of the environment and focuses on that.

In the great majority of analytic patients, of course, the interpretation offered by the analyst is heard. But it is heard selectively. It is put to use in the service of the patient's defenses rather than in the careful working through of his anxieties.

Thus it can be said that few interpretations are heard by the patient in the same way that they are offered by the analyst. They are first sifted through the patient's unconscious resistances. Out of this comes one point or another, usually related to what the analyst has said, but considerably altered. In effect, the patient's illness consists of conducting a monologue (which helps to account for the persistent feelings of rejection and of being misunderstood), while the analyst's efforts are aimed toward convincing him that he should engage in a dialogue.

A patient, obviously in strong transference, would wander around outside the analyst's office for hours after her sessions were finished. During these meanderings she hit upon various insights. In fact, she said, her best insights came outside the analytic situation, and she was beginning to wonder why she had to bother with me at all. First, I inquired what her feelings were about me. She had been referred by another therapist, who had worked with her supportively over a period of many years. Here, too, she had strong affection and admiration, but verbally she maintained that she had no feelings about him. My question about her feelings about me was interpreted by her as a request that she should enter into a relationship with me. It was only after the question had been repeated a number of times that she grasped the idea that she could express any feelings she wanted to about me, and could begin to probe into the transference.

A man, in treatment with a woman analyst towards whom he felt great sexual attraction, was being seen twice a week. At one point he ran short of money and said that he had to cut down to once a week. The therapist said that she thought it better for him to come twice. He disappeared. When she finally called him, he said that it was his understanding that she had dismissed him from therapy because he could not comply with her demand that he come twice a week. The misunderstanding was straightened out, and he continued his treatment.

Both of the above examples indicate that the careful analysis of the listening process leads directly into a discussion of transference and resistance. It could even be said that the switch from rational therapy to analytic transference therapy arose because Freud went beyond the other therapists of his day in recognizing that the patient, instead of listening to him objectively, entered into an immediate emotional relationship, i.e., the transference.

II. ACCEPTANCE-REJECTION

Assuming now that the patient pays sufficient attention to the analyst's interpretation to grasp it, how does he handle it further? Many variations occur here, and the remainder of this paper will be devoted to a discussion of these.

On the surface at least, the analyst's main concern around an interpretation he offers is whether the patient accepts it or rejects it. If it is accepted, he tends to feel successful; if it is rejected, unsuccessful. This is the reaction of most analysts when they begin.

Experience indicates that it is by no means so simple. Actually it is often the reverse. Mere acceptance of an interpretation does nothing until the patient incorporates it into his psychic makeup. If this incorporation does not take place, verbal acceptance is quite meaningless.

Paradoxically, one of the most difficult of all patients to treat is the one who agrees too readily. These are the people who say: "Yes doc, you're so right—anything you say, doc," and then go their merry way. To them the analytic relationship is like the parent-child relationship of early childhood, in which they receive approval for agreeing with what mother or father wants of them, and this approval solves all their problems. Very often this surface compliance covers up an underlying rebelliousness, which the patient is extremely afraid to bring to the surface.

This point leads to a principle which will be alluded to many times in this paper: The decisive question with regard to interpretation is not whether it is correct or not, but how the patient reacts to it, and in turn how the analyst reacts to these reactions of the patient. Most interpretations by trained analysts, even by relative beginners, are correct; the problem is rather that insufficient attention is paid to how they are elaborated upon by the patient.

A patient had great difficulty putting her brassiere on, and decided that she could do it only with her son's help. When the incestuous character of this action was brought out, and tied up with various incestuous conflicts in her childhood, she readily agreed, and shortly thereafter informed me that she had stopped. Years later it was accidentally discovered that she had not really stopped at all, but had merely told me that she had; this in turn was a repetition of an infantile pattern with father.

Just as acceptance is no proof that the interpretation will be worked out properly, rejection is no proof that it will not. Actually, many analysts have been so impressed by the negativistic element in every patient's neurosis that they have even set up a rule that an interpretation cannot be considered successful unless the patient disagrees with it. The rationale behind this statement is that if the interpretation is sufficiently important, it will run up against deep-seated anxieties which the patient cannot be expected to bring to the fore; hence, on the surface there is resistance and rejection. This point of view goes too far toward the other extreme; rejection is not a proof of adequacy, but it should not be considered a sign of failure. What is decisive is how the patient handles the total interpretative process, how he incorporates the dynamic ideas into his psyche, how he tries to effect changes, and the ways in which he does actually change. From this larger point of view acceptance and rejection are but surface manifestations; it is what comes later that really counts.

A gifted patient who was making excellent strides in his analysis had a rather odd way of rejecting almost categorically any significant interpretation offered. This rejection was accompanied by a short, angry blast at the analyst, who was described as biased, incompetent, unable to listen, and too intent on injecting his own numerous problems into the analysis. Some time after this happened, usually within a week or two, the patient would come in, state that he had on his own just discovered a most revealing and remarkable insight, and then reel off the interpretation which he had rejected a week or two before, completely oblivious of what had happened. What was important here was not his repetition of this pattern (which was not analyzed for quite a while because it was helping rather than hindering the analysis), but the fact that he was going ahead in his emotional growth.

It is because rejection is by no means an indication of the failure of an interpretation that resistance analysis can be conducted. Sometimes interpretations have to be offered in the face of intense resistance over a long period of time before they become really meaningful to the patient.

III. Production-Repression

A third dimension along which the patient responses can be classified is that of production of material as opposed to repression or, in some cases, suppression. One of the theses of this paper is that production is in some respects the most desirable of all responses, and the one that leads to the most successful analyses in the long run.

A more careful examination of the process of improvement as it occurs in the patient is needed at this point. The patient is faced by a variety of interpretations, some of which seem preposterous, some plausible, some possible. Before he can choose those which will be worked out, he has to have some *inner conviction* about what is being offered to him. The question then is: how will this inner conviction be brought about?

The conviction is greatest when it is based on material that he himself produces. Ideally the process involves three steps: (1) production of fantasy material, (2) reflection on what has been produced, and (3) change. This is only an ideal, which serves more as a guideline to practice than as an outline of what always, or even generally, occurs. What usually occurs is a considerable working through of resistances before the inner convictions really take shape and become the base for future actions.

The analytic situation is set up to facilitate the production of fantasy material. This is done in various ways: privacy, the use of the couch, the darkened room, the consistent probing into fantasy material ordinarily kept out of polite conversation or even consciousness.

Freud combined the two steps of production and interpretation, which is why the significance of production has generally been underestimated in analytic thinking. Thus, in the dream he showed how the dream is the royal road to the unconscious (which it still is in most cases); but he did not consider in detail the fact that before you can interpret a dream, the patient has to produce one and bring it to the session. To a considerable extent this blurring of the two steps was due to his own extraordinarily facility in producing fantasies, a facility not shared by many of our patients.

In analytic practice today patients with various degrees of capacity for fantasy production are encountered. Few possess the easy or prolific fantasy richness of Freud. In the great majority of cases the patient needs considerable encouragement to reveal what is on his mind. Some people dream frequently and readily; others dream little but remember much of their childhood. Still others are rich in daydreams. Some are meager in dreams, memories, and fantasies. All kinds of combinations are found.

In all of these, two principles must be observed. First, each patient's mode of production has to be ascertained and respected. If a patient does not dream much, we cannot expect him to start bringing in four or five dreams a night, as some patients do. If a patient remembers little of his childhood, more will eventually come out, but usually not as much as the patient who from the beginning has many clear memories. Analysis increases productivity, but the increase depends on the base from which it starts. Patients often have the idea that they cannot be analyzed unless they dream prolifically or remember their first five years in detail; these patients have to be reassured on these scores. The scope of analysis must be adapted to the capacity of each patient to comply with the basic rules.

The second principle is that while the analyst must respect the patient's capacity to produce, he should not be satisfied with it. Consistent application of analytic principles, in most cases, leads to a considerably increased productivity. Thus the patient who dreams little at the beginning will learn to dream more, though not as much as some others. In one sense this is a simple application of the psychological principle of individual differences.

Analyzability in the classical sense can roughly be equated with this kind of productivity. The patient who dreams, has childhood memories, free associates—all to greater or lesser degree—can succeed in a classical analysis, regardless of the clinical diagnosis. The patient who does not produce material requires some variation in technique, though the underlying principles remain the same.

Productiveness goes on all through the analysis; it is not a matter of having told one's story, and then being through. There is a continuing need for material which will, in the long run, lead to that sense of inner conviction which can result in real change. That is why the best solution to the analytic impasse is generally one of more analysis.

The patient is not *per se* interested in producing material. His concern primarily is to get some relief from his symptoms, and the fact that the analyst asks for dreams or childhood memories often strikes him as strange, if not absurd. It is this difference in interest which adds to the continuous tug-of-war which characterizes most analyses, or, more technically, the continuous need to analyze resistances.

In general, interpretations which are too deep or too complicated cannot be grasped by the patient. Interpretations have to be relatively simple, compact and to the point. Frequently, when the patient comes out with some hitherto repressed or suppressed fantasy, the interpretation is obvious. But before the material came out it would have been useless to offer the interpretation.

A young man with an obvious homosexual problem comes to analysis for a variety of reasons. He expresses great fear of starting because the analysis might reveal him to be a homosexual and he knows that he is not. Reassured on this score, he starts. After about a year he has a dream that he comes to the office and overhears the analyst seducing one of his female patients. When asked what comes to mind, spontaneously he says that he is the girl being seduced. The dream here brings out his homosexual wishes toward the analyst. After this his homosexuality can be discussed; before, it would have been fruitless.

It is also useful to inquire from a metapsychological point of view why production is so important. Dynamically the analyst is a superego figure; the patient projects his superego to the analyst. In the course of analysis, by the consistent working through of transference interpretations, this superego is broken down and the patient can reintegrate his life in a more satisfactory way. These interpretations require the offering of some fantasy around and to the analyst-superego, who must then show that he is different from the original parent-figures. In this way the patient gradually frees himself from the inhibiting influence of the introjected parents. The building blocks in this freeing process are the demonstration, over and over again, that the analyst is different from the parents. In order to provide this demonstration the patient must repeatedly produce some fantasy which the analyst handles in a way that differs from the pattern employed by the parents.

The question arises here: what about the overproductive patient? There are patients who deluge us with dreams. A colleague in our analytic institute used to bring his dreams to seminar, and often they were four or five typewritten pages long and took half an hour to relate, much less interpret. Some patients can talk endlessly about their childhood without making the necessary connections with the present-day difficulties. With these patients the problem is to organize the material and its meaning for them, or to help them organize it. Sometimes certain types of material are used as a defense against others; e.g., occasionally patients dream excessively in order to cover up embarrassing everyday material. Many times, too, the excess of material is a prelude to superego punishment, manifested in strong resistances:

A fantasy-ridden woman produced innumerable dreams, childhood memories, transference fantasies—everything that seemed desirable for analytic purposes. When the analyst announced, two months ahead of time, his summer vacation plans, she flew into a violent rage. She said that she could just as well tell her dreams to her girlfriend, whose interpretations were just as good as the analyst's, and that all the interpretations of the analyst were old hat anyhow. In spite of interpretation of the negative transference, she insisted on taking her vacation a month before the analyst left and on coming back a month later. It took a long time to get to her feelings about separation.

This case brings up the point that it is not merely the quantity of production that counts, but also its nature. When a patient is blind to one area of her life, as in the above example, special measures have to be taken to help her become aware of it. In some cases, for example, it is necessary to ask patients not to bring in dreams for a while, or to stay away from other kinds of material. But all this does not alter the main theoretical emphasis on the central significance of productivity.

If production is so important, the question may well be raised why analysts remain so adamantly opposed to bringing in material obtained from other sources? For example, why not use projectives to help the patient see a homosexual conflict, or interview relatives to clarify the childhood situation?

The answer is that the ego is not ready for this material, and will therefore be unable to work it through. In addition, the introduction of foreign material of this kind rarely leads to any inner conviction about its content. And finally, productiveness is a process that goes on all through the analysis. If projectives are introduced, the patient will want more projectives later; these external stimuli are then relied upon to do the freeing for them again and again. In certain cases, however, hypnosis or projective devices may be called upon to break an impasse; but many times they will not succeed, and the impasse will still have to be worked out in other ways.

IV. Action-Discussion

A fourth kind of reaction to interpretation revolves around action. Some patients take interpretation as a command to action, while others find great difficulty in acting and engage instead in endless discussion. Historically these two contrasting reactions are mirrored in two contrasting approaches to analysis. Freud originally placed much more emphasis on discussion, but his personal experiences, which provided the basis for his theoretical views, played the decisive role. In his own life he had had no difficulty getting the things that he wanted; his problem was more an internal one of inner conflict. In his 1914 paper on remembering and working through, he laid down the principle that remembering was more important than action.

Some ten years later Ferenczi and Rank took the opposing view. They felt that the patient should be encouraged to act out in whatever way he wanted and that he should then try to learn from his mistakes. It is again of some interest that, historically, Ferenczi was a man who could not act much in his own life, for he courted a woman for 18 years before he could make up his mind to marry her. Rank on the other hand, after an early life as a scholar, evolved a new kind of analytic movement when he came to this country. His kind of analysis, however, is so doctrinaire that it has few adherents left.

In popular language, these two opposing positions could be described as (1) Go out and do things, then learn from your mistakes. (2) Look before you leap. Don't make a move until it is well thought out.

It is clear that both of these points of view can be incorporated into analytic theory today, but as heuristic principles rather than as absolute commands. To one type of patient action is most tempting, because they are constantly looking for suggestions about what to do. To them the careful perusal of fantasy material in analysis is highly irksome; they want immediate action. The contrasting type of patient is the one who delights in excessive discussion; he can go on for years without any resolution. Nowadays many scholarly and academic personalities present this problem in analysis.

The resolution to the conflict lies in helping the patient acquire a proper sense of *balance*. In some cases action is called for; in others, discussion. The patient who acts too much has to be helped to curb his self-destructive action, but the patient who acts too little has to be helped to translate his insights into activity.

Approaching the problem in this way leads to a useful technical modification. The ultimate goal is change; interpretation is only the tool. Early in the analysis it quickly becomes clear what the predominant pattern of the patient is—action or talk. The job of the analyst then becomes one of redressing the balance. Almost from the very beginning, interpretations can be geared toward this balance; the degree of success depends on the extent to which this balance is reached.

Two contrasting cases of young men illustrate this principle in practice.

One man came to analysis with a history of excessive sexual activity. For years he had been having sex with two or three girls a night; quite often he would then go home and masturbate. There was little satisfaction in his conquests. Actually the stimulus toward analysis came when a homosexual acquaintance told him that he (the patient) was really a homosexual at heart, which made him panicky. Here the interpretations were geared toward calming the patient down and allowing him to choose one woman, which he eventually did.

The second patient was one who was extremely withdrawn from the world. For a period in his life he had spent his time sitting in his room drinking tea and listening to records. His income came from part-time jobs and unemployment insurance. He had few human contacts. In this case the interpretations helped him to see how afraid he was of contacts with girls and encouraged him to experiment with various contacts, until he was eventually able to achieve some kinds of relationships.

These two examples bring up the interesting question of whether we do not in our analytic work deal in suggestion more than we are willing to admit. Glover considers that every inexact interpretation is a suggestion; since he has extraordinarily stringent requirements for "exactness," in his opinion most analysts do rely mainly on suggestion. Silverberg has made the point that interpretations, by the way in which they are slanted, do carry a strong suggestive element.

I think that a distinction must be drawn between suggestion and direction. A suggestion is given to a patient without much explanation; it is a command. Direction, however, is achieved after the analyst gets to know his patient fairly well. Direction is an essential part of the analytic process; without it the patient rightly feels lost. At various points there frequently is a consensus between analyst and patient that certain directions will probably bring fruitful consequences, while others will repeat the old neurotic stagnation. Even when the patient is in sharp disagreement, it is important that the analyst take a clear stand on major life issues. This does not mean that the analyst dictates the details of the patient's life, for there are many life situations in which any one of a number of choices would be quite adequate. The problem is rather to make a choice.

Looked at in this light, both action and discussion may be productive of good results in the long run, or may be used as resistances. What is decisive is the working through of the total design of the patient's life.

V. THOUGHT-FEELING

This category is related to the previous one, but there are important differences. The contrast is between an intellectual and an emotional reaction to an interpretation. This contrast has long been noted in the difference between obsessional (thought) and hysterical (feeling) patients. Ideally the analyst wants release of emotion, yet he also wants the patient to have reasonable control. It has been pointed out that, in this respect, analysis attempts to combine the classical and the romantic views of life in the concepts of the ego and the id.

The patient whose response to an interpretation is one of excessive thought is typically someone who also has great verbal command over analytic theory. He can talk about the oedipus complex, aggression, castration, orality, anality, etc., with great facility; but the trouble is that this facility goes too far and becomes too one-sided. He goes on and on about childhood, complexes, and the like, but there is an absence of feeling about what he is saying. Knowledge produces no significant change; there is merely interpretation and more interpretation. Often outsiders who fail to understand the real role of interpretation in analysis are antagonized by these people and see them as living proof that "insight doesn't work."

Closer examination of these patients reveals that while they can intellectualize a good many insights, certain ones are invariably missing. Basically, of course, they do not genuinely appreciate the significance of feeling. In addition, other insights are missing, particularly those related to the transference. Most people who come to analysis confuse true analytic understanding with a series of intellectual insights and fail to grasp both the role of feeling and the significance of transference and resistance. Also, certain other insights are generally simply bypassed by the intellectualizer. For example, a homosexual patient who could spout analytic theory with great ease completely failed to understand the basic analytic theory of homosexuality.

Another patient who could verbalize analytic theory with great fluency, but felt nothing, completed all his communications about himself in one session. After that he either theorized or talked about other people. Much of his energy went into convincing other people that they had problems. Some of his intellectual insights were fairly good but his affect-block made him blind about himself.

The opposite response is shown by the person who emotes all the time. Usually the previous type is a man, this type a woman. There is hardly any attempt to think about her situation. Interpretations do not interest her, and often such patients scarcely listen. Analysis for them is a chance to release their feelings. One patient would come and spend half the hour crying. Then she would dry her eyes, say she had had a good cry, and leave. Hardly any interpretations were offered in her therapy. In spite of this, she felt somewhat relieved by the process.

Popular literature on psychoanalysis is misused by this kind of patient. They read that analysis encourages the release of feeling, which is what they are doing all the time. Why don't they get better? The answer to this requires first a small theoretical detour. A theoretical distinction must be drawn between *manipulative* and *expressive* emotion. A manipulative emotion involves an unconscious effort to manipulate some other person; an expressive emotion is a direct release. Neurosis relies on manipulative emotion, going back to childhood, for to manipulate is the child's only weapon against inadequate parents. Once the manipulative pattern is set, it becomes internalized and the person then goes through life unconsciously using his emotions to manipulate other people. The release, in such cases, brings some temporary relief followed by a resumption of the old pattern. This is because the internalized object, which is the real target of the emotion, remains untouched. There is, as a result, a long-standing repetition of one unsatisfactory emotional experience after another.

An example can be taken from the affect of anger. Many people look upon analysis as a means through which they need only relieve their anger, and then they will be better. Quite often they consciously try to make the analyst into a target for their anger, sure that all they have to do is "bring it out." The anger is brought out, but the patient does not improve. In these patients, anger was a potent weapon the parents used against them in childhood, and now they are taking revenge against the parents by doing this to other people. But the internalized angry parent-figure is not exorcised by this procedure.

This dynamic can be contrasted with the situation in which anger may really be released with positive results. This occurs in patients who are chronically afraid that if they ever yell at anybody, the roof will fall on them. By venting their anger on the analyst, they discover that this fear is groundless—that it is a neurotic distortion which goes back to childhood. In this case, a modification of the superego takes place. What is decisive in this, as in the previous instance, is the inner dynamics of the process, not the release as such.

As before, analytic technique here requires the development of a proper sense of balance. The pale cast of thought must be warmed by passion; hysterical release must be calmed by cool reason. As Fenichel comments, the analyst must always steer between the Scylla of intellect and the Charybdis of feeling; too much of either and the patient will be shattered on the rocks.

VI. SELF-INVOLVEMENT—OBJECTIVITY

Finally, the patient may respond to an interpretation with excessive self-involvement or with objectivity. In theory, the nature of analysis is stated in terms of a pact between the healthy part of the ego and the analyst. When this pact or working alliance takes place, the patient is able to maintain a certain degree of objectivity about himself which makes for the optimal change. All too often, however, the objectivity is lost in a sea of excessive self-involvement.

The most common form this takes is that of self-blame. Instead of listening to an interpretation calmly, the patient seems to say: "That shows what a bad person I am. How can you ever expect such a person to get anywhere in life?" Often this happens with dreams. The patient comes in saying that he has had a "bad" or a "good" dream, depending on the wishes brought about—thus forgetting that a dream is basically a wish, neither good nor bad.

A young woman who had been brought up in an atmosphere of constant and intense quarreling between mother and father showed such a pattern. Her immediate response to any interpretation was to say: "If I have such wishes, how can you ever expect to help a person like me?" At the beginning of the analysis she gave up masturbation (which she had never practiced to excess anyhow), vowing that as long as she was in analysis she would never masturbate again. This was done to placate the analyst-superego, although he had never said anything about it, and when it was brought up had assured the patient that he did not feel at all disapproving of the practice.

Later, when she had children, the self-blame took a somewhat different form. She began to retract all the negative insights about her mother, because she was afraid that she might be doing the same sort of thing.

In patients with such extreme self-blame, there is a harsh superego and very often, in analysis, a negative therapeutic reaction. In these cases analysis of the superego is more important than any libidinal interpretations. The patient has to be reassured, over and over, that she is worthy of happiness in life, no matter what happened with her parents.

On occasion, the opposite may take place as well: an unrealistic self-approval. One such patient felt that he was somehow special in this world and that the analyst *really* appreciated him, unlike other people. This special feeling concealed a good deal of hostility, which came out only when the positive transference did not resolve his real life difficulties. Before then, his characteristic reaction to an interpretation was to use it as confirmation of his unusual role in the world.

Summary

The analytic stiuation is a dialogue, not a monologue. In this dialogue the patient's reactions to interpretations must be subjected to careful examination. Six dimensions along which such an examination can be conducted have been proposed. In general, the primary emphasis must be placed on the ways in which the patient responds to interpretations, rather than on whether the interpretations are correct or incorrect.

CHAPTER 19

The Therapeutic Act

John L. Herma, Ph.D.

This paper, and the one by Jule Nydes (Chap. 15), constitute the last written contributions of two of the most gifted psychologist-psychoanalysts who originally gathered around Theodore Reik when he formed the first institute in this country for the training of psychologists as psychoanalysts.

Dr. John L. Herma died of a heart attack at the age of 55 in his home at Mohegan, N.Y. Among his professional activities, Dr. Herma was a Research Associate at Columbia University, where he collaborated with Dr. Eli Ginzberg, the famous economist. Together they wrote Talent and Performance, *a study of the most highly talented graduate students and how they fared after leaving the campus. Along with other books, he is co-author of the forthcoming* Making Your Way in a White Man's World, *to be released by Columbia University Press.*

Dr. Herma had written a number of psychoanalytic papers, and he expressed to me his particular pleasure in this, his latest one. Thanks are appreciatively extended to Miriam Landau, psychoanalyst and close friend of John, for her editorial assistance with the finishing touches on the manuscript left at his death.

We are accustomed to respond to a patient's communications on two levels: to the literal meaning of what he is saying and to a meaning which he is not conscious of but which underlies his verbalizations like a *cantus firmus*. The overt meaning can be compared to the manifest content of a dream, the covert one to its latent meaning. Indeed, the associative connections between a series of thoughts are at times as surprising and as difficult to track down as those thought sequences which give the dream the appearance of incoherence or even irrationality.

We also take for granted that there is a counterpart to this dichotomy which exists also in the analyst's responses, except that we assume that only those unconscious responses operate in him which are conducive to the progress of the therapy. If unconscious tendencies other than those obtrude themselves into his therapeutic activity, we speak of countertransference reactions.

In the absence of such intrusions we assume, then, that the unconscious processes in the analyst which operate during his work are predominantly in the service of the therapeutic task and, hence, that his communications are relatively free from undesirable unconscious elements. Under such ideal conditions, the therapeutic situation could be described as one in which the analyst's verbalizations have predominantly only one level of meaning, the intended one, which is inspired by his rational understanding of the therapeutic task. The analysand's verbalizations, however, have two meanings—the manifest and the latent one. The latter is brought into sharper relief by the free-association process and therefore eventually becomes more clearly discernible.

Meaning Intended and Misintended

It is a commonplace observation that even the most carefully worded interpretation is not always received by the patient in the sense it was intended. Instead of being acknowledged as merely a translation of the latent meaning of a given set of the patient's associative material, the interpretation offered may be reacted to by the patient as though it were a criticism, threat, praise, reward, or any number of other things. This is easily recognized if the patient responds with a startling nonsequitur, an apologetic defensiveness, or a counter "accusation"; or if he, for example, insists that the analyst had encouraged some action of his of a dubious character (and it turns out that he had interpreted the short-cut question "Why not?" not as an inquiry about his motives, but as an exhortation, "Why did you not go ahead and do it?").

Even though such occurrences are quite familiar to us, they deserve to be more carefully examined. There are situations in which it is not easy for the therapist to see that his statements have assumed a meaning to the patient which he had not intended—a state of affairs of no small practical significance. But of equal importance, this constitutes an aspect of the analytic situation deserving inspection from the point of view of the *theory* of psychoanalytic technique. For while psychoanalytic theory provides the theoretical basis and the rationale for analytic therapy, the linkage between the two is often not as close as we assume or wish it to be. This sometimes gives too great a latitude to the therapist if he tries to account theoretically for what he does practically—a condition which at times leads to rationalizations for his actions rather than to providing a rationale. This gap is at the basis of the misleading notion that analytic therapy is also an "art," an implication that it is therefore less scientific. The real opposition is not between more or less scientific disciplines, but between a theoretical and an applied science.

All practical applications of scientific knowledge introduce personal factors such as experience, skill, intuition, and invention—thus introducing an element of the creative. This is the only set of factors which justifies the comparison with art.

As to the practical problem, the situations which may escape detection by the analyst may come about in various ways. The patient's attributing "special" meaning to the analyst's comments is not confined to the distortion of an interpretation, as in the above examples, but may attach itself to casual or routine statements, such as "We have to stop now." Even the analyst most attuned to the possible latent meanings of his statements would hardly suspect that the patient might react to such an innocuous remark with the fear that the analyst meant, not the end of the hour, but the termination of the analysis. Even had the analyst been aware of his patient's fear of being discharged prematurely, he would not ordinarily expect this fear to attach itself to this remark. A concluding remark, "We don't understand this fully as yet," was taken by one patient to mean that he had not performed as well as he had thought a good analysand should. Another patient took a similar phrase at the end of the hour, "Well, we have to look into this more closely," as a veiled threat of the analyst's intended intrusion into his private life to discover some guarded secret. Such reactions may remain subliminal and therefore not communicable. If anxiety is built up in response to such remarks over a period of time, the anxiety may become conscious, but the source may be lost. Because of the very "harmlessness" of the remark, as well as its obvious and clear-cut intention, it is likely to escape analytic scrutiny, for a short or extended period, by both analyst and patient.

Moreover, the patient may not only distort the analyst's statement, but he may also misinterpret around the fact that he made it—or failed to make it if one were expected. An appropriate remark may mean, irrespective of its interpretative content, that the analyst tries to understand the patient, that he shares his knowledge with the patient, that he is concerned, that he approves, or that he loves him. A remark expected, but not forthcoming, may mean to the patient disapproval, disinterest, criticism, or rejection. A man about to get married reacted to his analyst's comment as though it expressed dissatisfaction with him. At the time the patient had no conscious inkling of his feelings either of being criticized or of any criticism in connection with his marital plans. The observable manifestation was merely a slowing down of the therapeutic progress. At a much later phase of the analysis, it emerged that he had had an expectation that the analyst approve of his marriage explicitly, and hence he had been waiting for it. The "withholding" of the approval was interpreted as disapproval. This was not due to any doubt he had as to the appropriateness of his choice or its timing in terms of his analysis, but was related to his mother's half-jocular remarks, heard throughout his childhood, that he would never marry and leave his mother.

The unfulfilled expectation of an interpretation or comment from the analyst giving rise to unsuspected reactions of this type is a topic related to the more general one of the analyst's silence assuming unconscious meaning to the patient. Here again, the whole gamut of meaning can attach itself to the analyst's act of being, or remaining, silent: from the reassurance the patient feels that he will not be pressured into discussing subjects he is not ready to, to the feeling of a benevolent concern for his troubles or well-being; from a feeling of lack of interest in him, to one of silent contempt; from a sense of scornful rejection, to one of outright condemnation. Silence, therefore, is not necessarily the refuge for the analyst who wants to avoid those pitfalls of verbal communication where even the most innocuous remark may be twisted and held against him—usually years later. Silence, too, can speak to the patient, often as loudly as the spoken word and sometimes more convincingly.

CONTAMINATION OF COMMUNICATION

What we can learn from such observations (if fortuitous circumstances lead us to understand the miscarriage of communication at some point) is that the analyst is in the situation of a surgeon who fancies himself working with sterilized tools, when actually a contamination had occurred inadvertently. Furthermore, he cannot count on his instruments ever being sterile or remaining so, since it is the patient's unconscious which contributes a dimension of meaning, beyond the one intended by the analyst, to either the act of communication or to its content. What we call interpretation, then, is not as simple a psychological instrument as we would wish it to be, i.e., basically nothing but a "translation" of an unconscious content into a conscious one; nor is the analyst's activity adequately described when we conceive it as the performance, essentially, of just such a job of translation, appropriately timed and appropriately phrased.

The potential contamination of the tools of communication, of course, is not an "either-or" problem but a "more-or-less" one. There are situations in which communication on the rational level does break down because the means of communication are taken over by id derivatives and used as channels of expression. On the other end of the continuum, there are situations where communication proceeds with a minimum of interference from the patient's unconscious undertow. It becomes, consequently, necessary to consider under what conditions the one or the other situation tends to predominate.

CONTAMINATION AND REGRESSION

In the most general formulation, we may say that communication, like any other ego function, is more or less susceptible to interference by irrational forces. The degree of such interference is a function of the strength of the ego and, for any given moment, the balance between id tendencies and the defending forces of the ego. This implies that effective communication is determined either by the general state of maturity of the ego or, conversely, by a state of regression. The therapeutic situation alters this balance and, in addition, tends to foster a regressive trend of a particular type—the transference.

A woman patient, for instance, was not disturbed by the analytic silence until a father transference recreated a similarity to a childhood situation in which the family had to sit around the table in utter silence, the father only occasionally making a comment, usually of a critical nature or a reprimand. At this point in the transference, the analyst's silence assumed to her the significance of a prohibition to talk. First she became inhibited, then she felt increasingly embarrassed, and gradually she became more and more angry at the analyst if he did not break the silence by some comment which would rescue her from her stage of paralysis.

Certain tendencies toward distorting the communication process may be correlated with a given clinical constellation. An obsessive compulsive person, for example, not only may use his verbal expressions as an instrument of aggression, but also may similarly ascribe aggressive intent and meaning to the analyst's comments. In a psychotic person, the usual levels of communication may become totally submerged in id derivatives and he may respond to the analyst's remarks as though he was being fed, loved, attacked, and so on.

THE PROBLEM OF COUNTERTRANSFERENCE

There is little difficulty in recognizing the gross manifestations of the effect of the regression on the process of communication. It is a different matter when we are confronted with the more subtle, subliminal effects. The patient may develop diffuse states of anxiety which cannot be readily connected to anything discernible; resistances may be mobilized for which no adequate explanation is available; or a negative therapeutic reaction may appear which undercuts all therapeutic efforts and even endangers the very continuity of the analysis. When we cannot account for the patient's reaction in terms of his unconscious, we are inclined to look for indications of some interference emanating from the analyst. We are then apt to confuse (a) the effects of contamination of the analyst's communications with the patient, with (b) manifestations of countertransference.

Reich, for example, objected to prolonged silence and stated that allowing such a silence to continue for too long was nothing but an expression of the analyst's sadism toward the patient. An inference is drawn here from the patient's assumed reaction, his pain, to a countertransference reaction of the analyst. The motive for the analyst's silence need not be the one Reich mentions, but it is nevertheless possible that a patient who is pained by such a silence may attribute such hostile intention to the analyst. The same patient, when in another mood, feels quite differently. He might feel, for example, that he is not being forced to comply with the basic rule; or that he is given the freedom to keep his thoughts to himself; or that his privacy is being respected; or that he is given a chance to think something out independently. This all adds up to the point that the unconscious meaning which a given act of communication, including silence, has to a patient need not be a response to some unconscious attitude of the analyst; it may be one of the manifestations of the patient's unconscious.

At this point a confused, "chaotic" situation may provoke a variety of reactions in the analyst. He may feel critical of himself, inadequate, guilty, or suspicious of some undetected countertransference reaction. This in turn may touch off irrational responses to the patient. It also may manifest itself in a certain helplessness in an otherwise experienced analyst; in transferring a case to another analyst without sufficient justification; in terminating prematurely, and so on.

One patient developed a persistent anxious tension during the analytic session and complained that he felt deprived of his freedom to express his own ideas and arrive at insights on his own. He expressed a fear about communicating his associations because he feared being interrupted prematurely by some interpretative remark of the analyst. When the analyst focused his attention on the patient's needs to rely on his own efforts, the patient responded to this as to another interference and felt increasingly inhibited in verbalizing. The anxiety and the corresponding resistance reached a level of intensity which finally led the analyst to refer him to a colleague. The analyst thought that he had touched off the unmanageable anxiety reaction by an ill-timed interpretation. This proved to be only partially true, for it was not predominantly the content of the interpretation which had precipitated the overwhelming anxiety.

The new analyst, who was appraised of the situation, avoided interpretative comments as much as possible, particularly those that might have contained an element of surprise for the patient. The new analyst assumed, on the basis of some biographical data, that it was the act of interpreting which had a traumatic impact on the patient. He behaved so as to remain in continued verbal contact with the patient so that he could always be in tune with the patient's thoughts and feelings and thus avoid any unexpected move.

The infantile situation which led to the patient's oversensitivity to interpretative comments revolved around his relationship to his father. The father was given to entirely irrational outbursts of anger or criticism for which there was no recognizable connection to anything the patient had done. The patient had no way of anticipating his father's reactions, but he did feel responsible for them because of his mother's frequent warnings not to upset his father. This situation engendered in him both a feeling of power over others as well as a fear of power. Because there was no intelligible connection between cause and effect, there was also no control over this magic power of his. When he began to be afraid of his own associations in the analytic situation, what he was really afraid of was touching off a reaction in the analyst—an interpretation—which he could not anticipate and therefore not control. The danger was avoided as long as he could make an interpretative connection himself, for then the situation remained intelligible to him and therefore within his control.

THE THERAPEUTIC ACT

The above case illustrates that in situations where communication by means of language is of no avail, or is temporarily interrupted, the analyst is not necessarily rendered helpless if he understands how to divest the means of communication of the symbolic significance which had made it useless as a therapeutic tool. The second and forewarned analyst followed a procedure that aimed to replace interpretation by a specific kind of behavior on his part. This behavior was not merely designed to postpone interpretation for a more auspicious time, but it aimed rather at restoring to the patient a sense of control over the situation, the loss of which had thrown him into a panic of such intensity that the function of communication could not hold up against the regressive pull. It is not the handling of the transference itself which is of interest in this context, but the specific means which were employed. It was a particular way of acting, on the part of the therapist, which assumed a therapeutic function. Inasmuch as an act of this kind is specifically geared to the particular therapeutic situation as is an interpretation, we may speak here of a "therapeutic act" in parallel to, but as distinct from, an interpretation.

There is a certain semantic difficulty in making such a parallel. An interpretation is usually thought out in advance and therefore is relatively less likely to have an unexpectedly disruptive effect upon the therapeutic situation. A form of behavior on the part of the analyst, however, which is not considered by him in the context of the meaning it may take on for the patient, may more readily have an unanticipated consequence. Just as an interpretation remains an interpretation whether it has a good or a bad therapeutic effect, so we may call a particular way of behaving on the part of the analyst a therapeutic act not so much on the basis of whether or not it is therapeutic, but whether or not it plays a role in the therapeutic process. If it assumes such a function unintentionally, or even without anyone becoming aware of it, the therapeutic act is comparable to the interpretation which assumes a symbolic meaning not intended by the analyst. In practice, therapeutic acts are intuitively expressed by the experienced analyst. Only in unusual situations is one forced to separate conceptually the content of an interpretation from its aspect as an act, or to consider the possible secondary meaning of normally neutral activities—such as closing an hour, opening the window, recording a payment, or making an extraneous remark. Only when the patient's unexpected reactions attract our attention do we usually become aware of this. In practice, we are likely to make deliberate use of it only when difficulties arise.

In his second analysis,[1] a patient complained that his first one had remained unsuccessful in spite of a promising beginning. He said he began to feel somehow left out of it, as though he had been only partly there. As it turned out, this feeling arose in an early phase of the first analysis after a psychodiagnostic report had been sent to his analyst. After a short discussion of its content, the analyst retained it in his files. Acting on a hunch, the new analyst prevailed upon his colleague to send the report to the patient. The subsequent analysis of the incident bore out what he had surmised: the retention of the report had meant to the patient that the analyst had gotten into possession of part of the patient's personality, that somehow he had been robbed of his identity.

This example is instructive in terms of technique. The second analyst did not communicate his understanding of the situation to the patient: he did not "interpret," nor did he wait for a later phase of the therapy to do so. Instead, he told the patient he would arrange to get the report back into his possession and did so. That is, he took a particular action, the therapeutic significance of which was to release the patient from a defensive stance which would have doomed any of the second analyst's interpretations just as effectively as it had those of the first.

---

[1] I am indebted to Dr. Martin Bergmann for this case illustration.

THE WORD AND THE ACT

In general, the "parameters" of the analytic situation are such that the scope of action on the part of the analyst is minimized and limited. This is rightly so, since action is a carrier of meaning, a mode of communication which suffers from certain deficiencies as a tool of analytic therapy. It is more global, less differentiated, less specific, more ambiguous. Action is open to attributed meaning more readily than verbal communication because of its ambiguity; and if it derives a higher degree of specificity of meaning to the patient, it does so only from the context of the situation.

In the analytic situation, the unconscious of the patient determines the contextual meaning of the analyst's action to a much higher degree than is done with others in everyday situations. On the other hand, action is more penetrating, it makes more of an emotional impact, and it is closer to perception and functionally more primitive than is verbalization. In analytic therapy, relatively more reliance is based on the verbal mode of communication with its higher degree of specificity, plastiscity and subtlety. Yet, even the carefully controlled analytic situation allows a certain amount of "action" to enter the situation; and even the psychoanalytic intervention in its purest form, the interpretation, is at the same time also an act—an act of communication.

TRANSFERENCE AND THE THERAPEUTIC ACT

Taking this aspect of the therapeutic situation into account in the formulation of a theory of psychoanalytic therapy does not mean that the scope of the analyst's action is widened, nor does it introduce an element of manipulation foreign to its spirit. On the contrary, awareness of possible secondary meanings of the analyst's actions may, under certain circumstances, limit him more and make him more circumspect in the use of his analytic tools. On the other hand, it may also make him do certain things with deliberateness which previously he may have done intuitively. In any case, a careful assessment of the phenomena described in this paper should give a place to the therapeutic act in the framework of a theory of technique. This in turn, may make us perceive therapeutic possibilities where they had previously been defeated.

Thus when we speak of the therapeutic act, we merely give a name to an aspect of the therapeutic process which is well known but the significance of which is not fully appreciated. In one form, however, we are quite familiar with it, except that it goes under another name, that of "handling the transference." The very fact that we make a distinction between handling and interpreting transference shows that the analyst's activity is not confined, strictly speaking, to "interpretation." Aside from the act-aspect of the latter, there are a number of things which the analyst says or does that are not interpretations in our sense of the word, yet have a specific function in the total therapeutic process. Allowing for variations to fit particular conditions, he adjusts his behavior, his silence, and his interpretating or not interpretating of certain material toward a particular goal. Such goals might be: establishing a transference, or safeguarding it, or reducing it and generally utilizing it for therapeutic purposes. These activities, sometimes verbal, are designed to facilitate, influence, or interfere with the development of transference reactions. They all fit our definition of the therapeutic act, for none are interpretations in the sense of "translation." As a matter of fact, we often use the term "intervention" so as not to get caught in the narrower concept of interpretation, when we are actually doing something other than interpreting. Nor are such noninterpretative interventions a kind of manipulation. On the contrary, they are legitimate forms of behavior required by our understanding of the nature of the therapeutic process.

The following example illustrates how easily the one concern with "countertransference," loosely defined, can make an analyst lose sight of the significance his own actions may have for the patient:

Returning from an excursion to the Near East, a patient began to tell enthusiastically about his experiences, and at some point he asked whether the analyst was interested in hearing all about the trip. His analyst affirmed his interest, and later felt he had agreed primarily to satisfy his own curiosity. Hence, he suggested that this session be considered a social call; he would not charge the patient for the session. The patient responded with increased anxiety. He took the analyst's action as a reprimand for having stepped out of his role as a patient and having talked to his analyst as an "equal." The offer of suspending the fee for the session meant to him that his behavior had not been appropriate to the therapeutic situation and that this was not acceptable to the therapist. He therefore feared criticism and rejection.

The fact that transference reactions develop in the course of an analysis means that the patient endows the therapist with a meaning which does not correspond to reality. This is a parallel phenomenon to endowing the process of communication on the part of the analyst with meaning beyond the one intended. If this happens without the analyst taking theoretical cognizance of it, he is liable to look upon this phenomenon as an interference with the therapeutic work. It is reminiscent of Freud's reaction when he first encountered transference. Perhaps we will never be able to turn the process of contamination to similar advantage for the therapeutic task as he did with transference; but if we learn to recognize it as one of the many ways in which unconscious mental processes manifest themselves, we will at least be in a more favorable position to deal with them.

CHAPTER 20

On the Dialogue in Classical Psychoanalysis

Donald M. Kaplan, Ph.D.

Donald M. Kaplan has studied at the City College of the City University of New York, Columbia University, and New York University. He is a graduate of the Psychoanalytic Institute of the National Psychological Association for Psychoanalysis (NPAP). Dr. Kaplan has been on the staffs of several outpatient clinics in New York City and was a supervisor in the clinical psychology internship program at the Long Island Consultation Center. Presently, he is on the faculties of the institute of the New York Society of Freudian Psychologists and the Washington Square Institute for Psychotherapy and Mental Health. He was, for some years, associate editor of The Psychoanalytic Review *and is currently an associate editor of* The American Imago. *Nonclinical applications of psychoanalysis have been of longstanding interest to him. He is a contributing editor to the* Tulane Drama Review, *where several of a series of his articles on psychoanalysis and theatre have appeared, and he is a co-author of* The Domesday Dictionary (*Simon and Schuster, McGraw-Hill and Jonathan Cape, London*).*

Kaplan writes so effectively that I, for one, would read him for his prose alone. But what Kaplan has to say, under the articulateness of the way he says it, is reflective, wide-ranging, and substantive. He is an analyst who deals with complexities and who does so in graceful style. Within the spectrum of analytic positions, Dr. Kaplan is known as a vigorous and uncompromising orthodoxist.

> ALL HUMAN ERROR IS IMPATIENCE, A PREMATURE RENUNCIATION OF METHOD.
> —Franz Kafka

> I SHALL NEVER BE TIRED OF REPEATING THAT WE ARE BOUND TO ACCEPT WHATEVER OUR PROCEDURE BRINGS TO LIGHT.
> —Sigmund Freud

Chapter VII of *The Interpretation of Dreams* (Freud, 1953) was a pinnacle of more than ten years of the clinical observation and intellectual struggle of a genius who was to impart to our present century a significant piece of its modernity. In that famous chapter, Freud arrived at a psychological theory that encompassed not only his observations of dreams, but also of other states and activities of mind ranging from the uncommon to the most ordinary. The scope of Chapter VII, with its elegantly conceived relationships among perception, memory, affect, attention, consciousness and action, amounts to nothing less than an innovated image of man. Thus the adoption of the model of mind that Freud constructed in that chapter signifies, really, an agreement with a particular point of view about the nature and trials of human existence.

Since interpretation is the most significant instrumentality in that clinical technique deriving directly from Freudian psychology, the very act of in-

---

This paper was read before Faculty and Fellows of the Menninger School of Psychiatry, Topeka, Kansas, October 30, 1967.

terpretation—which includes the intentions, goals and preparations behind the act—presupposes certain strong partialities in the analyst. Moreover, it presupposes, in that aspect of the public willing to become analysands, a capacity to be educated into and to work with the analyst's partialities. Whatever the parametrical necessities may be in a particular case, a normative concept of "analyzability" is never entirely absent from the analyst's procedural judgments. The neutrality that the analyst strives for toward his patient's conflict resolutions does not extend to his choice of technical measures. To the analyst, the outcome of a conflict—that is, whether the ego ultimately accepts or rejects an instinctual demand—is a matter of indifference; but the manner in which the conflict is conceived and examined in the clinical situation is anything but arbitrary (Freud, 1964c).

I am reminded of a paper by Kurt Eissler (1963) in which Eissler describes a severely neurotic patient he treated for three years. The patient left treatment to go on to achieve in her life all that she had wished for upon entering treatment—marriage, motherhood, position in the community, even the remission of a painful erythrophobia. Yet, despite this stupendous clinical success, Eissler reviews the case with misgivings, berating himself for a technical error that sabotaged a successful treatment. Eissler remain unimpressed with a behavioral outcome that would immensely gratify most therapists. According to Eissler, this particular patient "adhered to what psychoanalysis offers at a social level—a therapy," and responded to treatment with the principle, "I would rather act sanely than face the truth about myself."

To nonanalytic clinicians the psychoanalytic dialogue has always seemed a bit of much ado about nothing, so much in the dialogue does a particular concept of mind pale all else—the traditional healing function of the therapist, our common sense of the time factor in these matters, not to mention economics, even questions of action—what the patient actually should do at one point or another in the course of things. The psychoanalytic dialogue seems to revise the rank-order of what is important in life. A patient, whom I intend to return to further on, came to a session one day and reported at the outset that, during her walk to my office some moments before, she had passed a brownstone whose charm had caught her gaze. She went on to say that approaching it she was conscious of a wish to know the technical name for the doorway's distinctive architectural shape. We were to spend several sessions on this incident. But the point here is that the patient happened to be at this moment in her life in the throes of a serious vocational crisis (and I must add that she is not an architect).

Of course, to maintain that such revisions of seeming import as take place in the analytic situation are the result simply of the unqualified primacy of mind in psychoanalysis would be cavalier, not to say foolish. Granted the centrality of mind, why shouldn't the investigation of the patient's mind proceed by means of issues strongly attractive to the patient's attention in his everyday life, such as financial worries, sexual adversities, interpersonal antagonisms? To be sure, the patient will begin with such issues. But why should he not be encouraged to proceed with them exclusively?

Considering the well-reputed fact that psychoanalytic therapy makes a great deal of the patient's early history, the answer consists in a rather surprising paradox: The patient's chronologically most recent, and subjectively most trivial, thoughts are the harbingers potentially of his most profound self-explanations. I should add that among the reasons for the comparatively frequent sessions in psychoanalysis and the priority of the relationship to the analyst is the insurance of recent and experientially trivial topics in the patient's monologic self-reporting.

Let me quote a bit of Freud from Chapter VII (pp. 263-264):

> The reason why these recent and indifferent elements so frequently find their way into dreams as substitutes for the most ancient of all the dream-thoughts is that they have least to fear from the censorship imposed by resistance. But while the fact that *trivial* elements are preferred is explained by their freedom from censorship, the fact that *recent* elements occur with such regularity points to the existence of a need for transference [between the mental systems]. Both groups of impressions satisfy the demand of the repressed for material that is still clear of associations—the indifferent ones because they have given no occasion for the formation of many ties, and the recent ones because they have not yet had time to form them.

Though Freud is here speaking of the formation of dreams out of day-residues, what he says has to do also with processes of mind in general: The perceptual attention that imbues experience with felt importance reduces, at the same time, the likelihood of alterations within the psychic apparatus. To put it another way, the stronger the feeling about a perception, the less chance there is to discover alternative solutions to the conflicts in which the perception participates. And I am relieved to be able to say that psychoanalytic therapy is concerned with solving conflicts.

One of the advantages of using Freud's writing for a discussion such as this is that, Freudian or not, we all know Freud in some detail. I shall unravel a final string of reminders about his theory: Freud came to conceive of the psychic apparatus as a compound instrument. The compounding of the apparatus is an adaptive expedient, for the operation of a neonatal (wish-fulfilling) mentality alone cannot guarantee supplies appropriate to needs. A fantasy of food has no nutritional value. A fantasy of warmth does not regulate room temperature. Hence, in addition to wishing, a second mental activity must come into the service of the organism, an activity that will address itself to the actual localities of the wished-for supplies. While wishes are experienced as internal, the localities for their fulfilling supplies are soon perceived as external, and the psychic apparatus begins to negotiate its wishes in accordance with perceptions of external circumstance. The infant's first perceptions that many of its wishes are being fulfilled through the cooperation of an agent separate from himself—an external mother—is an extraordinary event in the maturation of his psychic apparatus. At this point, we begin to speak of the infant's acquisition of a sense of reality, and we go on to distinguish two mental processes in reciprocating relationship, to which Freud assigned the names "primary" and "secondary" processes. He spelled out the energic economics obtaining between these two processes and outlined a theory of psychopathology based upon the articulation of the processes (rather than upon the interaction, say, between a patient and his social environment, which is also a legitimate basis for a theory of psychopathology). The theory of psychopathology, however, is merely a special instance of a general theory of mind.

Now what does all this suggest for a technique? I have mentioned the possibility of recent and trivial thoughts reaching across intrapsychic topographies otherwise closed to thoughts carrying higher degrees of "habit" and import. I have also suggested that these topographies of mind are shaped by a developmental distinction between wish and circumstance. Psychopathology is a special instance of failure of the apparatus to acquire a facility with circumstance sufficient to fulfill (through activity) crucial amounts of specific wishes in accordance with the modalities of secondary process. In psychopathology, the primary process has gained direct access to action, but the fulfillment in this action is in conflict with circumstance, now in the form of present reality, or the superego, or both. The fulfillment creates the intractability in the pathologic process, while the conflict creates the suffering. The psychoanalysis of such a state of affairs demands a current circumstance with an explicit and enduring identity against which the original circumstance can be compared. This current circumstance is the set of arrangements about the time and duration of appointments, the fees, the functions of the analyst. The analytic situation is an experimental circumstance.

As for the wishes, if they are to come under the regulation of the secondary process, they must be deprived of their most powerful sponsor—direct action and, through direct action, direct gratification. They must suffer a provisional loss of importance. In the analytic situation there are numerous opportunities for action. The most eminent involves the person of the analyst.

The activity of the analyst is restricted to the preservation of the analytic circumstance and to the encouragement of the patient to report recent and trivial thoughts. The analyst's explanatory verbal allusions to all unsolicited modifications by the patient of both the analytic circumstance and the analytic task are called interpretations of resistance. In view of the common, erroneous assertion that "resistance analysis" is synonomous with psychoanalysis, it should be stressed that the term "resistance" is literally gibberish in a therapeutic situation in which no rule of free association—the reporting of recent and trivial thoughts—is being enforced. The term "resistance" only acquires meaning in connection with an effort to alter conditions between primary and secondary processes through a method involving free association. Where the resistance takes the form of an interaction with the analyst, the analyst's verbal allusion to it goes by the name "transference interpretation." The entire labor is to maximize thought by minimizing action.

It is clear that the analytic endeavor is quite different from the kind of therapeutic endeavor aimed at discovering what the patient wants and then going on to prescribe strategies with which the patient can get what he wants. It is also different from those endeavors that provoke vitalities in the patient deemed absent but worthwhile by a chemotherapist, active therapist or sexologist.

Although an analysis can be conducted in a variety of human styles and temperaments, it cannot be conducted by a clinician whose personality simply cannot tolerate being in a room with another human being without affectual interaction. A clinician who cannot abstain from an opportunity for verbal and emotional give and take cannot conduct an analysis. Anything spectacular in the analytic situation is a sure sign that something has gone wrong. An older colleague of mine, who is now deceased, was fond of relating an incident in which he had gotten into a physical brawl with a patient in the midst of a session. He had subdued the patient finally through great physical effort and was proud to describe how he converted the incident into therapeutic gains for the patient. It was out of affection for this colleague—and respect, for he was not a fool—that I never shared my thoughts with him on the matter. If an analysis was taking place, the incident could not have happened. Things could never have gotten that far in an analytic situation.

On several occasions, Freud (1958a, 1958b, 1964a) counseled wariness against an emotional overloading of the therapist-patient relationship. He advised interpreting derivatives of hatred before a negative affect gained the momentum to sweep away the analysis. He gave the same advise in regard to derivatives of love, for too much love can also freeze the dialogue by destroying the patient's perceptual flexibility. Optimally, the dialogue is contemplative and unhurried. Passion invests the task, not the persons collaborating in the task.

The psychic apparatus has a strong propensity for imparting sense and meaning to experience. The secondary revision in dream recall is an example of such propensity. We revise dreams in their telling because our resistance to leaving experience meaningless is aroused. In reporting a dream, the patient says, "It was a men's room, so I couldn't have been urinating in a toilet. I must have been standing at a urinal." Here the patient discards a fleeting notion and replaces it by something that makes more sense. Only in cooperation with a second person, such as an analyst whose training has created in him an interest in such things, can an individual be held to an examination of fleeting notions, the sense and meaning of which are not yet apparent.

Not long ago, I moved from an office I had been using for a number of years. The move was anticipated about seven months in advance. I was aware of the significance of the move (more accurately, I couldn't see how the move would not be filled with significance), so I was prepared to watch for psychological eventualities. They began almost immediately, including an incapacitating lumbosacral sprain. But I was not to understand these eventualities, including the sprain, until a month after I had established myself in my current office, and the understanding began only in my effort—an extraordinary effort, indeed—not to ignore my dialing a particular phone number incorrectly twice in succession. A review of the past eight months brought into connection a series of unconnected events, each one having possessed at the time it occurred a meaning and justification quite irrelevant to any meaning my office move consciously had for me.

For example, an argument with the agent of the building in which my new office was to be situated was entirely plausible to me at the time it happened, though in retrospect I recognized how I had provoked it. I am certain that, had I been in a formal analytic situation, I would have been held by my analyst to examine innumerable subjective irrelevancies at the outset of the period of the office move and would thereby have gained a comprehension of the situation in a matter of weeks, rather than the eight months it took on my own. I have good reason to believe that my sprained back would also have been averted. (I wonder whether we don't overlook among the benefits of psychotherapy the question of what would have happened to the patient without it. The prophylactic value of therapy may be quite as important as its ameliorative value.)

I have been emphasizing the prominence of thought as against action in the psychoanalytic situation. I have been speaking of turning the patient's consciousness away from the perceptual and motor end of the psychic apparatus, where it mainly resides, toward the preconscious system, that psychic zone in which the primary and secondary processes interact. I want to return to the patient I referred to earlier and show how the analytic dialogue nevertheless leads to the possibility of spontaneous actions, actions informed by thought but, in my opinion, free of the intellectualized quality of action-oriented psychotherapies.

I mentioned that the patient was preoccupied with a vocational crisis. The patient was a 30-year-old woman, a biochemist who had entered therapy in connection with a longstanding but painful love affair with a married man much older than herself.

After two years of treatment, she extricated herself from the affair and then a year later married a man more consistent with her age and interests.

Throughout all this, her career created persistent dissatisfactions that were never altogether clear. She was respected for her knowledge and competence, but no amount of advancement and study would rid her of the apprehension that she was a novice and a fraud. From time to time, these feelings dissolved in excruciating boredom.

An unexpected shake-up in the hierarchy of the pharmaceutical company at which she worked thrust her into a rather high position. This precipitated an anxiety reaction. Anxiety and derivatives of it preoccupied her for months, especially paranoid derivatives having to do with the incompetence of her colleagues. It was in the midst of this that I suggested to her, at the end of a session, that she had drifted into this repetitive preoccupation because there was something she was afraid to tell me. This was not a shot in the dark: There had been two dreams to which she had had, for her, remarkably weak associations, and both dreams had been stridently sexual. She agreed that there was something she had been keeping from me.

She returned for her next appointment to tell me, with difficulty, that of late she had been performing fellatio on her husband. Yet, she had no idea why it was so difficult to tell me. Nor could she say why she had used precisely her job anxieties in connection with suppressing the information about the turn in her sexual life.

I have already mentioned the incident of her wanting to know the architectural term for the doorway of the building she admired during her walk to my office. Following her telling me about this, she was silent for some time and then said parenthetically and with a trace of sheepish humor that she knew from reading a psychology text that a building symbolized the human body, and that therefore the doorway would represent probably the female genital; whereupon she was again silent, as though waiting for permission to proceed with what felt to her an obvious intellectual train of thought—or permission not to proceed. I told her that she hesitated because she was embarrassed at stealing my thunder. She went on to report a memory of her father's slamming the bedroom door against her when she had happened upon him dressing, a memory she had brought up several times previously. She then spoke of the time she had approached her mother with a question about the mechanics of conception and pregnancy, though already fully informed by clandestine reading in various medical books. Initially, her mother put her off awkwardly, but then went into a rage at the question.

I reminded the patient of her persistent feelings of possessing knowledge without permission and authority. Now the connection between her anxieties at being promoted at work and her withholding her sexual activities from me could be made. For several weeks thereafter, a phase of the transference underwent clarification.

But the action arising from this piece of analytic work was unpredictable and, thus, beyond what any coercive technique could have accomplished. You can't manipulate behavior in a prescribed direction, if the behavior falls outside the realm of specification. This patient's principal professional responsibility involved a kind of trouble-shooting examination and modification of experiments conceived and proposed by others, a function the patient executed with such resourcefulness that it was never an issue of psychopathology. Her professional performance was a network of virtues created out of the necessities of infantile circumstance. An important by-product of this phase of the analysis was that additional functions came into existence with additional gratifications. For example, the patient has since published two papers on original work of her own. However, none of the changes were spectacular. Their subtlety protected them from intellectualization. By-products of the analytic process rather than definite goals, these changes were in every sense of the word spontaneous.

Let me give another example of spontaneity of action. A female patient in treatment for a number of years for an obsessive-compulsive psychoneurosis reported a repetitive sexual fantasy she would have during sexual relations with her husband. The fantasy involved her being sexually molested by a horde of truck drivers on the floor of a commercial garage. The sexual fantasy (I shall pass over the analytic steps) was the manifest content of a latent fantasy containing the wish for a private sexual experience with a particular sibling. The patient had been the only girl in a family of five brothers and had participated in the years of her growing up in a great deal of group sexual play. The fantasy accompanying her sexual relations with her husband served to assuage her guilt at the fact that she was having sex with only one person, rather than with several persons. The lack of privacy in the manifest fantasy had reference as well to her ritual of carefully locking up prior to going to bed, a ritual involving a fantasy of sexual invasion and its prohibition.

While the ritual continued to be a painful compulsion, a behavioral outcome of the analysis of these matters was her ridding her rather large apartment of what sounded to me like tons of old, useless furniture and paraphernalia, thus providing a luxury of living space. Again, this action was not previously stipulated by the patient, nor was the condition of her apartment a conspicuous complaint in her remarks. She went on to refurnish the apartment. I suspect these actions of the patient in respect to her apartment would not have been taken into account in a before-and-after experimental design investigating the effectiveness of treatment; yet, in retrospect, I count these actions as having far-reaching effects upon this patient's sense of herself. Though behaviorally unspectacular, they were among the most courageous actions of her adult life.

These examples also illustrate the evocative character of the analytic dialogue.[1] Provocativeness is alien to the spirit of the undertaking, much as a sledge hammer would be the wrong sort of probe for a pocket watch.

Psychoanalysis regards consciousness as a series of mental events, fugitive and incomplete, yet all that the patient has to go by (Freud, 1964b). The analytic situation does not aim to deprive the patient of consciousness, as, say, a hypnotic situation does. It aims rather to degrade the syntactic, logical, rhetorical and other formal properties of language through which consciousness is conventionally reported to a listener. Free association possesses less formal properties than does conventional speech, but it is not less conscious. However, free association resembles more closely the actual nature of consciousness, and it is something about the patient's consciousness that the analyst wishes to interpret.

Interpretation can be thought of as mending the incompleteness of a portion of a conscious series of mental events. But not only must the analyst locate the disconnections in the fabric of consciousness, he must also go on to mend them with material of like substance. Alien material won't do. Interpretations must be made

---

[1]For a discussion of the concept of evocativeness, though in a somewhat different sense, see Applebaum (1966).

from data evoked in the patient by the process. (With due regard to this business of "listening with the third ear," what is evoked in the analyst—his feelings, fantasies and associations—are at most clues to a larger meaning in what the patient is reporting. Clues, however, are not equivalent to solutions.)

To listen, to wait, to gather data and to inhibit active interventions until a solution is achieved regarding a segment of observation are not easy tasks. Harold F. Searles (Scarizza, 1965, p. 14) has commended this stance even in the therapy of deeply regressed patients:

I have some comments on the therapist's responsibility. It seems to me that this is where Freud made one of his very great contributions, with the free association method, which calls for the patient to take part in therapy. Even a schizophrenic patient can do well to follow this procedure, even if he is not able to talk. If we leave in the patient's hands a comparably high degree of responsibility for setting the tone of what happens between himself and the doctor, for bringing up his ideation—whether by verbal or nonverbal means—it is this kind of setting which promotes the patient's exercising of the degree of responsible initiative which needs to remain in his own hands. I have frequently found myself trying, or have found my colleagues trying, to actively rescue the patient from the illness. It seemed to me that the patient never did open up and make moves toward the therapist, and toward the world of reality, until the therapist finally had tried everything active that he knew, and eventually had given up, had sat back, and thus had given the patient room to reach out.

Elsewhere, Searles (1964) takes exception to John N. Rosen's therapeutic stance, pinpointing the difference between psychoanalysis and therapies based upon substantive preconceptions. Rosen approaches all patients with expectations that the therapeutic relationship will duplicate a specific pathogenic infantile relationship. Hence Rosen can begin "interpretations" immediately, since he carries with him bottled truths about every patient's pathology. Every patient is virtually the same; the patient need not generate the substance of the dialogue; no transference need evolve. Searles scores this as indoctrination. Rosen's is not "an investigative approach in which patient and doctor are engaged in a mutual exploration of what is transpiring in the patient. . . . His approach is, by contrast, a message-carrying approach, a forcing-into-a-preconceived-mould approach, in which the initiative rests not primarily in the patient's hands, as is the case in truly psychoanalytic investigation, but, obviously, in the hands of the therapist" (p. 600).

I like Rudolf Ekstein's comparing the psychoanalytic undertaking to a Pirandello situation (1965): "We might say that the patient . . . is in search of a plot. . . . [In] order to find the plot, he goes to a psychotherapist whom he mistakes in the transference for an author" (p. 163). The therapist's interpretations are ultimately the plot describing the patient's past. Psychoanalysis is thus concerned with producing a script which the analyst ghost-writes, to be sure, but only from what the patient tells him. That a script is to be fashioned is determined by the analyst's theoretical commitment, but the content resides entirely in the patient.

At those fortuitous moments in the dialogue when a verbal relationship is made among the patient's interactional effort with the analyst, a piece of current triviality and a memory, we speak of analytic insight (Kris, 1956). Under analytic auspices it is more usual, however, for insight, like action, to occur as an experientially elusive process, identified in retrospect. The notion of a profoundly felt confrontation of the patient with a fragment of personal truth is much more a lingering social mythology about psychoanalysis than an actuality. Such possibilities of cathartic experience tended to disappear from the analytic situation before the turn of the century, with Freud's technical recommendations in the final chapter of *Studies on Hysteria* (Breuer & Freud, 1955). Like the patient who wonders about the status of his analysis because he has not yet burst into tears, as he imagines other patients doing, a therapist may also be the victim of notions about cathartic events in the practice of his colleagues and may provoke such events in hopes of confirming the legitimacy of the therapy. With such attempts to keep up with the Jones's we might compare psychoanalysis with certain current social and professional trends.

In a publication of a large community mental-health clinic, there is an article by a famous psychotherapist-hypnotist (Greenwald, 1966), who reports that he is using hypnosis to simulate the hallucinogenic effects of LSD. He hypnotizes the patient and suggests that the patient is under the sway of LSD. I quote a typical result of this technical procedure. The patient in question was an overt homosexual. "The results in his case were dramatic. Within a period of three months, from having been a lifelong homosexual, he became exclusively heterosexual and, at the age of fifty, reported that he was having full pleasurable intercourse with his wife, six and seven times a day" (p. 47).

In the context of my previous discussion, what is notable about this report is the unscripted quality of both the therapy and the outcome, and also the direct connection between the presenting diagnosis of the patient and his post-treatment behavior. I do not think the author would be inclined to dispute my conclusion that the patient got precisely what he (the patient) thought he wanted in the quickest way possible with the least exposure to what could be called an investigation of his thought processes. Although the author would probably maintain that a complex explanation of what had happened could be furnished with some amount of retrospective thought on his part, I have every reason to believe that he would consider the request for such an explanation a sign of professional anachronism in the asker, if not a sign of pathologic intellectualism.

Anyone who has kept abreast of the proliferating literature on psychotherapy must recognize that this author could go just about anywhere in America at this moment and find himself entirely at home professionally. Unscripted, interactional psychotherapy is not the vision of the future, as Philip Rieff sees it in *The Triumph of the Therapeutic* (1966). It is presently the largest movement among us.

My sense is that this state of affairs in psychotherapy is in rapport with the most prevalent modes of thought in the community. The hypnotic conversion of the homosexual patient is an example of a socialization of both therapist and patient. I quote from an item in *The New Republic* (1966):

The day before the elections, November 7, the Voice of America began using a brighter, faster broadcasting technique aimed primarily at the world's speakers of English, who now number more than a billion. Announcing this as "the new sound," the director of the government's overseas broadcasting agency, John Chancellor, explained . . . our broadcasts . . . must sound American and reflect the current image of the United States as an interesting, dynamic, and up-tempo place. Giving examples of the "new sound," Chancellor said that the longest single item in the first hour of the day's revised programming was an interview with Secretary of State Dean Rusk that lasted only 4 minutes 38 seconds. . . . Richard Krolick [Chancellor's chief consultant] declared that the "new motto" of the Voice of America is "think short."

This new Voice-of-America technique is in full accord with Marshal McLuhan's now famous dictum, "The medium is the message," the corollary to which is the motto of a mushrooming theatre and mass media of happenings and events: "Art is anything you can get away with." In this view of process and outcome, the concept of error virtually disappears, and with it the concept of responsibility. I am reminded of the psychotherapist who told of his having been in a patient's neighborhood in the dark hours of the morning and his yielding to an impulse to drop in on her. "I decided to do it because I'm a doctor and therefore anything I do is therapeutic."

Bell (1965) cites the "eclipse of distance" as the underlying reality of contemporary society, "an effort to annihilate the contemplative mode of experience by emphasizing immediacy, impact, simultaneity, and sensation" (p. 220). The eclipse of distance,[2] Bell suggests, originates in such facts as overpopulation and increased interpersonal interaction due to urbanization. The mass media enhance our interactions symbolically. Individuals today know of countless other individuals. We know not only what others possess and achieve, but also what others seem to experience, for the mass media penetrate traditional barriers of privacy. It is no longer enough to compete with the other fellow's acquisitions and achievements; we must also feel what we think the other fellow feels. Our self-esteem seems to reside at the frontiers of our personal sensual capacities.

Bell's eclipse of distance finds a psychoanalytic counterpart in Spitz's "derailment of dialogue" (1964), an ego-disrupting consequence of overpopulation and urbanization. Spitz, like Bell, observes the widespread lack of privacy and contemplative activity in contemporary society and relates this to a growing inability among the population to complete "action cycles." Mothering that is constantly interrupted by social interactions tends to produce a child unfit for partnership in any kind of dialogue. "With the derailment of dialogue," Spitz adds, "the appetitive branch of the action cycle comes to replace the consummatory one." (I wonder whether our psychedelic hypnotist had not redirected his patient's appetitive impulses, while leaving untouched his consummatory abilities.)

Ellul (1965) regards propaganda as our present environment of instant information, a solvent of ideology, morality, art, individuality. The fantasies in the poetry of the French Symbolists are at the service of art partly because of the contemplative quality of the creative labor. The fantasies reported by "hippies" are like disposable novelties; they supply the environment with propaganda.

Any psychotherapy that emphasizes immediacy, impact, simultaneity and sensation is consistent with the most prevalent current processes of socialization. The medium of every such therapy is social propaganda. No matter how uplifting the jargon, the participants in such therapies are attempting to replace the responsibilities of individuality by the advantages of adjustment to the social moment. The painful ambiguities and dialectics of the social role-personal identity dichotomy are mercifully postponed.

I am sure I need not belabor my opinion as to where psychoanalysis stands among such matters, and where the analyst stands in relation to our present society when he maintains that the individual can be regarded intrapsychically—that is, in terms of that elemental system of mind distinguishing each of us from the family we

---

[2]In this regard, see also "The Role of Interpretation in Therapy," Chapter 2 in this book.

come out of and the society we enter into, that small station of mind where individuality resides.

There is a current idea that psychoanalysis no longer suits our present patient population. But this has always been the charge. From the beginning, if psychoanalysis was not outright nonsense, it was impractical. Reisman (1954) has referred to Freud as a " 'rate buster'—a person who violated 'production norms' as to how much sympathy and time were to be given to patients" (p. 271). Reisman counts among Freud's greatest contributions Freud's "willingness to spend years if necessary with patients who were neither fatally ill nor important people. . . . Today, it is just this luxury aspect of psychoanalysis—its prolonged concern with individuals as such, and for their own sake—that is sometimes under attack" (p. 272).

Psychoanalysis has always distinguished between what the public wants and what the public needs. Since needs are not as capricious as wants, psychoanalysis, in addressing itself to needs, has enjoyed an eventful but not at all frenetic evolution as an intellectual movement. Its insulation against transitory social fads and against the opportunism that comes into play when a doctrine seeks widespread approval has insured psychoanalysis the orderly development that many condemn as parochial, rigid, or outmoded—the pejoratives vary with the values of those who apply them.

REFERENCES

Applebaum, S. A., Speaking with the second voice: evocativeness. *J. Amer. Psychoanal. Ass.,* 1966, 14, 462-477.

Bell, D., The disjunction of culture and social structure. *Daedalus,* 1965, winter, 208-222.

Breuer, J., and Freud, S., Studies on hysteria. In S. Freud, *Standard edition,* Vol. II. London: Hogarth Press, 1955.

Eissler, K., Notes on the psychoanalytic concept of cure. *Psychoanal. stud. Child,* 1963, 18, 424-463.

Ekstein, R., General treatment philosophy of acting out. In L. E. Abt, and S. L. Weissman (Eds.), *Acting out: theoretical and clinical aspects.* New York: Grune & Stratton, 1965, pp. 162-172.

Ellul, J., *Propaganda: the formation of men's attitudes.* New York: Knopf, 1965.

Freud, S., The Interpretation of dreams. *Standard edition, Vol. V.* London: Hogarth Press, 1953.

——, Remembering, repeating and working through. *Standard edition, Vol. XII.* London: Hogarth Press, 1958a, pp. 147-156.

——, Observations on transference love. *Standard edition,* Vol. XII. London: Hogarth Press, 1958b, pp. 159-171.

——, Analysis terminable and interminable. *Standard edition,* Vol. XXIII. London: Hogarth Press, 1964a, pp. 216-253.

——, Constructions in analysis. *Standard edition, Vol. XXIII.* London: Hogarth Press, 1964b, pp. 257-269.

——, An outline of psychoanalysis. *Standard edition,* Vol. XXIII. London: Hogarth Press, 1964c, pp. 144-207.

Greenwald, H., Hypnosis and hallucinogenic drugs. *J. Long Island Consultation Center,* 1966, 4, 46-51.

Kris, E., On preconscious mental processes. In *Psychoanalytic explorations in art.* New York: International Universities Press, 1952, pp. 303-318.

Reisman, D., The themes of heroism and weakness in the structure of Freud's thought. In *Individualism reconsidered.* New York: Anchor Books, 1954. Pp. 246-275.

Reiff, P., *The triumph of the therapeutic: uses of faith after Freud.* New York: Harper & Row, 1966.

Scarizza, S., *Proceedings of the first international congress of direct psychoanalysis.* Doylestown, Doylestown Foundation, 1965.

Searles, H. F., Book review of direct psychoanalytic psychiatry. *Internat. J. Psychoanal.,* 1964, 45, 597-602.

Shakow, D., and Rapaport, D., *The Influence of Freud on American psychology* (Psychol. Issues, monogr. 13). New York: International Universities Press, 1964.

Szasz, T. S., Behavior therapy and psychoanalysis. *Med. Opinion Rev.,* 1967, 2, 24-29.

Spitz, R. A., The primal cavity: a contribution to the genesis of perception and its role for psychoanalytic theory. *Psychoanal. Stud. Child,* 1955, 10, 215-240.

——, *A genetic field theory of ego formation.* New York: International Universities Press, 1959.

——, The derailment of dialogue: stimulus overload, action cycles, and completion gradient. *J. Amer. Psychoanal. Ass.,* 1964, 12, 752-775.

The New Republic, November 19, 1966, p. 3.

Wallerstein, R. S., The current state of psychotherapy: theory, practice research. *J. Amer. Psychoanal. Ass.,* 1966, 14, 183-225.

CHAPTER 21

Interpretation and Language

Susan Deri

Susan Deri was educated in Budapest and worked in Szondi's laboratory after obtaining her "matura" certificate. In 1938 she obtained her final diploma in medical psychology and became a teaching staff member of Szondi's clinic. Her psychoanalytic training, obtained at the Hungarian Psychoanalytic Institute, was completed in 1941 when she came to America and to the State University of Iowa to work with Lewin. She has written widely in the field-theoretic tradition and on psychoanalytic theory and technique. Since 1945 she has been in private psychoanalytic practice in New York City and is on the teaching faculty of both the Training Institute of the New York Freudian Psychologists and of the National Psychological Association for Psychoanalysis. She was formerly on the faculty of the Graduate School at C.C.N.Y. and of the New School for Social Research.

> THE GOOD ORDER OF THE WORLD DEPENDS ON
> THE DISCIPLINE OF LANGUAGE.—Confucius

Psychoanalytic treatment is essentially *language treatment.* In analysis patients learn to *speak* correctly; they learn to *name* the previously unnamed content of their inner world as well as to communicate and share their experiences with others through the consensually accepted language common to their surrounding culture. Whatever the form of neurosis or psychosis, language is always impaired. So is the patient's relationship to time, to the sequence of past, present and future. The meaningful articulation of time into its three main segments is contingent upon the proper function of language. Realistic relationship to time and proper use of language equal good ego functioning.

The interaction between patient and analyst is nonverbal as well as verbal. Verbal communication implies nonverbal elements such as tone of voice and rhythm which to a great extent determine the effect of communication. All of the analyst's verbal interventions depend on timing, dosage, level of conceptualization and his particular language patterns. I shall concentrate on the last one, on the role of language in the therapeutic dialogue between patient and analyst.

Keeping in mind that the aim of analysis is to enhance the effective sphere of the rationally functioning ego within the total functioning of the patient, I shall subsume under the concept "verbal therapeutic intervention" the various subconcepts used by different authors, such as: reconstruction, interpretation, preparation (Loewenstein), confrontation (Devereux), clarification (Bibring), and indication (Fenichel). Delineation between these various technical tools is often spurious. In one way or the other they all use language for the purpose of directing the patient's attention toward noticing and verbalizing previously unrecognized mental content. In this sense all verbal interventions serve interpretation, since they all aim at making something previously not understood understandable. Words are the lever for bringing about this transformation. In psychoanalytic terminology, words are the lever for lifting psychological processes from the unconscious, or from the primary process image world into the organized, secondary process functioning of the preconscious and the conscious.

It is more than coincidence that Freud's first major, but seldom-quoted, psychophysiological work deals with the pathology of language and the misfunctioning of the preconscious. It reflects the central role of language in all of Freud's writings. *On Aphasia* (1891) foreshadows much of Freud's later recurrent efforts to formulate a model which illuminates the role of language in consciousness, in thinking, and in the structurization of the mental apparatus. Probably the most systematic discussion of the relationship between language, thought and consciousness is to be found in the "Project" (Freud, 1895). Freud's catharctic treatment of hysterical patients reflects the clinical application of this early model for a language theory (Breuer & Freud, 1895). Patients were led to recall forgotten visual memories, the pathological effect of which was then assumed to be dissipated by means of the energy discharge function of verbalization. Language served as "abreaction." As Freud put it, "The strangulated affect needs exit through speech."

This catharctic function of language, however, would not suffice to explain the curative function of "talking therapy." We know from our daily work that the amount and intensity of highly emotional speech, far from being an index for cure, can well serve the purposes of resistance. The curative effect of speech is to be accounted for by at *least* two of its dynamic and economic functions: (1) abreaction or discharge of energy, and (2) the transformation of freely mobile primary process energy into *bound* energy, which is the raw material for secondary process functioning.

Neither the energy discharge aspect of language nor the binding aspect of it explains by itself the curative function of "talking therapy"; only the interaction between the two brings about a beneficial synthesis of mental processes.

In his final but unfinished work, *An Outline of Psychoanalysis* (Freud, 1940), he speaks of the "hypercathexes of the material of the mind" which "brings about a sort of synthesis of different processes—a synthesis in the course of which free energy is transformed into bound energy." He states further: ". . .we hold firmly to the view that the distinction between the unconscious and the preconscious condition also lies in dynamic relations of this same kind, which would explain how it is that whether spontaneously or with our assistance, the one can be changed into the other."

To this we can add that the "hypercathexis of material" means that the patient's attention cathexis gets directed upon previously unformulated, nevertheless effective, mental phenomena. Whatever form the analyst's verbal intervention may take, it should always result in directing the patient's attention so that it will throw light upon a hitherto dark or hazy mental territory. *Naming* and words do function as light. The function of the therapeutic dialogue is to raise the level of psychic organization by naming the previously unnamed with words, thereby establishing well organized relationships through the proper syntax and correct use of tenses.

Picture memories, like dream imagery, do not convey logical or time relations among the various elements. These can be established only through the syntax of language. Interpretive interventions elicit verbalization which, in turn, brings order, continuity and proportions into the disjointed image material. Because of their unindexed, chaotic nature, image memories are more frightening and less tamed than language memories. Nonverbalized picture memories, like preverbal visual impressions, have a mythical quality of the "uncanny." This explains why traumatization is most likely to occur in the preverbal stage. The naming and unifying function of language holds in check the frightening nature of the image world. Cassirer (1946) derives the origin of language from man's awe and fear when faced with the nameless object. Picard (1963), in *Man and Language,* says: "Something of the object is taken into the word, and therefore when he speaks man is related to the object because something of it is contained in the word."

This beautifully formulated statement also expresses deep psychological truth. It points out the interdependence between man's experiential world and his language. If, for whatever reasons of traumatization or fixation, a patient's experiential world gets distorted this will be reflected immediately in his language. This is why schizoid, borderline or schizophrenic patients find verbalization in psychotherapy so torturously difficult. Their eternal complaint is that they can never convey what they really mean. Communal language feels quite inadequate for expressing their private, idiosyncratic experiences. If therapy succeeds in helping these patients to develop more realistic and constant object relationships, then the categories of communal language will be experienced as more fitting means of expression and communication.

The reverse, however, is also true. Acquiring language, or even a new language, changes the child's or the adult's relationship to his object world. Since each language implies a more or less different *Weltanschauung,* a different relationship to inner and outer reality, personal identity does change when one speaks a new language. For example, when one is forced to give up his mother-tongue, one feels initially somewhat depersonalized, since the new language does not seem to match one's experiences. The unity between object and word feels broken, and one feels as if he is playing an arbitrary lotto-game, attaching prefabricated labels to things. Slowly, as new object relationships accrue and solidify, the new language acquires its organically natural, expressive and representational functions.

My first-hand experience and struggle with adjusting to a new language environment sensitized me to the idiosyncratic language problems of my patients. The mutually interdependent relationships among language, perception, thinking, emotional balance and the quality of object relationships were self-evident. So was the recognition that, under the aegis of the transference, the psychoanalytic setting closely parallels the conditions of the early mother-child relationship in which speech was originally learned. Thus the analyst's speech patterns acquire crucial significance, since the patient, in a sense, is learning to speak from him.

The physical setting of the analytic session and the rule of free association are devised to encourage the patient to break with his usual speech patterns. The demand for free association puts the patient in the attitude of picking up mental content previously unlit by his attention, thus changing unformulated psychic background into delineated "nameable" figures in the foreground. Figures are "things" with outlines which can be clearly perceived and consciously manipulated, at least in some respects. This "nameable" foreground in our mental apparatus is called the preconscious. The preconscious consists of mental things which have been named already and which are ready to be named, i.e., verbalized any time should the searchlight of attention cathexis fall on them.

I have tried to explicate, in terms of Gestalt perception, the function of language as an ordering and clarifying agent in mental life, and thereby clarify Freud's famous statement in *The Unconscious* (1915): "The conscious presentation comprises the presentation of the thing plus the presentation of the word belonging to it, while the unconscious presentation is the presentation of the thing alone." Earlier, in *Interpretation of Dreams* (1900), Freud had postulated that speech serves as a source of internal excitation which is able to attract consciousness, thereby producing subtle psychical qualities. Consciousness is thus able to follow intricate thought processes independent of perception of external objects or crude sensations of pleasure or pain. Through the medium of speech—spoken or silent—thinking becomes objective.

I think the conceptual approach of Gestalt psychology helps in the understanding of the full meaning of the above quotations. It clarifies the nature of what Freud calls the "quality" provided by language which makes thought processes available to consciousness.

In other words, we find that free association extends the realm of the patient's preconscious spontaneously, even without any interpretive intervention from the analyst. However, thinking of the effects of free association without its complementary counterpart—the analyst's interpretive activities—is obviously a theoretical abstraction. Yet it is useful to differentiate the function of speech within the closed psychic system of the patient from the function of language as shared experience. This is so particularly since Freud's model of language, like his theoretical models in general, refers almost exclusively to the supposedly-closed energy system of a single individual.

The function of free association within an analytic session, however, is also communicative. By talking in the presence of the analyst, the patient's private reality becomes communal, shared reality. Sharing experiences with others by means of a common language is an essential part of the socialization process, i.e., of maturation. A shared reality means victory over primary narcissism and autism. To believe in the possibility of shared reality is not an easy task for the schizoid, borderline and schizophrenic, nor even for many hysterics and obsessional neurotics. The analyst's technical skill and empathy are needed to convince these patients that their verbalizations are understood. Actually, it *is* often difficult to understand them, since they at times use words as magic gestures, even in instances where the manifest language pattern gives the impression of regular secondary process communication. This is the trickiest speech pattern to decipher, more so than if primary process verbalization openly prevails. Seriously schizoid obsessionals excel at this deceptive pseudo-secondary process talk.

The aim of the analyst's verbalizations with all these patients is (a) to convince them that they *are* understood, and (b) to lead them gradually into the use of communally shared secondary process language. Regarding the former, the patient must register the information that no matter how unique and strange he feels his experiences and verbalizations to be, the analyst understands him. To achieve this aim, it is helpful if the analyst couches his remarks in the words or metaphors the patient has just used. Entering the metaphors and using the patient's words not only facilitates recognition, but also, particularly in a schizoid patient, gives him a feeling of reality, a certification of his existence. Hearing his own words repeated by the analyst furnishes substance and reality to these words as well as to the locus of origin of these words—namely, the mental "inside" of the patient. Sometimes a patient will ask the analyst to simply repeat what he, the patient, has said without adding anything to it. In extreme cases it might be advisable for the analyst to simply fulfill this requirement; in other cases, interpretation of the remark in the above sense is more helpful. One thing, however, is sure: it should never be interpreted in terms of the patient's wish to manipulate the analyst. The need for a mirror to convince oneself of one's existence is not manipulation of the mirror.

Even though actual mirroring in language is only asked for, or needed, in extreme cases of schizoid depersonalization, the analyst still has to find the fitting style of language for each patient. This, by the way, is not a matter of conscious choice of language construction, but is taken care of by the analyst's preconscious, hopefully a well-functioning one. The analyst, in some sense, lives in as many different keys as he has patients, for which he needs the paradoxical combination of an easily fragmented, yet sturdily integrated, character. A slight depersonalization, if not a prerequisite, is certainly a professional risk in this type of work. But fortunately there is also a built-in safeguard: Besides entering primary process metaphors and developing tailored language, the analyst also has to induce the patient to communicate in his culture's generally accepted secondary process language (aim "b").

This consensually-accepted language pattern is referred to by de Saussure (1915) as "la langue," in contradistinction to the individually-used "la parole." I believe the communal language should be used by the analyst with the utmost simplicity. It is in this context that the patient has to learn to "de-magicize" language, as well as "de-magicize" his analyst. Words and syntax should be simple, and the tone of voice should be casual and unemphatic, void of personal emotions.[1] At times, one can sound as if he is just thinking aloud. This style of speech is designed to convey the message that neither the analyst nor language is magical.

At this point, some of the more usual forms of the analyst's verbal interventions should be mentioned. Dictionary-type interpretations, of the immediate-translation type, should of course be avoided. Unfortunately, they often appear in Freud's clinical illustrations, thus serving as faulty models for analysts of subsequent generations. Genetic reconstructions often represent similar dangers. I wholeheartedly agree with Devereux (1951) who, quoting Jokl, states: "A genuine interpretation is an act whereby the *quality of intelligibility* is added to the patient's own statements and acts. *Substantive* additions are not interpretations, but an attack upon the patient's autonomy as a person." He says further that ". . . an interpretation must add *nothing* to that which is being interpreted, and must be intelligible to the listener." Yet a good interpretation, by rearranging known material, does yield new insight to the patient, while a confrontation merely focuses the patient's attention on something which he perceived but failed to register properly.

No doubt, reconstructions are needed at times during an analysis. I can even see the occasional necessity for the analyst to offer, modestly and tentatively, a rounded-out version of potentially crucial segments of the patient's past history. This can be done in the form of a question or a tentative hypothesis which might or might not be valid. The word "might" is important in these interpretive formulations. One tries to enumerate all the evidence making the construction probable, but one should never offer it as "This is *it*." Constructions should, instead, invite the patient to think about and arrive at his own decision as to the construction's probable validity.

I think this type of communication from the analyst is important for developing

---

[1] I do not believe in the "cherish your patients; be warm to them" type of theory of technique advocated by some analysts. I think our "cherishing" should be implied in our respect for the patient as a person and in our steady effort to do good work.

calm, secondary process language in the patient. In this atmosphere, as in the original infantile setting of speech development, the primitive instinctual demands are tamed through the medium of language. Structured language gradually enhances the ego's sphere over the compulsively repetitious clamorings of the id.

The analyst's spoken language can contribute greatly to the creation of those propitious conditions which, according to Kris (1950), make recall and recollection possible. That is the reason we ask the young analyst in supervision for the exact wording and tone of voice of his therapeutic interventions. Textbooks unfortunately are of little help in this respect. Time-worn advice—such as, "Always interpret the resistance before content," or "Avoid deep interpretations at the beginning," or "The oedipal identifications should be interpreted before proceeding to the deeper layers"—does not teach the analyst *how* to make his verbal interventions in the optimal therapeutic manner.

I think it possible to write a textbook in this helpful, concrete manner, but at present, there is none. Therefore, we have to rely solely on supervision for conveying the importance of exact wording. Supervisors have to know whether the interpretive remark was worded directly, addressed to "you" (the patient), or offered by using the general subject "one" in the tentative hypothesis. Did the analyst-in-training offer an imagined scene as one describes a picture, or did he offer a piece of theoretically-formulated information such as, "Children are likely to feel resentful at the birth of a sibling"? These and other possible formulations can have very different effects in bringing about appropriate or inappropriate conditions for recall and insight. They also differentially affect the prevailing transference reactions. In my experience the less all-knowing and emotional the interpretation offered, the less of the patient's mental energy will be wasted in transference-resistance, and the more the analytic work becomes truly a shared project of investigation.

The matter-of-fact calmness of the analyst's statements can, nevertheless, have emotionally significant therapeutic effect upon the patient. In fact, it is exactly this matter-of-fact quality of the statement which can sometimes have more therapeutic effect than its content. Often the analyst's tone of voice can erase some of the worst effects of a sadistically-inclined, infantile superego. A patient, who was a prostitute, once asked me: "Are you *never* shocked at anything?" I told her that I *can* be shocked, but that it usually happens when I read about Vietnam in the newspaper, not when I listen to patients.

Valenstein (1962) mentions the "redemptive capacity of humor," and I find this very true. One should, however, be cautious in talking about it lest he finds it soon formulated as a technical tool of "being funny." Humor *can* have an integrating as well as a tension-releasing function, *if* it naturally fits the analyst's personality and *if* it comes at the psychologically-right moment. Humor always implies a certain distance and objectivity; it orders the content into a larger framework of human experiences, sometimes even into the category of "human folly or comedy." One should be sparing with humor, though, since some patients use it for isolation or distancing as a habitual mode of resistance.

A few final remarks about two often-quoted dangers in interpretation. We are often warned that picking up emerging "deep" material early in analysis might jeopardize the whole analytic process, and Glover (1931) warns us against the irreparable harm caused by vague or inexact interpretations. I think any urgent material has to be dealt with if it emerges, no matter in what phase of analysis.

There are several ways of "dealing" with "deep" material emerging early which take the edge off the danger of either causing an unmanageable outbreak of anxiety or threatening the analysis with premature interruption.

A brief acknowledgment of the emerging impulse is definitely indicated, or else the patient will feel that his impulses are too frightening for the analyst to recognize. In these instances it can be quite helpful to formulate the recognition in unspecific, general terms, indicating the hope that "we will understand more about this problem later." A nonspecific recognition provides opportunity for the patient's ego to keep up the necessary layer of defense as a guard against any untimely outbreak of affect, while at the same time it enables him to feel accepted by the analyst. The fact that *the* dangerous topic has been recognized, in a general way, by the analyst and that there have been no shattering consequences will bear fruit in keeping the avenues open for further recall and associations.

In conclusion, a successful analysis results in the patient's improved ways of dealing with reality—which will be reflected, among other indicators, in his ability to express himself, to communicate, and to think objectively in secondary process language.

This does not mean, however, that patients are expected to come out of analysis as prototypes of "the normal" person, "the man in the grey flannel suit" who is "well adjusted" to our great society. I rather hope that in analysis patients also develop their idiosyncratic uniqueness—that they, in de Saussure's terms, develop their individual "la parole" as well as the consensually accepted "la langue."

Hopefully the method of free association has taught them to reach, with language, to their ever-existing primary process world, keeping thereby their creative potentials functionally alive. Yet this easy contact with the deeper layers of experiencing should not inhibit, but be well-integrated with, secondary process language where categories of communal consensus and causality prevail.

The deadness of empty, mechanized language, the ever-present verbal-sound noise, and the lack of fruitful silence in our society are as much the symptom of a sickness of gradual wholesale depersonalization as is the autistic language of a schizophrenic the sign of an individual sickness.

REFERENCES

Breuer, J., and Freud, S., *Studies in hysteria* (1895). Boston, Beacon Press, 1961.

Cassirer, E., *Language and myth*. New York, Harper, 1946.

Devereux, G., Timing of confrontations and interpretations. *Internat. J. Psychoanal.*, 1951, 32.

Freud, S., *On aphasia* (1891). New York: International Universities Press, 1953.

——, Project for a scientific psychology (1895). In *The origins of psychoanalysis*. New York: Basic Books, 1953.

——, The interpretation of dreams (1900). *Standard edition,* Vols. IV-V. London: Hogarth Press.

——, The unconscious (1915). *Standard edition,* Vol. XIV. London: Hogarth Press.

——, *An outline of psychoanalysis* (1940). New York: W. W. Norton, 1949.

Glover, E., The therapeutic effect of inexact interpretation. *Internat. J. Psychoanal.* 1931, 12.

Kris, E., On preconscious mental processes. *Psychoanal. Quart.*, 1950.

Picard, M., *Man and language*. Chicago: Henry Regnery Company, 1963.

de Saussure, F., *Course in general linguistics* (1915). New York: Philosophical Library, 1959.

Valenstein, A., The psychoanalytic situation. *Internat. J. Psychoanal.*, 1962.

CHAPTER 22

The Use of Imagery in Interpretive Communication

EMANUEL F. HAMMER, PH.D.

An interesting congruence between a dominant aim of the creative artist and a central intent of the psychoanalyst may be discerned by the reader of the works of both.[1] The task of the poet is expressed by A. E. Housman (1933): ". . . I think that to transfuse emotions—not to transmit thought but to set up in the reader's sense a vibration corresponding to what was felt by the writer—is the particular function of poetry." Ruesch (1961), in *Therapeutic Communication,* writes: "It is the task of the therapist to choose words and gestures which, when combined within the head of the patient, will produce something that is alive. Unlike the scientific expert who chooses his words in such a way that the dictionary definition corresponds to the state of affairs to be described, the therapist cares for the impact words have upon

---

[1] There are two allied disciplines, one on either side, from which analysts might learn: (a) the *molecular,* such as the neurological and the experimental, and (b) the *molar,* such as the naturalistic, anthropological, philosophic, artistic, literary or poetic. In this latter direction a special affinity has often been felt between psychoanalysis and art. Perhaps one reason is because both share a common goal. It is true that no single theory on the function of art will suffice, yet one of the ultimate ends of art is to humanize life—to show and absorb one in experiencing its fullness and richness. Similarly, one of the ends of psychoanalytic treatment is also to enable the patient to get in touch with this richness, to experience a full immersion in existence.

In the shadow area at the edge of consciousness lie the feelings without which a person can neither relatively know nor be himself. Beyond the removal of symptoms, an ideal goal of depth psychotherapy is to assist the patient's inner self to stretch, breathe, look about, and grow. In the service of this goal, what is therapeutic is "feeling"—to quote e. e. cummings, "not knowing or believing or thinking." Perhaps one of the deeper aims of therapy, like that of this poet for himself, is to enable the patient, on increasingly more basic levels, to express, as cummings continues, "nobody-but-oneself in words, because when you think or you believe or you know, you're a lot of other people: but the moment you feel, you're nobody but yourself."

Artistic and psychoanalytic procedures also share in common a search for the truth, and a desire to make a statement of any increasing approximations to the goal of so arrogant and noble a quest. The novelist, playwright or poet seeks to recognize the universal in people. Here, too, the goal is a common one with that of the analyst. At the same time the writer also charts the particular, the unique in a character. Similarly, the psychoanalyst orients himself to recognize in his patient those personality elements given to the latter to a degree which are his alone. The analyst, like the writer, strives for the vision to see what others do not see, the courage to face and speak that vision, and a fullness of being a person himself. From this last-named, even more than from the rest, the artist builds his craft and the analyst builds his treatment.

Both writer and analyst share the intent of extending, respectively, the reader's and the patient's reality. Both value, and centrally engage in, a probing experience. Malamud, the writer, asserts, "Art must interpret, or it is mindless." So, too (with the singular exception of the Rogerian), must all psychotherapies.

Warmest appreciation is extended Drs. Daniel W. Schwartz, Max Deutscher, Dorothy Bloch, and my wife, Lila, for their sensitive reading of this paper and their many fruitful suggestions.

people . . . [a task of the psychotherapist] is to produce an effect." (On the side of the difference, of course, the poet communicates his own feelings, although he hopes to strike a universal cord and thus make a statement of those personal to the reader too. The analyst for the most part—there are instances of exceptions—communicates predominantly what is within the patient, although he sometimes knows this because it resonates within him.)

In a letter to Robert Hutchins, Dahlberg stated, "A writer should employ a language that can pierce the heart or awaken the mind" (Seaver, 1966). So, too, often should the therapist. Perhaps we can learn from the creative individual many things for our work, especially in the realm of communicating. It is here that we might profit from what the novelist or poet demonstrates to us of the value of imagery—the special value of images for concentrated effect, for pithy communication, and for vehicles to touch feelings and contact affective regions. What is presented in this paper is a method of interpretation *which employs imagery* in the service of achieving insight by establishing more immediate connection with feelings.

To step back briefly first, a large number of clinical papers are written about the initial phase of treatment, and almost as many about the terminal phase, but it is striking how few there are written about the vast middle phase. Somehow the feeling the reader gets from the publications in the area of technique is an attitude that if the patient is handled well in the beginning phase, and that if considerably later the therapist knows how to terminate with the patient, somehow, in the sprawling ground between, they will both muddle through.

In the middle phase of therapy, however, as the patient sometimes experiences it, the therapist speaks in the too-familiar tongue—reflecting, commenting, categorizing, describing, interpreting. The sense of inner resistance, of the patient half-dismissing it all, can be felt by the therapist. Here, not only the patient's resistance but also the problem of the therapist's imprecision of his own communications must be confronted. Is there another way to put things? In the therapist's search for serviceable instrumentalities, is there some small innovation in the existing interpretive approach which he can use to make psychoanalytic technique more effective.

Frequently, the analyst observes that interpretations are going in one proverbial ear of the patient and out the other. However, an *occasional* one will strike sparks in between. The analyst can, in this latter instance, then sense the patient's feeling of conjunction between what was said and something within.

To accomplish this, Strachey (1934) says, "Interpretation must be emotionally 'immediate'; the patient must experience it as something actual." Well, admittedly none of this is new. But how?

To quicken the process of assisting a patient to sense himself at and beneath his defenses, both within himself and in the relationship with the therapist, I have found one emphasis particularly helpful. This emphasis is one of striving, wherever possible, for conjoint vividness, which I find can be approached by using images. Communication to the patient in the form of images offers the advantages of (a) economy of words, (b) directness of meaning, (c) basic pictorial expression, and (d) density of affect—the latter perhaps the most important of the four.

To a masochist I once observed, "How nice to get a wound you can lick." "Wham! That connected," he said. I was struck with the degree to which this communication reached the patient as other conventional interpretive explanations had not.

Another patient, an intellectualized, obsessive-compulsive individual, "always," in his words, "told the 'truth' to everyone, no matter what!" I had earlier expressed to him the understanding that under the guise of truth he was often really releasing hostility. He agreed from the top of his head only. One day when he was telling me a story of how he had just "told the truth" to a colleague of his about this colleague's faults, I commented, "With that one you really *hit him right on the jaw.*" At another time when he used the "truth" as a weapon, this time against his father, I commented, "That must have landed squarely *between his eyes*"—suggesting the David and Goliath image in addition to the aggressive one. Images have as their objective the production of an effect through *multi-layered communication.* These images, in two consecutive sessions, succeeded (where more conventionally expressed interpretations had not) in transposing the discussion of the patient's underlying anger to the interior plane on which it raged. For him, the insight was then not in the nature of something *inferred* but something *experienced*; it was not merely cognitive, but affective. For the first time the patient could feel the anger, which had been deflected into his intellect, closer to home: as he reported, in his "muscles" and in his "gut."

A colleague (my wife, Lila) supplies another example of communication on multilayered levels which images allow. She commented to a female patient of the hysteric type, "You seem to comfort yourself by hugging your misery like a teddy bear?" Images may do service, as the above one did, in referring in concentrated fashion to *both* the childishness and the woe of the patient as they were exploited for secondary gains. Such interpretations may be used also when the therapist wishes a comment to be either sobering or to possess some element of surprise, or both. It can be compelling, as can few other styles when a therapist feels a need for a mode of expression, during sluggish phases of the treatment, to focus attention to an interpretative possibility.

To a young psychiatrist in analysis who was "interpreting" to his wife almost everything she did at home, I found the most effective thing I ever communicated to him about it to be: "It's important not to get so used to tearing away people's masks that you no longer hear the rip." Here, auditory *and* visual imagery were jointly employed to put the patient in touch with the affect of hurting others.

In general, resorting to auditory imagery can be as effective as visual. To a 36-year-old male patient, I once commented that he seemed continually to pretend boyishness to feel safe. The patient showed no real grasp of what was meant until I added, "I hear a 'Gee Whiz' and a 'Golly Gee' in between the lines whenever you talk." As treatment went on from there to address his character armor, he would refer to this defense as his "Golly Gee role," and in doing so seemed to feel its texture and meaning.

The sense of taste may also serve, as in the comment to a relentlessly Pollyannish person regarding his tendency to put "such gobs of gooey whipped cream on everything."

When the interpretive communication is shaped into a pictorial expression, an otherwise abstract or intellectual idea is given flesh by the concrete example. The image employed is not only a symbol, but it is also a more active participant than is more conventional verbalization in bringing the patient's feelings to *felt* awareness. Arieti (1966) offers an illuminating explanation with the parallel of imagery in poetry.

Art, indeed, is founded to a great extent on *paleological reinforcement.* At the same time that the work of art elicits the abstract concept, it sustains itself upon the paleologic reinforcement, or identification with a concrete example. There is almost a perfect welding of the abstract concept with the concrete example, of the replaced object with its metaphor. The concrete object of the metaphor is not only a symbol, it is a participant in producing the effect.

Interpretation is most usable by the patient when, in its presentation by the therapist, it incorporates the actual experience of its referents. Loewenstein (1957) says that when actually interpreting, we must retranslate concepts into the patient's concrete experiences.

Particularly with the obsessional, isolated, and alienated patient (and this lifeless defense has over the years become a more and more frequent syndrome), images supply desired affectively-richer stimuli. Obsessional individuals reduce the exchange of language, in therapy or out, to the emotionally sterile, to the experiencially rarified. The ritualistic and rigid quality of their linguistic operations fend off feelings. Responses from the therapist to thaw out the patient should themselves be warm, alive, and concrete.

Isolated patients can best be reached by an emotional encounter or, on an interpretive level, by a vivid, emotion-tinged image. Images are more *experienceable* than are other forms of communication. When the analyst can locate and employ an image umbilical to the patient's affect, then he moves the patient closer to his feelings. In images, thought and affect merge instead of staying separate. They help the patient to *think-feel* the interpretation.

It is, moreover, not only in instances of the patient requiring assistance to feel kinesthetically, in his muscles, the affect beneath his words that an imaged communication has advantages.[2] Sometimes it effectively clarifies. It may send something home in a way that registers with the patient. One woman in treatment engaged in a continuous stream of rapid chatter without pausing for breath. This allowed neither the patient to reflect on what she was saying nor the analyst to comment. I interrupted one day to say, in a somewhat different style than I had expressed it previously, that her defense was much like that of a sentry frantically doing double time to allow no one across the border from either side: She did not allow me to express any observations from one side nor allow any thoughts to leisurely emerge from within her which might take her by surprise from the other. The idea had earlier been expressed to her without the image of a border sentry doing double time, but with the assistance of the image she was able to see more clearly what she was doing. Her speech settled to a more natural pace and treatment could proceed. She had been able, as are other patients, to try on the image more easily than she could mere words. If the image then fits, a deeper identification in the patient with the interpreted content results.[3]

One point of clarification: a patient should not be inundated with images. This

---

[2] I find, however that this area is where it *is* most valuable.

[3] On the negative side, it must be observed that greater caution is necessary here by the therapist to be sure he is offering a valid interpretation. I find that in interpretations the effect. of suggestion, on suggestible patients, is greater with imagery.

type of interpretative style should be used judiciously. Generally, the proper quality of the analysts' responses are simple and should be, as Menninger (1958) says, that of "quiet observers, listeners, and occasionally commentators" (p. 129). Against this backdrop, however, the occasional image which might occur to the analyst in reference to any single patient has the additional advantages of a change of pace and an enlivening quality. It additionally serves the goal Applebaum (1966) speaks of as *evocativeness* in treatment.

DISCUSSION

Words are more distant abstractions than are pictures. Pictures are closer to the concrete, to the actual. And word-pictures fall between these two communicative levels.

There is neurological confirmation in the view of the hierarchy of neurological functioning, as first suggested by Jackson (1926, 1958): that the abstract is a more surface and later evolutionary acquisition than is the concrete. Additional support may be found in the work of Goldstein (1942, 1948, 1963) with aphasics during, and since, World War I.

The experimental area also supplies congruence. An interesting study invites our special attention. Three groups of boys were employed in a dart-throwing procedure. One group practiced throwing darts at a target, another group imagined throwing darts, and a third did neither. After this, all three groups threw darts and were judged for accuracy. The intriguing finding is that the group who imagined throwing darts fell midway between the group which actually practiced this activity and the group which neither practiced nor imagined doing it. Apparently, imagining is a midway procedure, approaching the actual (Arnold and Gasson, 1954).

There are data offering support from still another direction, the physiological. Subjects who were asked to imagine various activities—for example, riding a bicycle—showed EEG patterns and physiological responses more like that of individuals actually bicycling (in place), and less like that of a control group (Arnold, 1960). Trying on the image, as the clinical examples cited and also Arieti previously suggested, is not a passive, but is a *participating*, experience. It is this which explains the report of the patient offered the interpretation that his telling the "truth" must have hit his colleague "right smack on the jaw": that he then felt the sensation in his muscles.

There are lessons also to be learned from our academic colleagues. Arnheim (Kepes, 1965) discusses the significance of perceptual, imaged articulation in the development of conceptual thought. The significance of images in thought and perception is not relegated to childhood but is seen as an equally necessary component of adult logical and creative activity.[4]

Within our own field, Bruner (1966) presents the first major theoretical assessment of the process of cognitive development since the pioneering work of Piaget. After six years of intensive research, Bruner and his colleagues examine the growth of three systems of representing information, two of which are through imagery and through the symbolism of language. In line with their work, the present writer has

---

[4]Kepes called an earlier book of his *The Language of Vision,* and his interest all along has been in the syntax of that language—the syntax of the visual world and the intricate interrelationships between its syntax, denotation and metaphor.

elsewhere (Hammer, 1958) expressed the points that pictorial thought precedes verbal expression and that it more readily reaches unconscious receptors of communication.

The individual begins to use graphic communication early in life. Children draw before they can write. In terms of negative content, when one observes the drawings of children, one sees things that the children would never have been able to express in words even if they had been fully conscious of some of these feelings which toss and distress them.

In dreams, the language is predominantly a pictorial one. The unconscious expresses itself in images. As stated by Naumburg (1955), "Intellectualization and the exaggerated verbalism of our culture have been imposed on the deeper and more primitive levels of our unconscious mode of imaged expression." In accord with this, anthropologist Lewis Mumford (1967) points out that in man's development dreams preceded speech.

Freud (1933) had earlier found that patients could frequently express themselves more easily through graphic means of communication than through verbal ones. In speaking of the difficulties patients often have communicating their dreams, he wrote, " 'I could draw it,' the dreamer frequently says, 'but I don't know how to say it.' "

The case of August Strindberg also illustrates the greater affinity between feelings and images than exists between feelings and words. This dramatist, so extraordinarily able in verbal areas, made use of drawings during periods in which he felt unable, because of depression and other psychic disturbances, to express himself adequately by words. He tried to "say" his otherwise inaccessible mental experiences in pictorial ways (Hildebrand, 1932).

The child tends naturally to order his experiences visually. Once he is in school he is compelled to translate his experiences into more indirect symbols, to reduce reality to an abstract code. The relation of perception to conception is strained, and a whole mode of education, the most natural way to understand complex forms, is forsaken.[5] The child, like the artist, perceives order and relationships in a pictorial Gestalt, to which he tunes in more easily than to words; and the child lives, "as father to the man," beneath the adult layers in the grownup. As such, a more effective communicative avenue to the child within, to the deeper regions below the rational (or pseudo-rational) adult surface, would appear to be by way of imagery.

Kepes (1966) also suggests that the proper use of visual perception would reopen the innocent eye and so, in a sense, rejuvenate the mind.

In a reductionist form, we might say that psychotherapy is a conversation, albeit quantitatively one-sided, between two persons. "Essentially," says Shaffer (1947), "they communicate, mainly by the use of words, although other media of communication, including . . . gesture, facial expression, and tone of voice are also present. . . . Movement, tension, visceral and glandular changes, attitudes, postures, images . . . are among the secondary responses evoked by the interchange of

---

[5]A young poet patient of mine once expressed:

> "Extend to me a picture of almost things
> Of things not quite expressed . . .
> Abide with me awhile
> To unlearn words."

words." Since the intent is to evoke such images (among other responses) within the patient, to start with images as one of the communications sent serves two overlapping purposes. It puts the interpretive message one step closer to being received and enhances its possibility of such reception.

We can draw similar implications from Freud's observations of the primary process. In speaking of these primary processes which define the depths in people, Maslow (1957) observes: "Deep down, we look at the world through the eyes of wishes and fears and gratifications. . . . Think of the way in which a really young child looks at the world, looks at itself and at other people. . . . It has nothing to do with time and space or with sequence, causality, order, or with the laws of the physical world. This is a world quite other than the physical world. When it is placed under the necessity of disguising itself from conscious awareness to make things less threatening, it can condense several objects into one as in a dream." Maslow concludes the point by underscoring the quality of primary processes as "preverbal, very concrete, closer to raw experiencing and usually *visual*" (italics supplied). Since the natural language of the primary processes and of the raw experiencing within is preverbial and visual, therapists "speak the language" when they employ the imaginal to communicate to the deeper regions of a patient.

CONCLUSION

When interpreting, the analyst often subordinates image to idea, so that what emerges is treatise, polemic, or catechism—anything but revelation or a deeper vision.

The use of imagery in the interpretive communication, by contrast, may serve to facilitate the patient's locating a pertinent feeling inside himself. It may more easily carry the communication of the therapist through the interstices of the patient's intellectual layers. A pictorial mode of communication, leaning toward the preverbal, may constitute a more effective vehicle for lifting the psychological processes out of their preconscious state onto the plane of consciousness.

Through imaged communication, we move closer to where the patient's affect resides. This provides another advantage. The feeling below the surface can be reevoked on the surface by an accurate, focused image.[6] Reevoked, it is now accompanied by an echo or tone of familiarity. At this point, surface and subsurface feelings, when congruent, move to join—*and in uniting, they make an avenue of contact through the defensive layer of repression.*

An image provides an extra dimension; it can be seen as well as heard.

REFERENCES

Appelbaum, S. A., Speaking with the second voice: Evocativeness. *J. Amer. Psychoanal. Ass.,* 1966, 14, 462-477.

Arieti, S., *American handbook of psychiatry,* Vol. III. New York: Basic Books, 1966.

Arnold, Magda, and Gasson, J. A., *The human person.* New York: Ronald Press, 1954.

Arnold, Magda, *Emotion and personality,* Vols. I & II. New York: Columbia University Press, 1960.

---

[6]Since imagery strengthens the communicative effectiveness by supplying an affective undercurrent to accompany the cognitive meaning, the impact for the patient is a little like the experience of responding to that occasional dream Herma (1967) speaks of, in which the latent content coincides with the manifest. Somewhat similarly, Arieti (1966), speaking of the use of imagery in poetry, sees its special impact as coming in part from the agreement between paleologic and logic: "Paleologic actually reinforces logic" (p. 733).

Brunner, J., *Studies in cognitive growth*. New York: John Wiley & Sons, 1966.

Devereux, G., Some criteria for the timing of confrontations and interpretations. *Internat. J. Psychoanal.*, 1941, 32, 19-24.

Freud, S., *New introductory lectures on psychoanalysis*. New York: Norton, 1933.

Goldstein, K., *Aftereffects of brain injuries in war*. New York: Grune & Stratton, 1942.

——, *Languages and language disturbances*. New York: Grune & Stratton, 1948.

——, *Human nature in the light of psychopathology*. New York: Schocken Books, 1963.

Hammer, E., *The clinical application of projective drawings*. Springfield, Ill.: Charles C. Thomas, Publisher, 1958.

Herma, H., The therapeutic act. In Hammer, E. (Ed.), This book, 1968.

Hildebrand, A., *Problems of form, painting and sculpture*. New York: Julian Press, 1932.

Housman, A. E., *The name and nature of poetry*. Cambridge: University Press, 1933.

Jackson, J. H., *Eine Studie uber krampfe*, Berlin: Karger, 1926.

——, *Selected writings* (Edited by Taylor, J.), Vols. I & II. New York: Basic Books, 1958.

Kepes, G. (Ed.), *The nature and art of motion*. New York: George Braziller, 1965.

——, *The education of vision*. New York: George Braziller, 1966.

Loewenstein, R. M., Some thoughts on interpretation in the theory and practice of psychoanalysis. *Psychoanal. Stud. Child*, 1957, Vol. XII.

Maslow, A., Emotional blocks to creativity. Lecture to *Creative Engineering Seminars, U.S. Army Engineers*, Ft. Belvoir, Va., April 24, 1957.

Menninger, K., *Theory of psychoanalytic technique*. New York: Basic Books, 1958.

Naumburg, Margaret, Art as symbolic speech. *J. Aesthet. Art Crit.*, 1955, 13, 435-450.

Ruesch, J., *Therapeutic communication*. New York: Norton, 1961.

Seaver, E. (Ed.), *Epitaphs of our times. The letters of Edward Dahlberg*. New York: George Braziller, 1966.

Shaffer, L., The problem of psychotherapy. *Amer. Psychol.*, 1947, 2, 389-342.

Strachey, J., The nature of the therapeutic action of psychoanalysis. *Internat. J. Psychoanal.*, 1934, 15, 127-159.

CHAPTER 23

Varying Technique in Treatment

EMANUEL F. HAMMER, PH.D.

"Psychotherapy," Wolberg (1966) comments, "is no mining operation that depends for its yield exclusively on excavated psychic ore. It is a human interaction. . . ." Nevertheless, we often seem to overlook the implications of psychotherapy as a human enterprise. We are prone, for example, to be parochial and unrealistic in our tendency to ignore the fact that different patients require different styles of approach. Each case is different, of course, but to some degree we uncritically assume one perspective is suitable (ruling out the borderline and schizophrenic patients) for all the neurotic ones.

The various symptom groups are too numerous to consider individually in this chapter. Rather than take up the whole tree, then, we will touch upon several diverse branches to illustrate the principle of shifting one's interpretive approach.

OBSESSIONAL PATIENTS

Individuals who fall in the obsessional category are generally those not buoyed by any connection they feel with existence. They seem to live beside life more than in it. The therapist feels as if their vital processes run sluggishly, as if the sap of affect has run thin.

When communicating, the obsessional individual employs language more to fend off feeling than to express it. Communication from the therapist should all the more, then, be warm, alive, concrete, and strive to deal with the actual.

The isolated or obsessive-compulsive patient, estranged as he is from his own emotions, is, I find, best approached both through emotional encounters in the treatment process and by the route of imaginal interpretations described in Chapter 22. Whether through the use of such images in the interpretative communication and/or through direct emotional engagement, the intent with the obsessional patient especially is to evoke an alive, richer, less diluted experience by providing an exchange contributing to an eliciting of affect.

The obsessional individual lives in a state of isolation from himself, and this inner vacuum also puts him at a distance from others. While there is considerable overlap, to be sure, the aim of emotional encounters between therapist and patient is more to establish interpersonal contact, while the use of images is somewhat more in the service of enabling the patient to establish contact with himself.

The adjunct use of group therapy in the treatment program of the obsessional individual has demonstrated itself valuable in rekindling within such people a state of involvement and response, in assisting the isolated patient over the threshold to where he can feel more a part of experience. What the obsessional sometimes profits from is being immersed in a vibrant group process, soaked to the marrow in an atmosphere rich in affect.

What Appelbaum (1966) speaks of as "evocativeness"—i.e., drawing forth, opening up—is a particular quality to strive for in working with the obsessional and the isolated. In this regard Butler (1962) classifies therapists' comments or interpretations according to three qualities of expressive style:

1. *Freshness of words and combinations.* The most highly connotative language possible seems to be poetic, metaphorical language in which much sensory imagery is used . . . the use of metaphor which adds vividness and color to the primary experience.

2. *Voice quality.* Is the therapist actually bringing something as a person (to the relationship), something that provides or generates new interpersonal experience for the client? . . . Is he simply present and accounted for . . . or is he actually removing something from the situation through dullness, weakness, or through empty and forced attempts to be something which at that moment he isn't?

3. *Functional level of responses.* How much are the therapist's remarks directed at the meaning or impact of experience?

Butler's classification is in accord with Sharpe's (1951) position that the language of clinical psychoanalysis should be closer to poetry than science. Because of his diluted emotional tone, with no patient more than with the isolated or the obsessional is this as important. (We here temporarily leave the considerations of treating obsessional patients, to return to them in the later section of this chapter on length of the session.)

DEPRESSED PATIENTS

In *The Public Happiness,* Heckscher states that the proper, vigorous connection to life can be found in relating to it as "a kind of game, a conviction that everything we do is a half-serious search [for] the elusive reality we can never quite touch. . . . If [an individual] finds a humor which serves him and keeps him whole, it will be a kind of tentativeness, a playfulness in the face of the world." Those therapists who are fortunate in having this quality will find that it can sustain and invigorate their patients.

These ingredients are of particular value with the depressed ones. Fisher (1966) asks, "Shall the therapist laugh, spoof and tell stories? Indeed, there is nothing better at moments. Opportunity for light-heartedness should not be passed over. Generally, patients need to be cheered up, to have a counter to their choking self-concern, their feeling that life is too much to bear." Greenwald (1967) speaks of what he whimsically refers to as "play therapy for adults." Fisher (1966) qualifies, "The therapist's compassion and taste for comedy desirably will intermingle."

The therapist need not be afraid to be animated. With depressed patients, a sombre approach only serves to depress them further. Allowing himself playfulness, spontaneity and expression of what richness of emotional tone he possesses, the therapist can lead the way for the patient while, at the same time, the more basic work continues. The example thus set for the patient is that work and play should harmoniously coexist.

In making a point with depressive individuals, it is helpful to reach for jokes when available. There was one despondent young lady who had finally been admitted into college after maintaining that she was too stupid to be accepted. She then stated, however, continuing her despairing mood, "All this proves is that *anyone* can get into college." I quoted neither the wise philosophers nor the psychoanalytic greats, but rather Marx—Groucho Marx. I told her the story of Groucho being invited to join an exclusive country club. He sent back an immediate telegram: "I WILL NOT JOIN ANY COUNTRY CLUB THAT WOULD HAVE ME AS A MEMBER."

The patient not only saw the point but, in doing so, emerged from her despondency to laugh. But what is more important is that she laughed *at herself*. The capacity to laugh at oneself is a step toward maturity and, I find, a stirring out of the grip of one's neurosis.

At other times, something else which proves helpful with depressed patients is, paradoxically, telling them just how depressed they are. When this is done, they no longer have to go on demonstrating it so hard. For this same reason, at times, the therapist might be slow to point out progress or signs of the depressive individual's feeling better. To do so only tends to throw him in the other direction, and into denials.

When depressed patients are suicidal, the therapist can, where indicated, be supportive by gratifying their voracious oral needs. One might offer cigarettes, gum, a cough drop, or, on a cold day, coffee. When such patients receive this in the context of emotional warmth in which the offer is extended, it helps to sustain them through the suicidal period while the deeper treatment concurrently proceeds.

An important qualification, however, is to be noted. A balancing consideration in the approach involving the above-described use of humor with the depressed patient is that this emphasis remain a secondary one, lest the more basic therapeutic work be thrown off its main course. Depressed individuals have their own private furies which immobilize them. The basic goal, of course, is to help such a patient experience the underlying rage against which his depression is so frequently a defense. For the therapist to create too jovial an atmosphere does, of course, make it difficult for the patient to experience his anger. A balance is therefore necessary. The use of humor is effective in providing momentary relief or "first aid" during the difficult times when the patient's depression is deepest. Bellak (1952), who also speaks of a "light touch" in interpretive work with depressed individuals, combines this quality with the goal of helping them to get in touch with their underlying anger in this way. What he does is employ a method he refers to as *indirect catharsis*. This consists of the therapist putting the patient's feelings into words for him in a viable and earthy manner. "It has been helpful to use strong vernacular expressions for aggressive sentiments, for example, 'I bet you really wished the goddamsonofabitch would drop dead!' This method permits the patient vicarious gratification without his quite having to take the responsibility for these feelings" (p. 331). Simultaneously, we might add, the patient finds reassurance in hearing the therapist, as an authority, feel free to express such affect. It is frequently helpful to add reassurance to the patient that just about everyone feels this sort of intense rage at times, even toward, if not particularly toward, those whom they also love.

It is important to attempt, next, to go past Bellak's suggestion, to move the patient beyond the stage where he requires *indirect catharsis* to one where he can eventually release his own anger. The depressed patient's movement from this earlier position to the later one is frequently over a long and brambly path. The blocks against experiencing aggression are strong in those who suffer significant depressive symptoms. The depressed patient frequently becomes quite dependent, while simultaneously exuding discontent and complaints that nothing is being done for him. The therapist must keep a finger on the pulse of his countertransference reactions in order to handle his tendency to be alienated by the patient's "nagging."

The usual uncovering approach has to be tilted in the direction of maintaining an atmosphere supporting a positive transference for an extended period, particularly when suicidal possibilities infiltrate the depressive picture.

The delicacy required in balancing lightness of approach with seriousness of intent, and the frequent complications of suicidal possibilities, create a trying situation where the therapist must be prepared to suffer disquieting anxiety, drained feelings and strain more frequently than with most other patient groups. At the same time, however, there are few patients who suffer so acutely, nor more urgently need professional help. A willingness to extend the length of session time where appropriate, to increase their frequency with some, to schedule emergency sessions if necessary, to know when not to discourage phone calls even at night, and other uses of flexibility under the direction of the therapist's empathic feeling with the patient through suicidal crises are the factors upon which a successful treatment program are to be built.

Paranoid and Masochistic Patients

Because of the common sharing of overloads of guilt by paranoid and masochistic patients, there are common denominators in the special approach applicable to their treatment. Both, hence, will be considered here in one section. Paranoid and masochistic patients share a tendency to respond to interpretation with an attitude of "Ouch!" and "How can you say that to me!" Both hold their scars high, one accusingly, the other pleadingly. The paranoid then capitalizes on this to justify his previously existent anger and hostility, and thereby gives license to his attack. The masochist uses his contrived and/or felt hurt as a subtle bill of demands now for protection, sympathy, being taken care of, and as insurance against other hurts. These reactive patterns have to be dealt with, of course, if treatment is to accomplish any goals of central magnitude, but to trigger off these respective mechanisms early in therapy only endangers the treatment itself.

With paranoid individuals, the use of proverbs and aphorisms in interpreting is stylistically preferred (Nydes, 1968). Rather than employ direct or pointed statements with the paranoid patient, it is desirable for the therapist to couch what he has to say in more generalized terms. This may be so with the masochistic individual as well. With patients who tend to receive what the therapist says as either an accusation or a hurt, it is often less threatening or otherwise preferable for the communication to be in the form of fables, generalities, or truisms. Interpretations via such channels are easier confronted by the patient, since the aphorism or fable implies that what he may consider to be his own singular flaw or defect is instead part of a more universal human condition.

One patient, a T.V. performer, was having considerable difficulty asserting himself because of his fear of "hurting other's feelings." As he discussed his wish to break off arrangements with his agent and find a better one, he responded to the support of a truism, "One can't make an omelette without breaking eggs." Another patient experienced a dream in which a gang beat up his older brother. When the therapist inquired into the anger the patient experienced toward his brother, the patient commented, "*I* didn't have him beat up." The patient was then told the following story: A woman dreams that a tall, dark, handsome slave pulls her, a princess, up into a secluded tower of a castle, throws her onto the bed, takes his shirt off, and looks lustfully at her. "What are you going to do next?" she cries with mixed fear and anticipation. "I don't know, lady," he answers, "it's your dream." Then the patient understood.

To illustrate the patient's selective or biased perceptions, for example, one might tell him this story I find helpful: There were once two knights who were sent around the kingdom with respective missions. One was to count all the flowers and the other all the weeds. When they returned from the lengthy task and reported their counts, the knight who was commissioned to count the flowers was asked by the king how many weeds there were. "I noticed none, your Majesty," he answered. Conversely, the knight who was asked to count all the weeds noticed no flowers.

When this story is then related to the patient's particular selective perceptions, he can less defensively face the possibility as one not necessarily a mechanism of his alone. The mellowness of a reference to a fable or story reassures the patient that the therapist is not "out to get him."

Patients with significant paranoid trends tend to perceive almost every interpretation as an indictment. With them, it is best to employ generalized statements, introduced with a phrase something like "Most (or many) people. . . ." Illustrating a combination of the concepts of employing generalities and humor, Theodor Reik (1963) would say to a patient suffering over death wishes, "A thought murder a day keeps the analyst away."

To convey to a patient an awareness of his use of projection, the therapist might employ the following joke: A man goes toward his neighbor's house to borrow a lawnmower, thinking how nice his friend is to extend him such favors. As he walks along, however, doubts concerning the loan begin to gnaw at him. By the time he arrives, the doubts have given way to rage, and as the friend appears at the door the man shouts, "You know what you can do with your lawnmower; shove it!"

The therapist might be cautioned against interpretive use of his observation of the patient's waiting room behavior, the patient's interaction with other patients there, or *direct* reference to his manner of walking into the therapy room. This is particularly so with patients possessing paranoid elements. Such patients feel judged, criticized, or spied upon when the therapist uses material they have *not elected* to bring into the session.

Now such material, when valuable, does not necessarily have to be altogether lost. The patient can be put in touch with it by asking him how he feels when he comes into the session, or asking him how he feels when he is in the waiting room interacting for a moment with the patient who is leaving. That way the patient has a choice of whether he will bring out his feelings at this time. But for the therapist to observe directly to the patient what he has sensed of that which went on outside the office is only likely to trigger off from the patient's arsenal of accumulated grievances, an eruption of paranoid reactivity and self-righteous vindictiveness. Although this may sometimes be useable in treatment, with the person who sustains himself on persecution it usually releases more intense irrational feelings and accusatory mechanisms than can be employed effectively for the analysis; and the danger always is that the patient may precipitously lunge out of therapy before what he is reacting with can be usably clarified.

Another danger with the paranoid is that valid inferences on the therapist's part might be taken by these people as confirmation of a belief that he can read their minds. With them, it is particularly important to share an explanation of how the therapist was led to his hunch, the basis upon which he drew his conclusions, and the steps along the way.

In the treatment of the masochistic patient, Reik (1963) would use an attitude he said he learned from Freud—an attitude of "no pity!" or as Nydes (1965) would say, "No rachmunis!" Here, the therapist addresses the patient's strength rather than becomes unduly supportive, gentle or protective (as the masochist attempts to arrange). The pity for which the masochistic patient underlyingly but relentlessly appeals must be denied. Thus, rather than satisfy that which the patient wishes to derive from his suffering, his efforts here are to be defeated so that he must address more constructive sources for obtaining satisfactions.

This is part of a general principle: If the patient's defensive strategy gains him nothing, he is more inclined to try other means. For example, the patient who defensively must continually joke during the sessions in an effort to be liked, to feel lovable and entertaining, if not rewarded with the therapist's laughter, then begins to feel anxious. As the therapist maintains his neutrality, the patient may next grow angry. When his feelings are received, accepted, and responded to, when they are not punished as he had anticipated, he can then dare to allow still more to show. He can, in doing so, lay aside the defensive role of the entertainer.

Schizoid Individuals

With schizoid patients whose defenses shelter them from others, it is helpful to comment and react, but quite casually at first and without any interpreting. This is crucial for an extended beginning phase of treatment.

Fromm-Reichmann (Bullard, 1959) cites the personal experience of Christopher Burney, who was confined for 18 months in solitary confinement by the Germans during World War II. Following such a solitary stretch, Burney commented that on the few occasions when there was an opportunity for communication, he found that the muscles of his mouth became stiff and unwilling, and thoughts he wanted to express sounded within his head as if they would be ridiculous if he voiced them. "Solitude," he said, "had so far weaned me from the habit of intercourse, even the thin intercourse of speculation, that I could no longer see any relationship with another person unless it was introduced gradually by a long overture of common trivialities." Similarly, with a highly schizoid, isolated subject, to spend the beginning phase of treatment in discussing the mere surface of things is frequently the only approach eventually and gradually to allow for more contact. Such a patient's fear must be gradually allayed by long periods spent dealing with the impersonal.

Dr. Fine, in Chapter 18 of this book, cited the case of the schizophrenic patient, withdrawn into silent and cushioned retreat, who did not speak a word to his therapist while the latter spent session after session talking to him. Then finally, one day, when the therapist walked out without his usual farewell, the patient spoke for the first time to say, "You didn't say goodbye." I differ with Fine's interpretation of this. It seems to me that the patient *was* reached. He did have a need for continued contact, and any diminishment of the experience of that little which was going on had suddenly become intolerable to him. And so he spoke up to ask that the present allotment not be curtailed or rationed further. The contact had begun to matter, but it was only because of an extended, peripheral relationship, long maintained by the therapist, that this was finally made feasible.

After the schizoid patient is more deeply into the relationship, only then can the style of relating to him be slowly shifted. With the schizoid patient, encapsulated in a shell of detachment and hermetically sealed, it is necessary for the therapist eventually to shift his style to the one he will then maintain to the end—one in which he strives to be almost exquisitely personal. The aim here is to enable the patient to become increasingly aware of his own identity and reality as a human being.[1]

Although it is most important to let any patient see that the therapist does not regard him as a "case," it is even more vital with schizoid persons. This is one of their overriding fears in the therapy relationship. It is also most important to be sure to not give any impression of probing or quizzing. Such is apt to be interpreted by them as efforts to pry into their secret fantasies or thoughts, and they are likely either to withdraw further or to back out of treatment altogether.

It is better not to use fables, proverbs or the like with a schizoid individual, but instead to couch interpretations in a form which uniquely and personally relates to just him. The style of communication should be simple, specific, and particular to this individual.[2] The aim is to put him in touch with what he feels (anger, tenderness, longing, etc.) more than why he feels it. This is what is necessary to reach across the kind of desert zone the schizoid person has established around the central stronghold of his personality, to assist thereby the individual who somewhere feels, "I am not what you think I am. I am not what *I* think I am."

DELINQUENT CHARACTER DISORDERS

In treating the patient who suffers from a character disorder, there is special difficulty. Character disorders are essentially ego-syntonic in nature; and ego-syntonic symptoms, by definition, are not experienced by the patient as an unwelcome set of traits or patterns to be discarded. Rather they are something the patient feels the need to hold on to, to preserve, to save, so that in turn it may save him.

Significant change here demands more than insight, which, however, can be the first step. The pattern of a character disorder must be demolished and a healthier pattern reconstructed. The treatment approach calls for a continual and firm unmasking and bankrupting of the character-disorder pattern, to the point where the patient experiences the meaning and destructiveness (particularly toward the self) behind what he is doing. Only then can the healthier components emerge.

How is this work begun? A young man once phoned his father, who lived in another part of the country, to explain that he had learned he was dying of a brain tumor. He explained that he had one year to live and utilized this picture of his limited future to extract money from his father for spending this "last" year in Europe in luxurious style. When he came back twelve months later, he informed his

---

[1] With this type of patient, Deri in Chapter 21 suggests that it is helpful for the analyst to couch his remarks in the words or metaphors the patient has just used. "Using the patient's words and metaphors not only facilitates recognition, but also, particularly in a schizoid patient, gives him a feeling of reality, a certification of his existence. Hearing his own words repeated by the analyst furnishes substance and reality to these words as well as to the locus of origin of these words—namely, the mental 'inside' of the patient."

[2] As examples we may recall two cited in Chapter 6: (1) the woman to whom the therapist commented that it seemed she felt anxious whenever she acted as if she wore feminine clothes, not the "torn undergarments" her mother prescribed; and (2) the man whose father had been a professional ballplayer and to whom it was interpreted that he seemed to be afraid whenever he contended with males to see who had the "more powerful bat."

father unconvincingly that a physician in Europe had brought about a "miraculous" cure, and he was joyful to report he was to live after all.

The reader may rightly wonder what brought this patient into treatment. As far as the patient was concerned, the psychopathy was not *his* problem (it never is), but he did have marital difficulties. If there was anything he wanted in the area of his psychopathic symptoms, it was not a resolving of them, but only a concealed wish to have the analyst teach him how to be more effective at it, how to accomplish his *conning* more smoothly with less chance of it boomeranging.

What I did with him was what I do with juvenile delinquents in general. I tried to "top" the patient so that he would begin to respect me within the context of his own values. Then, and only then, can the psychopathic patient be slowly led from his to the therapist's actual value system. (And let's face it, that's actually what we want to do, in spite of all that has been written in the past about the therapist not imposing his values on the patient.) In this case, health, honesty, facing the truth, the reality principle, and more constructive self-fulfillment were the values needed.

One might thus, following Aichorn's (1936) lead, tell a psychopathic character something like: "You think *you* have it made. I have a deal for life. People come and talk. I lean back in a comfortable chair. And they pay me. They don't come for weeks, but years. Unlike the average doctor or the dentist, I invest in little equipment." And so on.

There is a proportion of such patients, when the psychopathy is partial, with whom direct confrontation can be helpful. With one openly flirtatious and frankly seductive woman, after pointing out the way she always threw her skirt up when she got on the couch, the thing which worked was to call her bluff and offer her the confrontation: "I would like to see all of your thighs; why don't you lift your skirt higher?" Only that therapist can do this effectively, however, who would be comfortable with the role. Then he can say with Ferenczi, as he moved to unbutton his clothes in offering a similar confrontation to a continually seductive female, "All right, let's go." It goes without saying, of course, that this approach is recommended only when the therapist feels reasonably sure the patient is masquerading a bluff.

With the psychopathic patient, once a positive relationship is established and some desire to emulate the therapist becomes operative, interpretative confrontations then can be employed. Confrontations are helpful at this stage with character disorders in order to accomplish the task of making the ego-syntonic symptoms ego-alien. (See also Chapters 4 and 15.)

The efficacy of confrontation for moving an ego-syntonic symptom into an ego-alien position can be illustrated with the following example. A 20-year-old Jewish girl was taking drugs and dating members *only* of other races. The therapist expressed to her his sensing that she was not dating these boys *regardless* of their being Negro and Puerto Rican so much as *because of it*. It was pointed out that her need without exception to do the opposite of what her mother wanted is no more freedom than is doing exactly what one's mother wishes. This eventually enabled her to address her pattern in terms of its compulsive hold on her rather than as a reflection of merely an idealistic value system. She could then see that, quite the opposite of being free of color and religious restrictions, she was actually exerting inverse prejudice.

SPECIAL SITUATIONS AND VARYING APPROACHES

Having discussed several diagnostic types of patients requiring special approaches, we might now note that the special *situation* of a patient also, of course, warrants a shift in the therapist's stance. To restrict ourselves to just one example of this, it may be profitable to examine the situation of the "second-hand patient," the person who has previously been to one or more therapists. The term "second-hand patient" is one lately used by Marie Coleman Nelson (1965), and before her, she reports, by Oberdorf. It is used here not in any sense to denigrate this type of patient, but rather to convey *his* image of himself. Such patients often experience themselves as an unwanted or hand-me-down type of individual, not so much *because* they have gone on from one therapist to another, but because of the other arrangement of cart-and-horse. So often it is the depreciated, shabby image of themselves as unwanted which causes them to "shop around" from one therapist to another.[3] Feeling incapable of being appreciated as persons, they "quit" one therapist after another before they are "fired." They break off treatment before the therapist, they feel, will discover how awful and worthless they are, only to initiate therapy with another in the vain hopes of finding someone they can feel is *all*-accepting and *all*-loving.

With such patients, what is generally most important is for the new therapist to clarify quickly their tendency to employ various degrees or combinations of an essentially paranoid-masochistic strategy. On the paranoid side, they may (1) reject before they are rejected; they accuse and disqualify lest they be accused and disqualified. On the masochistic side, such patients may (2) defeat themselves in order to avoid expected defeat by another, or reject themselves in order to weaken the impact of rejection before it is dispensed to them; or (3) they may amass secondary gains of maintaining their role as "victims" (including the feeling of thus having earned the right to be taken care of, to have compensatory privileges and indulgences, to indict the enemy with their mute hurt, or to feel that this latest injustice scores yet another point of moral superiority over the "oppressors").

The second-hand patient might expend considerable effort to persuade the new therapist of the ineptness or even villainy of the previous one. This is done to convince himself and the current therapist that it was not the patient who was a "failure." The "mistreatment" at the hands of the former therapist(s) may have been real, or it may be a distortion by the patient, or it may have occurred but have been unconsciously stage-managed and provoked by him. Admittedly a difficult task, it is important to attempt to distill the various factors in these possibilities, to try to clarify quickly over the beginning months of the new treatment, just what the earlier treatment situation was. This problem must be given interpretive priority before distortions or provocations (if such there were) bring the new therapeutic collaboration to wreck on the same rocks.

Timing, of course, is a consideration here as elsewhere. With one patient who repeatedly maligned her first therapist, her current one waited until a situation was described by the patient in which she was being particularly "castrating" in attitude toward her husband. When, in confirmation of this, she brought forth memories of

---

[3]Many, of course, break off treatment for the more simple reason that their resistances are heightened against some threat in the analytic work, but fewer of these people then go on to a next therapist.

how she had acted similarly with other men before she was married, the therapist then related this to her possible attitude toward her previous therapist. The immediate intent, at this point, of course, was to safeguard the treatment against a repeat performance; the long-range intent was to clarify and eventually resolve this pattern in general.

Along with exploring what went wrong in the previous therapy, it is frequently necessary to correct unrealistic expectations and to orient the patient explicitly. One may have to explain to the patient why a therapist doesn't, as the previous therapist didn't, tell the patient exactly what to do—whether, for example, to move out of one's parents' house. In this instance, the patient has to be helped to grasp the point that the more ambitious goal of therapist and patient is to help the latter to learn to weigh, to reflect upon, to sense his needs, and then evolve his own decisions, rather than to be told which decision is the "right" one for him. With such patients, it frequently has to be stated specifically that *growth,* rather than *not making the wrong move,* is the central therapeutic purpose.

With the same patient mentioned above, the first treatment situation floundered, ostensibly, on the question of missed sessions. The first therapist had not charged her if her son was sick and she had to stay home on this account. But, according to the patient, this former therapist then began to doubt her and to feel she was lying when she began to use this reason more and more frequently for missing appointments. When the current therapist heard this in the first session, and the patient asked what his policy was, he stated simply that he charged for all sessions. No interpretation whatsoever was made at this point. The patient expressed thanks for the clarification of the situation and thereafter rarely missed an appointment.

Considerable opportunity should be given for catharsis regarding the previous therapist. The central temptation at this point for the current therapist to resist is one of being set up by the patient as in competition with earlier ones. The therapist may have to sense within for possible subtle signs of a desire to outshine his colleague. As the patient defines the new one as the "good parent," the therapist has to avoid being maneuvered, for this reason, into being "more giving" than the one before.

In terms of frequency of interpretation, by and large the second-hand patient has been interpreted to enough, but he may not have experienced enough in therapy. Therefore, the current therapist might use his understanding of what is going on to define how he might *react* to the patient, rather than risk overinterpreting to him. The therapist frequently experiences a tendency to react in an opposite way to the manner in which the previous therapist handled the patient. That is, if the earlier therapist was said to talk too much, the current therapist tends to talk less than he ordinarily does. If the complaint was that the first therapist was "too silent," the current therapist finds himself less silent than usual. Here, *to a degree,* the feelings of the therapist are not inappropriate, and the relationship which then evolves between patient and new therapist is often workable. What is important is that the manner of the new therapist not be such that the patient take it as merely an extension of that of the old. Further into the middle phase of the collaboration, of course, this leaning over backward to be sure that one is different from the previous therapist has to be broken away from. Then the previous complications are to be analyzed as they begin slowly to reappear when the therapist no longer operates in an antithetical style to the earlier one.

One second-hand patient, Martin Bergmann (1965) reports, had broken off treatment in the midst of a transference neurosis, telling her first analyst, "It was just my luck to find the one analyst in the city who is *just* the way my father is." While it is remotely possible that he was so totally like her father, the probability is that the observing functions of the patient's ego had lost distance from or been submerged in the experiencing ego. The feeling of "I feel as if you are like my father" gave way to "You are exactly like my father." With such a patient, particularly, the new therapist has to be sure that traits which may be somewhat similar to those of the previous therapist or to those of the patient's parent be played down initially, and that their opposites, if they exist in the therapist, be brought relatively forward. This can be done only to a limited degree without seeming phoney, and usually only for a certain time. It should, of course, not be pushed past the limits of authenticity.

With patients who have hopped back and forth between other therapists and one particular therapist, it is appropriate to set firm limits. One patient returned to his initial therapist for the third time, after trying two others in between. With him the rule was set that this would be the last time he would be accepted back, that it was a case of either settling down to finish the treatment, or leaving for good. This time, under such structuring, he was able to make a go of the treatment.

If a patient, after an apparently long and deep analysis with someone else still remains quite neurotic, terminates with that person and comes to me, with whom he is then "cured" in a relatively short time, my self-congratulations are muted by a certain reality. The reality is that the patient, often to spite the first therapist with whom the negative transference had not been sufficiently analyzed, now has been motivated to progress mostly *to show* him. In such instances it is wise to attempt to maintain the patient in treatment after "cure" appears to have been attained, for clinical experience is that what has occurred is predominantly a transference cure and not reliable in terms of permanency.

MODIFICATIONS OF SESSION LENGTH

There is one last type of modification we might consider here: one involving the *length* of the standard therapy session (Hammer, 1965). In terms of frequency of session, we have inaugurated various modifications of the classic model of five or six sessions a week, but in terms of the 45- or 50-minute "hour" there seems to have been little experimentation other than that of the reduction to a 30-minute hour offered by clinics in the interests of economy. In the field of pharmaceuticals or of x-ray treatment, we find that dosage is tailored to the needs of the individual patient. In our field, however, for some strange reason we give the same length of session to all patients regardless of their diagnosis, age, or other variables.

To mention but two proposed exceptions, my experience is that (1) extending the time to a 75-minute "hour" for obsessional patients and (2) reducing the time to a 30-minute "hour" for a specific type of adolescent patient tend to produce better results than does the more usual session. The 30-minute session was inaugurated with one unreflective adolescent boy, possessed of a relatively barren inner life, who would continually run dry half-way through the time. What was tried was a splitting up of his hour into two 30-minute sessions during the week. The results were heartening. Continuity was improved, the relationship "took," and now in place of one half-usable session there were two usable ones.

The last 20 or 25 minutes of the original session had become a period that degenerated to strained clock-watching by the patient, and an undoing of a good deal of the relationship achieved (and having to be rebuilt) in the first portion of each session. The change, however, moved us away from the mounting danger that this boy would break off his treatment. Adolescents, being too old for play techniques and frequently too young for verbalizing at length, are one group for whom the shortened session frequently works more effectively.

This is not to deny that for some of the adolescent patients it isn't preferable to keep them in the longer, for them more painful, session, utilizing the stress period as grist for the therapeutic process and thereby attempting to work out the difficulty. With others, however, this begins to emerge as a losing battle, and it may be advantageous to think of variability in session length as one of the tools in the therapist's armamentarium.

With the obsessional adult patient, just as he begins to break through the crust of his intellectualized, unemotional rationality—a crust developed to control and hide the impulses and throb of life within—the usual standard session ends. It takes this full session to thaw out the obsessional's cool, affectless defense and just begin to get to the person beneath. By working with this type of patient for a longer time at each sitting (my practice is to use a double 45-minute session), we may note that his ordinarily guarded prognosis is generally improved.[4]

Goldfarb and Turner (1958) and Wolk (1967) report positive results when the length of sessions was altered with geriatric patients, some requiring longer sessions and some being more comfortable and less anxious with shorter.

SUMMARY

Varying therapeutic approaches suggested by the personality integration of different types of patients were discussed. With the obsessive-compulsive, consideration was given to emotional encounters, the use of images in interpreting, evocativeness in terms of freshness of the therapist's language and voice quality, and group therapy; with the depressive—the use of humor, the offering of oral gratification, telling the patient how depressed he is so he might ease off demonstrating it, and indirect catharsis; with the paranoid and the masochistic—the use of fables, proverbs, and generalities, avoidance of direct interpreting of waiting room behavior, and a sharing with the paranoid patient of the steps along the way of an interpretive inference; with the schizoid—a long initial phase devoted predominantly to the impersonal, and then eventually a gradual shift to the personal, the specific, and (avoiding fables and generalities) the unique in the patient, all guided by an intent to assist him to get in touch with what he feels more than why he feels it; and with the character disorders of psychopathic leanings—the direct use of confrontations, the use of interpretations designed to enable ego-syntonic symptoms to become ego-alien, and simultaneously a strategy of "topping" the patient in order to encourage identification and a desire to emulate and learn from the therapist.

Special situations also require modification of approach. This was discussed with

---

[4]The possibility that the patient is manifesting treatment rather than characterological resistance should always first be considered and explored. If such turns out to be the case, there is certainly a question, of course, about whether altering the session time is the most effective way of handling it.

the situation of the "second-hand patient" serving as illustration. Perhaps, too, it is time to recognize that there is nothing sacrosanct about the 45- or 50-minute "hour."

What is here proposed is a search for guidelines which can serve to orient us, as therapists, to one approach working better with one type of patient or situation and another with others. Thus, the therapist may be oriented the better to relate to—and in relating, to honor—both the diversity among patients and the particular, dominant psychic constellation in the individual patient.

REFERENCES

Aichorn, A., *Wayward youth.* London: Putnam, 1936.

Appelbaum, S. A., Speaking with the second voice: Evocativeness. *J. Amer. Psychoanal. Ass.,* 1966, 14, 462-477.

Bellak, L., In Bychowsky, G., and Despert, J. L. (Eds.), *Specialized techniques in psycho-therapy.* New York: Basic Books, 1953.

Bergmann, M., Professional Meeting, National Psychological Association for Psychoanalysis, New York City, 1965.

Bogard, H. M., Psychotherapists reactions to suicidal patients. *Prof. Dig., N.Y. Soc. Clin. Psychol.* 1967, 2, 6-9.

Butler, J., On the naturalistic definition of variables: an analogue of clinical analysis. *Res. Psychother.* 1962, 2, 178-205.

Choron, J., Suicide and the meaning of life. New York Society of Clinical Psychologists symposium, "Suicide: Its Meaning and Implications," New York City, March 24, 1967.

Federn, P., *Ego psychology and the psychoses.* New York: Basic Books, 1952.

Fenichel, O., *Psychoanalytic theory of neurosis.* New York: W. W. Norton and Co., 1945.

Fisher, K. A., Psychotherapy as play. *Arts & Sciences, N. Y. U. Bull.* 1966, 66, 28-33.

Fromm-Reichmann, Frieda, *Principles of intensive psychotherapy.* Chicago: The University of Chicago Press, 1950.

Goldfarb, A. A., and Turner, H., II, Utilization and effectiveness of "brief therapy." *Amer. J. Psychiat.,* 1953, 109, 792-799.

Hammer, E. F., President's column: Of diagnosis, research, and the therapy hour. *N. Y. Soc. Clin. Psychol. Newsletter,* 1965, 13, 1-2.

Nelson, Marie C., Symposium on "Second-Hand Patient," New York Society of Clinical Psychologists meeting, 1965.

Nydes, J., Personal communication, 1965.

——, Interpretation and the therapeutic act. In Hammer, this book, 1968.

Reik, T., Personal communication, 1963.

Sharpe, E. F., *Dream analysis.* London: Hogarth Press, 1951.

Tirnauer, L., Notes for a happy psychotherapy. *Voices.* 1967, 3, 63-64.

Wolk, R. L., The Kernal interview. *J. Long Island Consult. Cent.* 1967, 5, 45-51.

CHAPTER 24

Two Proposed Alternatives to Psychoanalytic Interpreting

Harry Bone, Ph.D.

"Harry Bone was born in 1899 in Topeka, Kansas. His father was a lawyer and politician, earthy, quick-witted and humorous, who gave Harry too little attention. His mother, who was educationally limited like her neighbors, was a definite personality, true to her code and a loyal wife and mother, who gave Harry too much attention. Like everyone, they did the best they could and, in addition to receiving life from them, their son and daughter were more fortunate in them than otherwise.

"At adolescence the boy had an intense religious experience which did him so much good and so much harm that, to this day, he cannot evaluate it definitively. It had two permanent values for him. One was acquaintance with the Bible (that paradigm of human experience and one of the taproots of Western civilization regarding which many therapists, both Jewish and Christian, seem to be illiterate). The other was his introduction to the social facts of life under the influence of Socialist associates in the Student Christian Movement. In 1920 a brilliant teacher, Karl Menninger, who taught a few courses at Washburn College in Topeka, mediated to him the Freudian Enlightenment.

"Too nonconformist for a religious vocation, whether Christian, Freudian or Marxist, he went to Paris to be analysed by Otto Rank. He had two other reasons for going to France. He was 33 and he thought he could get a doctorate more easily there than in the United States—even though he had to learn a foreign language (at which he was not apt) in the process. And he had observed that people who have lived in more than one culture are likely to be less provincial than stay-at-homes.

"He considers that his chief resources as a therapist stem from having lived and worked at various jobs with all kinds of people in different localities, and from the partial success he has had in overcoming his originally severe personality conflicts. Like everybody he is full of contradictions, but both his assets and liabilities are greater than average. He is somewhat detached and not highly social, but he has an elemental respect for everybody and he greatly enjoys some people. He is over-sympathetic with the underdog and those under authority (for "the superior virtue of the dispossessed" is an illusion), and this trait has made him a headache to colleagues who have carried more responsibility for organizational functioning. In spite of his generally mild manner he has a tough, logical mind, which is sometimes capable of bright insights. He has enough culture to know that his own is not very broad or deep. Very fearful in the past, he is no longer intimidated by anyone. Once moth-eaten with anxiety, he now enjoys considerable serenity. He is incredibly inefficient. His obsessional slowness is an exasperation to his friends and intimates. He took so long to write the present paper that he will probably never write another—out of consideration for his tolerant, loving wife, Virginia.

"His penchant for heresy sometimes lands him on the beach, and sometimes enables him to enjoy the wave of the future before it has fully arrived. (He expects that the somewhat unconventional commitments in his current essay will be an instance of the latter.) He is spiritually as well as literally left-handed, a condition he attributes partly to his anatomical dysplasia (left-sided dominance), and partly to the severity of his struggle for autonomy. His friend and colleague, Erich

Fromm—to whom he owes much, including encouragement to think independently —was especially helpful when he reassured him that his style was "slow growth." As a 1-1-7 ectomorph he has found (as Sheldon would predict) each decade of his life more satisfactory than the preceding one. In view of the gross injustice, from the human point of view, of nature and circumstance, he considers himself an exceptionally fortunate human. A current major satisfaction is fathering his third daughter, Wendy, who has just turned four.

"Unidealized as this biographical sketch is, it is probably unduly flattering since it is autobiographical, having been written by the subject himself."

The editor would like to add that Dr. Bone is a Training and Supervising therapist at both the Postgraduate Program at New York University and at the William A. White Institute of Psychiatry, Psychoanalysis, and Psychology. Harry Bone ranges in his presentation below to include a comparative evaluation of three major schools of therapy. In addition to breadth, there is a profundity in what follows below; Dr. Bone touches upon the philosophical depths beneath the issues of therapy and technique.

Interpreting is the chief function of the therapist in most systems of psychotherapy. Psychoanalysis, in which it is the *sine qua non* of technique, has brought it to its fullest and most refined development. My contribution to this volume will be to compare psychoanalysis with two other therapies, each of which offers an alternative, or functional equivalent, to the psychoanalytic interpretive procedure. Before discussing any of the three therapies, however, I wish to present a general context for my *essai.*

The purpose of psychotherapy is change—change in a person's living through change in his experience of himself and his world. It is generally agreed that in the therapeutic process the therapist and the person are co-agents, that the therapeutic agency resides partially in each of them. Therapists differ, however, in their conceptions of the respective tasks of the two co-agents, in their conceptions of the kind and degree of initiative and responsibility which each of the two parties to the enterprise can and should assume. No therapist does everything, and no therapist requires or permits the patient or client to do everything, but between these (nonexistent, heuristic) extremes there is a continuum from predominant emphasis on therapist-initiative to predominant emphasis on patient- or client-initiative. *Helping the other person,* and *helping him to help himself,* are distinguishable therapist functions which may be combined in various ways and proportions. A few clinical examples will illustrate what I have in mind.

1. A client enters, highly agitated, and tells the therapist he wants to be hospitalized —he is now convinced that he is really insane. *Therapist:* "What makes you think so?" *Client:* "When I went into my apartment this afternoon, I had a feeling that an enemy was in hiding there. I had to look in all the closets. Of course I found no one, but the feeling persisted. That's *crazy!*" The therapist, knowing that the client had fears of injuring himself by his compulsive sexual solitaire, said: "It seems to me that your perception was essentially correct, that there *was* an enemy in your apartment—as soon as you entered it. Something that is going on between you and yourself was experienced by you as going on between you and somebody else."

2. A man who, after a traumatic experience, was overtaken by paralysis of both legs, was taken to Otto Rank in Paris. *Patient:* "I didn't ask to be brought here—you can't help me." *Rank:* "Well, since you're here you might as well tell me what happened." *Patient:* "There's nothing to tell except what my relatives have probably told you. Five of us tried to get out of Nazi Germany into Switzerland. The others were all caught. Only I escaped." *Rank:* "But you didn't."

3. A patient of Harry Stack Sullivan recounted a dream. "I was in lovely rural country, admiring a beautiful old-fashioned, wind-propelled flour mill. Then I was inside, and I found the machinery dilapidated, rusty and covered with cobwebs." Sullivan abstracted the dream: "Outside, very impressive; inside, not much use." The patient exclaimed, "Mother!"

4. A woman client was full of antipathy to men in general and to her husband in particular. She said: "It isn't fair! A woman's brains are as good as a man's but *he* can have a profession and a home; *she* has to sacrifice one or the other. Men have all the fun while women have to bear children in pain and at the risk of their lives." (More of the same for twenty minutes.) The therapist, without approval, disapproval, evaluation or interpretation, consistently gave her evidence that he was understandingly with her in what she was feeling. Her tirade reached a crescendo and collapsed of its own weight.

None of the foregoing examples is intended to illustrate any of the three therapies on which we shall focus, though example 4 is a suggestive example of client-centered therapy.

[NOTE:— Probably the most extreme instances (also not included) of *helping the person* (as distinguished from *helping him to help himself*) are provided by the various therapies which deny or minimize the importance, for personality change, of the person's own *awareness,* or which accept behavioral change in place of, or as a sign of, personality change. I am not well acquainted with them and I have an *a priori* prejudice against them because their manipulative style is uncongenial to my philosophy of man. However, their reports of striking results and their enthusiastic reception by not a few therapists call for more study of them than I have yet given them. (In Jay Haley's brilliant—perhaps too brilliant—*Strategies of Psychotherapy* (Haley, 1963) the paradoxes often seem to me more cleverly verbal than actual.)

The practitioners of these forms of therapy admit frankly that they are manipulative, but they claim that all therapies are manipulative, whether admittedly or not. If any effect one person has on another were tantamount to "manipulation," one would have to agree. But surely it is important to distinguish between influencing a person (behind his back, as it were) to change in a way that the therapist has previously decided would be desirable for him and, on the other hand, providing a person with a context in which he can find his own path. The former may solve a problem for him; the latter envisions his becoming a problem solver.]

The first of the foregoing clinical examples is a pure instance of direct *helping* by interpreting the patient to himself. The fourth example is a pure instance of *helping the client to help herself* by providing a favorable context for her to achieve her own "self-interpretation". The Rank slice of therapy illustrates interpretation by the therapist, but interpretation of such a nature that the creative activity of the patient is permitted and required. The Sullivan example is an instance of "setting the stage" for the patient's initiative; it is not necessarily a "leading" procedure in which the patient is subtly directed to a realization that has already occurred to the therapist: a therapist may abstract a dream from its latent content without knowing what the patient will come up with.

All of the procedures illustrated are, in my opinion, just so many methods of *interpretation* (Example 1), or its functional equivalent, therapist-facilitated *self-interpretation* (Example 4), or some *combination* of the two (Examples 2 and 3).

In all cases the purpose is the same—to increase the person's effective experience of himself and his world.

Psychoanalytic interpretation is too complex to be exemplified in capsule form, but its essence may be briefly indicated. Louis Paul says: "The source of clinical-interpretation statements and all therapeutic interventions is the *psychoanalytic appraisal,* the unspoken assessment of the analytic situation which the analyst has more or less formed in his mind" (Paul, 1963, p. 249). In other words, the analyst comes progressively to understand the patient and, periodically, tactfully reveals him to himself. He is occupied with preparing the patient for his interpretations and with the *what, when,* and *how* of interpreting. Thus emphasis is predominantly on the analyst's *interpretations* and the patient's *acceptance* of them, which must be demonstrably genuine. Primacy is given to *helping.*

CLIENT-CENTERED THERAPY

In terms of the suggested continuum, psychoanalysis gives relatively greater emphasis to the analyst's initiative and responsibility. The client-centered therapy of Carl Rogers, the first of the two proposed alternatives we shall consider, gives relatively greater emphasis to the client's initiative and responsibility. [NOTE:—The following opinions are strictly personal; they are not necessarily those of anyone else in either of the two training schools with which I am connected. Furthermore, as regards client-centered therapy, I do not wish to appear in the light of an unsolicited and embarrassing spokesman. Rogers and his associates have not expressed opinions on many of the matters I shall discuss; in these matters I do not presume to speak for them.]

It would be a misleading oversimplification to say that psychoanalysis espouses *interpretation* and that client-centered therapy repudiates it. The phrases "interpretation by the analyst" and "therapist-facilitated self-interpretation by the client" require explication. Psychoanalytic and client-centered procedures have more in common than is generally recognized, and it may be well to begin with their conjunctive aspects so that when the differences are specified, they will be real, not merely apparent, differences. Now *empathic understanding by the therapist of the patient's or client's inner world is considered indispensable by both systems.* Fenichel (1945) has said: "Since interpretation means something unconscious becomes conscious by naming it at the moment it is striving to break through, effective interpretations can be given only at one specific point, namely, where the patient's immediate interest is momentarily centered."

Rogers, commenting on this statement, says: "The client-centered therapist works somewhat similarly. He does not merely repeat his client's words, concepts, or feelings. Rather, he seeks for the meaning implicit in the present inner experiencing toward which the client's words or concepts point. As Gendlin has put it: 'The client-centered response at its best formulates something which is not yet fully formulated or conceptualized. . . . It formulates the meaning which the client has not yet symbolized explicitly but which he does now feel and which is implied in what he says. Sometimes it formulates the felt whole which the client has been trying to get at by various verbalizations' " (Rogers, in Arieti, 1966, p. 190).

Fromm, whose version of psychoanalysis is an extensive revision of the standard doctrine, states his position as follows (Evans, 1966, p. 46):

Unlike the Freudian analyst, I must feel within myself what the patient is talking about before I have any real understanding of the patient as a person. The patient himself may not be aware of what he is saying, but I must feel it. This is what you might call a humanistic premise: that there is nothing human which is alien to me. Everything is in me: I am a little child, I'm a grown-up, I'm a murderer, and I'm a saint; I'm narcissistic, and I'm destructive. There is nothing in the patient which I do not have in me. And only insofar as I can muster within myself those experiences about which the patient is telling me either explicitly or implicitly, only if they arouse an echo within myself, can I know what the patient is talking about and give back to him what he's really saying. [It then happens that] the patient . . . does not feel that . . . I'm talking down to him—instead he feels that I'm talking about something we both share.

While Fromm thus disagrees with Freudian analysts, he also disagrees with Rogers because, he says, "the client-centered therapist becomes a sort of mirror to reflect the patient to himself, rather than interpreting his behavior for him" (Evans, *ibid.,* p. 34).

But "reflecting," in client-centered therapy, is not as radically different from "interpreting" as Fromm assumes it to be. The client-centered therapist *verbalizes* (symbolizes, formulates, conceptualizes) what he believes the client is *feeling,* some aspects of which the client cannot fully verbalize. Since the therapist does not depart from the client's feelings, since he does not attribute to him any feeling that the client is not *experiencing,* he may be said merely *to reflect* the client's *feelings.* But since the therapist helps the client to *become more fully aware of what he is feeling* by verbalizing more than the client has *verbalized,* he may be said to be *interpreting.* Like Fromm he reflects or "gives back to him what he's really saying."

[NOTE:— An unclarified issue is involved here. There is much we don't know about the nature of unconscious experience before it becomes conscious. (Various authors list from eight to 16 definitions of "unconscious" which are not exclusive of each other.) Is the unconscious "physiological" or "psychological"—or something that escapes our dualistic mind-body concepts? Gendlin is contributing fruitfully to this important issue (Gendlin, 1962).]

In sum: Fromm's and Rogers' "interpreting" have much in common; and there is less difference than is often supposed, in regard to "interpreting", between the standard psychoanalysis of Fenichel and client-centered therapy.

Other changes in both therapies over the years have reduced the disparities between them. Originally Freud and Rogers represented, respectively, minimal and maximal estimates of the general human potentiality for autonomy and self-direction. Such estimates ultimately determine one's views regarding what the analyst must do for the patient, and what the client can do for himself, given an optimal context for his initiative.

[NOTE:— This is not a moral issue. It is not a disagreement between "bad misanthropic therapists who do not believe in man" and "good philanthropic therapists who do believe in man." There is no more virtue in overestimating human nature than in underestimating it. Rather, the problem is one of accurate assessment, which will be progressively established as we become increasingly able to determine the respective consequences of acting on these different estimates of human potentialities. This raises the question of the applicability of science to the therapeutic process (it will receive attention later).]

Psychoanalysis (as represented by ego analysts, among others) and client-centered therapy have both qualified somewhat their original estimates of individual autonomy. The following quotations will indicate recent modifications in client-centered procedure.

In explanation of his "unorthodox" responses to "Mr. Vac," Rogers says: "The responses are clearly client-centered in their respect for the person of the client, but the categories are no longer those of the earlier period of concern with standardized technique" (Rogers, in Arieti, 1966, p. 190). "Along with the recent stress on the importance of the therapist's genuineness, has come a corresponding divergence in method among client-centered therapists. . . ." As our interest has turned "from a central preoccupation with the technical problem of getting inside the client's frame of reference to the broader concern that the therapist use his whole person in the relationship, we have moved toward a greater variety of techniques among individual therapists" (*Ibid.*, p. 188). "It is helpful to be genuine even when negative feelings toward the client are involved"—not as good as not having negative feelings but better than hiding them if they do occur (*Ibid.*, p. 185). With some schizophrenic clients, especially at the beginning, "a conditional regard may be more effective" than unconditional regard. "This [very tentative] speculation is an example of the way in which our theoretical formulations have at times changed on the basis of more complete experience" (*Ibid.*, p. 186).

"Some of our therapists go further in their behavior. One in particular is moving more and more toward allying himself with the hidden and unrevealed person in the schizophrenic, and openly 'clobbering' the defensive shell. In his work there is a real similarity to Rosen and Whitaker. He is sensitively and obviously committed to the person who is in hiding but he is quite violently and sometimes sarcastically critical of the psychotic symptoms, the fear of relating, the defenses and avoidances. Perhaps partly because this approach is congenial to him as a person, he is finding it effective. As we listen to the recorded interviews of the various therapists in our group, we are gradually broadening the repertoire of behaviors which are real for each of us in dealing with our psychotic clients, and we are slowly hammering out ways of facilitating movement in the unmotivated person" (Goldstein and Dean, 1966, p. 10).

In sum, client-centered therapy has qualified somewhat its former extremely high estimate of the client's capacity for autonomy; the therapist is more self-expressive in the relationship as a separate person: he is not exclusively an *alter ego* of the client; he does somewhat more *helping*; and at least one client-centered therapist attacks the client's defenses vigorously. These developments are limited and tentative and should not be exaggerated, but they nevertheless tend to reduce the disparity between client-centered therapy and most other therapies, including psychoanalysis.

Having noted the similarities, we now turn to the disagreements between psychoanalysis and client-centered therapy. We will be occupied predominantly with an interpretive exposition of the latter since it is not only less well known, but when it is known it is often seriously misconstrued. [NOTE:— As far as I know, in no psychoanalytic training center are the candidates, either M.D. or Ph.D., officially exposed to it. This practice is contrary to Rogers' own principles. He says that in this time of confusing but fertile proliferation of therapeutic procedures, any training center which taught only client-centered therapy would be seriously depriving its students. Furthermore, many Ph.D.'s who studied it during their doctoral years do not understand it, as my supervisory experience has taught me.]

The unique features which, 25 years ago, made "nondirective therapy" (as it was then called) a radical departure from all existing therapies still essentially characterize client-centered therapy today. In the first book-length presentation of his viewpoint (Rogers, 1942), the main features of psychoanalysis were conspicuous by their absence. There was no diagnosis, no treatment plan, no *basic rule* of *free association,* no induction of a "transference neurosis" and the analysis of it, no analysis of resistance or of dreams ("the royal road to the unconscious") and no interpretation, reassurance, philosophical guidance or termination-timing by the therapist. The function of the therapist was, almost exclusively, to "reflect" the client's momentary felt experience. The "incredibility" of Rogers' proposal does not *ipso facto* invalidate it. All systems of knowledge progress partly by developing the implications of their basic assumptions and partly by a periodic more or less radical, revision of their basic assumptions.

L. L. Whyte has said, "Discoveries in physics fall into two classes; those that produce delighted surprise by confirming in some unexpected manner ideas that have already become familiar, and those that at first appear incredible or intellectually shocking to the majority of competent physicists because they refute principles that are still taken for granted. . . . The big pause that has occurred in relation to [a certain fundamental problem] suggests that some mental block, in the form of a deep-lying traditional assumption . . . must be preventing a more rapid advance. . . . Only one thing is certain regarding the next major step: it will present a shock to minds trained to accept existing methods as absolute" (Whyte, 1961, pp. 94-96). In 1945 Brock Chisholm (1946), in view of the insanity of the Second World War, and with the hearty endorsement of Harry Stack Sullivan, bade us call in question *every thing we have believed* (my italics).

Gardner Murphy has reminded us that three centuries ago Robert Boyle, in "The Sceptical Chymist," showed his overconfident colleagues that they "had established no firm basis, not even a method for achieving such a basis, for a new science" (Murphy, 1947, p. 914). In the role of "skeptical psychologist" Murphy refers to a number of well-known scientific revolutions, including the revolution in psychiatry precipitated by Freud. He then says: "Despite all these lessons, we write and speak today as if at last the full context and stature of man were known. But like our predecessors, we shall rectify mistakes not primarily by the minor readjustment of the lines of the argument but by recognition of the fundamental limitations of *the whole present system of conceptions* [italics mine]. It is preparation for this destruction and rebirth of knowledge to which serious research should be directed" (*Ibid.,* p. 927). Murphy says further: "The abyss of our ignorance cannot be spanned by philosophies of human nature, however profound. The scientific method has begun to take shape and it will be heard. Although not ready today, eventually it will be ready to integrate with older insights of an intuitive or poetic sort, which, though pointing the way, will reach effectively into the unknown only when supported by the methods of a future science" (*Ibid.,* p. 925).

In my opinion, client-centered therapy is one of those fundamental reorientations of knowledge, the most seminal contribution to psychotherapy since Freud's. For it has given evidence of achieving, more effectively and economically, a central aim of its predecessor, that of radically expanding the patient's self-experience and thus enabling him to change his living. This is accomplished by the apparently simple and innocent therapist-activity of entering empathically into the phenomenal world of the client, and convincing the client that he is actually doing this—a procedure often referred to as "reflecting his feelings". This procedure does not produce an exhaustive, objective, research knowledge of the personality of the client; but it does elicit those past and present experiences that are pertinent to constructive personality change.

The naturally integrative mental processes, which Freud tapped by his *free association* technique, are activated without imposition of the *basic rule*. No inclusive heap of unweighted "archeological" findings is desired or acquired, but the client's significant early experiences are automatically selected (by the client's "unconscious") for emergence into awareness when and as the client is able to deal with them. Dreams sometimes occur, unasked for by the therapist, and advance the process. Intense *transference* phenomena are rare but, when they do occur, are more amenable to constructive resolution than by traditional methods. (For an example see the case of "Miss Tir," Rogers, 1951, p. 210.) The necessary reassurance and guidance are provided by the client himself. The client knows within himself when to terminate, when he has gotten all that he can take of what he wants—and when to return later, if necessary. In this therapy the first feeble, sporadic, awkward, distorted expressions of egoism and altruism are considered to be the raw material of the responsible autonomy that is the goal of the therapy. Acceptance of them, by nonevaluative reflecting, from the beginning of therapy, is considered the necessary and sufficient means for their transformation (concomitant individualization *and* socialization).

At a professional society meeting many years ago Sullivan made a remark that has stayed with me. The topic of the evening was, "How can psychotherapy be made more effective and more economical of time?" Several participants related experiences of unusual effectiveness and speed in their work, but invariably they expressed doubts about the validity of these experiences—that maybe they were "transference cures," or maybe they were "flights into health." Finally Ben Weininger told of a schizophrenic boy who had made phenomenal progress in a relatively short time. Sullivan asked him, "Do you believe it was real?" Weininger answered, "Yes." Sullivan said, "Thank God, somebody believes in what he is doing." The group was skeptical: "But *that much* can't happen in *that short a time*," they said. Sullivan responded, "I would agree with you if we really knew how much of any 'therapeutic' hour is genuinely therapeutic."

I believe that client-centered therapy has greatly contributed to the problem of effectiveness and speed. (See Rogers' case, which is far from typical but nevertheless instructive, of basic personality change in eight sessions; Rogers, 1951, pp. 88-130.) After all, what could be more likely to maximize therapeutic effectiveness than for the therapist to connect continuously with the ongoing, underlying current of feeling in the other person? In that current are the sources and issues of the person's life. If the therapist accepts it, *as it is* (which the client does not do except selectively and partially), he will not be kept out. If he does not *have* to help the client in order to avoid a feeling of impotence, if he does not try to change his feelings except to help the person become more aware of them, they will change of themselves, autonomously, from the inside. Furthermore, the client will be experiencing the most basic of the satisfactions that humans can experience, in therapy or out—that of *being oneself* and *being related,* simultaneously.

If Rogers did have a contribution to make toward Sullivan's quest for greater effectiveness and economy of time, Sullivan did not hear it. He once said (in a seminar, in criticism of client-centered therapy, without naming it), "When a person goes to an expert, he has a right to expect expertness." In other words, for Sullivan therapeutic expertness meant understanding the patient in an objective framework (meaning: the therapist's presumably objective subjectivity) and bringing the patient to self-understanding through this means. He could not conceive of a different kind of expertness, one that "merely" imaginatively empathizes with the patient's subjective world. Nor could he conceive that such a procedure could enable the patient to do for himself what it is assumed that only the "expert" can do for him.

Anyone who thinks that expertness of this sort is not exacting should try it; actually it requires all the understanding of oneself and of human experience that one can bring to it, and (until it becomes natural) severe self-discipline.

[NOTE:— George Lyman Kittredge said, in his Harvard address on Shakespeare, that sympathetic knowledge of human nature and the gift of expression are rarely found together. "Shakspere (sic)," however, "could enter . . . into the thoughts and feelings of a wide range of human beings . . . and then he could make them speak . . . as they would have spoken if they had been Shakespeare. That [with the gift of the poet and the craft of the playwright] is all there is to Shakespeare". Empathy with the felt experiencing of the client and expression of it (effectiveness in which requires genuineness and unconditional positive regard) is about all there is to client-centered therapy.]

Just what is it that Rogers discovered? For myself, I put it as follows: He discovered that, in spite of discouraging appearances to the contrary, most people have a powerful, inherent, "autotherapeutic" urge toward maximal personal development, and that it tends to become actualized in a specifiable kind of interpersonal environment. He discovered that unconditional acceptance (or unconditional positive regard), made convincing by the therapist's nonevaluative verbalized empathy with the client's subjective experiencing, enables the client (more satisfactorily than hypnosis, free association, tactful interpreting, permissiveness, encouraging reassurance, "parental" guidance or drugs) to communicate freely with the therapist and with himself—the last of which is the precondition of everything desirable that is possible, psychologically.

I consider myself very fortunate in having learned fairly early in my career that potential self-direction may hide in the most unlikely places. I had a client who would have been diagnosed as extremely morbidly dependent. He was a theological student who, after mother, had had an unbroken series of helpful minister's wives to run his life for him. At the beginning he presented me with two "dilemmas": should he go home over Thanksgiving? and should he sell his bicycle? Without excessive confidence in my principles, I nevertheless resisted his urgent demand for my opinion and consistently conveyed my understanding of his feelings. He went along with this for a while, but when he realized it was not merely preliminary to my eventually giving him the answer, he issued an ultimatum. "I'm asking you what *you* would do." I answered, "I would gladly tell you what to do if I could believe that there is a right decision apart from your ability to make it—and if I knew what that right decision is. But, frankly, I haven't found it really helpful to tell a sane, intelligent adult what to do." He immediately relaxed, became sober, and said quietly, "I can see that." (After all, his own experience had long been trying to teach him that unwelcome truth.) A few sessions later the "computer" in his skull was clicking in a way that made me blink. He was registering and processing the pertinent data and he ended by resolving his "dilemmas." The payoff is that the *way* he resolved them would never have occurred to me!

Client-centered therapy, in spite of its apparent (and in some respects real) simplicity, is widely misconceived. According to my observation there are seven reasons for this, two of which have been discussed: (1) its sharp departure from principles generally taken for granted as permanently established, and (2) the erroneous belief that the client-centered therapist gives back or reflects only the *verbalized* feelings of the client. I wish to comment on the remaining five: (3) the assumption of its limited applicability, (4) the belief that it is "too soft," (5) the idea that it overestimates the client's capacities, (6) its unconventional picture of the end-product of therapy, and (7) the assumption that its scientific self-testing is ill advised or unnecessary.

Reason 3. Robert Harper (1959, p. 146) is not alone in his opinion that this therapy may be effective "with some *slightly* disturbed patients and even with some categories of severely disturbed patients"—though even *these* need something more (see 5 below). Research on client-centered therapy with schizophrenics (the most impressive instances of which postdate Harper's observation) are convincing indications of its very wide applicability (Rogers et al., 1967). I believe it has not often been used with mental defectives.

Reason 4. Harper (1959, p. 147) also speaks for many others when he says: "The person who experiences an approximation of unconditional positive regard and empathic understanding of all his characteristics is getting the closest he will ever get in adult life to the completely satisfying, undemanding environment of prenatal life." [NOTE:— Actually the idea of therapy as a provisional psychological womb is a rather helpful metaphor—if one does not latch onto only one aspect of it. The literal womb provides the zygote with the conditions necessary for the accomplishment of its incredible task. True, the task is unconsciously fulfilled, but just as unconsciously are the privileges "enjoyed." As Bernard Shaw has said, we never again manage our lives as well as during our first nine months. Undoubtedly the reason is that at that time "the wisdom of the organism" meets with no outside interference—"help" or hindrance. And the aim of client-centered therapy is precisely to enable the client to utilize, for *post partum* living, this very "wisdom of the organism," or "organismic sensing." But more to the point, no doubt, are the clinical facts.]

The voluminous verbatim reports of client-centered therapy do indeed reveal a striking dearth of those violent conflicts between patient and therapist which many believe to be indispensable for deep therapy, but they also clearly reveal rigors for the client of a different sort. The client-centered axiom, "No tension, no therapy," is amply illustrated. Both the bitter and the sweet issue from the therapist's allowance and requirement of virtually complete freedom and virtually complete responsibility on the part of the client. Clients are naturally deeply gratified at not being diagnosed or educated, but they find the hardships of freedom and of responsibility —which they quite promptly become aware of—something they would prefer to escape from. A client of mine once said, "You have a reputation for being soft, but I find you damned hard; I have to make my decisions on my own and I can't blame the consequences on anybody else." In this respect client-centered therapy treats the client exactly as the universe treats all of us: we may do anything we want to but we cannot escape the consequences of our actions.

Harper's failure to recognize the rigors involved in this "womb-like" therapy is eloquent evidence of the extent to which client-centered therapy is misconceived, for Harper generally has an objective and penetrating appreciation of all the therapies. In his unrivaled compendium (Harper, 1959), he obviously makes a strenuous attempt to be just to those therapies, such as client-centered therapy, which are personally uncongenial to him. His illuminating insights regarding the cultural and personal matrix of Rogers' achievement, and its significance in the current history of psychotherapy, are well worth consideration.

Reason 5. Does client-centered therapy overestimate the capacity of the neurotic for self-direction? Not, I believe when he is given a proper interpersonal context for his initiative; in that context his initiative tends to expand. Rogers is not unique in this assumption—Goldstein and others also share this view. The predominant opinion is well stated by Harper (1959, p. 147):

To a considerable degree . . . acceptance and reassurance may be considered helpful *pre*-conditions to the serious, often cognitive, sometimes directive business which then needs to follow . . . This "further business" of therapy is the help needed by an individual who has seriously failed to adapt himself to life as an adult. A brief sojourn in the womb-like atmosphere of Rogerian therapy may give such a person the recuperative strength he needs to face the job of learning how to handle the problems of the very unwomblike, nontherapeutic world of adult reality. But many such persons need direct guidance, specific education, in how to utilize their energies in effective, rational, realistic adaptation to interpersonal actualities.

It *is* frequently asked: What about the responsibility of the therapist to the client and to society? What if he is contemplating suicide, homicide, or seduction of a minor? These are important questions and Rogers does not claim (nor do I) to have assured answers for them. However, I might mention several pertinent considerations. First, while the principles of interpersonal relations are basically the same in and out of therapy, some distinction must be made in their application. When a person contemplates self-destructive or antisocial acts in therapy, he is in conflict about them or he wouldn't be discussing them with the therapist. The assumption of the client-centered therapist is that moral influence, however slight and subtle, is likely to mobilize negativism and exacerbate the conflict, while with no therapist's thumb on the scales the client is likely to make a decision that is personally and socially adequate.

Jessie Taft's child client who teetered threateningly on the sill of an open window illustrates the point. Taft, doubtless not without some uncertainty and discomfort, resisted the inclination to grab her, and succeeded in conveying to her that her life was her own to do with as she wished. Freedom and responsibility being given to and required of her, the child mobilized her self-protective resources and the danger passed (Taft, 1933). If there is no risk taken, there is no genuinely autonomous decision.

In the second place, the fateful situations we have been discussing are rare as compared with those ever-recurring incidents in which the therapist feels called upon to guide the patient. In so doing, he is acting on the assumption that making the right decision (right according to the therapist) is more important than that the person shall make it himself, right or wrong. The therapist believes that with his guidance the person will learn to do "right" and will then continue to do it, instead of merely substituting the beneficent authority of the therapist for the less beneficent authorities of his past. As I review my experiences as a patient with a half dozen rather eminent analysts, I believe their most frequent errors were of that sort. If they had stayed with me without trying to save me from error, I would have had more help in becoming authentically myself (which wouldn't have been saintly but not criminal either).

One of my analysts was "very accepting" but subtly moralistic. In several years' time she drove me, with the cooperation of my own masochism, of course, to the verge of psychosis. I became a "good boy" but it almost cost me my sanity. After several months of more anxiety than I had ever known, the mere reading of *Counseling and Psychotherapy* (Rogers, 1942) got me back to where I had been, and beyond, though it didn't constitute definitive therapy for me. Incidentally, one of my colleagues, an exceptionally eminent analyst, thought my high valuation of "nondirective therapy" was due to the urgency of my need at the time; his preconceptions would not permit him to entertain

the possibility that it was due to the authentic potency of such an "obviously superficial" therapy.

Twenty years ago I had two clients who succeeded exceptionally well in therapy.
Both came to me after analyses which left them almost hopelessly discouraged about
themselves. Now, people *can* fail with one analyst and succeed with another for a variety
of reasons extraneous to the character of the therapy. In these cases the reasons were
not extraneous. Early in the analysis of one of them, the analyst felt it desirable to
save him from a "misstep" and thereby became "mother," whom the patient could
never contravene. The analysis continued several years but no therapy took place.
The guidance tendency in the analyst of the other patient was just suggestive enough
of the "beneficent sadism" of the most important woman in the girl's life (*not* her
mother) that "transference" obstructed all progress. (The turning point of this person's
therapy with me is indicated above in "Example 4.", p. 171.)

The previous therapists were training and supervising analysts, and both analyses
involved more frequent sessions and more overall time than the therapy with me.
I was no brighter than the others and probably less bright at diagnosis and figuring
out the patient's psychodynamics. But my therapy had one asset that made the
crucial difference: I more accurately estimated the hidden strength of the initiative of
these clients and so I did not try to instruct them in living.

We all seem to have a tremendous urge to "do it ourselves," as illustrated by the
anarchy that must be tolerated by parents if children are to develop properly. This
indestructible, autonomous itch is vividly illustrated by an anecdote of Frieda
Fromm-Reichmann: Two schizophrenics made no progress whatever during extended therapy and the staff decided to give them up. The therapist reminded the
staff that much had been learned from them, and wished to continue purely for
research purposes. She was allowed to continue, and thereafter there was some
movement.

Reason 6. A major reason for rejection of client-centered therapy is its conception of the good life, of the "fully functioning person," of the desirable outcome
of therapy. Harper (1959, p. 156), again giving clear expression to the almost
universally held view, says: "Psychotherapy is a contemporary means for individuals with poorly functioning value systems to (learn) . . . a new value system
. . . [Although] none of these value systems learned in therapy may be considered
totally satisfactory for meeting the problems of present day social turbulence."

Harper predicts, correctly I believe, that the therapy of the future will render current therapies obsolete, but apparently he believes that the improved therapy-to-be
will consist of more satisfactory value systems and more effective means of inculcating them in patients. The intent of client centered therapy, on the contrary, is
not to replace less adequate value systems with more adequate ones, but to replace
any and every *value system* with a *valuing process*—a continuous, spontaneous,
organismic sensing (unconstricted by defensiveness) of oneself and the world. Actually these two conceptions of the source of guidance for living do not constitute a
radical dualism; they are not entirely mutually exclusive. But their different orientations are of crucial importance, for they concern one's most fundamental
assumptions about life and personality, and they express one's existing level of
development toward responsible autonomy.

What is involved here (and what was involved in the previous topic, Reason 5), is
one's assumptions regarding human nature. Does one assume that with an adequate
opportunity to be aware of and assess all the pertinent data, the individual is likely
to come to conclusions that are personally and socially viable? Or does one assume

that "narcissism" and egotism are more innate than the capacity to enjoy others (i.e., to love others) so that the individual's "natural" destructiveness must be restrained and reeducated from outside? This latter view is common and may be represented by a contemporary automobile, which has an engine to propel it and brakes to restrain it (society must inculcate restraint of the "irrational passions"). The estimate of man that underlies the alternate view is like the auto anticipated by H. G. Wells. Powered by compressed air, its propulsive and braking functions are integral: its starting and stopping and all forward and reverse speeds are responsive to a single lever. While all analogies have their limitations, this one suggests rather accurately the nature of the self-regulating personality. (More will be said below about morality as a system of values and trans-moral ethics as a valuing process.)

Reason 7. A final variable which determines one's evaluation of any therapy is the degree of importance one gives to scientific research. Psychoanalysts, for the most part, employ "clinical methods," that combination of empiricism and rationalism which until recently made all of the most important contributions. They neglect more rigorous methods as inapplicable to depth psychology. For instance, Fromm (1966) says, "The psychoanalyst . . . cannot use the methods of experimental psychology because his data do not lend themselves to this simplistic model of scientific procedure." Fromm's belief that his methods of research are significantly analogous to those of contemporary physicists is questionable. My impression is that while hypothesis formation in physics is freely empirical, rational, or intuitive (as Fromm implies), the rigorously controlled experiment is still considered decisive.

Fromm's assertion that psychoanalysis is unamenable to strict scientific treatment may be true—in view of the nature of its theoretical formulations—but it is not true of all formulations of depth therapy, and his picture of experimentation in present-day social science is accurate only to a very limited degree. Science develops by the periodic detachment from philosophy of perennial problems which become amenable to more exact treatment through the invention of novel methods (Berlin, 1956, p. 13). There is presently an efflorescence of this kind in the social sciences, and client-centered therapists are in the vanguard of the psychology sector.

"The amount of research aimed at understanding and controlling the variables involved in psychotherapy has increased in geometric proportions over the last fifteen years" (Stollack et al, 1966, p. V).

"The well-designed, rigorously controlled investigation of psychotherapy is still a relative novelty on the psychological and psychiatric research scene. Nevertheless a great deal of research has been carried out, and from the welter of studies that have been reported since the pioneering efforts of the Rogerian group in the late 1940's it is possible to discover several clear trends and developments" (Goldstein and Dean, 1966, p. VII).

A number of client-centered therapists have formulated precise definitions of terms (e.g., Gendlin, 1964, pp. 100-148, 26 definitions of distinguishable aspects of the therapeutic process) and have developed various measures of process which make empirical observation more amenable to objective testing. (See reports and bibliographies in Rogers, 1954; Stollack et al, 1966; Goldstein and Dean, 1966; and Rogers et al, 1967.)

The superiority of client-centered therapy to psychoanalysis in the matter of investigation concerns not only the methods of research, but also the *focus* of the studies. No doubt, *theory of personality* and *theory of therapy* are sources for each other, but the former sheds less light on the latter than the reverse sequence. But psychoanalysis has always given relative priority to personality theory; client-centered therapy, to theory of therapy.

[NOTE:— Of course, Freud's personality theory was based on the previously unavailable material afforded by his unprecedented therapeutic procedure, but his lack of means for rigorous scientific checking resulted in an excess of theory over assured empirical data. The wonder is that he achieved so much with such limited means. His overall experience, however, presents a clear indication of the need for more scientific research methods in psychotherapy if theory of personality is not to influence theory of therapy unduly.]

Rogers (1966, p. 194) says, "It seems to us that far more intelligent and answerable questions can be raised in regard to the *process* of personality change than in regard to the *cause*s of the person's present personality characteristics." He considers his theory of therapy much better-established experimentally than his theory of personality. By contrast, Freud's contributions to therapeutic *procedure* would be equivalent to only one or two of his many volumes. Contemporary examples of this emphasis may be found in Rollo May and Erich Fromm, whose copious output is distinguished by its variety of subject matter (which claims authority from their professional activity), yet neither has systematically presented his therapeutic procedure. Ferenczi and Rank (1925) tried to correct this imbalance in psychoanalysis, but their attempt has been slow in bearing fruit.

In brief: disbelief, in some circles, in the possibility and the importance of scientific research in psychotherapy, with study of process given priority over personality study, is one reason for insufficient appreciation of the significance of client-centered therapy.

The foregoing interpretive exposition of client-centered therapy, and reminders of the major features of psychoanalysis, may perhaps be suggestively schematized. Many of the differences highlighted by the schema are *not* entirely mutually exclusive alternatives, but rather indications of comparative emphasis.

1. Philosophy of human nature
   Psa: Man is inherently good and evil and in need of conditional acceptance (acceptance of the good and rejection of the evil, to overcome his innate narcissism and egotism and become socialized).
   Cct: Man is inherently morally neutral and in need of unconditional acceptance (as the precondition for self-learning of freedom and responsibility).
2. Structure-function interrelations
   Psa: Emphasis is on theory of character *structure* (personality theory), analytic *procedure* being relatively more derivative from it than determinative of it.
   Cct: Emphasis is on theory of personality *change* (therapeutic procedure), theory of *personality* being relatively more derivative from it than determinative of it.
3. Perspective
   Psa: Oriented toward the objective world, represented by the analyst.
   Cct: Oriented toward the subjective world of the client.
4. The context of the analyst's (therapist's) activity
   Psa: The analyst's assessment of the analytic situation.
   Cct: The client's felt and partially verbalized experiencing.
5. Subjectivity-objectivity balance
   Psa: Therapeutic change is from distorted subjectivity to objectivity in the patient.

       Cct: Therapeutic change is from distorted subjectivity to less distorted subjectivity in the client.

6. Moral-ethical emphasis
   Psa: Change is from a less adequate to a more adequate system of values.
   Cct: Change is from a value system to a valuing process.

7. The primary therapeutic agency
   Psa: Resides in the analyst, in his discriminating or conditional acceptance of the patient, and his capacity for empathy, diagnosis, and direction of the analysis.
   Cct: Resides in the client, in his vitality (growth tendency, self-actualizing tendency, "autotherapeutic" impulsion, or—what you will!).

8. First major function of the analyst (therapist)
   Psa: To interpret the patient to himself.
   Cct: To facilitate the client's "self-interpretation" (by verbalizing his empathy for the client's felt experiencing, including those aspects of it that the client cannot verbalize).

9. The secondary or auxiliary therapeutic agency
   Psa: Resides in the patient, in his capacity for therapeutic response to the analyst's interpretations.
   Cct: Resides in the therapist, in his use of his initiative to foster the client's initiative.

10. An additional major function of the analyst (therapist)
    Psa: Guidance or education of the patient for living.
    Cct: (Not performed—successful performance of the "first therapeutic function" is considered sufficient to establish the client's capacity for self-direction.)

11. Analyst's (therapist's) estimate of the patient's (client's) capacity to direct his life after therapy
    Psa: High.
    Cct: High.

12. Analyst's (therapist's) estimate of the patient's (client's) capacity to direct the analysis (the therapy)
    Psa: Low.
    Cct: High.

13. Preferred method for correcting and developing the system as a theory of personality and as a therapeutic procedure
    Psa: "Clinical research" on the analytic process.
    Cct: "Experimental research" on the therapeutic process.

Two points of disagreement regarding interpreting emerge from these summaries: "Interpretation" as a tool in psychotherapy is of basic importance in both therapies but (1) their *modes* of interpreting differ, and (2) the *part* interpretation plays in their respective total procedures is not the same. Psychoanalysis interprets from an objective, macroscopic cognitive frame of reference; client-centered therapy interprets chiefly in the sense of expanding the cognitive aspects of concrete microscopic instances of the client's immediate felt experiencing. Secondly, in psychoanalysis successful interpretation is supplemented by instruction in living; in client-centered therapy successful "interpreting" is all there is to therapy, since it enables the client to reconstruct his living quite unaided.

RATIONAL-EMOTIVE THERAPY

We now come to another proposed alternative to psychoanalytic interpreting which raises intriguing questions because it is strikingly similar to client-centered therapy in some respects and strikingly different in others. I refer to the rational-emotive therapy of Albert Ellis.

[NOTE:— I am vividly aware of the widespread antagonism toward Ellis. Nine out of every ten colleagues and students to whom I have recommended his unique contribution to therapy have thought me "nuts." (They hadn't read *Reason and Emotion in Psychotherapy.*) Ellis' excellent exposition of his highly original system (Ellis, 1963) was never reviewed in a certain important review-journal: it was deemed too late for review by the time a succession of prospective reviewers had refused the task. They could hardly have missed the values of the book—but what about their reputations! Ellis himself has said privately that he is the most hated psychologist in the field. He doesn't seek nor enjoy his inverted distinction, but it doesn't disturb him. I do not wish, at this time, to give my opinion regarding what grounds Ellis may give for the antipathy he inspires. I do wish to record my considered opinion that it is not essentially due to his "aggressive manner," his "bad taste," his "lack of sensitivity to the higher values," or his extremely unconventional views of sexual ethics, but rather to the radical (etymological sense) nature of his contribution. Ellis has said, "I stubbornly decided never to feel guilty." Rogers speaks of "no conditions of worth" and "unconditional positive self-regard." Are not these two very different persons *both* exponents of "trans-moral ethics"?

Aside from his contribution to therapy, Ellis has made many important, thoroughly scholarly researches which do not have as many readers as they deserve because of incidental considerations. For instance, his unparalleled study, *The American Sexual Tragedy,* carries the "undignified" dedication, "To John Ciardi, one hell of a fine editor" (to me a touching expression of sincere appreciation). Is it surprising that a dedicated iconoclast doesn't bother with kid gloves?]

It seems to me that Ellis' basic principle of *complete absence of blame,* of "not blaming *any one,* for *anything,* at *any time,"* is essentially identical with Rogers' principle of *unconditional positive regard.* The *thoroughness* with which they espouse this principle and its *implications,* together with their respective ways of effectively *implementing* it, distinguishes their systems from other systems. This is the source of their potency and economy, and at the same time the underlying cause of inadequate appreciation of them.

There are other respects in which rational-emotive therapy is like client-centered therapy and distinguishable from psychoanalysis and psychoanalytically-oriented therapies. It "works from the surface" (to borrow a phrase from Gestalt therapy); i.e., it focuses sharply on relating to the here-and-now person, regardless of how he came to be the person he is. It gives scant attention to past history and to dreams, and it tends to discourage the development of a transference relationship.

[NOTE:— Too much should not be made of the fact, but it is interesting and of some significance that Rogers and Ellis both originally got valuable leads from two members of Freud's original group who later became heretics. Adler's directness and his rejection of "muck-raking in the unconscious" appealed strongly to Ellis, but Ellis emphasizes rational self-interest over social interest as the preferred emphasis in therapy. There are two respects in which Rank's influence can be seen in client-centered therapy: his deviation in putting more emphasis on therapeutic procedure than on personality theory, and his unprecedented confidence in the latent capacities of the individual. Rank might have accurately called his therapy "client-centered" if he had chosen to do so. His quotation from Kant on Copernicus' replacement of the geocentric theory of the solar system by the heliocentric theory, as analogous to his own replacement of the therapist by the *patient* as the *center* of the therapeutic process, may be considered the original "manifesto" of patient- or client-centered therapy. Fromm has said, "I think [Rogers'] expression 'client-centered therapy' is rather strange because every therapy has to be client-centered" (Evans, 1966, p. 34). That is quite true, but it neglects the *widely diverse ways* in which therapy can be client-centered. No therapy, to my knowledge, is client-centered in the sense of giving the client the direction of it to the extent that Rank did, and, even more, that Rogers does.]

While the similarities in these two systems are often unrecognized, the two major respects in which they differ cannot be missed. In rational-emotive therapy the therapist is *directive* in two ways: He promptly and vigorously attacks the client's irrational ideas, and he encourages programs of action. At the beginning of the first hour with the client, the aim of the therapist, apart from starting to develop a working relationship, is to discover how the person unwittingly but *constantly re-creates* his low self-esteem. (This is assumed to be present, whether apparent or masked by blatant "self-assertion," and it is assumed to be the matrix of all the person's personality disorders. A further assumption is that every feeling and emotion has a cognitive aspect, however unconscious, and that if the cognitive factor is recognized and changed, by reason, the feeling or emotion will change of itself.) Ellis believes, with Epictetus, that it is not facts and events that disturb us neurotically but the *non-sequitor* meanings we irrationally give to them. When he sees an instance of this pathology in operation, he attacks it head on. He reveals in the momentary functioning of the client what the latter is gratuitously doing to himself—namely, actively, at that very moment, *creating* a sense of worthlessness by recriminating himself under the influence of groundless but unquestioned criteria of worth. This perpetually re-created self-rejection is his chief misery and the source of all his other miseries. Now this is certainly *interpretation* and *direction,* but it is not what is generally meant by these terms, as the following considerations, taken together, will show.

1. First of all, it is more microscopic than macroscopic. It is more concerned with concrete, immediate instances of the ongoing pathological process, than with general traits of the personality.

2. It is not cautious, tactful, and carefully prepared for in advance; yet clients react to it as though it is *not* an attack on their foundations. This is clear from a careful study of the verbatim transcriptions of therapy-in-process which are included in all of Ellis' writings on therapy. The client rather promptly comes to appreciate the fact that the therapist is hacking at his *chains,* not at *him.* Ellis' success with this procedure is due, I believe, to the fact that his nonblaming attitude is authentic to the marrow of his bones. Thus he can *criticize* the ideas without *blaming* the person, and the client feels this.

3. This disintegrative interpreting is directed against the client's irrational self-*de*flation, not, at first, against his irrational self-*in*flation ("narcissism," "idealized self-image"). This latter component enters the picture secondarily as the client's irrational "ought's" and "should's," submission to which is the cause of the low self-feeling. Thus the "narcissism" is more readily disintegrated because it is then less necessary as a defense against the feeling of worthlessness which has already been reduced. (Therapists who primarily attack the client's "narcissism" inevitably mobilize strong "resistance.")

4. This procedure is not manipulative. It matter-of-factly reveals what *is* in the

client; what *should be* emerges from that. Furthermore it is not authoritarian, for it rests not on the therapist's status but on his logic. The self-destructive mental mechanisms are demonstrated on the basis of data that are as immediately available to the client as to the therapist. Consequently the client rather readily learns to observe his habitual neurotic "self-talk" and thus progressively becomes his own therapist.

Therapist-encouraged real life action by the client, even against strong inner reluctance, is a prominent feature of rational-emotive therapy. It has an explicit rationale which is highly convincing, but I shall confine myself to commenting on an aspect of this procedure which Ellis takes for granted but has not, to my knowledge, explicitly stated. Generally when a therapist encourages a patient to take action, it is with the unquestioned assumption of both of them that taking action will raise the patient's self-respect by giving him a new reason for self-respect. This self-defeating principle of gaining self-approval by one's extrinsic achievements is automatically obviated by the rational-emotive ethos. Since, according to Ellis, the person is worth while whatever he does or does not do (Cf. Rogers' "no *conditions* of worth"), his "ego" is not at stake. He then acts *not* to raise his self-esteem (which has already been increased prior to any "improvement" in his living, by exposure of the irrational causes of his earlier low self-feeling), but for the sound and uncomplicated reason that he will thereby have less factual, practical frustration and more concrete satisfaction in living.

When, with the characteristic features of rational-emotive therapy in mind, we remember the current flexibility of client-centered procedures, including one therapist who "clobbers" the client's defenses (which is what Ellis does characteristically), we must conclude that these therapies are far from antithetical. They are based on the same ruling attitude, and the procedures by which they implement it display overlap, in spite of obvious differences which I have no wish to deny.

What are we to do with all of this? Perhaps Pascal's dictum, "Love God and do as you please," points a direction. Perhaps an axiom for psychotherapists might be, "Become real and acceptant, and free from any trace of blame, and do as you please." Perhaps, in an unqualifiedly-acceptant context, criticism, sarcasm, and many other "negative" forms of expression may be genuinely therapeutic. *It is the therapist's subtly evaluative attitude that is obstructive.* However that may be, the crucial questions I have raised cannot be resolved by easy generalizations of this sort. For myself I am wrestling currently with such questions as these: Are these procedural differences of Rogers and Ellis differentially applicable to temperamentally different therapists? Are they applicable, respectively, to different kinds of clients? Or (as I am inclined to believe) are they potentially variable resources of a potentially integral procedure?

[NOTE:— I make no apologies for my "eclecticism." If I were better acquainted with more of the worthy therapies now available, and if there were more space in this paper, I would probably be even more eclectic. But aren't we all, in varying degrees? It seems to me that all therapists fall in one or another of about five categories: (1) The (relatively few, and never absolutely original) originators of systems that become widely influential; (2) their docile, doctrinaire disciples; (3) their independent associates; (4) indiscriminate eclectics; and (5) discriminating eclectics. Categories 1, 3 and 5 are all respectable habitations. I should probably be located in 3—somewhat "trigamously," since I recognize the well-deserved mentorship of Rogers and Ellis as well as of revised psychoanalysis. But since I learn many things from many therapists, I may be said to have some of the characteristics of category 5.]

Unconditional Positive Regard

In the remainder of this paper I wish to call attention to some widely-diverse considerations which, in my opinion, constitute presumptive support for the principle of unconditional positive regard, or complete absence of blame, as a desirable principle of life and of therapy. The topics are: the idea of human equality; a certain potent historical doctrine; fictional treatment of the theme of "the double"; the theory of psychological determinism; and several illustrations of the negative effect of conditional acceptance in therapy.

Rogers defines *unconditional positive regard* as follows: "If the self-experiences of another are perceived by me in such a way that no self-experience can be discriminated as more or less worthy of positive regard than any other, then I am experiencing unconditional positive regard for this individual." Clinically, "It is the fact that he (the therapist) feels and shows an unconditional positive regard toward the experiences of which the client is frightened or ashamed, as well as toward the experiences with which the client is pleased or satisfied, that seems effective in bringing about change (Rogers, 1959, p. 208).

The Idea of Human Equality

William James has pointed out "the blindness with which we are all infected in regard to the feelings of creatures and people different from ourselves," feelings which determine "judgments of the worth of things" (James, 1899). He reverts to this favorite theme in another lecture: "The first thing to learn in intercourse with others is noninterference with their own peculiar ways of being happy, provided those ways do not assume to interfere by violence with ours" (James, 1899). James is expressing an aspect of the Christian principle of the equal worth of all persons, a principle which must be included in the desired world consensus that is necessary for peace and social development (Whyte, 1948, p. 34). In spite of the innumerable *natural* inequalities of men, and of the inequalities required by the necessary hierarchy of *social organization,* everyone has an equal right with all others to his own "judgment of the worth of things" and "his own peculiar way of being happy." No one has any rational grounds for assuming that his values, however admirable, are applicable to the next developmental step of anyone else.

I once had a client (he entered therapy a bank employee and left it a painter) who discovered in a popular "psychology" magazine the phrase, "All egos are equal." It seemed effectively to conceptualize what he had been coming to in his therapy and it had a profound effect on him. It meant to him, I believe, that he could be *himself* without feeling *inferior*. The principle of human equality has much in common with the principle of unconditional positive regard toward self and others.

A Certain Potent Historical Doctrine

Recognition of the need of people to be accepted while still "unacceptable" is probably common to sotereological religions of the moral type. In Christianity it is recognized in the doctrine of *salvation by faith* rather than by "works" (ritual and moral obedience)—the doctrine of Paul, Augustine and Luther. Its promise of *acceptance, unconditioned* by conformity to the Law has, over the centuries, saved innumerable Christians from hopeless feelings of worthlessness and has produced numerous transformations of character. Luther said that if he had continued his rigorous moral efforts he would have killed himself, whereas when he became convinced that he was "justified," the gates of Paradise swung open for him. Francis Thompson's "The Hound of Heaven" (Catholic) and John Masefield's "The Everlasting Mercy" (Protestant) are two poetic records of the experience, among numerous others.

The doctrine had different meanings for different persons. It did not involve "masochistic submission" for those to whom "the Will of God" symbolized the necessary conditions of human development. For the majority, however, it probably represented neutralization of the illusion of worthlessness by the illusion of supernatural acceptance, conditional on submission to Authority. But experientially the consequence was more positive than negative and perhaps the best that was possible in a fundamentally dualistic culture. (See Whyte, 1950, on *Paul*, p. 161*ff*.) Furthermore, it is not entirely true that Christianity and the other redemptive religions *created* the problem for which they offered a *solution*; their "good news" was, in large measure, a response to an antecedent, general human experience of irrational fear and guilt.

I have referred to the doctrine (which few informed people find tenable today), because it provides a convincing demonstration of the tremendous power of self-evaluation, both positive and negative.

Historically, the idea was "You are accepted, just as you are, with all your sins upon you, *not because you deserve acceptance* but because of God's invincibly loving nature. Your part is to submit to His Authority" (however that might be conceived). A contemporary homologue might be (for a therapist vis-a-vis a client, for instance), "My unconditional acceptance of him is a belated response to what he has always needed and deserved, and it entails no submission on his part."

The Theme of the Double in Literature

This theme has occurred at least once in the writings of most of the giants of literature, and it has characterized much of the work of some authors. Otto Rank (1914) assembled, and analyzed in depth, an astonishing number of examples. A certain common structure underlies many—perhaps most—of them. Edgar Allen Poe's tale, "William Wilson," is typical of the genre. The titular character, bedeviled by his double to the point of desperation, finally stabs him, whereupon the blood spills fatally from his own heart. The psychological truth is that attempts to amputate a rejected part of a person (by himself or by another) is, if successful, disastrous. ("Resistance" during therapy is often the patient's self-protective struggle against the therapist's misguided efforts which would destroy him, or a vital part of him, by destroying his bad self. Cf. below, the discussion of the therapy of several dual personalities.) Nothing can be done with a bad self but to accept it. If it is treated like a bastard, it will continue to be "a bastard" (the twofold usage of the word is significant). If it is accepted, it may change and contribute a necessary or valuable component to a more satisfactory eventual personality.

The Theory of Psychological Determinism

Strict, universal causality may be an unproved assumption (as Hume insisted), but such command as we have over ourselves and our world, and all of our scientific discoveries, presuppose it. Integral to Freud's achievement was his demonstration of its operation even in "irrational" mental processes. Now, few people who witness a hypnotic experiment will blame the subject for the posthypnotic misbehavior which had been suggested during the trance. But compulsive behavior that is consciously and voluntarily "acted out," though it is due ultimately to early "waking hypnosis" of the child by the parent, is often viewed as arbitrary irresponsibility. If causality is universal, then what a person *has been* and *has done,* he *had* to be and he *had* to do. Since blaming assumes that the individual "could have" been or done differently (without some determinant in the situation including, especially, himself, having been different), blaming is irrational.

The causal factor that the blamer assumes could have been different is the *will,* supported by *conscience* and *reason.* This view, however, implies that the will and its supporters are *unconditioned,* somehow able to determine, without being determined by, the process which is the personality. Hence the theories of *vitalism* and *free will,* which are supposed to save us from *mechanism* and *determinism.* There are valid considerations involved in that view. Every *organism,* because of its *organization,* has some freedom (capacity to realize its wishes). Even the ameba accepts food and rejects not-food. The whole is greater than the sum of its parts; some classes of effects are greater than their combined causes (Whyte, 1949, p. 16); and *con-sciousness* is not merely a mechanical vector of its constituent causes but also a new causal factor. Thus, organisms, and especially persons, are, in some sense and degree, free or self-determining. However, *it would seem logical to assume that in any given act the will was no freer than the act indicates.* To assume the contrary is to deny psychological determinism, an assumption that issues in punitive blaming and moral exhortation (which may produce apparently desirable results but which is ultimately unconstructive). The individual himself is commonly victimized by the erroneous assumption, and one of the most important tasks of therapy is to disabuse the client of his overestimation of his past and present degree of freedom, and thus to free him from his irrational self-recrimination. Blamers and self-blamers alike attribute "sins" to an illusory and arbitrary "free" choice of "evil."

I believe the theory of psychological determinism is commonly qualified—watered down and softened up, as in *blaming*—because its implications are commonly misconceived.

1. It is often assumed that to affirm determinism is to deny freedom. Actually freedom, as well as unfreedom is strictly determined. Freedom is a form of determinism, namely, self-determinism. One is free (i.e., "able to realize his intentions"—Macmurray), to the extent that his intentions are expressions of a unified self. (I refer to *psychological* freedom, for there are also biological and social conditions of freedom.) Psychological unfreedom, the intrapsychic inability to realize one's intentions, is due to the existence of mutually contradictory intentions, as a result of which the satisfaction of a wish automatically frustrates its opposite. Inner contradiction *is* personality conflict *is* self-frustration *is* unfreedom. (Psychotherapy expands freedom by resolving personality conflicts.)

2. It is widely assumed that without blame, self-blame and guilt feelings there would be no motivation for development. The fact is that feelings of guilt *only activate attempts to realize one's neurotic idealized self-image.* Freedom from feelings of guilt leaves one in full possession of the motive of becoming more sane and mature for the simple and sound reason that life is more satisfactory that way.

3. It is widely and rightly assumed that people should be held responsible, but it is widely and wrongly assumed that *holding responsible* and *blaming* are synonymous. Actually *one may be held responsible without being blamed.* A person may be permitted, or even required, to undergo the consequences of his acts in spite of the fact that he *had* to act as he did. As Dewey and Tufts say (in their "Ethics"), a person

is held responsible not because he *could have been* responsible, but that he *may become* responsible.

Morality involves blaming, but morality is man's basic problem today. *The idea of moral good and evil is the source of most of our worst problems.* Brock Chisholm (1946, p. 7), former head of the World Health Organization, has called it *poison*— "the poison long ago described and warned against as 'the fruit of the tree of the knowledge of good and evil.' In the old Hebrew story God warns the first man and woman to have nothing to do with good and evil. It is interesting to note that, as long ago as that, 'good' is recognized as just as great a menace as 'evil.' They are both fruit of the one tree and are different aspects of the same thing."

The principle of living that is made possible by freedom from the poison of morality is sometimes called "trans-moral ethics" (e.g., by Paul Tillich), but different thinkers name it and describe it in different ways.

For Brock Chisholm it is simply *being sensible.* "Freedom from moralities means freedom to observe and to think and behave sensibly to the advantage of the person and the group, free from outmoded types of loyalties and from the magic fears of our ancestors" (Chisholm, 1946, p. 9).

For Carl Rogers it is *functioning fully.* "The fully functioning person . . . will be open to his experience . . . will exhibit no defensiveness . . . will experience himself as the locus of evaluation . . . will have no conditions of worth . . .[and] will experience unconditional self-regard" (Rogers, in Koch, 1959, p. 234).

For Albert Ellis it is *living rationally.* He believes [with Walt Whitman of modern times and Jesus of Nazareth of ancient times] that the worth of a person is intrinsic and inalienable—that no one is to be condemned, rejected or blamed regardless of his physical, mental, moral or any other condition (Ellis, 1965). Living rationally consists in affirming one's worth, in eliminating one's irrational sense of sin and guilt, and in freeing oneself from the lethal nonsense that was inculcated during one's defenseless nonage (Ellis and Harper, 1961).

For L. L. Whyte it is *direction by the unitary process* which is conceived as inherent in nature, including man. This outlook "substitutes development for moral progress, formative tension for static harmony, continuing transformation for permanence, the unitary social hierarchy for the ambiguous conception of democratic equality, and unitary balance for the subject-object dualism. It replaces the illusory ideal which neglected its shadow by the proper spontaneity of integrated man" (Whyte, 1950, p. 231). "Unitary thought is concerned to facilitate the development of each along its proper path within the whole, and not to make ethical or other relative valuations which neglect the differences between the histories and present situations of one country and another," or between one person and another (*Ibid.*, p. 233).

[NOTE:— The outlook of "trans-moral ethics" (with its implied attitude of unconditional positive regard) is congenial with unitary views of nature and life, with the aims of general system theory, and with "evolutionary," "emergent" and "synoptic" naturalisms. It is uncongenial with all dualisms and with reductive monisms of mind (idealism) and matter (materialism). Its scientific base is expanding with the progressive resolution of the vitalism-mechanism dilemma (by Whyte, Bertalanffy, et al.). We are here concerned only with "trans-moral ethics" (under whatever designation) and the associated attitude of unconditional positive regard. The thinkers quoted above are the representatives of "trans-moral ethics" with whose work I am most familiar.

The outlook of Erich Fromm appears to be congenial to these views. He says that "humanistic conscience is the reaction of our total personality to its proper functioning and dysfunctioning" and that "the authoritarian conscience is derived from the commands and tabus" of external authority. His exposition of humanistic ethics is deeply insightful. He explicitly repudiates the various forms of radical dualism that characterize, or infect, many religious, philosophical and scientific systems, including Freud's. However, in the formulation of his position he prefers to retain the concept of morality and to distinguish between rational and irrational morality. This is in spite of his statement that "most of the religious and political systems of history" are authoritarian. His terminology represents a plausible (in fact, the most frequent) mode of expression. I believe, however, that more than a mere semantic preference is involved, for Fromm is intensely occupied with good and evil. He conceives the dualities (aspects of an inclusive process) in his "existential dichotomies" in such a way as to make them into radical dualisms (mutually exclusive opposites), notably in his extreme dichotomization of *life and death,* and of *good and evil,* and his identification of these two pairs of concepts with each other. As a result, his outlook has a distinctly moralistic cast (Fromm, 1964).

Humanism was progressive as a solvent of supernaturalism, but today it is limited by its philosophical and moral idealism, which in practice, if not in theory, spawns dualistic dilemmas. Twenty-five years ago, in *Selfishness and Self-Love,* Fromm freed himself from Freud's dualisms (life and death instincts, individual-society) by a profound and brilliant stroke of reconstruction (Fromm, 1939); but he has since retreated, implicitly, not explicitly, from that position instead of maintaining it and carrying out its implications.]

In sum, the theory of strict determinism is quite consistent with a *conditional* view of human freedom and responsibility, and with an ethical philosophy of living. Also, it involves an attitude of unconditional positive regard, and freedom from blame, toward self and others.

Conditional Acceptance in Psychotherapy—Three Illustrations

I now invite you to consider three reported instances of therapy with dual personalities which I believe reveal the antitherapeutic influence of conditional acceptance of the patient by the therapist. Cases of therapy with this condition afford an excellent opportunity to observe the consequences of selective acceptance because here "socially acceptable" traits predominate in one personality while "socially rejectable" traits predominate in the other. Each of the cases I have chosen received long, intensive therapy, and each of them has been excellently and copiously reported: Eve White (Thigpen and Cleckley, 1954, 1957; Lancaster and Poling, 1958); Doris Fischer (Prince, W. F., 1915, 1916); and Miss Beauchamp (Prince, Morton, 1905, 1957).

In each of them there is a conforming self (A) and a nonconforming self (B). Eve *White* (A) was conventionally good, dutiful and self-abnegating; Eve *Black* (B) was gay, pleasure-loving, bold, and irresponsible. *Doris* Fischer (A) was sober and compliant and studied her lessons faithfully; *Margaret* Fischer (B) was mischievous and rebellious and generally refused to do school work. *Miss* Beauchamp (A) was prim, pious, fearful, studious, submissive and morbidly conscientious; *Sally* Beauchamp (B) was carefree, fun-loving, assertive and adventuresome. It would seem that the three conforming selves were actualized to gain the acceptance of a rejecting parental authority, under the imposed conditions. It seems equally likely that the three nonconforming selves were actualized in loyalty to the native self, to one's organic integrity, as far as possible in the circumstances. I hypothecate that the (A) personality is a means of *belonging,* while the (B) personality is a means of *being oneself.* I hypothecate further that (A) represents a distorted form of *socialization* while (B) represents a distorted form of *individualization*.

Eve. Eve was strictly raised by authoritarian parents. She suffered serious psychological deprivation and several severe traumas, the memory of which was dissociated until reintegrated during therapy. With a few exceptions (due to the breaking out of Eve Black, as was discovered later), she was always a rather colorless "good" girl. In marriage she was a dutiful wife and a self-sacrificing mother. She entered therapy because of migraine and other ailments, and because she was mystified by her husband's accusations—namely, that she charged expensive party-girl clothes to him and that she tried to strangle her daughter! As was later found out, these acts were perpetrated by Eve Black. During therapy Eve Black "came out," to the astonishment of the therapist, who realized that she was an entirely different person from Eve White. She excoriated Eve White for her "disgusting" self-abnegation and for having married "that jerk," Ralph White. She was boldly "palsy-walsy" with the therapist and wanted him to go dancing with her. The therapist considered Eve White to be his patient, and was often exasperated at Eve Black's interference with his aim of curing Eve White. He had a certain sympathy for Eve Black, but persisted in his efforts to "liquidate" her. After many dramatic vicissitudes, including hospitalization, and several almost fatal incidents, *Jane,* a third personality, appeared. She seemed to the therapist to be superior to both of the Eves and he now took *her* as his patient. In time he established Jane's exclusive possession of the organism by the extinction of the two Eves.

Jane divorced Ralph and married Earl. Two years after therapy she and Earl had several long conferences, together and separately, with the psychiatrists. They were convinced that her happiness was genuine and that she had been able to make a happy life for her husband and child (Thigpen and Cleckley, 1957, p. 273). They hoped, but were not sure, that this would endure. Some tests made at a later date suggested increasing improvement, but one of them suggested an increasing degree of emotional disorder. In view of the selective accepting and rejecting that had characterized the therapy, the principle of unconditional acceptance implied that Jane had not sufficiently incorporated the potentialities that had existed, in a distorted form, in Eve White and (especially) in Eve Black; that she was in large measure a synthetic construction of the therapy; and that thus she must necessarily be unstable. That is what I reluctantly but quite confidently suspected.

A year or so later my suspicions were confirmed. A book appeared entitled *The Final Face of Eve,* by Evelyn Lancaster, the "final face" herself. In it I learned that "Jane" had become increasingly disturbed and desperate but did not reenter therapy, that finally she tried to kill herself and, in a sense did so, because she was extinguished; but the organism was saved from the poison Jane swallowed by the emergence of Evelyn, who got rid of the poison. In this instance a spontaneous, authentic integration occurred (or so it seems to me). The steadfast loyalty of the husband was probably indispensable. For the rest we can only cover our ignorance by assuming that the "autotherapeutic" resources of persons are tremendous and that in Evelyn they were sufficient for the task.

Three brief but eloquent items will indicate Evelyn's quality. Her little daughter said to her, "You *really* love me now, don't you, Mommy?" Earl (who had previously encountered a hornet's nest on entering the house) said, "I look forward to coming home to you, Evelyn." He also said, after intercourse with his formerly frigid wife, "Well, *I'll be damned!*"

Later, when Evelyn informed the psychiatrist of what had happened, he felt he had "deserved" to have her return to him when she became desperate. Evelyn agreed and was apologetic for not having done so! In my opinion, she was not guilty of "resistance" but was following an unconscious inner wisdom. If she had returned, would she not have subjected herself to more of the same misguided therapy that had produced the artificial "Jane."

Doris Fischer. W. F. Prince hypnotized Doris and said to her "bad" self, "I am going to take away your power." The girl's pulse weakened and she turned blue. The voice of a previously unsuspected personality, "Sleeping Margaret," spoke out and said, "You must get her out of this! Walk her! Walk her!" (Quoted by Murphy, 1947, Chap. on Multiple Personality.) The therapist walked her and she was restored. The wisdom of the organism had saved her from the therapist's misguided efforts. But he did not learn from this incident what might have been hoped. Progressively, by allowing more and more time in control of the body to Doris, and increasingly less to Margaret, he consolidated the "good" self and destroyed the "bad" one. The case report occupies several volumes and is very complicated: dogmatic judgment is not called for. I believe, however, that the data presented by the therapist himself reveal that the outcome was restricted because not enough of the independent, self-affirming aspects of the Margaret self were permitted to be incorporated into it.

Miss Beauchamp. As a child she experienced extreme rejection. She reacted in the way that produces neurosis: she idealized her mother and blamed *herself* for being rejected. As one would anticipate, she became artificially and compulsively "good." But an enclave of independence was maintained in the personality in the person of Sally, whose existence was discovered only during therapy. Sally, from early years, had precisely the realistic appraisal of the mother that therapy attempts to achieve, but she was "bad." I am simplifying a very complicated history. During therapy, 18 more or less fragmented "selves" appeared. In the course of time the therapist decided that the *original* Miss Beauchamp had been, and that the *eventual* Miss Beauchamp should become, a composite of B-I and B-IV, each of which was a relatively comprehensive and functional self. Sally, who opposed that program, was condemned to extinction. (But not, be it noted, until the therapist had used her for his purposes which, of course, he thought were the interests of his patient. The "rejectable" personality often—always?—has the greater lust for life and the fuller and more accurate sense of the situation.)

The therapist finally succeeded in combining his two favorite personalities. He extinguished Sally (or rather, as later appeared, drove her underground) by strenuous means, which included deception, psychological coercion, and deep etherization! The new Miss Beauchamp appeared to be a great improvement over all of the previous personalities. Unfortunately, however, stress would reduce her again to the three contradictory selves. It would seem that the integration would have been more authentic and stable if Sally's resources had been permitted to participate in it. Before she was suppressed, Sally had said some profound words to the therapist: "I know the difference between *real* people and the kind you *make up* [my italics]. This one is made up. You forget the *willing* part." A residue of cultural preconceptions did not permit the wise and kind therapist to hear her. What he heard was not a voice of "the wisdom of the organism," but the selfish petulence of a "subconscious state." He advised his synthetic Galatea, and he advises the reader of his report, not to take her seriously!

Gardner Murphy has said that the alternate personalities in dual personality are not stereoscopic (Murphy, 1947). That is certainly true of the existing distorted selves, but if my theory is accurate, the respective *motivations* of the two developments *are* stereoscopic, for they are simply the universal duality of needs for *individuality* and for *relatedness*.

My criticism of the therapy of the three cases of dual personality is based on the following assumptions: that the distorted aspects of the personalities were (to a determinative degree) caused by parental rejection of selected aspects of the child during the formative years, and that acceptance of them in their distorted form by the therapist was necessary for them to change so that each might contribute constructively to the realization of the potential eventual personality.

The foregoing interpretation of the three cases seems to me unavoidable. In the case of Eve, especially, item after item in the detailed records falls into place on this interpretation. Yet, as far as I know, it has never been advanced. I am inclined to attribute this to the pervasive but dubious assumption that *antisocial* traits—narcissism, egotism, selfishness and sadism—are immoral, while *anti-self* traits—self-rejection, compulsive altruism, selflessness and masochism—are not. This is hardly surprising, since people are not *as obviously and directly* frustrated by the overcompliance of others (in fact it is *apparently* to their advantage) as by self-assertion in the other person (This bias is embedded in the vernacular: "selflessness" is generally taken to mean "unselfishness," for instance. Dictionaries offer hardly any terms for self-regard that are unambiguously commendatory. Most of them are pejorative, and the few that *may* have a positive connotation can also be employed with a negative connotation.)

If attitudes toward self and toward others are conjunctive, improvement in either will lead to improvement in the other. However, it is preferable to focus first on improving one's self-regard, since it would seem to be more feasible to replace irrational self-interest (selfishness) with rational selfinterest (self-love) than to replace dislike for others with liking for others while one still basically dislikes himself. This is especially pertinent to our culture in which moralists generally believe that self-interest should be restrained rather than developed.

Kant, "the father of modern philosophy," held that morality is concerned with one's obligation to others while obligation to self is morally neutral—presumably because of the supposition that selfinterest is *natural*, while social interest must be *acquired* by moral effort. This view (which Kant formulated rather than created)—that attitudes toward self and others are disjunctive rather than conjunctive—was shared even by revolutionary champions of the rights of the individual. Max Stirner and Nietzsche, for example, could conceive no alternative to altruistic self-abnegation but aggressive egoism. They advocated self-interest while Kant advocated social-interest, but both they and he agreed that the two attitudes were antithetic. So did Freud in his theory of ego-cathected versus object-cathected libido (the more one loves himself, the less he loves others; the more one loves others, the less he loves himself).

The deep-lying tendency toward approval of altruism (whether morbid or not) and disapproval of self-regard (whether healthy or not) is reflected in the respective acceptances and rejections of the therapists of the three cases of dual personality to which we have referred. In my opinion, the best defense against that antitherapeutic bias is an attitude of unconditional acceptance, or complete absence of blame for any aspect of the personality.

SUMMARY

The purpose of "interpreting" in psychotherapy is to expand the patient's (client's) experience of himself and his world. This purpose can be achieved by psychoanalytic interpreting and by certain alternatives to it, or equivalents of it, notably by the procedures of client-centered therapy and of rational-emotive therapy.

One's evaluation of these three ways of "interpreting" is determined by one's assumptions regarding the patient's (client's) capacities, and one's conception of the attitudes and activities of the therapist which will most satisfactorily foster them.

The attitude of unconditional acceptance (positive regard) is the most desirable therapist attitude because it expresses the most accurate evaluation of the patient's (client's) potentialities, and it most effectively establishes the conditions for the realization of his potentialities. If the idea of unconditional acceptance and its implications are taken seriously, certain fundamental characteristics of contemporary culture, philosophy and psychotherapy must be questioned. Not only are popular moral assumptions criticized, but along with them all philosophical and scientific assumptions involving philosophical and moral idealism.

The implications of these views for psychotherapy are that there are procedures which can enable the patient (client) to take the major part in the direction of his therapy; and that if, by these means, he acquires sufficient access to his subjective organismic experiencing, he can direct his own further development more satisfactorily than can anyone else.

Standard psychoanalytic procedure is criticized because, since it assumes that the primary therapeutic agency resides in the analyst rather than in the patient, it does not provide the optimal conditions for the functioning of the patient's potential capacity to direct his own therapy and to direct his own living.

REFERENCES

Arieti, S. (Ed.), *American handbook of psychiatry*. New York: Basic Books, 1966.

Baruch, Dorothy, *New ways in discipline*. New York: Mentor, 1956.

Berlin, I., *The age of enlightenment*. New York: Mentor, 1956.

Bertalanffy, Ludwig von, General system theory and psychiatrry. In Arieti, *op. cit.* (Contains an extensive Bertalanffy bibliography.)

——, *Problems of life*. New York: Harper Torchbooks, 1952, 1960.

Chisholm, B., The psychiatry of enduring peace and social progress. *Psychiatry*. 1946 (Feb.), 3-34.

Ellis, A., *Reason and emotion in psychotherapy*. New York: Lyle Stuart, 1963.

——, Intellectual fascism. In *Suppressed*. Chicago: New Classics House, Novel books, 1965.

——, and Harper, R. A., *A guide to rational living*. Englewood Cliffs, N.J.: Prentice-Hall, 1961.

Evans, R. I., *Dialogue with Erich Fromm*. New York: Harper and Row, 1966.

Fenichel, O., *The psychoanalytic theory of the neuroses*. New York: W. W. Norton, 1945.

Ferenczi, S., and Rank, O., *The development of psychoanalysis*. New York: Nervous and Mental Disease Pub. Co., 1925. (According to William Menaker, *The Developmental Goals of Psychoanalytic Therapy* would be a better translation of *Entwicklungsziele der Psychoanalyse*, as more accurately indicating the intention of the authors.)

Fromm, E., Selfishness and self-love. *Psychiatry*. 1939, 2, 507-523. (Also in Ruitenbeek, Ed., 1964. A version with some additions and some subtractions is "Selfishness, Self-Love, and Self-Interest," in Fromm, *Man for Himself*, 1947.)

——, *Man for himself*. New York: Rinehart and Co., 1947.

——, *The heart of man: Its genius for good and evil*. New York: Harper and Row, 1964.

——, Scientific research in psychoanalysis. *Contemp. Psychoanal.*, 1966, 2, 168-170.

Gendlin, E. T., *Experiencing and the creation of meaning: a philosophical and psychological approach to the subjective*. New York: Macmillan, The Free Press of Glencoe, 1962. (This book, except the Introduction and Chap. 7, assumes a philosophical background in the reader. It develops the idea of *felt experiencing* as a conceptual tool for the social sciences and for philosophy. The author applies it to psychotherapy, and indicates how it may permit acceptance of the values of both logical positivism and existentialism.)

——, A Theory of personality change. In Worchel and Byrne, *op. cit.*

——, Therapeutic procedures in dealing with schizophrenics. In Rogers et al., *op. cit.*

——, Values and the process of experiencing. In Mahrer, *op. cit.*

——, Experiencing: A variable in the process of therapeutic change. *Amer. J. Psychother.*, 1961, 15, 233-245.

Goldstein, A. P., and Dean, S. J., *The investigation of psychotherapy*. New York: John Wiley, 1966.

Haley, J., *Strategies of psychotherapy*. New York: Grune & Stratton, 1963.

Harper, R. A., *Psychoanalysis and psychotherapy: 36 systems*. Englewood Cliffs, N. J. (A Spectrum Book): Prentice-Hall, 1959.

James, W., On a certain blindness in human beings, *and* What makes a life significant. Both in *Talks to teachers on psychology and to students on some of life's ideals*. New York: Henry Holt, 1899; New York: Dover Publications, 1962.

Koch, S., *Psychology: a study of a science*. New York: McGraw-Hill, 1959.

Lancaster, Evelyn, and Poling, J., *The final face of Eve*. New York: McGraw-Hill, 1958.

Mahrer, A. H. (Ed.), *The goals of psychotherapy*. New York: Appleton-Century Crofts, 1967.

Murphy, G., *Personality: A biosocial approach to origins and structure*. New York: Harper and Bros., 1947.

Paul, L. (Ed.), *Psychoanalytic clinical interpretation*. New York: The Crowell-Collier Pub. Co., 1963.

Prince, M., *The dissociation of a personality*. New York: Meridian Books, 1957.

——, The Doris case of multiple personality. *Proc. Amer. Soc. Psychical Res.*, 1915, 9, and 1916, 10.

Rank, O., *Don Juan: une étude sur de double*. Paris: Denoel et Steele, 1914.

Ruitenbeek, H. M. (Ed.), *Varieties of personality theory*. New York: E. P. Dutton, 1964.

Rogers, C. R., *Counseling and psychotherapy*. Boston: Houghton Mifflin, 1942.

——, Significant aspects of client-centered therapy. *Amer. Psychol.* 1946, 11, 415-422. (Reveals the early scientific structuring of the procedure.) Also in Ruitenbeek, 1964. (But it concerns process, not personality theory. The editor's introduction is full of errors. Rogers was born in *1902*. He has never called himself a psychoanalyst. Though he credits psycho-analysis with important clues, originally, there has not been a direct and unilateral dependence on the clinicians mentioned by the editor. Rank, on the other hand, is *not* mentioned though Rogers has been explicit regarding his original important debt to him and to Jessie Taft and Frederick Allen, both followers of Rank.)

——, and Wallen, J. L., *Counseling with returned servicemen*. New York: McGraw Hill, 1946. (Good, short account of client-centered procedure.)

——, *Client-centered therapy: Its current practice, implications, and theory*. New York: Houghton Mifflin, 1951. (Best comprehensive exposition Chapters 2-5 especially valuable.)

——, and Diamond, Rosalind (Eds.), *Psychotherapy and personality change*. Chicago, Univ. of Chicago Press, 1954.

——, A theory of therapy, personality, and interpersonal relations, as developed in the client-centered framework. In Koch, *op. cit.*, pp. 184-256. (Precise definition of terms and formulation of hypotheses.)

——, *On becoming a person*. Boston: Houghton Mifflin, 1961. (Selected papers, 1951-1961. Wide range of topics. Excellent brief accounts of major contributions. Complete bibliography through April, 1961.)

——, Client-centered therapy. In Arieti, *op. cit.*, pp. 183-200. (A brief up-to-date exposition which clarifies some important issues.)

——, Gendlin, E. T., Kiesler, D. J., Truax, M., and Charles B., *The therapeutic relation with schizophrenics*. Madison: Univ. of Wisconsin Press, 1967. (Report of a five-year research: plan, instruments, methods, results, and samples of the therapy. Includes evaluations by outside experts.)

Ruitenbeek, H. M. (Ed.), *Varieties of personality theory*. New York: E. P. Dutton, 1964.

Stollack, G. E., Guerney, B. G., Jr., and Rothberg, (Eds.), *Psychotherapy research—selected readings*. Chicago: Rand McNally, 1966.

Tigpen, C. H., and Cleckley, H. M., A case of multiple personality. *J. Abnorm. Soc. Psychol.*, 1954, 49, 135-151.

——, *The three faces of Eve*. New York: McGraw-Hill, 1957.

Whyte, L. L., *Everyman looks forward*. New York: Holt, 1948. (Out of print.)

——, *The next development in man*. New York: Mentor, 1950.

——, *The unconscious before Freud*. New York: Basic Books, 1960.

——, *Essay on atomism from democritus to 1960*. New York: Harper Torchbooks, 1961.

Worchel, P., and Byrne, D. (Eds.), *Personality change*. New York: John Wiley and Sons, 1964.

CHAPTER 25

Interpretation as Active Nurture:
An Interpersonal Perspective

Edwin Kasin, M.D.

Dr. Edwin Kasin received his medical degree from New York University College of Medicine in 1938, began psychiatric training in 1940, spent four years in the army during World War II, and subsequently completed his training as a psychoanalyst at the William A. White Institute in 1948; he has been an active teacher on their faculty, as well as a training and supervising analyst. His own teachers included Drs. Harry Stack Sullivan, Frieda Fromm-Reichmann, Janet Rioch, Erich Fromm, and Clara Thompson.

He is a member of the Washington Psychoanalytic Society, a charter fellow of the Academy of Psychoanalysis, and an Adjunct Professor of Psychology in the N.Y.U. Post-Doctoral Psychology program. He is mainly engaged in teaching and private practice but manages to find a little time to pursue what he refers to as "the frustrating challenge of the oboe."

From his very beginning, either as a phylum or as an individual, the behavior of man has been trying to catch up with his philosophy. As soon as he appears to have done so, he invents new possibilities and is off again. Man changes his environment and in turn finds himself needing to change to deal with this alteration of environment. In the individual this process is called mental growth; for the phylum it is called civilization.

Freud gave us a tool, psychoanalysis, the first draft of a method to investigate the meaning of mental disorder. As frequently happens, the use of a tool reveals something yet unknown about the problem to be solved. Increased knowledge of the problem suggests new tools. In turn, these illuminate new aspects of the problem, and eventually a great many new unsolved problems must be handled with as yet undevised tools. What has happened, however, is that the operation can be continued in a richer, broader context.

From the study of symptoms, and diagnosis of particular varieties of neurosis, we were led to the elucidation of character structure, to the general structure of personality, to the study of the interpersonal nature of personality, to the adaptive nature of mental illness, to the illness of society, and to considerations of identity and values in the life of each man and the very questioning of the sanity of anyone.

With these developments it became necessary for many psychoanalysts to modify their notions of the boundaries of the field and especially their role in the therapeutic relationship. We know that patients are genuinely helped regardless of the theoretical orientation of the therapist. Perhaps not enough attention has been paid to the meaning of this phenomenon in the process of evaluating what is more readily apparent—one body of theory as against another.

In trying to orient myself in this growing field (in my work generally with patients, and from what I have read and heard from colleagues), various thoughts began to organize themselves and to lead to the notion of interpretation as active nurturing. I have found it convenient to consider persons for treatment from two different aspects: (1) What signs and symptoms are present (under the general category of the manifestations of anxiety)? (2) How far has the individual developed along the stages of growth or maturation? It is this second category that I wish to dwell upon in this paper.

Stated differently, each person arrives with a particular diagnosis, but in the course of getting to know him we discover he manifests particular patterns of relatedness which stem from disturbances in development and have their origin predominantly in infancy, childhood, the juvenile period, preadolescence, or early and late adolescence. Furthermore, we discover an intimate connection between the presenting symptom and the lack of preparation necessary for the fulfillment of the requirements of the current life situations. It is this lack of preparation, which may be restated as a failure of growth or the failure to have had the necessary preliminary preparatory life experience, which will become one of our central preoccupations in treatment.

Any success in psychotherapy relies on the fact that in each individual there is a force variously described as vitality, the will to live, libido, life energy, or a drive toward mental health. The biological organism, impelled to fulfill its potential, grows, and in the course of its growth it manifests the wonder of life. The human organism develops in an environment which must include other persons, and the organism demonstrates an expanding, complicated fabric interwoven with biologic needs and social requirements. In an unfavorable environment the possibilities for simple maturation of capabilities are interfered with, and to the extent that these interferences distort behavior, the individual becomes a candidate for psychotherapeutic intervention. This statement is scarcely news to anyone; but with the wealth of theoretic formulation in this field, it is all too easy to lose track of the requirements of this simple human potential which is our greatest ally in treatment.

In this paper, following Sullivan's heuristic classification of the stages of development of the human organism, I wish to focus attention on (1) the particular quality of the active role of others which is necessary at each stage, and (2) the orderly progression of growth, each stage preparing the way for the next. Throughout the entire process a general rule applies: that first the biologic capability must mature, and then one must have appropriate experience with people to manifest this capability.

I also wish to point out how frequently the role of the other person, especially the parent and the chum, is strikingly similar to what the therapist finds himself doing in his daily work. I propose the notion that there is a favorable climate in which the growth of an individual proceeds in life generally; and I would like to consider the climate of therapeutic relationship and its relation to what we say and how we say it.

Although we deal continually with the context of anxiety in the difficulties of our patients, I would like to consider the broader context, the climate in which we as therapists function, in which the process of communication between patient and therapist ensues. I would also like to review at some length the stages of development as described by Sullivan. At each point I have had to resist the temptation to expand the thesis into greater depths and dimensions. This would lead us off into diversions and side issues. I can only suggest that when I state a fact it is the briefest summation of an active, vital, intense, interrelated life situation. This problem is well expressed in the story of the scientist and the poet who were passing a flock of sheep grazing on a hill side. The poet said, "It is spring; look, the sheep have just been sheared." The scientist looked over and replied, "Yes—on the side facing us." So, while I make these rather dry statements, according to the best scientific tradition, I trust the reader may bring to them the poetic side of his experience as well as his scientific skepticism.

The period of infancy begins at birth and continues to the appearance of the beginning capacity to use language. Shortly after birth all evidence of needs on the part of the newborn evokes a response of tender cooperation from the mothering one. The organization and proper functioning and development of the organ systems, the gastrointestinal tract, the respiratory tract, the skin, the neuromuscular apparatus, and so forth, all require the tender administrations of the mother. Studies have amply demonstrated the lasting effects of deprivation of tender loving care in these preverbal stages of development, as well as the optimistic and hopeful outgoingness which appears directly attributable to early sufficiency of attention and affection. I primarily wish to note that successful infancy is linked to the willing acceptance, the alert ministrations, the reliability, and the security in the love of an ever-present, nonanxious, attentive mother—in brief, the interpersonal nurturing atmosphere.

We know that deprivation of a mothering figure, despite the presence of all physical requirements, once led to marasmus. This means that, to survive at all, one's first interpersonal experiences must be good ones, that the earliest prehended relationships of the infant must include a prehension of "optimism" concerning the fulfillment of needs. I believe that what we later call "hope" is essentially the felt aspect of the satisfaction of needs and the process of growth, and with this notion alone, one could project a biologic basis for a brotherhood of man. It is only because of this early full cooperation for the fulfillment of need that life could at all proceed.

The period of childhood, the next era, begins with the development of the language faculty and continues until the maturation of a need for compeers. Now the child begins to be trained in the requirements of the culture—more specifically, the parent's version of the culture. We see a continual nurturing of the aspects of behavior which they believe will be useful and necessary for living in their world. The constant total acceptance of all needs of the infant is replaced by a conditional acceptance. The child receives approval or tenderness to the extent his behavior conforms: conversely, he receives disapproval for performances which would violate the mores of the culture. Providing the climate for learning is favorable, this conditional acceptance is the primitive basis for what later will become the individual's sense of responsibility—namely, that modifications of his own behavior will have an effect in securing the satisfaction of his needs. This learning takes place by rewards, punishments, and human example. The parents are the teachers.

There are some general rules for good teaching that are applicable not only in the classroom and in the raising of children, but also in the treatment of patients. Good teaching requires consistency, repetition, and sanity. By sanity is meant behavior which is geared to the capacity or ability of the child to analyze, observe, and elab-

orate. This requires that the parents be attuned to the needs and frustration tolerance of the child. The child learns by play and through curiosity, experimentation
and elaboration in fantasy. A highly complex process (called "eduction" by
Spearman) proceeds out of the capacity of our nervous system and enables us to
pull out the durable and dependable relationships in the world. All of this is very
susceptible to parental approvals or disapprovals. Should a particular gift appear
but go unrecognized by the parents, it might succumb to the hazards of indifference.

The child learns foresight and how to arrive at particular goals, and he gets a
sense of happiness in successful achievements of behavior. A general sense of self-
esteem develops out of the realistic pleasure the parents reflect for his
performances. He seeks out information about the behavior of the parents, because
he needs to know and learn about some of the puzzling meanings of certain complex behavior on their part. The parents' honest and sane cooperation is necessary
for this development.

A sense of maleness or femaleness arises out of the tender appreciation of aspects
of behavior which emerge in play and imitative behavior. Usually the more accepting attitudes of the parent of the other sex will stamp in the feeling of the value
of being a little boy or girl.

The negative aspects in this era that result from failures of nurture emerge in the
personality as attitudes of marked obedience or rebelliousness. Experience with
fear-provoking situations lead to preoccupations which, if major, may severely crip-
ple maturity. The child may develop handicapping patterns of concealments and
deceptions, as well as great confusions in foresight. Most destructive of all is the
development along the lines which Sullivan describes as the "malevolent
transformation of personality," in which chronic experience with rebuff of one's
needs leads to behavior calculated to call out rebuff.

So, in this period we see the continued need for tenderness, sane regard, and
participation in the child's development. As a protection against ridicule in the next
period, the child must be taught to distinguish between fantasy and reality, since he
is likely to suffer at the hands of the more mature juveniles if he is allowed to remain too infantile.

The juvenile period arrives when the need for people his own age matures. Fantasy life diminishes and he becomes more occupied with fellows like himself. The
child leaves the sole environment of the family and enters a world which includes
other authorities (the policeman, the teacher, other parents) and similar juveniles.
He learns the skills of social accommodation with others of his own age. He com-
pares, noticing even slight differences in the behavior and attitudes of others, both
adult and juvenile. He learns the skills of cooperation and competition—winning
one day, losing the next, but generally getting along.

The juvenile develops a cleverness in dealing with people of all sorts. So many
new people arrive in his life that they have to be dealt with by the construction of
stereotypes. This is clever, but not wise. Cleverness characterizes much of the quality of the relatedness in the juvenile era. Cleverness is manipulative, for one
enhances one's prestige at the expense of people or things. Wisdom, on the other
hand, has as its central quality the inclusion, appreciation, and understanding of the
humanity of others. (I cannot resist the temptation at this point to say that civiliza-

tion as we know it is now in its clever stage and has not yet reached its preadolescence, which is the period that follows this one.)

At the end of the juvenile period, the parents are no longer perceived as god-like. Enough experience has been lived through so that the juvenile has formed what might be called an orientation to living. This important development involves a knowledge of his needs and how to get them satisfied fairly simply, plus an ability to postpone immediate satisfaction for the sake of future satisfaction.

In the negative aspects, as the result of failure in this period the parents remain god-like. One may avoid competition entirely and settle everything for peace and quiet, or be completely involved with being better than others. Or one may be simply eager to be liked, or to amuse for the sake of the uncritical regard of insignificant people.

Juveniles are likely to be insensitive to the needs of others; and in the process of learning a great deal about getting along with a group, under threat of ostracism, they may lose a lot of potential. Juvenile society reflects the larger society, and the richer, fantasy life is discouraged in this culture. (This is an unfortunate consequence, and perhaps can be viewed as an object lesson of the point I am trying to make concerning the importance of nurturing climates.) This era is therefore not likely to be particularly enhancing creatively, but rather more adjustive. I think it partially explains why it has been labeled the "latency period."

Preadolescence, the next period, arrives as a new type of need matures—the need for personal intimacy, for a chum of the same sex. Sullivan refers to it as "a quiet miracle." The significant positive effect on development of this experience serves to doubly draw our attention to the importance of nurture. I see the "chumship" as a renewal of the exclusive mothering relationship of early life, but now on a higher level. In infancy, it was in relation to general body needs; in childhood, to the need for acculturation. Then, having been exposed to the wear and tear of the juvenile era, having achieved some separation from parents, the need now appears as the need to be nurtured as an individual.

One needs to be nurtured in one's new adaptations. Successful chumships are marked by such care in protecting each other's self-esteem that all areas of personal experience are opened for comparison, and the evaluation of the real worth of both other's and one's own endearing and nonendearing traits is possible. An ideal society of two is formed in which the illusory feeling of being different is dissipated. Out of this collaboration each gains the feeling of belonging to the wider human race. This period includes the first development of real concern for another person; this is love and in it are the anlage, the model, for humanistic ethics and values and wisdom. When the other person is as important to you as you are to yourself, conditions of status are secondary. The satisfaction of genuine sharing and concern is so rewarding that all other considerations pall. I believe that this relationship, in its deepest possibilities, occurs relatively infrequently, or that what develops is a diluted version of what might be. This is due to the massive intrusions of the larger, essentially-juvenile society to which we all belong.

Early adolescence is ushered in by the puberty developments and the possibility for lust, with movements for development of chum relationships with the other sex, and the gradual inclusion of others of one's age in forming young societies modeled on the adult society. This blends into late adolescence, where definitive patterns of sexual relatedness are formed.

Concerning human maturing, Sullivan (1953) states:

The most mature are the least accessible for study; each of the outstanding achievements of the developmental eras will be outstandingly manifest in the mature personality. The appearance and growth of the need for intimacy with at least one other
includes a lively sensitivity to the needs and security of the other. The mature individual will be quite sympathetically understanding of the limitations, interests, possibilities, anxieties and so on of those among whom they move. By widening and deepening interests, life, far from becoming a bore is always increasingly important.

This description of development would be incomplete without some reference to
the important phenomenon of loneliness. Sullivan considered its roots to be
fourfold: (1) out of the infantile and continuing need for physical contact with
other humans, (2) out of the childhood need for audience participation, (3) out of
the juvenile fear of ostracism, and (4) out of the preadolescent need for intimate
exchange. This can be reformulated as the need to nurture whatever one has
developed or is developing, be it physical or mental. Loneliness in this consideration
is the felt aspect of the lack of a nurturing other person. Just as deprivation at the
beginning of life can lead to death (which would indicate how imperative the need
is), so in later life this driving force of loneliness can lead to complicated involvements with others, despite the severest anxiety.

I have followed the individual briefly through the various stages of growth and
maturation, emphasizing the essential role of others who appear as active nurturing
figures in this development. Growth occurs primarily out of experiences with them
where needs are fulfilled, and frustration or deprivation of such experience is
destructive of smooth development. The key words are *active nurturing*.

There is a curious and remarkable discrepancy on the whole, between the public
statements, theoretical attitudes, and the facade which many therapists assume, and
the reports of patients who have worked successfully with them. I have been particularly impressed that the patients' reports emphasize the warm nurturing aspects
of the relatedness. When they needed help in a crisis and when they needed a kind
word, reassurance, or sympathy, apparently they felt the humanness of their
therapist. Yet, in their public mode, these very therapists often seem to reject the
notion that they played such a nurturing role. I believe there is a confusion between
being simply human and somehow contributing to the perpetuation of a dependent
relationship. I wish to disassociate myself from any notion that I am suggesting that
one should baby one's patients. On the contrary, I believe one must be firm with the
neurosis, but at the same time one must keep in mind the defensive nature of the
neurosis which is protecting the person beneath while also preventing new experience and growth.

Nurturing varies considerably with the level of maturity which the individual has
achieved, and this is why it makes considerable sense to obtain a complete history,
if possible, at the beginning of the work. We learn what experiences patients have
had and we can make intelligent assessments of what they have missed. An individual living predominantly in any particular era of development needs a
particular response from the world in order for it to make any inner sense to him.

A 45-year-old woman was involved in a marriage which had been marked by continual fighting for over 20 years. She couldn't tolerate her husband's indifference, for
which she would attack him. In turn, he would withdraw and become icily punitive.
She was as impulsive as he was controlled. Her previous therapy had concentrated

on her destructive attitudes to her husband, and came to include destructive attitudes to the therapist.

Her history was one of utter neglect and indifference by her parents. We therefore concentrated on her central feeling of neglect and its sources. I made every effort to emphasize her positive potential, which was real; in other words, I was the good parent. I asked her to take a look at who her husband was, to understand that he had not had enough in his life even to begin to make up for her tremendous need. It was the first time she had ever considered this. Like the child, she had been unable to discriminate.

After a separation from her husband, she was intolerably lonely; I was the only one she could talk to, and I made myself available during this crisis. She experienced the grief of a child separated from a parent. After some time she began to see other men, and on the basis of comparison gradually began to be able to evaluate them as they really were. She learned who were detached or empty and unrelated, and eventually she made friends of both sexes. At this point then, she developed an orientation to life (which brought her to the end of the juvenile stage). She could now see clearly the infantile nature of her marriage relationship, her inordinate demands, and so forth. She had acted out an early pattern directed at an apathetic parent in connection with her husband and her previous therapist. I was not apathetic to her needs on the whole, although I frequently was not completely with her, but was frank to say so. I nurtured the neglected child in her. Later she found her own sources, and we were involved in a chumship type of relationship, in which I sensed her growing feeling of equality and related to it.

This patient was a real infant. She was certainly destructive, and she knew it. But what does it mean to an infant to say, "See here, be reasonable and act grown up." As far as she was concerned, her husband had everything she wanted and was just being spiteful, and she could not accept that. Nurturing in this case included an acceptance by the therapist of the fatherly role, spreading the context of the patient's unlived life in front of her, and sharing with her the struggle to reorganize and modify her life through her own growth.

Early in my work, I was under the influence of the notion to be quite formal and removed and to pay strict attention to the so-called transference aspects of the work. Any feelings of my own, I felt, belonged more appropriately in my own analysis, and although noted by me were not to be used directly in the work. During this period, a number of patients would from time to time have rather similar dreams, all variations on a repetitive theme: They would be with me in the office. We were not alone, however, because various members of my family were there with us. "Nothing much more happened," they said.

These dreams would usually occur in the course of their discussions to clarify their relationships with their own parents. At first I was puzzled. We tried various interpretations, none of which rang true, until one day it occurred to me that this was their way of reporting their experience of this artificial separation. I was with them and yet I wasn't, which actually was exactly what I had been trying to do. All of them had had the common experience of deprivation, of personal and singular attention from their parents. They had missed this exclusive relationship in their early lives. Since then, I have changed my approach and have become much more responsive and free in expressing my feelings about them and the work. What has impressed me is that in the last ten years I have never had a single similar dream reported. I have theorized that, in the interest of their needs, they were calling to my attention something about me which deprived them of something they lacked and wanted. As far as I can tell, this change in my availability as a human being has not interfered with our work; rather, it has nurtured their need and has made it more possible for them to relinquish these infantile, unsatisfied yearnings.

This is not the only technique, I am sure, but it is one that I have found will frequently work. For instance, there are many women who are quite uncertain and unsure of their attractiveness as females. In a number of cases, where we worked through their childish attitudes toward themselves and the world, they began to experience me no longer as purely an authority figure, but frequently entertained a variety of romantic notions. This would stimulate reciprocal feelings in me. I generally viewed this as a healthy development toward maturity and found that some acknowledgment to them that they are able to do this proved very nourishing to their self-esteem. (Of course, I must add that I do not believe that any acting out in this area should be encouraged.) I have not found this to be a hazard; instead, it is an impetus for them to use this newly-felt power to develop relationships with men outside the therapy hour. I rather believe that failure to acknowledge such bids for validation tends to perpetuate seductive behavior. It is rather similar to the child who clings to the mother who wishes to reject him, but feels free to go when he is secure in her acceptance.

What I am suggesting is that after, or in the course of, discussing the neurotic problem as such, these patients tried to get something they were entitled to as children. Having gotten something of a small sample from me, they could go on from there. I became aware of the personal importance that I had to them as a reality figure. They wanted and could use something that I really could give them—not my soul, nor an opportunity to manipulate me, but a chance to experience my undivided and concentrated interest as well as my human reactions to their behavior. At this point, they were usually more ready to move toward others. They seemed to soak up something, which, if they had originally experienced it, would have averted the neurotic problem.

Another patient who puzzled me for a long time was a vague, evasive young woman who spoke in an affectively flat tone. For a number of months, I could get no handle on what she was talking about in the hours. It included vague reports of vague events with rather bizarre people. Her life seemed lived in a very unrelated way, in a series of continual parties which kept her exceedingly busy. The only information I had about her which might have had some reliability were her dreams, of which she had a moderate number. There were, however, few associations, and these were offered with very little conviction. A few, which I interpreted for myself, gave me some clue to her inner conviction that she could get help from no one, and that if she tried, she would make things worse.

What concerned me was that I found myself quite bored and that I wasn't able to get interested in anything she had to say. She was so dull in delivery that, although she did not lack words, it was hard listening to her. She was not very much impressed by any interpretations I had to make. My concern was that she was a dull, empty, hopelessly uninteresting person. I find it very necessary for me to feel some interest in my patients, so I spent a great deal of time worrying over this and finally discussed the problem with a colleague. I seriously considered transferring her.

I disclosed to my colleague my concern that she did not arouse my interest. In other words, I could not find where the person was. His reply was, essentially, that considering how much thought and time I had spent on her outside the hours, I must find her of more interest than I was aware. At this I felt encouraged, so I told her, "Look, I don't know what's going on with you, what you want for yourself or from me. You avoid saying anything very real, and that is very dull for me to listen to. You seem to say nothing about yourself, and the way you say it lulls me to sleep. However,

I have spent a great deal of my time thinking about what's going on here, and to me that means that there's something about you that's alive and could grow, but God knows what! You work full time to hide it."

This roused her considerably. Tears came to her eyes and she said, "You mean, you think about me?" I asked her what was so surprising about that. She then appeared quite moved and began to tell me about the indifferent surroundings in which she had spent her childhood. Her parents had both been caught up in a social whirl. Their children had never been real to them and had been raised mostly by a series of casually-hired servants.

It is not relevant to go on with the details, except to say that she eventually turned out to be an immensely rewarding creative individual. I believe that this sudden dramatic presentation, which I delivered quite emphatically, supplied her with the beginnings of an experience which she had unfortunately been deprived of in her early life. What I had been dealing with were the transference aspects, but it was the human approach which nurtured the person within.

Another example of the salutary effect of a simple human response in the course of therapy occurred many years ago. A patient began an hour by asking me if I would write a note for him on my stationery stating that he had been ill, so that he could use it to collect sick pay. He had been ill for one day, had not seen a doctor, and it was on a day when I would ordinarily not see him. I knew nothing about the illness, therefore, until his arrival on this particular day. For numerous reasons, I said, "No, I couldn't; it would make me too uncomfortable." The matter was dropped and we went on with some work that had been under discussion. I was preoccupied to some extent with my own problems which he had aroused, and I spent much time later trying to clarify what I really felt. I was secretly ashamed to discover that it was not so much an ethical problem, but my own fears.

Subsequently, he told me that as he left the office that day he found himself singing and happy, in an elated mood and feeling suddenly released. As he thought about it, to explain this feeling, his mind settled on the beginning of the hour and he suddenly realized that he knew what had happened. Any request he had ever made to his mother was likely to get answered in such a sticky, manipulative fashion, with such resentfulness, suspicions, and so forth, that he would always leave feeling guilty and confused. She had taken no responsibility in any of these encounters and resented his demands as an intrusion on her life. She would get anxious and turn on him for making her feel inadequate. In an accidental way my answer had made it clear to him that we were separate, that he was he and I was I, and that I had my problems and did not have to make them his problems. This new experience opened the world for communication. Formerly, all he had expected was recrimination and guilt.

With regard to the foregoing example, I might have responded that I felt he was manipulating me and putting me on the spot. One of the hazards of our work is that we can never know what might have happened had we acted differently. However, in general, people don't stop manipulating when they are caught at it; they get more refined at it. They stop when they've grown beyond the need to relate to the world as children or juveniles. Significantly, I did not feel he was manipulating me, but rather I experienced my own conflicts which he unwittingly had precipitated. It was this feeling to which I responded.

Our society is notoriously unnurturing. In this way, I believe, it is responsible for a great deal of alienation. Sullivan has described how the infant, failing to have his needs responded to, develops a state of apathy or somnolent detachment. This response to the lack of nurture exists on a broader scale in society because of society's indifference to general human needs. There is a tendency for tenderness to be confused with weakness, nurturing to be confused with infantilizing, and concern to be confused with overprotection. The therapeutic situation has, as its purpose, the growth of the individual; and this growth requires a climate of nurture. This points out the way, the flavor, of communicating with patients.

Classical psychoanalysis, with its emphasis on the events of the first six years of life, implicitly recognized the need to make up the deficiencies incurred in this period. The developments of family and group therapy, I believe, have occurred in response to a felt need for individuals to get a second try at the childhood and juvenile experience they have missed. Existential therapy, concerned with values and identity, is also a current development out of the sense of the need to nurture the more mature aspects of life.

With the reader's indulgence, I would like to make an extremely hypothetical formulation to help illustrate what I have been trying to say. Let us suppose an individual, because of his previous history, manifests what I believe is a terribly serious distortion in living—namely, the malevolent transformation of personality. By this I mean that he has been so humiliated and rebuffed in his early movements for tenderness that he manifests hateful behavior whenever the need for tenderness is felt.

By some miracle, let us transport this person to a society of individuals of the utmost maturity. Given sufficient lifetime, I believe we would witness the dissolution of this pattern and the eventual development of this person to a maturity approximating that of the rest of the society. Driven by his needs for interpersonal relatedness, he would eventually notice the massive experience of their behavior as so different from his. He would have to reformulate some of his notions of reality; he would test our reality, as it were, trying to make it conform to his early notions of the world, but his environment would be so sensitive to the meaning of the malevolence, so understanding of his difficulties and needs, that this would be impossible; and eventually he would change his inner construction of the world and his expectations thereof. Somewhere, sometime, he would expose the person within at the level he was in development, accept the nurture of society, and go on to become like them.

If, by some further miracle, there were a therapist in this society, I believe the chief difference would be that the whole process I have described could be immeasurably speeded up. Utilizing his specific training, he would nurture foresight in the patient (according to the principles of consistency, repetition, and sanity that characterized the desirable parental attitude previously discussed). The presence of a mature climate in the larger world would simplify this task to a great extent.

In the course of training for a therapist, we insist that it include both formal training in a theory of human development and possibilities, and a personal analysis to develop the underlying person (which exists in each one of us). We advocate a full understanding of how one came to be the person one is, and our selection of students is based on their potential for full and rich emotional development. We value strong and vital feelings as opposed to weak and superficial ones. Ideally, we emphasize all those qualities which lead to warm, spontaneous relatedness. It would seem to me to follow that such a person (the therapist), in the course of a growing relationship with a patient who necessarily starts out as less mature, would find himself experiencing a whole gamut of emotions in some way reciprocal to that which the patient is experiencing.

How these are used in the therapy is another story, but I believe it matters very much that we have them. It is what makes the relationship, at its root, real and vital. As our patients grow, we must have a response of pleasure and pride, such as we have in the growth in our own children or loved ones. Similarly, when it comes time to separate, we must experience the pangs of grief that accompany separation—in the same way that the departure of anyone we have come to know intimately can affect us. These are not countertransference phenomena as I view them. To the extent that the relationship is real, these responses seem to me inevitable. They are part of the nurturing climate in which we exercise our main skill, the resolution of anxieties.

REFERENCE

Sullivan, H. S., *The interpersonal theory of psychiatry*. New York: W. W. Norton, 1953.

CHAPTER 26

The Experiential Response

EUGENE T. GENDLIN, PH.D.

Dr. Gendlin was born in Vienna, Austria, came to this country, and received his masters and doctorate at the University of Chicago. There he studied under Richard McKeon in philosophy and Carl Rogers in psychology. At the University of Wisconsin he directed a research project on psychotherapy with hospitalized schizophrenics. He is concerned with theory of personality and personality change, and with the philosophic bases for the new trends in psychology. He is now in the Philosophy and Psychology Departments at the University of Chicago, where he teaches and is engaged in research in "focusing" on feeling in relation to outcome in psychotherapy. He is Editor of Psychotherapy: Theory, Research and Practice, *the quarterly journal published by PIAP, Psychotherapy Section of Division 12, American Psychological Association.*

While keeping one foot planted in the client-centered domain, Dr. Gendlin is reaching into existentialist territory with his other foot. Midway between the two, he is developing a system which may prove to be the forefront of the continually-evolving Rogerian and existential orientations. Gendlin's chapter represents a comprehensive rethinking and systemization of just what works in therapy, and why.

RULES FOR RESPONSES

Felt Meaning

Personal problems and difficulties in living are never just cognitive, never only a question of how something is interpreted or understood. There is always an affective, emotional, felt, concrete, experiential difficulty. The individual's thoughts and interpretations flow from, and are largely influenced by, his affective ways of living in his situations.

A helping person's responses, therefore, must at least sometimes have an affective experiential effect,[1] if they are to have any problem-resolution effect at all. The question, "What is the best sort of therapist response?" leads us to the question, "How can a therapist's response have a concrete experiential effect in the individual?"

---

[1] In these footnotes, I will comment on the relations between psychoanalysis and client-centered or experiential psychotherapy. My view is that, when effective (and done as the best practitioners of each orientation prescribe), the two modes of responding are extremely similar. However, the way in which the optimal therapist response is conceptualized in the two schools is very different, and hence, the typical ways of misunderstanding it are also different. Thus, different pitfalls arise in the two orientations.

An "experiential effect" is also the aim of good psychoanalytic interpretations. Fenichel (1945) says: "In giving an interpretation, the analyst seeks to intervene in the dynamic interplay of forces, to change the balance . . . . The degree to which this change actually occurs is the criterion for the validity of an interpretation. A valid interpretation brings about a dynamic change . . . ." Thus, an interpretation must not only be correct, but must produce a dynamic change. In the above, I employ an experiential vocabulary, and I term what I take to be the same event an "experiential effect." It is an effect which the individual can feel, concretely.

The client-centered type of therapist response used to be called "reflection of feeling." Considering how it has since evolved (Rogers, 1958, 1961, 1963; Gendlin, 1955-66, Gendlin and Zimring, 1955; Butler, 1958), it is probably better termed an "experiential response."

"Reflection of feeling" emphasized feeling, affect, and concrete experiencing; but, the word "feeling" seemed to refer to very specific emotions, such as love, hate, joy, anger, fear. Of course, there are times when one does feel quite distinct emotions of this sort, but much more often one feels nothing as clear as that. Instead, one is up against a complicated and somewhat unclear situation. Rogers (1951) explains "reflection of attitudes" (which soon came to be called "reflection of feeling") with examples such as, "This makes you feel helpless." "Helpless" is not really an emotion. Similarly, most often one feels, for example, "upset," "uncomfortable," or "resentful because . . ." or "worried that . . ." or "hoping for . . . but discouraged that. . . ." These more common conditions are not really "emotions" but complicated ways we react and ways we see ourselves in situations.

From these examples we can form three conclusions: First, what the experiential response refers *to* is not usually sharply clear emotions, but rather a more complex experiencing. We may feel all this very strongly, even though we may not know clearly what we feel.

Second, what we feel is not an internal object (an "affective state" as something *only* inside us), but a felt sense of a whole situation—how we are in that situation, what we bring about, perceive, and feel we are up against.

Third, this felt sense also involves how we have interpreted and construed the situation. Therefore, such a felt sense isn't something *only* felt, but is also intellectual. We may be quite confused about what it involves, but at least *implicitly* it always involves aspects of interpretation, i.e., thought, learning, perception, and construing.

Thus, the "feeling" we respond to in another person is not usually a sharply-defined emotion, not usually separate from the situation, and not without some implicit intellectual cognition. For the therapist to respond, "You are worried that . . ." refers to an experiencing of the individual which includes, in one felt whole, his feeling of an intellectually interpreted situation.

Of course, as therapists, we may not be mainly concerned with the individual's specific present situations so much as with the personality difficulties he brings into all his situations. These difficulties should not be conceptualized as though they were little things inside him. They are real, noticeable, and felt by him only as he lives in situations (with others, or alone in his room). The experiential response on the part of the therapist aims at the patient's concrete feeling which always implicitly includes the situational and intellectual aspects, i.e., how the individual sets up and construes situations, his maladjusted learnings, past experiences, and ways of perceiving and creating situations.

Typically, by the time one is "up against" a situation, one has *already* brought the situation about, set it up and construed it with one's emotions, learnings, past experiences, and hence with one's personality difficulties. Thus, it is correct to say that the specific situation doesn't matter; only his personality difficulties really matter. It would be an error, however, to conceptualize personality difficulties in terms of internal entities and to seek to respond to such entities while ignoring the way in which they are actually manifest and felt in the individual's experiencing. Experiencing always involves, not emotion-entities, but detailed person-situation complexities which are concretely felt.

Although felt by an individual, all this may not yet have been carried into words and may not have been directly viewed in terms of general cognized meanings or patterns. A great many facets—all in one—are often strongly felt, but as yet only implicit.[2] The first rule is that *we respond to felt meaning* (this is very much in the individual's awareness, but it is felt and may not be at all conceptually clear).

Explicating the Felt Meaning

The client may *say* something like this: "She isn't willing to look for an apartment where I said she should. She went every other damn place except there, and so we won't be living there." These two sentences are perfectly clear. The client-centered reflection of feeling would involve the therapist sensing anger here. ("You are angry that she deliberately didn't do what you asked," might be a reflection of such feeling.)

We can always assume that the experiencing of the problem is more complicated and that hence the present feeling implicitly involves much more. Yes, there is anger here, but not *just* anger. Anger (any emotion) is not an inside thing, but a way we are interactively. We are never just angry, always angry *at*. Experiencing is an interactive process (Gendlin, 1964). The situation in which we are angry, and the other people we are angry at, always involve many more specific facets. "Angry" is only a short-cut word—a broad, crude classification of feelings.

In our example, the therapist responds to the felt meaning and uses some word like "angry" or "furious" or "mad." But it makes all the difference if the therapist, in responding, points at a felt sense that is really more complex. No matter how precise and clear what the client says may be, we must always *assume* and refer to a concrete felt sense. As experiential, the client can refer to it *directly,* and it always involves many implicit[3] aspects and complex reactions. If the therapist's response

---

[2]Some therapists might insist that the actual realities they work with are dynamic entities. They would consider the experiential complexity the person experiences as only a superstructure. Others, myself for example, might insist the opposite: the dynamics are only our (often excellent) generalizations of what really exists only as the detailed experiential complexity.

This issue need not be settled so far as practice is concerned, since, whatever our view, it remains the fact that we employ dynamic knowledge to understand and sensitize ourselves to the individual, whereas with him we must "work through" the difficulty in the concrete experiential way, the only way in which he can feel and work with it.

Perhaps the only real difference is that psychoanalysts consider it valuable to teach the patient the generalizations first, so that he can then search for his own concrete experiential versions. In contrast, experiential therapists see this as "intellectualizing" and getting the individual off the track of his experiential focus, which alone has value. The individual can produce his own conceptual generalizations directly from his experiential process, and these are more specific and better suited to each individual.

[3]What I term "implicit" would be conceptualized by psychoanalysts as "repressed" or "subconscious," but they would add that felt anxiety or complex discomfort indicates that the repressed is close to the surface and might be about to emerge. It is only to such "unconscious" matters as are "about to emerge" that *effective* psychoanalytic interpretations can be given. Fenichel says: "Since interpretation means helping something unconscious to become conscious by naming it at the moment it is striving to break through, effective interpretations can be given only at one specific point, namely, where the patient's immediate interest is momentarily centered" (*op. cit.,* p. 25).

points to the implicitly complex experiencing, it is much easier for the client to continue to feel and search into what he is up against. He may soon say: "And *that's* really what makes me mad about the whole thing; it's her ignoring me. I see now that I'm not so angry about our not living where I wanted, but rather about her way of ignoring what I ask for." Whatever the therapist's next response is, he ought to be aware that more is implicitly present. He can expect that there might now come up facets about needing to be loved, or perhaps understood rather than ignored, or perhaps new and old feelings of being hurt. Then, again, perhaps none of these facets will come up, but instead something about the client's having prematurely given up and assumed that he cannot in any way enforce his wishes. If his wife didn't look where he wanted, then they won't be living there. Perhaps he gives up too fast; or perhaps he doesn't try to enforce his wishes, because anything you have to force someone to do doesn't count as love or understanding.

The therapist's experiential responses draw the client's attention directly to his own felt meaning. The therapist merely aids. Only as the client "focuses" on his felt meaning, can it shift, and only *from it* can further facets emerge.[4] Some individuals come into psychotherapy with a great ability to engage in this experiential "focusing" (Gendlin, 1968), while with others the therapist must struggle to draw their attention again and again to the felt sense they concretely have. Sometimes the client acts as though he had no idea that he has access to anything but his words. Nevertheless, the therapist must assume and imagine that the client has a directly *felt* sense of the whole complexity of the problem, and the responses must be pointed at such a felt meaning. If necessary, the therapist can imagine for the client many general directions into which the client's further explicating might lead him, but these are only examples of what the client *might* find if he attends to his felt meaning. The therapist will try these in a form in which they take only a small step further from what the client says. All such responses have the intent to invite the client to see for himself what will actually be there for him if he attends to what he can concretely feel. On the other hand, if the client already "focuses" directly on the felt meanings of his experiencing, the therapist must follow by responding exactly

---

Thus, while the psychoanalytic theory of the unconscious differs in many ways from client-centered theory, *that* unconscious to which an effective interpretation refers is exactly what I term "implicit felt meaning."

Thus the client-centered reflection and the psychoanalytic interpretation are quite similar, *when done effectively.* On the other hand, when done poorly, they differ: the psychoanalytic interpretation done poorly tends to lead the patient into intellectualizing and away from his concrete concerns, while the client-centered reflection done poorly tends to repeat what the client said.

[4] In psychoanalysis "free association" can be concretely similar to the above, but it is not always so. Two uses of free association exist in psychoanalytic practices: In one use free association consists in the patient voicing associations until the analyst notices something he can interpret. The analyst then interprets it, often without effect. There is little here that is experiential for the patient. What is interpreted exists primarily as an inferred connection the analyst thinks of.

A second use of free association corresponds much more to the experiential process outlined above, and is also much more exactly what Freud intended. In that use, the patient free-associates until he runs into a block. The patient feels this block quite concretely, but is unable to explicate what it is. The analyst then points his interpretations directly at the patient's concrete, experiential sense of the presently felt blockage.

(though sometimes more explicitly) to the felt meaning on which the client is "focusing."

The term "focusing" seems like a "looking at" a felt datum. Really it is a process in which focuser and datum are one, and both change, as focusing is ongoing. One cannot attend to a feeling without thereby feeling it in a way one didn't moments earlier. To "focus on" is also a "feeling further" which explicates what is felt.

A second rule: *We try to explicate felt meaning so that new facets emerge concretely from it.*

Sensitivity: Trying Out Directions for an Experiential Advance

That felt meanings are implicitly complex is well known, but what is usually said is only that a therapist must be "sensitive," must "listen with the third ear," and hear all these facets so that he can help the client to become aware of them. However, in telling therapists to be "sensitive," we don't really tell them how this is done!

Everyone wishes to be sensitive, but what if he isn't? What does he do to be sensitive? Does sensitivity "just come to us"? No; I propose to tell how this "sensitive" responding is done. It is, in fact, done experientially, whatever the theory.

First of all, let us admit that we are often mistaken in what we expect the client to come up with. We are often wrong from moment to moment, and also sometimes wrong from month to month. No "x-ray" sensitivity is really involved. Nor does the secret lie in brilliant dynamic or insightful thinking. That usually gives us *many* leads, not just one. If we try out one lead very gently, whatever *then* comes up usually gives us more, different, or more detailed understanding. We may try out several varied leads, or expectations, based on different thoughts. These thoughts occur in us in a swift and sketchy fashion, as we practice. Thus, it is rarely the case that we have a single, sure, x-ray type sensitivity, whether intuitive or dynamic.

Knowing that the client's concrete felt sense is always complex and implicitly full of many facets, we try out this or that, and often nothing happens—no experiential effect. Occasionally, something does happen: the client is enabled to feel more intensely, or to formulate further or more clearly what he does feel. One *feels* the "knowing more clearly."

A third rule: *We try various tentative directions for an experiential advance.* Thus, the therapist aids the client's explication by tentatively trying out various directions until the client finds himself experiencing further. By "further" we mean either new relevant facets, or a clearer feeling.

Staying on the Experiential Track

If the therapist is going to try out various (often wrong) directions, he must know what to do (a) if the client does react in some important way, and (b) if the client has no experiential reaction to what the therapist said. Sensitivity is not really a magical source for the right therapist response; rather, it consists in carefully noticing the client's *next* reaction to what the therapist says.

(a) Although what the therapist's response has stirred in the client may be nothing like what the therapist expected, he is now going to respond to *that*. The secret of sensitivity is not in knowing what to say, but in guiding oneself to *then* respond to the subsequent reaction. No matter how relatively obtuse or wrong something the therapist is about to say, he can say it, if he will *then* respond to, ask about, and seek to understand the client's resulting experiential reaction.

(b) On the other hand, if the therapist's response turns out to have been merely irrelevant, the therapist must know how to return the client to his own experiential track. It is important that the client not think he must discuss and pursue something irrelevant just because the therapist brought it up. For example, if my client's answer to me is "Yes, that *must* be true . . . er," I know that my response is no good. People say something *must* be true if they have to *infer* it—i.e., when they don't feel it directly. The "er" also indicates that there is nowhere to go with what I said. Now I reply, "That sounds sort of right to you, but it isn't what you mainly feel now." And I thus invite him to attend, once more, to what he does feel, so that he won't get hung up on my useless response.

The purpose of therapist responses is not being right; therapist responses aim to carry the client's experiencing further. This can be done as well at the second opportunity as at the first.

Our fourth rule is: *We follow the client's experiential track.*

Experiential Reference: Our Responses Point

In the very simple description which has just been given, a fifth rule is already implied. Our responses point at the felt sense of it all, which the client now has. The response itself might turn out to be wrong or beside the point, but that is not as important as its aim. A therapeutic response always aims at the client's own directly-felt sense of what he is talking about. This aim is what makes it an "experiential response." This aim also implies that only the client's experiential reaction is the basic indicator of what is valid. My response may be true, wise and accurate, but it is useless[5] if it misses its main aim, which is to point to the client's directly-felt sense of all that he is up against.

We can always imagine an experiential felt sense of a more complex "all that" (even if the client has stated something quite specific), and imagine ourselves aiming to respond to the broader whole. We do so by quite specifically understanding what he says, for without such *specific* understanding, one doesn't get more deeply into the felt sense of the whole problem. Therefore we must grasp exactly and specifically all he says just as he intends it. Taking every highly specific facet the client can verbalize, we still imagine that even all this specificity tells us but one instance, or aspect, of the problem which he now explicates, as he directly feels the whole implicit complexity.

It is possible to respond "experientially" only because *one* felt meaning (one concretely felt "all this") can contain so *many* implicit facets, whereas what one says is always very limited. The whole dynamic tissue which a theory might infer is implicitly here, in this directly-felt sense the individual has as he speaks and says these limited things; but it is felt, not known. It is felt in an incomplete, incipient way. To lay it all out in words would be to cope with it. His problem is that he cannot. Hence, to actually succeed (over a period of time) in differentiating and explicating

---

[5]Psychoanalysts would argue that some interpretations that produce no result in the hour are to be taken home by the patient and worked on as "homework." It is true that this often happens in psychoanalysis, but doesn't it mean that the therapist has failed to aid the patient in the working through? If the client couldn't do it with the therapist, is he really likely to be able to do it, in a real way, alone?

it verbally and interactively requires further experiencing than he can now do. It is to resolve the problem.

Therefore, when our responses point at the client's felt sense of the problem, and when we respond as exactly as possible to state more explicitly what he has explicated, we aid him to feel more, and so again to become able to be aware of more. As we respond by explicatively pointing at what he *now* concretely feels, he becomes able to feel, and therefore then able to explicate still more.[6]

The fifth rule is: *Responses point.* The response must point at just exactly that felt sense the client now experiences. We aim at just that felt sense, the one he has as he struggles to make what he says as specific and clear as possible.

Carrying Further

An experiential response points at, and brings the client's attention to, his felt experiencing so that his felt experiencing is thereby carried further. Thus, one of the best possible client reactions to what a therapist says is: "No, not at all, it isn't like *that*; it is rather more like. . . ." Often, my saying how I guess "it is" enables the client to say much more exactly how it really is. And that is what I want, for my response is not a factual statement that seeks to be true, but a pointing statement that seeks to bring into clarity and help carry further what he feels.

When an individual has a problem, he is always partly confused and stuck. To clarify what is wrong, he must *further* define his reactions and situations. Without defining *further*, he cannot "clarify" at all! Thus, not all that the individual says now was already there in him, complete, before he says it. What we seek to do with therapeutic responding is not at all a mere fact-finding or explaining. Instead, we seek that sort of clarifying which involves *more and further* living and feeling than the individual was able to do when he was stuck or suffering.

A sixth rule is: *We try to carry experiencing further.* Explicating brings about a further experiencing which had not, until then, been possible.

"Carrying Further" Guides the Therapist, Not Vice-Versa

We don't seek any old "more," but only that "more" which will resolve or clarify that which was previously hung up, impossible or confused. How can we tell what that is? Again, only by the client's actual experiential reaction. Thus, our responses must be guided by the client's moment-to-moment reaction, not only to find out when what we say is valid, but to open an avenue into which he can move, to establish therapeutic direction.[7] This is shown by the direction of the client's ac-

---

[6]The psychoanalytic formulation of the above would be: As we respond to what is in the preconscious, more and more material rises into the preconscious from the unconscious. However, it does not seem accurate to term "preconscious" something which is very directly felt *in awareness,* often painfully so, even though it is not conceptually clarified and consists only of incipient inhibited reactions. To term this "preconscious" formulates it as if the process had already fully occurred, but in a hidden way, *when in fact it has not yet fully occurred.*

[7]Intellectually, one can often state (the client can, or the therapist can) what the client's problem is, why it is, what the etiology, past experience, participations of others and of the client is. One can even specify what would be solutions for anybody else in such a predicament—although, of course, such people as could avail themselves of these solutions wouldn't long find themselves in such predicaments anyway. One finds that these solutions don't work for this client. Given the individual's past and the sort of emotional and interactive inabilities he has, we can often see why no thinkable solution for him exists, why

tually-sensed new bits of experiencing (and thus newly-clear interpreting and defining) which were previously impossible for him in the situation.

Thus, a seventh rule: *Only the individual knows his track*; *we go by his sense of his experiential track*. But how can our responding be guided by his experiencing, when at the same time I have also said that what we seek is not all already there? Isn't this a contradiction? On the one hand, I say that only the client's experiencing can guide the therapist, and on the other hand I say that genuine clarifying is always partly a further defining and a further experiencing.

Cannot anything be further defined in thousands of different ways? How does one choose the direction? The answer lies in the fact that we seek not just any way of further defining and further experiencing, but only *just that* way in which there occur bits of experiential resolving of just that which felt so hung up, confused or unbearable before.

Referent Movement: *the "Felt Give"*

We must now look more exactly at how we recognize when a bit of experiential resolving or clarifying occurs in that which the individual feels as a problem. How

---

he must indeed be and remain as he is. And there you have the dead end of the purely intellectual approach. Now what?

The purely intellectual "clarification" of the client's personality problem fails when it has not carried *further* his feelings, his experiential process. A mere fact-finding does not change anything. In medicine (as in car repairing) diagnosis and cure are two separate phases. First, one must know what's wrong, then one can decide what to do. With personality change, however, this two-phase distinction doesn't apply. If the clarification process has not itself already altered the client, we can deduce nothing from what we learned which can help him. We can only explain more exactly how he came to be as he is, why he has to be that way, why he can't change. The best we can do, when we arrive at this stuck point (knowing it all, but having changed nothing) is to invite the client to explore further, to go over again what we both already know, hoping this time to involve his feeling life, to carry it further and thereby resolve something, to do what psychoanalysts call "working through."

The experiential approach can also be viewed as offering a systematic method for what psychoanalysis terms the "working through" process, something remarkably rarely discussed systematically in psychoanalytic literature. The therapist may feel that he knows the overall general direction of therapy, but the specific steps of "working through" are not known to him in advance and cannot be intellectually determined. Both client and therapist must follow where the experiential steps lead—which the client actually senses when they occur. Both may be surprised by the turns which these steps take, and by the eventual resolution.

Even if the therapist is concerned that the client reach certain outcomes, he must be able to stand it that experiential steps, for some time, go in quite a different direction than he might like. If he can follow where the experiential steps go, then either eventually the goal he predicted is reached (despite many turns in the direction), or, if the outcome resolution surprises him, the therapist learns very convincingly that a resolution very different from the one he expected, is possible (Gendlin, 1967a).

A therapist who refuses to follow where the client's experiential steps lead usually stops his client from engaging in a genuine resolution process. This is not to say that the therapist's presence and responses as another person leave the client unaffected. On the contrary, resolution could not occur without the fact that to explicate with—and expressively toward— this person is a very different sort of process from thinking or feeling by oneself. The attitudes and responsiveness of the therapist fundamentally affect what the client finds and is, but, as this emerges experientially, both persons must follow the concrete steps which occur and are directly sensed.

can we tell when he experiences further? Is just any new experience a "further" experiencing? No, it isn't. By "further" we always mean just in that respect in which he was hung up before, stopped, puzzled, confused, inhibited, incapable of going on in a way that felt all right, adequate, or bearable.

When experiencing is carried "further," there is a very distinct and unmistakable feel of "give," easing, enlivening, releasing. I call it "referent movement" because there is felt movement in the felt direct referent. It may arise at times when something seems solved or resolved, but also when a feeling becomes clearer or when some new facet emerges.

The individual has a certain troubled but unclear felt sense of what he discusses. Quite often he explains, describes events, understands origins, invents how he wishes he were, says much that is true and wise—and yet, nothing is concretely changed. His felt sense, after all the talking and effort, is just as it was before. No "referent movement" has occurred. There has been no experiential effect.

In contrast, it is unmistakably different when even the slightest bit of felt "give" or "referent movement" occurs. It may seem only as if that simply indicates the truth of whatever was just said; but as he continues to explore his experiential felt meanings, everything is now a little different. New facets arise. Much that seemed relevant before is now suddenly beside the point. The little bit of felt "give" now turns out to have been a real step. He again refers directly to a felt sense of the whole problem he is talking about, but this felt referent is now slightly altered.

The newly-emergent facet may seem to solve nothing, may be worse than anything the individual had expected. He may say "How awful! Now I *really* don't know what to do." But if it is an aspect that genuinely emerges from his felt sense of what he is up against, if it is an aspect that genuinely emerges from his experiencing, then he feels that distinctive "give," a felt shift, an experiential effect which I call "referent movement" (Gendlin, 1964). After a moment's felt referent movement, everything is usually slightly altered, and new verbalization usually arises.

Our eighth rule is: *Only referent movement is progress.* (The direction in which the process should go is indicated by the client's directly felt experiential "give" or "referent movement.")

The Experiential Use of Concepts

Theoretically we have implied (see also Gendlin, 1962, 1964) that "becoming aware" of something one was previously unable to be aware of, always first or simultaneously involves further felt experiencing. We have also implied that any negative "hung up" condition or problem carries within itself implicitly the directions for its own positive solution, even if that solution must be created and cannot merely be "found." Thus, a therapist must pay very close attention to the possible positive aspects incipient in maladjusted negative behaviors and feelings. Felt experiencing is the bodily feel of being alive, and as animals we stay alive only because our animal bodies are organized in life-maintaining biological systems. Any human animal is vastly elaborated by culture and individual learning, and with these elaborations the body tends to remain organized. (If it didn't, we would fall apart very soon.) Given our elaborate learning of what we can and cannot do, a situation can easily become an "impossible situation" for us, one in which we can find no way of interpreting or acting that feels life-maintaining. But the impossibility of the problem itself is made up out of positive tendencies and positive life-maintaining avoidances.[8] When new modes of interpreting that are useful to the individual are discovered, they are clearly marked because they permit a bit of further experiencing to occur, and this is always releasing and "feels good," even if one also feels awful about much that is newly visible after such a small, further experiential step.

It goes without saying that these "steps" and "further experiencing" cannot be deduced logically. None of our theoretical concepts are nearly specific and complex enough to come even close to the facets one feels. Logic and theory merely reconstruct some aspects of experience into a general pattern. *After* some experiential hang-up has been resolved, we can always explain what happened. We can explain it in a few brief sentences, or elaborately in a long novel. But during the process of resolving, in therapy, our theoretical concepts are only tools that point, and thereby aid in referring to experiencing and thereby carrying it further. This is not to say that our concepts are in any sense useless or unimportant. The more accurately and well we can use concepts (whatever set we use), the better we can point at and help carry further the client's experiencing.

The ninth rule is: *Therapy requires the experiential use of concepts.* In therapy, our words and concepts should be used not only factually and logically, but experientially, to point at felt experiencing.

Perhaps most importantly, the experiential use of concepts involves, not logical steps, but experiential steps. The crucial difference is that if we intend a concept experientially, then we intend it to point at what is felt, and *whatever* new facets may thereby emerge. Should these new facets not fit our construct, we aren't surprised. We only used it to help us point. The new facets may now generate a *different construct* in us, and one which doesn't at all fit with the earlier. If we have a lot of time, we might try to reconcile the two in a theoretical way, but usually we don't have time for this in ongoing therapy. Certainly there is a continuity, and it can be made explicit. We weren't wrong before, at least not in every way, for what we then said or thought has helped us get to this, now. But now we will freshly use the total of our theoretical, diagnostic and interhuman knowledge to grasp this new moment, these new facets. Something quite contradictory to the earlier implications may now

---

[8]The psychoanalytic way of formulating this is: The energy that maintains the repression comes from the repressed itself. This statement means that the energy which now prevents the release one seeks in the psychotherapy, is actually the energy of that which one seeks to release.

It was Rogers' (1951) central discovery that "resistance" could be obviated if the therapist responded with, rather than against, the client's felt desires, perceptions and self-protecting urges; i.e., the client soon moves through steps by which the "repressed" emerges (Rogers termed it the "denied to awareness") in its positive, or life-maintaining, character, even if it began by being extremely negative or self-defeating. But this change requires that the therapist respond to the client's actual felt intent, and not in terms of an external evaluation.

The psychoanalytic version of this basic fact sounds extremely different, as though it were only a theoretical statement of the source of energy. On the other hand, Rogers' formulation ("faith" in the individual; "growth principle," "self-actualization") has given this fact a seemingly idealistic and optimistic cast. The experiential formulation not only clarifies this as a basic organization aspect of any living thing, but also shows why full symbolization of a problem is possible only as the further experiencing. The blocked tendencies toward this further experiencing, culturally elaborated to the point of conflict and not further elaborated to resolution, constituted the problem in the first place.

be what we think and say next. The experiential step is between the last conception and this one. It is not only a logical sequence from one to the other.[9]

Therapists sometimes have difficulty learning this experiential use of concepts. One easy way of conveying what it is, is to turn the tables: What sort of use of concepts do you wish the client to use? Do you wish him to talk to you only conceptually, theoretically, going from one step to the next by sheer factual and logical implications? No. You want him to use his concepts not at all for their conceptual interest and logical implications, but as pointers to, and expressions of, his affective and interactive life. Very well, and that is just how anyone who aids him to do that must use *his* concepts.

You don't mind your client talking politics or religion or psychological theory, as long as what he says is really pointing at, and knowingly tied into, his own struggle to clarify and move beyond his troubled feelings and reactions. If this is the direct reference of his talks, if these abstract topics are just vehicles with which to express his emotional meanings, then such talk can be therapeutic. But if he takes these concepts at face value and not as pointing at experiential facets of his own, then therapy is at a standstill and he is "intellectualizing." The same condition applies to the therapist's use of concepts. Whatever theory the concepts stem from, if they are used

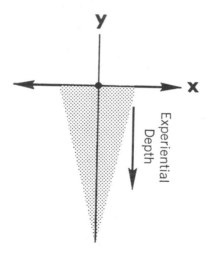

[9]The experiential use of concepts has also been illustrated in these footnotes concerning psychoanalysis: When I have said, in these footnotes, that some client-centered formulation could be stated psychoanalytically, I didn't mean that the two formulations were really identical or the one reducible to the other. On the contrary, I am aware of enormous differences in each term and its theoretical implications, but it is just these latter which the experiential use of concepts allows me to shelve. I can use these very different theoretical conceptions in their experiential reference, which they also have. Then I discover that their experiential reference is the same!

For example, aside from theory, what is the term "dynamic shift" concretely? What, that occurs in practice, does it refer to? That is very nearly the same as what is concretely referred to by my quite different term "referent movement."

To use concepts in this way requires willingly shelving their theoretical contradictions and employing only their experiential reference. It means moving from one step of thought to the next via what each concept experientially refers to, and via whatever we make of that (how we differentiate that further), rather than moving only along the theoretical implications. This is the experiential use of concepts, which in the theory of experiencing (Gendlin, 1962a, 1962b, 1966) has been developed as a method of thought.

experientially, as the client seeks an experiential "carrying further," then they can aid. But, of course, that means they must be guided by, and altered by, the very next concrete facets which develop.

Experiential Depth

One meaning of depth (which I deny has any use in psychotherapy) is the "depth" of generalized theoretical implications. Let us plot this on a diagram along an "X" axis, horizontally. From a given point at which the client now feels, we diagnosticians can move away to deduce many other traits and ways of this client. If he is as he now says, then it is likely that he also is this and that other way. Thus, we can move left and right on my diagram and say all sorts of (perhaps quite correct) things about him. This usually distracts the client, if he was about to go deeply into what he now feels.[10]

There is another dimension, however, more truly termed "depth." We plot it along the "Y" axis of the diagram. It is depth *into* the point at which he now is and feels. Along this dimension he (and we) can say more and more and more, but always exactly (always more and more exactly) explicative of just this feeling that he has now (as it thereby changes).

What, then, distinguishes "depth" along the "Y" axis? What will be pertinent to the individual's present felt experiencing? How can one tell what is really "in" this, and what isn't? The answer is *only via a series of experiential steps.* Experiential depth may produce facets which sound much like our theoretical deductions would have sounded, or it may produce facets which we could never have produced ourselves. Whichever it is, *we* cannot take another person's experientially concrete steps. Even when we are fortunate and respond perfectly so as to help carry his experiencing further, what counts is not the response itself, which we produced, but his concrete movement.

Thus, the tenth rule is: *"Depth" is into the point, not away from it.* I can now sum up the principles of experiential responding which I have stated so far:

1. We respond to the felt meaning.
2. We try to explicate felt meaning.
3. We try various tentative directions for an experiential advance.
4. We try to follow the experiential track.
5. Responses point.
6. We try to carry experiencing further.
7. Only the individual knows his track: we go by his sense of his track.
8. Only referent movement is progress.
9. Therapy requires the experiential use of concepts.
10. Depth is into the point, not away from it.

---

[10]In the client-centered usage of words, "interpretation" stands for a bad response. The term refers to that sort of response which introduces intellectually or diagnostically relevant material which actually moves the client away from his experiential track and into intellectualizing. So as not to become confused by mere terminology, I have chosen to write this chapter on our conception of the most effective sort of therapeutic response. I take that to be the topic to which this book's title refers.

"Interpretation" in our usage refers to what is defined by the "X" axis in the diagram above. We seek to avoid it. I assume that effective psychoanalysts also seek to avoid it, as the earlier quotations from Fenichel have shown.

EXPERIENTIAL INTERACTION

Very often the best response can arise for us if we, as therapists, pay attention to how we ourselves are feeling and reacting just then. There are a number of reasons for this. First, what the therapist *says* has only a limited effectiveness. His personal presence and interactive response is more powerful. Let us suppose that there were no real therapist, only his words projected on the wall before the client who reads them. Would therapy be equally effective? No, it would not (and even then, the client would rightly have strong feelings toward the unknown but real other person who is reacting to him and making these statements). The fact of there being a real other person is an essential part of the effectiveness of therapeutic responses. The client's present experiencing is always concretely with and toward that real other person, even if verbally he seems only to explore himself.

To some degree, the client can carry his experiencing further even when he is alone and responds to himself, thinks about himself, or talks silently to himself. By merely laying out in words what he feels, he clarifies and carries his experiencing further. If the client talks out loud to himself, this effect may be maximized. By doing it out loud, he tends less to fall into a vague, mind-wandering slump. By writing things down to himself, he may maximize this even more. If he speaks into a tape recorder and plays it back, there is an even stronger effect. Most people, on first hearing their voice played back, are startled and embarrassed because they hear aspects of themselves which they usually don't hear. How is it possible for them to "hear" in the tape-recorded voice what they fail to hear while speaking? Experiencing is basically interactional. To hear the voice from the tape recorder is to perceive external environmental effects of aspects of ourselves which usually never receive feedback. But without feedback there is no interaction process (no chain of reaction, effect, and reaction to that) and hence usually only the implicit and painfully inhibited condition; there is no actual experiencing. Thus, environmental effects carry experiencing further. However, far most powerful in this regard is a real other person who responds not merely like a tape recorder, but who is himself still another dimension along which the client's incipient reactions are carried further into lived-out interactions with an environment.

A therapist's responses fit into the above list of environmental interactions only if he responds *to the client*. As a therapist, I can usually tell the difference between those of my felt reactions which are really irrelevancies from my own personal troubles, in contrast to those that are relevant to our interaction here. *If my feeling is relevant to what we are now doing, I must respond from it.*

My reactions are part of our interaction. I owe it to the client to carry further that part of our interaction which is now occurring in me. If I don't, we will both be stuck in that respect. Of course, I am responsible for *how* I respond. This means that I must respond in such a way as to be giving my reaction honestly back to him, making it visible, acting so that he can in turn respond to that in me which he has set off.

Thus, I will not simply "act out" in therapy; or at least I won't only do that, but I will also carry my own feelings further in me, to let them become more fully what they are, since at first they are often only incipient. I will not express my defensive covering reactions, or at least (if I find I have already done so) I will go on to express myself aloud until what is actually happening in me is visible.

It is of little importance how good, wise, strong or healthy the therapist is or seems. What matters is that the therapist is another human person who responds, and every therapist can be confident that he can always be that. To be that, however, the therapist must be a person whose actual reactions are visible so that the client's experiencing can be carried further by them, so the client can react to them. Only a responsive and real human can provide that. No mere verbal wisdom can.

The therapist should be stable enough not to be destroyed. However, this is usually more truly conveyed if he is open about his reactions than if he covers them. When the client senses that the therapist is covering, the client cannot clearly react, nor can he tell whether the therapist could stand to have the client react to him. In being open, the therapist easily shows that the extent to which he is bothered, angry, hurt or upset is quite bearable.

The therapist and his reactions should not become the central focus, however. As a therapist, I am willing to be the focus for a brief time. I am willing that we notice and resolve my reactions, if they are part of what we together must become able to carry further. I do not believe that I should take up my "countertransference" outside the hour where the client can't see it and react to it. I must make available to him anything in me which could concern him. But the client remains the center. I make it possible for any of my reactions to be explored if that is needed, and to the extent it serves our purpose. This purpose is to clarify our interaction and carry it further, not to obstruct it with any new complications.

Many therapists have questioned this aspect of experiential interaction. How is it different from therapy for the therapist? At rare times and for some minutes, it might be just that; but the purpose is to make my feelings accessible so that *the client* can move freely and further. We are not likely to get stuck on me. As my openness carries the client's experiencing further, *he* is now more likely to move on, if I don't stop him.

Most clients need a long period (months) of persistent therapist-response to exactly what the they feel, perceive, and imply. During such periods the therapist's use of his own feelings is for the purpose of imaginatively sensing the client's felt meanings. More personal reactions of the therapist will be expressed, at most, only very rarely.

What has been said here should not have the effect of propelling therapists into expressing themselves very often and dramatically, when what the client needs is aid in developing a gentle and slowly-developing process of experiential focusing.

The sort of client who is not on any experiential track at all may need a great deal of therapist-expressivity (Gendlin, 1962) so that an experiential interaction will first arise. On the other hand, when the client is pursuing an experiential process of differentiating and carrying further his felt sense of his difficulties, then an absolute minimum of therapist interruptions of this process is best. Then, it is usually best for the therapist to follow gently and precisely, understanding every turn and every main facet, and adding nothing that might throw the client off his track and lead him into a different and extraneous train of thought.

The therapist keeps a special lookout for reactions of his own that are uncomfortable (feeling "on the spot," embarrassed, impatient, or otherwise troubled). Almost always the therapist will discover these reactions in himself at a time when he has already behaved so as to cover them up, cope with them, suppress them, or try to get away from them. It is natural that we tend to "control" such reactions, and usually they are slight enough to make control very easy. Nevertheless, they contain important information about what is just then happening in the interaction.

It is natural for a therapist to feel a little incompetent or maladjusted himself when he has these reactions. Certainly such reactions will often involve whatever is incompetent or maladjusted in him, and no human lives without such aspects. But to see only this is to miss an essential aspect of psychotherapy: If the client is a troubled person, he cannot possibly fail to rouse difficulties in another person who relates closely with him. He cannot possibly have his troubles all by himself while interacting closely with the therapist. Necessarily, the therapist will experience his own version of the difficulties, twists, and hang-ups which the interaction must have. And only if these do occur can the interaction move beyond them and be therapeutic for the client.[11]

Thus, feelings of difficulty, stuckness, embarassment, being manipulated into a spot, resentment, etc., are essential opportunities for the relationship to become therapeutic. But this cannot happen if the therapist knows only how to "control" these feelings in himself (i.e., force them down). Of course he can control them, since usually they are not very strong. On the contrary, the therapist must make an extra effort to sense them in himself. Certainly he must (and usually can easily) stay in control of such feelings and not be undone or unduly upset by them; but he must also see them as his valuable concrete sense of the now-ongoing difficulty, the now-manifest hang-up of the interaction and of the client's experiencing process.

Only much later can the therapist (and the client) see clearly just what was involved. One cannot expect to grasp clearly what the trouble is while it troubles. As I said before, grasping clearly is possible only as one experiences fully, and for that one must experience beyond the hang-up which constitutes a problem or difficulty. Thus, the therapist cannot expect always to be comfortably in the know. He must be willing to bear being confused and pained, to feel thrown off his stride, to be put in a spot and not find a good, wise, or competent way out. Only if he can develop open and visible ways to carry his interaction with the client further in these respects, does he carry the client's experiential process further.

---

[11]Throughout this paper we are discussing what a therapist response must be in order to engender a "working through process." Most therapists agree that psychotherapy cannot be only intellectual, but also must involve a "reliving," an "emotional digesting," an interactive "transference" process in which the patient not only talks about his feelings but relives them and feels them *toward* the therapist.

But, even this, although very true, doesn't yet characterize the change process. It isn't enough that the patient *repeats* with the therapist his maladjusted feelings and ways of setting up interpersonal situations. After all, the patient is said to repeat these with everyone in his life, and not only with the therapist. Thus, the sheer repeating, even when it is a concrete reliving, doesn't yet resolve anything. Somehow, with the therapist, the patient doesn't *only* repeat; he gets *beyond* the repeating. He doesn't only *re*live; he lives *further,* if he resolves problems experientially.

Psychoanalytic literature is elaborate about personality contents and conflicts, but sparse on how the "working through" process occurs. Similarly, it is elaborate about the repetition and reliving of "transference," but sparse on how the "handling" or "overcoming" of transference concretely occurs. But this latter is, of course, also a concrete living interaction as transference is. It is part of transference, the latter stages of it, and the only aspect of transference which changes anything, rather than merely repeating experiences.

If the therapist cannot be more visible, unhurt and open than most people in the client's life, and if the therapist cannot permit the client to see what he has stirred in the therapist, then the client won't be able to carry his experiencing further and differently than he usually can. Many of the client's interactive behaviors are troubled, self-defeating and negative in how they affect others. Hence the client lives in troublesome situations. When the therapist himself becomes such a situation (and at times he will), he can help only if his reaction is more open than the usual person's reaction.

The therapist rarely needs to state reactions of this sort as "only my feelings." If he will notice such reactions in himself, he can then question himself "why?" Very shortly he realizes why, as he attends to his felt sense and carries it further. Then, he can respond directly and clearly to that facet of the interaction which has given him this feeling. The hard part is noticing that one feels the discomfort. Once noticed, it generally explicates itself.

The trouble is usually not the therapist's main personality difficulty, and therefore he is much more able than the client to carry further his felt meaning. Thus the therapist becomes able to respond in a way which moves beyond precisely this hang-up. If the therapist were not to use his momentary troubled feelings in something like this way, he would be leaving unused the main advantage which his greater strength or better adjustment (in these respects) can offer for the client. This advantage is precisely that the therapist probably *can* carry further his own felt sense of what is wrong, whereas the client, thus far, cannot.

However, one is usually turned away from such feelings and in the habit of ignoring them. I have gradually learned to turn toward any such sense of embarrassment, stuckness, puzzledness or insincerity which I may feel. By "turn toward it," I mean that I don't let it simply be the way I feel, but I make it into something I am looking at, from which I can get information about this moment. Thereby I first carry it further in thought and feeling, before I respond from it.

The therapist pays attention to his own reactions and explicates them to himself before he states them. I don't usually express reactions that are as yet totally unclear. (I will do that only if, after trying, I see that I can't get them clear and yet I sense that they are relevant. Then I will say something, even if I am confused.) I will not know exactly what and why, especially not all about how the client engendered my reaction—or even if he did. But I can most often clarify my own feelings to myself, and thus I am able to express them clearly and simply with brief words. Usually, I can simply say to what present events I am referring.

Does such self-attention by the therapist preclude his attending to the client? Not at all. Hundreds of things course through our minds. Only by strenuous effort can we suppress everything so that we don't notice what is happening in us. It is true that the first priority for my attention is to the client, to what he is saying and doing, but that leaves me plenty of room to attend also to my own reactions. As long as they are not relevant, they simply "go by"; but if they seem relevant, I must note them, carry them further. Eventually, I may decide that they must be given voice. My decision depends upon whether I then believe that these, my reactions, belong to the interaction, i.e., are needed by the client. If he needs them to see more clearly what he is up against, what he does, then I must somehow respond from them to enable him to experience further or more optimally with me than he does with others.

What the client stirs in me is always partly me. (In a different person he might stir different reactions.) But my reactions are also partly a function of the client and his way of setting up situations and interactions. Whatever of me might be revealed thereby, I must insure that he can react to it and carry his experiencing further with me than he usually can with others.

While the client's maladjustive behaviors may stir rejection in most people (and have just made the therapist uncomfortable, let us say), the very fact that a personality problem is involved means that positive, life-maintaining tendencies are being thwarted in these patterns. The behaviors are negative. But here, in *this* interaction, the therapist's aim is to enable the positive tendencies to succeed nevertheless. The individual reaches out to others, but perhaps he does it in ways that must fail to reach others and bring only rejection. (Here, however, in therapy another person *will* be reached.) The client seeks to express himself but perhaps he sounds "phony." (Here, the therapist's response will attempt to insure that the client *has* succeeded in genuinely expressing himself, nevertheless.) The client seeks to assert himself, but perhaps the resulting behavior is really only passive resentment. (Here, his self-assertion will be taken as such and hence can develop and emerge more directly.) There is always a positive tendency which we can "read" in the negative behavior. Such reading isn't a Pollyanna invention of ours. It is, rather, that something of importance is always just then being defeated, making for a problem. If this were not the case, there would not be discomfort, anxiety, and tension.

Whatever is being defeated in the client's usual behavior and interaction pattern must not be defeated here, in this interaction with the therapist. It must instead be carried further and beyond the usual self-defeating pattern. It must succeed here, whereas it usually fails elsewhere. This, however, applies only to interactive behaviors of the client which affect the therapist. Usually the therapist will help interpret whatever the client feels and is up against, be it good or bad. He must help phrase and explicate many bad, negative, defeating, hopeless, hostile and sick facets the client feels and to which he refers. No positive, reassuring, whitewashing attitude can help. What is bad must be expressed as just as bad as it then is or seems.

It is something quite different, when the therapist takes it upon himself to respond with his own troubled or annoyed feelings at what the client is doing to him. When the therapist uses his own negative feeling response and makes it more visible, it is not at all enough if the result is only that the client notices what he has done, or how negatively he behaves. How can the client change this in himself? Even if he now sees it, he cannot change it. It is an interactive mode of his, and it can usually change only in a further and different concrete interaction process. If this *newly different* interaction process won't happen here and now, where and when will it?

Thus, the therapist must first and foremost respond to the positive tendency which needs to be carried further from out of the negative pattern. But this positive tendency may not be visible. The therapist may have to imagine it, then respond to it, then wait to hear the quite different actual positive tendency which then concretely emerges.

For example: I am being pressured by my client to aid her in some enterprise which I know I won't feel honest taking part in. I don't like her pressuring. First and foremost, I must respond to her trying to help herself, and thereby carry further the constructive component in her plan. If I so respond, she may then explain that this isn't what she is doing at all. She is really just trying to get even with someone, assert herself for once, stop taking everything lying down. All right. I didn't imagine correctly what the positive urge was, but here is some of it concretely. I say "We certainly have come far enough together that you could expect me to help in this way. We're getting to be allies." She may again explain that this isn't the point for her. Rather, she wants to know when I am ever going to do anything for her except talk. Here, then, is the real relating to me to which I hoped to respond. I imagined it incorrectly. Actually, it is resentful, angry and challenging. All right. I can respond to that. "So, you're mad at me! I haven't been doing anything? Me, I think I feel pretty strongly for you. You think I've got it soft, just sitting and talking. My life is easy. Well, it is true that you have to bear up under it mostly all by yourself. And, you're daring me to get into it with you, for real." Her reactions as I speak will indicate what aspect of this response begins to carry anything further.

The effort is always to complete the incipient, positive, interactive tendencies, to make them succeed and not remain in the self-defeating forms in which they first arise. In the context of that sort of always-positive carrying further, the therapist can and should voice his own actual reactions. In that context he can, and certainly should, say (for example) that he feels pressured, sat on, pushed, and doesn't like it—that it makes him want to push her away. He cannot *merely* react as most other people do. That has already not helped the client.

The positive interaction process must come first, but if it is already ongoing, then the therapist can immediately (for example) express the feeling of being pressured, even without first seeking positive responses. But even then the tenor of this self-expression will be, "I am feeling pressured by you, and that makes me feel like pushing you away, but that isn't how I usually feel or want to feel with you. So, we'll do something to clarify it, resolve it, since that isn't really how you and I are."

Because the details I have described above are difficult to describe, this aspect of psychotherapy is one of the least well understood. There is much discussion in general about "confronting" the patient with the therapist's real reactions; but if one did this as it is usually described, one would only react to the patient as most people in his life react. His wife and his friend often enough tell him what's wrong with him, and how he makes them feel. He can stand it from the therapist, not because he trusts the therapist's respect for him in a general way, but because with the therapist this specific negative pattern is being (or immediately will be) carried further to a positive, life-maintaining, experiential completion which was only implict and had been stopped and troubled until then.

THE EXPERIENTIAL METHOD AND THEORY

In the preceding two sections I have presented two aspects of experiential responding: (1) the therapist's efforts to respond to the client's meanings and thereby to carry the client's experiencing further, and (2) the therapist's efforts to respond openly to the client's interactive behavior. The second effort is also designed to carry the client's experiencing further. What now is the relationship between these two aspects of psychotherapy?

First, we might note that along both lines client-centered therapy has become experiential. Whereas a relatively formal focus on the client's expressed meaning used to be required, now the therapist seeks to respond to the felt, as yet implicit, experiencing. The expressed meaning is viewed as only one explicit facet. (But while this was not clearly stated before, this always was the client-centered therapist's aim.) Similarly, the therapist's interactive behavior used to be limited to a relatively formal role of "reflecting" only the client's feelings. The therapist refused to react from his own person, sometimes to the point of complete exasperation and despair on the part of the client. (But again, such sheer role playing never was Rogers' intention or practice. It wasn't stated clearly, but the therapist was urged to devote his actual feeling life to a sensing of the client's feelings.) Despite the underlying intention, there frequently occurred wooden repetition of what the clients said, and obviously artificial refusals to interact openly.

Currently, the emphasis is on *experiential* responding, both in regard to what it is in the client to which we seek to respond, and in regard to what of ourselves we express and show in the interaction. The theory of experiencing (Gendlin, 1962a, 1964, 1966a, 1966b, 1968) develops a method of thought and theory which enables us to differentiate and formulate what concretely and experientially occurs.

Why is it that different orientations to therapy look so similar when they are examined experientially? It is because we are then looking at what actually occurs in psychotherapy, concretely, when it works. The events which then happen are not always exactly the same in each therapy orientation, but they are very largely the same. There are only so many (quite few) concrete processes which are therapeutic, although there is an endless variety of ways of conceptualizing them. Thus the similarities between different orientations become visible when each[12] orientiation is reformulated experientially.

The experiential theory permits differentiation of the concrete processes of therapy. Rather than leaving them as some *one* vague term in our theory (for example, "working through," or "self-actualizing" or "emotional digesting"), we can and must specify what occurs with us and the client very much more specifically and with many more terms and steps. Then we can hope to develop a vocabulary which will permit us to formulate further the psychotherapy process, to communicate how we practice it so that we can train new therapists more effectively, and to define specific observable research variables (Gendlin, 1968) whose associations will be both replicable and meaningful.

The fact that so much of what we really mean turns out to be concretely the same in the various orientations does not imply that we can settle in to some comfortable relativism where we all speak vaguely and differently, but are confident that we mean the same things. Rather, it means that the older issues between the different methods have been transcended, and a new universal experiential method of theory opens the new opportunities for which we have been hoping.

---

[12]Thus the experiential formulations of psychoanalysis which I have been offering in these footnotes have illustrated that psychoanalysis can become experiential, just as client-centered therapy has already done. We can retain the various theoretical concepts in all their precision and the differences among them (so that we can reason logically and theoretically when we wish), and still formulate and differentiate the experientially concrete events to which we refer. Such experiential precision also develops sufficiently specific terms to lead to operational research variables, so that differences on the theoretical level become capable of being settled both by more specific observational reporting and by research.

REFERENCES

Butler, J. M., Client-centered counseling and psychotherapy. In D. Brower and L. E. Abt (Eds.), *Progress in clinical psychology*. Vol. III: *Changing conceptions in psychotherapy*. New York: Grune & Stratton, 1958.

Fenichel, O., *The psychoanalytic theory of neurosis*. New York: W. W. Norton, 1945.

Gendlin, E. T., and Zimring, F. M., The qualities or dimensions of experiencing and their change. *Counseling center discussion papers*, Vols. 1, 3, 1955. University of Chicago Library.

Gendlin, E. T., Initiating psychotherapy with "unmotivated" patients. *Psychiat. Quart.*, 1961, 34, 1.

——, Experiencing: a variable in the process of psychotherapeutic change. *Amer. J. Psychol.* 1961, 15, 233.

——, *Experiencing and the creation of meaning*. New York: Free Press of Glencoe, 1962.

——, Need for a new type of concept. *Rev. Existent. Psychiat.*, 1962, 2, 37.

——, Client-centered developments and work with schizophrenics. *P. Counsel Psychol*, 1962, 9, 205.

——, Subverbal communication and therapist expressivity. *J. Existent. Psychiat.*, 1963, 4, 105.

——, A theory of personality change. In P. Worchel and D. Byrne, (Eds.). *Personality change*. New York: John Wiley, 1964.

——, Schizophrenia: problems and methods of psychotherapy. *Rev. Exist. Psychol.*, 1964, 4, 168.

——, Research in psychotherapy with schizophrenic patients and the nature of that "Illness". *Amer. J. Psychother.* 1966, 20 (1), 4-16.

——, Experiential explication and truth. *J. Existentialism*, 1966, 6, 22.

——, Values and the process of experiencing. In A. Mahrer (Ed.), *The goals of psychotherapy*. New York: Appleton-Century, 1967a.

——, and Tomlinson, T. M., The process conception and its measurement. In C. R. Rogers (Ed.), *The therapeutic relationship and its impact: a study of psychotherapy with schizophrenics*. Madison University of Wisconsin Press, 1967b.

——, Beebe, J., III, Cassond, J., Oberlander, M., and Klein, Marjorie, Focusing ability in psychotherapy, personality and creativity. In J. Shlien (Ed.), *Research in psychotherapy*, Vol. III, 1968.

Rogers, C. R., *Client-centered therapy*. Boston: Houghton Mifflin, 1951.

——, A tentative scale of the measurement of Process in psychotherapy. E. A. Rubenstein and N. B. Parloff (Eds.), *Research in Psychotherapy*. Washington, D.C.: American Psychological Association, 1959.

——, *On becoming a person*. Boston: Houghton-Mifflin, 1961.

——, Toward a science of the person. In T. W. Wann (Ed.), *Behaviorism and phenomenology*. Chicago: University of Chicago Press, 1964. Reprinted in *Midway*, Number 20. Chicago: University of Chicago Press, 1964.

CHAPTER 27

A Transactional View of Interpretation

LAWRENCE E. ABT, PH.D.

Dr. Abt's graduate work in psychology was divided about equally between Columbia University and New York University, culminating in a Ph.D. from the latter school. Following World War II he received psychoanalytic training at the William Alanson White Institute after a year of training at the New York Psychoanalytic Institute. Dr. Abt has taught at Brooklyn College and at New York University, and is presently visiting professor at the New School. With Leopold Bellak he edited Projective Psychology *in 1950, and with Stewart L. Weissman* Acting Out *in 1965.*

In addition, he has edited the well-known seven volumes of Progress in Clinical Psychology, *first with Daniel Brower and, in more recent years, with Bernard F. Riess.*

His proposed three dimensions in the paper below, "Relevance," "Directness," and "Distance," emerge as incisive and heuristically useful concepts to the technique of interpretation.

For years there's been a story going around in analytic circles that I feel is pertinent to our present interest:

One hot Summer afternoon, analyst and analysand were both finding the going quite difficult, for the material they were going over was old and was being reworked for the Nth time. Feeling that he could risk it, the analyst slipped out of his chair, left his office, and proceeded to the coffee shop that was conveniently located on the first floor of his office building.

Ordering a glass of iced coffee, the analyst drank it, musing as he did so about how the therapeutic work with his patient was going, and why things seemed bogged down at that particular point. Looking up during his musings, the analyst was quite startled to see his patient, whom he had left on the couch only a few minutes before, sitting across the counter sipping a Coca Cola.

At about the same time, the patient caught the analyst's eye, and said, "Don't worry, Doc, my tape recorder is talking to your tape recorder!"

Now, apart from the humor of this little story, I think there's something in it of importance in relation to the topic of our symposium. Its humor, I believe, lies in the fact that psychotherapy is a process occurring between two or more human beings, and it is something that we necessarily presume cannot occur between two tape recorders, however well they may be programmed to respond to each other! The sharp transition between the serious collaboration of the analyst and his patient and the later "collaboration" of the two tape recorders is what makes for the essential humor of the story—if you find that it has this quality for you. The more serious aspects of the story may now be made explicit.

First, there is recognition in the story that whatever else psychotherapy is, it is essentially a process of communication. Although communication is not the property of the human animal alone, it is certainly one of the most distinctly human characteristics. As a second aspect of the story, the tale places emphasis on the basically *human* qualities of both the psychotherapist and the patient, suggesting that each can become tired of the therapeutic work and bored with each other, and that each can become desirous of escaping, ever so little, from the joint effort. Third is the suggestion, however humorously it has been put, that somehow psychotherapy continues, even though the collaborators are not directly working on material that furthers it.

There can be little question that interpretation is a therapeutic tool, and it may well turn out to be the quintessential one. For me, interpretation is related to the process of searching for the least common denominators in all of the client's communications and with putting such material to him in a form, and at a suitable time, so that it stimulates him to go beyond the facade of his manifest thinking, feeling, and behavior into less apparent meanings and motivations. But my present bias is that of looking at interpretation—and indeed of the whole psychotherapeutic enterprise—in *transactional* terms.

The unit of my inquiry, for this purpose, I have elsewhere called *the interpersonal transaction*. We may define this as any proceeding between two or more persons, who may be either real or illusory. Since human organisms cannot usefully be considered apart from their social environments, the interpersonal transaction is always embedded in, and is a part of, a larger social process of which it may be regarded as the most significant expression or component. Psychotherapy, as a collaborative process, may be looked upon as a series of recurrent and incomplete interpersonal transactions carried on between two persons, one of whom functions in the role of the psychotherapist and the other of whom plays the role of the client or patient. The interpersonal transactions constituting the therapeutic process tend to be recurrent because they are derived from material that is historically relevant to the patient that is never fully exposed, ventilated, and worked through; they tend to be incomplete because, although they have a contemporary reference point, their historical character fails to allow any given transaction to be definitive.

If our therapeutic bias is psychoanalytic (as is mine in the broad sense), we observe that our patient's or client's therapeutically significant interpersonal transactions are those that involve transference and resistance, and that the therapist's are those of *countertransference*. The interweaving complex of transactions—transference-oriented and resistance-oriented ones that stem from the patient, and countertransference-oriented ones that come from t h e psychotherapist—constitute the total, ongoing, therapeutic process. When this process is viewed within a transactional frame of reference, the two operations are seen as complementary and, therefore, represent the essence of the therapeutic collaboration.

The interpersonal transaction itself develops from the confrontation of two or more persons that constitutes the therapeutic encounter, and the transaction represents what both the patient and the therapist bring, at any given time, to the therapeutic collaboration. The interpersonal transaction, as I have just described it, considered not only in its verbal but also in its nonverbal manifestations, is the unit of psychotherapy.

I view interpretation as the effective tool for moving forward the therapeutic undertaking. Considered in transactional terms, interpretation is one of a number of responses made by the psychotherapist to the communications of his client. From my point of view, it is the patient himself who establishes the effective basis for interpretation through his efforts to confront his conscious and unconscious thoughts and feelings and to communicate as many of them as possible to the therapist.

We may approach an understanding of the transactional nature of this relationship by means of the analogy of the buyer and the seller. It is virtually impossible to define the functional nature of the buyer, *as buyer,* apart from his series of transactions with the seller. It is likewise just as difficult, if not impossible, to define the seller, *as seller,* apart from the transactional nature of his relationship with the buyer.

I have so far made reference briefly to the nature of interpersonal transactions in psychotherapy and have suggested that it may be useful to look upon interpretation in transactional terms. It is now useful, too, I think, to consider more fully the nature of interpretation and to explore the ways in which a skilled therapist uses it as a tool for the furtherance of psychotherapy.

There are a number of dimensions of interpretation, of which we will consider several. In each instance, we seek to understand interpretation as a transactional response by the therapist to the communications of his client, both those made by the client and those stimulated by the psychotherapist. In the continuing search for the least common denominators in the patient's communications, the therapist seeks to use interpretation as a tool for moving forward into new areas of insight and understanding. We may discern three dimensions: relevance, directness, and distance.

1. *Relevance.* As a response by the psychotherapist, interpretation may be relevant in at least two senses. It may be relevant to the material *per se* or it may be relevant to material previously offered but now properly related in the sense of timing. Skilled psychotherapists have become increasingly aware of the importance of having their interpretations relevant, both in time and substance, to their clients.

2. *Directness.* It is useful to look upon this dimension as lying along a continuum from tentative interpretations, at one end, to authoritarian ones at the other end. Tentative interpretations are put to the client by way of summarizing the bits and pieces of his communications. Further along this continuum are interpretations calculated to help the client himself formulate his own interpretations to the materials he has provided. At the other end of this continuum lie the strong, authoritarian forms of interpretation employed by the psychotherapist to overcome deep and pervasive repression which might otherwise not yield.

3. *Distance.* This dimension has reference to the extent to which the therapist, in his interpretations, remains close to the data of communication from his patient or departs significantly from them. The process of departing significantly from the communications to form interpretations involves extrapolation and has to be undertaken with caution and care. Extrapolated formulations necessarily involve the therapist in working with a theoretical system of personality or psychotherapy, no matter how implicit or explicit.

Whatever the therapeutic strategy, provided it uses interpretation, it is clear that interpretation has an instrumental quality that makes it possible for the therapist to use it for conducting a dialogue with his patient. The instrumental nature of interpretation is seen in the fact that the therapist aims it at achieving changes in the behavior of his client. Moreover, it is well known that interpretation, especially when skillfully used, has important affective consequences.

Interpretation also requires a common language between therapist and client, and where such does not exist, it becomes one of the tasks of psychotherapy to establish a semantic bridge. Indeed, it is a common experience of psychotherapists that they must develop a groundwork of understanding between themselves and their clients before they can usefully employ interpretation.

SUMMARY

The therapeutic enterprise depends heavily upon the instrumental use of interpretation. It is aimed at effecting forward movement in the therapeutic work, and its outcome cannot always be reliably forecast by even the most skilled therapist. Although it is clear that we are beginning to understand a great deal about the role and uses of interpretation in psychotherapy, a full research program is necessary which will have as its primary objective a sounder and fuller statement of the interpretation process in psychotherapy with respect to definition of dimensions, methods of use, and bases for forecasting outcomes of its instrumental use.

CHAPTER 28

A Rational Approach to Interpretation

ALBERT ELLIS, PH.D.

Albert Ellis has his Ph.D. in clinical psychology from Columbia University and is famous—or, as he describes himself, infamous—on at least two major counts: He is the founder of rational-emotive psychotherapy and the author of several best-selling books in the field of sex, love, and marriage relations. On the former count, he is Executive Director of the Institute for Rational Living, Inc., which trains professionals in rational therapy and educates the public in "rational living." He has authored several volumes on psychotherapy, including Reason and Emotion in Psychotherapy. *In the second area, he has made many public appearances, in person and on radio and television, has frequently published in popular magazines, and is the author of over a dozen books, including* Sex Without Guilt *and the* Art and Science of Love. *He devotes his spare time to carrying on probably the busiest private practice of psychotherapy and marriage and family counseling of any New York City therapist. Some day he "threatens to retire—and really get some work done."*

In the relation between reason and emotion, between the logic and the psychologic of the person, Ellis operates on the principle that faulty logic initially pro-duced the emotional disturbance rather than that the emotional disturbance led to maladaptive, faulty logic. As an extension of this, he consequently approaches the patient on the logical, as well as the psychological, level.

Practically all schools of psychotherapy take a distinct approach to interpretation, even if they mainly caution against it (Ford and Urban, 1964; Harper, 1959; Munroe, 1955; Wolberg, 1954). In my practice of rational-emotive psychotherapy, I also take a definite stand on many problems of interpreting the patient's verbalizations and behavior: I employ interpretations so that he comes to understand much more fully what he is thinking and doing and uses his insight into his own (and into others') behavior to change fundamentally some of the aspects of his functioning and malfunctioning (Ellis, 1962, 1963, 1965a, 1965b; Ellis and Harper, 1961, 1966). Many of the things I do in regard to interpretation are similar to, or overlap significantly with, the approaches of other schools; but many of them are also radically different. In this present paper, I shall stress the differences rather than the similarities, in order to highlight the fact that there is a clear-cut attitudinal or philosophic school of psychotherapy which follows rational lines and whose adherents take a somewhat unique attitude to interpretation.

KINDS OF INTERPRETATION

Let me indicate, first, the kinds of interpretation which are usually *not* emphasized in rational-emotive psychotherapy, although they are highly important in psychoanalytic and neopsychoanalytic therapies.

1. The rational therapist for the most part ignores connections between the patient's early history and his present disturbances. He does not believe that the patient was made neurotic by his past experiences, but by his own unrealistic and

overdemanding *interpretations* of these experiences. He therefore spends little time in digging up and interpreting past occurrences and events; rather, he *interprets the interpretations* of these events. Thus, instead of showing the patient that he feels angry at dominating women today because his mother dominated him when he was a child, the therapist shows him his irrational thinking processes which made him, when he was young, *demand* that his mother not be dominating, and which in the present are still leading him childishly to demand that women be passive or warm rather than ruling and cold. The rational therapist consistently keeps interpreting the patient's *responses* to his history, rather than that history itself and its hypothesized intrinsic connections with his current behavior.

2. Most analytic schools of therapy spend considerable time interpreting deeply unconscious or repressed material to the patient (Freud, 1963). The rational-emotive school holds that there is no such entity as *the* unconscious or *the* id; and that although thoughts, feelings, and actions of which the individual is partly unaware frequently underlie his disturbed behavior, practically all the important attitudes that exist in this respect are not deeply hidden or deliberately kept out of consciousness because the patient is too ashamed to acknowledge them. They are, rather, just below the level of consciousness or (in Freud's original formulations) in the patient's preconscious mind, and they are relatively easy for him to see and accept if the therapist will forcefully, persuasively, and persistently keep confronting him with them. The rational therapist, therefore, probably does more interpreting of unconscious or unaware material to the patient than do most other therapists; but he does so quickly and directly, with no mysticism or mumbo-jumbo, and with no pretense that this material is terribly hard to discover and face.

3. Most contemporary psychotherapists appear to make a great stir about the transference relationships between themselves and their patients, and expend much energy interpreting to the patient his deep-seated feelings for the therapist. The rational therapist believes that the patient's relations with other human beings are normally far more important than his relations with the therapist, and that how he likes or hates the therapist has little to do with his basic problems, although it may well be an illustration of his difficulties. He therefore ignores most of the feelings which the patient has about him, the therapist, and selectively uses only those aspects of these feelings which truly seem important and which may be employed to teach the patient to relate better to people in the outside world. Instead of interminably analyzing the patient's attitudes toward him (and his own attitudes toward the patient), the rational therapist interprets and attacks the general philosophy which the patient employs to *create* his transference reactions—namely, his irrational belief that he *needs* the therapist's approval and that he cannot accept himself without it.

4. A great many therapists concentrate on interpreting to patients their resistances and defenses: showing them how they rationalize, project, repress, compensate, and resist getting better (A. Freud, 1946; Reich, 1962). The rational-emotive psychotherapist probably overlaps with analytic therapists more in this than in any other respect, since he particularly shows his patients their rationalizing, inconsistent, and illogical modes of thinking. Going much further than most other therapists in this regard, he directly and vigorously *attacks* the patients' illogicalities and evasions and forces them, by giving activity homework assignments, into posi-

tions where the patients no longer can get away with these kinds of crooked thinking.

5. Many schools of therapy today, such as the Freudian (Freud, 1963; Stekel, 1961) and Jungian (Jung, 1954), emphasize the interpretation of dreams. The rational therapist does not believe that the dream is the royal road to the unconscious, nor that it usually gives very important aspects of the patient's thoughts and wishes which are not easily available from an examination of his waking life and fantasies. He consequently spends little time on dream analysis and prefers, instead, to examine the patient's current nondreaming thought and behavior, to see how it reveals (as it almost invariably does) the patient's underlying irrational philosophies and self-defeating attitudes toward himself and others. By the same token, the rational-emotive therapist rarely interprets the patient's obscure symbolisms, whether these occur in sleeping or waking life, because he believes that there are too many allowable interpretations to many symbolic processes, and that it is often impossible to divine exactly what a given symbol means. He would rather stick to specific events in the patient's life and the patient's concrete responses to these events; and from these (and especially from the responses) the therapist can determine exactly what the patient's basic postulates about himself and the world are, how irrational these postulates are, and what can be done about changing or eliminating their irrationality.

6. Some schools of psychotherapy, particularly the experiential and the Gestalt schools (Perls, Hefferline, and Goodman, 1965), emphasize interpreting to the patient the meanings behind his physical gestures and postures. The rational therapist does some of this kind of interpretation, but in a minimal way in most instances, because he is more interested in attacking the ideas behind the patient's gestures rather than in demonstrating their mere existence. Thus, if he sees that the patient is holding himself back physically or is speaking in a stilted manner, he will not only point this out, but will try to get him to see that this posture or gesture is a direct result of his believing that he dare not let himself go because then people would find out what he was really like and would hate him. The rational therapist questions and challenges this hypothesis that the patient holds about himself, rather than emphasizes the symptomatic results, such as postural inhibitions, that result from it.

7. The psychoanalytic, experiential, and expressive schools of therapy tend to interpret almost *all* the patient's expressions, fantasies, and behaviors as significant, and they tend to show him the unconscious meanings behind these manifestations. Thus, they will make an issue of his being late to the therapy session, or his slips of the tongue, or his writings or drawings, and will find notable underlying meaning in all these kinds of productions. The rational therapist will ignore much of this activity and expression and will highly-selectively interpret what he considers to be the most meaningful aspects of the patient's life, such as his procrastination at work or at school, his problems relating to others, and his evaluation of himself. It is not that he thinks various of the patient's behaviors unmeaningful, but that he selects some of them as being much *more* significant than others; he prefers to concentrate the therapeutic work, in the interests of efficiency, in these more important areas.

So much for what the rational-emotive therapist tends to deemphasize or not do in the realm of interpretation. What, now, does he tend to emphasize and do? First, his main interpretations are invariably philosophic rather than expository or even explanatory. If the patient, for example, is unaware that he is overly dependent on others, the rational therapist not only shows him that he is, but also shows him that dependency is the result of an idea, a belief, or a value system—namely, the belief that he *must* have other people's help or approval in order to like himself. The therapist then forces him to question and challenge this hypothesis, to prove to himself how invalid it is, and to replace it with another hypothesis—e.g., that it is nice to have other people's approval but that he is a perfectly valuable person in his own right *whether or not* he does have it.

The main philosophic ideologies which the rational-emotive therapist keeps showing the patient, as the underpinnings of his disturbed behavior, are the irrational ideas (a) that he must totally condemn himself and others for wrong or inefficient conduct; (b) that he must attain a high degree of perfection in his and others' eyes; (c) that he must be absolutely certain that specific desirable events will occur and other undesirable events will not; (d) that he and others are utter heroes when they follow proper line of conduct and complete villains when they do not. The rational therapist, in other words, continually shows the patient that he is an absolutist, a bigot, a moralist, a perfectionist, and a religious dogmatist; and that only by accepting reality, uncertainty, and tolerance is he likely to surrender his emotional disturbances.

The therapist who takes a rational approach to interpretation keeps showing his patient that there are inevitable consequences to his irrational premises: that if the patient believes that others must approve him, he *will* become anxious and depressed; that if he intolerantly condemns people for their mistakes and failings, he *will* become incessantly hostile and suffer pains in his own gut. The therapist continually proves, by the laws of logic, that certain unrealistic philosophies of life *do* result in self-defeating symptoms—such as phobias, obsessions, and psychosomatic disorders—and that only if the patient changes these philosophies is he likely to get significantly and permanently better.

Instead of interpreting to the patient the historical causation of his present aberrations, the rational therapist shows him that *he,* the patient, is in the saddle seat ideologically, that *he* brought on the original inappropriate responses to failure and frustration, and that *he* is continuing to respond destructively in the same basic manner in which *he* chose to respond years ago. The therapist fully acknowledges that the patient's biological inheritance as well as his sociological conditioning make it very easy for him to get into certain dysfunctional habit patterns and to continue to behave in self-sabotaging ways. But he shows the patient that *difficult* does not mean *impossible;* that he *can* change, with sufficient work and practice on his part; and that he had *better* force himself to do so if he wants to live with minimal anxiety and hostility.

The rational therapist, in other words, interprets the patient's essential *two*-sidedness which underlies his past, present, and future behavior. He demonstrates how, on the one side, the patient is biosocially predisposed to allow himself to sink into neurotic pathways, and how, on the other side, he has a special faculty, called reason, and an unique ability (self-propelled effort and practice) which he can employ to largely overcome his oversuggestibility, short-range hedonism, and rigid thinking. He interprets to the patient not only how the patient got the way he is, but exactly with what kinds of irrational beliefs he keeps reindoctrinating himself to keep himself that way; and how he can logically pause, reflectively challenge, and then ruthlessly uproot these beliefs. His interpretations, therefore, go much deeper and make wider inroads against disturbed ideas, emotions, and actions than do the interpretations of many other therapists.

The rational-emotive therapist also interprets and teaches the general principles of scientific method and logic to his patients. He shows them that false conclusions, about either objective reality or oneself, stem from (a) setting up false premises and then making reasonably logical deductions from these premises, or (b) setting up valid premises and then making illogical deductions from them. He shows his patients exactly what are their false premises and illogical deductions from valid premises. He teaches them to accept hypotheses as hypotheses, not as facts, and to demand observable data as substantiating evidence for these facts. He also shows them how to experiment, as much as is feasible, with their own desires and activities, to discover what they truly would like to have out of life. He is, in many such ways, a scientific interpreter who teaches his patients—who in many ways resemble the pupils of other science teachers—how to follow the hypothetico-deductive method and apply it to their own specific value systems and emotional problems.

The rational therapist interprets to patients how their ideas and motivations are unconsciously influenced by their actions, and how they can consciously change the former by forcefully changing the latter. He urges them not only to question and challenge their irrational philosophies of life on theoretical or logical grounds, but he also gives them practical homework assignments so that they can *work* against reimbibing these false and inimical values. In the course of so doing, he interprets to them what happens in their heads when they overinhibit their activities—for example, when they withdraw from social relations because of their inordinate fears of rejection—and what likewise happens in these same heads when they force themselves to do things which they have been afraid to perform. Instead of endlessly-interpretively connecting the patient's past with his present, the rational therapist more often focuses on connecting the patient's present with his present—that is, his current inactivity with his contemporary uncritical acceptance of unvalidated hypotheses. And he tries for reciprocal change in the patient, by inducing him to two-sidedly modify both his thinking and his motor behavior.

METHOD OF INTERPRETATION

In several important respects, then, rational-emotive psychotherapy encourages interpretation which is rather different from the kinds of interpretation which occur in most other forms of therapy. *The way in which interpretation is given* by the rational therapist also tends to differ quite markedly from the way in which many other therapists interpret. How so?

1. Interpretation is usually made in a highly direct and not particularly cautious manner. The rational therapist feels that he knows right at the start that the patient is upsetting himself by believing strongly in one or more major irrational ideas, and the therapist usually can quickly surmise which of these ideas a particular patient believes. As soon as he does see this, he tends to confront the patient with his irrational notion, to prove to him that he actually holds it, and to try forcefully to induce him to give it up. Where the majority of other therapists tend to be namby-pamby, passive, and nondirective in their interpretations, the rational-emotive therapist is almost at the opposite extreme, since he believes that only a direct, concerted, sustained attack on a patient's long-held and deep-seated irrationalities is likely to help uproot them.

2. Most analytic therapists follow Wolberg's (1954) rule that "it is important to interpret to the patient only material of which he has at least preconscious awareness," but the rational therapist has no hesitancy in trying to show him, from the first session onward, material of which he may be totally unaware, and that even may be (on occasion) deeply repressed. He frequently directly confronts the patient with two conflicting behaviors or values to show him that the position that he says he consciously believes in or follows obviously is coexterminous with an opposing, and presumably unconsciously held, position which he also follows. The rational therapist is not intimidated by the patient's possibly becoming temporarily more upset when he is confronted with some of his own covert thoughts and feelings, since he then immediately goes to work on showing the patient how he is *creating* his own upsetness, and precisely what he can do to calm himself down again by changing the ideas with which he is creating this state of disorder.

3. Most psychotherapists only dare to make deep interpretations when, as Wolberg again states, "the therapist has a very good relationship with the patient." The rational-emotive therapist, however, usually starts making direct, depth-centered interpretations from the very first session, long before any warm or intense relationship between him and the patient may be established. He is frequently highly didactic and explicatory, and relies much more on the patient's potential reasoning powers than on his emotional attachment to the therapist to induce him to accept his teachings and explanations.

4. While rarely being warm, fatherly, or loving to the patient, the rational therapist consistently has what Rogers (1961) calls "unconditional positive regard" for him, in that he is quite nonjudgmental. The core of rational-emotive therapy consists of teaching the patient that no one is to be blamed, condemned, or moralistically punished for any of his deeds, even when he is indubitably wrong and immoral—because he is a fallible human and can be accepted as such even when he makes serious blunders and commits crimes. The therapist, following this philosophy that an individual has intrinsic value because of his being, his aliveness, and not because of his performances, thus fully accepts all his patients, even when he has to point out to them that their deeds are irresponsible and reprehensible. Giving them unconditional positive regard, he can afford actively-directively to confront them with all kinds of undesirable aspects of their behavior, since his interpretations in this connection are quite consonant with his own tolerance for *them*, as individuals, in spite of their deplorable *ways*.

5. Because, again, the rational-emotive therapist keeps forthrightly and ceaselessly attacking, not the patient but his feelings of guilt and shame, he does not have to watch the timing of his interpretations too carefully. He does not wait for the patient to be ready for major interpretations. Instead, he usually *makes* the patient ready by presenting the realities of the patient's presumably shameful ideas and feelings, and concomitantly fighting against the belief that they need be shameful. Occasionally, with an especially anxious patient, the rational-emotive practitioner may have to wait to make certain revelatory interpretations; but most of the time he quickly jumps in with them, and not only gets them, but the irrational ideas that induces the patient to keep himself from facing them, out of the way.

6. Much of the time, the rational therapist puts his interpretations in questioning form rather than as declarative statements—not because he is afraid to upset the patient by being more direct, but because one of his prime goals is to teach the patient to question himself and his own thinking. Thus, instead of telling the patient what

he is saying to himself to make himself anxious, the therapist will say to him: "What could you be telling yourself? . . . Why would you think that this event, if it occurred, would be terrible? . . . What evidence is there that it would be catastrophic if you failed at this task?" By these leading questions, the patient is led to make his own interpretations of his behavior—and, more importantly, to keep making these interpretations when the therapist is no longer present.

7. Like many other therapists, the rational-emotive practitioner frequently makes the same interpretation repetitively. He deliberately does this, knowing that the patient has been repeatedly overlooking this interpretation, or pushing it out of his mind, or making some false interpretation instead. He therefore wants to give the patient an opportunity to go over the same ground, again and again in some instances, until he begins to see that the interpretation is really true and workable, and not something to overlook or merely something to which to give lip service.

8. The rational-emotive therapist is unhesitatingly vigorous about many of the interpretations he makes. He believes that the patient sticks to his self-defeating irrationalities partly because he has very strongly kept reindoctrinating himself with them over the years, and that he is not going to give them up if he wishy-washily gives himself some alternative ideas. The therapist, therefore, vehemently shows him that he *cannot* be happy with some of his silly values, that he had *better* give them up if he wants to become less anxious, and that *there is no other way* than steady work and practice on his part if he is to truly surrender his superstitions and become less disturbed.

Summary

The rational-emotive approach to psychotherapy takes the position that it is not the event or stimulus at point A that bothers or emotionally disturbs the individual at point C, but that it is his philosophic attitude or response at point B which really upsets him. This position suggests little point in interpreting to the patient what the details of A are, how they originated in his early childhood, and how they have affected him ever since. The rational-emotive therapist thinks that this is not only a waste of therapeutic time, but that it is acutally misleading and harmful in that it diverts the afflicted individual from looking at the true cause of his neurosis—namely, his own attitudes, values, or philosophies about the events of his life, and his own tendencies to perpetuate these attitudes even when they lead to pernicious results.

The rational therapist, therefore, quickly and persistently interprets to most of his patients the philosophic sources of their disturbances—namely, the specific irrational ideas that create and maintain their psychological aberrations. He active-directively explains exactly what these ideas are and how they are biologically rooted as well as sociologically instilled. Thus, he shows the patient that he is born with a tendency to desire approval from others and to mistakenly believe that he absolutely *must have* that approval and is a worthless individual without it; and that, in an other-directed society, such as our own, he is raised to accentuate rather than to minimize this tendency, and is conditioned to feel that prestige and popularity are all-important. In addition, the therapist shows the patient that he is physiologically predisposed to be a short-range hedonist (or to adhere to what Freud called the pleasure principle, and to strive for immediate satisfaction rather than future gain), and that in our culture, and with his particular set of parents, he is usually also socially conditioned to believe that he *must* have what he wants and that it is awful and *terrible* when his desires are not fulfilled.

More importantly, the rational therapist indicates to the patient what these biosocial irrational beliefs inevitably *do* to the person who believes them, how illogical and self-defeating these ideas are, and how they can be attacked and uprooted by the patient's challenging and questioning them (in theory as well as in practice) and working against them to the best of his ability in ideomotor ways. Because of his theory of human disturbance and its philosophic causation, his content and manner of interpretation is in many respects quite different from that of most other psychotherapists.

His interpretations tend in many ways to be largely concerned with material that is unconscious, although not always deeply repressed; not overly involved with transference phenomena; directly attacking in regard to resistances and defenses; little concerned with dreams and obscure symbolic processes; highly selective in regard to what is significant in the patient's life; very concerned with the fundamental irrational ideas which underlie the patient's disturbed emotions; emphasizing of the inevitable consequences of his false premises and illogical deductions from sensible assumptions; strongly favoring general principles of scientific method; and distinctly involved with impelling the patient into action which will help him change his value system. Because of their strong philosophic flavor, rational-emotive interpretations are usually made in a manner which is exceptionally direct, independent of the therapist's warm relationship with his patient, conducive of a nonjudgmental attitude on the part of the therapist, not particularly dependent on any kind of special timing, largely given in the form of forthright questioning, quite repetitive in many cases, and unhesitatingly vigorous. Both the content and the form of rational-emotive interpretation unquestionably have dangers and drawbacks and may be pragmatically and experimentally modified as time goes by. But so far they have proved to be unusually effective with all kinds of psychotherapy patients, particularly when compared to the results obtained by other interpretive methods. Let us hope that they can be still further improved.

REFERENCES

Ellis, A., *Reason and emotion in psychotherapy*. New York: Lyle Stuart, 1962.

——, *If this be sexual heresy . . . .* New York: Lyle Stuart, 1963.

——, *Suppressed: seven key essays publishers dared not print*. Chicago: New Classics House, 1965a.

——, *Homosexuality: its causes and cure*. New York: Lyle Stuart, 1965b.

——, and Harper, R. A., *A guide to rational living*. Englewood Cliffs, N.J.: Prentice-Hall, 1961.

—— and ——, *The marriage bed*. (Original title: *Creative marriage*.) New York: Tower Publications and Lyle Stuart, 1966.

Ford, D., and Urban, H., *Systems of psychotherapy*. New York: Wiley, 1964.

Freud, Anna, *The ego and the mechanisms of defense*. New York: International Universities Press, 1946.

Freud, S., *Collected papers*. New York: Collier Books, 1963.

Harper, R. A., *Psychoanalysis and psychotherapy: 36 systems*. Englewood Cliffs, N.J.: Prentice-Hall, 1959.

Jung, C. G., *The practice of psychotherapy*. New York: Pantheon, 1954.

Munroe, Ruth, *Schools of psychoanalytic thought*. New York: Dyrden, 1955.

Perls, F., Hefferline, R. and Goodman, P., *Gestalt therapy*. New York: Delta, 1965.

Reich, W., *Character analysis*. New York: Noonday Press, 1963.

Rogers, C. R., *On becoming a person*. Boston: Houghton Mifflin, 1961.

Stekel, W., *Interpretation of dreams*. New York: Universal Library, 1961.

Wolberg, L. R., *The technique of psychotherapy*. New York: Grune & Stratton, 1954.

CHAPTER 29

The Problem of Interpretation from the Point of View of Existential Psychoanalysis

HERBERT HOLT, M.D.

Dr. Herbert Holt, in speaking of his background, says:

"As a graduate of the Universities of Vienna and Lausanne, with their tradition of humanism, the concept of the patient as first of all a human being—who is ill— was introduced naturally to me. In this atmosphere Freud was on the periphery and was, at this time, considered by teachers and students in the medical school as something of a purely technical nature.

"It was during my years at the University of Lausanne that I became aware of Binswanger and his emphasis on the concept of the human being living in the world and giving his world meaning by selecting out from the totality of functioning that which would supplement his basic character structure and personality, thereby reinforcing his world view."

Dr. Holt is presently Dean of the New York Institute of Existential Analysis and President of the New York Ontoanalytic Association, of which he was one of the founders. In his presentation in this book, he focuses not only on individual therapy, but also on group therapy. He does so, as one of its most articulate spokesmen, from the existential point of view. In the process, he ranges broadly from epistemologic questions to problems of psychotherapeutic technique.

What is the distinctiveness of existential analysis as a therapeutic technique? On what basis may its proponents support a claim that it may provide a more direct and more effective treatment than other forms of therapy? Is it a selective method, valid for certain difficulties but of no help in others? These are the questions which come to mind as a background for considering any problem of technique in therapy from the standpoint of existential analysis. Unfortunately, they are not easy to answer, for to do so involves a host of scientific and philosophical problems, both directly and indirectly related to questions of technique. This is because, on the one hand, the whole subject of psychiatry as a branch of medical science can well be questioned, while, on the other, the nature of the relationship of patient and physician in psychotherapy is such as to call into question some of the major premises of scientific investigation—certainly many of those on which Freud based his method. Thus, a proper presentation of the problem must be understood to require a far more extensive inquiry than any we can attempt here. We must confine ourselves as much as possible to the major considerations.

Freud, of course, provides us with a central reference point (Gurwitsch, 1966), for existential analysis would have been unthinkable if there had not been his commanding position to react against. Existential analysis was initially a reaction to Freud, although it must be emphasized that the beginning of the movement involved no such dramatic break with the founder as marks the origins of Adler's Individual Psychology or Jung's Analytic Psychology. The pioneer of existential analysis was Ludwig Binswanger. He died in February 1966 at the age of 85, which means that he was almost a generation younger than Freud. Yet because both of them lived so long, they shared a considerable span of working years, and the fact that psychoanalysis was a comparatively late product of Freud's life allowed Binswanger to be a contributor to the movement at a very early stage of its development. His major contribution, which became the starting point for succeeding existential analysts, was the assertion that Freud's frame of reference was too severely restricted. Binswanger knew that in private Freud was open to the indeterminate possibilities of a very wide range of human experience. He did not share Freud's sense of necessity in making a public stand on the basis of a very few fundamental ideas to which he stubbornly adhered. Binswanger, in becoming the recognized but unofficial spokesman for a number of creative men who reacted similarly to the public dogmatism of the Freudians, himself stubbornly insisted on erecting a therapeutic technique on his less determinate view of human experience; but he never did so in such a way that Freud's contribution would be minimized or his fundamental ideas denied.

The nature of the relationship between the two men, and perhaps by extension between the two schools of psychoanalysis as well, may best be illustrated from a celebrated account of a meeting of the two. Binswanger discussed with Freud the puzzling phenomenon that many patients who seemed well on the way to recovery were unable to make the final step and give up their illness. He declared that he believed in those undefinable qualities which can only be called "spirit." To his surprise, he tells us, Freud agreed with him. "Yes," he said, "spirit is everything. Man has always known he possessed spirit: I had to show him there is such a thing as instinct" (Gurwitsch, 1966). Interesting as this is in itself, it also symbolizes the issue in which we are interested here; for the implication of "instinct," as Freud understood it, was that it was something given, something inaccessible to cultural influences in its fundamental energy. Both the most basic and the most complex mental functions were reduced conceptually to certain autonomous "natural" processes of a few hypothetical agencies of the mind. Binswanger raised basic questions about Freud's procedure, but in the context of mutual respect which reflected both men's high regard for each other's work.

In part, the difference may be defined by the statement that Binswanger (1963) was less driven to round off his theory into a system. He was aware, I believe, that it was then much too soon for anyone to conclude that a clear answer to all human mental difficulties was available. He sought to initiate a mode of inquiry which would yield an anthropology in the broad sense, a scientific understanding of the ways of human action and interaction. He realized, however, that the kind of observation which would make this possible is a special problem for psychotherapy, since the observer is one in species with the object of his observation. The therapeutic situation may not be such that the participation of the physician as an observer can yield "objective" data. Worse, the very quest for objectivity in many cases may be far from therapeutic. The needs of the therapeutic situation, then, caused Binswanger to ask radical questions about consciousness and human relationship in order to find out how they could best be understood and changed. For its vocabulary and philosophical apparatus (which, after all, are fundamental considerations in any science of man), existential analysis, following Binswanger's lead, turned to the method of phenomenology and the existential assessment of man's human situation, particularly as they were related in the work of Heidegger.

Heidegger's basic concept, *Dasein,* or "being in the world," gave the German name of *Daseinsanalyse* to the rather unorganized "group" which formed around the new therapeutic position.

The basic point can be stated very simply. It is that ordinary scientific knowledge, according to the nineteenth-century model, is achieved on the basis of certain common-sense assumptions which are rarely questioned. Mental life in its basic forms, however, brings these assumptions into question to a radical degree. As Marvin Farber puts it, "A world existing continuously and independently of our experiencing is the natural basis for nonphilosophical thinking." Philosophy, however, called this assumption into question as it does all assumptions. The modern tradition which attempted to deal most radically with the phenomena of conscious awareness, the *Lebenswelt,* was that of Husserl's phenomenology, which was of major importance in the foundation of Heidegger's thought. To say it in another way, our consciousness at its deepest levels, makes no such assumptions. To recall Descartes, to whom Husserl also looked back, consciousness assumes only itself. What is more, there is no assurance that any individual consciousness is like any other. In fact, the experience of each is unique. There are, however, similarities of shared response which argue the existence of certain basic structures of mental functioning. The real issue is whether these are best revealed by analyzing them into basic functions after the manner of the physical sciences (whether, indeed, they are adequately revealed at all in this way), or whether the structures of an individual consciousness are not rather to be dealt with in the unitary way in which they are experienced by each of us. If so, how are they to be approached methodologically, and what are the implications of this philosophical methodology for the conduct of therapeutic work?

In the first place, the focus is not, as in the classical Freudian method, on the etiology of the disease, on the traumatic recovery of lost emotional crises. Each patient is considered as a unique individual who enters therapy with an individual structure of experience. Like all of us he experiences the world not "as it is," however that is, but as "his" world, the world in which he has his experience. But it is the very quality of this experience which is the problem for him. He does not like it. Often he is only too anxious to have the analyst "interpret" for him, to provide him with the key concepts which will explain all, which have been there all along but which he, the patient, has somehow managed to overlook. Neither the diagnosis nor the cure is as simple as this, however. Thus the patient's pressure must be resisted, because the primary goal of the initial stages of therapy needs to be discovery of a comprehensive expression of how the world "appears" to the individual—how it makes him feel because of the way in which he, as an experiencing subject, chooses to experience it. Clinical examples of what I mean will readily occur to any practicing therapist. Patients obviously do have idiosyncratic world-views, which are at variance with the way in which the world appears to others.

Classical Freudian analysis attempted to use a biological model of disease for mental illness (Boss, 1963). Assuming that "reality" was a given entity which could be tested, Freud wished to establish a pathology of faulty reality-testing. The therapist as objective scientist passes judgment on the progress of his patient. He defines normality and recognizes when the patient succeeds or fails in apprehending it correctly. Connected with this view of the nature of mental illness is therefore a need to investigate the onset of the disease, to measure its progress, and to recognize its termination. There must be a symptomatology, a well-defined set of disease categories, and, if possible, a technique specific for each.

The fact, that in many of these respects the achievements of psychiatry are negligible, is admitted even by those who think that this way of attacking the problem is, alone, the scientific way. But it is just here that existential analysts believe that a fundamental mistake is being made. The primary question they raise is the one as to the way in which consciousness relates to "reality." Are we really concerned with finding out what the world actually is like? Can we hope to do so with any adequacy? Finally, does it matter for psychotherapy if we do? To all these questions, existential analysis gives a negative answer. In the first place, we cannot wait until all the knowledge is in, and we do not expect that it ever will be. We must act in an effort to help concrete individuals, whether there is a cure for them or not. But even if reality could be adequately defined and explained, it is apparent that no one can possibly know it all, but can know only a part of it, which therefore becomes "his" world.

At this point, existential analysis makes an assumption of central importance. It is an assumption which resembles some of the cardinal principles of classical analysis, but which is given a distinctive interpretation and considerably more weight in the theoretical structure we work with. It is that these individual worlds are also individually selected, even chosen, and that there is an intimate relationship between the world which I perceive and the structure of my own consciousness. In philosophical terms, one of our central methodological principles is the idea that consciousness is "intentional." This notion of the intentionality of consciousness was adapted by Husserl from the Catholic philosopher Brentano, and it is, according to Maurice Natanson, "the central theme of phenomenological philosophizing." Natanson states the thesis very well. It is "that every act of conscious life is directional in its very structure—that every act of thinking, willing, remembering, sensing, and so forth, must point to some object (whether real or not), must intend something thought, willed, remembered, sensed, and so on."

Two consequences follow from this initial assumption. The first is that the reality of a patient's situation is less important to establish than the structure of his intentionality. This is the basis for our use of the phenomenological technique of "bracketing." To bracket reality means to set the whole question aside, to put it within mental brackets for the sake of clearer focus on other considerations. Philosophy asks how we can ever establish beyond doubt the existence of a world outside consciousness, and it therefore has often studied mind while leaving to science the study of the world as it is or may be assumed to be. But phenomenology calls this an abstract division, and so leaves aside the question of what reality is in itself, in order to study how consciousness establishes itself always as a relation between a mind and a context. In therapy, of course, as opposed to philosophy, there is such a thing as illusion, and it is important to know whether a given individual knows the difference between, for example, what another person said and what he only thinks the other said. Nevertheless the basic point still holds. What is of prime importance is to discover how an individual relates himself to the contents of his consciousness, because there will be no essential difference between the patterns of reaction to what we may call "real" and what we may call "imaginary" events.

The second implication is that what is intentional is also selected, and that what is selected, at whatever level of being, is also chosen. That is, one of our primary assumptions in existential therapy is that the patient has chosen his world, the world as he wants to view it. It is not too much exaggerated to say that unless we believe this, a cure for mental illness is a logical impossibility, for if we think of it as caused by prior events, which are immutable, all we can hope for is an unhappy compromise with that "reality." From our point of view mental illness is not caused by events, but is a more or less successful response to a mode of perceiving events and relationships in a characteristic way. It can also be regarded as a psychological process with survival value—at least a survival value in a certain kind of situation. In many individuals the question of childhood etiology can profitably be raised in this connection. What appears now as a neurotic response, seriously defective as a mode of approach to the world in which the patient has situated himself, was originally developed in a situation where it was the appropriate response, or perhaps one of the few appropriate responses within the range of childhood powers. But because the situation is no longer the same—because death may have altered the family structure, or the individual has grown up, or motives have intervened to cause the individual to try to place himself in another kind of situation—the old response is no longer appropriate.

Once again two possibilities present themselves. A new mode of response may be chosen, one which is more appropriate to the life-style an individual wishes to establish for himself and which is more consistent with his purposes (Heidegger, 1962); or an individual may discover that the internal cost of such a change is greater than that which he wishes to pay. This implies another assumption which we make in practice. It is that although consciousness is intentional, people are far from being always conscious of these intentions. They do not know why they react as they normally do; they do not know the purposes served by the structures of their consciousness; and they are not aware, except at the cost of various neurotic symptoms which trouble them and which seem to them to be central to their problem, of the ways in which the inconsistency of their modes of perception complicate their existence, costing them also countless deep emotional reactions which they cannot deal with except by the classic patterns of denial and repression. It is a matter of choosing one set of consequences or another. Once aware of the pattern which his consciousness expresses and the devices he uses to maintain it as it is, an individual will at least understand why he chose it and what it does for him. He may not want to do anything about it, but even in this there is a gain, for he can deduce the cost of holding out against cultural or family pressures to be something else than what he is. He can be freed of his resentment and at least take responsibility for his choice, hopefully without recrimination, without the disabling cost of dealing with his internal anger.

In other words, successful therapy need not be a "cure" by any "objective" standards; that is, it need not necessarily issue in radically different behavior or the cessation of symptoms. Since consciousness is intentional and behavior to the same degree is purposeful, it is entirely possible that illumination of the reasons for characteristic modes of behavior may not result in the cessation of what we regard as deviant patterns. On the contrary, they may convince patients to do what the prophets of LSD now preach, namely to "drop out" of committed participation in the structure of our society. From our point of view, however, to maintain the forms of conventional behavior without commitment to them by internal choice is fraudulent—a self-deceiving life-style. To choose with responsibility to oneself and to those to whom one relates, an eccentric pattern of behavior may well be a responsible choice. By traditional standards such a person will not be "cured," but there may well be a considerable difference in the degree to which he attempts to impose his standards on others.

Naturally we prefer a more socially responsible course of action, but we do not make it an index of the success of therapy. In fact, our approach makes it possible in many cases for people to choose more constructive behavior than might otherwise be the case. We do not identify the power-holders in society with parent-surrogates, nor postulate an inevitable conflict between individual self-assertion and repressive social forces. Our ideal is a social world, a *Mitwelt* of self-chosen relationships which are characterized by willingness to let others be themselves, by refusal to set up, or be set up by, patterns of dominance and submission. Conscious always of the internal marks of his own identity, the existential analyst thinks of himself not as the passive vehicle for his patients' distorted imaginings, but as an active co-participant in the agreed-upon task of achieving for the patient a corresponding personal integrity.

Thus, we do not feel that we can impose standards of health upon patients, for we believe it to be insufficiently appreciated how much it costs them—not only financially, of course, a problem large enough in many cases, but in terms of emotional isolation—either to maintain their habitual patterns *or* to give them up for others. It is at this point that we have learned much from the existentialist philosophy, which emphasizes man's precarious condition at the point when his developed consciousness discovers that its uniqueness is also separation from all external support. Neurotic defenses are costly, since they involve perceiving others according to patterns which falsify the facts of their individuality. They also mean living with the consequences of unfulfilled demands, which the neurotic is unaware that he has no right to make. On the other hand, to emerge from these patterns of consciousness is to become aware of them, to feel the guilt of what they have tried to do, but most of all to discover that one is entirely alone in the universe, responsible to do something, to make a place for himself in a tumultuous world which is basically neither friendly nor hostile, but simply there to be lived in (Spiegelberg, 1960).

A simple, clinical example will illustrate all these dynamic processes in action:

A woman—let us call her Mary—reports that she is perpetually overcome by fatigue, so much so that she cannot do the minimal necessary housework. She can't even make the bed in which her condition forces her to spend much of her time. Fortunately, Mary has a loyal and generous husband who is willing to come home and do the cooking, clean up, wash the dishes, make the bed, comb her hair, and generally be sympathetic to her need. Now it is quickly apparent that Mary's feelings for her husband and his devotion are anything but grateful. It turns out that she had a father whom she "loves," but who always knew better than she what she ought to want. If Mary wanted a certain doll, her father would spend more to buy her one which would be more educational—that is, requiring a more adult kind of care. Naturally this made Mary furious. Now at least she can get what she wants, the kind of control which means that her desires are taken seriously. But both sides of the control-pattern take their toll. In psychotic moments she spurts out her hatred of her father-husband and "confesses" her zeal to control his behavior, her contempt for his subservience. Yet at other times, when this is recalled to her by a well-meaning therapist, her need for self-esteem takes over. Mary cannot have said such things, for she has the kindest of husbands, whose help in her tired times is invaluable. Only the suggestion of such things is an accusation, an attempt to destroy a happy marriage. She continues in this vein.

It may be argued that we understand the dynamics of such a case in fairly conventional ways; this is the meaning, after all, of the psychoanalytic origins which we have never repudiated. However, we interpret it somewhat differently both to ourselves and to the patient. If awareness of one's patterns of consciousness is the primary goal, how is it best achieved? The point is not that Mary's father initiated a pathological pattern of reaction in her to other human beings, but that she intends a world in which her need and her fear that it will not be met combine to create an internal tension which literally leaves her weak. What she wants to do is humiliate her husband in order to escape the terror of her weakness, and in a way she is fortunate that he is content to live with a contrapuntal conflict of his own. But Mary cannot be told outright that this is what she is doing, for she could not afford to accept the interpretation. She must discover it for herself and then decide whether this is the way in which she wants to go on living. These results will not be accomplished most expeditiously, I believe, by therapeutic detachment, for Mary and those like her need to know the possibility of real human relationship quite as much as they need to get out from under the burden of their ways of experiencing the world. They need to experience the care and concern of someone who nevertheless refuses to fall into the pattern which they impose on the world of their relationships, on their internal consciousness and even on the field of their perceptions. In simple words, they need most to discover that there are other worlds than their own.

To adopt another world-view, however, is another step altogether. Such a change involves, literally, the loss of one's own world. How can we expect anyone to make it? Certainly no one can make it easily. We must assume, of course, that what prompts some individuals to seek psychotherapy, while others remain in the crazy worlds which they have structured for themselves, is a desire to reduce the cost of conflict, to bring some harmony between the three modes of experience—the interpersonal, the internal, the biological—out of the midst of a condition in which incongruities are dimly perceived. In effect, we ask for a reexamination of a whole lifestyle, which may entail the destruction of old work-patterns, friendships, marriages, but most importantly the very fabric of the world as it is experienced. For example, one may look out over a modern city and be depressed by its squalid aspects or exhilarated by its size and variety; or one can imagine a web of conspiratorial power-structures or crimes waiting to happen, or, on the other hand, one can be terrified of its impersonality, complexity, and problems. All such perceptions can acutally constitute the world which we perceive; yet to purge our vision of all such internal elements involves throwing the burden back on ourselves to create our own meaning out of the welter of human possibilities. Little wonder then that the first sign of change, of truly individual experience, is anger that the old ways are being disturbed. As therapists we must be aware that it is not just the patient's fancy. We really are agents of change, and their anger is in this sense justified, even while we maintain ourselves free from a reactive anger which would indicate that our own identity is somehow threatened by the new turn of affairs (Husserl, 1962).

The first stage of therapy is therefore properly a one-to-one relationship in which the therapist tests the capability of his patient, not by any concrete behavioral standards, but by the general criterion of ability to exist for himself, to stand out from his surroundings and neither insist on his private construction of the world nor persist in being an unwilling partner in others' constructions. One judges what is going on, of course, by patients' reactions to what they recount to us of events in their daily life, as they speak to us in the context of the therapeutic relationship. Since we assume that experience is integrated, whether consciously or not, such communications are as important for their manner as for their content. We observe the tone of voice, posture, and so forth, and relate them to what is being told, in order to discover phenomenologically the way this particular world of experience "feels."

In addition, we permit ourselves to verify these perceptions of our own by what I call "set-ups," verbal cues designed to elicit the old patterns of response or to demonstrate a certain freedom from them. I would not permit myself to give the impression, for example, that I could give Mary a diagnosis of her condition or an authoritative clinical definition of its causes, its cure, and the progress she was making. It is part of many patients' neurosis, of course, that they want answers of this kind in a situation in which such answers are not possible. Thus it must be made explicit that, on the contrary, all statements made by the therapist are *not* the truth, but "working statements" calculated to give the patient a choice, the possibility of a new mode of relationship, or at least an awareness that the one he chooses at that moment is not the only one which might be made available to him. The purpose of the therapist for his patient is therefore not to tell the truth, or to be "true" in the sense of responding consistently in an expected manner, but instead to give options, to play different roles which may be responded to in new ways, to enable his patient to experience the possibility of making substitutions of new perceptions for old.

If it be objected that we therefore deceive our patients or tell them lies in response to their genuine cries for assistance, we must reply that the crux of the matter of interpretation is not the truth-value of what the therapist says to his patient, or its credibility, but what it enables the patient to do about his situation. In practice it is not a matter of choosing a truth or a falsehood as an appropriate response to a patient's demand for a definition of his condition; it is rather the channeling of therapeutic communication into more productive directions. Thus in existential analysis the problem does not often come up. The therapist makes it clear from the start that he is interested in discovering with the patient the ways in which the latter experiences the world, his personal relationships, and himself in relation to them. This is what consciousness means, and until some degree of it is realized no individual can believe that he has genuine alternatives to the ways in which his life habitually moves. Since often the first step in such an achievement is the experience of individuality through anger, it may well be appropriate in some cases to say things which are calculated to make the patient angry. In such a situation, so long as the offer of a genuine relationship is made, it is not important to be able to feel certain that anger is a projection of the patient. Rather one looks for ways to help him stand out for himself.

Once again, however, it must be emphasized that this experience of existential identity is not easily or permanently achieved. Insofar as it requires opening oneself to relationships of real mutuality, it may be said to be virtually inevitable that identity includes a dimension of suffering, one which in some ways may be more acute than what was experienced before, when one paid for distorted relationships at the cost of fantasy-wishes for something else. Thus, any change is experienced as a matter of choice, and it is fully possible, and even acceptable as a therapeutic goal, that the choice may be refused.

A woman of means had a deep need to feel that she was creating around herself an atmosphere of family loyalty and affection. In reality she had married a much younger man who coveted her money and spent his affection elsewhere. She had never had such an atmosphere in her own life and was satisfied, more or less, with the illusion of it. She made explicit, as a matter of fact, what we have been saying is implicit in the therapeutic relationship. She made it clear that she did not want to change, for she felt, at least at that point in her life, that a real change would be too costly to her emotional equilibrium. Under such circumstances it would be a hostile act on the part of the therapist to destroy the illusion she wished to preserve. It was the therapist's duty, I felt, to agree that she had the right to make this choice, so long as she recognized her need and knew her intentions. It had survival-value, as it had had for years. If she were to give it up for a new choice, the decision was not mine to make through "interpretation," but only hers (Holt, 1965).

To be clear about it, one may consider what the patient would have had to give up in making the choice of a new life-style. Living as she did to support, and be emotionally supported by, a younger husband and an adopted child who had no real affection for her, she would have had to deal with the underlying fear that she might never find relationships which she did not buy in the old way. She was old enough not to be especially attractive to men, yet she valued the illusion of being the object of a young man's desire. To recognize the financial factor in this relationship would be a deep self-humiliation, and no one, I believe, would have the right to demand this of her or, what is more, to look on unmoved as she tried to take the consequences of becoming fully aware of the quality of her relationships if she decided to do so. One can only admire the courage of some who undertake to reorient themselves.

If and when reorientation occurs, when it becomes apparent that a patient has achieved some degree of ability to correlate his internal processes of mind with his sensory and interpersonal experience, it becomes necessary for him to find new people to relate to, in ways which will not call up again the patterns which he is trying to overcome—assuming, of course, that he is trying to do so. At this point it cannot any longer be simply a matter of one-to-one therapy, not only because the time is usually so limited but also because the therapeutic relationship is not friendship. It is at this point, I believe, that group therapy on an existential basis is an integral part of the healing process. If it is possible to do so, people can be matched according to age or neurotic pattern or intelligence; but this is not essential to the possibility of significant group experience. Its premise is the achievement of a certain minimal "separating-out" of the individual from identification with the things of his world.

Mary's denial of her problem, for example, took the form of identification with her verbal statements, which were themselves expressions of an internal imagery which would not allow her to recognize, under ordinary circumstances, the anger which she expressed by her behavior. She heard herself saying that her husband was patient, loyal, helpful, and that theirs was a wonderful marriage. She wanted so much to believe this that she forgot the rest. As I have said, the suggestion of the possibility of something else by the therapist in an individual session would rightly bring anger, perhaps with the lingering suspicion, which no assurances to the contrary could quite dispel, that the therapist is only expressing his own pre-judices.

Group experience, however, provides at least two general benefits in this regard. There is, on the one hand, a sharing of common views of experience. It need not be identical experience for the members of the group to be able to realize that others survive equally drastic events. In fact, it is often valuable to have patterns which differ in kind, if not so much in degree, because once again the demonstration of other possibilities for living experience is a necessity. Thus the therapist may remain the catalyst, but he is not the test of "reality." This reality is provided by relationships with others within the group experience.

Secondly, those who have some self-awareness are not easy to fool about what someone else is really saying, not nearly so easy as the person himself when he wants to convince himself against the facts of his actual relationship to others in the group. The other group members can therefore articulate their reactions to what someone contributes to the group, and there can be no question in regard to them, for example, of the self-interest of the therapist who makes a living from others' distress (Holt, 1965-66). Finally, the group provides a disinterested concern and mutual encouragement which is free from the intensity of family conflicts and their inescapability. The group is a temporary gathering from which social friendships may arise but from which no permanent relationship need be expected by any.

To sum up our general aims, what existentialists teach is primarily a method for bringing intentionality into conscious awareness through the experience of in-dividuality in an interpersonal relationship. We know that, in taking on the new identity which this awareness implies, many patients may experience the loss of their old neurotic identities as a lapse into non-being, no-thingness. To lose what one has been living *against* is not to be provided with something to live *for*. That lat-ter condition will be realized only after a serious confrontation with the range of potentialities available in any individual's historical and social situations. One separates out one's own identity with, first, a sense of naked responsibility and a new apprehension of existential, as opposed to infantile, loneliness. This self-separa-tion includes the renunciation of a host of fanciful or even real possibilities, which remained comforting in the time before commitment. Thus, movement to the choice of a life-style of one's own offers repeated opportunities for regression to earlier modes of being, modes which served one well in childhood or later.

The steps toward self-awareness follow similar courses in terms of work-rela-tionships, group life, and the closer ties with those who live in the patient's everyday world. Relationships which were taken for granted suddenly appear in a new light; for when a person begins to take himself seriously, he finds that he must take others into account as well. One who becomes a being for himself, in recognizing his own individuality and uniqueness, comes to understand that others too have an identity for themselves and are no longer controlled by the fantasies which once confined them into regular patterns. They must be allowed to be themselves; but before this takes place, the turning of attention from internal imagery to the *Mitwelt* of rela-tionship entails practicing in our perceptions of others the same new awareness we have of ourselves.

We need to add to our store of illustrative detail on how the existential approach facilitates the achievement of identity, without simultaneously creating new emo-tional patterns which, in turn, need to be overcome. A major advantage of the mode of relationship which we have been describing here is that it anticipates many of the difficulties of classical analysis where the relationship of analyst and patient is concerned. The existential analyst is active, as we have said, although not always in the same manner. He gains the advantage that he does not become the passive object of fantasy-projection on the part of the patient, as in the Freudian model for analysis. As a consequence, the transference problem is minimized, since the existential analyst presents himself always as a unique individual, a human being who has his own structures of intentionality, who is interested in helping others to discover their own individuality, but who is not a substitute parent or even a friend. Other problems, like those of resistance and termination, are also transformed by being related to the patient's own power of decision. When they are the analyst's responsibility solely, or are considered to be so, it is almost inevitable that his interpretation will be experienced as a coercion which the patient has every right to regard as such, and to counter by a reluctance which the analyst, from his point of view, must then label "resistance" and proceed to overcome.

To be sure, the revelation of much in one's internal structure is painful, but the cultural situation has changed so much since Freud's time that there is much less to be overcome on this count. The image of resistance perpetuates a therapeutic relationship which in many ways is not therapeutic at all, as we have suggested. Instead of "overcoming resistance," I would speak of the "unfolding of self-awareness" as a patient comes step by step to recognize the implications of the ways in which he experiences his being in the world.

Our difficulties may come earlier in the course of therapy than they do for Freudians, because we so often violate the expectations in our attempts to add more dimensions to our initial experience of them and to provide the basis for new experience on their part (Holt, 1966). Does this imply an inconsistency? The method is troubling to many, especially those who are accustomed to patterning their behavior on emotional initiative which they have called up unconsciously in others but which they find missing in the existential therapeutic relationship. The existential analyst refuses to become a foster parent, because that is not what his patients need. Yet there is considerable doubt that this lack of predictability is experienced as any more destructive than a Freudian impersonality or than the neurotic equilibrium for which the patient already pays a heavy price. In addition, the rewards are many, for there is no need for a tactic to resolve an artificial transference relationship, and the patient in a successful analysis finds his perception of his therapist beginning to approach the kind of individuality which others also begin to have for him.

In turn, the problem of termination is minimized, for the patient comes to know what he has to deal with in his daily life. He learns how he tends to perceive others; but since this way of experiencing them is his own, he need not act, in Kantian fashion, as though his rule ought to become a universal law. He can begin to let them be themselves, to recognize where his responsibility ends and theirs begins for any situation of conflict. Since the therapist has maintained no mystique of apartness from the life of common mortals, the patient can participate in the decision to conclude therapy either temporarily or for good.

Thus, to sum up, the primary focus of existential analysis is not a concentrated attention to finding the proper explanation and interpretation of the patient's internal vision, for it is all too easy to take a verbal conceptualization or a recorded perception as some essential element of his individual reality (Husserl, 1962). Instead, we think of bringing to light the ways of a patient's individual experience, illuminating it in depth as well as on the surface as something which he has and which he produces for himself, but from which the center of his identity is somehow free. That is, the things we do can be acknowledged as our own, as our responsibility, which we can choose to take, however, only if we are secure in the knowledge that they do not exhaust our meaning or commit us to an unredeemable future. In becoming conscious of his individuality, a person becomes capable of experiencing his view of reality as a choice. This experience in turn forms the basis for a new choice which only he can make—that of maintaining an old and perhaps inappropriate mode of experience or choosing one which better suits his present realities and opens to him a more promising future.

A few further implications of this position may be suggested in conclusion. If there is any principle which all therapists may be said to have in common, it is that a higher level of conscious awareness is an achievement which may help a person to lead a more meaningful and purposeful life. What we disagree about (and properly so at our present state of knowledge) is the best way to help others make the achievement. We ask ourselves what theoretical assumptions on our part will help us communicate most effectively—both to patients and to our fellow physicians and therapists—the set of attitudes which will help others to bring themselves, by their own capacities, to a more authentic and self-conscious mode of existence. As we have suggested, this is a matter of choice at some of the deepest levels of individual existence, and so we are obliged to recognize that the only valid interpretation is that which is done by the patient rather than the physician (Spiegelberg, 1960).

Secondly, whatever the role of other therapeutic aids (such as drugs and perhaps unused modes of sensory stimulation), it seems likely that we shall have to conclude that human beings achieve consciousness only in a verbal world, a world of language. The very existence of the practice of therapy as talking testifies at least to the partial validity of such a postulate. There is, however, more to be said. Since language is social, consciousness also is inevitably social to the degree that it depends on verbal forms. This means in turn that the social context of therapeutic language is wider than the one-to-one relationship of individual therapy. If therapy is, in a sense, communication about how words are understood, the need expressed in the request for treatment is the need to find a new language for all relationships. The therapist therefore concerns himself not just with internal fantasies, but also with ways in which his patients link their fantasies with words and the ways in which they communicate with others in the affairs of their everyday lives. Since therapy is a unique, even artificial, mode of relationship, it is important to discover whether it is consistent with relationships to others in family and working situations.

For such purposes, group therapy is an important instrument (Van den Berg, 1955). It is not only that group work helps us to satisfy the pressing demand for psychological assistance; there are more positive reasons for encouraging patients to enter a therapeutic group. In relationships which are relatively free from anxiety, (since primary-group obligations are absent and all are recognized as people who have no stake in the milieu, in maintaining a false image of themselves), it also becomes possible to verify some of the discoveries of individual therapy and to give people the possibility of becoming aware of the similarities and the differences between the ways in which they and others relate through language and through nonverbal forms of communication. We advance the possibility, in fact, of an existential group therapy which may be more effective, at least in many cases and at the appropriate stage of therapy, than an unduly-prolonged course of individual analysis.

The techniques of existential analysis are related to a theoretical framework which is applicable with great flexibility to the whole range of neurotic problems, which are understood as particular styles of being and experiencing an individual's world. To my mind, existential analysis constitutes the most effective set of procedures currently available for both group and individual therapy.

REFERENCES

Alexander, F., et al. (Eds.), *Psychoanalytic pioneers*. New York: Basic Books, 1966.

Arlow, J., and Brenner, C., *Psychoanalytic concepts and the structural theory*. New York: International Universities Press, 1964.

Binswanger, L., *Being-in-the-world*. New York: Basic Books, 1963.

Boss, M., *Psychoanalysis and Daseinsanalysis*. New York: Basic Books, 1963.

Gurwitsch, A., Edmund Husserl's conception of phenomenological psychology. *Rev. Metaphysics*, 1966, 19 (4), 689-727.

Heidegger, M., *Being and time*. New York: Harper and Row, 1962.

Holt, H., The psychiatrist: an alienated being in our time. Lecture delivered at the Fourth Annual Meeting of the Society for Phenomenology and Existential Philosophy at the University of Wisconsin at Madison, 1965.

——, Existential psychoanalysis in groups. *J. Psychoanal. Groups*, 1965, 1 (3), 37-45.

——, The hidden Roots of aggression in American society. *J. Exist.* 1965/66, 6 (22), 225-234.

——, The case of Father M. *J. Exist.*, 1966 6 (24), 269-395.

Husserl, E., Phanomenologische Psychologie. In W. Biemel (Ed.), *Husserliana*, Vol. 9. The Hague: Martinus Nijhoff, 1962.

Spiegelberg, H., *The phenomenological movement*, Vol. 1. The Hague: Martinus Nijhoff, 1960.

Van den Berg, J. H., *The phenomenological approach to psychiatry*. Springfield, Ill.: Charles C. Thomas, 1955.

CHAPTER 30

Remarks on Insight and Interpretation

Paul Cornyetz

Paul Cornyetz has been practicing psychoanalysis and psychoanalytic psycho-therapy since 1950 in New York City, where he teaches at the Training Institute of the National Psychological Association for Psychoanalysis. Before 1950, he was active in various positions at the New York Psychodramatic Institute, taught undergraduate psychology classes at Brooklyn College and graduate psychodrama workshops at the University of Denver, and practiced Rorschach psychodiagnostics for psychiatrists in New York. All this has left him with a deep interest in inter-personal perception, transference-countertransference, and the judgment we call "clinical." This interest extends to a lively curiosity in epistemology and the theory of knowledge generally. On the more immediate side, he is concerned with the formulation of logical connections between personality theory, theory of person-ality change, and procedures in psychoanalysis and psychotherapy.

From his exquisitely sensitive description of the free associative process (so that you are there, on the inside), to his lucid demarcation of what free associa-tion is and is not, to his charting of the analyst's role, Paul Cornyetz offers us a masterful understanding of the meaning of the analyst-analysand collaboration.

Cornyetz' section below, "The Error of the Emotionalist View," enters a dialogue, on the one side, in response to the existentialist position presented by Holt, while his section, "The Error of the Intellectualist View," takes up the challenge, on the other side, of the rational-therapist position of Ellis' chapter.

THE PSYCHOANALYTIC SITUATION

Insight and interpretation cannot be discussed outside a description of the psychoanalytic situation. If we interrupt an ongoing analysis to make a *structural* examination of the moment, we find that insight and interpretation have forms particular to the selected instant. If we examine an ongoing analysis in terms of *process,* we find that an insight or an interpretation has origins, passes through phases of preparation, varieties of manifestation, and perhaps vanishes in some transformation or assimilation. Either approach to an examination requires a thorough appreciation of the changing environment helping to shape insight and in-terpretation.

Eissler (1965) and Stone (1961) have contributed good discussions of the model psychoanalytic situation. No attempt is made in this paper to go over the ground so well surveyed for us; we shall rely on these surveys to provide our context.

The Location of Insight and Interpretation within the Situation

What takes place in the setting of the psychoanalytic consultation room? Each of the two participants has his distinct role to perform in the ongoing situation. The task first assigned to the analysand is to speak his mind, to report everything he notices to be happening to or within himself. We refer here to the ground rule of psychoanalysis (Freud, 1913, p. 134f). Is this effort by the analysand to associate freely an intellectual endeavor? Far from it. He is not giving utterance to indifferent matters and we expect him not to suppress how he feels about what he tells us. Every rush of emotion and every ripple of feeling of which he is capable are in-gredients in the stream of associations.

Is free association then a flood of emotion and desire? Again, no. The analysand is productive of ideas, small and great; of thought, specific and general; and of schemes, mean and grand. All his thinking from loosely-connected fragments of fan-tasy to logically constructed plans of reality-oriented action also is in the stream of associations.

The task first assigned to the analyst includes listening to what is reported in a way that corresponds to the way in which the report is made. "It will be seen," says Freud (1912, p. 112), "that the rule of giving equal notice to everything is the necessary counterpart to the demand made on the patient that he should com-municate everything that occurs to him without criticism or selection." There is a literature on the analyst's way of listening. Theodor Reik's description (1948, pp. 157-172) has not been surpassed for conveying the attitude of the psychoanalyst. At present, we only wish to note that as the analyst is not hearing about indifferent matters, not uncaring about the person on the couch, and is trained for an attentive listening that at times approaches empathic understanding, he finds himself participating in the situation. He is not observing and looking in; he is inside the situation. He participates fully rather than intensely, however. As the psychoanalyst has a professional rather than a personal intention in the situation and is trained to practice his skills, he does remain outside the drama limiting the life of the analysand.

It soon becomes evident to the analysand that he cannot accomplish the task he voluntarily accepted, often with enthusiasm. More than this, he finds or reveals an inner drag against continuing the effort. Experience has taught us how often this is a signal of disturbing thoughts about and feelings toward the analyst. As pointed out by Strachey (1937, pp. 142-143), an extratransference interpretation will soon have to be followed by a transference interpretation. Sometimes we observe only silences, evasions, and desultory talk of indifferent matters. It becomes the responsibility of the analyst to intervene and to see that the difficulties besetting the analysand are reduced in as economical a manner as possible. The analysand, let us note, is expected to be, to feel, liberated from that inner drag against the moving current—to again speak his mind and to resume his effort at self-disclosure. As long as the analysand is able to go on, willingly, the analyst has no reason to speak. It would not be an intervention, but an intrusion.

The foregoing remarks serve to locate the time or place of insight and in-terpretation within the psychoanalytic situation. It is obvious, we believe, that the analysand and analyst are interacting in an atmosphere laden with affect, and that they are moving together along paths of associations. Occasionally, the analysand, who is leading the way, seems unable to proceed and, at such times, the analyst reminds him of the way he has gone thus far—which generally is sufficient help. Usually, the analysand's difficulty is a confusion over the nature of the analyst's participation in the exploration.

THE ERROR OF THE INTELLECTUALIST VIEW

"It is true," notes Freud (1913, p. 141), "that in the earliest days of analytic technique we took an intellectualist view of the situation. We set a high value on the patient's knowledge of what he had forgotten, and in this we made hardly any distinction between our knowledge of it and his."

Thus does Freud begin an answer to his own question: "Are not the patient's ailments due to his lack of knowledge and understanding and is it not a duty to enlighten him as soon as possible—that is, as soon as the doctor himself knows the explanation?" But simply to tell the analysand what we have learned about his unconscious motives—in advance of his readiness to assimilate such information, while he has only a vague sense of his inner reluctance, and before he has prepared his own recognition of or approach to such revelation—is simply to intensify and complicate the aroused resistances, to ignore the analysand's unidentified fears and anxieties, and to postpone or even endanger favorable outcome. An analyst can help or harm the analysand's chances for a successful exploration; the so-called "stalemate" imperils the next game, if the analysand attempts a second game. In itself, intellectual acceptance fails to advance the analytic exploration. The conviction in the analysand, which is necessary, has to arise from within him. Such conviction is connected intimately with an experience of insight and this cannot be replaced by successful arguments from the analyst. An analysand who has been persuaded by his analyst is far different from an analysand who has been convinced by his own experience.

It is not difficult to see how an intellectualist view can develop despite warnings against it. Only two of the many possibilities will be touched upon here. (1) The analysand's reporting may assume gradually the character of self-examinations. No matter how sincere, honest, and penetrating, self-examination is an evasion of the fundamental rule. We do better to understand it as part of the trouble for which the analysand seeks analysis. (2) Reciprocal to self-examination by the analysand is theoretical instruction by the analyst. For other reasons also, the analyst's comments may assume gradually the character of lectures on theory. No matter how excellent his teachings, he is disrupting the process of psychoanalysis. Despite Freud's detection of and warning against the intellectualist view, such a view was widespread among psychoanalysts and "followers" exist still.

Some analysts slid away from listening to their analysands. Ferenczi (1919, p. 180n) explains that if an analyst dozes, it is because the analysand's associations are worthless, and he avers that ". . . at the first idea of the patient's that in any way concerns the treatment we brighten up again." It is to be doubted that when Freud (1912, 111f) recommended an evenly-suspended attention, he meant to include drowsiness. Also, some analysts allowed the effort at free association to be replaced by a cold recital of happenings, past or present; they exerted themselves only to discover and communicate causal connections between current difficulties and past events, even bypassing the transference aspects of the analytic situation. In such an atmosphere, the delicate reconstruction by the analyst of the analysand's past must have been a strange, affect-alien piece of academic work.

The intellectualist view of the psychoanalytic stiutation was opposed most energetically by Ferenczi and Rank (1924). They assailed "descriptive analysis" for neglecting the dynamic factor of experience, "collecting of associations" with little interest in underlying affects and motives, and "fanaticism for interpreting" regardless of the total analytic situation. They rediscovered, it appears, the preanalytic findings of Breuer and Freud (1893-1895), perhaps reading again that "each individual hysterical symptom immediately and permanently dissappeared when we had succeeded in bringing clearly to light the memory of the event by which it was provoked and in arousing its accompanying affect, and when the patient had described that event in the greatest possible detail and had put the affect into words. Recollection without affect almost invariably produces no result." (See p. 6 of "Preliminary Communication".) It was the ambition of Ferenczi and Rank to restore to psychoanalysis the emphasis on recollection with affect.

The Error of the Emotionalist View

On the one side, there is the error of the intellectualist view. This error consists in overlooking the fact that a recognition or acceptance by the analysand of a probably true statement is not the same as an *experience* of the truth of a statement. On the other side, there is the no less grievous error of the emotionalist view. We start again from the psychoanalytic situation and its two participants. The analysand is trying to put into words what he is experiencing: ideas, impulses, feelings. The attempt itself is an emotional as well as an intellectual activity. The analyst is providing all of himself to the experience of hearing what the analysand has to say, feeling into how the analysand is saying it, and responding both intellectually and emotionally to this stream of associations and the person who is speaking his mind.

Having reminded ourselves that we must not neglect the way in which the analysand behaves for an interest in what he is saying, the opposite error confronts us. (See Reich, 1933 and 1949, for an early, valuable emphasis on the manner of the analysand's participation in the psychoanalytic situation.) We may begin to overvalue the quality, so to speak, of the analysand's emotional expressions. Thus Ferenczi and Rank soon seem unsatisfied with a mere *recollection with affect*. They require a reliving of the events of the past and they require this with such an emphasis and to such an extent that, it may seem, if only we could provoke the analysand to a veritable reproduction of the events which were factors in the development of his troubles, we shall have done enough and what is necessary. In such a view, the significance of an intervention by the psychoanalyst is reduced to its use as an encouragement to profound explosions of affect. The intellectual meaning of the analyst's communication is drowned in the tides of emotion. If the three aspects of repetition, remembering, and working through (Freud, 1914, pp. 147-156) are to be acknowledged as characterizing psychoanalysis, then the active therapy advocated by Ferenczi and Rank—having ignored working-through and having subsumed remembering under repetition—is not a modification of but a departure from, psychoanalysis. (See the 1957 Paris symposium, "Variations in Psychoanalytic Technique".) Is this particular departure a constructive one?

Glover (1924) has given us a balanced evaluation of the active measures advocated by Ferenczi and Rank. It should be clear that at the very point where it is essential for the analyst to intervene with comments directed at the transference-resistance in order to reduce the difficulties encountered by the analysand in his effort to speak his mind, the use instead of active therapy would (1) obscure the analysand's developing misconception of the relationship he has with his analyst, (2) complicate the resistances, (3) disrupt the exploratory progress of the analysis, and (4) risk rendering the analysand passive before an encouraged, if not provoked, inundation by unexpected affects and desires.

Both the intellectualist and the emotionalist sidetracking of the psychoanalytic situation force the analysand into a passive position. It is frequent, under the first regime, for the analysand's dry recitals to serve only as an introduction to the analyst's dry speculations. The analyst then persuades his analysand to a passive acceptance of his academic conclusions. Under the second regime it can happen that the analysand passively becomes more or less a stage on which exaggerated versions of past events are enacted to the analyst, who increasingly directs the drama. Each scene follows on the one before with not even an intermission for discussion. Of course, it is all far more complex than these caricaturing remarks suggest; nevertheless it remains fair to criticize both views as unduly restricting the participation of the analysand and as unduly aggrandizing the part played by the psychoanalyst—all to the detriment of the analysis, to the prevention of a more favorable outcome for the analysand.

THE BIPHASIC PARTICIPATION OF THE ANALYSAND

In proceeding from our comments about the intellectualist view to our comments about the emotionalist view, we started with some consideration of the analysand's reception of the analyst's intervention and ended with some remarks about the analysand's task—to recollect with affect with the ultimate purpose of its assimilation into the ego. To continue with the main issue: Fenichel (1941) recognized the importance of Sterba's 1929 paper on the dissolution of the transference-resistance and, in his own discussion of psychoanalytic technique, he made extensive use of Sterba's idea of the splitting of the ego.

In the psychoanalytic situation, the analysand is called upon not only to experience what is happening to him, but also in a special way to side actively with his analyst in reviewing his own reports, particularly when encountering difficulties in continuing with his associations. We are all familiar with the idea of the split of the ego into a reasonable, judging portion and into an experiencing portion. It is unnecessary to repeat such familiar accounts. We may point out, however, that this idea remains useful, as a point of departure to additional ideas, when we are confronted with analysands who at the start of their analytic venture require the analyst to be the judging ego until they have developed these skills themselves. We can approach to the center of our concern by the light of Sterba's (1934) lucid presentation of his idea: "Through the explanations of the transference-situation that he receives, the patient realizes for the first time the peculiar character of the therapeutic method used in analysis. Its distinctive characteristic is this: that the subject's consciousness shifts from the center of affective experience to that of intellectual contemplation."

We can add that the analysand shifts *between* two positions. In the one position, he is speaking his mind, experiencing and communicating the flow of ideas, urges, feelings, images, and sensations. He reaches an obstacle and cannot get through it. His associations go into swirls and backwaters and, if encouraged, the analysand will bypass this obstacle. The responsibility of his analyst is to insist upon the encounter with the obstacle. The series of interventions on the analyst's part go through a process from simply noting the stoppage to an interpretation.

In the other position, the analysand is joined with the analyst in the endeavor to deal with the difficulty. Sterba (1934) says: "The transference-situation is *interpreted*"; that is, an explanation is given which is uncolored by affect and which shows that the situation has its roots in the subject's childhood. Through this interpretation there emerges in the mind of the patient, out of the chaos of behavior impelled by instinct and behavior designed to inhibit instinct, a *new point of view of intellectual contemplation."* Gradually, as the analysis proceeds, the islands of intellectual contemplation are enlarged. There comes into play what Nunberg (1929) calls the synthetic function of the ego, what Sterba (1934) calls assimilation. Since then, we have learned that, quite often, the recovery of a memory may follow upon the analyst's comment about the transference-situation, a comment which itself does not attempt a reconstruction of childhood events. Such recollection is *with* affect; it is related to the affect in the transference-situation to which the analyst directed his remarks.

The point is plain. If the analysand follows the fundamental rule—to say everything he thinks and feels, censoring nothing—his associations will range over the events of his life, disclosing the connections between current problems and earlier developmental situations. It becomes an affect-laden account. Many of the connections will be observed by the analysand, without any intervention from the analyst, and these observations are accompanied by affect. Some of the connections will not be noticed by the analysand, and eventually there will be a piling-up of these very connections. As mentioned, analytic experience has shown us that these stoppages involve the relationship to the analyst. The transference-situation has to be disclosed to the analysand. Such disclosure produces an experience difficult to describe except with such words as "revelation," "light," or "relief with understanding." It is an experience of insight.

If we formulate the insight as a gain in intellectual understanding, then we must add, however, that it is accompanied by affect. If we formulate the insight as an experience of relief, then we must add that it is accompanied by revelation. Undoubtedly, sometimes an insight is more the one than the other. Undoubtedly, too, particularly during the working-through, when the analysand himself confronts and is confronted by us over and over again with the disclosure of the same forces in new guises, the analysand may experience not relief, but chagrin, disappointment, and annoyance with himself, as well as a full variety of feelings toward the persistent analysis. We may as well admit that we do not know of a psychoanalysis which has proceeded from peak to peak, which has not led through the valleys, along difficult ridges, and with many falls along the way.

Throughout the process of an analysis conducted in the way suggested here, the analysand is *both passive and active* before his own associations. As the analysis nears its termination, the reasonable ego of the analysand has less and less need for the intervention of the analyst. Some analysands—but this is not a requirement—can at the end assume a role impossible to them at the outset, the role of self-analyst.

REFERENCES

Breuer, J., and Freud, S. (1893-1895), Studies in hysteria. *Standard edition,* Vol. II. London: The Hogarth Press, 1955.

Eissler, K. R., *Medical orthodoxy and the future of psychoanalysis.* New York: International Universities Press, 1965 (especially pp. 58-76).

Glover, E., Active therapy and psychoanalysis: a critical review. *Internat. J. Psychoanal.,* 1924, 5, 269-311.

Fenichel, O., Problems of psychoanalytic technique. *Psychoanal. Quart.,* 1941.

Ferenczi, S. (1919), Child analysis in the analysis of adults. *Problems and methods of psychoanalysis,* Vol. III. New York: Basic Books, 1955.

——, and Rank, O. (1924), *The development of psychoanalysis*. New York: Dover Publications, 1956.

Freud, S. (1912), Recommendations to physicians practicing psychoanalysis. *Standard edition*, Vol. 12. London: The Hogarth Press, 1958.

—— (1913), On beginning the treatment. *Standard edition*, Vol. 12. London: The Hogarth Press, 1958.

—— (1914), Remembering, repeating, and working-through. *Standard edition*, Vol. 12. London: The Hogarth Press, 1958.

Nunberg, H. (1929), The synthetic function of the ego. *Practice and theory of psychoanalysis*. New York: Nervous & Mental Disease Monographs, 1948.

Reich, W. (1933), *Character analysis*. New York: Orgone Institute Press, 1949.

Reik, T. (1936), *Listening with the third ear*. New York: Farrar, Straus, & Company, 1948.

Sterba, R., The fate of the ego in analytic therapy. *Internat. J. Psychoanal.*, 1934, 15.

Stone, L., *The psychoanalytic situation*. New York: International Universities Press, 1961.

Strachey, J., The nature of the therapeutic action of psychoanalysis. *Internat. J. Psychoanal.*, 1934, 15.

——, On the theory of the therapeutic results of psychoanalysis. *Internat. J. Psychoanal.*, 1937, 18.

1957 Paris Symposium: Variations in classical psychoanalytic technique. *Internat. J. Psychoanal*, 1938, 39, 200-242.

CHAPTER 31

"... More Than One Way to Skin a Cat"

MARIE COLEMAN NELSON

Marie Coleman Nelson, a psychologist and therapist for some 20 years, is perhaps best known for her innovations of paradigmatic techniques in psychoanalytic psychotherapy. She is the Managing Editor of the Psychoanalytic Review, *a faculty member of the Training Institute of the National Psychological Association for Psychoanalysis, and former Associate Chief of the Psychology Department of Stuyvesant Polyclinic in New York City. Mrs. Nelson engages in private practice and is a Director of the Smithtown Consultation Center on Long Island.*

In the paper below, she cuts through to basic levels of communication between therapist and patient in a way which promises to stand as a significant contribution to the field. The transcription of a therapy interaction reflects the practice of treatment moved to the plane of art. One may find oneself stirred by its imagination and uniqueness as "one way to skin a cat."

The presentation which follows, simultaneously published in Israel,[1] also displays the author's forthrightness and courage in reporting verbatim what the dialogue is in session, and, at each step, why.

As a child I was happily endowed with one superlative uncle. He played the banjo, hunted bears, built me a crystal radio before other ordinary mortals had them, and made ice cream in the hand freezer on Sunday mornings. Best of all, he initiated me into the mysteries of odd-job repair. Trailing about after Uncle Joe, I discovered that the more he was able to "make do" with some unlikely leftover intended for an altogether different purpose, the happier he was with the result. After such triumphs of ingenuity, he would exclaim, "There's more than one way to skin a cat!"

Since I was passionately fond of cats, his grisly imagery stuck in my throat when I tried to repeat the saying, but its essence filled my being. Through my uncle, as time passed, I was to develop a set of appreciations. First I came to understand the joys to be derived from focusing disparate elements toward one end, using for one task objects intended for another, and adapting a single implement to several purposes. Later I came to perceive the relationship between these solutions and the creation of poetic phrases which condense several levels of meaning. It is not surprising that I have found a multipurpose clinical orientation so helpful in the formulation of therapeutic communications as to warrant this suggestion: Wherever disturbed thought processes are part of the clinical picture, analytic verbalizations, by and large, should be overdetermined—deliberately structured to offer not one, but several options of meaning to the patient.

The classical analyst is schooled in the simple, straightforward interpretation on the premise that it is less likely to be distorted by the patient's projective fantasies if it is clear in meaning and rational in content. The tripartite principle governing this style of interpretation is as follows: (1) The patient voluntarily and involuntarily

[1]*Israel Annals of Psychiatry and Related Disciplines*, 4, No. 2, Autumn, 1966.

presents psychic material rooted in past and present, with varying degrees of understanding as to the economic, structural and topographic import of these constellations. (2) The therapist, perceiving more clearly than the patient the patterning of psychic events in the latter's history, processes the mass of data into simpler inferential units which, when communicated properly, can be grasped piecemeal and eventually ordered by the patient. (3) The therapist offers his understanding of the dominant presenting theme by means of spare, factual and homogeneous interpretations which neither tax the patient's intellectual or emotional readiness for conscious awareness nor threaten heavily-defended areas.

Freud's concept of hierarchical psychic structuring based on the lawful succession of libidinal stages presupposed a retrograde interpretive process which moves from the characterological surface downward to the earliest developmental levels of the psyche. That the unconscious (or to be more precise, the *repressed* unconscious) requires to be made conscious for depth change to occur in the psychic structure is an accepted dictum. What *is* debatable is the implicit assumption that the repressed unconscious will become known to the patient only through rational explication by the analyst (Menaker and Menaker, 1964).

Is it not possible that our therapeutic necessity to decode the symbolic language of the patient generates in us a certain bias against symbolic formulations *per se* when they occur in the framework of interpersonal communication, rather than in the more formal contexts of literature and poetry? We tend to view symbolic condensation as the antagonist standing between the patient's unconscious and the therapist. The ambiguous expressions, sexual allusions, and "word salad" of the psychotic are seen almost exclusively in their defensive aspect. The patient who employs them is seen as a hapless victim whose ability to communicate is impaired by the fear of destroying or being destroyed by others, should he venture to express himself directly. This is all very well, but on the other side of the picture—as we experience in our appreciation of wit, humor and the comic—are the autistic delights of word-play, substitution, condensation, neologisms and obscenity without moral stricture. To these may be added negativistic, and outright aggressive, object-related satisfactions derived from frustrating the listener and obliging him not merely to hear, but to work overtime to decode the cryptic communications.

Playing variations on language and the word is such universal music that, even allowing for the aim of therapeutic neutrality, one cannot help but wonder why a simplistic principle should continue to govern the analyst's formulations. By analogy, can one conceive of the sophisticated physical scientist preserving an irrational loyalty to the principle that simple chemical substances varying only in strength of concentration, in quantity, or in frequency of application will be more effective in achieving desired results than compounds of several ingredients? The determining factor in psychotherapy as well as in chemistry obviously lies in the nature of the substance to be acted upon.

The style of interpretation (I should really say, intervention) that I suggest here finds its theoretical affinity in Glover's (1939) concept of developmental ego nuclei which are not presumed to supersede or eclipse one another historically, but rather to coexist as primary affect-ideational constellations originating in various early experiences and undergoing different degrees of elaboration, encapsulation and linkage, one with the other, with the passage of time. Bion's (1962) formulations concerning the formation of thoughts and the process of thinking also have relevance to this discussion. Bion perceives thinking as composed of *alpha* and *beta* function. In his system, alpha function consists of attention, notation and deposition by means of the various offensive and defensive mechanisms known to psychoanalysis. Beta function comprises elements which, through fear and/or hatred (i.e., disruption of alpha function), cannot be processed or digested into memory, but are more like "things-in-themselves" which must be evacuated by means of projective identification and acting out. An outstanding characteristic of beta elements is their incapacity for associative linkage, such linkage being a characteristic of alpha function. Bion (1962) and Fairbairn (1954) are in essential agreement that internalization of the good object (Klein's view, 1958) is not necessary for positive ego growth; that only the bad object requires internalization—internalization being viewed by both as a pathological process (Guntrip, 1961).

From my standpoint, one of the essential goals of therapy is externalization of (in Bion's language) the introjected beta elements and, since these are not capable of being associatively linked *intrapsychically*, they must undergo extrajection and through the transference become available to fresh observation and reordering via the alpha system.

For patients with high beta residue in the psychic structure, therefore, the therapeutic communication must aim for a number of discrete elements rather than integrated or associated mental products, for the rational synthesis implicit in the standard form of interpretation has no counterpart in those areas of mentation harboring the most pathological imprints. By contrast, communications whose content does not bear the stamp of formal logic, but which *may* or *may not* mean a number of things, more closely resemble the products of unconscious mental activity (i.e., fantasy and dream). Overdetermined communications may also be compared with classical interpretation as follows: Following the classic model, the analyst abstracts meaningful patterns from the patient's productions and communicates these to the patient at appropriate points. Following the principle of overdetermined intervention, the analyst's response will be a sort of cryptogram, an encoded message which touches upon, but does not make clearly manifest, the meaning of the patient's productions.

A verbatim portion of a therapeutic session has been selected to demonstrate the above points:

Harold, 34 years old and unmarried, had pronounced schizoid traits with bizarre mentation. Many of his hours dealt exclusively with the nonhuman environment. He harbored thinly concealed paranoid attitudes toward men, and his limited social life seemed to revolve almost entirely about three "Nancies"—girls named Nancy in whose apartments he spent a good deal of time, ate a great many dinners, repaired an infinite number of leaky faucets, and had little or no sex. At first I mistakenly concluded that the three Nancies were actually one Nancy delusionally perceived by the patient as having a variety of contradictory traits, as well as several occupations and numerous ethnic origins. Only later did I realize that they actually were three distinct individuals.

Unknown to the patient, but evident in his productions, was the double purpose these maidens served as mother surrogates and as a collective bulwark against Harold's strong unconscious homosexuality. When I had been exposed for a period to the patient's affectless mumbling and concretistic thinking, I realized that his predilection for Nancies quite probably involved a symbolic displacement of homoerotic impulses toward "Nances"—male homosexuals.

An interpretation to this effect would not only have been repudiated, but might well have driven this patient, with an already limited capacity for object relations, to avoid even his three Nancies. The problem that was more focal was the nature of his transference. Harold's mother had always seemed "dead" to him, and so did I. We were two cardboard cutouts; our words strung out one after the other like beads on a long rope necklace, or they bubbled up from our lips and floated along the ceiling like the word balloons in a comic strip. The chief therapeutic task was to help the patient to talk about his preference for the inanimate and his manipulation of human relationships as if other persons were inanimate things. His accumulation of Nancies was a case in point. The secondary objective was to learn more, if possible, about the symbolic meaning of these Nancies. To promote the transference, a third objective was to convey (noninterpretively): (a) narcissistic mirroring of the patient's resistance; (b) alleviation of his unconscious anxiety that I would break through the resistances with direct inquiry and interpretation of painful material; (c) through my evasion and denial of motivation, stimulation of the patient's curiosity about my thoughts. This would channelize aggression toward me, promote its eventual discharge as an object-related feeling, and thereby establish me as a more significant object in the patient's life.

To understand Harold's responses, it is necessary to know that the major portion of the session preceding this exchange consisted almost entirely of a detailed monologue about his current carpentry project, his furniture, the ingenious use of a piece of mesh fencing as a room divider, the exact dimensions of his apartment, and so forth. So thorough was his exclusion of the human factor that even he commented on his preoccupation with mechanical things in the hour. Harold then made vague reference to a dinner engagement:

P1: (mumbles)

T1: What did you say?

P2: Her friend, another Nancy, I've forgotten her last name, is coming over for supper.

T2: (cheerfully, brightly): Well, that will make four that you know.

P3: Well this other Nancy is married, to some Australian. She's visiting the United States. Married, has a couple of children. (pause) I sense you feel there is too much of an accumulation of Nancies.

T3: Why shouldn't you have an accumulation of Nancies? A person has a right to collect something.

P4: Then you take me to be just a collector?

T4: You wouldn't consider yourself to be a collector of Nancies?

P5: No.

T5: Well, not everybody knows so many Nancies. Why wouldn't you consider yourself a collector?

P6: Well, one can know a group of girls—it just so happens—their names are different.

T6: So, they are not collectors.

P7: Certainly not collectors. Or they are not collectors of any one kind of name.

T7: Why? Do you feel there is something wrong with it?

T7: His projection: that I disapprove of his role as a collector. Actually, I have expressed only a benign interest. If at this point I were to remain silent, he would probably resume his autistic monologue. My question as to whether he disapproves of it, delivered ingenuously, allows him to go forward. (In classical interpretation, analyst might ask patient why he feels analyst disapproves, or interpret that it is actually he, the patient, who is projecting the disapproval.)

P8: Well, Nancy does . . .

T8: Which Nancy?

P9: Barnes.

T9: So why doesn't she change her name?

T9: A reversal technique. I deliberately employ paleologic reasoning, which places the patient in the logical position.

P10: Well, I don't think it's so much the name "Nancy" that's the thing that bothers her. It's two Nancies that seem rather . . . rather close to me, or close enough to me that—she feels sort of insecure. She feels agitated—or—competitive—or. That doesn't make me a collector. (mumbles) You don't like the name Nancy?

P10: Notice that Harold finds nothing strange in my faulty *T9* logic. A patient with less disturbed thought processes would correct me or criticize my proposal. His reply suggests that girls tend to be more jealous of rivals who bear the same name. After thinking of Nancy Barnes' disapproval, he attaches the disapproval to me—a common mechanism of displacement.

T10: I?

P11: Yes.

T11: *Should* I not like it?

T11: My asking, *"Should* I not like it?" is an open-ended substitute for the classical interpretation, which (assuming one were given) would be in the nature of a declaration: "You would like me to be jealous over you, like Nancy Barnes."

P12: Well, I don't know whether you should or you shouldn't. I—I assume you don't, following your comment.

P12: A noncommittal and noninterpretive attitude on my part encourages the patient to venture an opinion.

T12 (pause): Well, why don't you think I like it? Or why do you think I don't like it?

T12: Again I withhold confirmation or denial. This perpetuates his curiosity and thereby his contact with me. By my not taking a position he feels free enough to make a little joke.

P13: I have no idea. (laughs) Maybe you were bitten by a Nancy.

T13: Do you think I ran into a Nancy-nest or something?

T13, 14: We play a game—

P14: Well, it's possible. As a small child—somebody by the name of Nancy bit you. (pause) I don't know—I just throw that out. I don't understand why you don't like Nancy.

T14: Well, it's an excellent hypothesis; where do you think I was bitten?

P15: I don't know. I was thinking about your ankle or legs. (long pause) I'm thinking of the student center—models they have—artist's works—Nancy Barnes down there—I think of your comment about being a collector of Nancies—Why a collector?

P15: —which he terminates when fantasy leads him to think of my legs. He flees to a distant place that is filled with inanimate sculpture and the reassuring presence ("spiritual" presence—*cf. P27.*) of Nancy Barnes.

T15: What's so terrible about collectors?

T15: The patient is a collector. By defending collectors I become the one who resists insight. By my reversal of roles the patient is freed to take the analytic initiative. (In the classical mode the analyst might well offer an interpretation of collection as a symptom of the patient.)

P16: Well, it seems a little inhuman.

P16: It is the patient, not I, who offers an interpretation. He speaks from the standpoint of a human, evaluating inhuman symptomatology.

T16: Why? A great many people collect postage stamps and you collect human beings. What's so inhuman about that?

T16: This is a highly overdetermined comment. On one hand, I defend collecting; on the other, I lump human and nonhuman objects together in the category of material to be accumulated. My words reflect his own undifferentiated perception of the world.

P17: Well, I don't think that people are collected, really.

T17: Maybe they gather around you? Maybe you collect them involuntarily. Maybe they gather around you as bees to honey?

T17: Also overdetermined, this comment is designed to acknowledge at one and the same time his feminine passivity and his masculine attractions. In its very structure the remark encompasses the bisexual principle. (A classical interpretation might be, "You would like to escape responsibility for collecting [i.e., being active] and present yourself as passive and innocent.")

P18: Well, a lot of them *do* pass through my life one way or another.

P18: He is static, others are active—they "pass through." (Harold's father was invalided by an accident in the patient's tenth year.)

T18: Maybe if you had your blood typed you'd find it wasn't universal, but something like being Nancy or something. You match to them, maybe.

T18: Therefore (I imply), perhaps this association with Nancies is one of feminine identification. Perhaps he, too, is a "Nance."

P19: (long pause): Well, I guess I don't like the word *collector*. The word collector makes me feel a little uncomfortable. Perhaps it's because Nancy Barnes has already brought that point out in my mind. I seem to know too many women.

P19: Unconsciously and perhaps consciously he understands the innuendo. Hence, the long pause. But because I have made no interpretation he cannot be absolutely certain. In uncertainty, he retreats to safer ground.

T19: Too many women?

P20: Yes.

T20: Well that's not what *I* said. I said its interesting that you know so many Nancies. I think it's very interesting. (enthusiastically) And now you're going to know another one.

P21: Well, that seems to be purely coincidental. Certainly this other one whom I met once before happens to be—ah—Nancy Barnes' former classmate, coming over for supper.

T21: Then she collects Nancies too!

P22: Well, that's the only Nancy I know that she knows though. I don't see how she can collect one item.

T22: Maybe that's just the first one. After all she collected you, and you've got three others (correcting) two others—two others.

P23: Well, what's behind this word "collect"? You seem to be using . . .

T23: (interrupts): Does something have to be behind it?

P24: Well, yes.

T24: You're always looking for deep, dark meanings in things.

P25: (long pause): Well, I thought since it's such an unusual way to explain this sort of thing that there must be something behind the word "collect." That doesn't seem to be a deep, dark meaning.

T25: So, what do you think is behind it?

P26: Well, I don't know. Collection seems to be collection of something in-human. Nonhuman.

T26: Why? Why—does it have to be that way?

P27: Well, let's say the connotation is certainly in that direction. Collecting rocks or stamps—or tools—I think—Well, I don't think that's the word comes to mind. (long pause) The idea sort of occurs to me now that maybe the opposite of collection is concentration—concentrating on one Nancy only. Somehow Nancy Minkowsky is so useful. Finding out things about myself—terrific. Nancy Posten is very useful in supplying me with material things. Nancy Barnes seems to supply spiritual things.

P27: He is saying: The opposite of collecting, using people as tools or lifeless things, is concentration. Concentrations means a significant love object, a permanent relationship with one woman. The image of the mother as part-object is especially clear here. He seems to be saying that the fragmentation of the mother-image has made it impossible to care for one woman, but that he does the next best thing, which is to find women by the same name who together can supply the qualities he seeks.

T27: She knitted a scarf for you, too.

T27: My "chatty" addendum is intended to suggest that it is not the girls whose specialized qualities fill separate part-object needs, but his *perception* of them, which assigns to each an independent nurturing function. (A classical interpretation at this point would undoubtedly incorporate the points in above paragraph, *P27.*)

P28: Oh yes. Well, material *and* spiritual.

DISCUSSION

Two questions arise: First, was the session therapeutic, and if so, how? Second, if so, what specific therapeutic interventions or units of interaction made it so?

1. Viewed in comparison with the first portion of Harold's session (not given), which was filled with a monologue concerning the manipulation of things, the patient's interest in expressing thoughts and feelings about human object-relationships was sustained, much of it in the context of transference. Although Harold at no point confirmed anything the therapist said or acknowledged his accumulation

of girls named Nancy, his final statement (*P27*) differentiating "concentration" from "collection" signified recognition of a new vantage point from which to evaluate these relationships. That the therapist's hypothesis was not confirmed by him is of no consequence, for there is no reason to assume that insight achieved in an oppositional spirit is less potent than insight achieved in a spirit of mutuality. In the light of the particular difficulties of this patient, especially his withdrawal pattern and the engagement with his problem and with his therapist, leads to the conclusion that the session was, from a therapeutic viewpoint, advancing.

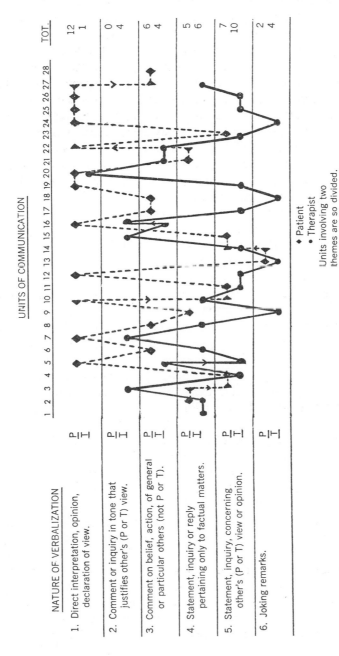

Fig. 1. Sequence of Type of Interaction between Therapist and Patient

2. In Figure 1 the therapeutic dialogue has been classified into six general types of communication. While such typing is admittedly crude, it nevertheless suffices to demonstrate: (a) the contrasting ratio of opinion *expressed* between patient and therapist (12P:1T); (b) the relatively high proportion of opinion *inquiries* by both participants (7P:10T); (c) the distribution of joking remarks in the series; (d) that the only opinion commitment (not actual interpretation) by the therapist (*T20*) was made within the last third of the total series of exchanges; (e) that the session ends with a cluster of four opinion statements by the patient, and two derivative references by him to the characteristics of another person in terms of need satisfaction—showing a relatively high degree of affect and ego cathexis.

In general, the accumulation of ego cathexis is facilitated by the therapeutic policy of keeping the patient in a state of frustration, either by not answering questions, by answering them humorously, or by overanswering them to the point where the patient regrets having asked. With Harold, the analyst usually turned the question or answered jokingly. Ego cathexis is also maintained and can be increased by sustaining patients' curiosity about the analyst's thoughts and feelings—since curiosity, like love, tends to become an intensely object-bound attitude (whatever or whoever the object may be). Elsewhere I have discussed the value of keeping the patient slightly in pursuit, because it generates activity and aggression rather than passivity and compliance (Nelson, 1962). Thus, even the decision of whether or how to answer a question is governed by the principle of overdetermination, by multiple factors related to affect and the disposition of energy, and not merely by considerations of whether or not the content of the patient's inquiry warrants an answer or whether the act of questioning stems from resistance.

In conjunction with the foregoing observations, another aspect of the therapeutic role warrants attention. On four separate occasions (*T3, T7, T15, T16*), the analyst adopts the position that even if Harold *is* a collector of Nancies, having three and about to acquire a fourth, there need be nothing wrong or odd about it. The same supportive theme colors other analytic interventions (*T10, T11, T19, T20, T26*). This is a technique of paradigmatic psychotherapy (Nelson and Nelson, 1957): When the analyst defends the pathology, the patient's need to oppose (i.e., negativism) can only find expression in countering and analyzing his *own* resistance as it is enacted by the analyst. Here again, as in the maintenance of transference curiosity, the patient is induced to function actively, rather than passively, in relation to the therapist.

Turning now to the joking interventions, it has been this writer's experience that manic and depressive personalities need to develop tolerance for the middle range of feeling, while many other patients need to develop tolerance for the extremes of feeling, whether this tolerance be acquired remedially or be analytically reclaimed from repression. Whereas a certain number of patients never do acquire the *élan vital* that signifies the capacity for a wide range of feeling, it is nevertheless the ultimate task of analysis to enable patients to express in treatment all affects of which they are capable.

Quite apart from the insights that naturally accrue from patients' analysis of reactions to absurdity, the experience of fun and nonsense lightens the therapeutic atmosphere and increases the patient's tolerance for the suffering that also comes with self-revelation. Moreover, humorously euphemistic constructs such as *T17* and *T18* permit the therapist to test dangerous ground without frightening off the patient. For example, a serious suggestion to Harold that his association with Nancies was a proxy association with "Nances" would have plunged him into severe anxiety and withdrawal. Proposed in the manner that it was, I am quite certain that this paranoically-sensitive patient sensed the implication, but since my words involved no overt insult to his heterosexual self-image, he was able to relate to the far less offensive concept, "collection," and propose an explanation which dynamically was much closer to the heart of his difficulties: the internalization of part-objects.

Harold's dawning recognition of the autonomous "uses" to which he put his respective Nancies was an important transitional step toward the therapeutic ejection of beta elements—the undigested internalized part-objects associated with the mother figure. The fact that he felt no discomfort or guilt in characterizing the three girls as "very useful" for different purposes testifies to the archaic quality of his object relationships. They were useful in the same way as a fine tool or a piece of wood. Yet, when *I* had calmly condoned this attitude earlier in the session (*T16*), he was able to recognize its peculiarity. Thus, by externalizing the ideational representations associated with beta residue, they become available for alpha processing.

In conclusion, open-endedness is the prime characteristic of the interventions I have described. Through being essentially noncommital, they offer more than one way to "skin a cat." Reality has many faces, and people experience it in different ways with varying emphases (Nelson, B., 1965). Every documentary film producer knows that a powerful public scene can be built with completely untrained extras by simply instructing them to do nothing but watch the main action; their physical immobility and lack of facial expression provide the blank screen onto which the viewer projects and amplifies his own emotions. Similarly, communications which say nothing that constitute a focused response imply whatever is projected into them by the listener. By the same token, communications which typify or symbolically embody several meanings—proverbs, allegories, bits of rhyme, exaggerated phrases, neologisms—not only activate curiosity, but also provide the patient with options for creative response.

REFERENCES

Bion, W. R., *Learning from experience.* London: Heinemann Medical Books, 1962.

Fairbairn, W. R. D., *An object-relations theory of personality.* New York: Basic Books, 1954.

Glover, E., *Psychoanalysis.* London: Staples, 1939.

Guntrip, H., *Personality structure and human interaction.* New York: International Universities Press, 1961.

Klein, M., On the development of mental functioning. *Internat. J. Psycho-anal.,* 1958, 39.

Menaker, E., and Menaker, W., *The ego in evolution.* New York: Grove Press, 1964.

Nelson, B., The psychoanalyst as mediator and double agent. *Psychoanal. Rev.,* 1965, 52 (3).

Nelson, M. (Coleman), Effect of paradigmatic techniques on the psychic economy of borderline patients. *Psychiatry,* 1962, 25 (2).

——, and Nelson, B., Paradigmatic psychotherapy in borderline treatment. *Psychoanalysis,* 1957, 5 (3).

DREAM ANALYSIS

CHAPTER 32

Free Association and Interpretation of Dreams: Historical and Methodological Considerations

Martin S. Bergmann

Martin Bergmann is consultant to the Arthur Lehman Counseling Service, where he conducts weekly seminars. He is also on the faculty of the Mental Health Consultation Center and the N.P.A.P., where he teaches a course on "The Impact of Psychoanalytic Ego Psychology on the Interpretation of Dreams". The paper below was given as a lecture to the Professional Association of the Post-Graduate Center for Psychotherapy as one of eight lectures delivered as the recipient of the First Chair for Advanced Psychoanalysis (1966-1967). A previous paper on the dream, "Intrapsychic and Communicative Aspects of the Dream," appeared in last year's International Journal of Psychoanalysis.

In this chapter, Bergmann enumerates and squarely faces some of the difficulties that have emerged in the application of free association to dream interpretation. This is clearly an important paper, by an important psychoanalyst, inquiring into a significant dimension of the treatment process.

When Freud's *Die Traumdeutung* was translated as *The Interpretation of Dreams,* some of the original meaning of the word was lost. The English term, "interpretation," connotes something subjective and relative. For example, the Supreme Court interprets the Constitution, and we take it for granted that another generation of judges will interpret the Constitution differently; or we speak of an original interpretation given to *Hamlet* or to a familiar piece of music by a new director or musician. The German *Deutung,* on the other hand, connotes the revelation of a mystery (Ekstein, 1966). It is closer to divination than to interpretation. Freud wrote to his friend Fliess, only half in jest, of a tablet that will read: "In this house on July 24, 1895, the mystery of the Dream unveiled itself to Dr. Sigm. Freud" (Freud 1954). The metaphor of nature as a book written in a secret script that can be deciphered, animated the leading scientists from Galileo to Einstein, as it did Freud. Contemporary science reluctantly gave up this heroic metaphor. Scientists no longer believe that nature is written in any kind of language, be it mathematical or logical (Munitz, 1961). This new scientific relativism is relevant also to the interpretation of dreams.

When Freud, shortly before the turn of the century, discovered the Oedipus complex as the nucleus from which the adult neurosis will develop, he made the discovery with the aid of a new technique of investigation, called by him "The Technique of Free Association."

So important was this technique that Freud called it the fundamental rule of psychoanalysis and even referred to it as the "sacred rule" (*S.E., Vol. 16, p. 288*). Half a century later, Lewin (1954, 1955) speaks of the psychoanalyst as "the guardian of the free association," and Bellak (1961) was to call free association "the cornerstone of psychoanalytic technique and the main instrument of psychoanalytic research." On the other hand, Kubie (1959) is of the opinion that one of the major deficiencies in the development of psychoanalysis as a science is its failure to study free association more objectively and precisely. Indeed, the literature on free association is not extensive (Lowenstein 1963).

It is fascinating, even after 70 years, to follow the path that led Freud from hypnosis to free association. If we read the studies on hysteria (Breuer and Freud, 1893-95) in the light of subsequent developments, we will be struck by a basic difference. Breuer, the older and more authoritarian, treats his patients as the recipients of his medical knowledge. Freud, the younger and more curious, listens to the patients and, so to speak, makes them his teachers; step by step, he learns from them the technique of free association.

Nor is her conversation during the massage so aimless as it would appear. On the contrary, it contains a fairly complete reproduction of the memories and new impressions which have affected her since our last talk, and it often leads on, in a quite unexpected way, to pathogenic reminiscences of which she unburdens herself without being asked to.

I had interrupted her after her first story, that the patients were tied on to chairs. I now saw that I had gained nothing by this interruption and that I cannot evade listening to her stories in every detail to the very end.

If she stopped talking but admitted that she still had a pain, I knew that she had not told me everything, and insisted on her continuing her story till the pain had been talked away. Not till then did I arouse a fresh memory. (Breuer and Freud, *S.E.*, Vol. 2, pp. 56, 61, 148.)

While the discovery of the unconscious preceded that of the technique of free association, the technique made the discovery of the Oedipus complex and the interpretation of dreams possible. In 1914 Freud said: "I need say little about the interpretation of dreams. It came as the first-fruits of the technical innovation I had adopted when, following a dim *presentiment,* I decided to replace hypnosis by free association." (Italics mine; *S. E.,* Vol. 14, p. 19.)

The first formulation of the basic rule appears in the interpretation of dreams, and it also illustrates how closely Freud linked free association with dream interpretation:

My patients were pledged to communicate to me every idea or thought that occurred to them in connection with some particular subject; amongst other things they told me their dreams and so taught me that a dream can be inserted into the psychical chain that has to be traced backwards in the memory from a pathological idea. It was then only a short step to treating the dream itself as a symptom and to applying to dreams the methods of interpretation that had been worked out for symptoms. (*S.E.,* Vol. 4, pp. 100-101.)

When Freud demanded this pledge from his patients, the psychic territory from which free association emerges was, as yet, unexplored. Freud had not yet understood the intrapsychic constellation that makes free association possible or fruitful, nor was he aware of how difficult, if not impossible, it is to free-associate in the presence of another person without what Erikson called "basic trust." The decision to demand that the analysand obey the basic rule from the very beginning had a profound impact on the subsequent history of psychoanalytic technique.

If we study free association in a historical perspective, we can differentiate three distinct periods. During the first period, psychoanalysts are almost exclusively preoccupied with the problem of how to insure compliance with the basic rule:

The first thing we achieve by setting up this fundamental technical rule is that it becomes the target for the attacks of the resistance. The patient endeavours in every sort of way to extricate himself from its provisions. At one moment he declares that nothing occurs to him, at the next that so many things are crowding in on him that he cannot get hold of anything. Presently we observe with pained astonishment that he has given way first to one and then to another critical objection: he betrays this to us by the long pauses that he introduces into his remarks. He then admits that there is something he really cannot say—he would be ashamed to; and he allows this reason to prevail against his promise. (*S.E.,* Vol. 16, p. 288.)

For two decades, psychoanalysts were preoccupied with what Ferenczi in 1919 called "the abuse of free association." Even Wilhelm Reich (1928) says that "few patients are disposed to follow the basic rule," and his character analysis was specifically designed to circumvent the difficulties posed by those patients who could not or would not follow the basic rule.

The publication of Anna Freud's classic marks the beginning of a second phase in the history of free association:

Even to-day many beginners in analysis have an idea that it is essential to succeed in inducing their patients really and invariably to give all their associations without modification or inhibition, i.e., to obey implicitly the fundamental rule of analysis. But, even if this ideal were realized, it would not represent an advance, for after all it would simply mean the conjuring-up again of the now obsolete situation of hypnosis, with its one-sided concentration on the part of the physician upon the id. Fortunately for analysis such docility in the patient is in practice impossible. The fundamental rule can never be followed beyond a certain point. The ego keeps silence for a time and the id-derivatives make use of this pause to force their way into consciousness. The analyst hastens to catch their utterances. Then the ego bestirs itself again, repudiates the attitude of passive tolerance which it has been compelled to assume and by means of one or other of its customary defence-mechanisms intervenes in the flow of associations. The patient transgresses the fundamental rule of analysis, or, as we say, he puts up "resistance" (Freud, A., 1937.)

What Anna Freud says of the beginners in analysis was true of all psychoanalysts until a few years before the publication of her book. The new emphasis and interest in the ego greatly reduced the angry confrontation between the demanding analyst and the reluctant patient. Until now, one may say that an unrecognized alliance had existed between the psychoanalyst and the superego of the patient. The demand to free-associate was the old demand "to be good" disguised in a new vocabulary. The inability to free-associate often added new guilt to the guilt with which the patient already came to the psychoanalyst.

A third phase in the understanding of the nature of free association came with the attempt to widen the application of psychoanalytic therapy beyond the boundaries of the classical neuroses. Federn (1952) recognized that making the unconscious conscious need not always liberate and strengthen the ego. In preschizophrenics it can weaken the hold of the ego upon reality.

Eissler (1953) described a schizophrenic patient who feared to look at another person because he was afraid that his soul would go over into the other person. Such patients with a weak ego boundary should not be encouraged to free-associate. Parents who insist that they can read the child's thoughts and who tolerate no secrets create special obstacles in the ability to free-associate. In a subsequent paper, Eissler (1958) observed that delinquents, even if they could be induced to free-associate, would produce only undisguised derivatives of the id. This discharge of id wishes does not contribute to the curbing of delinquency. Finally, severe melancholics, if they free-associate, produce little but a monotonous repetition of the reproaches coming from their superego. It is evident, therefore, that the technique of free association, if it is to be beneficial, depends not only on the ability of the ego to abstain from interfering, but also on an interplay between ego, id and superego. The situation is favorable for free associations when none of the three institutions dominate the total scene to the detriment of the other two. It operates best when, at different times, one "hears the voice" of the ego, id and superego.

It is interesting to compare Freud's demand for free association in 1900 (quoted earlier) with Eissler's statement (1963, p. 198) written 63 years later:

In the psychoanalytic process "saying everything" includes not only reporting every event past and present, every feeling, impulse, fantasy, but also that which is considered by the patient to be a lie, a falsification, unimportant, unnecessary. In order to reach the point of bringing all this material into analysis certain changes must take place in the patient. Strange as it may seem, to live up to this requirement is one of the most difficult tasks and it is questionable whether anyone has ever lived up to it completely.

Eissler's statement raises some disquieting questions. If he is right, then most psychoanalytic patients free-associate, if at all, toward the end of their analyses. By then, the bulk of the work of interpretation has already been made, and it was obtained on the basis of data less trustworthy than Freud had believed. In addition to the difficulties coming from the analysand, there are those which emanate from the psychoanalyst. These have so far not received the consideration they deserve.

The emphasis that Freud put on free association could lead one to believe that the patient, insofar as he free-associates, determines the drift of his own analysis. But this is not entirely the case. In 1910 Freud said, "We give the patient the conscious anticipatory idea [the idea of what he may expect to find] and he then finds the repressed unconscious idea in himself on the basis of its similarity to the anticipatory one." In one of his last papers on technique, Freud (1937, p. 260) described this process in greater detail, now calling the "anticipatory idea" a construction: "The analyst finishes a piece of construction and communicates it to the subject of the analysis so that it may work upon him; he then constructs a further piece out of the fresh material pouring in upon him, deals with it in the same way and proceeds in this alternating fashion until the end."

Freud was not disturbed by the possibility of a construction being an inaccurate one. When the wrong construction is given, "the patient remains as though he were untouched by what has been said," but no discernible harm has been done. Ekstein (1966) has pointed out that Freud was interested more in the effectiveness of our interpretation than in the historical accuracy of the interpretation—that is, whether it opens the gates to new associations, new memories, or leads to a change in symptoms. By contrast, Glover (1931) raised the disquieting question that an inexact interpretation may lead to a premature closure and act as a new defense blocking further free associations.

The case history of the Rat Man (Freud 1909b) offers many illustrations of how such constructions work out in practice. The patient had just finished telling Freud a childhood memory associated with strong guilt feelings. The patient, as a boy, induced his brother to look into the barrel of his gun and then pulled the trigger, hitting the brother on the forehead rather than the eye. If after this disclosure the patient had been left to free-associate, he may have been led to speak more of sibling rivalry, or possibly the sexual symbolism of the act may have become conscious. Freud, however, intervened with the statement: "I took the opportunity of urging my case. If he had preserved the recollection of an action so foreign to him as this, he could not, I maintained, deny the possibility of something similar, which he had now forgotten entirely, having happened at still earlier age in relation to his father" (*S.E.,* Vol. 10, pp. 184-185).

Freud here clearly deflects the feeling of the patient from the brother onto the father. He uses the memory as if it were only a screen memory for oedipal hostility. Such interventions direct the analysis away from where the free associations would have led it and toward the preconceived goals of the psychoanalyst. In the notes to the Rat Man published now for the first time in the *Standard Edition,* we find that Freud himself did not, at least unconsciously, always feel justified in making constructions, for he prefaced one with the statement, "I could not restrain myself here from constructing the material at our disposal into an event" (*S.E.,* Vol. 10, p. 263). Freud's emphasis on reconstruction, so strongly worded in this paper, is mitigated by a statement in another paper (Freud, 1920):

. . . an analysis falls into two clearly distinguishable phases. In the first, the physician procures from the patient the necessary information, makes him familiar with the premises and postulates of psychoanalysis, and unfolds to him the reconstruction of the genesis of his disorder as deduced from the material brought up in the analysis. In the second phase the patient himself gets hold of the material put before him; he works on it, recollects what he can of the apparently repressed memories, and tries to repeat the rest as if he were in some way living it over again. In this way he can confirm, supplement, and correct the inferences made by the physician. (*S.E.,* Vol. 18, p. 152.)

Freud then goes on to compare the first stage to the buying of the ticket, the second stage to the actual journey. The ticket alone "does not get one a mile nearer to the destination." In this paper, we see, the role of reconstruction is somewhat mitigated.

It is well known that Freud (1937) was deeply interested in archaeology, and his concept of construction was derived from it: "But just as the archaeologist builds up the walls of the building from the foundations that have remained standing, determines the number and position of the columns from depressions in the floor and reconstructs the mural decorations and paintings from the remains found in the debris, so does the analyst proceed when he draws his inferences from the fragments of memories, from the associations and from the behaviour of the subject of the analysis."

Since the concept of construction, or reconstruction, is taken from archaeology, I will permit myself a short digression. The archaeologists of Freud's generation—Violet LeDuc, the reconstructor of Carcasson, and Sir Arthur Evans, the reconstructor of the palace of King Minos in Crete—freely mixed the remainders of the old structure with their reconstructions so that the observer today cannot tell the line of demarcation between what was there and what was added by the archaeologist's fantasy. By contrast, current archaeologists in their work of reconstruction (for example in the beautiful museum in Heraklion in Crete) leave the original findings and only indicate by fainter colors what they propose as a reconstruction. I believe that the analogy has relevance also for psychoanalytic reconstructions.

I believe that if the psychoanalyst is not interested in persuading the patient to accept a particular psychoanalytic postulate, he will use constructions sparingly. If recall is not forthcoming, I question the wisdom of telling the patient how it must have been. The unknown can be tolerated, but wrong reconstruction will block further curiosity.

There is, however, one area in clinical work where construction is justified. A number of clinical studies have shown that dreams contain disguised memories. This hyperamnesic quality of dreams had already been noticed by Freud (1900). Under normal conditions these disguised memories emerge by themselves in the process of free associations, but there are special situations when the superego, or some defense mechanism, blocks the translation of a dream into a memory. Here constructions have proved themselves to be fruitful (Fenichel, 1925; Rider, 1953; Rosen, 1935).

Freud's early analytic technique before the advent of psychoanalytic ego psychology can, I believe, be described with the aid of a metaphor. The patient, like the old Colonial countries, produces the raw material which here takes the form of free associations. The psychoanalyst listens to these free associations with an "evenly suspended attention" (Freud, 1912). He then imparts to the patient the interpretation just as the industrialized countries shipped back to the Colonial countries the manufactured goods made out of their own produce. Freud (1912, pp. 111-112) said:

> The Technique is a very simple one. As we shall see, it rejects the use of any special expedient (even that of taking notes). It consists simply in not directing one's notice to anything in particular and in maintaining the same "evenly suspended attention" (as I have called it) in the face of all that one hears.
>
> It will be seen that the rule of giving equal notice to everything is the necessary counterpart to the demand made on the patient that he should communicate everything that occurs in him without criticism or selection.

The technique that Freud described as a very simple one proved to be rather difficult to follow and gave rise to an interesting controversy on technique. Ferenczi (1919) described the difficulties inherent in following this recommendation.

> Analytic therapy, therefore, makes claims on the doctor that seem directly self-contradictory. On the one hand, it requires of him the free play of association and phantasy, the full indulgence of *his own unconscious;* we know from Freud that only in this way is it possible to grasp intuitively the expressions of the patient's unconscious that are concealed in the manifest material of the manner of speech and behaviour. On the other hand, the doctor must subject the material submitted by himself and the patient to a logical scrutiny, and in his dealings and communications may only let himself be guided exclusively by the result of this mental effort. In time one learns to interrupt the letting oneself go on certain signals from the preconscious, and to put the critical attitude in its place. This constant oscillation between the free play of phantasy and critical scrutiny presupposes a freedom and uninhibited motility of psychic excitation on the doctor's part, however, that can hardly be demanded in any other sphere.

More was involved in the question of the "evenly suspended attention" than Freud could have then realized, as the controversy between Theodore Reik and Otto Fenichel brought out. To Reik (1935), the unconscious of the analyst is the most important instrument in the understanding of the patient. To him every analysis is, to some extent at least, a self-analysis of the psychoanalyst. By putting himself in the position of the patient, the therapist "co-free-associates." If the analyst's "moral courage" (Reik's term) in the face of his own unconscious is superior to that of the patient, he will go on when the patient might falter. Reik divides the process of understanding into four stages: guessing, surmising, grasping, and understanding. (In German: *ahnen, erraten, erfassen, verstehen*).

The analyst can be all the surer that he is on the right track when the interpretation comes to him as a surprise. Fenichel (1939, p. 5) criticized Reik as follows:

> There are doubtless some analysts who would like to substitute knowlege for experiences and who therefore do not dissolve repressions but rather play thinking games with their patients. There are perhaps at least as many analysts who commit another equally serious error. They misuse the idea of the analyst's unconscious as the instrument of his perception so that they hardly do any work at all in analysis but just "float" in it, sit and merely "experience" things in such a way as to understand fragments of the unconscious process of the patient and unselectively communicate them to him.

Behind the controversy between Fenichel and Reik lie differences in personality structure. Indeed, my experience as a teacher has convinced me that students of the dream show two opposing characteristic difficulties. There are those who have difficulty, when listening to a dream, in forming a hypothesis as to what the dream means, while other students have the opposite difficulty. These latter students grasp, or believe they have grasped, the meaning of a dream and have difficulty in waiting until further material either confirms or disproves their hypothesis. But even if we make allowance for differences of style, the question may still be asked, "What are the differences between a 'floating' and 'working' analyst?" If both are equally endowed and have the same mastery of psychoanalysis, the difference will nevertheless be marked. The "floating" analyst has established a temporary narcissistic relationship with the patient; he assumes that what seems beyond doubt to him must also be true for the patient. By contrast, the "working" analyst follows the same technique in order to arrive at the hypothesis. Having reached this stage, he now checks for further evidence whether his hunch will be corroborated by the patient. This waiting and checking, this sifting and weighing, this recognition that an inner certainty need not be correct, requires the overcoming of omnipotence and narcissism in the analyst himself and is subjectively experienced as work.

Free associations only rarely lead to clear and unequivocal answers, in most cases, and particularly in dreams; the process ends in a number of diffuse associations from which the interpretation can be made. I have already indicated that one source of illumination, as well as error, is the unconscious of the psychoanalyst; but another serious source of error is the excessive investment in psychoanalytic theory. Freud's work offers examples of sudden insights that emerged in the course of his clinical work. One example is found in the *Analysis of Little Hans* (Freud 1909a, p. 42):

> As I saw the two of them sitting in front of me and at the same time heard Hans's description of his anxiety-horses, a further piece of solution shot through my mind, and a piece which I could well understand might escape his father. I asked Hans jokingly whether his horses wore eyeglasses, to which he replied that they did not. I then asked him whether his father wore eyeglasses, to which, against all the evidence,

he once more said no. Finally I asked him whether by "the black round the mouth" he meant a moustache; and I then disclosed to him that he was afraid of his father, precisely because he was so fond of his mother.

Theoretically this was not a new discovery. However, it was the clinical material, not the theory, that led Freud to the conviction that behind the phobic animal stood the father. There were, however, other instances in which the theoretical position blocked insight. In a recent paper, Zetzel (1966) showed that in Freud's notes on the Rat Man (1909b), he made more than 40 references to the mother, and yet that in the analysis the mother was entirely ignored.

To give another example: On the basis of hitherto unpublished letters between Freud and Fliess, Schur (1966) demonstrated that the famous Irma dream, with which the *Interpretation of Dreams* opens, was not, as Freud thought, dreamed in order to shift responsibility from himself to a colleague, but rather to protect the dreamer from the growing recognition that the esteemed colleague in whom Freud had put so much trust has been responsible for a serious iatrogenic illness. The paper of Schur is of particular interest here because it shows that even a conscientious application of the technique of free associations may end in the upholding of a defense rather than in significant insight, if the insight is too painful.

Melanie Klein (1940, pp. 332-333) offers a particularly striking example of the dangers of the psychoanalyst seeing the dream only as a confirmation of a previously held position:

He then told me a dream of the previous night: He saw a bull lying in a farmyard. It was not quite dead, and looked very uncanny and dangerous. He was standing on one side of the bull, his mother on the other. He escaped into a house, feeling that he was leaving his mother behind in danger and that he should not do so; but he vaguely hoped that she would get away.

He then spoke of buffaloes in America, the country where he was born. He had always been interested in them and attracted by them when he saw them. He now said that one could shoot them and use them for food, but that they are dying out and should be preserved. Then he mentioned the story of a man who had been kept lying on the ground, with a bull standing over him for hours, unable to move for fear of being crushed. There was also an association about an actual bull on a friend's farm; he had lately seen this bull, and he said it looked ghastly. This farm had associations for him by which it stood for his own home.

In the following paragraph Klein uses free association as a confirmation of a previously held position. When the analyst uses the imagery of the patient to make his own interpretation, his power of suggestion is thereby greatly increased.

I then reminded him of the dream of the bull, interpreting that in his mind his mother had become mixed up with the attacking bull-father-half-dead-himself and had become uncanny and dangerous. I myself and the treatment were at the moment standing for this combined parent-figure. I pointed out that the recent increase of hatred against his mother was a defense against his sorrow and despair about her approaching death. I referred to his aggressive phantasies by which, in his mind, he had changed his father into a dangerous bull which would destroy his mother; hence his feeling of responsibility and guilt about this impending disaster. I also referred to the patient's remark about eating buffaloes, and explained that he had incorporated the combined parent-figure and so felt afraid of being crushed internally by the bull.

Readers familar with Melanie Klein's theories will note that the interpretation of the dream is a restatement of her positions on paranoia and depression, clothed in the imagery supplied by the patient's associations. I am here not concerned with the correctness of these views, but rather with the danger that a dream, even with free associations, can so easily be made to fit a preconceived frame of reference.

If the commitment of the analyst is to the discovery of the unknown rather than to a dogmatic refinding of a previously held position, how can he avoid this error? I believe there are two ways. The first way is to ask more questions, such as: "Who do you think the bull stands for?" or, "In your associations, you spoke of buffaloes, but you dreamt of a bull, what is the difference between the two?" These and similar questions give the psychoanalyst a chance to test the correctness of his hypotheses. The other possibility will consist of trying to formulate an alternate hypothesis and see if the free associations will confirm one or the other, or perhaps necessitate a third hypothesis. The buffalo, for example, could represent the Far West—the land outside the law and therefore the id. The formulation of alternative hypotheses will tend to militate against a premature closure.

It will be recalled that Freud called the interpretation of dreams the "royal road to the unconscious." The expression "royal road" is, according to Sarton (1959), borrowed from Euclid. Allegedly, Euclid was visited by the then-reigning Ptolemaios Soter, who wanted to know whether there is a shorter way to geometry than Euclid's book. The proud mathematician is said to have replied, "There is no royal road to geometry." It is understandable that Freud, besieged by so many uncertainties, reversed Euclid's statement, but we who are no longer pioneering in an unknown territory can, I believe, return to Euclid and acknowledge that the interpretation of dreams has given the Freudian analyst a unique and important tool, but it is far from being a royal road.

REFERENCES

Bellak, L., Free association: conceptual and clinical aspects. *Internat. J. Psychoanal.*, 1961, 42, 9-20.

Breuer, J., and Freud, S., Studies on hysteria. *S.E.*, Vol. II. London: Hogarth Press, 1893-1895.

Eissler, K. R., Notes upon the emotionality of a schizophrenic patient and its relation to problems of technique. *Psychoanal. Stud. Child,* Vol. 8, 1953.

——, Notes on problems of technique in the psychoanalytic treatment of adolescents: with some remarks on perversions. *Psychoanal. Stud. Child.,* Vol. 13, 1958.

——, Goethe, a psychoanalytic study 1775-1786, Vol. I. Detroit, Mich.: Wayne State University Press, 1963.

Ekstein, R., The nature of the interpretive process. In *Children of time and space of action and impulse.* New York: Appleton-Century-Croft, 1966.

Federn, P., *Ego psychology and the psychoses.* New York: Basic Books, Inc., 1952.

Fenichel, O., The appearance in a dream of a lost memory, 1925. In *Collected papers, first series.* New York: W. W. Norton, 1953.

——, Problems of psychoanalytic technique. *Psychoanal. Quart.*, 1939.

Ferenczi, S., On the technique of psycho-analysis (1919). *Further Contributions to the Theory and Technique of Psycho-Analysis.* London: The Hogarth Press, Ltd., 1951.

Freud, A., *The ego and the mechanisms of defence.* London: Hogarth Press, 1937.

Freud, S., The interpretation of dreams (First Part). *S.E.,* Vol. IV. London, Hogarth Press, 1900.

——, Analysis of a phobia in a five-year-old boy. *S.E.,* Vol. X, 1909a.

——, Notes upon a case of obsessional neurosis. *S.E.,* Vol. X, 1909b.

——, The future prospects of psycho-analytic therapy. *S.E.,* Vol. XI, 1910.

——, Recommendations to physicians practising psychoanalysis. *S.E.,* Vol. XII, 1912.

——, On the history of the psycho-analytic movement. *S.E.,* Vol. XVI, 1914.

——, Introductory lectures on psycho-analysis (Part I). *S.E.,* Vol. XV, 1916-1917.

——, The psychogenesis of a case of homosexuality in a woman. *S.E.,* Vol. XVIII, 1920.

———, Constructions in analysis. *S.E.*, Vol. XXIII, 1937.

———, *The origins of psychoanalysis*. London: Imago Publishing Co., 1954.

Glover, E., The therapeutic effect of inexact interpretation: a contribution to the theory of suggestion. *The Technique of Psycho-Analysis*. New York: International Universities Press, Inc., 1955.

Klein, M., Mourning and its relation to manic-depressive states (1940). *Contributions to Psycho-Analysis, 1921-1945*. London: The Hogarth Press, 1948.

Kubie, L. S., Psychoanalysis and Scientific Method. In S. Hook (Ed.), *Psychoanalysis, scientific method and philosophy*. New York: New York University Press, 1959.

Lewin, B. D., Sleep, narcissistic neurosis, and the analytic situation. *Psychoanal. Quart.* 1954- 23, 487-510.

———, Dream psychology and the analytic situation. *Psychoanal. Quart.*, 1955, 24, 169-199.

Lowenstein, R. M., Some considerations on free association. *J. Amer. Psychoanal. Ass.*, 1963, 2, 457-473.

Munitz, M. K., In S. Hook (Ed.), *The relativity of determinism in determinism and freedom*. New York: Collier Books, 1961.

Reich, W., On character analysis (1928). In R. Fliess (Ed.), New York: International Universities Press, 1948.

Reider, N., Reconstruction and screen function. *J. Amer. Psychoanal. Ass.* 1953.

Reik, T., *Der Überraschte Psychologe*. Leiden, 1935.

Rosen, H., The construction of a traumatic childhood event in a case of derealization. *J. Amer. Psychoanal. Ass.*, 1955, 3.

Sarton, G., *A history of science*, Vol. 2. Cambridge, Mass.: Harvard University Press, 1959.

Schur, M., Some additional "day residues" of "the specimen dream of psychoanalysis." In R. M. Loewenstein (Ed.), *Psychoanalysis—A General Psychology* New York: International Universities Press, Inc., 1966.

Zetzel, E., Additional notes upon a case of obsessional neurosis. *Internat. J. Psychoanal.* 1966, 47, 123-129.

CHAPTER 33

The Place and Use of Dream Interpretations in Therapy

RICHARD C. ROBERTIELLO, M.D.

Richard C. Robertiello, M.D. has been a practicing psychoanalyst in private practice for the past 15 years. He is Director of Psychiatric Services at the Long Island Consultation Center, Forest Hills, New York, and is on the executive committee and the teaching staff of the Institute for Practicing Psychotherapists. He is supervising psychiatrist at the Community Guidance Service, a Diplomate in Psychiatry of the American Board of Psychiatry and Neurology, and a Fellow of the American Academy of Psychoanalysis. Dr. Robertiello is a Member of the Society of Medical Psychoanalysts and the National Psychological Association for Psychoanalysis. He has written four books: Voyage from Lesbos; A Handbook of Emotional Illness and Treatment; The Analyst's Role *(co-authored with Dr. Bertram Pollens and David Friedman); and* Sexual Fulfillment and Self-Affirmation.

The interpretation of a dream is similar to the translation of one language into another. There are many basic similarities between dreams, so there are rules that can be applied generally that aid the translation greatly. However, each dream is also extremely personal and individual, so that a proper translation requires not only a knowledge of the general rules about dreams, but also a very intimate knowledge of the dreamer. This requires knowing not only what kind of person he is and what his character structure and psychopathology are, but also where he was in the continuum of his emotional development at the exact instant of the dream.

There is no such thing as analyzing a dream "blind." By this, I mean that one is given a dream without any knowledge of the dreamer and asked to interpret the meaning of the dream. The same manifest content can mean something completely different if dreamed by different persons. Beyond this, the same manifest content can mean one thing at one point in the life of a patient and something quite different at another point in his life; so it makes no sense to attempt an analysis of a dream without knowing a good deal about a patient, including his history, pathology, associations, and what issues were emerging in treatment at the time of the dream.

On the other hand, I find that investigating the day residue is often relatively fruitless. In my opinion, the dream is determined much more by intrapsychic forces in the patient than by what his particular experience was during the day of the dream. It is true, however, that where the patient *is* intrapsychically will determine to what he will be selectively attentive or inattentive during the course of the day. This, however, can frequently be determined just as well by the general trend of the content of the session without a specific search for the day residue.

As a student of Freud's ideas about dreams, I am led to the conclusion that his ideas have essentially stood up over the years. The recent work on the physiological aspects of dreaming is certainly interesting in making us aware of just when dreams take place and of how this is brought about, but such aspects have added little to our understanding of the meaning of dreams. I think dreams can still be best explained as an attempt by the mind to preserve sleep, and I feel it is important for us to remember that function. Our use of them to understand what is in a patient's psyche is purely a by-product. When an impulse arises in sleep that produces emotional conflict—that is, when the fulfillment or gratification of the impulse would lead to anxiety—then the dreamer has a tendency to awake in order to escape from the anxiety. Instead of waking, he may have a dream that deals with the impulse in a way that partially gratifies it and partly defends against the anxiety which the full gratification of it would produce. Therefore the pattern we see in dreams generally falls under the scheme of interaction of (1) impulse, (2) anxiety, and (3) ego defense against anxiety.

For example, a girl may dream that a man is chasing her down the street. She feels attracted to him but also afraid of him. She calls for help and a policeman arrests the man. In this dream the girl was expressing a sexual impulse to be chased by an attractive man. This produced anxiety in her. Her defense was to call forth her superego forces (the policeman) to inhibit gratification of the impulse and therefore reduce anxiety. The impulse arises in the id and is an impulse from childhood that has been frustrated by the environment of the dreamer and has been pushing for release from repression and also for gratification. The anxiety that is aroused by the impulse is the danger signal that was initially released in the ego of the child at the time that the impulse emerged, given the level of ego development at the time of the impulse. The defense is those mechanisms which arose in the ego to help keep it repressed, or at least partially repressed, and thus defend the ego against harm. If the dream can produce a partial gratification and an adequate mechanism of defense against the impulse, then sleep will be preserved and the dream will have succeeded in its function. If not, the dreamer will try to avoid the anxiety by awakening, as occurs in nightmares. The dream seen from this point of view is an autonomous mental function.

The dream is not *dreamed* in order to communicate something to the therapist or to another person. However, whether or not the dream is *remembered* has a great deal to do with *communication with another person.* Patients whose therapists show an interest in hearing dreams are apt to remember many more dreams than they did before they went into therapy. And patients whose therapists are adept at dream interpretation and use this as a major tool of therapy are much more prone to remember dreams than patients whose therapists either do not emphasize the use of dreams or are not skillful in interpreting them.[1] The conflictful material in the dream also may have a great bearing on the last analytic session, since resistance interpretations and analysis of ego mechanisms of defense can help bring a hitherto unconscious impulse out of repression.

Universal symbols are very helpful in analyzing dreams. One must always keep in mind that they are not *truly* universal and that in any particular instant they may have another personal meaning specific to the particular dreamer. Nevertheless, most of the time they aid interpretation greatly. For example, a snake will usually

---

[1] Also, patients sense the analyst bringing himself to attention to address the complexities of a dream, or his remaining as is, or his discomfort and retreat. The patient may also report more or less dreams at times depending, for example, on whether he wishes to please, bore or threaten the therapist. (Ed.)

indicate a penis, but to some patient it may indicate an animal that bites, and the oral, sadistic meaning may outweigh the phallic one.

Another key point in deciphering the meaning of a dream is to try to establish the level of psychosexual development from which the major wish in the dream derives. Usually—if we are analyzing the dream of a neurotic patient in a reconstructive analysis—this level will be the same as the one that dominates the patient's recent dreams and associations. Sometimes in a dream there is a major wish at a certain level—for example oedipal—and then the rest of the dream contains elements of defensive regressive levels of adaptation, either anal or oral. Once the basic level of the wish has been established, it becomes much easier to determine the nature of the anxiety in the dream and the manner in which the ego defends itself against this anxiety. For example, there may be a dream in which the dreamer has a sexual wish for a maternal figure (oedipal), then has to run to the bathroom (anal), and then goes to eat (oral).

I do not put as much stock in the patient's associations to dreams as many others have done. First, even if the dream is reported correctly, the associations can be determined by the resistance as well as being in the service of uncovering. Second, with some exceptions I think a good dream analyst should be able to analyze and interpret most dreams a high percentage of the time, without day residue or associations. He is not working in the dark. He knows the patient intimately and he knows exactly which conflicts the patient is in the process of uncovering or working through. I believe the therapist should make every effort to interpret the dream to himself while he is in the process of hearing it. With good training, he should be able to have the meaning of the dream most of the time by the time the patient is finished telling it. If he does not, he has to judge whether it is profitable to continue working on it through the patient's and perhaps his own associations.

Let us assume that he has arrived at the meaning of the dream accurately by the time the patient has finished presenting it, or shortly thereafter. Now what does he do? The answer to this question is really quite complicated. It involves knowing the kind of patient, including an assessment of his ego strength, the goals of therapy (especially whether reconstructive or supportive), the degree of closeness to consciousness of the material in the dream, and, of course, the competence of himself, the therapist, in dealing with unconscious material. We will deal with some of these issues later. For the moment let us assume a competent therapist, a neurotic patient with a strong ego in reconstructive analysis, and material that is preconscious and quite close to consciousness.

A more traditional approach is to let the patient struggle with his own dream until he has understood it himself. I disagree vigorously with this approach. I think it has been sustained mostly to hide the analyst's lack of skill in interpreting dreams. If the analyst is fairly sure he understands the meaning of the dream, I think he should make a brief attempt to see if the patient can get to it also. First, he can ask such broad, general questions as, "What do you make of it?" or "Do you have any idea what it could be about?" If these fail to bring much of a response, the therapist can then begin to ask leading questions based on his own interpretation of the dream.

Let us assume this does not bear much fruit. Then at this point, given the outlined conditions (competent therapist and reconstructive analysis of patient with a strong ego and material close to consciousness), I would interpret to the patient what I thought the dream meant. Usually I would do this shortly following the recounting of the dream. I usually stop the patient after he has told one dream and make him *and myself* deal with that. Even having another dream or two after the first is likely to cause confusion in both analyst's and patient's minds. With very few exceptions, I think a dream should be dealt with in the session it is told and not carried over into the next session. As far as my point about the analyst's taking the lead in interpreting the dream, I feel dream interpretation is a very special skill that requires specific talent and training. I do not feel we should require this skill of our patients. Most of them will not have such skill, and if a less direct approach is used by the therapist, a great deal of very rich meaningful material may be lost. Also, if the patient sees no evidence of the fact that he is communicating something important to the analyst by remembering and reporting dreams, shortly he will stop doing so and the "royal road to the unconscious" will be closed off. In the kind of therapy I have outlined above, dreams can be invaluable, especially with patients who may be blocked otherwise in expressing their unconscious or deeper feelings.

Now let us consider the use of dream interpretations in patients other than neurotics or neurotic characters who are in a reconstructive analytic kind of therapy. Here the use of dream material varies considerably, and it becomes somewhat difficult to generalize. Let us take first a very sick patient, one with little ego strength, who for whatever reasons (age, diagnosis, rigidity of character structure, organic pathology, mental retardation, etc.) we have decided will only respond to supportive therapy and for whom even the mildest attempt at insight would either be threatening or at the least useless. With this kind of patient, as with *all* patients, the therapist should attempt to understand the dream in terms of the patient's unconscious. But how shall the therapist use the dream in the therapeutic session? Once the dream is understood for the therapist's benefit, the real meaning with this type of patient may be completely hidden from him. Instead, certain parts of the *manifest* content can deliberately be used as starting points for superficial discussion or ego support. This is done with the therapist's full knowledge that the manifest content is only a disguised expression for the real, latent meaning of the dream. Here the therapist deliberately decides *not* to use the real meaning of the dream because it would serve no useful purpose for the patient.

Let us take another type of patient, a pseudoneurotic schizophrenic who is very bright, sensitive and insightful, but who has a basically weak ego. Here the therapist may have decided to strengthen the patient's intellectual defenses, thus aiding repression of impulses that cannot actually be worked through because of ego deficit. In this instance the therapist may want to interpret all the dream material extensively, even if it is not particularly close to consciousness. The purpose here, however, is not to aid the uncovering process, but to do the opposite. It is to put the patient's id into a neat, intellectual package, remove anxiety from it by reassurance and support, and then help the patient to re-repress it after having desensitized the patient as much as possible to the material of its content.

Another type of patient is the one who is within the neurotic range—that is, one who is not schizophrenic, psychopathic, etc.—but for whom we have decided that a reconstructive analytic approach is not feasible. This decision may be based on limited intelligence, personality rigidity, age, minimal commitment to treatment, or outside forces which limit the amount of time a patient can be in treatment. With these patients we may have to set limited goals for our treatment. There may be certain areas of the unconscious we feel would be better left unexposed. With these patients, then, we can limit the dream material we interpret to them to these areas which we feel they can deal with profitably. We may be deliberately inattentive to those areas which *we* choose to keep unconscious in them. Again the therapist should try to understand the meaning of the dream, but choose to communicate only certain aspects of it to the patient.

The issue of the selective use of dream material is the important issue in the technique of interpreting dreams to any patient. Even with a neurotic patient in reconstructive analytic therapy who possesses a strong ego, not all aspects of any dream are given the same weight by the therapist. For instance, in the case of the patient who expresses an oedipal wish in the dream, but who also included anal and oral material as regressive levels of adaptation to defend against oedipal anxiety, it would be incorrect for the therapist to pay as much attention to the regressive defensive levels as to the major wish. Obviously, regression here is being used as a mechanism of defense against oedipal anxiety. What the therapist wants to aid to come out of repression here is the oedipal wish. The patient wants to avoid the anxiety by anal and oral regression; and if the therapist deals mainly with the pre-oedipal material in the dream, he will be doing the same thing as is the patient's ego. He will be supporting the repression of the wish which has the maximum anxiety by stressing the ego mechanism of defense—in this instance, regression.

Another choice the therapist must make in deciding what material in the dream should be communicated to the patient is based on the factor of the closeness to consciousness of the material in the dream. Here we often have an excellent clue from the degree of distortion, abstraction and symbolization through which the id wish is presented. If the wish is presented in an extremely obscure manner, then we are usually better off waiting until the wish is closer to consciousness. As it becomes so, it will be less and less disguised in the dream material. Although at times we may choose *not* to interpret the unconscious id wish in the dream, we may often very profitably deal with the part of the dream that emanates from the ego and exposes the mechanism of defense against the wish. Analysis properly deals with a simultaneous exposure of the id and the mechanisms of defense in the ego, and the analysis of the mechanism-of-defense part of the dream will be a preliminary step in aiding the id impulse to emerge from repression.

In summary, then, I have attempted here to deal briefly with the framework for analyzing dreams and to focus on the therapist's choice in deciding what dream material should be interpreted to the patient and under what circumstances. The correct interpretation of a dream is the classic keystone for the utilization of dream material in analytic therapy. Beyond the correct interpretation, however, the therapist must make a great many decisions (based on the kind of therapy, goals, diagnosis, ego strength, and closeness to consciousness of the material) which will determine whether he should be selectively attentive or inattentive to this or that layer and portion of the material as far as his communicating it to the patient is concerned. It is the use and purpose of the interpretation, in that session, which defines appropriate technique.

CHAPTER 34

Interpretation of Dreams on the Subjective Level

Its Application in Diagnosis

RENEE NELL, ED.D.

Renee Nell has specialized in doing things that others have told her cannot be done. Her latest activity is the creation of The Country Place, a halfway house for bright and creative borderline cases, based on milieu therapy. She functions as its chief executive, therapist, and "cook and bottle washer." "It can't be done" led her into making a film for a doctorate: "The Initial Interview—A Teaching Aid in the Education of Marriage Counsellors." She also wrote and produced other films in the mental health field: "It Takes All Kinds," "Marriages Are Made on Earth," and "Divorce," in which she also acted.

"I made a career of being a black sheep," she said; "I studied with Jung when everyone wanted to be a Freudian." She was most impressed with Jung's use of dreams and their applicability to diagnosis, assessment of the treatment process and also to guidance in reality situations. She has done considerable work on dream interpretation and likes to teach its art in seminars.

The interpretation of dreams on the subjective level is possibly Carl Jung's most useful contribution to psychotherapy. Although all dreams are interpreted objectively as well, the interpretation on the subjective level is generally more interesting to the dreamer and is considered more important. Suppose someone dreams, "I unexpectedly met Aunt Mary." His association is: "Aunt Mary was my father's oldest sister. I never liked her. She was known as penny-pinching and suspicious." Recalling the event from the previous day, the dreamer adds that he met a woman who for some unknown reason was repellent to him. In discussing the dream, he suddenly feels that the woman he met resembles his Aunt Mary and that he now understands why he disliked her. This is the interpretation of a dream on the objective level. On the subjective level, however, the dream informs him of something much more important. Aunt Mary is seen as the dreamer's own tendency to be penny-pinching and suspicious, a quality he dislikes in himself and tries to rationalize away. My interpretation would be that the day before he was unexpectedly confronted with this trait through the woman he disliked, and repressing this awareness, he then dreamed about it. Where, on the objective level, the dreamer became aware only of why he took a dislike to a fleeting acquaintance, on the subjective level the dreamer was confronted with a negative characteristic of his own.

In Jungian dream interpretation, long chains of association or enforced search for childhood material are discouraged. The emphasis in association is on specificity: Who was Aunt Mary? What did she mean to the dreamer? What were important character traits? The dream is always seen as an immediate corrective response to thought, actions and feelings of the previous day. The function of the dream is therefore homeostatic: Jung believes the psyche and the unconscious to be a self-regulatory system, working toward balance and normalcy, just as the body does. In dreams our unconscious finds many ways to show us how we could establish homeostasis. In "Aunt Mary," the dreamer meets his own stinginess; working this trait through makes the dreamer not only more acceptable in his own eyes, but generally in those of others too.

Another example of the homeostatic function of the dream and the psyche: a man who aggrandizes himself had a dream of dwarfs, or, at another time, that his apartment is much smaller than he thinks. There is no supposition for a hidden wish-fulfilment. On the contrary, the dream confronts the dreamer with aspects of himself of which he least wishes to be conscious. On the other hand, a man who found new strength in himself, but did not quite dare yet to take psychic possession of this quality, found reassurance and encouragement in his dreams: he lifted a great burden with amazing ease.

Taking the symbols literally is only one of the many ways in which Jung differs from Freud and from all other psychotherapeutic theoreticians. These differences are essential. Jung sees the dream as a Gestalt—i.e., a coherent configuration like a piece of music, a poem or a painting. Each part of the dream is seen in interaction with its other components. Just as one sees a red car in a painting, one sees, too, how the object and the color red relate with the rest of the painting. Is the color dominant, or is it nearly blocked out by another color, or a composite of colors? Similarly, a car appearing in a dream interacts with other components: Is the car parked, or racing with other cars? Is it old or new? Who is in the driver's seat? All such factors have to be taken into consideration.

The principle of interactional field theory underlying Jung's interpretation of dreams is quite the opposite of Freud's cause-and-effect theory. Their difference extends to the area of general symbolism. Freud uses mostly the symbols of the Oedipus and the Electra legend which support his reductive theory leading to the biological family drama. Jung finds in the unconscious all the symbols and images that have been part and parcel of mankind's mythology. These age-old properties of man's history Jung calls the archetypes. They comprise the seasons and the elements (sun, moon, summer, winter, water, fire, etc.), animals (lion, snake, mouse), basic human figures (father, mother, child), and recurrent symbolic representations (angel, devil, hero, witch). They appear as mythologic, religious or fairy-tale figures in dreams, drawings and fantasies.

These archetypes do not become part of a reductive theory. On the contrary, they widen the personal drama to become part of the psychologic drama of all mankind, while by the same token, the drama of all mankind finds its specific, unique and individual echo in the dreamer. In the interpretation of dreams, the general meaning of the archetype has to become significant in very specific ways to the individual dreamer, his every day life, his immediate psychologic problems. Only when the archetypal image has been related in its specific meaning can the dream be understood on the subjective level.

Snake dreams by two different dreamers will illustrate this theoretic point. "I see two snakes, one white, one black, entwined as in the staff of Aesculapius. One is poisonous, the other is not. I do not know which is which. Though somewhere I think I do know." The dreamer, a woman in her late twenties, who likes the outdoors, says she likes snakes and is well acquainted with them.

Association to the previous day: She had been reprimanded in group therapy for remaining so silent. Her explanation was that she did not know what to say and was never quite sure whether her remarks might be helpful or harmful: "I do not know enough about the person, or about therapy." The group did not accept the explanation and asked her to find the real reason for her silence. She thought about it before falling asleep without arriving at any conclusion.

The dream tells her that right and wrong, good and bad are intertwined; that it is difficult to predict which remark will be helpful or harmful to another group member. Furthermore, she herself has good and bad qualities; she does not know whether the source of anything she might say is a good feeling or a poisonous one. But somewhere she is sure she does know. The dream makes her aware that she imposes censorship on her spontaneity in group as well as in other social situations in order not to reveal inadvertently that she, too, has bad feelings; the awareness of these two qualities is part of the healing process—two snakes wrapped around the staff of Aesculapius.

The other dream is from a young man in his early twenties: "There is a huge but not evil snake on a mountain. I am driving up in my car. The snake's face is like mine and he wraps himself around my car, drinking all the liquid that is in the car." The association of the dreamer was one of a guilt feeling regarding compulsive masturbation which had interfered with his studies. Here the dream tries to make the dreamer aware that the guilt feeling is gratuitous, that the snake is really not evil, but nevertheless, robs him of energy necessary to do his homework.

The snake as an archetypal symbol stands for earth-wisdom. In Eastern philosophy, the winged snake is a symbol of the sun, of goodness and strength, and is used as a good luck charm. In Western philosophy or mythology, it symbolizes that same knowledge seen as evil; the dragon is representative of all the forces of the underworld. Though the archetypal meaning of the snake is apparent in both dreams, the significance is the specific application to the dreamer and the use that is made of the symbol in the interpretation of the dream on the subjective level.

One of the most frequent archetypes is that of the masculine and the feminine function. In mythology, this dualism is often represented by earth goddesses and sky gods. In Jungian psychology, the feminine component in man has been termed the anima and the masculine component in women, the animus. Anima is a Latin word for psyche and represents the qualities of subjectivity, feeling, imagination, receptivity. The animus represents woman's objectivity, thinking function, activity drive, organizational ability. In the dreams of man, the anima appears in the form of a woman. A man under thirty, dreaming of nothing but diseased women and prostitutes, not only sees women in this light, but has treated his own inner woman, his anima function, the same way. He has prostituted his feelings, probably using them only to get things—money or sex. A man who dreams of the weak and clinging adaptive woman is overidentified with his feminine side and appears in life as the effeminate man. A man who is infantile in his emotional reactions and human relations will dream of young or even baby girls.

The animus function in women appears in dreams in a similar light. If a woman dreams of overly strong men whom she tries to reach or embrace or imitate, she will in reality try very hard to act as a man. Women of this type are often described as "the boss lady" or "the woman who wears the pants." In Jungian language, she is referred to as a woman who is overidentified with the masculine side of her personality, her animus, and who has developed it at the expense of her feminine side.

The following dream dealing with the crippled animus function of an intelligent professional woman exemplifies how the interpretation of dreams on the subjective level can be used in diagnosis and the development of a treatment plan, even before anything is known of the person's history. The dream went as follows: "There were a number of crippled men, and I was to take care of them, but I didn't want to and felt rather repelled by it." She added that before going to bed she had worked on a research paper on male cripples hospitalized in a rehabilitation center for several years. Although she liked the work itself, she was bored with the paper and wished she didn't have to do it.

As the woman was not a patient and the situation was not a therapeutic one, I suggested that for the sake of the experiment, I would tell her everything I could read of the dream.

It is my guess that you have crippled the masculine side of your personality for many years. You have not developed your ability to think as much as you could have; you have prevented yourself from being as active in your profession as you could be. You are by nature much more of a doer than you are actually doing. The reason for this situation in your life might be due to a family war in which you were wounded. I don't know whether it was father, mother, brother or life's circumstances alone that crippled this function of yours. Though your achievements might be excellent, even superior, in the eyes of others, you know that you are only getting by and could do much better if you did not feel so crippled.

Your wish for rehabilitation is great, but you often suspect, perhaps rightfully so, that you have used your lameness as an excuse to remain in your confining situation. This I deduced from the association: cripples hospitalized for a long time. I interpret your confirming situation as teaching or working in an institution rather than something freer and more daring such as private practice. You probably think you are not strong enough or capable enough to stand on your own two feet outside of an organizational setup. To compensate for this feeling of lameness you must have developed or perhaps overdeveloped, your feminine side by the unusual attention you apparently give to dress, hairdo and makeup. By this you aim to attract, but then get scared. My guess would be that you keep yourself removed from other people, partly because you do not want them to know the secret of your lameness and partly because you know consciously or unconsciously that your animus—your own masculinity—will not protect you well. A man crippled in a wheelchair is helpless, and without self-assertion your logical defense mechanism would become withdrawal or denial.

There is another danger in your relationship with men. In order not to feel your inferiority, you will either be attracted to a man who is more impaired in his masculinity, in his ability to stand on his own two feet, to handle life, to speak up, so that you can feel stronger. Such men become dependent and exploitative, and you get hurt. The other danger is that in maintaining your own crippledness, you are still looking for the knight in shining armor. Your masculine function is not protecting you and you are willing to project this needed protection to any man who is halfway able to carry the projection of the knight—the strong man. Then you are the one who becomes dependent and you probably suffer severe anxieties over whether you will be good enough to hold him. Again you give service, this time not as a maternal woman to a crippled man, but as the doormat to the strong man, a masochistic game by which you are bound to lose the man and get hurt again. The result would be further withdrawal.

At this point, the woman interrupted and confirmed the accuracy of her professional and personal dilemma. She wanted to know the principles involved in arriving at my diagnosis. I will now name some of the questions I asked myself as I worked on the dream. In what state is her animus? What is his action in the dream? What must logically result in life if a woman's intellectual and self-assertive function is passive? What possible compensations would an intelligent woman resort to if she feels intellectually inferior? Is an impairment of one side of the personality possible without creating feelings of insufficiency in other parts of the person? Though the dream speaks about an impairment of her animus function, this must lead to feelings of inferiority as a woman and the difficulties with men mentioned above.

Understanding how like a blueprint her inner Gestalt emerged, she wanted to know whether the dream gave any direction in regard to treatment and restoring balance to her personality. The remedy to her dilemma was expressed in the dream as a demand that she take care of the crippled man, i.e., her own crippled masculinity rather than turn away from it as she did in the dream and in reality.

In the following dream dealing with an overdeveloped animus function, the same principles of interpretation can be applied. The dreamer, a woman in her middle thirties, whom I had known slightly, called me in a state of panic. She was paralyzed in regard to a final paper required to obtain a most desirable professional position. The deadline was only a few days away and she saw no way to finish her assignment. After an overwhelming anxiety attack, she had the following dream which she had come to tell me in the hope of receiving some insight: "I was visiting my therapist, a brilliant man who asked me to dance with him. My intention seemed to be more than just dancing; I wanted to have intercourse with him. When I put my arms around him, he grew very tall so that I could barely reach his waist. I thought I would never be able to have intercourse, at best fellatio, but I was not interested in that. Another man entered the room. He did not seem as bright and attractive as my therapist, but he was jovial, friendly and relaxed. I turned to him and danced with him. He was my size; we danced well together, and I felt at ease and secure with him. We had intercourse, which was like an enjoyable continuation of the dance. I experienced an orgasm in the dream."

It seemed that she had tried to model her own masculine side, her animus function, on that of her therapist; but her unconscious told her that she was not his match. No feeling of completion or orgasm could come from fellatio. At the very best, she would swallow the semen and then spit it out again, which would mean mouthing his intellectual conceptualizations. If she could think of her intellect as being of more average size, as was the other man in the dream, she would have a more harmonious interaction between herself and her thinking function. This made sense to her, and she amplified it by childhood experiences.

She then showed me the partially completed paper that had caused her all the trouble. It was dry and pedantic, which I told her. She thought that she was too stupid to write a better paper. I encouraged her to tell me about her topic in the way her intelligent, relaxed and jovial partner in the dream might talk. To begin with, I asked her what feelings had prompted her to choose the topic. She gave me a colorful and interesting presentation of the subject matter with which she wanted to deal. I interrupted her after a few minutes and asked her to write down immediately what she had told me.

The next day she proceeded in the same vein without my being present, and, for the first time in her life, there was no writing block. On the contrary, writing was enjoyable and flowed easily. There was a continuous interaction between her feminine feeling and masculine thinking side, as exists in a dance between two partners moving together in a harmonious manner.

These examples were employed to demonstrate why dreams are viewed as the most important available guide for therapist and patient alike. The interpretation of dreams on the subjective level is used from the moment of the first encounter, and later on in the evaluation of the treatment process itself. It accompanies the therapy until the person's life and its reflection in the dream indicate that the time for the termination of therapy has been reached.

THERAPY MODIFICATIONS AT DIFFERENT AGE LEVELS

CHAPTER 35

Interpretations and Child Therapy

Haim G. Ginott, Ed.D.

Haim G. Ginott is Adjunct Associate Professor at the Graduate Department of Psychology, New York University, and Associate Clinical Professor at the Post-Doctoral Program in Psychotherapy, Adelphi University. He is consultant to several schools and mental health centers and is on the faculty of the Metropolitan Institute for Psychoanalytic Studies.

In 1964 and 1965, Dr. Ginott served as a UNESCO Consultant to the Government of Israel, Ministry of Education, in Jerusalem. He is the author of numerous articles on child therapy and parent guidance. His books, Group Psychotherapy with Children *(1961) and* Between Parent and Child *(1965), have been translated into several languages. The latter is currently on the "Best Seller" list.*

Examining anxiety, transference, and defenses, Ginott has, in the following paper, thought through and organized his extensive experience in treating children. He offers a systematized discussion of the where *and* when *of offering interpretive illumination to the child patient. In doing so, he takes up, one by one, the special considerations attached to the treatment of children with character disorders: effeminacy, immaturity, schizoid personalities, chronic inhibitions, overmaturity, conduct disorders, the overanalyzed child, and those who disproportionately rely on projection or on rationalization.*

His chapter and that of Dorothy Bloch (Chap. 36) present a forum of somewhat different approaches and emphases in meeting the challenge of treating children who need professional help.

Child therapists of different theoretical orientations make use of toys and play materials in the treatment of disturbed children. Play is the symbolic language of childhood. In play, a child can communicate more vividly and less self-consciously than in words how he feels about himself and his world. He can state hidden feelings, act out forbidden dramas, and rehearse and resolve interpersonal and intrapsychic dilemmas. The role of the therapist is to comprehend play language and to communicate his understanding to the child. The child's play messages and the adult's verbal decoding constitute a healing dialogue.

There are sharp disagreements in the literature, however, concerning the meaning of the child's play and the content of the therapist's response. On the one extreme, the Melanie Klein school advocates deep interpretations in play therapy. The symbolic meaning of his play is interpreted to the child in the way dreams and free associations are interpreted to the adult. In contrast, a nondirective therapist uses no interpretations; he concentrates on recognizing and reflecting the feelings behind the play.

Both systems adhere to a dogma: One always interprets; the other never does. In each system, a certain procedure is used with all patients—the same melody for every malady. The insertion of a pencil into a pencil sharpener will always be interpreted as sexual intercourse by a Kleinian therapist. A nondirective therapist will merely mirror the fact that the pencil needed sharpening. Either of these approaches will prove wrong if applied to all children.

The essence of scientific therapy is individualization. No one procedure is effective with all children. Not all children need verbal interpretation; some require it, many do not. For some children, it is a method of choice; for others it is counterindicated. To some children it brings insight and strength; in others, it creates confusion and disorganization.

Criteria are needed for identifying children who can and cannot use interpretive therapy. A process akin to matchmaking is required to match patient and procedure. We may never have a perfect blueprint, yet guidelines need to be formulated, tested, and refined. The guidelines offered here are educated hypotheses, derived from theoretical considerations and practical experience.

INTERPRETIVE THERAPY AND NEUROTIC CHILDREN

Theoretically, interpretive therapy is indicated for psychoneurotic children. By psychoanalytic definition, neurosis is the result of unconscious conflicts over the handling of sexual and aggressive impulses toward parents. Though repressed, the conflicts are active and anxiety-producing. Defenses and symptoms are formed to ward off anxiety, but the conflicts remain unresolved. The internal battles and the efforts to keep them underground drain the ego energy of these children.

Interpretations, properly timed and phrased, can bring insight and relief. Only when the child trusts the therapist, and is able to regress in his presence, can he accept an interpretation and see its relevance to his life. To be effective, an interpretation must relate to the child's specific disclosures, not to universal textbook aims. This process is slow. The child leads and the therapist follows; the child hints and the therapist responds. In therapy, as in traffic, speeding is dangerous. In child therapy, interpretations touch on three areas—anxiety, transference, and defenses. Each area requires different handling.

ANXIETY

In adult therapy, anxiety is allowed to run its course. In child treatment, the therapist attempts to reduce anxiety with deliberate speed. For adults, anxiety is painful; for children, it can be devastating. As a rule, the neurotic child should leave every therapy session less anxious than when he came. Many neurotic children have not yet developed stable defenses, and suffer from vague anxiety and fear of impending doom. They need the sympathetic acceptance, understanding, and interpretation of their condition.

TRANSFERENCE

Interpretation of transference is the most risky part of child treatment. Children do not come to therapy week after week because they seek mental health. They come because of their relationship with the therapist. Therefore, errors in relationship may bring an end to therapy. Not infrequently, parents are only too glad to comply with their child's vocal demands to terminate treatment.

Although risky, interpretation of transference is necessary. The exploration and interpretation of attitudes toward the therapist serve to clarify for the child his feelings toward his parents. When hostile and libidinal urges are uncovered and worked through, the child starts seeing his parents in a new light. He develops "transference in reverse" (Slavson, 1952). Just as in the beginning of treatment he saw the therapist through the mirror of his past experience with his parents, he now sees his parents in light of his new experience with the therapist. He discovers in his parents the human qualities and humane characteristics that he found in his therapist. Jerry, aged seven, said to his therapist:

> It used to be I thought everybody was out to get me, but I guess I been wrong. All people aren't bad people . . . you're good. Sometimes I'm good. . . . Maybe— all people are some good and some bad. . . . Maybe *even Mom!* (Axline, 1950, p. 55)

DEFENSES

Any direct attempt to analyze defenses is experienced by a child as an attack on his personality. Even sympathetic exploration is often taken as implied criticism. Whenever feasible, it is better to strengthen a child's ego than to interpret his defenses. A strengthened ego can deal effectively both with inner conflicts and defenses. Defenses disappear when the child no longer needs them. Time must be allowed for this process to occur. However, when defenses are continued out of habit rather than need, exploration and interpretation may be indicated. This step is left advisedly to the last phase of therapy. Defenses can be examined only when the therapeutic relationship has been solidly cemented and when the child's ego has grown strong. Only then is the child ready to give up his self-defeating mechanisms.

EGO THERAPY AND CHARACTER DISORDERS

Character-disordered children benefit little from verbal interpretation. Character is shaped by experience with persons and situations; it is not changed by words. It can be modified only by corrective emotional experiences.

Interpretations *are* useful when the ego can be employed to modify another part of the personality. Thus, in the neuroses, guilt and anxiety over libidinal and aggressive strivings are dissolved when, in the security of the therapeutic relationship, repressed conflicts are brought to the awareness of the ego and are worked through. In character disorders, the entire structure of personality, *ego included,* needs modification. Therefore, the ego cannot be mobilized to reconstruct other parts of the personality.

Children with character disorders do not suffer great intrapsychic distress. Their traits are ingrained and their behavior is ego-syntonic. They gain little from exploration of primary process thinking, or from interpretation of libidinal strivings. They are not helped by taking the lid off their id.

This condition is frequently overlooked by sophisticated therapists who come to child psychotherapy with a rich background of adult psychoanalysis. Often, they tend to assume that depth psychology is the treatment of choice for all disturbed children. Sooner or later they begin to probe the unconscious, analyze the defenses, and interpret the resistance of every child patient. This approach cannot but cause damage. A therapist must pursue therapeutic aims tailored for a particular patient. He must resist the temptation to use his skills "to gratify his curiosity in the mystery of the human psyche" (Des Lauriers, 1962, p. 198).

The specific therapeutic aim in treatment of character-disordered children is to build ego and correct character. This task cannot be accomplished by the employ-ment of transference and interpretations. It requires contact that compels and presence that demonstrates. It requires not only an adult who accepts and un-derstands, but a peer group that makes demands, offers rewards and encourages corrective identifications (Ginott, 1961).

Unlike adults, children internalize experience, assimilate it, and make it part of their personality. Children are pliable; their identifications are fluid, their defenses unstable, and their growth uncompleted. They change with their life mold. To a large extent, children become what they live (Ginott, 1965).

> If a child lives with criticism, he learns to condemn.
> If he lives with security, he learns to have faith in himself.
> If he lives with hostility, he learns to fight.
> If he lives with acceptance, he learns to love.
> If he lives with fear, he learns to be apprehensive.
> If he lives with recognition, he learns to have a goal.
> If he lives with pity, he learns to be sorry for himself.
> If he lives with approval, he learns to like himself.
> If he lives with jealousy, he learns to feel guilty.
> If he lives with friendliness, he learns that the world is a nice place in which to live![1]

To play upon words, one can say that, for adults, character determines ex-perience; for children, experience determines character.

CHARACTER DISORDERS AND GROUP THERAPY

Where ego functioning and character formation are defective, interpretations and insight are of secondary importance. The main curative elements are example and imitation, internalization of remedial experiences and identification with corrective models, the nurture of autonomy and self-reliance, and the enhancement of self-im-age. For the large number of children who need ego repair and character correction, group therapy is the treatment of choice.

The basic prerequisite for admission to ego-oriented group therapy is a capacity (actual or potential) for social hunger—a need to be accepted by peers and a desire to attain status and maintain esteem in a group. In return for peer acceptance, the child is willing to modify impulses and change behavior. He begins to play, talk, and behave like other group members.

The desire for acceptance stems from satisfactory primary relations with a mother (or substitute) who, by fulfilling the infant's needs, imprinted him with the value of, and craving for, affection and approval. Children who, in infancy, missed sustaining contact with a mother figure are not suitable candidates for group therapy. Because their first relations have failed them, they suspect all relations. Having had no experience which made delay or sacrifice worthwhile, they find it dif-ficult to delay gratifications and modify behavior in exchange for acceptance. Anna Freud (1949, p. 60) states: "If infants are insecure and lacking in response owing to a basic weakness in their first attachment to mother, they will not gain confidence from being sent to a nursery group. Such deficiencies need attention from a single adult and are aggravated, not relieved, by the strain of group life." This statement

---

[1]This formulation of mental health concepts appeared as an editorial, "Children Learn What They Live," in *Florida's Children*, 1959, 10 (10).

holds equally true for therapy groups. In the following sections are brief descriptions of children for whom ego-oriented group therapy is the treatment of choice.

Effeminate Boys

In psychotherapy, one encounters some boys who have been brought up like girls. They usually come from matriarchal households, where the father is either weak or absent or where they were the only boy in a family of many females. Since their primary identifications have been with nonmasculine models, these boys cannot help but assume some feminine roles. They may lack the characteristic aggressiveness expected of boys in our culture. They may shy away from rough games or be unable to mingle freely with other boys. They feel more comfortable in the company of girls. Such boys usually receive rough treatment from other children. They are negatively nicknamed, attacked, and abused. They are socially stigmatized and emotionally scarred, and they often grow up to be inadequate adults.

Ego-oriented group therapy with a male therapist is the preferred treatment for such boys. Individual therapy is counterindicated, because a close relationship with a male therapist may activate latent homosexuality, while a female therapist cannot meet the boy's needs for masculine identification. A nonintense relationship with a male therapist, masculine toys and activities, and the company of boys provide the optimal curative elements for treatment of effeminate boys. The group therapist serves as an identification model without strong libidinal ties. The materials and group members call forth the masculine components of personality without arousing anxiety. The setting as a whole encourages assertiveness without fear of retaliation.

Immature Children

Some children have been so overindulged and overprotected that they are unprepared for the realities of life outside their family. They have had little opportunity to develop sensitivity to the needs and feelings of others. They find it difficult to share possessions or to delay gratifications. These youngsters are spoiled, and want what they want when they want it. They show excessive dependence upon parents and siblings and annoy everyone with constant demands for attention and assistance. Instead of exerting their own efforts, they want to be served. Even outside their homes, they demand to be waited on and catered to. Children who remain infants are constantly involved in conflicts. They create tension at home, turmoil in school, and quarrels in the neighborhood.

When the core problem is immaturity, therapy must concentrate, not on probing the unconscious, but on maturing personality. Therapy must do for the infantile child what his parents have failed to do. It must encourage self-reliance and limit acting out. A misconception prevalent among some child therapists is the belief that all acting out has therapeutic value. Acting out is of value only when it represents working out of inner difficulties. For infantile children, acting out has no curative effects beyond pleasure. It does not lead to self-evaluation, recognition of motivation, constructive guilt, and attempts to alter behavior. Their weak superego and strong narcissism, in such instances, instead lead only to perpetuation of acting out and to further disorganization of personality.

The main task of therapy with infantile children is to strengthen their ego and help them complete age-appropriate psychosocial tasks. Therapeutic limits help prevent these children from becoming victims of their own destructiveness and omnipotence. Such limits enhance the ego and lead to self-discipline; through identification with the therapist and the values he personifies, the child achieves greater powers of self-regulation and self-control.

Ego-oriented group therapy is a treatment of choice for infantile children. The group offers them what they need most: growth producing experiences. The group makes demands, invokes restraints, offers corrective identification models, and encourages new modes of behavior. In the group, they learn what aspects of their conduct are socially unacceptable, and what behavior is expected. As a result, they make an effort to adjust to the standards of their peers. In the group, they acquire essential social techniques: they learn to share materials and activities, as well as the attention of a friendly adult. They learn to compete and to cooperate, to fight and to settle fights, to bargain and to compromise. These techniques prepare them to deal with peers on an equal footing.

Schizoid Children

Schizoid children are isolated and isolating, withdrawn and detached, cold to their parents, and distant to their peers. These children seem unperturbed by their isolation and find consolation living in fantasy and daydreams. They have a limited capacity for emotional experience, and they have great difficulties establishing relationships and forming attachments. They feel ill at ease in close interpersonal situations and are unable to express ordinary feelings of affection or aggression. They have no friends or playmates, and they avoid social give-and-take.

Schizoid children find it difficult to relate to a therapist in individual treatment. They continue their habitual withdrawal patterns in the therapy setting. They spend many silent hours in a corner of the room, choosing quiet and safe activities and avoiding spontaneity and risk. Some of these children have a fear of handling tools and of finishing projects. To them tools represent aggression, and completion symbolizes sexual culmination. Such children are threatened by achievement. It brings anxiety rather than satisfaction.

Probing and interpretations are contraindicated in the treatment of schizoid children. They experience exploration as attack. Treatment has to be directed toward ego strengthening and reality testing. They are reached more readily in group therapy. The friendly adult, the interesting materials, and the groupmates make it difficult for them to stay withdrawn. The whole setting entices them into activity and lures them out of their isolation.

Inhibited Children

Unlike schizoid children, these children crave warm relationships but are too shy and too inhibited to initiate them. They do not take part in sports or social activities. Some of them even diminish their verbal participation. A few show elective mutism; they talk only to family members and not at all to strangers.

Interpretive therapy is handicapped because these children are unable to relate even minimally to a strange adult. They avoid verbal communication with the therapist. An active approach threatens their main line of defense. Even a friendly conversation may be frightening to such children since for them any social contact calls for assertiveness which they cannot afford. Interpretations of their unconscious fears of losing control of aggressive or sexual impulses drive these children into further withdrawal and silence. What these children need is a mild group where they will be able to relate at their own time and pace. Only when their own observations have convinced them that relating is safe, will they be ready to risk giving up their protective mechanisms.

"Overmature" Children

Some children are referred to therapy because they are "too good." They are obedient, orderly, and neat. They are concerned about mother's health, father's finances, and little sister's safety. Their whole life is oriented toward pleasing others. A frequently noticed symptom in such children is chronic fatigue. Under the "goody-goody" mask, many a bad impulse is hidden. The effort of transforming hostile impulses into angelic behavior, and the eternal vigilance required to maintain a facade, consumes the life-energy of these children.

Children who overrely on reaction formation benefit from ego-oriented group therapy. In individual treatment, they may continue their established pattern of "altruistic surrender." They are meek and gentle, and spend much of the time propitiating the therapist, whom they fear. They bring him gifts, sing him songs, draw pictures for him, and volunteer to clean up the room. They tell him how nice a person he is, and how much they like him. This is their way of saying how afraid they are of their aggressive impulses and of the therapist's expected retaliation.

An interpretive approach is counterindicated. Any attempt to unmask their hostility toward their parents brings denial, resistance, and refusal to come to therapy. Even a slight hint is rejected. They react as though their lives depended on the conviction that their parents were perfect. Any interpretation to the contrary results in resistance or flight.

Group therapy provides an effective setting for modifying reaction-formation behavior. By observing the aggressive behavior of groupmates and the consistently nonretaliatory reactions of the therapist, these children slowly begin to allow their own impulses to gain some expression. First through "spectator therapy" and then through actual experience, they learn that there is no need to be ingratiating and self-effacing. They are able to give up dutiful compliance toward adults and to assume normal assertiveness.

Children Who Overrely on Projection and Rationalization

Children who use projection and rationalization as their main adjustment technique are helped in noninterpretive groups. In individual therapy, they may continue for a long time to resist facing any unpleasant truth about themselves. They are experts in excusing failure, in blaming others, and in deceiving themselves. Any attempt by the therapist to analyze these defenses will only reinforce them. The therapist himself would become a target for accusations, projections, and blame.

In a group, these mechanisms are effectively unmasked by other members. Their reactions are often powerful and penetrating, as the following example illustrates.

George, aged ten, is always complaining that the teacher picks on him, and makes his life miserable.
David (aged 11): What does she do?
George: She says my homework is sloppy, and she sends notes to my mother.
David: Is it sloppy?
George: She doesn't like the special handwriting that I use, and she picks on me.

David: You are full of shit! You are asking for trouble, and gettin' it. Don't write sloppy, and she'll leave you alone.

For a minute George stood dumbfounded. The words hit him like a bolt of lightning. Then he said, "You're right. Anything to get her off my back!"

Many children who resist interpretations, insight and limits from adults are willing to accept them from members of the group.

Children with Conduct Disorders

Many children are referred to therapy because of conduct disorders, including fighting, cruelty, truancy, and general misbehavior. But they engage in aggression only on a part-time basis. The aggressive behavior occurs at home but not outside of it, or vice versa. Their misbehavior is a reaction against real or imagined mistreatment by parents. Their core problem is an unconsciously retaliatory way of life against all authority. Because their parents failed them, they are suspicious of all adults.

The most difficult task in treating these children is to establish a relationship of trust. They fear the therapist, distrust his kindliness, and cannot tolerate his permissiveness. They aggressively avoid close relationship with him by acting obnoxious and hostile. Any attempt to interpret their behavior will backfire. The directness of individual treatment is too intense for them, even without probing and analyzing. What they require are relationships of lesser emotional intensity. Because of its diluted relationships, group therapy offers them a more appropriate treatment method. "The group acts as an insulator for them, diluting much of the tension that would otherwise exist if the children had no means of escape from closer contact with the worker" (Schiffer, unpublished).

The group helps these children in several ways. They feel reassured by the support of other members. Their guilt is diminished when they discover that others also harbor hostility toward adults. Since their attitudes and behavior are not met with retaliation, the emotions underlying the behavior are affected. There is less self-blame and more self-worth. There is more expression of self and less suspicion of others. The groupmates' support and the therapist's timely interventions help these children achieve a healthier balance between acting out and self-control.

Overly Independent Children

Some children rush toward autonomy. Childhood is too long a period for them. They show impatience about growing up. They deny feelings of dependency and have difficulty accepting help or instruction from adults. Although they are not ordinarily destructive, they resent and resist limits or advice from grownups. Verbal interpretations about their need to overcompensate are met with ridicule. They reject any insights about dependency conflicts, castration fears, or fantasied defects. These children are best treated in group therapy with boys older than themselves. The group members unmask their omnipotence and convince them that age is a reality that cannot be denied.

Overanalyzed Children

Some children become allergic to words. They come from pseudosophisticated homes and have been reared according to various misconceptions of Freudian theory. From early infancy, they were overexposed to "analysis"; their personality was invaded, their motivation questioned, and their conduct explained. They were fed "scientific" jargon with their mother's milk. Some of the parents were themselves in analysis, and were eager to apply their newly-acquired insights to their own children.

A therapist who tried to interpret the play of a young patient, the son of a clinician, heard the following plea: "All of my life I've been psychologized. Please don't you do it." Interpretive therapy is counterindicated for such children, at least until later stages of therapy.

SUMMARY

This paper maintains that interpretations, like surgery, are not for everyone. For some children, interpretations are psychotherapeutic. For others, they are psychonoxious. Guidelines are formulated to identify children who need and profit from interpretive therapy. Descriptions are also given of children for whom ego-oriented therapy is the treatment of choice.

REFERENCES

Axline, Virginia, Play therapy experiences as described by child participants. *J. Consult. Psychol.*, 1950, 14, 53-63.

Des Lauriers, A. M., *The experience of reality in childhood schizophrenia.* New York: International Universities Press, 1962.

Freud, Anna, Nursery school education: its use and dangers. *Child Study,* Spring 1949, pp. 35-36, 58-60.

Ginott, H. G., *Group psychotherapy with children.* New York: McGraw Hill, 1961.

——, *Between parent and child.* New York: Macmillan, 1965.

Slavson, S. R., *Child psychotherapy.* New York: Columbia University Press, 1952.

CHAPTER 36

The Use of Interpretation in the Psychoanalytic Treatment of Children

DOROTHY BLOCH, M.A.

Dorothy Bloch is a psychologist, certified by the state of New York, and a psychoanalyst in private practice. She received a B.A. degree at Hunter College, an M.A. at New York University, and is a member of the faculty at the National Psychological Association for Psychoanalysis. She began her career as a child analyst and although she later expanded her practice to include adult patients, she still devotes a major part of it to the analytic treatment of children. This range of experience has provided valuable opportunity for studying the interrelationship of parent and child.

In her papers, "Feelings That Kill: The Effect of the Wish for Infanticide in Neurotic Depression," and "Some Dynamics of Suffering: The Effect of the Wish for Infanticide in a Case of Schizophrenia," she presents a theory concerning the genesis of emotional illness in which the child's response to the parent's concealed wish for infanticide plays a major role.

In the chapter which follows, she extends these contributions further and at the same time relates them to the interpretive-illuminating interaction between therapist and child patient. Uniting scholarship and clinical perceptiveness, integrating theory and practice, her writing challenges established viewpoints, stimulates new ones, and at the same time, as an extra dividend, satisfies aesthetically. As Erik Erickson came to analysis from art, Miss Bloch was previously in literature and writing. Her remarkable sensitivity, patience and skill as a child analyst are apparent in her several cases, but especially so in her treatment case of Patty presented below.

Consideration of the question of the use of interpretation in the psychoanalytic treatment of children inevitably involves an examination not only of the basic premises of psychoanalytic theory, but of their application to the particular world of the child. Although the use of interpretation is a matter of major importance, a prior concern is always the comprehension of the patient's communication, a problem which is complicated in work with children both by the special language which they employ and by the theoretical assumptions which have determined to a large degree our approach to its meaning. A child speaks to us through fantasy and through play, and his direct verbalizations frequently make use of the symbolism of primary process thinking. In order to chart a course through these complexities, we use—among other things—whatever guideposts theory offers us. It might be helpful therefore, before embarking on a discussion of the use of interpretation, to examine these theoretical concepts in the light of our experience and to explore the world which requires such special means of communication.

Because Freud's theory of the Oedipus complex as the nuclear concept of the neuroses was so fundamental to the structure of psychoanalysis, the shift in the nuclear role to the parent-child relationship with its accompanying emphasis on pre-oedipal experience has left scarcely any area of psychoanalytic thought untouched.

Not only has it resulted in a revision of our concept of the very nature of man, but it has illuminated in a new way almost all aspects of emotional illness—its dynamics, its function and the meaning of its symptoms—and provided a new framework for the comprehension of the patient's communications. Inevitably it has also called for a reappraisal of our theory of the technique of treatment, involving our concept of interpretation and its use.

Freud's theory rested on several major assumptions. In addition to the nuclear role which it assigned to the Oedipus complex, it held that "what decides the purpose of life is simply the program of the pleasure principle" (Freud, 1933), and ascribed to man what appears to be a basically destructive nature. It viewed emotional illness as the result not only of the frustration of the child's "excessive demands" for instinctual gratification from the parents, which gave rise to "an unconscious sense of guilt" and "a need for punishment" by a parental authority, but of the presence of a "tendency to self-destruction," "the manifestation of a death-instinct" (Freud, 1949).

Regarding instincts as "the internal foe," a major source of psychic difficulty, and a threat to society, Freud saw the child as the author of its illness and the enemy not only of itself, but potentially of mankind. "In a few short years," said Freud, "the primitive little creature must grow into a civilized human being." "Civilization" was defined in terms of "prohibitions and punishments and . . . repressions," the implication being that without them, the ego would emerge "powerful and uninhibited" and "in the profoundest sense antagonistic to civilization" (Freud, 1949). Fear was explained, for the most part, on the basis of castration anxiety in men, "one of the most frequent and one of the strongest motive forces of repression, and therefore of the formation of neuroses," and on the basis of "the fear of the loss of love" in women (Freud, 1933). In his final work, Freud (1949) extended this concept to include fear of "the external world."

Suffering was understood in terms of gratification and of reversals. "We have long known that no neurotic harbors thoughts of suicide which are not murderous impulses against others redirected upon himself," Freud stated. He saw "self-torments" as "without doubt pleasurable," a gratification of sadistic tendencies and of hate, both of which relate to an object and in this way have both been turned round upon the self." The function of the suffering was "taking revenge . . . on the original objects" and "tormenting them by means of the illness" (Freud, 1919). In *New Introductory Lectures* Freud (1933) offered another reversal, this time of an opposite character: "We have to destroy other things and other people in order not to destroy ourselves, in order to protect ourselves from the tendency to self-destruction."

The theory of treatment which stemmed from these concepts regarded "the advantage through illness" provided by the neurosis as "on the whole and in the end detrimental to the individual and to society" (Freud, 1950a). Freud (1919) admonished, "You will remember that it was a *frustration* that made the patient ill, and that his symptoms serve him as substitutive gratifications." What this meant in terms of the analyst's role is explained in the statement, "Our hope is . . . to induce the patient to adopt our conviction of the inexpediency of the repressive processes established in childhood and of the impossibility of conducting life on the pleasure-principle."

Although these explanations did not wholly satisfy Freud, it is possible that the framework of the Oedipus complex scarcely permitted any real exploration of some of the questions which he himself raised or their incorporation in any dynamic way into his theory. As far back as 1910, he had inquired, "Is there one of you who has not at some time caught a glimpse behind the scenes in the causation of neurosis and had to allow that it was the least of the evils possible in the circumstances?" The observation in *The Ego and the Id* (1927) that "There is no doubt that there is something in these people that sets itself against their recovery as though it were a danger," is also reechoed in his later years when he stated, "But it must be confessed that these are cases which we have not succeeded in explaining completely" (Freud, 1949).

The concept of man that was the warp and the woof of the oedipal theory inevitably engendered an attitude that was in many instances detrimental not only to an understanding of the dynamics of emotional illness but also to the theory of its treatment. The view of the patient as the victim of his instincts, the object of the pleasure-principle, and as fundamentally destructive by nature, not only beclouded and distorted the meaning of the patient's communications, but tended to insulate the analyst from him. To the degree that these concepts diminished the patient's stature and his strivings, they also served to inspire feelings of disrespect for his suffering. Freud's emphasis on reversals of meaning in addition encouraged an attitude of skepticism on the part of the analyst and the creation of untherapeutic distance between him and the patient. Such an approach frequently resulted in merely reinforcing the patient's illness.

The inescapable impression that emerges from a study of Freud's work is that the child is the agent of his illness and that the parents are passive, kindly figures, the innocent recipients of the child's aggressive drives. This created particular havoc in the work of child analysts. Since they were in a position to observe very readily not only the interaction of parent and child, but also the dynamic process of the child's development, they experienced enormous difficulty in reconciling their observations with psychoanalytic theory. This was especially true of Melanie Klein, who was led by the logic inherent in Freud's concept of the child's nature as basically destructive to say, "This brings us to the consideration of a very obvious objection that may be raised against child analysis. It might be asked, would not too great a reduction in the severity of the superego—a reduction below a certain favorable level—have an opposite result and lead to the abolition of social and ethical sentiments in the child?" Her reassurance stems from the conclusion that "so great a dimunition has never, as far as I know, happened in fact" (Klein, 1933). She found it possible to retain the theory of the nuclear concept of the Oedipus conflict only by moving its timetable back to the first year of life and linking it to the weaning process. That this scarcely sufficed is reflected in her constant questioning of her perceptions.

The magic circle which Freud had drawn around parents, excluding them from any but a passive role in the creation of the child's neurosis, presented her with a protean task. At one point, she stated, "There seemed to be no bridge over the gulf which separated the loving and kindly mother of real life and the monstrous persecution and humiliations which 'she' inflicted on the child in play" (Klein, 1929). At another point she said: "We get to look upon the child's fear of being devoured, or cut up, or torn to pieces or its terror of being surrounded and pursued by menacing figures as a regular component of its mental life. . . . I have no doubt from my own analytic observations that the identities behind these imaginary, terrifying figures are the child's own parents, and that those dreadful shapes in some way or other reflect the features of its father and mother, however distorted and fantastic the resemblance may be. . . . How does it come about that the child creates such a fantastic image of its parents—an image that is so far removed from reality?" She dealt with these phenomena by structuring a "terrible, menacing superego which is wholly divorced from reality" (Klein, 1933).

Her explanation of castration anxiety is perhaps an even more dramatic illustration of the intellectual feats to which Freud's theory of "reversals" led. She stated, "In my view, castration fear starts in infancy as soon as genital sensations are experienced. The boy's early impulses to castrate his father take the form of wishing to bite off his penis, and correspondingly castration fear is first experienced by the boy as the fear lest his own penis be bitten off" (Klein, 1945). Her exclusion of the parents from the child's treatment is possibly still another facet of the application of Freud's theory and may have served to perpetuate an idealized image of the mother and father.

In my treatment of both child and adult patients, I have found that the nuclear problem is the parent-child relationship, and that behind the child's fear which Freud explained on the basis of castration anxiety and the terror which Klein characterized as "a regular component of its mental life," is what the child appears to experience as the threat of annihilation at the hands of the parents. It is very likely that our preoccupation with the Oedipus complex has impeded any realistic appraisal of the child's relation to the world, or a consideration of the actual dynamics of his position and the psychological truths that may flow from it. The child's defenselessness and helplessness scarcely need establishing, but the effect on his psychic processes of his early awareness that in fact his existence may depend on the good will of his parents surely requires exploration.

In his *Outline of Psychoanalysis,* Freud refers to the threat of annihilation from the external world as a major concentration of the ego's defense. It is important to note, however, that for Freud, the "external world" excluded parents. He stated, "Children are protected against the dangers threatening them from the external world by the care of their parents; they pay for this security by a fear of losing their parents' love, which would deliver them over helpless to the dangers of the external world" (Freud, 1949). For the infant and the young child, however, the "external world" is synonymous with "the parents," and the fear of annihilation therefore appears to be experienced in relation to them. The tenacity with which children attempt throughout their lives to deal with their need to feel loved by the parents may indicate that they are convinced that their lives depend on it, and here suggests a link with their fear of annihilation.

It therefore follows that far deeper concerns than the pleasure-principle dominate the child's psychic processes. Rather than instinctual gratification, his major preoccupation appears to be survival. This latter seems to rest on two related elements—the fear of annihilation at the hands of the parents, and the need to feel loved by them. It is my impression that these two components form the basis for a major part of neurotic symptomatology.

The implications of this concept in regard to the meaning of his defenses are also far-reaching. In her major work, *The Ego and the Mechanisms of Defense,* Anna Freud (1946), tying her concept to the nuclear theory of the Oedipus complex, confined her discussion to defenses that were directed against instincts and affects. In order to supply a motive for the defense against instinct, however, she found it necessary to introduce the concept of "objective anxiety," which she equated with "dread of the outside world," further defined in her discussion of reality as "those responsible for the child's upbringing." In the *Outline* Freud (1949) had already suggested an extension of the concept of defenses to include the defense against perception in relation to the external world. He stated, "We can now supplement this by a further assertion that during the same period of life, the ego often enough finds itself in the position of warding off some claim from the *external world* which it feels as painful, and that this is effected by *denying* the perceptions that bring to knowledge such a demand on the part of reality." If we extend the phrase "external world" to include the parents, that is, those who are in most cases "responsible for the child's upbringing," it becomes clear that the defense against perception is a major task of the ego. Rather than denial, however, I have found the concept of "self-deception" a more useful description of the mechanism of defense employed.

This concept was defined for me by two adult patients whose cases I discussed in "Feelings That Kill" (Bloch, 1965) and "Some Dynamics of Suffering" (Bloch, 1967). At a certain point in their treatment, they both formulated their insight in identical terms, stating, "I must not know what I know," and "I must not see what I see." In those two instances, as well as in the others referred to in those papers, the perceptions that were warded off were also identical—the parents' concealed wish to commit infanticide. In each, the self-deception enabled the patient to cope with the feeling which he had absorbed—and with the equally murderous feeling which it had elicited—and to survive. In explanation of the patient's defense against his perceptions, I stated in the latter paper (Bloch, 1966):

Under such conditions, these children bend all their efforts towards creating the illusion of being loved. Self-deception is their major tool and self-defeat their primary investment. In order to persuade himself that his parents "really" love him, but that he "makes" them hate him, the child prefers to believe that everything is wrong with him. He represses the knowledge of the parents' feelings which he has absorbed, searches for the defects within himself and willingly makes himself the cause. He devotes his life to establishing his worthlessness, accuses, vilifies and involves himself in a massive engagement in self-defeat, all in the service of justifying his unconscious knowledge of his parents' feelings and of proving that they are right, thereby providing the hope without which he cannot live—that since his worthlessness has provoked their hatred, if he can change and become more worthy, he may win their love.

His struggle, however, is complicated by another factor: his parents' murderous feelings evoke similar feelings in him. In order to conceal his own murderous wishes, he develops a sensitivity to criticism lest the acknowledgement of any fault within himself expose his inadmissible hatred and with it the buried knowledge of its cause, the parents' destructive feelings. In a case of schizophrenia the intensity of the feelings that had to be concealed was of such magnitude that this did not suffice. They had to be dealt with by "going out of contact" and by experiencing the world through "glass walls." In addition to establishing his worthlessness in order to justify his unconscious knowledge of his parents' feelings, he must also therefore maintain a sense of his worth.

This need to assert both his worth and his worthlessness simultaneously becomes a major source of his suffering and keeps him in an inextricable bind.

The concept of a defense against perception provides us with a major key to the understanding of children's communications, a prerequisite for any formulations concerning the use of interpretation. The type of thinking which he employs has been described simply as "characteristic of childhood" (Hinsie and Campbell,

1960) and its resemblance to the primary process of the dream merely noted. If we pursue the similarity further, however, and consider that in the dream primary process has the function of enabling the unconscious to evade the "censor," we must allow that it may serve the child in a similar way. An analysis of the child's thinking reveals that, like the dreamer, he makes use of "allusion, analogy, displacement, condensation and symbolic representation" (Hinsie and Campbell, 1960) in place of conveying his meaning directly. My observations lead me to believe that his unconscious purpose in doing so is to keep his perceptions a secret both from himself and from threatening adults, so that he may survive.

The dynamics underlying the child's employment of this process are suggested by Freud's description of the dreamer. He states, ". . . if the unconscious makes use of its relative freedom and enters on some activity, it finds the avenue to motor expression stopped up, and only the innocent outlet of hallucinatory satisfaction open to it. It can now, therefore, dream . . ." (Freud, 1933). In a similar sense we can say that, confronted by the overwhelming and threatening power of the adult, the child's "avenue to motor expression" is also "stopped up" and only the "innocent outlet" of primary process thinking and fantasy are "open to him." His fear of annihilation is apparently so intolerable to him, and his need to feel loved by the parents so overriding, that he must devise whatever means he can to defend himself against his perception of their destructive feelings and their power, and of his own helplessness. Not only does the "fantastic image" to which Klein refers seem to be very much a part of the child's emotional reality and "a regular component of its mental life," but his use of a vast range of "menacing figures" reveals the child's profound investment in displacing his fear from the parents, in concealing and camouflaging their identity and in hiding his perceptions.

This process invests almost all areas of his functioning. His fantasies, his play, his verbal communications—all seem to reflect it. Although it has been assumed that the child's method of communicating stems from an inability to express himself clearly, it appears that there is "method in his madness," and that his unconscious objective is nothing less than to conceal what he finds unbearable in his experience or impermissible in his thoughts and feelings—mainly, his parents' murderous feelings and his own murderous response to them. That adults frequently tend to misinterpret children's communications or to find them completely mystifying may therefore reflect neither their shortcomings nor the child's inability to make his thoughts and his feelings known. I have the impression that like the symbolism of the dream, in a hostile atmosphere the child's communications are designed not to be understood.

The suspicion that the child's ability to give verbal expression to his thoughts and feelings had been vastly underestimated, and that the fear of annihilation is a universal preoccupation, first suggested themselves to me in my treatment of very young patients. I should like therefore to present brief illustrations of this phenomenon with just enough background to make them understandable.

During her initial session, a girl 3½ years old stated with startling urgency, "I don't like to think of myself as a giraffe." Questioning elicited only that "giraffes don't bite," but when she announced by the beginning of her third session, "I don't think of myself as a giraffe today," it became clear that Ellie thought of herself "as a giraffe" when her father's murderous rage evoked similar feelings in her. The father, whose work required periodic absences from home, was particularly irate because when he returned, frequently in the early morning, he would no sooner have fallen asleep than Ellie was up and calling for him. He then responded as though propelled by lightning, bounded out of bed in rage and roared at her to keep quiet. This was frequently the character of their reunion. The morning after one such encounter, she arrived at her session wearily singing a repetitive song, "If you don't love me, then I don't love you." The murderousness of the rage which his attacks elicited could apparently be expressed only via a figure as enormous and as phallic as a giraffe. Her need to protect him against it, however, was also served by her selection of a species which she had been told "don't bite."

The image of the giraffe alternated with that of "baby monster." On seeing a whole brick lying on my terrace and beside it, a half brick, she automatically dubbed the whole brick "a mean monster," and the half-brick "a baby monster." Her play was constantly punctuated with the cry, "He's after us! We have to run!" After many months of fleeing from him—in which I was invited to join—only then did she feel strong enough to challenge his power, declaring, "We're not going to let him get away with it—right?" When it had become apparent after a while that the monster had several moods, I took to inquiring about him as one would about a member of the family, and learned that sometimes he felt "friendly" or was even "nice and cuddly this morning." At no time, however, during the duration of the fantasy, was he identified as the father.

In another instance, Ronny, 5½ years old, matter-of-factly and without comment presented, during his first session, three events of his life which preoccupied him. A year before, he had fallen out of the second-story window of his house and had been caught by the bushes. When he was "small," his father had put him on a big horse and had let him ride all by himself. His father had also taken him on a roller-coaster and they had sat on the front seat.

Ronny had been referred because his behavior had made life at home unbearable, especially for his mother. His birth had constituted an untimely interruption of her singing career, which she found very difficult to forgive. His father, an engineer whose growing dissatisfaction with the marriage subsequently led to divorce, delighted in using his son as a weapon against his wife. His continued exposure of him to one perilous situation after another, which preoccupied Ronny and which the father tried to justify on the grounds of "toughening" him, inevitably raised the question of whether he were not trying unconsciously to destroy the boy. Ronny took refuge from the dangers of his world in the fantasy of a "germ," microscopic, but deadly. He inhabited an invisible empire which, he explained, was small enough to fit inside the setting of his ring.

In another instance, Danny, 5½ years old, during his first session presented the hopelessness of his situation in his expressed wish to make every weapon that he saw, from a plastic water-pistol to an air-rifle. He was the preferred younger child whose older sister secretly threatened to kill him. His parents saw nothing more than normal rivalry in their children's relationship and despite Danny's appeals for help, treated it lightly. The father's favorite game with Danny was feeding him misinformation and then roaring with laughter at his confusion. Danny's relationship with his mother was defined by his fear that she would not remember to pick him up after the session, a feeling that was substantiated by events.

Danny's play commenced with his putting me "in jail," then wandering off at some distance and reclining in a lounger for many minutes. When I finally commented that he must be very tired, he replied, "My enemies are far away, and I'm resting." After several sessions, we started on a routine that was to last for many months. He became a sheriff and I his deputy. Our work consisted of the murder and disposal of multitudes. After each killing, we had to "clean up," a ritual in which we carried the "corpses" to the edge of my roof-terrace and dumped them over the side. We then returned, brushing the "blood" and "dirt" off our hands. Both my manner of carrying corpses and my method of brushing my hands rarely met with approval; each time he imitated my "clumsiness" and instructed me in the proper way. My shooting and fighting were also below par. He was never too absorbed in the struggle to spare one eye for my performance, which invariably drew his scathing criticism. Surrounded by enemies who were out to kill, he could expect only the most ineffectual help from others, and therefore had to rely on his own extraordinary powers, which he could believe in only in fantasy and which usually failed him in reality. Danny's hopelessness about any favorable solution was expressed in a pre-occupation with suicidal wishes. When he turned from the game of sheriff and deputy to play with soldiers, the soldier who was "himself" was inevitably destroyed.

The cases of these three little patients, in addition to demonstrating the fear of annihilation and the defense against perception, suggest that the handling of fantasy is a major aspect of work with children. Before discussing interpretation proper, therefore, it may be helpful to survey this world and to establish what we can about its character. To understand how fantasy deals with fears and perceptions, it may be useful to return once more to the dream. Like the dream, fantasy is a "royal road to the unconscious." We can therefore expect that inhibition has the same meaning and the same relationship to the production of fantasy as it does to the creation and the recollection of dreams. With younger children, fantasy is such a necessary part of their functioning that when we encounter a child who excludes it, we can suspect—as we also do with the child whom it dominates—that fear of annihilation has reached monumental proportions.

This was vividly illustrated in the case of Joan, 4½ years old, to whom I referred in "Feelings That Kill." Her mother had admitted a constant preoccupation with a wish to kill her and had reported that after an incident at swimming, the little girl had stated, "Mommy really loves me. She didn't try to drown me; it was an accident" (Bloch, 1965). Joan responded to her mother's underlying feelings by repressing all awareness of them. Their magnitude was such, however, that in order to maintain the repression, she had to avoid play. She cut herself off from her deeper self and prevented a break-through by terminating any activity the moment it became involving. Like the insomniac who wages an exhausting battle against sleep rather than be engulfed by the unconscious, Joan constantly complained of boredom, but dared not submerge herself in a medium which might betray what was unendurable. She defended herself by excluding fantasy from her life.

Where fantasy flows freely, if one is correctly oriented, there is little difficulty in understanding the communication. A basic premise is that fantasy is never "divorc-ed from reality." The important frame of reference in any fantasy is the particular world of the particular child. Out of this raw material will be woven the child's perception of the feelings which he has absorbed from the parents and his struggle to deal with them. The first requirement therefore is to acquaint oneself fully with the nature of the child's real world and its history.

Armed with this knowledge, one is then prepared to enter this region of no dimension. Until the analyst is admitted, there are two major elements—the child and the world. The world is frequently an abstraction of overwhelming power, danger, cruelty, insanity, or whatever quality represents the child's perception of its reality. Or it may be the opposite; the child may initially supply in fantasy all that is lacking in the real world and devote himself to a continuous idyl. The possibility for variation is infinite. Nevertheless, a study of large numbers of fantasies reveals some common factors that separate them into recognizable groupings and suggests a relationship between the type of fantasy and the severity of the illness.

I should like to sketch briefly some dominant ones that have emerged in my own practice. It is my impression that where a sense of danger is almost unen-durable—usually where there has been an actual eruption of violence or where both parents communicate violently destructive feelings—the child may create distance and a sense of safety by displacing the danger onto an imaginary world. We saw this in the case of Sandra in "Some Dynamics of Suffering" (Bloch, 1967). Her "creatures" and "shades" and "black chiffon things"—and not the father—were "all especially bent on destroying children." Or again, in possibly less serious situations, the opposite may be true, and the "creatures" may become the allies of the child. One five-year-old boy peopled the regions "behind the clouds" with "spooks," creatures who, although no more than three feet tall, were the most powerful beings in the world and were all controlled by him. Whenever he felt he was in danger, he signalled them. Their failure to defend or rescue him at any time was usually explained on the basis of traffic delays or of their involvement in some unusually distant part of the universe. Another six-year-old, whose first drawings were labeled "Danger Sky" and "Danger City," was always accompanied by her "boys," who might number in the hundreds. In other instances, the child may con-jure up an idyllic world which becomes his adopted home. "Candyland," "Ted-dybearland," and "Mouseland" are a few whose geography I have come to know.

In a similar fashion, and depending on the intensity of his fears of annihilation, the child also transforms himself. At one extreme, where the child appears to be overwhelmed by his own murderous response, he may establish a sense of safety by depersonalizing himself and endowing objects with his feelings. This occurred in the case of a four-year-old boy whose mother's deepening depression was accompanied by spells of weeping when she experienced his demands as intolerable. She informed me that at such times she simply wanted to kill him. He dealt with the feelings which she elicited by beating himself over the head and compulsively masturbating. He abandoned the use of the pronoun "I," at first referring to himself as "he" and then transferring that pronoun to his toys. He selected one little car in particular, using it as a weapon against the other toys and exclaiming each time about its anger.

In other extreme cases, the child may create the illusion that he is shadowy or in-visible in order to protect himself against the parent's rage. In still others, he may assume a new identity. Larry, 4½ years old, who had witnessed violent scenes between his parents and experienced his mother as "wishing him dead," established his invincibility by proclaiming himself "Mighty-Mouse." Aside from his bullet-proof vest, he confided that the most important thing about Mighty-Mouse was that "he isn't afraid of the cat." He lived this identity, never appeared without the ap-propriate garb, assembled the related books and toys, and even invented a country of origin, "Mouseland, the most beautiful country in the world." Somewhat lower in the scale of intense need is the child who fantasies that he is some kind of superman but who never loses sight that it is a fantasy.

Sexual identity is another "variable" which serves as a refuge from the fear of an-nihilation. Children who feel exposed to annihilation at the hands of one or both parents frequently feel that their sex is at fault. In extreme instances, they may insist on an opposite sexual identity. This occurred in the case of a six-year-old boy who felt hated and ignored by a father whose violent depressions necessitated periodic hospitalization. The boy's mother used seduction as a way of relating to him. He created a sense of safety and of hope by insisting that he was a girl; he played with dolls, drew pictures only of girls (asserting he didn't know how to draw boys), "swished" when he walked, and dressed in feminine clothes whenever possible. In other, possibly still more serious situations when the threat of annihilation stems from both parents and is truly overwhelming, the child may relinquish his claim to any identity and experience himself as neither male, female nor human. Again, somewhat lower down in the scale of intensity, is the child who has vague feelings of "something wrong," which at a later age may become a preoccupation with homosexual fears.

In still other cases, children create another world or another identity inside of themselves. A four-year-old girl had a "tiny man" inside of her who guarded the door to a roof, a fantasy which may have had some connection with her defense against her knowledge of her mother's miscarriages. At other times she also thought there was someone else who repeated all her actions exactly as she performed them. The "tiny man" made her feel safe; her sense of reality may also have been reinforced and her feelings of desolation diminished by the presence of someone who duplicated her actions. With a boy who entered treatment at twelve, the original character of "the little man" could not be established. At the time of commencing treatment, his function appeared on the surface to be punitive. He was a critic and, by means of merciless ridicule, succeeded in keeping the patient perpetually on the verge of failure. Since the patient experienced success as very perilous and as exposing him to annihilation, however, "the little man" was underlyingly really a protector who defended him against dangerous risks.

To summarize what the fantasies and play have indicated thus far, it appears that all of these children felt threatened by annihilation and all found a way of thinking and feeling which enabled them to deal with this threat so that they could surmount or tolerate their terror. In order to accomplish this, they used some form of primary process thinking which made it possible to conceal their perceptions from themselves and to displace the source of their terror from their parents. To that end, they transformed the world by adding a new and magical dimension to it, or displaced their feelings onto objects, or endowed themselves with superpowers, or assumed a new identity or a different sex, or created companions who dwelt either inside or outside of them.

Since on an unconscious level each sought—and found—a way of dealing with his fear, these phenomena appear to suggest that the child is constantly involved in a struggle to safeguard its well-being—or its life—and under certain circumstances, perhaps inevitably, develops "illness" as a necessary part of that process. It seems permissible therefore to assume that survival is clearly a leading function of the psyche and that "neurotic symptoms" are its tools. If we see them in this context, we cannot fail to be impressed by the "health" of "illness," nor to marvel at the subtle, complex and devious methods, and the unfailing resourcefulness by which human beings seek to guarantee their existence. Since this process operated in a fully-developed form by the age of 3½, as the case of Ellie indicated, it might be safe to assume that it starts at a much earlier age. Mahler's (1965) studies suggest that it is already operative during infancy.

The implications of the child's use of his fantasy-making powers appear so profound that in order to probe their depths we must first return to the concept of the child which we have inherited from the nuclear theory of the Oedipus conflict. The child's absorption in attempting to structure a world which will give him a sense of safety throws into perspective the concept of our function as inducing him "to adopt our conviction . . . of the impossibility of conducting life on the pleasure principle" (Freud, 1919). The pleasure principle appears to be very readily abandoned in pursuit of the more basic need for survival. Only if we misinterpret his symptoms, can we also see the child as self-destructive, or as having "a need for punishment" or "a need to be ill," or revealing "manifestations of a death-instinct" (Freud, 1933). It was very likely the patient's mystifying investment in feelings of worthlessness and the dedication to a life that inevitably resulted in suffering which gave rise to these concepts. Once these are understood as defenses which are necessary for survival, it becomes clear that man's energies may be mainly devoted to maintaining life. In many instances it seems that only as a last resort, when his system of self-deception is threatened and his hope of winning his parents' love abandoned, does he turn to thoughts of suicide.

If our task is no longer seen as related to the pleasure principle or the death in-stinct, but rather to the fear of annihilation at the hands of the parents and the need to feel loved by them, a reassessment of the role of both patient and analyst in the therapeutic process becomes mandatory. Up to the moment when he enters the analyst's office, it appears that no one may have been as active as the child himself in providing a psychological framework to insure his survival. We can assume then that his psychic processes are extraordinarily reliable. The fact that they have enabled him to function in a situation which required that he produce neurotic symptoms in order to survive suggests that if psychoanalysis can offer a relationship in which this is no longer necessary, but in which he may operate in his normally constructive way with the assistance which he needs, the same psychic processes may enable him to set about the task himself to effect his own cure. He then becomes the guide and the analyst merely the adjunct or aid, whose major work is to liberate the patient's creative and curative powers and to allow them to function unimpeded.

Although this impression developed gradually over the years, as one child after another passed through my office, the case which offered the most dramatic demonstration of it and finally defined the concept for me was that of Patty. I should therefore like to present it at some length.

An only child whose father had died during her infancy, Patty was referred to me at the age of ten with a diagnosis of schizophrenia. Both her mother and her step-father described her as withdrawn and friendless and seemingly unaware of people, as an unhappy child who cried herself to sleep and whom they experienced as un-cooperative, negativistic and provocative. That she was unhappy and withdrawn was clearly indicated at a glance. In addition, her long, unkempt red hair and her unattractive dress reinforced an impression of general neglect. She spoke in a high-pitched, unreal voice as though she were perpetually on stage. Although she avoided looking at me when I asked if she knew why she was coming to see me, she stated, "There's one thing I know about you—you're nice." At the beginning of the second session, she drew a blur which she designated an angel, who, she said, "could turn bad people into good." With this clearly stated definition of what she hoped was my function, Patty set out on a path that led to the understanding and resolution of her unbearable feelings and her confrontation and handling of those of her parents.

As with Sandra, the threat of annihilation was so overwhelming that even in fan-tasy she could not risk the creation of figures that suggested any resemblance to the real world. Like her, she also distilled the essence of that world—the danger—and projected it onto "creatures," in this instance, poisonous animals. Unlike Sandra's world, however, which remained virtually static until her middle twenties, Patty's began to change as soon as I entered it. She started by announcing that she was "Clang," the clown, a primitive creation without any clearly defined sex or roots in reality. Immediately after her assumption of this identity, she stated that there was a lion outside on my terrace. My expression of mild alarm quickly drew the response that she was an animal trainer and assurances that I had nothing to fear. She became my protector and guarded me against all the dangerous and poisonous beings that were to inhabit my terrace for many weeks—snakes, alligators, hairy elephants, and fire-breathing dragons. When I commented that she lived in a very dangerous world, she stated very simply, "I am brave; I have courage."

During this period of her fantasy, like her, I remained vague and shadowy. I had no clearly-defined form, but was merely there. I waited for cues, however, and as I picked up first one and then another the fantasy began to evolve, and with it, both our identities. Before Patty emerged from her schizophrenia into the world of reality, her fantasy was to progress through three different phases and a coda, each one representing an advance on the way back to health, and each requiring a different set of identities for both of us.

It became evident at the very beginning that Patty's greatest need was approval and acceptance. Just as the clown had become an animal trainer merely in response to my acceptance of her fantasy and my willingness to enter her world, so the animal trainer also developed at my expressions of admiration for her extraordinary powers. She then became a circus performer, offering me an opportunity as her audience to shower her with praise. I applauded every act with enthusiasm and gradually assumed the role of barker. In that capacity I was in a fine position to proclaim all of Clang's virtues and to inform the world of her remarkable attributes.

Patty then began to talk about a horse that lived in their garage and took her to school, sometimes turning into a boy who wore her clothes, sat next to her, and gave her all the answers. The horse was then named, and as "Tiger" galloped in and out of Patty's real world with a leaping abandon that was an impressive spectacle. Sometimes I was informed that he had brought her to my office or was simply waiting outside on the terrace when she arrived. Tiger obviously called for praise, and I became very vocal about his prowess and beauty. During one session, Patty announced that she and Tiger had escaped from her mother and had found a water hole in the desert where they planned to live on camel's meat. Tiger also escorted us to the circus and blended in with the performers.

It was then that my first metamorphosis took place. Up until this time, I had had to fend for myself and to fit into Patty's fantasy as best I could. At this point, however, I received my first assigned role, that of Tiger's master. Patty informed me that I was the first master who was good to her. There had been two others who were mean; one had given her food, but no water; the other, water, but no food. At different times, they had locked her in the garage and planned to blow her up, but each time she had outwitted them and escaped. That's when I found her. She was very glad; I was the first master who treated her right and gave her the right food and the right bed—a human bed.

For the first time Patty not only structured our relationship, but found one which also brought her closer to me, an experience which gave her the strength to be even more daring. In the next stage, she not only risked greater intimacy, but abandoned roles that demanded praise and advanced to the next line of defense. From time to time she had spoken of a dog—the dog her mother had given away because it was bad, a "fairy dog" which she had brought with her occasionally, and then a highly versatile dog who had been a circus performer. Now, after some months of being Tiger, when summer and vacation had intervened, and a new season necessitated our playing indoors, Patty became a dog that, in her words, "didn't deserve to be a child," and I became her owner.

In this role, she pretended to be bad and demanded punishment. She went through the motions of biting me, running away and destroying the furniture. Under her constant prompting and direction, I had to make a show of beating her, muzzling her, putting her in a cage and starving her, shouting at her and denouncing her wickedness. Sometimes she had to be "beaten" so hard that a doctor had to be called to bind up her wounds. In that role, I was able to take advantage of the moment to be solicitous and tender, just as in the role of her owner, even while I had to inflict punishment under her direction, I could commiserate with her and express my hope that she would change and make such treatment unnecessary.

This form of the fantasy continued unchanged for several months. Then a gradual shift occurred; the wicked behavior was reduced and the punishment expanded. Our roles were reversed. From having been the bad dog with the good but necessarily punitive owner, she became the good, abused dog with the wicked owner. I was now directed to engage in erratic, irrational cruelty. At that point, a third character who actually evolved from the "doctor" was introduced and I was assigned a dual role. There were now two owners, a wicked one and a good one. The dog, who had had a series of feminine names, definitely became "Priscilla." She responded according to the treatment which she received. She was bad with the wicked owner, who neither understood nor appreciated her, so bad in fact that she was inevitably sold to the good owner, under whose kind treatment she blossomed and became a truly phenomenal dog. The punishment diminished and became only the point of departure for the second part of the fantasy and then was abandoned altogether. The bad dog and the bad owner disappeared.

The entire session was now devoted to the happy relationship of a dog whose only goal was to please and of an owner whose response was to reward. After many repetitions of an idyl in which Priscilla and her owner devoted their time first to shopping for new clothing for her and then to purchasing a dog license, this version of the fantasy also became too constricted. One day, despite her owner's warning, Priscilla went off by herself, only to be brought home severely wounded, once more requiring a doctor and bandaging and tender ministrations. Then the circumstances surrounding the accident began to evolve, from Priscilla's attempt to save at first one life, then five, then a dozen, and then hundreds. It finally appeared that by one heroic act, she had saved an entire city. She was acclaimed by the newspapers, and then the mayor himself, in a special award ceremony, made a speech praising her heroism and presented her with a medal. The awards then began to multiply. They arrived in such numbers from all parts of the country that warehouses had to be constructed to hold them. This version of the fantasy finally culminated in my marriage to the president and my move to the White House accompanied by Priscilla.

At this point Patty appeared ready to abandon the fantasy. She had been in treatment for a year and a half, during which many changes had occurred. Dynamically, she had advanced from a shadowy identity to one that was masculine, and finally to a feminine one. The drive to becoming "human" was also clearly established. During all the months when she was Priscilla, Patty had not permitted herself to speak, but only to bark, except when she had stepped out of her role to prompt me. When she carried the fantasy to the point where the mayor and the reporters interviewed her, however, it became clear that being a dog cramped her style. She obviously needed a more satisfying form of communication, and therefore promptly endowed me with magical powers; by performing a simple ritual, I conferred on her the ability to speak. That this also represented a profound inner change and a new stage in her development was signified by the fact that once it was introduced, it was not abandoned. Hereafter the ritual started each session, and Priscilla spoke. With cameras clicking and admiring crowds swarming—Patty conducted all interviews standing on the table—she also felt moved to perform, but as a ballet-dancer. She therefore endowed Priscilla with this unusual skill.

Although Patty's parents had changed very little, her reality situation showed improvement in other respects. After about a year of treatment, her creative powers had begun to emerge and her status among her peers to grow. Her musical ability began to produce impressive results. From having experienced herself as an outcast who had little connection either with people or their goals, she began to receive recognition and to develop an interest in achievement.

When she returned after another summer, she did not resume the fantasy, but instead discussed the real problems which occurred in relation to her mother and her friends. During one month in the winter, however, she was not brought for her sessions. When she finally arrived, she seemed withdrawn, again looked unkempt and spoke in an artificial voice. Her regression was expressed analytically by her need to return to the fantasy. At the end of the first session following her absence, she commented, "It's a long time since we talked about Tiger and Priscilla." Several sessions later, which continued somewhat irregularly, she asked if we could play "the dog game."

In this new and final version, her mean owner, now called "Meaninda," reappeared and gradually evolved into a witch. She left Priscilla outside my door in a basket which Patty instructed me to take in. Meaninda then reported the loss of her dog, informing me that I could keep her if I found her. Following this introduction, the session usually started with Priscilla's complaints to me of her mistreatment. Then Meaninda arrived and, after some disparaging comments about Priscilla, announced that she had changed her mind and wanted to buy her back. At no time throughout this new stage was Meaninda allowed to know that Priscilla had the power of speech. It became my role to assert unequivocally that I would never part with Priscilla and to demand that Meaninda leave, because the very mention of the subject was an affront. This version lasted several months and eventually became the game of "jailing the witch," and then after another summer, was finally abandoned. Patty was now ready to talk, and the use of the couch was in order.

The parents' pressure to terminate, which was played out in this last version, built up again once Patty had improved and resulted in her withdrawal from treatment before she had had an opportunity to establish on a verbal level what she had achieved in fantasy. Only in fantasy had she been able to confront her parents' wish to "blow her up" or "give her away," her rage at her mother and her worthless self-image. At the point where she abandoned the fantasy, however, she was ready to admit these feelings into awareness and to deal with them.

Only in retrospect, of course, is it possible to delineate so clearly the various stages of Patty's evolution. While the actual process was going on, I was frequently at sea. The soundness of my reliance on the principle of providing whatever was required within the limits of the analytic situation, however, was always evident. Even when I was uncertain about the direction of the fantasy, the positive changes in Patty's personality and her relationship to reality were a source of reassurance. After one year, there was a burst of creative activity that continued during the rest of her treatment. By the stage of "the dog that didn't deserve to be a child," the evolutionary character of her play was dramatically clear. There were also intervening sessions when Patty pursued other activities—drawing, painting, playing with dolls. From time to time she also devoted her session to having lunch and spent the previous session planning it. Inevitably, however, she picked up the fantasy again and stayed with it for months at a time.

Her need to direct everything herself was foreshadowed in the second session when she alone could control the poisonous beasts. She structured the entire session to the last detail. Like the prompter who reads from a script, she cued me in and gave me my lines. I elaborated on her directions only where I felt I could expand a feeling which she required. As long as she indicated that she needed a particular response, I provided it. When it had served its purpose—to strengthen her ego—she automatically abandoned it herself and through her own decision moved on to the next stage. Only after months of praise and acceptance had restored some small area of her ego, for instance, could she begin to confront what she had previously found unendurable and permit herself to experience the self-image which was the next line of defense—"the dog that didn't deserve to be a child." At that point I had to become the dispenser of justice; she was guilty and I punished justly and dispassionately. When she had received enough punishment, she was able to give up this defense and to confront in fantasy the nature of her "attacker." I then became irrationally cruel and impossible to please. She could then experience herself as good and her "owner" as bad. Having worked through first her self-hatred and feelings of worthlessness in fantasy, and then the hating character of her "owner," she was now ready to give expression to her yearning for love. The entire session was then given over to providing her with this new requirement, still under her direction. After having received a sufficient dosage of it, she was ready to abandon the fantasy. At that point, however, when the treatment situation was threatened, she regressed and returned to it, although on a new and thinly-veiled level.

Although the use of direct verbal communication does not necessarily indicate the child's emotional level of development, his use of play, fantasy and primary process thinking are generally dominated by pre-oedipal factors. It is in relation to these factors, therefore, that our formulations concerning the use of interpretation in the treatment of children must be made. In this connection I find myself in complete agreement with Spotnitz's (1967) concept of "the maturational interpretation." He states: "Preverbal patterns are responsive only to symbolic, emotional and reflective interventions, which are really primitive forms of interpretation. Affective, verbally not significant, communications, even the analyst's state of being, give the pre-oedipal personality freedom to grow." In discussing the method of creating insight, he questions the usefulness of objective understanding and stresses the importance of using interpretation "to create the precise emotional experiences which will resolve the problems. When the analyst operates in this way, insight emerges as a by-product of the connections established between the impulses, feelings, thoughts, and memories of the patient and his words."

In Patty's case, my meeting her emotional—or maturational—requirements with this type of intervention during each phase of her fantasy enabled her to move on to the next one, until she finally emerged. When at the commencement of treatment, her terror was so great that she could assume only a shadowy identity, I responded by also remaining shadowy. As she made known through her changing roles what her emotional requirements were, I attempted to fulfill them by supplying at first praise, then punishment, and finally love. I interpreted, clarified and established meanings always within the context of her fantasy. My first interpretation at her announcement of a lion's presence was simply my reflection that lions are frightening. When she described the poisonous creatures that surrounded us, I commented that she lived in a dangerous world. Both of these comments set up reverberations that touched on her perceptions of her real world, but were comfortably contained within the fantasy, so that she could respond, "I am brave; I have courage," and still maintain the distance from reality which she required. When she related the attempts of Tiger's previous masters to blow her up, I waxed indignant at such criminal behavior, thus establishing myself very clearly as her ally. I also returned repeatedly to questions of dynamics—why the dog was so bad, or the owner so mean. The clearest reply came in relation to the last stage of the fantasy when Patty stated in answer to my question about Meaninda, "She's a witch because her mother was a witch and now she's trying to do the same thing to Priscilla." Transparent as this reference was, Patty was still some distance from being able to acknowledge directly the smallest part of it.

My handling of Patty's case illustrates some of the principles which I consider essential in psychoanalytic work. Since the child is constantly engaged in defending himself, whether it be in fantasy or play or verbal communication that may employ primary process thinking, it follows that respecting his defenses means observing the level, the form and the language of his communication. In the main, I am in agreement with Melanie Klein's formulation: "One of the principal aims of analysis . . . is attained by the analyst's assumption of the roles which the analytic situation causes to be assigned to him." I would modify it only to stress that in most instances it is the child who assigns the roles and our task to discover what they are and to assume those that appear to lead to constructive solutions. I have not had Klein's experience with interpretation, however. She states, "From the start the child expressed his fantasies and anxieties mainly in play, and I consistently interpreted its meaning to him with the result that additional material came up in his play" (Klein, 1957). Whenever I have violated the framework of the fantasy or the play or the communcication which employed primary process thinking, and reached out into reality for the meaning of the symbols—or, in Freud's (1910) terms, "described his unconscious to the patient"—the child responded as Freud predicted. He usually broke off the fantasy and withdrew further, sometimes requiring many months before he dared to resume it. The argument against such an approach was illustrated very dramatically by a colleague who reported that when he asked the patient if he understood the meaning of the characters in his murderous fantasy, the analyst drew the immediate reply, "If I understood what they meant, I'd kill myself."

Because of the thinly-veiled character of the child's communications, it is particularly tempting to child analysts to violate this principle. Not only do "his affects betray themselves against his will," as Anna Freud (1946) points out, but also his thoughts and perceptions. In order to strengthen the child's feelings of security, it therefore becomes important to interpret within the framework which he offers us. Otherwise, in addition to having his defenses torn apart, he may come to regard us as very threatening beings who are apparently endowed with magical powers of insight from which he therefore has to defend himself even more vigorously.

By meeting Patty's emotional requirements at each stage—first with praise, then punishment, and finally with love—I enabled her to progress from one level to the next until she emerged from schizophrenia. Possibly because the world of her parents remained too threatening, Patty's growth continued to occur on a preverbal level and her insights to remain excluded from awareness. I would therefore like to cite more briefly an illustration of the occurrence on a verbal level of insight resulting from "the precise emotional experience."

This took place in the case of Larry, who assumed the identity of Mighty-Mouse. From the very beginning of treatment he had made requests for materials that reinforced this identity. When I introduced two very appealing little woolly mice, a white and a grey, their quality produced a significant change in his self-image. Whereas he had always previously stressed the mouse's power, he now saw him for the first time as loving and lovable. He became ecstatic when he first discovered them, danced around with one in either hand, making kissing noises and exclaiming, "They love each other!" The white one was immediately named "Mighty-Mouse" and a tiny red cape ordered for him; the grey one was called "Larry." While I was occupied with the cape, Larry, still on the crest of emotion stirred up by the "loving" mice, for the first time turned to the family of dolls. After banging the mother and father together, proclaiming their wickedness, he picked up the boy and charged, "They don't love their son!" The mother was singled out again with the indignant statement, "She wants her children to die!" He then confided for the first time that he remembered the day Mighty-Mouse arrived. It was a terrible day, he informed me, although he couldn't remember exactly what happened. The man was put in jail, however, and finally died because they didn't give him any food. "He was worse than a pirate!" he exclaimed, then added quickly, "It was twenty years ago." Thus for the first time, in response to his discovery that mice—and he—could be lovable, he was able to recall the trauma of his parents' violent battle the night they separated when he was about three.

This type of response was demonstrated even more dramatically at a later date. Although the mice remained the focus of his attention for many months, gradually the Mighty-Mouse identity began to yield, and following a very satisfying summer, his interest widened to include squirrels and hamsters, and involved him after his return in the construction of "Rodent Apartments." Then toward the end of about a month, he held up the grey mouse and asked, "Do you know how old Larry is?"—immediately following with, "Five months—no, I mean five weeks—no, five days—five minutes—he's just five seconds old!" "He was just born!" I cried. He agreed and began to coo and to make appropriate clucking noises. "What a beautiful baby!" I exclaimed. Larry was ecstatic, and since the session was drawing to a close he spent the last few minutes bedding the mouse down until the next session. As soon as he arrived the following time, he announced that Larry was now three days old, the exact time interval between sessions. He lifted him from his nest, and repeated the cooing and clucking and exclamations of wonder, all of which I shared. He than expanded the experience to include the hamster and the squirrel which he had constructed out of plastic materials. We both rejoiced in their babyhood, and this time he made a nest for each of them before departing. It was a session of indescribable rapture. As he was about to leave, however, he turned at the door and with an expression of utter desolation, stated, "But I'm five and a half!" And at that moment, the grim reality that had been his life seemed to come in on him, but for the first time, without his having to take refuge in a magical identity.

Fantasy is such a direct and important road to the unconscious that eliciting it becomes a major objective in treatment. With patients whose needs are as pressing as Patty's or Larry's, the dominant part of whose lives was given over to it, it presents little problem. One need merely establish a nonthreatening and receptive atmosphere for it to come pouring out. With other patients who are more rigidly defended against fantasy, one may have to wait longer. Once a secure feeling has been established, however, the child frequently begins to drop clues. In one instance, where the child's terror had found a carefully structured competitive game most compatible for many weeks, he finally permitted me a momentary glimpse into this other world. As he was bringing a piece of chalk towards him, he suddenly stopped his hand, looked at me in surprise and announced, "He's stuck in a traffic jam!" My immediate identification with the chalk and expression of sympathy for its plight satisfied him and encouraged him to take additional risks in the ensuing sessions, until fantasy was finally granted a dominant role in the treatment.

In situations that do not directly involve fantasy, whether it be competitive board or other types of table games, games of skill or actual combat involving weapons of one sort or another, or some kind of arts or crafts, our approach still rests in the principle of respect for the form, the level and the language of the child's communications and is dictated by our reliance on his own curative powers and on his dedication to survival. If we, in addition, offer a verbal response only when it is called for, leaving the initiative for the most part to the child, we free him to make whatever projections meet his needs and permit ourselves to discover what role is assigned to us and what the problems are, and to assume those roles which the child requires to facilitate his growth. Just as Patty found the exact ingredients which each stage of her development demanded, so will each child select the requisite activity and structure the analytic situation accordingly. Our goal continues to be the liberation in our analytic setting of those psychic processes which have worked so well for him in a setting that necessitated the formation of neurotic symptoms; our task is to elicit his rage, to direct it away from himself to its real target by way of the transference, and to train him to channel its expression. Interpretation then becomes a tool to help him to get where he wants to go.

Where children who suffer from a repression of their angry feelings confine their play to board or other types of competitive games, I have also frequently found it useful to translate the game situation as soon as possible into a battleground on which deadly enemies are pitted against each other, each seeking the other's destruction. Since my efforts to win are usually only effective enough to keep the child engaged, he begins to revel in his new powers and, in my definition within the context of the game, of his desire to "slaughter," "murder" and "kill." From there to the direct verbalization of his murderous feelings, sometimes via a detour of attempted acting out, is a matter of progression.

The problem of behavior disorder has frequently been cited as proof that the child's instincts are basically destructive and that only "prohibitions and punishments . . . and repressions" (Freud, 1949) can civilize him. This concept not only ignores the civilizing force of feeling loved and cared for, but also misinterprets the symptoms. Such responses most frequently occur in relation to murderous feelings which have been absorbed. The child who indulges in destructive, provocative behavior usually finds this the best possible defense. Although individual dynamics may vary, a regular factor in behavior disorder is the parents' failure to impose controls on the child. Whether this is due to a confusion between love and indulgence or to an inability to make demands on the child for whatever reason, the end result is usually the enslavement of the parents by the child's behavior and the consequent spiraling of hatred and the secret wish to kill. The child absorbs these feelings and attempts to justify them through further misbehavior. He is caught up in a vortex of feelings that must be denied in a pattern of continually escalating transgression. His sense of safety is completely undermined and his fear of annihilation almost unmanageable.

In treating this illness, a major goal is to replace the acting out with verbalization. One's own lack of anxiety is such an important factor in achieving this that all elements in the treatment situation must be harnessed to it. I have found it helpful, for instance, to remove from the room any object whose loss would affect me. The decision to terminate the session at the first infringement of the rules, to cancel the next session if need be, is also effective. One's own person, it goes without saying, must be inviolate. One is then free to analyze and interpret behavior without in any way getting involved in it. The resultant feelings of friendliness then help to reduce the child's terror and guilt. Since dominant features of the illness are the massive repression of feelings and the child's consequent lack of insight into the dynamics of his behavior, which produces only a continually reinforced conviction that he is "bad," the child appears to be a complete mystery to himself. Combining the imposition of limits with frequent references to his true feelings in an atmosphere which communicates understanding and acceptance therefore appears to be a very useful approach.

In summary, we can say that our theory of treatment and the use of interpretation has inevitably been influenced by the considerable growth in our understanding of the dynamics of personality and of emotional illness since Freud's original formulations. Once our thinking has been liberated from a concentration on the Oedipus complex as nuclear to the neuroses and from its conceptual ramifications, it becomes possible to examine in a new way the dynamic relationship of parent and child, to consider the reality of the child's position in the world and its psychological implications, and to distil from all of this a new approach to treatment.

It appears that a large part of neurotic symptomatology stems from what seems to be the child's universal fear of annihilation at the hands of the parents and his simultaneous need to feel loved by them, the intensity of which in most instances may indicate that he experiences survival as dependent on it. His defenses against his perception of his helplessness and of his parents' overwhelming power, as well as against his unconscious knowledge of his parents' destructive feelings and his own destructive response to them, become "neurotic symptoms." In his attempt to deal with these phenomena, he makes use of primary process thinking, fantasy and play. Like the primary process of the dream whose function is to evade the "censor," his thinking appears to have as its goal the concealment from himself and from the threatening adult of whatever is impermissible in his thoughts and feelings and inadmissible in those of his parents.

His "illness" can therefore be seen as a constructive, although frequently self-defeating, rather than a destructive adaptation which the human psyche makes to a neurosis-producing environment in order to insure its survival. Far from developing neurotic symptoms because of a frustration of instinctual gratification stemming from the Oedipus complex, or out of a "tendency to self-destruction, the manifestation of a death-instinct," the child expresses by means of a continuing process of modification and accommodation a profound and indefatigable will to live. In many instances, only when his defenses fail, exposing the murderous feelings of his parents and the hopelessness of ever gaining their love, does he seek death.

The scale of emotional illness thus appears in large part to be a measure of the task which confronts the child. Whether he can remain rooted in reality, or whether he must "change" his form and "redesign" the universe in order to contain his terror seems largely to depend on the degree of the violent and destructive feelings which he encounters in his parents, and his ability to deal with them. Where the danger appears to be truly overwhelming, he may respond by displacing his feelings onto objects, by creating the illusion of invisibility, by fragmenting his self-image, or by assuming another and all-powerful identity. He may project the danger onto imaginary creatures, thus keeping the loving image of the parents intact, or conjure up powerful allies who may dwell inside or outside of him and inhabit either earth or the sky. Whatever the adaptation, it appears to be accompanied by a repression of feeling and a denial of perception in a system of self-deception which may pervade every area of his life.

The implications for treatment and for the use of interpretation are far-reaching. Since the child's profoundest investment is in survival, it becomes the goal of the analyst to create a therapeutic atmosphere wherein his psychic processes, which have worked so effectively in an environment which required the formation of neurotic symptoms, can continue to perform their constructive task and restore him to health. Always guiding himself by the level, the language and the form of the child's communication, the analyst to a large degree leaves the initiative in the treatment to the child and merely lends his aid as it is needed in the child's own search for health. Interpretation then becomes a maturational tool which facilitates the emergence of the patient's creative and curative powers and permits them to function unimpeded.

REFERENCES

Bloch, D., Feelings that kill: The effect of the wish for infanticide in neurotic depression. *Psychoanal Rev.*, 1965, 52, No. 1, 51-66.

———, Some dynamics of suffering: The effect of the wish for infanticide in a case of schizophrenia. *Psychoanal. Rev.*, 1966, 53, No. 4.

Freud, A., *The ego and the mechanisms of defense.* New York: International Universities Press, 1946.

Freud, S., *The ego and the id.* London: Hogarth Press, 1927.

———, *New introductory lectures on psychoanalysis.* New York: W. W. Norton, 1933.

———, *An outline of psychoanalysis.* New York: W. W. Norton, 1949.

———, The future prospects of psychoanalytic therapy. *Collected papers,* Vol. II, London: Hogarth Press, 1950a.

———, Observations on "wild" analysis (1910). *Ibid.*

———, Turnings in the ways of psychoanalytic therapy (1919). *Ibid.*

——, Mourning and melancholia. *Collected papers,* Vol. IV. London: Hogarth Press, 1950b.

——, The economic problem in masochism. *Collected papers,* Vol. II. London: Hogarth Press, 1950c.

——, *Civilization and its discontents.* New York: W. W. Norton, 1949.

Hinsie, L. E., and Campbell, A. J., *A psychiatric dictionary.* New York: Oxford University Press, 1960.

Klein, M., The early stages of the Oedipus conflict. *Contributions to psychoanalysis, 1921-1945.* New York: McGraw-Hill, 1964.

——, Personification in the play of children (1929). *Ibid.*

——, The early development of conscience in the child (1933). *Ibid.*

——, The Oedipus complex in the light of early anxieties (1945). *Ibid.*

——, The psychoanalytic play technique: Its history and significance. In M. Klein, P. Heimann, and R. Money-Kirle (Eds.), *New directions in psychoanalysis.* New York: Basic Books, 1957.

Mahler, M. S., and La Perriere, K., Mother-child interaction during separation-individuation. *Psychoanal. Quart.,* 1965, 34, 365-410.

Spotnitz, H., The maturational interpretation. This book, 1968.

CHAPTER 37

Specific Forms of Interpretation in Psychotherapy with Adolescents

ERNEST HARMS, PH.D.

The therapist who meets the challenge of working with adolescents confronts through them the awesome complexities of issues facing the young today. Many of them are already worrying about the draft—not only about being killed but about killing someone not regarded as an enemy. Frequently, therapy must engage the adolescent and his exceedingly difficult array of choices when the time comes. What is involved in being a conscientious objector, inside one's self as well as outside? Will Canada be an answer? Or maybe jail? Do adults have the right to make you kill? And if not, how do you assert your right to live and let others live?

As people, they know who they don't want to grow up to be like—their parents for example, they frequently say—but they are far from certain they will find ways of staying as whole as they can, of avoiding being processed into gray-flannel suiters or "suburbanites" and losing their spirit, their honesty or their genuineness.

They ask, "Should pot [marijuana] be smoked? Should it not be legalized? If not, why not, when all of you smoke cancer, lift yourself through a day on pills and get to sleep with other pills or with liquor?" They are also concerned with such questions as, "Why should I have to marry a girl to sleep with her, if we both want to sleep with each other?"

On the other hand, for all their difficulties, teenagers are sheer poetry in their possibilities, spontaneity and sensuality. But to help them survive a transition to adulthood without being unduly stifled or spirit-broken—or to do successful therapy with them at all—the therapist must be young enough in spirit himself to enter a world that has something to with what the young feel, dream and fret about. What is needed in work with adolescents, in sum, is a still-active aliveness to the struggle with the questions of what life is, and a feeling that there are things one can still learn along with the young. For those fortunate in being able to enter such a dialogue with youngsters, the experience can be among the most satisfying and instructive of all those available to the therapist.

Ernest Harms is such a fortunate therapist. He is also a well-known figure and elder statesman in the field. We recognize him with the veneration we feel for our classical grandfathers. His chapter is steeped in the wisdom which has grown out of more than 40 years of clinical experience. In the following contribution, one noteworthy innovation is his described story-telling technique as a shaper and bolstering influence on the developing ego-ideal in adolescents. His differentiation of interpretation from explanation sharpens our thinking about the two, while his discussions of a "pretreatment" phase presents a basic condition of successful therapy with young patients.

Dr. Harms was born in Germany, studied psychiatry with Kraepelin in Munich, received his Ph.D. degree from Wuerzburg, and did graduate work with Blueler and Jung in Zurich, with Janet in Paris, and with Carl Spearman in London. He came to the United States in 1926 as a fellow of Harvard and Duke Universities, remaining for two years. On his return to Europe he started the International Institut fuer Volkspsychologie and the journals, Yearbook and Library of Idealism. The upheavals in Europe resulted in his coming back to the United States in 1936, this time to stay. He has served as a special adviser to the U. S. Government and has taught at the University of the State of New York and the

New School for Social Research. For two decades he was director of child guid-
ance clinics in New York City. He has worked as a therapist in private institu-
tions and in state hospitals. He edited The Nervous Child *and* Journal of Child
Psychiatry, *and he now edits the journal,* Adolescence. *He is the author of*
Handbook of Child Guidance *and* Handbook of Counseling Techniques, *several*
monographs on child psychology, and scores of scientific papers.

The writer has always viewed it as a basic aspect of psychotherapy that the patient be given as clear an insight into his condition as possible and also with an
understanding of the means employed in treating him and guiding him along the
road to mental health. The scope of psychotherapy, under the influence of the growing insights of psychology and social psychology, has widened in many directions.
Psychotherapy has become a field independent, in certain respects, even from
psychiatry. In the detailed working out of the relationship between therapist and patient, interpretation of the various aspects of this two-person process has developed
into the basic factor. Although many aspects of psychotherapy have been developed
in great detail, a technique of systematic interpretation still seems lacking. Whole
schools of psychotherapy produce therapists who appear to have a fear of letting the
patient in on their "trade secrets," of giving them awareness of what will happen to
them in the process of therapy. These therapists thereby deprive themselves of the
influence of an important therapeutic agent: the removal of the fear and the
establishment of security feelings in the patient in regard to his *role* as a patient in
the collaboration. The writer has often heard, from persons who have been in
psychotherapy for months, such comments as, "I really don't know why I am going;
I don't feel any different." "I am doing it because my best friend, who has been in
analysis for several years, told me therapy would make things easier for me."
Psychotherapy based, in part, on mere social confidence misses, to the degree to
which it is so based, giving the patient the benefit of the more important personal
aspect in the struggle to achieve mental health: real understanding of the *aim* of
psychotherapy and the *process* of improvement.

In this chapter we are also concerned with another element in psychotherapy: the
specific character of treatment of the adolescent and the specific aspects of interpretation in dealing with this age group. It must be accepted as a presupposition
of this discussion that psychotherapy with adolescents differs basically from
psychotherapy with children or with adults.

The upheaval and confusion in the life experience of adolescents, not only in this
country but throughout the Western world during the past quarter of a century, has
frequently been pointed out as a novel symptom of the inadequacies of the social
and educational fundaments of our civilization. This, at least, has been the opinion
of the critic with a narrow view. The cultural historian, who takes a wider view, instructs us that even ancient civilizations experienced serious problems in dealing
with the final maturation phase of life. The Eleusinian Mysteries, central cultic
rites of the most sensitive of all ancient cultures, the Greek, were an institutionalized
form of dealing with the basic problems of adolescence. Goethe, in his first major
work, *Die Leiden des jungen Werther,* provided one of the first serious treatments of
the special problems of adolescence.

Reducing our scope to the field of psychopathology, we find that British psychiatrists, who comprised the earliest school of psychopathology and demonstrated the highest degree of social-pathological sensitivity before the middle of the nineteenth century, formulated a concept of puberty neurosis. They were aware that in adolescence there occurred a specific pattern of psychopathology that called for specific methods of handling. Kraepelin, the formulator of academic psychiatry, believed that most psychotic and severe neurotic conditions had their onset during the early years of adolescence. Following in this tradition of cognizance of the psychopathological involvements of adolescents, we now face the task of reformulating our view of psychotherapeutic techniques with adolescents within the framework of current psychopathological and adolescent-developmental concepts.

No one denies that the adolescence problematic has been aggravated during the past decade as compared with what was designated, at the beginning of the century, as the "revolt of youth." Cherished concepts of the past must be recognized as obsolete. The relentlessly thrashed-out sociogenetic concepts of the Janus position of adolescence, as the end of childhood and the beginning of adulthood, must be replaced by broader totalistic concepts viewing adolescence as a stage in self-development and personality development, with differential phases of inner confirmation and outer social adjustment. We have learned from developmental psychology that, in children and in young adults, intellectual, emotional, and motivational-volitional psychological forces do not grow at the same pace. Recognition of this uneven development, which may be greatly influenced by physical or psychological illness, has basically changed our attitude toward problems of adolescence. We have now learned to understand that the reason for lack of success with merely rational "therapy" approaches is that the problematic is deeply rooted in emotional conflicts. Very frequently there is no comprehension on the part of the adolescent of any motivational impetus or of activity choices. This is not the case because of laziness, as parents will frequently label it, but is due to the inability to bring into sound relationship one's rational insight and the activity drives. The feelings of desperation so prevalent among adolescents arise out of such factors. A main tool in this relatively new, primarily psychological, approach to the adolescence problematic is *interpretation* as an aid in psychotherapy.

The concept of interpretation, even for many professional therapists, does not possess any clear connotation. We often hear the term used indiscriminately as synonymous with "verbal exchange" or "explanation." The difference between "interpretation" and "explanation" is one of major specific influence. "Explanation" is a rational attempt to convey the *meaning* of facts of external or internal experiences. "Interpretation," in contrast, is an attempt to make understood and *experienceable* one's relatedness to any factor of outer or inner awareness. The therapist not only adds rational perspective to the experience; he tries to share the experience of the patient, whether that experience be emotional, volitional, motivational, or unconscious. Interpretation, which when correctly practiced, has at its base the ultimate in empathy, is especially necessary, as we shall see later, in the case of the adolescent, with his unsettled mental and psychological state. Interpretation may be centered in rational factors, but there is much in it that provides contact with the deeper experiences, emotional and otherwise, in human relations.

Pretreatment Interpretation

One aspect of psychotherapy has only recently begun to take on clear outline in the minds of therapists. This is the matter of preparing the patient for and, as is frequently crucial with the adolescent patient, making him willing to accept psychotherapy. In a wider sense, this pretreatment is a part of psychotherapy, but not yet actual psychotherapy, since it does not have the therapeutic aim of cure, but only the aim of providing the patient with the insight needed to see where therapy might help him and to what extent. In some respects this period of pretherapy is parallel to another factor in psychotherapy: diagnosis. There is a view too widely held that diagnosis should precede therapy. Concretely seen, pretreatment is, to an extent, diagnosis—the difference being that diagnosis is directed mainly at establishing a synthesized view of pathological factors and the pathogenic background, while pretreatment aims at providing a lowered threshold to therapy for the patient.

Pretreatment with adolescents is probably the most difficult of all psychotherapeutic tasks. But then the achievement of acceptance by, and the right attitude toward, psychotherapy in the case of an adolescent is half the cure. Many desperate adolescents seek help, but what happens next in the majority of cases after the first few sessions? Frequently the adolescent comes to believe that therapy is wrong for him, or that the therapist is disagreeable or even malicious. Only a small number of adolescents, from the beginning on, accept therapy without distortions as to the kind of treatment it is. In the majority of cases it is almost "normal" to find elements of rejection; these, in a gradual pretherapy period, invite the focus of attention.

One reason for their doubts about therapy or therapist lies in the fundamental status of present-day adolescent youth. It is not our purpose here to present a cultural analysis of the present teen-age problematic; we are concerned rather with one aspect of the therapy needed by these teen-agers—psychotherapy. We must, however, give some attention to what might be called the psychoconstitutional circumstances of the puberty period and the inadequacies of our present approach to understanding the problems of the second decade of maturing. There are three special areas of default: (1) the adolescent's inadequacy of insight, resulting in his unsatisfactory handling of the factors of physical maturing (not simply the sexual organization and its psychological impact); (2) the overemphasis on social and professional adjustment and wage-earning to which the adolescent is subjected, to the neglect of first providing the opportunities needed by the young personality to complete itself properly and to acquire its own resources and recognition of its own capabilities; (3) society's overevaluation of intellectual development, and the near repression of the sound growth of the inner forces of emotions, motivations, and self.

This is the essential situation at the outset, and on into the actual therapeutic undertaking. Emphasis on these elements is of great importance; they are the factors toward which interpretation should be directed and upon which it must hover until an impact has been achieved.

To make the adolescent see and understand his inner state requires interpretation. Such interpretation cannot be simply a theoretical explanation. It must aim at more personal depth of insight. Only if we succeed in imparting this insight can we prepare the patient to accept, on a sound basis, whatever is deemed necessary by way of therapy to help restore him to further development.

The process of interpretation in the pretreatment situation is as difficult as it is important, because the therapist faces so many varied types of adolescent conditions. Although each individual presents a new and different task, we would be wise to reduce the difficulties of the task by placing each patient within some framework. Such classification, however, is not enough. To give the therapeutic attempt a complete relationship to the specific traits which are to be dealt with, we must identify the individual features in each case. Individuality is the noteworthy feature of the adolescent. The adolescent himself is strongly aware of this; we fail him if we do not acknowledge it openly every step of the way.

THE PATIENT AND THE THERAPIST

The second, although quite overlapping, step in establishing a treatment procedure with an adolescent is one of establishing a sound relationship between the therapist and the young patient. There is a sizable literature on the problem of transference and countertransference, a major part of which has been contributed by the psychoanalysts. Freud's emphasis on these problems has made it almost obligatory for his students to add new speculations. Oddly enough, there has been no really satisfactory elaboration of the subject of transference problems in the treatment situation with adolescents. Although psychoanalysis has given ample attention to the problems of infantile psychological development, it has not given proper study to adolescent psychological development or the impact of puberty.

Sexual maturation and its meaning for the psychological and mental reality of the teen-ager is, when properly viewed, the most intense and fateful episode in his life, entailing for him a completely new formulation of social concepts. Help at this stage is important for adolescents, whether such help comes from parents, siblings, peers, teacher, guidance counselor, or therapist. The essential consideration is what kind of agent the adolescent turns to, or is directed to, for help. To seek help voluntarily from a therapist implies a consciousness of need for expert help, or a lack of confidence in, or fear of being hurt by, familiar or social relationships. A certain amount of rational consideration, or desperation, induces a youth to seek out a therapist. Most young people come to the therapist with feelings of having been abandoned; they see no past, no future, and no one whom they can really trust. The therapist must become, so to say, everything. There is much less of the rational in the adolescent's reaching out for help than in any older age group, but the rational approach is the one along which most adolescents have been taught to relate. This is in part due to the intellectual pressures to which the adolescent is subjected at school during half, and perhaps more, of his waking life. The therapist who has worked with adolescents knows that the earlier he overcomes this initial period of intellectualization, the surer it is that he will be able to tackle the basic problem situation of his patient; and the surer he can be that he has made a dent in the pattern of fear and has woven the first threads of confidence between himself and his patient.

His decades of therapeutic experience have taught the writer that there are no greater effective results than that accrued by replacing intellectual, professional, explanatory rhetoric by interpretation based on emotional and motivational factors. To help a patient, the therapist must, of course, know something about the patient's problems and aims. This means that diagnosis must go hand in hand with preliminary, as well as more basic therapeutic processes. To understand another person's condition and to communicate in a workable way are important in the therapist-patient relationship. Communicating understanding goes far beyond offering theoretical explanation; it requires tactful interpretation of that just beyond the boundaries of the patient's consciousness. Bleuler once formulated the statement that empathy (*Einfühlung*) toward the patient is the most important tool in all psychotherapy. Such understanding of the patient is not achieved by intellectual means.

Especially important for the adolescent is the understanding of his fears and his feelings of insecurity. Interpretation has the particular task—which must be at the forefront of all others if therapy is to progress—of overcoming negative elements in the human relationship of the patient to the therapist which are expressed, at various phases, in distrust, insecurity, misunderstanding, and hate. Because the teen-age period of school activity is for the most part geared to intellectual learning, the adolescent seems to be open to an intellectual approach in interpretation. This appears to contradict somewhat our previous statements. However, the rational or intellectual coating of youthful mental life becomes thin ice when emotional disturbances occur. Interpretation, the reach of which is deeper than rationalism, provides a continuous bond between therapist and patient against the negative interfering forces of fear, doubt, and distrust. In many cases it must become a continuous procedure in the treatment to test and solidify this bond.

INTERPRETATION IN AIM-SETTING

Just as in pretherapeutic preparation, the attempt at aim-setting is a preliminary factor in psychotherapy. At least, it is a factor to be tackled at the beginning of the therapeutic relationship. Almost every disturbed person will, somewhere at the beginning of his contact with the therapist, come forward with the question, "Can I be helped?" This is even more frequently true in the case of the adolescent. Having been geared usually to pursue professional and social aims in life, the middle-class adolescent patient (and most of them are from this class) is afflicted with insecurity, fear, and inability to perform or to live up to standards. Aim is therefore a major issue in therapy with the adolescent, and interpretation has an especially important task in regard to the general question of aims in the adolescent's life as well as in regard to the aims of the therapy. As to the first, the issue of aims will in most cases remain alive throughout the entire therapeutic course, and may be the last issue the therapy will focus. The second aims of the treatment, presents one of the first tasks in establishing the course of psychotherapy.

Interpretation of the aims of therapy should not be an explanation to the patient of the theoretical points of view of the therapist concerning the goals of therapy with any patient who comes to him for help. Such theoretical presentation may be appropriate for a class of college juniors, but a patient is a more or less pathologically involved individual, in most cases not interested in such intellectual and generalized views. Even general interpretation must be accompanied by empathy toward what the patient is able to understand and accept in terms of aim-setting. Beyond this, of course, there is the issue of the personal aspect of aim-setting, which, in the case of some patients, may come up at the beginning of the pretherapeutic period and continue throughout the entire course of therapy, however long it may last. For many patients, finding and achieving a real aim in life is the deciding factor in final cure.

DIAGNOSTIC INTERPRETATION

A most difficult and special task in interpretation arises when we consider the question of how much, and when, interpretation of the patient's pathology should be attempted. This is a problem in which careful differentiation is required, depending on the kind of pathology involved and on the status of the patient. With certain types of pathology, especially with the depressive states, minimizing the felt pathology and directing the patient away from self-observation are almost essentials for success. With other types, especially paranoia, one must work away constantly at the patient's false thinking. Here, again, what is required is a great deal of empathy toward the emotional and motivational involvement in even the most abstract, irrational thinking of some paranoid patients. In other words, there must be not only abstract interpretation and discussion of "the nonsense," but also discussion of the wide area of psychological undertones and the emotional and unconscious relationship within this paranoid system.

Of special importance, in fearful or anxious individuals, is interpretive penetration of the area of phobic experiences which only too often, because of fear of experiencing fear, try to hide behind intellectualization. Diagnostic interpretation with adolescents encounters the same special difficulties, discussed above, connected with all work with adolescents. Adolescents are geared to want a rational interpretation, but rational interpretation, if offered, will mean very little because of the vast nonrational psychological elements which are difficult to reach in a satisfactory way. (More on this is offered in the following section on the therapeutic process.)

INTERPRETATION OF THE PSYCHOTHERAPEUTIC PROCESS

Confusion, fear, and indecision are the three major pathological factors that one faces at the outset in the therapeutic treatment of adolescents. These are the phenomenological elements behind which the factors of causation and underlying pathological functions reside. Whether one works simply to overcome the overt elements, or whether one proceeds from a formulated syndrome of the underlying pathology, one must plan a strategy, a therapeutic plan. In this strategy the personal relationship between the therapist and the patient is *the* basic element. The writer has always felt that the most fruitful, perhaps the only, approach is to make the patient a partner in the effort to bring him back to health and full functioning, rather than to treat him as the subject or object of the therapy. Such a partnership in therapy requires understanding and insight on the part of the patient, and the major tool in achieving this, again, is interpretation.

One of Jung's most important contributions to psychotherapy is his emphasis on the fruitfulness of viewing a psychopathology as a transient process, with beginning and end, bordered by a specific cause, and, if constructively grappled with in therapy, ending in cure. This point of view appears to the writer to have considerable importance in the strategy of therapy as such. It offers a total view and, so to speak, forces the aim-setting on the therapist. It is, however, also of basic importance in the interpretive relationship with the patient. The constant question, "Doctor, when will I be cured?" can be checked by the interpretive aim-setting carried on and modified constantly during the course of therapy. Giving the patient insight, not only into the method applied in therapy, but also into the planned effect of the treatment, removes to a large extent the most difficult early hurdle in therapy—namely, the overcoming of fear and distrust. It emphasizes the partnership aspect of therapy. It results, furthermore, in a much more intimate relationship between therapist and patient, which makes it possible realistically to reach into the deeper psychic regions of the pathological involvement.

It is necessary to apply such methods in dealing with all kinds of patients, especially those in a severely disturbed state. We will find that such patients have as part of their emotional-mental background a habitual social, often even a philosophical, life setting which they have been helped to develop; they have a definite system of concepts and attitudes toward life which continue more or less to exist in the background, although the patient may have momentarily lost his security in thinking, feeling, and sense of motivation. The therapist must tie his therapeutic measures to this more or less healthy background with the aim of restoring it.

The preadolescent, in contrast, has such a conceptual setting from the parental and family environment in which he has grown up and *to which he is still attached*. In any psychotherapy with children this factor exerts an influence, but the adolescent lacks anchoring in these settings. He has not yet acquired the adult setting, and is for the most part antagonistic and negatively inclined toward the family setting, from which he is though ambivalently, most anxious to continue to free himself. This means that the therapist must try to resolve not only the pathological functioning of the inner psychological mechanism, but also the negative attitudes toward the outer world. He must assist his patient to develop both his inner self and his sound relationships to the social world. Interpretation here reaches beyond the actual therapeutic boundaries and becomes instruction. Such instructive interpretation does not, within the therapeutic frame, aim at overcoming pathological intellectual and behavioral factors; rather it aims at orienting the patient toward existing independently in the normally functioning environment. These two things are, of course, most intimately connected.

Change and reorientation are basic functional elements in the process of psychotherapy. Their roles must be well understood by the patient. Around this changing state, constant interpretation and reinterpretation are required. Adolescents are anxiously observant of any change in their insights and feelings about themselves. There exists "by nature" a process of constant physical and psychological change, and, in connection with this change, there may be abnormal patterns of delay, too rapid advance, or actual defectiveness which may reach the point of acute or chronic psychopathology. It is the first task of the therapist to gain, through empathy, a clear feeling of the specific situation. In addition, the therapist must make up his mind about how he can apply his therapeutic strategy for the benefit of his patient. Interpretations may follow a specific sequence, beginning with interpretation of the normal problematic of adolescence and continuing with the presentation of the point of view of the therapist. Next follows a generic discussion of the endangerment of the pattern of normal development, ending with a presentation of the personal condition of the patient as he is able to recognize it. There may then follow an introductory interpretation of the first observation of therapeutic success in an improvement of the conditions as they occur. In this way a platform, so to speak, for the therapy is created on which the therapist and patient can proceed.

The therapist dealing with adolescents knows that there are two sets of stumbling blocks which he will encounter again and again. One is the patient's inability to comprehend or remember either advice or interpretation given. The other is the patient's insecurity, which is expressed, according to the kind of pathology and status of the patient, in waves of fear or distrust, and even in speculation about suicide. At every session the therapist may have to cope anew with these factors. There will be few sessions in which repetition of certain earlier interpretations will not prove necessary. A sketch, so to speak, must be drawn of where the patient stands, what is occurring, and what is to come, and, with changing conditions, new interpretation provided. In fact, the process of therapy becomes a continuous interpretive moving against these insecurities and difficulties in remembering, until both the latter are more or less removed or have lost their impact on the psychological life of the patient.

Unconscious functioning is a source of great trouble for the adolescent. One thinks immediately of the amount of turmoil that, viewed from the Freudian point of view, sexual problems and sexual-psychological interpretations create in the maturing youth. We should like here to widen the area of the problematic of the unconscious and point to the problems of developmental delay and conflicts, discussed above, in which unconscious functionings are appreciably involved. We recognize the enormous role played by repression and the need to repress impermissible conscious experiences in this belligerent age group. Although we acknowledge that interpretation in this area may be of great importance, and must be more sensitively applied than in any other area, the therapist is walking on thin ice when he tries to work interpretively with the unconscious element in the adolescent. The adolescent simply cannot, and will not, be properly rational about efforts to move him toward an examination of his unconscious functioning, and he has a tendency to become upset and even agitated if the therapist goes beyond explanatory presentation of the theory of the unconscious and tries interpretively to analyze unconscious conflicts in him. Insecurity, painful sensitivity, and fear are combined into a "don't touch me" state. Frequently it is wise not to approach moving toward the unconscious directly, but to "leave it alone" until the patient himself indicates a willingness to make advances in this direction. If our general therapeutic approach is correct and successful, patients will develop a positive attitude toward interpretation. It then becomes for them a therapeutic way which they can trust. At a certain point the patient himself asks for an approach to deeper, unconscious functioning. It is only at that point, and not before, that we have a possibility of being successful with adolescents.

There is another element, novel to interpretive treatment, which has often proved helpful in what is usually considered an analytical approach to the unconscious. This is the element of phenomenological self-interpretation. It consists in asking the patient to give a self-interpretation of his self-observation, which then is given reinterpretation by the therapist. Theoretically, this is a method by which the patient is helped to bring into focus those experiences which lie on the border between unconscious and conscious. The patient then discusses his self-observations with the therapist, who strives to eliminate the negative impact of these preconscious elements. By learning to observe and to understand this impact, the patient begins slowly to cope with it as well as with certain mechanisms of defense. This is perhaps the most activated form in which interpretation can be applied in psychotherapy with adolescents.

One element in psychotherapeutic procedure has not as yet been mentioned here: the application of analogy. Some emotionally disorganized persons are strongly inclined toward a kind of self-assertion through identification. They, particularly adolescents, find similarities between their own life experience and that of a living hero, the protagonist of a novel or a play, a screen actor, or some other prominent person. In the analogism, the patient "feels good" because others suffer as he does, especially if those others are high-placed or well-known personalities. The sameness exerts a soothing power and even evokes in the patient a feeling of heroism in his sickness and suffering.

In the therapeutic application of analogism, the patient is offered a "story"—made up by the therapist—about a person who found a way out of his mental disturbance or overcame his distress or his depression. The "story" may be imaginary or an abstract of the patient's own experience. Such an interpretive involving of a third person is especially helpful in the case of the adolescent, an individual acutely experiencing a sense of being unformed or of forming. The third-person image becomes a teaching tool, or a scaffold to hold onto, for demonstrating to the patient what he can do and become. Needless to say, the "story" is often forgotten before the session is over and needs to be repeated in whole or in part over and over, possibly with adjustments to fit the particular momentary status of the patient. A wide interpretive range is necessary in applying this method, since in working himself into such an educational-therapeutic image, the patient experiences and brings to discussion numerous aspects prominent or coming to the fore in the process of his individuation. A considerable amount of sensitivity, tact, and empathy must be applied in order not to "overdo" the storytelling technique.

INTERPRETATION OF DISENGAGEMENT

The opinion of the therapist, and even of the patient, that cure has been achieved when pathology is no longer present, does not necessarily mean a cutting off of the relationship with "the doctor." In one form or another, the human relationship continues, and even if the separation has been accompanied by anger and distrust, a relationship, though negative, frequently continues for a long time. Discontinuance of the primary therapeutic relationship between therapist and patient is in many cases a major phase of the work.

The main problem is whether the patient can exist and function in the remainder of the adolescent storm without the mental and social assistance the therapist has provided. Often a long interpretive process is necessary to disengage the patient and put him solidly on his own feet. Although a therapist should succeed in getting the patient to experience his improvement and return to normality during the process of treatment, in almost all cases a special interpretive process is needed to make the patient independent of therapeutic help. This interpretive process is in many cases much more complicated than was the formation of the therapeutic relationship at the beginning. There has developed a paternal and sometimes even latent erotic relationship which the patient does not want to relinquish. Often it is expressed as a merely pleasant social relationship the patient would miss if he could not visit his therapist for an hour or so each week. In many cases, subconscious emotional ties develop, even if the therapist has seriously attempted to avoid them. For the most part it will be interpretive approaches that assist disengagement by bringing these subconscious ingredients to light.

Again, this process of disengagement has very special features where adolescents are involved. First of all, the need for parental relatedness and guidance by the therapist are stronger in the adolescent than in any other patient group. Next to the basic inner confidence developed, the relationship between the adolescent patient and his therapist becomes the most essential part of the entire therapeutic process. The transition from immersion in the parental relationship to one of self-help and independence is a major step in the therapy of the adolescent treatment.

From the moment the process of disengagement is introduced, the main focus of interpretation must shift in a relative sense from the pathological to the healthful-living area. Introduction to social, school, and/or occupational life here becomes the main subject of the interpretive process. By now, the patient may have developed considerable emotional resistance to giving up his relationship with the therapist, which may be the only solid and trustworthy relationship he had and has. It must be made clear to the adolescent again and again where and when he is able to stand on his own feet. To get along without the therapist will go along with an enlargement of self.

A great deal of the interpretive task now focuses on demonstrating the appropriateness and advantage of now dissolving the bond. In some cases, serious consideration must be given to continuing social contact. Merely to understand is not sufficient; in some instances even a definite replacement must be arranged.

Lastly, there remains to be discussed one form of assistance in the process of disengagement that has recently acquired importance in aiding the readjustment of the patient to normal social life. This is what is known as aftercare. Aftercare is now used almost routinely with patients discharged after a more or less lengthy stay in a public mental institution. Since aftercare patients for the most part are not seen regularly by the same therapist, a deeply personal relationship is rarely formed, the relationship being more with the institutional setting. The writer has repeatedly heard from adolescents that aftercare clinics are no more than a meeting place for youngsters who have been "in." The main emphasis of explanation might be on the fact that aftercare is of assistance in finding solid ground in the social world. If aftercare is applied in private practice, the personal element will play a more central role. The change in the relationship with the therapist from therapy to friendship moves the relationship to a new level where it is possible for two people, if they like each other, to now find the other, man to man.

CHAPTER 38

The Role of Interpretation in Psychotherapy with the Aged

ROBERT L. WOLK, PH.D.

Dr. Wolk has worked in the field of aging for many years. He is currently a research psychologist for the Office of the Consultant on Services to the Aging, New York State Department of Mental Hygiene, and is employed studying specific problems of the older person. He is also Director of Research of the Long Island Consultation Center in Queens, New York. Dr. Wolk has taught at Brooklyn College, has been actively engaged in a number of research projects concerning drug addiction, penology and child care, and is also a psychologist with the New York City Criminal Court Psychiatric Clinic.

Dr. Wolk is the author of many papers in the area of gerontology and is currently working on a book, Psycho-Gerontology. *He has a private practice in Brooklyn, New York.*

From his specialized experience with the aging, he offers the presentation below, clear and to the point.

Literature in the field of psychotherapeutic techniques with the aged is relatively sparse. Until recently, treatment of the aged by means of psychotherapeutic intervention had not significantly emerged upon the contemporary scene. Freud (1924) placed little credence upon utilizing psychoanalysis with older patients, and this prejudice has remained. In the existing literature there are only passing references to the role of interpretation when treating the older person (Goldfarb, 1965; Rustin and Wolk, 1963).

Psychologically, the older person is complex. His fund of life experience is, of course, considerably greater than is that of the younger person. The older person has had the opportunity to synthesize his experiences, and in many cases he has integrated them in specific contexts, having had the opportunity to validate his judgments with the outcome of many past events. Because he has had more good and bad experiences than a younger person, he can sometimes take a perspective from a vantage point of occasionally deeper wisdom. The older person is the sum total of a long life and is a protaganist in more experiences that have run their course through a beginning, middle and end.

The older person frequently suffers from physical limitations. Having had many experiences he has had to relinquish, debilitation weighs heavily upon him. He finds he no longer has the strength, energy or physical stamina to fulfill a mode of life that has become familiar to him. He can be further burdened with the actual loss of thinking capacity, resulting from the deterioration of cellular brain tissue. If this deterioration is sufficiently progressive, he might suffer from a degree of chronic brain syndrome. The most notable sign of this phenomenon is mild to severe memory loss. The older person also suffers from encounters with depression, isolation and "kinwretchedness," the disruption of family intactness (Goldfarb, 1964).

He often feels worthless and fears helplessness in general, and specifically so at the immediate or close prospect of death. In most cases, the older person has difficulty in finding employment. If he cannot or chooses not to work, living frequently is on a marginal financial level. Unlike in some other cultures, the older person in our society often is not held in reverences or respect, and his opinions and judgments are disregarded.

It is within the framework of the impact of aging on the individual in our society that the psychotherapist must often interpret behavior, feelings and motivation. Interpretation in the treatment of the aging person, for purposes of this paper, is viewed as the explanation of the motives for particular behavior, and of the direct cause and effect of both feelings and actual acting out.

The goals of therapy with older persons must be focused upon the immediate problems of the person and the immediate relief of anxiety, rather than upon the development of deeper understanding of himself. This has been demonstrated in several studies and clinical papers (Goldfarb, 1953; Wolk, 1966; Wolff, 1962). Therefore, if the goals differ, the place and the importance of interpretation also must be differentiated in the treatment of the aged. The emotional need for getting a sense of security from the therapist and relief of depression and anxiety are universal needs of older people. In contrast to this group, there is a smaller number of aging patients with greater mental and emotional intactness where a more interpretative therapeutic approach can be rewarded by gains in insights.

Based upon the former point of view, where insight is desired, emphasis is focused upon immediate behavior, with little emphasis upon childhood experiences. Deep psychodynamic explanations are not ordinarily useful to a person at this stage of life. Psychosexual formulations tend to create anxiety and depression and are not usually expressed by the therapist. The older person seeks and requires *immediate* relief from his oppressive feelings. The tolerance of the older person to anxiety or depression is minimal.

Greater emphasis in the therapy is put upon time. The older person cannot afford the time expenditure of three or four years of treatment. Problems arise. Treatment of these problems must produce results rapidly. The older person manifests an *Einstellung* for time that usually docs not allow for long-term plans. Long-term development of a slowly uncovering, interpretive approach then has little meaning and no place in the psychotherapy of the aging person. However, when long-term treatment with the aging person does develop, and the use of interpretation is possible, it is generally because his immediate priority needs have been satisfied first.

Certain other considerations must be taken into account when interpretations are made to older people in psychotherapy. First, interpretation should never be made which may decrease self-esteem. With many older patients, self-esteem is one of the few remaining resources or ego props upon which they depend. The lowering of their fragile self-esteem tends to create or reenforce their extant feelings of inadequacy. Feelings of inadequacy are frequently the very major experience against which the patient is defending himself. For example, if the patient is relating an incident in which his behavior appears inappropriate to the therapist and would cast the patient in an unfavorable light if looked at more closely, to develop an interpretative theme might push the patient to withdraw or question his basic ability to handle situations. To an aging patient, this is destructive. The insight such an interpretation would achieve tends to be outbalanced by the negative self-esteem then created or reenforced. The approach, rather, should be supportive, recognizing in the patient the difficulty encountered when, with limited resources, he is faced with the harshness of his reality. Rather than dwelling on the unchangeable realities, interpretation is more helpful to the patient if focused on his feelings toward others under the present circumstances. In this fashion, his self-esteem is preserved and the patient can view himself in a process of continuous relation to others.

The therapist might, at times, point out to the patient the manner in which he responds to younger people because of his age and the self-concept aging creates. In his interpretations, the therapist would advisedly lean toward accentuating the positive and minimizing negatives.

A second overlapping "rule" is never to interpret material to a patient which may result in a loss of self-confidence for him. Interpretation should always be constructive to the patient's ego. Experience tells us that when the aging patient loses confidence in himself, depression tends to follow. For example, a patient should never be told that he encourages anger from others onto himself. Rather, the therapist's interpretation might center around the positive aspects of the patient's wishes or abilities to establish and maintain relationships. The anger the patient may solicit from others, and an awareness of how he does so, should be approached only if explained in terms of helping him understand the nature of his communication. The patient can then work through the problems of why he must communicate by utilizing his anger. If the patient is allowed to focus upon the breakdown in his relationships, confidence in his ability to communicate diminishes and he is likely to withdraw in the aforementioned ensuing depression.

In the treatment of younger people, if an interpretation is not assimilated in one session, the patient usually can leave, taking his anxiety with him and carrying it until the following session. In the treatment of the older person, if the patient's self-confidence is threatened, he frequently is unable to sustain himself until the next session.

The nature of the relationship the therapist has with his older patient is of special importance, *even* more so than when treating younger people. As reported elsewhere (Goldfarb, 1953; Wolk, 1967), the aging patient's dependency is utilized as the fulcrum of the treatment. The early therapy sessions are constructed so that the patient can begin to view his therapist quite earlier as a parent-surrogate, a person with whom he has established an alliance which has the necessary ingredients to allow the patient to recognize his realistic dependency and openly ask for support and help. This relationship is used as the focus of the entire treatment process because it frequently becomes the only "safe" dimension for the patient.

The patient may reveal specific behavior about himself or another person which is symbolic of his relations with previous parent-figures; this is dealt with at face value, in conversation rather than in light of its underlying meaning. Interpretations, however, often should center about the nature of the relationship the patient has with his therapist when applied to the very situation, not the transference aspects, between the two of them. The therapist, having established his role as parent-surrogate, trades upon this specific image. The patient, in turn, recognizes the often-unspoken alliance between his therapist and himself and perceives the therapist as a worthwhile authority, the parental figure who can help and be trusted.

Interpretation must be extremely direct, immediate and related to the situation at hand. At times, the therapist must be able to talk louder than the patient in order to interpret while an incident is recounted. Interruption of the patient can take place where indicated so that an interpretation can be made before the patient quickly moves onto some other subject matter, as the aged person is so prone to do. Interrupting has been found to be much more effective with an older patient than allowing him to go on with his story and then having to return to the points the patient made. It must be remembered that generally his memory is far from good. Also, since a flood of ideas frequently challenges the therapist on many fronts, he otherwise might not get back to an interpretative clarification until the material to which it relates is stale.

Interpretation should be complete within the session. As was discussed, one of the foci of psychotherapy with the aging person is the diminution of anxiety. It is harmful for the older patient to leave the therapy session more anxious than when he came. Interpretation, then, must encompass the subject under discussion, allowing little or no anxiety to flow over into his life until the next session. The patient cannot tolerate the additional anxiety for long, and one of several things may occur: The patient may become depressed, break off treatment, act out, regress, assume a "masked" depressive symptom, somaticize, or change his perception of the relationship between himself and his therapist. At the least, future sessions then might have to be spent diligently reestablishing the parental-surrogate role, treating the depression, and alleviating the accumulated anxiety.

The therapist must take into account the cultural aspects of the patient's background when treating the aged person; in application, cultural influences operate with far greater frequency than when treating younger people. The therapist, by and large, is used to treating a person of a culture similar to his own, but the aged individual who comes from Russia, Germany or Italy may have a value system exceedingly different from that of the therapist. A Sephardic Jew, for example, has specific attitudes toward his family somewhat different from those of many other cultures, attitudes which might be contrary to good mental health in an Americanized patient. To undermine them would lead to the patient's loss of self-image, loss of role within his specific subculture, and, pragmatically, frustration of the aims of the therapist. The patient might enter a depression or other defense against the threat of loss of the familiar—that which he has been integrated into and which sustains him through a great deal of his life experiences.

The following case study illustrates the technique of interpretation in the psychotherapy of an aging person.

Mr. B., a 74-year-old married man, was living with his wife in a three-room, low-cost "co-op" when he was referred to the geriatric clinic. His two married daughters lived close by. The patient had been referred for psychotherapy because he was irritable at home and was picking fights with other members of his Golden Age Club. A week prior to his referral, he had hit another man with his cane. When seen, Mr. B. was depressed, anxious, and troubled about whether his wife would continue to live with him or would, because of his uncontrollable rages, go live with one of his daughters. He also worried whether his daughters were planning to place him in a home for the aged. The patient had no previous mental hospital history. He had been employed as a printer until his sixty-seventh year and now lived on a small pension and Social Security payments.

No interpretation of any sort was offered the patient until he and the therapist established a sound, parentified relationship. Then, within this dependency relationship, interpretations were made. When the patient discussed, in some detail, his anger toward other members of his Day Center and his physical assault against one specific member, the focus of attention was upon the patient's feelings toward his antagonists and the immediate experiences the patient was encountering. At that time, no effort was made to interpret early feelings of anger related to his competitiveness, which the therapist had come to realize was the basis for the sudden physical attack. It was felt that an interpretation would only open a Pandora's box, and that the patient would be unable to "handle" such material, since interpretation would be prone to be perceived as an attack on his self-esteem and feelings of worth. Instead, the situation was related to the patient's feeling anger toward his therapist.

The scene which took place in the Golden Age Club was reenacted between the therapist and Mr. B. The method of interpretation was indirect; the therapist created a demonstration,[1] and the patient, by himself, was then able to make interpretations concerning his behavior. The patient recognized his irritation in regard to loss of self-esteem and worthiness, and he began to cry, seeing himself as a "fool" in the eyes of the other club members. It was then that the parental role adopted by the therapist came to use. The therapist was supportive, and the patient saw that the therapist still held him in high regard. At the same time, in recognizing his previous behavior for what it was, the patient was able to function better when he attended subsequent club meetings.

The patient frequently mentioned his irritable feelings and behavior toward his wife. He felt, it emerged, that he was unable to continue to live with her, as she was reflecting the fact that he was growing old. When he saw her as aging, he felt older and feared death. He recognized the irreversibility of his situation and saw, with a great deal of fear, that the only alternative to leaving his wife was residence in a home for the aged. He also recognized that if he lived in such a home with many other old people, his angry feelings at them would, for the same reason, become more intensified.

The patient's anger was becoming more uncontrollable as time went on. The concept of projection was introduced to the patient, but against the supportive context of the established wisdom and sobriety of the aged. Interpretation centered around the patient's feelings that as he grew older, his life was coming to an end. He felt that with the loss of his physical capacities, he could not function alone. It was pointed out to him that in reality he was managing his physical functioning quite well and that, in fact, his wife was dependent upon him. At the time, this reality was not apparent to him. The patient was then able to understand that the actual reason for his anger and irritability toward his wife was his own feeling of dependency upon her: as she aged, he was afraid he would have no one upon whom to be dependent. It was demonstrated to the patient—with the data of his everyday performance

---

[1]In view of the preceding discussion regarding the potential risk in interpretation and the lowering of the patient's self-esteem and sense of worth, the reader may wonder if this procedure of "reenacting" doesn't run a similar risk. The rationale is that the patient can act out his feelings with safety with his parent-surrogate figure, one whom he knows will protect him and will not consider rejection. The patient also usually feels the therapist will exercise the controls that he, the patient, may not be able to exercise himself.

—that while he was growing older, he still possessed sufficient strengths to function adequately. His daughters still sought him out to ask specific advice. The patient grasped this reality, found that he was unreasonable in his feelings toward his wife, and the fear of her loss became more manageable. As it did, he also felt less angry toward her. The therapist was careful not to interpret the patient's underlying feelings of long-term dependency needs, dating back to childhood and adolescence.

The therapist made it clear to the patient that he, the therapist, was always available. The dependency on his wife both diminished and was transfered to the therapist. Treatment was supportive and long-term. After seven months of treatment, the patient was then seen infrequently but still often enough to allow his feelings of dependency upon his therapist to be maintained.

The patient's wife was also seen in psychotherapy, since this frequently is the best procedure when treating older married people. Interpretations were made to her on the same surface level as to her husband. Focus of her treatment was on her relationship to her husband. She explored what she felt when her husband fostered his dependency upon her. Again, interpretation was in terms of immediacy. Thus, it was not interpreted that she manifested a need to foster this dependency because of her own feelings of insecurity (which was seen by the therapist to relate to the wife's early relationships with other men, primarily her father). To do so would have raised many other problems for this woman at this age.

The focus of psychotherapy with this patient and his wife was thus the resolution of immediate problems so that the couple could more adequately function. Brief therapy was the procedure and interpretation was offered within this framework. To rake up early experiences would have disrupted other aspects of the patients' functioning. At all times, preservation of the intactness of the fragile ego was central to therapy.

SUMMARY

In treating the older person as in treating any other patient, a variety of interpretations play a role. However, interpretations are here used somewhat differently. Therapy is usually brief. The immediate situations are primarily dealt with and little attention is paid to long-term, past experiences. At all times, the patient must be kept as continually ego-intact as possible.

Tolerance for depression or anxiety among older people is considerably lower than it is with younger patients. The aging patient, therefore, must not be left with excessive anxiety or be allowed to become depressed even transitorily as a result of the therapeutic process. Self-esteem and self-confidence must be consistently maintained and supported in the patient. In the therapy relationship the patient must feel the value of an alliance with a worthwhile person for its own therapeutic effect and in order for interpretation to be effective. Interpretation must be aimed toward the constructive and positive in the patient; it must be essentially supportive and at times directive. Often, what is not interpreted to the aging patient is more important to the therapy process than what is interpreted.

REFERENCES

Freud, S., On psychotherapy. *Collected Papers,* Vol. I. London: Hogarth Press, 1924, pp. 249-263.

Goldfarb, A. I., and Turner H., Utilization and effectiveness of "brief therapy," II. *Amer. J. Psychiat.,* 1953, 109. 916-921.

——, Psychotherapy of older persons. *Psychoanal. Rev.*, 1956, 42, 180-187.

——, Psychodynamics and the three generation family. In E. Shanes and G. Streib (Eds.), *Social Structure and the Family: Generational Relations*. Englewood Cliffs, N.J.: Prentice-Hall, 1965.

Rustin, S., and Wolk, R. L., The use of specialized group psychotherapeutic techniques in a home for the aged. *Group Psychother.*, 1964, 26, 25-29.

Wolff, K., Group psychotherapy with geriatric patients in a psychiatric hospital: six year study. *J. Amer. Ger. Soc.*, 1962, 10, 1077-1080.

Wolk, R. L., and Goldfarb, A. I., Results of group psychotherapy with institutionalized aged patients. *Amer. J. Psychiat.*, 1967, 10, 1251-1257.

——, The Kernel interview with older people. *Gerontology* (in press, 1967).

GROUP THERAPY

CHAPTER 39

Some Aspects of Interpretation in Group Therapy

LESLIE ROSENTHAL

Mr. Leslie Rosenthal received his early training in group therapy at the Jewish Board of Guardians under S. R. Slavson, world-famous pioneer in group methods. He succeeded Mr. Slavson as Director of Group Therapy at Jewish Board of Guardians, holding this position from 1956 to 1963. Mr. Rosenthal is currently Consultant in Group Therapy to a variety of hospital, educational and social agency settings, including Jewish Board of Guardians, Montefiore and Jacobi Hospitals, and the Bureau of Child Guidance. He is a Fellow of the American Group Psychotherapy Association, a member since 1955 of the Editorial Board of the International Journal of Group Psychotherapy, *and the author of more than a score of articles on various facets of group therapy.*

Rosenthal provides us with a compact synthesis, from a careful culling of the literature and from his own clinical experience with groups, of the use of interpretation in group therapy. In comparing its use in group and individual settings, he clarifies the issues around the special handling of the interpretive tool, retailored for group application.

The literature on interpretation attests to the rich variety of approaches to interpretation in psychotherapy. Glover (1955), in his well-known survey of analysts, found conditions of wide variability in the use of interpretation in form, timing, quantity, depth, order and content. Menninger (1958) observed that "for forty years there has been a running three-sided debate between proponents of *resistance* interpretation, proponents of *transference* interpretation and proponents of *content* interpretation." While similar variation undoubtedly exists among group therapists, the very nature of the group setting profoundly shapes and influences the nature, scope and depth of the interpretive tool.

In individual therapy the immediate problems confronting the therapist are those that are part of the patient's personality, shaped by his past experience, as they are reactivated in the presence of the therapist. The setting favors the concentrated study of the patterns of behavior of this one individual. His life story unfolds and the images of significant figures in his childhood are transferred in a generally sustained and consistent way. In the group setting by contrast, there are a number of individuals who are in different states of emotional adaptation to each other, and there is a therapist who is adapting to different individuals at the same time. The group members relive their experiences in dramatic form through their spontaneous emotional interchanges (via their multiple transferences to each other), as well as through their memories. Thus the learning experience is one which is communicated more through emotional impact than through insight.

In this context the definition of group therapy proposed by Mann (1955) is particularly relevant: "Group therapy is a method of psychotherapy in which the *emotional* reactions of members to each other and to the leader are understood as being reflections of interpersonal conflicts of the individuals comprising the group. The collection of individuals into a group provides a setting in which these conflicts are intensified and even exaggerated because of the number and variety of pressures exerted by the presence of a group of people. The leader of the group exploits the setting and the emotional reactions for the *direct* general benefit of the group *as a whole, indirectly* for the individual members of the group."

Interpretation then, as a cognitive process of imparting to the individual information about himself, is in group therapy subordinate to the primacy of the emotional reenactment within the "second family" of adaptational patterns which group members utilized in their very first group. The level, focus and aims of interpretation appropriate to the group therapeutic arena are clearly defined by Spotnitz (1961): "I concentrate as much as possible on the group and sub-group phenomena, making many interpretations of the pattern of *resistant* behavior which *all or most of the members* engage in. As much as possible, too, I interpret other patterns of behavior in relation to what is going on in the group as a whole. 'All of you are hating each other and trying to hide it,' I told one group repeatedly during its early sessions. When its members became irritated but voiced no objection to the tendency of one woman to grab the center of the stage. I brought this to their attention by asking: 'Why are you all so willing to let Hannah do all the talking and why is she so willing to oblige you?' "

That the group and the emotional forces it generates, rather than the individual and the content of his productions, are the focus of interpretive intervention is conveyed by Foulkes (1965): "The conductor's selective interpretations concern actions, behavior defenses, processes, content as voiced, all within the context of the group. An interpretation does not become a 'group interpretation' because it is given in the form 'we,' 'all of us.' Neither does it become an individual interpretation because it is directed to any particular individual. What is really decisive is whether the configuration, the gestalt is recognized in its conception and execution (timing, etc.)." Every event involves the whole group, even if apparently only one or two individuals are manifestly involved. Within this perspective Foulkes (1965) describes the use of dreams:

The dream as reported is left to the group to analyze. The dreamer often reports events in his dream which shed light on his own situation in particular in relation to the group, on the group as a whole, on events going on in the group, his unconscious reflections on group occurrences. This aspect of dreaming is of value in the context of group analysis, whereas the recounting of dreams—the product of withdrawal from human contact—becomes more significant from its aspect as resistance. This of course is quite different from the handling of dreams in the individual treatment situation where we seek to penetrate into the dream's latent meaning by means of free association. The foregoing is an example of the application of a group perspective and group concepts in practice, and the difference they make in respect to individual manifestations as compared with individual treatment.

In their book *Psychotherapy through the Group Process,* Whitaker and Lieberman (1964) offer the following example of a group-oriented interpretation:

In an out-patient adolescent group the prevailing conflict involved the members' sexual feelings toward one another with concurrent fear of retaliation from the therapist for these impulses. The group members became quite giddy and joked about sexual feelings and "phallic symbols." At the height of a rather hysterical period, the therapist said, "Now that we have dealt with this by reducing it to an absurdity. . . ."

The giddiness immediately subsided. One of the boys asked, "Yeah, why did we have to make fun of it?" and the discussion turned to examination of why it had been necessary for them to ridicule their own sexual feelings.

A major and unique characteristic of interpretation in group therapy resides in the number of potential interpreters. In the group setting the therapist surrenders the monopoly he enjoys in the individual relation as the only object available for transference, identification, and as the primary dispenser of interpretations. In group therapy all members can share in this function and the rendering of telling interpretations of each other's feelings, motives and needs is a commonplace. These statements from one's peers in the group are frequently more favorably received and more emotionally digestible than those forthcoming from the therapist-authority figure. While the transference relation to the therapist is a factor in this, it is also undeniable that the intuitive perceptions and identifications are frequently sharper among patients than between a patient and the therapist. Slavson (1950) cites an example from an adolescent girls' group in which one member, Betty, seemed to be striving to suppress certain feelings toward her mother and sister. Another member looked at Betty's doodling and commented that Betty hid her true feelings because she started out making geometrical designs but then immediately crisscrossed them so that no one could see what she was trying to draw.

Another example of peer interpretation is taken from a mothers' group:

Mrs. K. expressed concern and helplessness in relation to her son's constant embroilment in conflict with school authorities. She described his idea of bringing a teacher a "present" of an artificial piece of feces. Mrs. S. exclaimed to Mrs. K., "He knows you like the idea!" Mrs. K. reacted with denial, but Mrs. S. continued, "If the corners of your mouth turned up in front of your son like they're turned up now, he knew all right that you liked the idea." Mrs. K. grinned and acknowledged that it had been hard for her to keep a straight face.

The value of the interpretive aid rendered by the group members is attested to by Spotnitz (1961): "Group members assist me a great deal in analyzing as well as catalyzing feeling. The first phase of group treatment is much easier than that of individual treatment because they are quick to point out inappropriate attitudes and forms of resistant behavior which they themselves do not engage in."

Johnson (1963), in his text on group therapy, drastically inhibits the therapist's interpretive role in relation to individual group members and delegates this task wholly to the group: "The therapist does not make interpretations or point out to an individual member transference phenomena, anxiety acting-out or behavior patterns. Instead he asks the group members to discuss the thoughts and feelings that each member expresses and then to make the interpretations. An atmosphere of mutual analysis can thus begin early in group therapy and rise to a high, constructive pitch when the members have worked through the anxiety of the group process."

Various writers have recognized certain potential difficulties relating to interpretation in groups. Slavson (1961) observes that an interpretive obstacle not encountered in individual therapy is the varying differential in readiness for interpretation. "Since one cannot assume that all members have worked through their repressions and have overcome their anxieties at the same rate, an interpretation that is well-timed for one member may be out of place for another."

Levin (1963) notes that, as a consequence of patient participation in the role of interpreter, there is a danger of encountering "wild analysis." He suggests that this kind of unhelpful interaction is apt to stem from hostile and competitive impulses.

A significant aspect of the group therapist's interpretive activity (and perhaps a partial solution to the negative feature mentioned by Levin) is that of rendering group members emotionally comprehensible to each other. In seeking to achieve this, the group therapist may explain to a group that (1) a withdrawn, constricted member is in reality protecting the group from his aggression; (2) the anxiously hurried and anxiety-producing verbal staccato of a member's productions are a reflection of her feeling that no one would really care to listen to her; (3) the member who has presented only adequacy and has avoided asking for help is desperately seeking to avoid the pain of rejection.

The following illustration of this aspect of interpretation is from a mother's group:

Mrs. A. reacted with intense hurt and resentment to a seemingly minor criticism from Mrs. W. In turn, Mrs. W. reacted with astonishment and bewilderment to Mrs. A's intense response. The two protagonists withdrew into silence and the group atmosphere was one of anxiety. The group therapist explained that criticism was devastating to Mrs. A. since she was criticized from the moment she was born. Mrs. A. emerged from her withdrawal to amend the therapist's statement with, "From the moment I was conceived." She then told of having been frequently informed, in her childhood, by her mother of the latter's attempt to abort her. Mrs. W. then conveyed her understanding of how hurt Mrs. A. must have been by this. The group members then proceeded to discuss and examine their own intolerance of criticism in the light of their early familial relations.

It is, of course, a special feature of the group setting that a helpful and growth-inducing interpretation need not be directed specifically to the individual it will benefit most. This characteristic of the group is especially beneficent for those guarded, suspicious and constricted members who need emotional distance and to whom an indirect approach is often more emotionally palatable. The gains derived from vicariously achieved insight and catharsis can be considerable for those who tend to perceive a direct interpretation as an oral engulfment, as a demand for change, or as a sexual penetration.

SUMMARY

Group therapy offers a treatment setting in which emotional learning, attained in the living and reliving experience in a symbolic family, assumes priority over information and content. The group therapist's interpretive function is most usefully and potently directed to aspects of group functioning—to helping create an emotional arena in which members can put their feelings toward each other into language and help each other to do the same. The interpretive role (but not the underlying responsibility) is shared with group members.

The unique province of the group therapist is the study and understanding of the emotional forces within the group. When this is combined with an increasing understanding of the individual member's nuclear problem and defensive system, a harmonious balance of concern for the group and for the individuals comprising it is the means toward the therapeutic goal.

REFERENCES

Foulkes, S. H., *Therapeutic group analysis.* New York: International Universities Press, 1965.

Glover, E., *Technique of psychoanalysis,* 2nd ed. New York: International Universities Press, 1955.

Johnson, J. A., *Group therapy: a practical approach.* New York, McGraw Hill, 1963.

Levin, S., Some comparative observations of psychoanalytically oriented group and individual psychotherapy. *Amer. J. Orthopsychiat.,* 1963, 33, 148.

Mann, J., Some theoretic concepts of the group process. *Int. J. Group Psychother.,* 1955, 5, 235.

Menninger, W., *Theory of psychoanalytic technique.* New York: Harper & Row, 1958.

Rosenthal, L., Aspects of similarity and difference in levels of group treatment of adults in social agency settings. *J. Jew. Comm. Serv.,* 1961, 37, 358.

Slavson, S. R., *Analytic group psychotherapy.* New York: Columbia University Press, 1950.

Spotnitz, H., *The couch and the circle: a story of group psychotherapy.* New York: Knopf, 1961.

——, The maturational interpretation. *J. Long Island Consult. Center,* 1966, 4, 1.

Whitaker, D., and Lieberman, M., *Psychotherapy through the group process.* New York: Atherton Press, 1964.

CHAPTER 40

Clinical Interpretation in Hypnoanalysis

MILTON V. KLINE, ED.D.

Dr. Kline is Director of the Morton Prince Clinic for Hypnotherapy and is in private practice of hypnoanalysis and hypnotherapy. He is a Past President of the Society for Clinical and Experimental Hypnosis and has served as President of the American Board of Examiners in Psychological Hypnosis. He was the Founding Editor of the International Journal of Clinical and Experimental Hypnosis *and is currently its Editor Emeritus.*

In past years Dr. Kline has taught on the graduate faculties of Long Island University and Seton Hall College of Medicine. He currently directs the course in clinical hypnosis at the Dental School of Fairleigh Dickinson University. In addition to being a member of the American Psychological Association, Dr. Kline is also a member of the Academy of Psychosomatic Medicine, The American Medical Writers Association, and the American Association for the Advancement of Science. He has published more than 100 papers in the field of clinical and experimental hypnosis, and is considered by many to be the dean of American hypnoanalysis. His paper below focuses on the clinical nature of interpretation within the hypnoanalytic relationship.

Freud's (1916-1917) evolvement of transference stemmed directly from his own early experiences with hypnosis both as scientific observer and as a therapeutic participant. Although viewed originally as primarily libidinal, it was clear that this instrument, so vital in therapeutic process and result, was in essence bound up with the nature and process of suggestion, which Freud had ostensibly abandoned. Whereas Freud had used hypnotic suggestions essentially as a repressive mechanism, the use of transference and suggestive devices within the psychoanalytic experience was designed to deal with the resistance of the ego and with what eventually came to be considered the analysis of the resistance and the transference.

In relation to the psychological model within which interpretation and particularly the hypnotic process must be viewed, Freud's observation of the solution of the transference conflict, as expressed in his "Introductory Lectures" (seven, lecture 28), is of interest. This solution "is made possible by the alteration of the ego which is accomplished under the influence of the analysist's suggestion. By means of the work of interpretation which transforms what is unconscious into what is conscious, the ego is enlarged at the cost of the unconscious; by means of instruction it is made conciliatory toward the libido and inclined to grant it some satisfaction, and its repugnance to the claims of the libido is diminished by the possibility of disposing of a portion of it by sublimation. The more closely events in the treatment coincide with this ideal description, the greater will be the success of this psychoanalytic therapy."

It is clear that Freud, in formulating at this point many aspects of ego involvement and analytic procedure, was still clearly stating the role and importance of suggestion within the therapeutic process and relationship. Later on, he was to minimize the use of the term "suggestion" and to differentiate it from hypnosis, but he was to continue to invent and devise a number of therapeutic instrumentalities which, in essence, were developed from the substantial core of the suggestive process.

Although Freud (Kline, 1958) at one time had accepted Bernheim's implication that there was no hypnosis, but only suggestion, in a later review of the situation he rather clearly indicated that it was his feeling that suggestion is a partial manifestation of the state of hypnosis. The implication was evident that the invention of the interpretive process and of its essential role in psychoanalytic therapy was clearly related to a conceptual model of the role and significance of suggestion and hypnosis in relation to therapeutic effects and the treatment relationship. It is important to keep this theoretical concept in mind in understanding the manner in which interpretation may be utilized and intensified within a hypnoanalytic setting.

Depending upon the demands of the situation as well as the motivational constructs, suggestion may assume increasing degrees of potency that lead to varying degrees of hypnotic involvement and depth. The hypnotic relationship itself, producing a rapidly-emerging transference phenomena, enhances the suggestibility of the patient significantly and leads to a situation in which suggestions tend to produce increasingly greater degrees of hypnotic involvement. These degrees may fluctuate, depending upon the circumstance of the treatment situation (Kline, 1967). Nevertheless, the rapid emergence of the hypnotic transference makes possible the use of interpretive procedures earlier in the therapeutic process than in a nonhypnotic analysis. When interpretation is recognized as essentially a suggestive mechanism, its role in analytic therapy must be assessed not only in relation to this phase of transference, but also to those issues and behavioral effects associated with hypnosis.

Since suggestion, in its broader sense, is related to archaic and more primitive levels of psychological function, when repeatedly and selectively used it transforms the characteristic nature of the hypnotic experience and, in turn, the hypnotic relationship. One can, with the proper use of interpretive mechanism, evoke aspects of primary process and more regressive psychologic functioning; or on the other hand, one can reinforce and stimulate better ego defense and more emphasis upon secondary process. In contrast to the use of direct suggestions on a simple verbal level, the use of interpretation and the cues that interpretation imply, both verbally and nonverbally, become a potentiating mechanism in hypnoanalytic work.

Strachey (1963), in viewing the classical model of an interpretation, notes that the patient should first be made aware of a state of tension in his ego, next made aware that there is a repressive factor at work, and finally made aware of the id impulse which has stirred up his superego and so given rise to the anxiety in his ego. In actual practice, the analyst must work in all three phases at once, or at times in irregular succession.

A hypnotic model has been utilized by Strachey (1963). He states, "The patient in relation to interpretation will be behaving just as the hypnotic subject behaves having been ordered by the hypnotist to perform an action too much in variance with his own conscience, he breaks off the hypnotic relation and wakes up from his trance." This state of things, which is manifest when the patient responds to an interpretation with an actual outbreak of anxiety or one of its equivalents, may be latent when the patient shows no response. It is clear that interpretation, as invented by Freud, became a substitute for the use of suggestion within a relationship which contained many of the components of hypnosis through the emergence of transference.

The process and nature of interpretation in the therapeutic action of psychoanalysis is strongly dependent upon the susceptibility of the patient to suggestion, which increases in relation to transference phenomenon. The rapid emergence of transference phenomena through the specific use of hypnosis permits more control over interpretation as a means of enlisting the archaic use of suggestion in a way not alien to the patient's ego structure.

Fenichel (1953) emphasized that Freud considered "analytic interpretation, as well as the procedure of the analyst in general, as an intervention in the dynamics and economics of the patient's mind, and thus he demanded more of interpretations than that they should be correct as to content." Freud asserted that only a procedure which addressed resistances and utilized transference could be called psychoanalysis—that is, only a procedure which intervened in the dynamics and did not merely give "translations" of the patient's allusions, as soon as the analyst understood to what they alluded.

The indications are that Freud's conception of interpretation was one developed within his hypnotic experiences, one perceiving interpretation as the *modus operandi* comparable to the suggestive techniques of hypnosis. He was able to substitute the evolvement of a relationship between patient and analyst which duplicated that of patient and hypnotist. He substituted the use of regressive ego mechanisms approached by interpretation rather than direct suggestive devices. Since we know that symptom interpretations will at times produce symptomatic change, he probably also saw that through interpretation he could even make symptoms disappear directly, as he had formerly done in the older hypnotic approaches. Thus, the dynamic nature of interpretation is compatible to the model of hypnotic intervention. Many of the determinants of effective interpretation in analysis hold true also for effective suggestion, whether it be direct or indirect. Readiness to accept suggestions and to respond to them productively requires that such material not be ego alien. The organism will reject that which is alien to its own dynamic and economic system, and the task for the therapist utilizing interpretation is to intervene in a manner that deals with the resistance to ego-alien matter. This is frequently encountered in the hypnotic relationship when issues are amplified through the dynamics of hypnotic behavior.

In considering the utilization of interpretation as one considers suggestion, the therapist must be concerned with its function and its timing. The patient's response to hypnotic procedure frequently reveals his needs, his expectations, and his willingness to participate at various levels of ego functioning more clearly than occurs in the nonhypnotic state.

Since hypnosis is both a cognitive and affective state (Kline, 1963) and since hypnotic behavior is largely influenced by the characteristic of the hypnotic relationship, the hypnotic "situation" in treatment becomes rather unique for the effective utilization of interpretation. As Wisdom (1963) sees interpretation, in the association of a relationship between networks of ideas governed by one or another of the component systems, the short-term aim is to enable the patient to understand this relationship and, in terms of it, to understand his relationship to his environment. This is to understand his conflicts. In hypnosis, experiential involvement in both ideation and affect is intensified and enhances the process of clarification. Hypnosis is frequently structured by the patient to amplify what is being experienced in order to comprehend its essential meaning.

Thus, among the various techniques in hypnotherapy, and specifically in hypnoanalysis, we have (a) those dealing with the induction of dreams, (b) the revivification of past experiences, and (c) the ability to utilize sensory and ideomotor processes in order to clarify the meaning of conflict issues.

The hypnotic state enhances associative functioning. When symptomatic behavior is made a focal point, the patient is very often able to respond to interpretation with reactions combining dynamic and mechanistic factors. This can intensify the working through of neurotic symptom formation.

Loewenstein (1957), in reiterating the points already made about the parallelism between interpretation and suggestion extending from the relationship between transference and hypnosis, says, "From experience, we know that the effectiveness of interpretation as well as of the various interventions which prepare them is contingent upon certain conditions such as dosage, hierarchy, timing and the wording of interpretations." These are precisely the determinants which are the essential ingredients for the effective use of hypnotic suggestion on verbal and nonverbal levels. Hypnosis offers greater control and maneuverability over these characteristics than does the nonhypnotic treatment relationship.

Clinical experience with hypnoanalysis, and observation from experimental investigations, show that patients in hypnosis are more perceptive of the essential meaning of their response to the therapist and of the nature of their transference reactions. The meaningfulness of sensory, motor and imagery expression is frequently clear within a hypnotic relationship, and thus is capable of self-interpretating. For this reason, the subtle interaction between patient and analyst which is the *sine qua non* of the analytic process is heightened and more productive when experienced on hypnotic levels.

The behavior of the patient in hypnosis, when carefully observed at all levels of response ranging from sensory to verbal expression, reveals rather precisely what needs are present in him at a given time and what the focal issue may be. This narrowing and illumination of focal problems is one of the most productive aspects of hypnosis in the analytic process (Kline, 1953, 1960, 1967).

It is important for the analyst to know when interpretations are "too deep" or when they may be too disturbing to the patient. This requires knowledge of the patient's defenses and his capacity to deal with what may be forthcoming. The dynamics of the hypnotic transference frequently elaborate the readiness of the patient's defenses as well as the content of his needs, so that the giving of interpretation can be more carefully and adequately determined. Just as Freud indicated that important interpretations should not be made until a dependable transference has been established and until the patient is almost ready of his own accord to understand what the analyst is about to interpret to him, the hypnotic involvement prepares the patient and the analyst for this. An interpretation in hypnoanalysis becomes a somewhat calibrated technique for the amplification of the therapeutic process and, at the same time, for the management of many of the variables of the treatment situation.

CLINICAL ILLUSTRATIONS

A 26-year-old, married, female physician was seen for hypnoanalysis without prior psychotherapy. She sought hypnoanalytic treatment since she felt she was too capable of manipulating most other treatment situations. When first seen, this depressed young woman indulged heavily in alcohol and was panicked by her emerging promiscuous impulses. She displayed a variety of conversion reactions which, at times, included paresthesia of the arms, a paralysis of the hands which would last three or four hours, extreme agitation, and immobilizing depressions. Many of her reactions were episodic and could be replaced with feelings of excitement and, at times, euphoria. There was little stability in her everyday life. During the initial consultations, which did not include hypnosis, she found it extremely difficult to talk except to describe her own background as one in which she felt completely alienated from her family, including her husband, and was deeply concerned over her inability to accept him sexually. Her sexual history revealed a background of frigidity which was absent only during an initial sexual encounter with a stranger.

This case serves to illustrate the role of interpretation in the very early stages of hypnoanalysis in which interpretation is related to the patient's spontaneous reactions to the induction of hypnosis. The initial induction of hypnosis had produced a reaction which involved rather complete immobilization of sensory-motor phenomena. The patient indicated that she could not move her body and was terrified. The only evidence of her panic was hyperventilation. At this point in the induction, the interpretation was that she was repressing strong negative feelings and that the other reactions were a defense against these feelings.

A few seconds after this statement, the patient verbalized, with considerable emotion, the following material: "Felt like I was being forced to hold a penis tighter and tighter—it felt horrible. Then I felt dirty and then anger—felt like I would go completely out of control and kill you—felt like screaming and hitting, but couldn't move. Then felt like I wasn't really in the room—everything was black—like fainting —wanting to be completely unconscious. Then felt ashamed and frightened, like crawling in a hole somewhere. . . . Wanted you to move away because I was afraid you would take my hand, and then I felt I would get hysterical, crying or hitting you and not being able to stop. . . . At first it felt like the left hand wanted to smash something and the right hand trying to hold me back—like I feel a lot of the time— wanting to let something out and being held back so much that I feel immobile or paralyzed—then I feel like I want to tear at myself and hurt myself to get some relief."

Following this, the patient attempted to strike the therapist but succeeded in only a feeble gesture, collapsing into a state of childlike weeping. In subsequent sessions, without the use of hypnosis, this episode led to considerable clarification of her own infantile needs and of her transference feelings. It was possible to deal with transference aspects very rapidly in this therapy, and the patient continued to make good use of hypnosis for purposes of clarification and for linking up infantile needs with her current manipulations of people.

The following case illustrates a somewhat different approach in utilizing interpretation and suggestion for nocturnal dreaming to clarify a therapeutic reaction.

A 36-year-old man came into hypnoanalysis following five years of psychoanalytic therapy for impotence. The impotence persisted despite certain other gains which he considered to be of some value. Induction of hypnosis produced relaxation, followed by spontaneous hyperventilation and the emergence of sexual-like movements while on the couch. A rapid ejaculation occurred during these movements, followed by a rapid movement into a somnambulistic trance state. The patient was brought out of hypnosis and was rehypnotized into a light state in which only relaxation was suggested.

A discussion was then undertaken of what had occurred, and the patient failed to see any significance to it. It was interpreted that his reactions were strongly related to what he and the therapist were doing with the hypnosis and that this, in turn, was an integral part of his sexual problem. He rejected this idea and thought that what had occurred was simply a startle reaction. He had no recollection of the sexual movements and denied that there had been any sexual feelings. He did admit the fact that he had an ejaculation, which he attributed to tension. He remembered that at the age of 13 or 14 he would ejaculate when frightened by other boys. He was amused when he described this, because he said that this was the first time that he had recalled those experiences for many years. During the light, second hypnosis, it was suggested that he would have a dream which would clarify what had been interpreted about the reaction to hypnosis initially. The patient had a dream that night which he reported as follows:

"As you predicted, I had my dream last night. In effect, it was one dream divided into two parts. In the first part I was in the street, which is a frequent setting for my sexual dreams. This time, instead of stopping a woman and stripping her down, I stopped a man [again the confusion of the sexes—i.e., women with penises, etc.]. I reached for his penis and took it out. Then I recall a close-up of his penis. I recall seeing it in all details. There was nothing strange or unusual about it. Then I took the penis and put it in my mouth. I began sucking hard and continued to do so for some time. I believe—but I'm not sure—that I was going through some kind of sexual motion while doing this; I was either dreaming I was, or I actually was.

"In a sense this dream was quite similar in certain aspects to one I had last week, which I told you about. In that one, there was a woman with a penis pointing at me; in this one it was a man with a penis pointing at me. In the first one I was fighting to turn the penis around to face the woman. In the second, however, I accepted it via the mouth. There was no pleasure at all involved with the taking of the penis in the mouth, but I don't remember repugnance. I just accepted it.

"In the second part of the dream, a familiar pattern was repeated. I was in the street again and this time I stopped a woman. I began stripping her with the intention of penetrating, but I recall some resistance—not from her but from within myself. I recall trying to penetrate and then winding up penetrating not with the penis, but with my big toe. At least I recall seeing my foot around her sexual area instead of my penis; and come to think of it, I don't actually recall seeing penetration with the toe, just sensing that I was going to do it with my foot. That was it."

SUMMARY

Clinical interpretation is viewed as having evolved from Freud's prepsychoanalytic experience with hypnosis, and in relation to ego functioning from assuming many of the characteristics formerly attributed to suggestion. Within the framework of the therapeutic transference, interpretation takes on many of the motivational and "demand characteristics" implicit in the hypnotic process. Hypnoanalysis, with its rapidly-emerging transference phenomena, permits the clinical use of interpretation very rapidly in therapy, and in a manner that is more manageable than occurs outside the hypnotic situation.

Interpretation in hypnoanalysis makes available to the therapist a direct means of elucidating the more regressive components of neurotic behavior, particularly those segments that are linked to repressed elements of the sensory order. Abreaction and the clarification of resistance can be obtained within a treatment plan that emphasizes both dealing with characterologic issues and management of focal symptoms and problems. Insightful awareness can be integrated with sensory experience and psychophysiological response, linking clarification with desensitization. Clinical interpretation in analytic therapy can be significantly enhanced when incorporated within the hypnotic process.

REFERENCES

Freud, S., Introductory lectures on psychoanalysis (1916-1917). *Standard Edition,* Vols. 15-16. London: Hogarth Press, 1966.

Fenichel, O., *The collected papers: first series.* New York: W. W. Norton & Company, 1953.

Kline, M. V., Hypnotic retrogression: a neuropsychological theory of age regression and progression. *J. Clin Exp. Hypn.,* 1953, 1, 21-28.

——, *Freud and hypnosis,* New York: Julian Press, 1958.

——, Hypnotic age regression and psychotherapy: clinical and theoretical observations. *Int. J. Clin. xp. Hypn.,* 1960, 1, 17-35.

—— (Ed.), *Clinical correlations of experimental hypnosis.* Springfield, Ill.: Charles C. Thomas, 1963.

—— (Ed.), *Psychodynamics and hypnosis.* Springfield, Ill.: Charles C. Thomas, 1967.

Loewenstein, R. M., *The psychoanalytic study of the child,* Vol. XII. New York: International Universities Press, 1957.

Strachey, J., The nature of the therapeutic action of psychoanalysis. In L. Pane (Ed.): *Psychoanalytic clinical interpretation.* Glencoe, Ill.: The Free Press, 1963.

Wisdom, J. O., Psycho-analytic technology. In L. Pane (Ed.): *Psychoanalytic clinical interpretation.* Glencoe, Ill.: The Free Press, 1963.

ON THE THERAPIST'S SIDE

CHAPTER 41

Interpretation: A Psychoanalytic Dialogue

STEPHEN A. APPELBAUM, PH.D.

Stephen A. Appelbaum has studied at the University of Connecticut and at UCLA, and he received his Ph.D. from Boston University in 1957. After two years of postdoctoral training at the Menninger Foundation, he joined the staff there and is now Senior Clinical Psychologist. He is a Research Fellow at the Topeka Institute for Psychoanalysis and is especially interested in the evocation of experience and its influence on the psychoanalytic process. As a member of the Psychotherapy Research Project of the Menninger Foundation, he is investigating change in psychotherapy as reflected in psychological tests.

The presentation which follows is imaginative, alive and provides the interest of interaction between individuals as well as between ideas. It is also satisfying to read a paper laced with humor. The author's thinking on a variety of topics suggests that he is himself, in the words of one of his characters below, a "maverick" in terms of innovating conceptions, although "orthodox with respect to the essentials of psychoanalysis."

The characters in this dialogue are two students of psychoanalysis. One of them ("B") practices psychoanalysis. They identify themselves further as they speak.

A: I appreciate your being willing to take the time to talk with me about psychoanalysis.

B: You are most welcome. But I also expect to learn something from our discussion.

A: I guess you mean that psychoanalysis isn't a discipline that can be fully mastered by the end of formal training.

B: Is there such a discipline? Certainly psychoanalysis is a long way from that possibility for a number of reasons. It's a young science, and refinements in it have probably been slowed by an insistent demand for its practical application.

A: Well, I hope you don't expect that my questions will be about the far reaches of psychoanalysis.

B: Any body of knowledge profits from having its fundamentals examined anew. I think that is one reason why Freud was able to write again and again about such cornerstones of psychoanalysis as dreams, and each contribution was rewarding.

A: But wasn't that because his ideas continued to develop through the years?

B: Partly. But also I think it reflected his way of returning to direct observation of his patients for renewed inspiration. While he was tenacious in developing metapsychology, he seemed always aware of its human referents, and was evidently not afraid of becoming repetitious through reinvestigating his ideas. I can do no less than try to follow his example. I do learn each time I painstakingly reflect upon the actual events between people which we call *a* psychoanalysis. But, tell me, how do you come to be interested in psycho-analysis?

A: Please forgive my being cryptic, but my field is scholarship, and my interests are every man's. Psychoanalysis has presented itself to me through the popular communication media. I hear about it from many of my acquaintances. I've read some basic texts, some of Freud's writings, and some current professional literature.

B: What in particular would you like to talk about?

A: Taking a cue from your remarks about Freud's returning to basic data, I'd like to ask about the matrix of psychoanalysis—namely, what happens between patient and analyst. I am particularly interested in learning about interpretation.

B: Why are you particularly interested in that?

A: I think it is because I feel confused about it. At first it seemed simple when I saw in a movie that the analyst could explain something to a patient, and this cured the patient's troubles. But I have also read about psychoanalysis being a special kind of human relationship, which doesn't fit with my first impression that the analyst was rather like a decoding machine. Then, I learned that analysts hope the patient will make his own interpretations, so I thought there might be other ways for the patient to learn besides simply listening to the analyst's explanation. But before I get into that, is it still a major goal of psychoanalysis that the patient learn about himself?

B: Yes.

A: Assuming that what he learns about himself is generally correct, does this help him?

B: If you mean by "help him," is the treatment effective, then I would say generally yes, though one cannot answer the question without reference to particular patients, particular analysts, and particular objectives whose achievement may be considered "help." I mean by this that psychoanalysis, unlike aspirin, is hardly a medicine that can be prescribed for and administered by anyone. One has to select those patients likely to benefit, recognize that analysts probably vary in their skill and do better with some kinds of patients than with others; and we must bear in mind that all objectives are not equally obtainable. But, perhaps you meant in the first place to ask whether the desired result comes about simply through the accumulation of knowledge by the patient.

A: That is what I meant.

B: I don't know, for sure. Many things contribute to change in a person—the conscious wish to change, attempts to please the analyst, environmental changes; when the patient's behavior changes, that promotes other changes. What specifically makes for internal change in psychoanalysis is the coming about of knowledge. But knowledge in psychoanalysis emerges along with ventilation of feelings, and in the context of an emotional tie with an unintrusive and sympathetic listener who meets with the patient at regularly scheduled times in an atmosphere of serious reflection upon one's thoughts and feelings. Thus, it is difficult to say that knowledge alone makes the whole difference.

A: Could we return now to the question of what ways there might be of developing insight other than through listening to the analyst's explanations?

B: You may have learned a number of ways already in our conversation.

A: In addition to what you have said?

B: Yes. From my appearance and facial expression, grammar and delivery of my words, from what I have not said, and how you have "interpreted" what I have said.

A: Hmm.

B: Why not let yourself go a bit? Try to say what you have learned in one way or another.

A: All right. At the moment I am learning that this discussion is to be more personal than I expected. You are apparently not afraid of focusing attention upon yourself, and while it takes a bit of getting used to, I am beginning to feel more relaxed, less afraid—what was I afraid of?—than before. I did, in fact, note to myself that while you create an intellectually urbane and fair-minded impression, you are a bit critical; for example, your notation about psychoanalysis being practiced too much and investigated too little. I wondered, too, if you were talking down to me. Or maybe that's me, my problem. And in your remarks about Freud's way of working I felt an implicit criticism of other workers, perhaps those who are less inductive.

B: Any other thoughts?

A: Well, yes. I have read enough in psychoanalysis to know that Freud is often quoted in a reflexive way, "Freud *himself* said," with the implication that if Freud said it himself, the question is settled. Your mentioning Freud so early in our discussion may reflect a need to be in good standing with his followers, as well as perhaps a feeling of comfort in having such respected footsteps to follow. You're not offended?

B: You're doing fine, go on.

A: I appreciated your giving alternate answers to my somewhat ambiguous question about whether learning in psychoanalysis is helpful. You could have pinned me down as to what I meant, but by answering both my possible questions you took the opportunity to offer additional information. At the same time, I learned that our discussion might be more useful if I tried to be more precise. I think I may succeed in being more precise, partly because you didn't tell me directly to be so. Does that make sense?

B: Sure, tell me more.

A: Well, a couple of times I thought that although I was here as the supplicant—that seems a loaded word—I felt a pressure to answer questions as well as ask them, to display knowledge as well as get it. I guess it is difficult for me to put myself in a one-down position to you, to be the student rather than the teacher. . . . Evidently, these are some of the ways learning comes about in the psychoanalytic situation. It seems obvious to me now; yet I doubt whether, under other circumstances, I would have given these observations more than passing thought. Does it help to say them out loud?

B: It seems to.

A: Well, it feels better anyway. [Silence] Did you have a reason for asking me to tell first what I learned about you?

B: Yes, I thought that a man such as you might find it easier, at first, to be in charge of proceedings. Otherwise, you might have had to overcome your discomfort through various devices which could have interfered with further learning.

A: If I had been busy trying to stay one-up in spite of wanting to be your student, I might not have been able to learn what you meant if you had made an interpretation. Then your interpretations would not have interpreted anything to me. They would have been interpretations in intent but not in effect. But, as it was, you made it possible for me to enlarge some issues, and to stimulate further information from you. Maybe my response could be considered a part of the interpretation. . . . And the other things that you did that ultimately helped me gain some understanding, such as giving me the floor first, they might also be considered part of an interpretation.

B: [Silence]

A: Is it my imagination, or have you not said anything for awhile?

B: How did it seem to you?

A: As if your silence might be telling me something. When you didn't respond, the echoes of my words seemed to come back to me, and I thought I had gotten a bit wound up and wordy [musing]. So, silence too can be an interpretation. That's a far cry from the movie version.

B: "Interpretive process" might be the best name for the coming about of learning in psychoanalysis; it may or may not, in any given segment, include the kind of integrating explanation which is often called "an interpretation."

A: Then, the criterion of "goodness" or "badness" might include not only how correct an interpretation is, so far as the substance or content goes, but how much it facilitates the complex interactive process which you describe.

B: Yes, in fact some kinds of interpretation, while correct, may stop the process. One of the motives which keeps the patient struggling to free his "free" associations from inner pressures against such freedom is curiosity. Too many questions too fully answered may lessen that curiosity.

A: Let me think for a moment about what I have learned so far about myself. I noticed more than usual of my feelings, and silently remarked to myself that I feel those ways often. I learned something about my (preferred) image of myself and had a tinge of the feelings associated with it—fear, resentment, cockiness, and sheepishness when you pointed it out. What kind of learning would you call that?

B: Understanding behavior which is characteristic of you might technically be called character analysis. We don't have a one-word label for your recognition of feelings; it's certainly part of what we mean by insight. Of course you probably knew all along that you frequently have such feelings, but perhaps the characteristic feelings became linked more clearly in your mind with the characteristic behavior.

A: I feel persuaded by what has occurred, but it isn't what I thought interpretation would be about. Shouldn't my parents be involved?

B: Well they are, no doubt, and we could have said that you are living out with me a patterned relationship that was developed in your mind—and maybe in real life—with your father. That approach, depending upon how it was elaborated, might be labeled a genetic interpretation or a transference interpretation.

A: We have talked for some time without using the words "conflict" or "dynamics."

B: We could have noted as a conflict your contradictory wishes to maintain me as a teacher and to surpass me.

A: How about dynamics?

B: In physics, of course, "dynamics" refers to the pressures which produce work. The pressures in psychoanalysis, affects and impulses, are responsible for keeping the sides of a conflict in operation—for example, keeping you caring to be both teacher and student. If I may editorialize for a moment—you already know I am critical—"dynamic" is sometimes used as a jargonish half-word synonymous with the whole variety of intrapsychic facts or contents—images of oneself and others, styles of thinking, ways of avoiding discomfort, anything which is unconscious, and more.

A: I hope you won't misunderstand my motives if I ask whether you might offer an interpretation about how I have, so far, managed to keep on learning from you, while not giving up my objective of surpassing you.

B: Whatever your many motives, you are suggesting that we consider the adaptive point of view. It may seem rather unfair to the patient, but in practice attention to the maladaptive generally results in the adaptive's taking care of itself.

A: Then interpretations are not supposed to make the patient feel good.

B: Nor bad. One attends to how the patient does feel, encouraging fuller, more explicit expression of his feelings, rather than trying to get him to feel any particular new way at any particular time.

A: I think that idea moved past me too quickly. Let's see, you want the patient to learn how he does feel, which implies that he doesn't know how he feels or at least not how much he feels it. At the same time, you say that you do not want him to feel anything new.

B: Your wish to keep up with me was put to good use. You have quickly noticed the theoretical difficulty of "unconscious affects," a hoary problem in psychoanalysis. What I had in mind is that the patient has a repertoire of feelings linked to a variety of memories and states of mind of which he is often unaware. When he does become experientially aware of these forgotten memories and states of mind, the associated feelings may seem new to him, but they are not new. I wanted to emphasize that I try to help the patient rediscover feelings belonging to the forgotten past, but I do not try to bring about particular feelings anew.

A: Your task seems much like that of an artist—an actor or director, for example—whose task also is to sense an array of meanings and to bring these out in the most evocative way possible.

B: I find the analogy compelling [Appelbaum, 1966]. In 1899, when Freud was just formulating psychoanalysis, he called "provoking patients' feelings as well as their ideas . . . indispensable." At that time it was, for him, "a second part of the treatment" [Freud, 1954].

A: To get back to interpretations, how about id, ego, and superego? Shouldn't they be included in an interpretation?

B: That would be an interpretation using structural terms. The analyst might make a judgment to himself about the qualities or conditions of psychic structures which go by the names id, ego, and superego, in the process of deciding what, when, and how to say something. But for his remarks to be helpful to the patient he would have to find words from life rather than theory.

A: How about libido?

B: The intensity and compellingness of a thought or feeling do reflect the distribution of libido, but it's the language of thoughts and feelings which is used in the interpretive process rather than the language of psychic economics.

A: So the analyst's task is as much to choose what kind of interpretation to make, how to express it, and when to make it, as to be correct.

B: The correctness at a particular moment may even be less important in the long run than the encouragement of the learning process. We are always working with hypotheses which are dropped, amended, or which gather increased confidence as a continual process guides us toward the ultimate truth.

A: Let me check with you an experience that I seem to be having. Here and there I have read most of these ideas. Yet from this discussion, I am getting a sense of the psychoanalytic process which is new to me. It's as if I knew something, but now I really know it, or more really know it.

B: I think the word "know" is treacherously inadequate as it is often used in psychoanalysis, and for that matter as it is often used anywhere. It may simply mean a one-dimensional "yes" or "no," known or not known. But aren't there many degrees and kinds of knowing? You know the effects of alcohol, I assume, by first-hand acquaintance, but you probably know the effects of morphine only by description, analogy, inference [Richfield, 1954]. We may know the plot of a Shakespearean play, but we know it differently when seeing it portrayed in the theater. We know what love is, but we know it differently when we are in love. We know that life must end, but when a person dear to us dies, we really know it.

A: So, in addition to the different ways in which learning takes place in the interpretive process, there are different kinds of learning as well.

B: Perhaps you have some thoughts about your learning experience today.

A: I don't think I will forget this discussion with you as easily as I might have forgotten the same material if I had merely read it somewhere or, for that matter, if I had heard you give a lecture. For one thing, our discussion has encouraged introspection, and while I am thus turned inward your words have easier access to me. I think the concreteness of your examples about knowing made the idea come alive more vibrantly than if you hadn't given examples. Your referring to "death" and "love" stirred feelings which will help me keep the knowing as part of me; it now means more than just relegating it to a corner of my mind. It was not just the words you chose, but the inflection in your voice as you said them, that caught me up.

B: Choice of word, inflection of voice, the use of example, and reminding people of the primal themes of life are strategies of the artist, wouldn't you say?

A: The analyst as an artist certainly clashes with any view of him as simply an information giver, an "interpreter."

B: Possibly the word "interpretation" lends itself to needless confusion. The dictionary gives many definitions of it, including its use as a "translation" of meaning from one medium or language to another. So the analyst may take the patient's associations, dreams, metaphors, opinions, and so forth, and translate from that language of seemingly unconnected elements from different levels of awareness, into another form, or organization, which contains new meaning. That is, while the meaning may seem new to the patient at the moment, it may be an old meaning indeed. Another chief meaning of interpretation is, as in music or theater, for the performer to render what he takes to be the original artist's meaning, or what he thinks the original meaning should have been.

A: The first meaning of interpretation seems more like the delivery of information; the second, more like the stirring of an experience.

B: Your readings in psychoanalysis have perhaps inadvertently focused you on a distinction between information and affect. In the earliest days of psychoanalysis, as you have read, cure of a symptom was supposed to come about through the release of affect attached to that symptom. If the patient could relive affectively the moment in memory which had been emotionally intolerable and which resulted in the symptom, he could give up the symptom. This point of view survives in several ways, among which is our current understanding that early conflictual patterns (if not specific moments) are most likely to persist and cause trouble if they are suffused with feeling. In pursuit of recreating such feelings, we avoid the coldness of jargon; and we especially find the reliving of events between patient and analyst useful because of their here-and-now quality. But even in the early theory it was understood that the patient's characteristic premises, assumptions, observations and conclusions resulted in the meaning, which resulted in the affect, which resulted in the symptom.

A: I have also read that the task of analysis is to make the unconscious conscious, to learn the contents of the patient's mind and help him learn them as well, and to do so with such techniques as free association and translation of symbols.

B: In fact, what reads like a dry, Germanic intellectualism in the interpretations in the early days of psychoanalysis did seem to help patients.

A: I think that if I had not had some introspective experience during this interview, and we had not thought briefly about the psychoanalytic process as analogous to the artistic process, I might be more tempted to think of cognition and emotion as somehow being opposed, or at least alternate, approaches. Now, I think the problem lies more in recognizing and possibly exploiting their integration. But maybe that is easier said than done. As I think over my readings, I notice that this integration is inadequately achieved by some writers. Some write at such a level of abstraction that they may as well be writing about physics.

B: That kind of writing and thinking has its rightful place in psychoanalysis. Some of the other schools of personality and therapy would, in my opinion, present themselves more coherently and effectively if they, too, were more theoretical.

A: So psychoanalysis may seem excessively theoretical, with the connotation of being emotionally remote, simply through comparison with those less interested in theory-building. I understand that Freud wanted psychoanalysis to be a general system of psychology in which all psychic phenomena could be accounted for. This doesn't seem to be the goal of other analytic schools.

B: I gather that your slipping into the use of "analytic" for "psychoanalytic" when referring to some of these schools comes from some intimation that their therapeutic approaches may not be psychoanalytic. I think it's some measure of our youth as a science that there is much unclarity about what does constitute psychoanalysis. For myself, I welcome all contributors. I do wish, however, that contributions could be made on their own merits rather than as a correction to the supposed hyperintellectualism of psychoanalysis.

A: I have noticed that the papers of these self-consciously critical workers follow a kind of pattern—first an obeisance to Freud, then the assertion that psychoanalysis is asociological, preoccupied with the past, inhuman, pansexual, as well as intellectualized. The heat which I feel in some of this writing, and the polarization of ideas which you say is needless, seems rather unseemly for a scientific discussion.

B: It is difficult to be scientific. The "seemliness" of science is something that we all have to struggle toward. The study of psychoanalysis, possibly more than many sciences, makes for greater difficulties in such struggles.

A: Why is that?

B: Because the stuff of psychoanalysis is the very stuff against which we struggle within ourselves—forbidden impulses, painful memories, fears, remorse.

A: But surely this must be manageable by practicing analysts through their own analysis and through experience with patients.

B: All of that, of course, helps. Yet Freud recommended that analysts be reanalyzed periodically—and for good reason. He respected the powers of repression, especially in those reminded in their daily work of what they might like to forget. Most of us have to maintain faithful attention to what we have learned about ourselves in order to manage ourselves effectively as analysts.

A: Are there some typical ways psychoanalysts use to deal with this occupational hazard of the profession?

B: Yes, I think there are. It takes a certain kind of person to be able to hurdle successfully the requirements for professional training, a person who has developed intellectual skills and who tends to depend on them for his self-esteem. And such a person, as a psychoanalyst, has to guard against a tendency to intellectualize too much. This is human error, not error inherent in psychoanalysis.

A: Your remark about the kinds of people who are drawn to psychoanalysis leads me to think that psychoanalysis is even less a standard procedure than I had imagined.

B: While psychoanalysis is general and objective enough to be described and taught, each psychoanalysis is different in important respects from each other one, because there are different individuals involved.

A: What are some of the personal influences with which a particular analyst may struggle?

B: Most patients come to psychoanalysis with a feeling of being one-down. Even those who behave as if they are one-up have to ask for an appointment, submit to certain necessary arrangements, yield their innermost thoughts, and pay money. Implicit in this situation, and often made painfully explicit by virtue of the way the patient looks at himself and others, is the idea that he is coming for help from an expert. It usually takes much time and work before the patient stops feeling one-down about this. Meanwhile, the analyst may have to struggle against the temptation to enjoy the inflated picture of himself reflected in his patient's eyes. One of the motives for seeking advanced educational training is to be on the one-up end of doctor-patient, professor-student relationships.

A: That seems a somewhat harsh picture of the analyst. Don't many people get graduate degrees and become analysts out of a wish to bring the health, knowledge, security and stature of others up to their own?

B: Yes, but it is not always easy to know whether the gratification comes from the bringing up of another's stature or from the feeling of being in a position to bring someone else up to his own stature.

A: Wouldn't an analyst with the need to be on top be inclined to "give interpretations" in the old-fashioned sense, rather than to encourage a process which might lead to the patient's making his own interpretation?

B: I think so, especially if the patient is one who hides his light under a bushel, or who needs to nestle at the feet of a great man, or who likes to take in information without effort.

A: I begin to see more clearly what you meant by the uniqueness of the analysis according to the individual personalities involved. . . . I read somewhere that much behavior can be described with respect to levels of psychosexual fixation. Can one describe the making of an interpretation in such terms?

B: The phrase *"making* an interpretation" might be a clue, especially if it is followed up with the feeling that ideas can be organized into units which are displayed for admiration, bestowed upon one who expectantly awaits them, or gotten rid of, once produced.

A: At first, I thought of "make" in the sense of "being on the make"; but you were illustrating the anal mode, weren't you? I thought you did that admirably. Suppose I try the phallic one.

B: Sure.

A: Well, as I recall what Erikson wrote, I think I ought to include the word "intrude." Come to think of it, I rather did intrude on your answer to my own question. To say nothing of hearing "make" the way I did.

B: I'll refrain from intruding on your associations.

A: If I were to let my associations go, I might think of making an interpretation as being like rescuing the patient, slaying the dragons of illness while sweeping the helpless maiden onto my horse.

B: Yes, with those feelings determining what you did, you might be unduly active. The interpretation could become your crowning moment.

A: Having just played the analyst myself, even for a brief moment, leads me to think that it must be rather a temptation to look in on people's lives. I guess I would be curious, if not nosy.

B: You might feel in these ways but you need not necessarily act in these ways.

A: That time you got ahead of my question, as I was just going to ask if an analyst's personality need necessarily be a harmful influence upon his professional behavior.

B: Since psychosexual stages are gone through by everyone and are some of the ways by which personality is formed, behavior has to partake more or less of these early influences. But whether that is helpful or harmful to the patient is quite another question. To put it technically, we have been talking about drives alone, but behavior is an end product, shaped by experience in the environment and based partly on drives, partly on capacities. The ego, as we say, is in charge of behavioral decisions. Drive may be minimal or used for adaptive purposes.

A: Haven't we passed over the possible oral qualities of the interpretive process?

B: Is it my turn?

A: I'm glad to see the twinkle in your eye, as you say that. Please go ahead.

B: Currents of feelings and thoughts swirl around you in a never-ending supply. You drift and float in a sea of silent associations which blend with those the patient gives. Boundaries dissolve, as separateness is converted into a warm flow of sharing and helping. Like mother and child.

A: I was a bit embarrassed, just then. Could it be that it is easier on us to put things in developmentally later terms? Maybe that's why we were on the verge of ignoring the kind of experience you describe.

B: Psychoanalysis as a science, and the individuals who practice it, are hardly alone in the struggles against infantile life within us. These underlie, in my opinion, conflicts in science between the tough-minded and the tender-minded, in art between the classicists and the romanticists, in jazz between "cool" and "hot," in psychoanalytic theory between activity and passivity, manliness and womanliness. It has been said there was something of the receptivity which Freud pointed out as biologically characteristic of women in his own ability to listen to his patients rather than to take action. Eissler [1965] mentions that women are well-suited to the task of psychoanalysis, and he bemoans what amounts to exclusion, since so many of them seem not to be willing to get medical training.

A: But is psychoanalysis woman's work? Aren't there dangers as well as advantages in this kind of receptive approach?

B: Yes, indeed. The gentle, receptive women and men we are describing may find it difficult to be incisive, even intrusive, when the moment for that comes. They may be inclined to mother their patients, to fly to rescue at signs of distress rather than reserving such activity for times of realistic danger.

A: It sounds as if you need a kind of "man for all seasons." Are there enough of such people, especially as compared to the demand for them?

B: I don't think anyone knows the answer to that, because of the processes of selection which narrow the range of potential analysts.

A: You mean the medical requirement?

B: Only partly. Medical training and practice does put a premium on acting swiftly in emergencies, and it may encourage action as a way of dealing with the feelings of pity, disgust, or horror to which physicians are exposed. But action is only one way to minimize receptivity and feelingfulness. Thought is another way. We have mentioned the many remote, abstract articles that contrast with such sensitive and emotionally rich writings as those of Marjorie Brierley and Ella Sharpe. If we could select freely from medical people, historians, social scientists, English professors, from among all who are interested, we might be able to learn better what kinds of character structures, temperaments, or infantile fantasies go into the making of what kinds of analysts. With such information we would be in a better position to attempt to make training more available. That might be one of those researches we earlier noted as being left undone for too long.

A: How about your training practices? I gather from this discussion—the analogy with art, for example—that psychoanalysts are less practitioners of cut-and-dried techniques than people skilled in using themselves with others in relationships which, if not unique, tend to pose their own special problems. Doesn't this put singular demands upon training?

B: The training analysis is our general answer to your questions. When Freud referred to it as the "cornerstone" of psychoanalytic education, I think he meant that the analyst must first of all be a certain kind of person and that his technical skills would follow from this.

A: But surely there is much training in addition to the training analysis. Perhaps training which is helpful in other disciplines may even be injurious to what seems the psychoanalytic approach.

B: Yes, I am inclined to agree with you. Some institutionalized practices are tangential, if not antithetical, to the objectives of psychoanalysis—for example, categorizing "illness" with labels and describing patients with "official" and general terms rather than letting the particular qualities of the person dictate the terms; or treating all information, however gathered, as equally useful for all purposes. One of our scholars [Kohut, 1959] has reminded us that the true data of psychoanalysis are the yields of introspection and empathy, and that facts, as relayed to a social worker, or as learned through the taking of a history, are a different kind of information.

A: If I were being written about for psychiatric or psychoanalytic purposes, I'd rather it be in the form of a short story, a poem, or a character sketch. I hope it's not just my wish to be special or lovingly treated or something, but I think such a form might be more useful. I might have a macabre interest in how I'd appear in a technical psychiatric document, but I'd have more confidence in the treatment if you knew my point of view, my expectations, my hopes—how I had managed all these in the past, and what I needed to manage them differently in the future.

B: If you are not yet surpassing me, you are at least joining me. I remember trying to convey to my students what is meant by a "narcissistic character." I recommended the movie, "Alfie," which to my mind could help them to "know" through an empathic experience what I was trying to teach them by description. I remember on another occasion struggling with the problem of how to teach something of the quality of developing and shifting identities, the repertoire of organized and unorganized, integrated and separate identities which underlie our behavior. I recommended Erikson's work for a text, and it was invaluable as a way of organizing and integrating information. But the wonder of the many selves that live within us, the moments of not knowing which is which, or which to believe or rely on—the ebb, flow, jangle and surge of identities that may course through an analytic hour—was better portrayed by Karl Chapek in his novel, *An Ordinary Life*.

A: Apparently you are something of a maverick, though I gather that you are orthodox with respect to the essentials of psychoanalysis.

B: I don't think that I am much of a maverick with respect to the substance of psychoanalysis as it was formulated by Freud and extended by some others. I think some of our cultural and professional institutions may have become maverick in the sense of setting in motion certain currents inimical or irrelevant to psychoanalysis.

A: So, in your view, if one begins as we did—with questions about interpretation—one quite properly, and perhaps unavoidably, is led to the literary masters, to the patient and analyst as poets of experience.

B: You put it well.

A: I asked an intellectual question and I got a kind of "feeling" answer. I asked a scientific question, and the analogy between psychoanalysis and art was brought to my attention. I asked about an interpretation as an entity, and I learned about a continuous process. Could you have overstated your emphasis?

B: Yes. If I haven't, then those persuaded by it probably will, as those explicit professional humanists discussed by us overstated theirs. The human mind works in such dialectical ways.

A: I gather that even analyzed minds cannot be expected to be exempt from the common frailties of human thinking, polarizations, concretenesses, excessive doubts, and unwarranted enthusiasms. And the resulting shifting emphases on affect or cognition, subsumed under the term "interpretation," evidently have considerable consequences for theory, technique, and even professional identity.

B: At the same time, psychoanalysis has unique skills for becoming aware of, and thus controlling, its destiny.

A: Your secretary told me that I was to talk with you for an hour. I guess that means 50 minutes. Could it be that I needed to be the one to end our talk?

B: [silence]

A: My gratitude.

B: My gratitude.

REFERENCES

Appelbaum, S. A., Speaking with the second voice: evocativeness. *J. Amer. Psychoanal. Ass.*, 1966, 14, 462-477.

Eissler, K., *Medical orthodoxy and the future of psychoanalysis.* New York: International Universities Press, 1965.

Freud, S. In M. Bonaparte, A. Freud, and E. Kris (Eds.): *The origins of psychoanalysis. Sigmund Freud's letters.* New York: Basic Books, 1954.

Richfield, J., An analysis of the concept of insight. *Psychoanal. Quart.*, 1954, 23, 390-408.

CHAPTER 42

The Reluctance to Interpret

ERWIN SINGER, PH.D.

Erwin Singer is Professor of Education at the City College of The City University of New York. After receiving his Ph.D. from New York University, he received his Certificate from the William A. White Institute in 1955 and has been on its faculty and one of its Training Analysts since 1962. He has also held appointments at New York University and at Yeshiva University, and he has lectured and studied in Europe and in Israel. In addition to many articles, he has authored Key Concepts in Psychotherapy, *and his new book,* Diagnostic Testing for Psychotherapy, *will appear soon.*

In this chapter, Professor Singer advances the discussion of interpretation by taking up the needs and emotional factors on the therapist's side of the interaction: the therapist's feelings about being "wrong," his fear of being "right," and his fear of timing his interpretations inappropriately; lastly, Dr. Singer considers both the complications and the fruitful clues of countertransference.

Since the days when Breuer and Freud (1893-1895) first proposed that emotional disorders have their roots in man's tendency to make himself oblivious to the truth of his inner experiences, the very core of all psychotherapeutic systems, loosely referred to as uncovering or insight therapies, has been the effort to help the patient achieve awareness of those emotional constellations which affect him without his having knowledge of their existence. While in some systems—for instance, in that of Rogers (1942, 1951)—this consciousness is thought to come about without the active interpretive intervention of the therapist, actually, Rogers maintained that such active interpretive intervention interferes with the development of true knowledge of the self. Most authors, however, insist that interpretation is a *sine qua non* of the insight-producing process.

From the early days when he first began writing systematically on the technique of psychoanalytic treatment, Freud (1910) insisted that the analyst "cannot dispense" with giving information (p. 225); and in one of his last statements on the matter (1937), when he preferred to talk about "construction" rather than about interpretation, Freud again emphasized the importance of interpretation as the vehicle destined to bring about curative insight. Thus, the insistence upon the curative value of the interpretation runs throughout Freud's writings on therapeutic technique.

This conviction was shared by many others, even when they deviated from the mainstream of orthodox psychoanalytic theory (Alexander, 1946; Fromm-Reichmann, 1950; Sullivan, 1945). Of course, all these theorist-clinicians, inside or outside this mainstream, offered rules and suggestions defining the type of interpretation they deemed curative and the type they considered useless. In addition, they wrote extensively about the importance of the appropriate timing of such interpretations. On the issue of timing, however, practice often deviated strikingly from theory. For instance, anyone reading Freud's (1905) discussion of his work with Dora would be struck by his directness in interpreting her second dream without there having been much evidence that she had come close to those insights on her own before he presented to her his vision of what her psychological life "must" have been. In fact, Freud remarks with surprise that she accepted his thoughts as willingly as she did.

Yet, despite this common and well-known maxim of psychoanalytic therapy—i.e., despite the importance ascribed to interpretation as an instrument of therapy—painstaking observation and honest scrutiny of one's own work and careful listening to the reports of colleagues and students force upon one the realization that quite frequently the therapist hesitates and refrains from offering certain interpretive comments, even though they appear later to the therapist and to others as obviously in order. This chapter examines some frequently noticed foundations for such reluctance and hesitance.

THE FEAR OF BEING WRONG

Only a therapist devoid of any shred of humility can honestly believe that all his interpretations reflect a correct understanding of the patient's inner life. There is little doubt that his insights about the patient's experience all too often will be off the mark. But why should this be bothersome to him if in a genuinely scientific spirit he is eager to explore possibilities, hoping that such exploration will lead the patient and him closer to truth? After all, investigators in other curative arts also pursue what turns out to have been incorrect hunches. A reply frequently heard in response to such a comment is the horrified assertion that an incorrect interpretive comment does not simply represent inadequate diagnostic probing, but is already a therapeutic intervention. Such replies also stress that while it may not be too harmful to a person if his physician orders a particular blood examination which indicates that the diagnostic hunch was incorrect, it may be very harmful to the sufferer were he given an inappropriate drug, a prescription based on inadequate diagnostic understanding.

This type of argument, as I have discussed in a different context (Singer, 1965), is based on the erroneous assumption that the psychotherapeutic process differs essentially from the psychodiagnostic process and that the medical model in which there exists a highly appropriate division between diagnosis and therapy is conceptually adequate for, and applicable to, psychological healing. Isn't it abundantly clear that the ultimate aim of psychotherapeutic work is the expansion of the patient's horizons of awareness, the growth of consciousness expanding into where there was unconsciousness—in fact, the development of a state of affairs in which the patient becomes his own diagnostician *par excellence,* so that he may pursue self-examination fearlessly for the rest of his life? When one talks about character analysis and character change as the final goal of therapy, one talks about nothing more and nothing less than a change from avoidance of self-knowledge—i.e., from fear of self-diagnosis to courageous willingness to know the self. This encompasses an orientation of eagerness for penetrating and continuous diagnosis of oneself. And clearly the term "diagnosis," in its etymological derivation, refers simply to a process of discernment.

If the therapist has labored honestly, it is most likely that the patient will forgive him an interpretive speculation which is incorrect. But the patient will not forgive the therapist's inability to perceive him correctly, and the patient will be harmed by faulty interpretations if they are based upon the therapist's own fanciful speculations. This occurs when the speculations are not rooted in the immediacy of experience arising from therapeutic encounters and collaborations, but are merely reflections of the doctor's sterile and schematized approach to the understanding of human development and human affairs, especially when this is coupled with his insistence that he must be right and his demand that the patient accept sooner or later some theoretical credo cherished by the therapist. Under such circumstances, the therapist's fear of being wrong and his subsequent reluctance to offer an interpretation, lest his incorrectness be damaging to the patient, are highly valid; and one must deem it fortunate that he had enough sense to abstain from offering an interpretive comment. Self-evidently, such behavior on the part of the therapist indicates his lack of focusing upon the patient and his communications. Indeed, it reveals that the patient was disregarded for the therapist's focusing upon some preconceived and highly valued theoretical construct instead.

This is not to say that theory has no place in the preparation of the therapist. If the therapist's wider scheme of understanding is based on certain generalizations derived from many astute observations carried out and reported by a variety of investigators, then it will aid the clinician in viewing observable phenomena in perspective. But this is quite different from using theory as a mold to which experience and historical events must be shaped. Above all, any worthwhile theory must include provisions for its own revision; otherwise, it is just a closed system, dogma, or pronouncement. The analyst offering interpretations on the basis of some preconceived theory about presumed historical actualities, rather than on the basis of his direct comprehension and appreciation of the patient's psychological reality, to use Erikson's (1964) terms, is insulting. He degrades the patient. This humiliating behavior confronts the patient with an experience probably all too familiar to him: the experience of not being heard and of being exploited by another person for that person's needs. Under such circumstances, the reluctance to interpret is a blessing in disguise.

Such dangers are, however, absent when interpretive comments are offered in terms of genuine questions. Consensual validation (Sullivan, 1947) can take place only when the therapist truly wonders out loud. Besides the importance of couching interpretations in questioning terms so as to invite validation or refutation, it must also be recognized that an interpretation which springs from the therapist's thoughts and feelings vis-a-vis his patient is almost, by definition, beyond right or wrong. It simply *is*. If the therapist confides in his patient a thought, an idea, or a sense which crossed his mind while listening to the patient, then the patient can affirm the therapist's reactions, or he may even insist that the therapist must be crazy to react the way he does. But he cannot say that the therapist's interpretation was right or that it was wrong, for, strictly speaking, the therapist did not interpret anything but instead *confronted* the patient with his (the therapist's) own reactions—hopefully rational reactions—to the latter's behavior and communications; that is, the therapist told the patient how he strikes him.

The therapist interpreting his patient in this manner has no cause to be afraid of being wrong. His focus was his own reactions, which were based on attentive listening and cultivated sensitivity to the subtleties and nuances of human experience.

The Fear of Inappropriate Timing

Although therapists are frequently convinced that they understand an important aspect of the patient's life and feeling tone, they are reluctant to reveal their reactions because they do not think that the patient "is yet quite ready to hear" what they have to say. They feel that they have to wait for a more opportune moment to make their disclosures. Here the problems are similar to those suggested in the preceding section. If the therapist has gleaned his insights about the patient's experiential life simply on the basis of preconceived theoretical constructs, no matter what the nature of his theoretical adherence may be, then indeed the interpretation will be premature. Actually, if based this way, it will remain premature forever. If, on the other hand, the patient has presented material which in its directness and immediacy moved the therapist to authentic reactions rather than to speculatively-derived thoughts, then one can be relatively certain that the patient has talked about some important aspect of his life *for quite a while*. Although he may not be aware of the significance of his communications, he must have labored a good deal in trying to tell the analyst something which the latter now finally understands.

It is well to remember that the patient always knows more about himself, though sometimes in confusion and bewilderment, than the analyst knows about him. In his recounting of events and in his associations, the patient presents the material useful to therapist and patient in bringing meaningful order and clarity into the latter's jumbled and foggy experience. The appropriate confrontational comment will force itself upon the sensitive therapist precisely at the moment at which he has been able to see psychological rhyme and reason in the patient's communications—that is, only *after* the patient himself has struggled to see something. In effect, this means that the patient is in some way "ready" to deal seriously with this particular aspect of his affective life.

A simple and rather obvious example will illustrate the point.

A woman in her early thirties sought help in order to rid herself of severe depressions, her depressed moods presumably being triggered by the sudden disintegration of a love affair which she had carried on for over ten years. Investigation revealed that the relationship had never been really satisfactory—that she had felt terribly lonely for a long time, even when she and her gentleman friend had been on presumably loving terms. She insisted, however, that she would be ready to do most anything, and on any terms, if they just could go on the way they had. When the therapist remarked that he could not be of service, that mending broken love affairs was really not his *métier,* but that he would be glad to try to help if there was something the woman felt she experienced as troublesome about herself, at that point the woman quickly shifted her attention to a discussion of her own family background. In a relatively few sessions, it became apparent that the patient, although a woman of considerable abilities and training, behaved in relation to her folks and other people as if she were crippled, totally inadequate, and in need of constant support.

Despite the fact that she had her own apartment, she subtly invited her mother to prepare food for her, to take care of her laundry, to shop for her, etc. Although she claimed to have little affection for her mother, she commented on those occasions, when it became obvious that she had invited such little "favors," that "after all, my mother has nothing else to do, so I let her feel useful in doing such chores for me." On other occasions she had talked about some ladies she knew, always women significantly older than she was, and how she played cards with them and how they enjoyed each other's company.

One day when the patient opened the session by reporting on one of her frequent quarrels with her mother, how they had argued the night before and how she really could not stand her, the therapist asked for details as to how the telephone conversation which had ended in this quarrel had come about. The patient somewhat hesitatingly recalled that she had called her mother to simply chat with her, for she knew that her father was out of town on business and that her mother was once again all alone at home. Finally, the patient tried to conclude this little reportage by remarking that things were all right again, that her mother had called this morning and that they had made up, but that this of course would not change the sad fact that her mother was an impossible person and that the patient just could not put up with her any longer. But the therapist responded: "My God, it does sound to me as if you were deeply in love with the woman, as if it were dreadfully important to you to tell her in her loneliness that you are lonely too, and that you feel urgently called upon to have some sort of lovers' quarrel with her. After all, making up is so sweet. That's at least how it strikes my ears." The patient remained silent for a while and then remarked in subdued tone: "I hate the thought, but I am afraid it strikes your ears right. It's awful how I really long for her."

No "deep" insights occurred at this moment, although it was enough to help this woman address herself to the investigation of important aspects of her life and to reduce the length of her useless ruminations about the unhappiness with her man. Regardless of the depth of insight and/or change engendered by the therapist's remark, the point is that his confrontational comment was based on, and in direct response to, material that had been offered by the patient, not on any preconceived theoretical construct. Therefore, it could be offered relatively early in therapy, after about four sessions.

This brings one to the often-heard assertion that the therapist needs a lot of data so as to be able to "convince" the patient of the validity of a given interpretation. In truth, it seems much more likely that the therapist needs a certain amount of data before he can hear what the genuine experiential situation of his patient happens to be, for otherwise he deals but in abstractions and theory.

The fear to interpret because one's timing may be inappropriate, therefore, seems prominently based on the therapist's faint suspicion that he has not really paid attention to the reality of his patient's communication. In addition, his fear of being premature in his interpretations reflects the therapist's unjustified assumption that he has knowledge mysteriously gathered, when in fact all useful knowledge the therapist can have about his patient is based on information the latter has supplied. It also seems likely that a co-determinant of concern with timing is the therapist's sense that what he gleaned about the patient is so utterly terrible and revolting that the patient is likely to be thrown into panic and despair at seeing more clearly what he now only dimly perceives. Yet, as pointed out, the patient is at least tangentially concerned with, and has at least partially exposed, all these "horrible" issues. Therefore, it is much more plausible to assume that in reality it is the therapist who is not yet "ready" to further examine such troublesome problems with his patient.

THE FEAR OF BEING RIGHT

A fascinating and frequent observation by psychotherapists supervising the work of younger colleagues is how often their claims that they do not understand some communication of patients prove fictitious. In many instances, careful and encouraging inquiry reveals their clear grasp of what the patient had actually disclosed. While this reluctance to face his understanding can often be traced to transference reactions of the therapist to his supervisor, and while in other instances, as Searles (1955) and Tauber (1954) have shown, this reluctance represents an unconscious communication by the therapist to his supervisor concerning important psychodynamic aspects of the patient, frequently the therapist, having gleaned an important aspect of the patient's makeup, tries to avoid his insight lest he be called upon to comment to the patient on what was noticed. In his eagerness to avoid exploration of a given issue, the therapist reveals his hope *not* to understand and his fear of understanding correctly. Most therapists, when fully honest with themselves, will be able to recall instances of similar behavior from their own practice.

Obviously this hope not to understand is also likely to be the outcome of some countertransference difficulty. The therapist's fear of arousing the patient's anger; his desire to maintain himself as a "kind" and unthreatening person; his fear of causing the patient anguish in commenting on certain problems; or his own anxiety in relation to the patient, transformed into hostility which demands that important material be left unexplored so as to remain a pathogenic agent—these are some of the more apparent dynamics of this inability to understand. Ordinarily, however, the therapist will realize that his understanding is based on communications by the patient and that the patient must have worked on an issue before the therapist heard the message. Furthermore, the therapist will know that his basic responsibility to the patient is the fearless pursuit of truth and that sham and the undue protection of the patient, be they perpetrated by acts of commission or omission, have no place in the therapeutic enterprise.

Finally, the suggestion that the therapist does not care to face what he sees in the patient because it reminds him too much of himself, and that therefore he avoids bringing the issue to the attention of the patient, holds little water in the context of the present discussion. After all, this section deals with reactions to material the therapist *did* notice, at least tangentially, but fears to have noticed correctly. Of course, one could say that he hopes to have noticed incorrectly in order to avoid any further exploration, because further inquiry might touch on additional material in the therapist's own unconscious, material which he is not willing to face. But this type of defensive countertransference is relatively rare. It implies that the therapist resists fuller exploration of difficult issues in his own life which have been examined only partially, and that he aborts investigation of related or associated questions in his patient's makeup lest it boomerang and force him into additional self-inquiry.

However, even the most honest therapists exhibit this reluctance to pursue correct hunches, leading one to a rather parsimonious understanding of their hesitance to acknowledge as correct what they dimly see. This fear of being right and the subsequent hesitance to interpret may correctly rest on their penetrating realization that in any interpretation offered by the therapist, he not only talks about the patient but he inevitably talks about *himself*. Unless he tries to delude himself and unless he tries to fool his patient into believing that his correct understanding is derived exclusively from book learning or previous work experience, it must be apparent to both participants, therapist and patient alike, that the correct interpretation stems from the therapist's own inner experience and his thoughtful search for self-knowledge. The more to the point and the more penetrating the interpretation, the more obvious it will be that the therapist is talking and understanding from the depth of his own psychological life. To put the issue into the common *patois: It takes one to know one, and in his correct interpretation the therapist reveals that he is one.*

It seems that the reluctance to understand and to interpret correctly is most frequently based on this fear to be right in one's discernment, and that this fear in turn is occasioned by the therapist's qualms about revealing himself to his patient through meaningful and correct interpretations. When a therapist remarks, "You sound to me as if you were dreadfully envious," or when he comments, "This makes me feel as if you experienced profound longing feebly disguised by benevolent concern," he reveals that he knows something about how it feels to be dreadfully envious, that he knows how it feels to experience profound longing, and that he knows how it feels to be called upon to dissemble something. He reveals that he knows all these states because he is, and has been, in touch with his own psychological life and experience.

THE RELUCTANCE TO INTERPRET AND THE PROBLEM OF COUNTERTRANSFERENCE

An examination of some major causes of therapists' reluctance to offer interpretations suggests that the deeper roots of this hesitance are to be found in countertransference problems, the outgrowths of the analyst's own unresolved personality difficulties. But, as will be discussed, such reactions do *not* inevitably work to the patient's detriment.

Clearly, the therapist's fear of being wrong lest he not impress his patient; or his insistence upon offering essentially detached interpretations, i.e., reconstructive comments based upon some theoretical credo concerning personality development; or his frantic desire that the patient simply accept interpretations—these are obvious manifestations of a therapist's personality difficulties which can do little but interfere with his and his patient's growth. Similarly, the therapist's exaggerated *fears* about inappropriate timing are also conditioned by countertransference difficulties expressing themselves in his inability to hear that the patient has dealt for quite a while with the material to be interpreted; or expressing themselves in his basic lack of confidence in the patient's desire to learn something of genuine significance about himself; or expressing themselves in the therapist's tendency to offer interpretations which are based on "the book" and his reluctance to make comments rooted in immediate communicative encounters. Obviously, then, his reluctance to interpret because he feels that the time for offering a given interpretation is inappropriate, demands the therapist's most careful self-scrutiny so that he may notice whether there are, and if so hopefully reduce, personal difficulties which obviate the effectiveness of the therapeutic exchange.

While one may hope that these countertransference difficulties will be kept to a bare minimum, they may, under certain circumstances and when handled constructively, further the therapeutic progress. When a therapist observes within himself such a reluctance to interpret a person's communications, and when he realizes that this type of hesitance is rather unusual in his work, then he is put into an excellent position to examine just what in the interaction made him inclined to interpret in a sterile and mechanical fashion and therefore made him fearful of being wrong; or what made him inclined to be unaware of his patient's having talked a good deal about an issue and thus made him fearful of inappropriate timing; or just what in the interaction made him reluctant to interpret lest he reveal *himself* through the correctness of his interpretation. Scrupulous and energetic self-examination may then lead the therapist to important insights about the patient's makeup which, in turn, gave rise to tendencies within the therapist that were expressed in varieties of fear reactions vis-a-vis interpretations to be offered. This creative use of countertransference reactions, so well described by Tauber and Green (1959), takes the therapist's reluctance to interpret as its point of departure, and leads potentially to investigations of the relationship from which both patient and therapist can emerge as changing, growing, and maturing participants in an adventurous journey toward more profound self-recognition.

REFERENCES

Alexander, F., Efficacy of brief contact. In F. Alexander and T. M. French (Eds.): *Psychoanalytic Therapy*. New York: The Ronald Press Company, 1946, pp. 145-55.

Breuer, J., and Freud, S. (1893-1895). Studies on hysteria. In S. Freud, *Standard edition*, Vol. 2. London: The Hogarth Press, 1953.

Erikson, E. H., Psychological reality and historical actuality. *Insight and responsibility*. New York: W. W. Norton & Company, 1964, pp. 159-215.

Freud, S. (1905), Fragments of an analysis of a case of hysteria. *Standard edition*, Vol. 7. London: The Hogarth Press, 1953, pp. 7-122.

—— (1910), 'Wild' psycho-analysis. *Standard edition*, Vol. 11. London: The Hogarth Press, 1953, pp. 221-27.

—— (1937), Construction in analysis. *Standard edition*, Vol. 23. London: The Hogarth Press, 1953, pp. 257-69.

Fromm-Reichmann, F., *Principles of intensive psychotherapy*. Chicago: The University of Chicago Press, 1950.

Rogers, C. R., *Counseling and psychotherapy*. Boston: Houghton Mifflin Company, 1942.

——, *Client-centered therapy*. Boston: Houghton Mifflin Company, 1951.

Searles, H. F., The informational value of the supervisor's emotional experience. *Psychiatry*, 1955, 18, 135-46.

Singer, E., *Key concepts in psychotherapy*. New York: Random House, 1965.

Sullivan, H. S., *Conceptions of modern psychiatry*. Washington, D.C.: The William Alanson White Psychiatric Foundation, 1947.

Tauber, E. S., Exploring the therapeutic use of counter-transference data. *Psychiatry*, 1954, 17, 332-36.

Tauber, E. S., and Green, M. R., *Prelogical experience*. New York: Basic Books, 1959.

CHAPTER 43

Interpretation: Science or Art?

EMANUEL F. HAMMER, PH.D.

We live in an age in which some of the younger generation, intent upon surfing, search the world over for the perfect wave. Being of a relatively older generation and of a sedentary profession, some of us are content to channel our searching impulses in our work, and at times in the quest for the best way to express an underlying understanding. The questions, among others, this book has addressed include: How can the therapist best present to the patient the difficult truths of his nature? How can the therapist best put him in touch with the complexities of his defenses and what he defends himself against? How can the therapist best move him from his frequent surface confusion of reality and appearances to the relatively more real?

When interpreting, what ingredients would an ideal communication possess? Here is my fantasy. An interpretation would carry no surplus words, no excess baggage, and possess a precision of form and a logic with which it is ordered. It would be expressed at a time the patient could hear and in a manner to which the patient could resonate. Thus, the therapist would speak to the immediate and the personal, responding with things seen and felt by him just beyond the patient's awareness.

The interpretation would have the benefit of vividness.[1] It would be a refined statement, eliciting terms which connect fully and freshly with the patient. Hence, it would possess a sense of truth to the patient's state, and it would be one step of a process of steady movement toward the center of a genuine experience. The interpretation would be given in the midst of an actual occurrence, and would further constitute a *related* actual event of its own. This would be in the service of assisting its assimilation by the patient—an assimilation which would, in turn, enable an expansion of a dimension of his known self. The patient's participation in it would, in the long run, perhaps even make some small contribution to a life enhanced by this newly-discovered relationship.

All this is a pretty tall order. It is, as I said, a fantasy. But fantasies can at times do service as distant stars to aim for, as aspirations towards which to strive. My fantasy may correctly suggest to some readers that, above and beyond the empirical findings that interpretations "work" (and certainly stronger than the experimental data), perhaps there is also a personal attraction which draws us, as therapists, to embrace an interpretative approach. Interpretation, to follow Samuel Butler, like life "is the art of drawing sufficient conclusions from insufficient premises." In a sensitive, perceptive, accurate interpretation, the *art* and the *science* of psychology meet, and hopefully blend. It is here that the objectivity, the rigor and the discipline of science merge with the empathy, the daring, the sensitivity and the intuitiveness which is, and must remain, art. It is here, then, that a therapist functions at his fullest—here that he calls forth more of his range.

---

[1]See Chapter 22, "Use of Imagery in Interpretive Communication for one type of vividness."

Psychotherapy may be viewed as a ladder that runs from the ground to the air, from the scientific to the artistic. Actually, the best therapist takes his position midway up the ladder. This position is, however, as much a function of temperament as it is of theoretical belief. The middle position encompasses a capacity for both "tough-minded" and "tender-minded" approaches, for oscillating between obsessive-compulsive and hysteroid potentials in oneself, without getting stuck at either polarity.

Overemphasis on the "scientific and tough-minded" obsessional qualities in the therapist incurs the risk that the therapeutic experience will be reduced to an intellectual, emotionally rarified, detached exercise. Actual behavioral change for the patient never gets off the ground. At best, the process remains somewhat academic; at its worst it may become weighed down by tedium and pedantry.

On the other hand, too much "artistry" that is "tender-minded" in quality and hysteroid in emotional tone results in treatment which is impressionistic and impulsive. It results in the therapist releasing a hotbed of insufficiently-understood variables into the therapeutic situation. Intuition—if not appropriately balanced by the critical faculties shaping, selecting, and evaluating responses before they are released—produces a disruptive, disturbing experience for the patient. He may not stand still in therapy; in contrast, he may be chaotically tossed in all directions at once. There is no patterning of processes initiated and refined; there is little unfolding of a materializing direction. It may become a bit like art done by a chimpanzee with random impulses undirected by a guiding intelligence. (In Rorschach terminology, the process is that of *color* and *color-form* without the balancing effect of sufficient *form-color*. One thinks of that brand of Existentialist who shares even his "pathology" with the patient. Conversely, domination of the therapist by the "scientist" part of himself results in a treatment situation which leans toward being all *form* without any enlivening of the process by a *form-color* or even, at times, an occasional *color-form* response.)

To approximate being a full person within the therapist's role (and can anyone considerably less than a full person assist patients to become full as individuals?), it is essential to know how and when to suspend one's logic temporarily. It is a precondition first to suspend *momentarily* an ever-evaluative, criticizing, judging function of the mind. This is necessary in order to remain open to "receiving" uncritically the off-beat experience or the surprising idea which comes unexpectedly. Then, of course, the therapist must bring his critical functions back into play to evaluate the perceptions which occurred—to select those that he finds make sense and those he judges appropriate and helpful to share with the patient. The more adequate therapist is the one who is capable of loosening the brakes which hold back the irrational. Only then does he reactivate the critical functions to shape, to modify, or to discard. But he must then be capable of recalling this critical side, or the process degenerates into "wild" psychotherapy.

To remain too "scientific," to maintain a nonhovering, heavy rationality may inhibit the appearance of the occasionally-unerring intuitive hunch. Only when these hunches play their appropriate part in the process does psychoanalysis become more than the mere exercise of a craft; only then does it attain the level of a creative endeavor.

This point invites a few remarks beyond the special circumstances of the therapy room. Unrelieved rationality inhibits originality and an imaginative approach in general. Continuous rationality stifles the appearance of a novel, incredible, or "unheard of" perception; yet, this is what creativity really is—the *reception* of a new, fresh idea which is so preposterous that no one ever conceived of such a likelihood before. After all, it was just a "mad" idea that the world is not flat but round; that we are descended from a common ancestor to the monkey; that the earth is not the center of the universe with the sun revolving around it as we can plainly see; that there is an unconscious part of us; that the blood circulates rather than stays still as it should in our bodies; that it is intercourse which leads to babies nine months later.

To be creative, one has to be able to peel off and *momentarily* lay aside one's sensible layers. Otherwise, one stays, as a therapist and as a person, one of those "reasonable" people who never say a foolish thing, nor a brilliant one.

On the other hand, however, let us not overlook the possibilities of either extreme, the all "scientist" or the all "artist" type who may happen to be right for a *particular* type of patient. For the highly confused, labile, loosely integrated patient who could profit from a process assisting him in "binding" himself, the "scientist" type of therapist may prove very helpful. For the detached, incapsulated, schizoid, or obsessional patient, the all "artist" therapist might be right for liberating affect, for thawing out the patient, and for attaching him to a meaningful life experience.

For the majority of patients, the scientist-artist blend in a therapist is what is most effective. This integration offers the greatest versatility of approach and of resources in treatment strategy. No less importantly, it goes along with the therapist possessing authentic *range* as a person in the therapeutic exchange.[2]

Should therapy provide the patient with windows to look through or environs to react in? The best therapist is the one capable of supplying either—when, and to whom, appropriate. The therapist must be flexible enough to shift back and forth between the polarities of Sullivan's "participant-observer" role. The therapist should know when to move, and then be able to, toward the "blank screen" posture in treatment, but he should also be capable of what I might term *educated spontaneity,* i.e., selectively expressing his own feelings where appropriate and contributory to the goals of the treatment.

The art of being is an art of balance. Antithetical impulses must be held in an active, dynamic equilibrium. At neither polarity does one encounter the complexity, the creative tension, nor the capacity for vision we hope for in those who undertake to do psychotherapy. What is needed is a balanced mixture of the art and the science of psychotherapy, and a mixture of art and science in the psychotherapist.

---

[2]It is this capacity for active use of intellect *and* affect, and for experiencing a harmonious balance between the two, that I, as a faculty member of psychoanalytic training institutes, look for in candidates who apply. It is this use of both scientific and artistic sides, perhaps as much as any other goal, which we might strive to help analysts-in-training to liberate.

Index

Acceptance
  conditional, by therapist, 191-194
  of interpretations, by patient, 112-113
  unconditional, by therapist, 187-194, 237
Acting out, replaced with verbalization, 318
Action therapies, 9
Actions by patients
  encouraged by therapist, 186
  after interpretations, 116-118, 133
Acts, therapeutic. *See* Therapeutic act
Adolescents
  aftercare of, 331
  and aims of therapy, 326
  analogies applied to, 330
  development of, 201
  and identification, 330
  interpretation in therapy of, 321-331
    diagnostic, 327
    difficulties in, 329
    of disengagement, 330-331
    pretreatment, 324-325
    of therapeutic process, 327-330
  management of, 166-167
  relationship with therapist, 325-326
  self-interpretation by, 329-330
  unconscious functioning in, 329
Affect, with recollection, 256
Aftercare, in adolescence, 331
Aged persons
  aims of therapy for, 333
  and anxiety, 333, 335
  cultural aspects of, 335
  interpretation in therapy of, 332-337
  management of, 167
  relationship with therapist, 334
  time factors in, 333
Aims
  of interpretations, 23-25, 45
  of therapy, 8-9, 170-171
    with adolescents, 326
    with aged persons, 333
    in hypnoanalysis, 346-347
Alienation, factors in, 205
Alternatives to interpreting, 169-195
Analogy, applied in adolescence, 330
Anger, relieving of, 119
Animus function, in dreams, 287-289
Annihilation, fear of, 303, 305
Anxiety
  in children, 292
  in older patients, 333, 335
  symbols producing, 16-17
Archetypes, in dreams, 286
Artistic aspects of interpretation, 372-374

Attenuation of interpretations, 50, 52
Authority roles of therapist, 56-57, 101-102
Autonomy, capacity for, 174

Behavior change
  and existential therapy, 246
  and insight, 79-80
  after interpretation, 48
Behavior disorders, in childhood, 317-318
Blame, absence of, as therapy, 187-194, 237

Castration anxiety, mechanisms in, 303
Catharsis, indirect, 158
Cathexis, and hypercathexis, 142
Change. *See* Behavior change
Character disorders
  in childhood
    and group therapy, 294-299
    interpretation of, 293-294
  treatment of, 162-163
Children
  anxiety in, 292
  case history described, 310-315
  character disorders in, 293-294
  communications of, 305-307
  conduct disorders in, 298
  defenses in, 293
  development of, 199-200
  effeminate boys, 295
  ego therapy in, 293-294
  fantasies of, 308-310, 317
  and fear of annihilation, 303, 305, 308, 310
  Freudian view of, 301, 302
  group therapy for character disorders, 294-299
  immature, 295-296
  inhibited, 296
  interpretations in therapy of, 291-299, 300-319
  overanalyzed, 298-299
  overly independent, 298
  overmature, 297
  projection and rationalization in, 297
  schizoid, 296
  transference in, 292-293
Clarification of feelings, concept of, 43, 44-45, 61
Clarification of relationships, in early phase of therapy, 28, 30
Client-centered therapy, 1, 9, 14, 43, 55-58, 61, 63, 74, 172-183, 208, 237
  efficacy of, 20
  and experiential response, 208-226
Clues for use of interpretation, 50-52, 79

Cognitive learning
  and conditioning, 48
  development of, 20-21
  and insight, 77
Communications
  in childhood, 305-307
  contamination of, 123-124
  diagram of therapeutic dialogue, 267
  in interpretations, 228
  overdetermined, 262
  regression affecting, 124
  therapeutic, 10
  See also Dialogue; Language
Conditional acceptance, in psychotherapy, 191-194
Conditioning, and cognitive learning, 48
Conduct disorders, in childhood, 298
Conflicts
  in adolescence, 329
  intrasystemic, and interpretations, 81-89
  positive endings to, 39
  resolution of, 9
Confrontations
  efficacy of, 163
  example of, 97-98
Consciousness
  expansion of, 8
  intentionality of, 243
Constructions
  in free association, 273, 274-275
  offered by analyst, 145
Contamination of communication, 123-124
Corrective emotional experience, 39, 40
Cosmologies, personal, development of, 20-21
Countertransference
  problem of, 124-125
  and reluctance to interpret, 369, 370-371
Cultural aspects, in therapy of aging persons, 335

Decision-making, by client, 18
Defenses
  attacked by therapist, 174, 186
  in childhood, 293, 303-305
  interpretation affecting, 23-24, 32
  narcissistic, 93-94
Definitions of interpretation, 3, 27, 43, 44, 75, 86, 323, 357
Delinquency, and free association, 272-273
Delinquent character disorders, treatment of, 162-163
Depression
  and free association, 273
  treatment of, 157-159
Depth of interpretation, 31-32, 44, 52, 79, 146-147
  in experiential responses, 219

in hypnoanalysis, 347
in rational therapy, 237
Determinism, psychological, 188-191
Development, stages of, 198-202
Diagnostic categories, limitations in, 92
Diagnostic interpretation, in adolescence, 327
Dialogue
  evocative character of, 135, 152, 156, 351, 355
  psychoanalytic, 120, 129-139, 351-363
  therapeutic, 10
    diagram of, 267
  See also Communications
Directions by analyst, compared with suggestions, 117-118
Directness of interpretations, 230
Discussion, as response to interpretation, 116-118
Disengagement in adolescence, interpretation of, 330-331
Distance, in interpretations, 230
Dreams
  in client-centered therapy, 55, 176
  induction of, in hypnoanalysis, 347
  interpretation of, 234
    in early phase of therapy, 29
    and free association, 270-278
    Jungian approach to, 285-290
    place and use of, 280-284
    selective use of material, 284
    on subjective level, 285-290
  pictorial language of, 153
Dual personalities, therapy of, 191-194
Dynamics, personal, interpretation of, 46-47

Early phase of therapy, interpretation in, 27-30
Effeminate boys, management of, 295
Ego
  intrasystemic conflicts, 82-86
  synthesizing function of, 87
Ego-alien and ego-syntonic behavior, 26, 98-99, 163
Ego function and interpretation, 67-70
Ego therapy in childhood
  and group therapy, 294-299
  and interpretations, 293-294
Emotional and intellectual insight, 77-79
Emotional reactions to interpretations, 118-119
Emotionalist view, criticism of, 256-257
  See also Rational-emotional therapy
Energies
  closed system of patient, 144
  neutralization of, 82, 87
Equality of humans, idea of, 187
Ethics, trans-moral, 190
Evocative character of analytic dialogue, 135, 152, 156, 351, 355

Existential analysis
  basic points in, 242
  and group therapy, 249, 251
  interpretation in, 240-252
  resistance in, 250
  transference in, 250
Existentialism, 20, 38, 92, 104, 206
Experiential response, 208-226
  concepts used in, 216-219
  depth in, 219
  and direction of therapy, 214-216
  felt meaning, 208-212
  frequency of therapist interruptions, 221
  interactions in, 220-225
  method and theory of, 225-226
  and positive tendencies in client, 224-225
  and reactions of client, 212-213
  and referent movement, 215-216
  resolution process in, 215
  and sensitivity, 212
  and uncomfortable reactions of therapist, 221-222
  and working through process, 222

Fables, for interpretations, 159-160
Failures in classic analytic approach, 69
Fantasies
  in childhood, 308-310, 317
  production after interpretations, 114
  sexual, interpretation of, 94, 135
Faulty interpretations, 365-366
Fear
  of annihilation, in childhood, 303, 305, 308, 310
  of being right, and reluctance to interpret, 368-370
  of being wrong, and reluctance to interpret, 365-366
Feeling, as response to interpretation, 118-119
Felt meaning, responses to, 208-212
Fixed role therapy, efficacy of, 20
Forms of interpretations, 3, 46
Free association
  and dream analysis, 270-278
  function of, 144
  processes in, 253-258
  sources of error in, 276-278
  uses of, 211
Frequency of interpretation, 32-33, 165
Functions of therapy. See Aims

Generalized statements
  as interpretations, 160
  positive effects of, 94-96
Geriatrics. See Aged
Gestures, significance of, 234
Goals of therapy. See Aims

Gratification of wishes, 131-132
Group therapy
  and character disorders in childhood, 294-299
  and existential analysis, 249, 251
  interpretation in, 339-342
  for obsessional patients, 156
Growth, stages of, 198-202

Homosexual wishes, interpretation of, 46, 94, 96, 104, 115, 118, 137
Homosexuals, management of, 262-263
Horizontal interpretations, 3
Humor, role of, 146, 157, 268
Hypnoanalysis, interpretation in, 137, 344-349

Id-ego matrix, characteristics in, 82, 85
Identification
  in adolescence, 330
  with analyst, and therapeutic love, 100
  process of, 87
Identity, existential approach to, 249-250
Imagery, use of, 148-155, 157
Immature children, management of, 295-296
Impulses of patient, recognition of, 147
Incorrect interpretations, 365-366
Indirect catharsis, 158
Inexact interpretations, use of, 64
Infancy, development in, 199
Infantile children, management of, 295-296
Inhibited children, management of, 296
Insight
  and change, 79-80
  efficacy of, 13-15, 18-19, 22
  intellectual and emotional, 77-79
  and interpretation, 48, 253-258
  nature of, 75-76
  partial, 76, 78
  processes in, 136
  truth of, 76-79
  value of, 3
Intellectual and emotional insight, 77-79
Intellectual reactions to interpretations, 118-119
Intellectualist view, criticism of, 254-256
Intellectualized interpretations, 57
Intellectualizing, as resistance, 78
Intentionality of consciousness, 243
Interfering needs of therapist, 40-41
Interpersonal theory of psychiatry, 197-207, 229
  in experiential approach, 220-225
  See also Relationship, therapeutic
Intrasystemic conflicts, and interpretations, 81-89
Isolated patients, treatment of, 151, 157

Juvenile period, development in, 200-201

Language
in interpretations, 33-36, 141-147
secondary process, 144, 145
use of patient's own words, 35, 145, 162
Latent meanings, in responses of patients, 121
Learning theory, and interpretation, 49
Length of sessions, modifications of, 166-167
Listening
by patient, 110-112
by therapist, 2
Logic, faulty, and emotional disturbances, 232
Loneliness, factors in, 202
Love, therapeutic, and identification with analyst, 100

Manipulative therapies, 171
Masochistic patients, management of, 150, 159-161
Maturation, stages in, 198-202
Maturational interpretation, 107-109
Meanings attributed to interpretations, 121-123
Melancholia, and free association, 273
Mirroring in language, use of, 35, 145, 162
Morality, problems in, 190

Narcissistic defense, 93-94
Needs of therapist, interfering, 40-41
Neutralization of energies, 82, 87
Nurturing role of therapists, 202-207

Objectivity, as response to interpretations, 119-120
Obsessional patients, management of, 72, 144, 151, 156-157, 167
Oedipal theory, as concept of man, 302
Open-endedness of interventions, 260-269
Order, need for, 5-6, 21, 24
Overdetermined communications, 262

Paranoid patients, management of, 159-161
Parent-child relationship, problems in, 303
Pediatrics. See Children
Perceptions, defenses against, 304-305
Personality, concepts of, 68-69
Play therapy, and interpretations, 291-299
Pleasure-principle, struggle with reality-principle factors, 84, 87
Positive endings, to old conflicts, 39
Postures, significance of, 234
Preadolescent period, development in, 201
Pretreatment interpretation, for adolescents, 324-325
Previous therapists, attitudes toward, 164-165
Production, as response to interpretations, 113-116
Projection, in childhood, 297
Proverbs, as interpretations, 159
Psychoanalytic dialogue, 120, 129-139, 351-363

Purpose of therapy. See Aims

Questions by therapist, interpretive character of, 44, 45

Rational-emotive therapy, 183-187
efficacy of, 20
interpretations in, 232-239
Rationality, commitment to, 18-19
Rationalization, in childhood, 297
Reaction-formation behavior, in childhood, 297
Reactions
of analyst, compared with interpretations, 101-106
of patient, to interpretations, 66
See also Responses
Reality
confrontation of, 97-98, 163
existential view of, 242-244
Reassurance of patient
in early phase of therapy, 28, 30
through interpretations, 64
negative aspects of, 96
Recollection, with affect, 256
Reconstructions, psychoanalytic, 274-275
Reductionism, 92-93
Reflection of patient's feelings, 173, 209
Reflective responses, use of, 45, 57
Regression, affecting communication, 124
Rejection of interpretations, 112-113
Relationship, therapeutic, 2, 9-10, 15-16, 27-28, 46
in adolescence, 325-326, 330-331
analyst's role in, 56-57, 101-106
clarification of, in early phase of therapy, 28, 30
dialogue in, 120, 129-139, 351-363
in existential therapy, 246-247
in experiential approach, 220-225
in hypnoanalysis, 346
and identification with analyst, 100
with older patients, 334
in rational therapy, 237
and transference, 17-18
and value of interpretations, 43-53, 59-61, 62-66
Relevance of interpretations, 230
Reluctance to interpret, 364-371
and countertransference, 369, 370-371
and fear of being right, 368-370
and fear of being wrong, 365-366
and fear of inappropriate timing, 367-368
Repression
in adolescence, 329
and changes in behavior, 19
after interpretations, 113-116
Resistance
in existential therapy, 250

and experiential approach, 217
and intellectualizing, 78
interpretation of, 29, 30, 32, 46, 132, 233
and length of sessions, 167
mechanisms in, 188
Resistant responses, to interpretations, 47, 52
Resolution process, in experiential approach, 215
Responses to interpretations, 47, 66, 110-120, 121-123
Responses of therapist
  experiential, 208-226
  rules for, 208-219
Rogerian viewpoint. See Client-centered therapy
Roles of patient and therapist. See Relationship, therapeutic
Rosen, therapeutic approach of, 136, 174

Schizoid patients, management of, 97, 111, 144, 161-162
  in childhood, 296
Schizophrenia
  dream analysis in, 283
  free association in, 272
  management of, 174, 178
Scientific aspects of interpretation, 372-374
Second-hand patients, management of, 164-166
Secondary process language, 144, 145
Self-deceptive function of symptoms, 23
Self-direction. See Client-centered therapy
Self-interpretation, by adolescents, 329-330
Self-involvement, as response to interpretations, 119-120
Self-realization, value of, 8, 9
Sensitivity, and experiential responses, 212
Sexual fantasies, interpretation of, 94, 135
Short-term therapy, interpretations in, 25
Silences in therapy, 10-11, 123, 124
Socialization processes, and psychotherapy, 137-139
Speech patterns. See Language
Spontaneity in interpretations, 71-73
Style of interpretation, 33-36
Sublimation, concept of, 87
Suggestion
  and interpretation, 347
  role of, 67, 117
Superego, conflict with ego ideal, 83-84
Symbols, anxiety-producing potential of, 16-17
Symptoms
  relief of, as goal of therapy, 9, 74, 80
  self-deceptive function of, 23
Synthesizing function of ego, 87

Technique, interpretive, 31-41
  varying methods for different symptom groups, 156-168

Tension, effects of, 63-64
Therapeutic act, 125-128
  and interpretation, 91-100
  and transference, 127-128
Therapeutic plan, interpretation of, to adolescents, 327-330
Therapeutic relationship. See Relationship, therapeutic
Therapist
  as authority figure, 56-57, 101-102
  fear of being right, 368-370
  fear of being wrong, 365-366
  interfering needs of, 40-41
  in psychoanalytic dialogue, 120, 129-139, 351-363
  reluctance to interpret, 364-371
Thought, as response to interpretations, 118-119, 133
Time, realistic relationship to, 141
Time sequence, in interpretation, 36-37
Timing of interpretations, 31-32, 50, 79, 164
  inappropriate, fear of, 367-368
  of transference interpretation, 38
Transactional view of interpretation, 228-231
Transference relationship, 17-18
  in client-centered therapy, 176
  and countertransference problem, 124-125
  and existential therapy, 250
  and hypnoanalysis, 346
  interpretation of, 37-40, 46, 88, 132, 233, 257-258
    in children, 292-293
  and nurturing role of therapists, 203, 205
  and therapeutic act, 127-128
Types of interpretations, 3, 46

Unconditional positive regard, as therapy, 187-194, 237
Unconscious, adolescent attitudes toward, 329

Value of interpretations, 23-25
Values implicit in psychoanalysis, 96-98
Varieties of interpretations, 3, 46
Varying technique in treatment, 156-168
Verbalization
  of feelings of client, 173
  replacing acting out, 318
  value of, 5
Verbatim report of therapeutic session, 262-266
Vertical interpretations, 3
Visual impressions
  as imagery in interpretations, 148-155
  traumatizing effect of, 143

Wishes, gratification of, 131-132
Working through process, in experiential approach, 222